The Encyclopedia of
WORLD SEA POWER

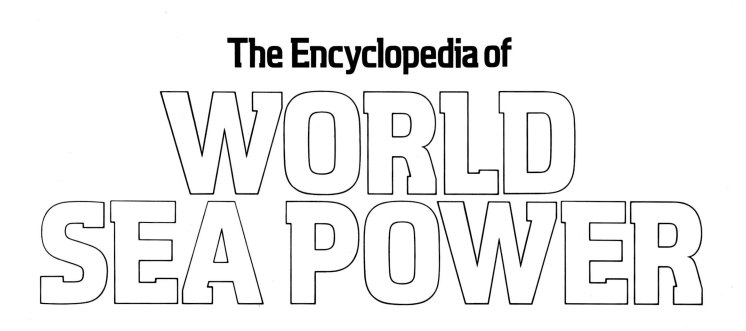

The Encyclopedia of
WORLD SEA POWER

Editor:
Chris Bishop

CRESCENT BOOKS
New York

Copyright © Aerospace Publishing Limited 1988

Produced by Aerospace Publishing Ltd
179 Dalling Road, Hammersmith, London W6 0ES

First English edition published 1988 by Temple Press
an imprint of The Hamlyn Publishing Group Limited
A division of The Octopus Publishing Group plc
Michelin House, 81 Fulham Road
London SW3 6RB

First published in book form 1988

This 1988 edition published by
Crescent Books and distributed by
Crown Publishers, Inc.

Printed by Mandarin Offset, Hong Kong

ISBN 0-517-65342-7

CONTENTS

Modern Missile Submarines

Silently through the depths, the most menacing leviathans the world has known make their stealthy way. For months at a time the missile-carrying submarines of five nations patrol the seas, their awesome destructive power concealed and protected by the vast spaces and depths of the ocean.

The missile control section aboard a British 'Resolution' class submarine does not look particularly dramatic, but in dozens of such places below the sea similar crews stand ready to unleash their mighty charges, hoping that they never have to put their equipment to the ultimate test.

The nuclear-powered ballistic missile submarine (SSBN) and the submarine-launched ballistic missile (SLBM) have become the shield of both the Eastern and Western power blocs. With vast areas of the world's oceans to roam on long lonely submerged patrols, the boats provide an almost totally immune second-strike capability against the opposing bloc's population centres and industrial targets and so keep the possibility of a first strike well in check.

The resources required to finance, build, outfit and maintain in service such a force mean that only a handful of countries can afford to operate these vessels. The largest operator by far is the Soviet Union which, after 20 or so years, has at last outstripped the USA in terms of total force levels and capabilities, with around 62 SSBNs of seven different classes in service. The Americans by contrast now field only 36 of three different classes. The Soviets also have five different missile types to the Americans' two, although the latter still lead in overall numbers of warheads carried. To back up the Americans in NATO and to provide an independent deterrent, the UK maintains one of its four Polaris-equipped SSBNs on patrol continuously, whilst France remains outside the NATO organization but still deploys one or two of her six-vessel SSBN force as part of her national strategic deterrent. In a bid to counter both major superpowers the People's Republic of China became the fifth SSBN operator recently when she deployed the first of at least four 'Xia' class SSBNs with an indigenously designed and built SLBM fitted with a thermonuclear warhead.

Because of this type of submarine's relative invulnerability to ASW countermeasures, it is expected that such boats will be around for many decades to come, although possibly in modified form as new missile types and defences evolve.

Larger than most cruisers of World War II, the current generation of ballistic missile submarines as represented by the massive USS Ohio are without parallel in their frightening destructive might.

‘Le Redoutable’ class SSBN

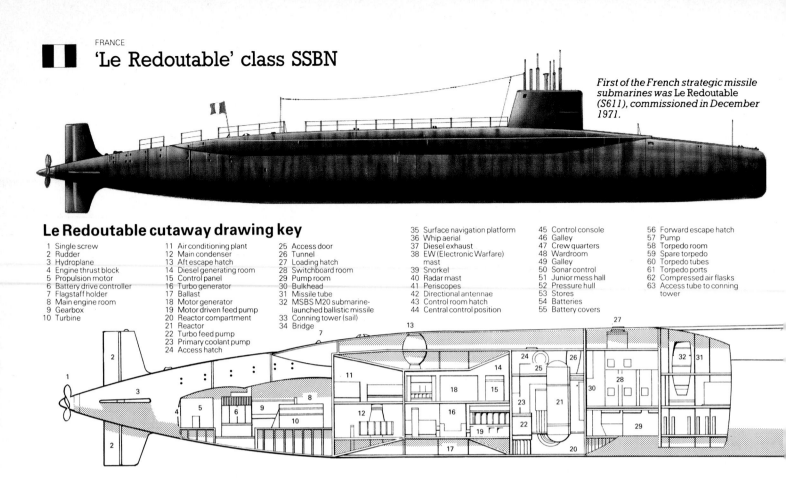

First of the French strategic missile submarines was Le Redoutable *(S611), commissioned in December 1971.*

Le Redoutable cutaway drawing key

1 Single screw
2 Rudder
3 Hydroplane
4 Engine thrust block
5 Propulsion motor
6 Battery drive controller
7 Flagstaff holder
8 Main engine room
9 Gearbox
10 Turbine
11 Air conditioning plant
12 Main condenser
13 Aft escape hatch
14 Diesel generating room
15 Control panel
16 Turbo generator
17 Ballast
18 Motor generator
19 Motor driven feed pump
20 Reactor compartment
21 Reactor
22 Turbo feed pump
23 Primary coolant pump
24 Access hatch
25 Access door
26 Tunnel
27 Loading hatch
28 Switchboard room
29 Pump room
30 Bulkhead
31 Missile tube
32 MSBS M20 submarine-launched ballistic missile
33 Conning tower (sail)
34 Bridge
35 Surface navigation platform
36 Whip aerial
37 Diesel exhaust
38 EW (Electronic Warfare) mast
39 Snorkel
40 Radar mast
41 Periscopes
42 Directional antennae
43 Control room hatch
44 Central control position
45 Control console
46 Galley
47 Crew quarters
48 Wardroom
49 Galley
50 Sonar control
51 Junior mess hall
52 Pressure hull
53 Stores
54 Batteries
55 Battery covers
56 Forward escape hatch
57 Pump
58 Torpedo room
59 Spare torpedo
60 Torpedo tubes
61 Torpedo ports
62 Compressed air flasks
63 Access tube to conning tower

The first French SSBN (or more correctly Sous-Marin Nucléare Lance-Engine or SNLE) *Le Redoutable* (S611) was authorized in March 1963, laid down in November 1964 and commissioned in 1971 after being employed for 2½ years on trials as the prototype for the French naval deterrent known as the Force de Dissuasion in official circles. She and her **‘Le Redoutable’ class** sistership *Le Terrible* (S612) were initially equipped with the 2400-km (1,490-mile) range two-stage solid-propellant inertially-guided M1 SLBM that had a single 500-kiloton thermonuclear warhead and a CEP of 930 m (3,050 ft). In 1974 the third unit, *Le Foudroyant* (S610), was commissioned with the improved 3100-km (1,925-mile) range M2 missile with a more powerful second-stage motor but carrying the same warhead and having a similar CEP. The two previous vessels were then retrofitted with the M2 system during their normal

overhauls. The fourth boat, *L'Indomptable* (S613), was commissioned into service in 1977 with the vastly improved M20 missile that has the same range and accuracy as the M2 but carries a new 1.2-megaton yield specially hardened warhead with what is believed to be chaff dispensing penetration aids to confuse defending radar systems. The last vessel, *Le Tonnant* (S614), was also completed with the M20 whilst the three units equipped with the M2 have now been brought up to the same standard. From 1985 the last four units built undergo yet another modification to carry the M4 SLBM that entered service in April of that year aboard *L'Inflexible*. All five boats are also being converted to carry the underwater-launched SM.39 Exocet anti-ship missile and the sonars of *L'Inflexible*. The planned deletion dates for the class are S611 1997, S612 1999, S610 2002, S613 2004 and S614 2008.

Le Foudroyant (S610) and her sisterships were designed and built in France without any help from the

Americans, unlike the British Polaris boats, which required considerable design assistance.

‘L'Inflexible’ class SSBN

Ordered in September 1978, the sole **‘L'Inflexible’ class** boat *L'Inflexible* (S615) is an intermediate design between the ‘Le Redoutable’ class and a new class of 14,000-15,000 tons planned to be operational around 1993-4 with new 6000km (3,750 mile) range M5 SLBMs equipped with MIRVs. She retains most of the external characteristics of the earlier class, but the internal fittings and sensors differ by taking advantage of the advances made in the propulsion system, electronics and weapons since the ‘Le Redoutable’ class boats were constructed. The rationale behind this intermediate boat lies in the fact that France requires three SSBNs to be continuously available, of which two are to be on

patrol. In order to achieve this the French navy has to have six submarines in service, a number one more than the ‘Le Redoutable’ class total.

Laid down in March 1979, *L'Inflexible* achieved operational status in April 1985 and is not due for deletion until 2012. Like all French missile submarines, she will have two crews, Bleu (blue) and Ambre (amber), to crew the vessel in rotation in order to máximize the time spent on patrol between reactor-refuelling refits. French SSBNs normally undertake patrols of two months' duration, with three months as the absolute maximum. All the vessels are based at Ile Longue near Brest and have special protection when transit-

ing to and from the port. This includes the French navy's sole Aérospatiale SA 321G Super Frelon ASW helicopter unit, Flottille 32F, which operates in groups of up to four helicopters to screen the boats, one helicopter dunking its sonar whilst the others stand back ready to attack if required.

Specification
‘L'Inflexible’ class
Displacement: 8,080 tons surfaced and 8,920 tons dived
Dimensions: length 128.7 m (422.2 ft); beam 10.6 m (34.8 ft); draught 10.0 m (32.8 ft)
Propulsion: one pressurized water-cooled reactor powering two steam turbines driving one shaft

Speed: 18 kts surfaced and 25 kts dived
Diving depth: 350 m (1,150 ft) operational and 465 m (1,525 ft) maximum
Armament: 16 launch tubes for 16 M4 submarine-launched ballistic missiles, and four 533-mm (21-in) bow tubes for 18 L5 ASW and F17 anti-ship torpedoes and SM.39 Exocet anti-ship missiles
Electronics: one DRUA 33 surface-search radar, one passive ESM system, one DLT D3 torpedo and Exocet fire-control system, one DSUX 21 sonar, one DUUX-5 ranging sonar and one underwater telephone
Complement: 127

Specification
'Le Redoutable' class
Displacement: 8,045 tons surfaced and 8,940 tons dived
Dimensions: length 128.7 m (422.2 ft); beam 10.6 m (34.8 ft); draught 10.0 m (32.8 ft)

Propulsion: one pressurized water-cooled reactor powering two steam turbines driving one shaft
Speed: 18 kts surfaced and 25 kts dived
Diving depth: 250 m (820 ft) operational and 330 m (1,085 ft) maximum
Armament: 16 launch tubes for 16 M4 or M20 submarine-launched ballistic missiles, and four 533-mm (21-in) bow tubes for 18 L5 ASW, F17 anti-ship torpedoes and SM.39 Exocet anti-ship missiles
Electronics: one DRUA-33 surface-search radar, one DLT D3 torpedo fire-

Above: The French try to maintain a minimum of two SNLEs on patrol at any one time, with submarines such as Le Terrible (S612) being screened on departure and return by French navy surface units, submarines and ASW aircraft in order to maintain security.

control system, one passive ESM system, one DSUV 23 or DSUX-21 sonar, one DUUX 2 ranging sonar and one underwater telephone
Complement: 135

FRANCE
M20 SLBM

The **Mer-Sol Balistique Stratégique M20** is essentially a variant of the earlier two-stage M2 with the Rita 11/P6 second stage converted to carry a single re-entry vehicle (RV) with an MR60 1.2-megaton yield thermonuclear warhead and associated penetration aids. Since initial deployment in 1977 aboard *L'Indomptable*, the missile has been refitted to carry the lighter but similar-yield MR61 warhead. Both types were specially hardened to resist damage from the electromagnetic pulse (EMP) and fast radiation produced when nuclear-tipped anti-ballistic missiles (from systems such a the ABM-1 'Galosh' network around Moscow) explode in their vicinity. The M20 is ejected by compressed air, and is the culmination of a missile programme that started design development in 1959 and entered operational service as the MSBS M1 in 1971. The development progressed through the uprated M2 that entered service in 1974 to the present M20. The whole 16 M20 missile outfit of a French SSBN can be launched within 15 minutes. From 1985 the M20 missile will be replaced aboard the last four of the 'Le Redoutable' class by the M4, which is virtually a new design for a MIRV payload. The last M20 missiles, however, will not be phased out until *Le Redoutable* herself is paid off in 1997.

Although due to be eventually superseded by the M4, the M20 will remain in service aboard the Le Redoutable. It is armed with a 1.2-megaton yield thermonuclear warhead that is specially hardened against the effects of defensive ABM nuclear weapon systems.

Specification
M20
Type: submarine-launched ballistic missile
Dimensions: length 10.4 m (34.1 ft); diameter 1.5 m (4 ft 11 in)
Launch weight: 20054.6 kg (44,213 lb)
Performance: range 3100 km (1,926 miles); CEP 930 m (1,017 yards)

Warhead: one re-entry vehicle with an MR61 1.2-megaton weapon and penetration aids
Propulsion: solid-propellant rocket
Guidance: inertial

FRANCE
M4 SLBM

Attaining operational capability with *L'Inflexible* in 1985, the **Mer-Sol Balistique Stratégique M4** was tested at sea in early March 1982 from the experimental missile submarine *Gymnote*. The design of the missile was started in 1976, and the missile was fired for the very first time from a land-based test pad in November 1980. The three-stage solid-propellant weapon has a payload of six multiple independent re-entry vehicles (MIRVs) of greater circular error probability (CEP) accuracy than previous French single-warhead SLBMs, with the added advantage of advanced penetration aids to defeat enemy ballistic missile defences. The interval between missile launchings is also shorter, and the possible launch depth is greater as a result of the use of powder charge injection, thus significantly improving the launch platform's survivability factor. All the French navy SSBNs except *Le Redoutable* are due to have the M4 retrofitted from 1985, and will thus have extensive modifications to their launch tubes, together with new fire-control and missile tube ejector systems. The refit schedule will be in the order *Le Terrible, Le Foudroyant, L'Indomptable* and *Le Tonnant*, and is to be part of the boats' normal overhaul cycles. The four 'Le Redoutables' are getting the improved M4.

The basic M4 entered service in April 1985. An improved version will arm four of the 'Le Redoutables'.

Specification
M4
Type: submarine-launched ballistic missile
Dimensions: length 11.05 m (36.25 ft); diameter 1.92 m (6 ft 3.6 in)
Launch weight: 35073.2 kg (77,323 lb)
Performance: range 4000 km (2,485 miles); CEP 460 m (503 yards)

Warhead: six MIRVs with TN-70 150-kiloton yield warheads
Propulsion: solid-propellant rocket
Guidance: inertial

Missile Submarine Development

With a genesis reaching back to German plans of World War II, the concept of the missile-armed submarine is not new. Both the American and Soviet navies made use of captured German technology in the post-war years, but it was in the 1950s that the modern conception of the nuclear-powered, nuclear-missile-armed submarine arose.

Although the precise origins of the American submarine-launched strategic missile programme cannot be traced, it is known that on 5 March 1946 the Chief of Naval Operations ordered the conversion of two World War II fleet submarines, the USS *Cusk* and USS *Carbanero*, to carry and fire two of the air-breathing Loon missiles which had been derived from the German V-1. At the same time as the first successful Loon was launched in March 1947 from the *Cusk*, development programmes for two indigenous long-range submarine bombardment missiles were in progress; these became the Rigel and Regulus. The former was subsequently cancelled in 1953 because of launcher problems, but in the year previous the fleet submarine USS *Tunny* had been converted to carry two Regulus I missiles, which could be fired from the surfaced submarine. An additional unit, the USS *Barbero*, was later converted along the same lines, and two more units, the USS *Grayback* and USS *Growler*, were completed on the stocks as missile launchers but with capacity for four missiles.

Nuclear power

With the advent of the nuclear reactor for submarine propulsion a further conventional boat, the USS *Halibut*, which had been ordered as a Regulus carrier, was reordered in 1956 with the new propulsion system and the ability to carry five missiles. She was to have been followed by a class of even larger nuclear-powered submarines each carrying four of the larger supersonic Regulus II follow-on missiles.

But in 1958 this new missile was cancelled and the submarines reordered as attack units.

The Regulus II had fallen foul of the Polaris ballistic missile. Evolved during the mid-1950s, this new type of underwater-launched missile required a projected force level of 30 submarines to be on station from a total of 45-50 units. To accommodate the 2220-km (1,380-mile) range interim Polaris A1 model a crash conversion programme was initiated in the late 1950s to install a 39.6-m (130-ft) long section for 16 missiles abaft the fin in the hulls of six 'Skipjack' class attack submarines to produce the 'George Washington' SSBN class. As these vessels were being launched so the six 'Ethan Allen' class vessels, designed from the keel up as SSBNs, were laid down. These were in effect ballistic missile versions of the contemporary 'Thresher' class SSNs and made effective use of that type's superior machinery-silencing techniques and deeper diving hull materials. Equipped with the Polaris A2 SLBMN they were rapidly followed down the production line by the still larger 31-strong 'Lafayette' and 'Benjamin Franklin' classes of SSBNs, the last 23 of which commissioned into service carrying the Polaris A3 missile. When the first Pacific Fleet SSBN carried out its first patrol at the end of 1964 so the five Regulus I submarines were phased out after seven years of patrols in the area. All of the 41 Polaris-equipped vessels were completed between 1959 and 1964, which still ranks as one of the major industrial and military achievements of recent times in the Western world.

One of the first launches of Polaris A3, in 1964, signalled the culmination of the astonishing scientific and industrial achievement which marked the Polaris programme. In the space of five years the USA had built 41 boats and established a strategic advantage over the USSR that was to last into the 1980s.

Now deactivated, the USS Robert E. Lee *(SSBN601), with four sister ships, comprised the 'George Washington' class of SSBNs that was converted from the 'Skipjack' class attack submarine design to give the world's first true ballistic missile submarines.*

Soviet systems

Meanwhile, in the Soviet Union during the 1950s the leadership, under Khrushchev after the death of Stalin, elevated Admiral Gorshkov to the navy commander-in-chief's post with the directive to build new missile-armed submarines and surface ships to defend the Soviet homeland. Before 1956, when Gorshkov became C-in-C, the Soviets had already had in development a submarine ballistic missile programme based on technology captured from the Germans at the end of World War II. This culminated in September 1955 when a conventionally armed R-11FM missile derived from the Soviet army's 'Scud' tactical ballistic missile was launched from a converted 'Zulu'

class conventional submarine. This was followed by five further 'Zulu V' conversions (1956-8, each with two missiles) and the 23 specially built Project 629 (built 1958-62, each with three missiles) 'Golf' class boats which carried the surface-launched R-13 (SS-N-4 'Sark') missile. In their usual manner of developing alternative strategic submarine systems the Soviets also designed and built the P-5 (SS-N-3C 'Shaddock') surface-launched inertially-guided 800-kiloton yield cruise missile which was tested in 1957 on a conventional submarine given the NATO codename 'Whiskey Single Cylinder'. This was followed by five 'Whiskey Twin Cylinder' (1959-61, each with two P-5s) and seven 'Whiskey Long Bin' (1961-

The follow-on class to the Soviet 'Twin Cylinder' conversions was the 'Whiskey Long Bin' type. This involved lengthening the hull and inserting a section into the sail to carry four SS-N-3C 'Shaddock' strategic cruise missile container-launchers at a fixed angle of 15 degrees.

5, each with four P-5s) conversions.

As these entered service so the Soviets also introduced their own nuclear-powered versions using a common design root. The SSBN class became known in the West as the 'Hotel I' (eight built 1959-62, each with three R-13s) whilst the SSGNs became the 'Echo I' (six built 1960-2, each with six P-5s). The latter was the only nuclear-powered class equipped with strategic cruise missiles because the Soviet navy was shifted from its strategic role in the early 1960s when the new land-based Strategic Rocket Forces assumed the task. Apart from deploying the submerged-launch R-21 (SS-N-5 'Serb') missile on seven of the 'Hotels' to give the 'Hotel II' subclass and on 13 of the 'Golfs' to give the 'Golf II' variant, the Soviet navy did not match the massive American SSBN build-up until the strategic role was reassigned to the navy as one of its primary roles. By this time Soviet military intelligence had obtained most of the relevant plans of the American 'Ethan Allen' class, together with British long-range sonar details. Thus in 1967 there entered service the first 'Yankee' SSBN that was very similar in appearance to the American class and equipped with a new long-range low frequency sonar of the type required for SSBN operations.

In a programme that matched America's SSBN construction rate, the Soviets built 34 units between 1967 and 1974 at two shipyards for

The first Soviet nuclear-powered ballistic missile submarine class was the 'Hotel' type. Reconfigured in the 1960s to carry the SS-N-5, these boats are now being phased out and are either being scrapped or converted to other roles such as submerged naval command posts.

Missile Submarine Development

eventual use off both coasts of the USA. However, because these vessels had to transit long distances through enemy-controlled waters to their patrol areas, the Soviets designed and tested new long-range SLBMs that could be fired from waters adjacent to the Soviet homeland and still hit targets in the USA. To accommodate these they simply took the 'Yankee' design and enlarged it to give the 12-tube 'Delta I' with the SS-N-8 and then the 16-tube 'Delta II' with the same missile. With MIRVing of submarine-launched missiles the Soviets again modified the 'Delta' to produce the 'Delta III' variant with 16 SS-N-18s.

As the Soviets introduced the first of the 'Delta' series the Americans began to deploy the Poseidon MIRV-equipped SLBM aboard their last 31 SSBNs to improve force capabilities. Its follow-on, the Trident, which offers longer range, was ultimately deemed to require a new submarine design with more missile tubes to obtain greater cost effectiveness. As an interim measure 12 of the Poseidon-equipped units were converted to carry the Trident I SLBM. The result of the new design programme was the 'Ohio' class which, with 24 missile tubes for initially the Trident I and then the Trident II when it becomes available, is the West's largest SSBN and will eventually be the only type in service with the US Navy.

As soon as the Soviets learnt of the new class they began design of their own counterpart, the incredibly large 'Typhoon' class, which attained operational status in 1983. With 20 missile tubes forward of the fin for the SS-N-20, the vessel is specifically designed for operations under the Arctic ice cap, a capability which is not matched by the West. In 1984, the Soviets launched their first of the 'Delta IV' class, also optimized for under-ice operation but armed with the SS-N-23 SLBM. Latest indications are that a new SSBN class will be built in the early 1990s, with the first 'Delta Is' retiring at about that time. Adhering to the SALT II Strategic Arms Limitation agreement, the Soviets have deactivated 14 of the 'Yankee' class while the Americans have retired all of their earliest SSBNs and are taking Poseidon armed boats out of service as each new 'Ohio' commissions.

Polaris and Trident

Of the other three SSBN operators, the UK built in the late 1960s the 'Resolution' class of four units with British technology but carrying the American Polaris A3 SLBM. These are due to be replaced in the mid-1990s by four 'Vanguard' class SSBNs carrying the Trident II missile system. The design will be larger than the current Polaris vessels but will have only 16 missile tubes rather than the 24 aboard comparable American submarines. France, the other European nation equipped with SSBNs, went her own way designing and building both the submarines and the missiles that they carry. The first class built was the 'Le Redoutable', the five units of which have been followed by a single interim unit, *L'Inflexible*, that is the forerunner of an entirely new design for the 1990s. More recently American intelligence has indicated that Communist China has made operational the first of the 8,800-ton 120-m (393.7-ft) long SSBNs known as the 'Xia' class. Fitted with 12 of the indigenous two-stage solid-propellant CSS-N-2 SLBM, a force of up to six units is expected to be operational by the late 1980s, targeted primarily against the Soviet Far East.

A 'Yankee I' class SSBN runs on the surface. The Soviets keep several units of this type off each coast of the United States to provide a minimum warning attack on time-sensitive targets such as Strategic Air Command bomber bases in the event of a nuclear war.

The 'Ohio' class of SSBN, much larger than its predecessors, is to be armed with the Trident II missile system. The D5 missile in that system will for the first time be accurate enough to allow submarines to attack 'hard' targets.

'Yankee' class SSBN

The **'Yankee' class** was the first modern Soviet SSBN to be built. The design was apparently based on the plans of the US 'Benjamin Franklin' and 'Lafayette' classes that were covertly obtained by Soviet military intelligence (GRU) in the early 1960s. Thirty-four units were built between 1967 and 1974 at the shipyards in Severodvinsk and Komsomolsk, the peak year being 1970 when 10 vessels were completed. The 'Yankees' are distinguishable from the later 'Deltas' by having a smaller rise to the 'turtle-back' missile compartment abaft the sail. In 1976 one unit was converted to a **'Yankee II'** class configuration in which the original 16 missile tubes were replaced by 12 larger units for the experimental solid-propellant SS-NX-17 SLBM. The 'Yankee II' also differs from the similar 12-round 'Delta I' by having a sloping forward edge to the 'turtle-back' casing of the missile tubes.

In order to comply with the SALT agreement a number of 'Yankee I' SSBNs have been deactivated as SLBM carriers. By early 1987 14 had been so treated, a number being converted to SSNs by the complete removal of the missile section of the hull. Another has become the trials platform for the new SS-NX-24 cruise missile.

At present three or four of 14 'Yankee I' boats, plus the odd 'Yankee II' in the Northern Fleet, are on station at any one time off the eastern seaboard of the USA, with a further unit either on transit to or from a patrol area. Overlaps do occur, and these occasionally raise the number of boats on patrol. Of the 10 'Yankee Is' in the Pacific Fleet two are on permanent patrol off the USA's western seaboard with another on transit to or from the patrol zones. The forward-deployed 'Yankees' are assigned the wartime role of destroying time-sensitive area targets such as SAC bomber alert bases and carriers/SSBNs in port, and of disrupting the American higher command echelons as much as possible to ease the task of follow-up ICBM strikes. More recently, NATO sources have in-

dicated that several of the 'Yankees' in each theatre have been switched to operate against theatre nuclear targets, with the submarines operating in sanctuary areas closer to the Soviet homeland. These vessels are thought to have replaced the older 'Hotel II' and 'Golf II' submarines in this role.

A Northern Fleet 'Yankee I' was scuttled on 6 October 1986, some 800km (500 miles) east of Bermuda. The boat had been severely damaged by what appeared to have been an explosion in one of the missile tubes.

Specification
'Yankee' class
Displacement: 7,700 tons surfaced and 9,300 dived
Dimensions: length 130.0 m (426.5 ft); beam 11.6 m (38.1 ft); draught 8.0 m (26.3 ft)
Propulsion: two pressurized water-cooled reactors powering four steam turbines driving two shafts

Speed: 20 kts surfaced and 27 kts dived
Diving depth: 400 m (1,315 ft) operational and 600 m (1,970 ft) maximum
Armament: 16 ('Yankee I') or 12 ('Yankee II') launch tubes for 16 SS-N-6 ('Yankee I') or 12 SS-NX-17 ('Yankee II') submarine-launched ballistic missiles, and six 533-mm (21-in) bow tubes for a maximum of 12 533-mm (21-in) weapons, though the normal load is eight 533-mm (21-in) ASW/anti-ship torpedoes and six 406-mm (16-in) ASW torpedoes

A total of 34 'Yankee I' class submarines were constructed in a relatively short space of time at the Severodvinsk and Komsomolsk shipyards. Some 14 units of the class have now been converted to other duties.

Apparently built with the aid of Polaris missile submarine plans stolen from the Americans, the 'Yankee I' class, with its SS-N-6 missiles, formed the major part of the Soviet SSBN fleet in the early 1970s.

Electronics: one 'Snoop Tray' surface-search radar, one low-frequency bow sonar, one medium-frequency torpedo fire-control sonar, VHF/SHF/UHF communications systems, one VLF towed communications buoy, one ELF floating antenna, one 'Brick Group' ESM suite, one 'Cod Eye' navigation system and one 'Park Lamp' direction-finding antenna
Complement: 130

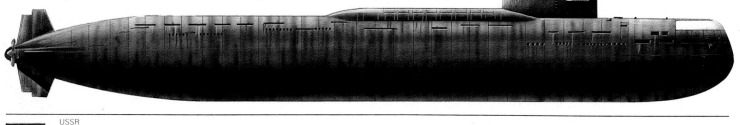

 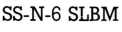

SS-N-6 SLBM

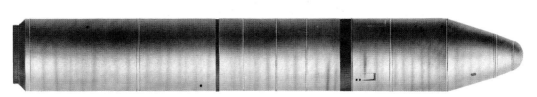

The photographs that have been released of what was thought to be the SS-N-6 are in fact of a competitive prototype that was never taken into service. Such ruses are a common part of Soviet disinformation exercises. The actual **SS-N-6** was tested on a diesel-electric 'Golf' class submarine that was converted around 1970 to carry and fire six such weapons in a lengthened sail structure that was added to an 18-m (59-ft) extension to the hull. Being a third-generation weapon, the missile is actually something of a hybrid as it utilizes components and technology derived from the land-based SS-11 ICBM. It is a single-stage SLBM with liquid-propellant propulsion. The original 2400-km (1,490-mile) range SS-N-

6 Mod 1 with a single 700-kiloton yield warhead entered service two years before the 'Golf' trials boat used to test the much improved and lighter **SS-N-6 Mod 2** variant in 1972. This missile uses a 650-kiloton warhead instead of the previous one and has a 600-km (375-mile) increase in range, which enables 'Yankees' cruising off either US seaboard to provide full target coverage from the 183-m (600-ft) contour. At the same time the **SS-N-6 Mod 3** began

development, initial deployment happening in 1974, one year after the SS-N-6 Mod 2. This third variant has the same range as its predecessor, but the single RV has been replaced by two 350-kiloton yield multiple re-entry vehicles (MRVs) for use against large area targets such as cities. By 1985 those 'Yankee Is' that were left in service had either SS-N-6 Mod 1 or SS-N-6 Mod 3 missiles in their tubes.

Now being used in its Mod 3 version with two Multiple Re-entry Vehicle warheads, the SS-N-6 arms the 'Yankee I' class of SSBN.

The 'Yankee I' class SSBN that was scuttled in mid-Atlantic in October 1986 was severely damaged by a fire in one of the missile tubes. It is likely that an accidental ignition of the liquid propellant in the SS-N-6 caused an explosion, which killed three of the crew according to Soviet sources. After a short salvage attempt, the boat and it's dangerous cargo was scuttled in over 5000m (more than 16,000ft) of water.

Predecessor to the SS-N-6 SLBM was the SS-N-5 'Serb'. This utilized a cold gas ejection system to fire the missile clear of the launch platform, where the main rocket motor was ignited. The 'Yankee' class SSBNs use a similar system to eject the SS-N-6 missiles from their launch tubes.

USSR

'Delta I', 'Delta II' and Delta III' class SSBNs

The **'Delta I' class** design was an enlargement of the previous 'Yankee' class design. Built initially at Severodvinsk and then at Komsomolsk in the Soviet Far East, the 'Delta I' was the world's largest undersea craft when the first unit was completed in 1972. The eighteenth and last of the class was completed at Komsomolsk in 1977. Designated a ballistic missile submarine (*podvodnaya lodka raketnaya krylataya* or PLRK) by the Soviets, the class carries two parallel rows of six missile tubes for the SS-N-8 missile aft of the sail, which is set forward with diving planes on each side.

In 1975 at Severodvinsk an interim batch of four **'Delta II' class** units was constructed. These were essentially the earlier design lengthened by 16.2 m (53.2 ft) to make possible the incorporation of a further four missile tubes to match contemporary Western SSBNs. These boats were followed in 1976 by the first units of the **'Delta III' class**. They are similar to the 'Delta II' boats but have the 'turtle-back' structure aft of the sail increased in height to accommodate the longer and more capable SS-N-18 in the missile tubes. A

total of 14 were built before production ended in 1984, and the improved **'Delta IV' class** emerged. At least eight of these boats are expected, with four having been launched by early 1987, all serving with the Northern Fleet. The 10 'Delta I', four 'Delta II' and 10 'Delta III' class vessels in the Northern Fleet have patrol areas in the Greenland, Norwegian and Barents Seas with one vessel normally on patrol in each location. More recently it has been revealed that a further unit is deployed in the eastern Atlantic, probably as far south as the Azores, in order to complicate yet further the task of US defence radars. In 1986, American intelligence revealed that the 'Delta IV' is designed for operations around and beneath the polar ice. It can surface through *polnyas*, or weak spots in the ice, to fire its 8300km (5,200 mile) range SS-N-23 missiles. In the Pacific Fleet only two of the eight 'Delta I' class and four 'Delta III' are on patrol at any one time, one in the Sea of Okhotsk and the other in the Bering Sea. However, in time of tension the number of units on patrol would be increased considerably so that an effective second

strike force would be available in a protracted nuclear exchange. The Soviets have been practising SLBM missile resupply from tenders in protected areas, whilst those submarines in port or under refit would for protection either be dispersed to concrete-hardened tunnels built into cliffs or be submerged in the deep fjords that lie just off their piers.

The first unit of the 'Delta' class (later to become known as the 'Delta I') was completed at Severodvinskin 1972. These boats, the largest submarines ever built up to that time, are likely to start being replaced by a new SSBN class in the 1990s.

Above: The ominous shape of a Delta III is similar to that of the Delta II, but with an even higher 'whaleback' to house the longer-ranged and larger SS-N-18 missiles.

Only four 'Delta II' class submarines were built, as an interim design. The only difference between the vessels and the earlier 'Delta Is' is an increase in hull length.

'Typhoon' SSBN and SS-N-20 'Sturgeon' SLBM

A true monster of the deep, the Typhoon has been designed for operations under the polar ice. Its huge size enables it to be armed with missiles capable of hitting the continental USA without ever having to leave northern Soviet waters.

The **'Typhoon' class** nuclear powered ballistic missile boats are by far the largest submarines ever built. They are thought to have a triple pressure hull – two 'Delta' type hulls side by side surmounted by a third, smaller pressure vessel from which the large sail, or fin rises. This third hull probably contains the control section. The whole is enclosed by a single outer skin, and the construction gives considerable protection against current Western ASW weapons. In overall size a 'Typhoon' is almost half as long again as the US 'Ohio' class Trident missile-carrying submarines, and has a displacement some 9,500 tons greater when running on the surface. It is thought that the class has been built specifically for operations with the Soviet Northern Fleet in the Arctic icepack. The two parallel rows of missile tubes fitted forward of the stub-like sail aft of the craft's centre point, together with the high-rise hull and retractable bow hydroplanes, allows the submarine to break easily through the spots of thin ice (known as *polnyas*) within the Arctic ice shelf.

The first unit was laid down in 1975 at Severodvinsk and launched in 1980. It achieved operational status in 1983. A total of four have now been completed, whilst there are at least another four under series construction in a special covered shipyard.

To arm the 'Typhoon' the Soviets started to design a fifth-generation SLBM, the **SS-N-20** (Soviet designation RSM-52), from 1973. First-flight tested in 1980, the SS-N-20 is a three-stage

solid-propellant MIRVed missile with a range of 8300 km (5,160 miles). This allows the submarine to fire the weapon from within the Arctic circle and still hit a target anywhere within the continental USA.

Specification
'Typhoon' class
Displacement: 26,000 tons surfaced and 30,000 tons dived
Dimensions: length 170.0 m (557.7 ft); beam 23.0 m (75.5 ft); draught not known
Propulsion: four pressurized water-cooled reactors powering four steam turbines driving two shafts
Speed: 20 kts surfaced and 30 kts dived
Diving depth: 400 m (1,315 ft) operational and 600 m (1,970 ft) maximum
Armament: 20 launch tubes for 20 SS-N-20 submarine-launched ballistic missiles, and six 533-mm (21-in) bow tubes for a maximum of 24 533-mm (21-in) weapons, though the normal load is 16 533-mm (21-in) ASW/anti-ship torpedoes and 14 406-mm (16-in) ASW torpedoes
Electronics: one 'Snoop Pair' surface-search radar, one 'Rim Hat' ESM system, one low-frequency bow sonar, one medium-frequency torpedo fire-control sonar, two VLF towed communications buoys, one ELF floating antenna, one 'Park Lamp' DF antenna, one 'Shot Gun' VHF communication system and one 'Pert Spring' Satnav system
Complement: 150

The mammoth Typhoon SSBN is thought to be comprised of two 'Delta' class hulls in a side-by-side configuration with the missile tube compartment forward of the sail.

Such submarines are being built for operations beneath and within the polar ice regions of the northern hemisphere.

Specification
SS-N-20
Type: submarine-launched ballistic missile
Dimensions: length 15.0 m (49.2 ft); diameter 2.0 m (6 ft 6.7 in)
Launch weight: 60000 kg (132,000 lb)
Performance: range 8300 km (5,160 miles); CEP 600 m (565 yards)
Warhead: nine 500 kiloton MIRVs
Propulsion: solid-propellant rocket
Guidance: stellar-inertial

SS-N-8 'Sawfly', SS-N-18 'Stingray' and SS-N-23 'Skiff' SLBMs

Introduced into operational service in 1972 aboard the 'Delta I' class SSBN, the **SS-N-8** is a fourth-generation SLBM that began flight trials back in 1969 aboard a lengthened 'Hotel' class nuclear-powered ballistic missile submarine (codenamed 'Hotel III') converted to carry and fire three of the missiles in an enlarged sail. A second trials vessel was converted in the early 1970s from a diesel-electric 'Golf' class ballistic missile submarine. Code-named 'Golf III' and fitted to carry and fire six SS-N-8s, the vessel has now been dismantled under the SALT limitations. The SS-N-8 is a two-stage liquid-propellant missile that, in its SS-N-8 Mod 1 form, has a range of 7800 km (4,845 miles). To ensure accuracy over that range, stellar-inertial guidance is used to update the navigation computer by utilizing two 'star fixes' for mid-course flight profile corrections. In 1977 an engineering improved variant, the **SS-N-8 Mod 2**, entered service with

a range of 9100 km (5,655 miles) and the same warhead.

However, two years before this the Soviets had begun flight testing of the two stage fourth-generation 6500-km (4,040-mile) range storable liquid-propellant **SS-N-18** (Soviet designation RSM-50) which became operational on the 'Delta III' class in late 1976. The SS-N-18 Mod 1 version was also the first Soviet SLBM to feature MIRV capability. This was followed in 1979 by the **SS-N-18 Mod 2** with a single warhead but much greater range. The SS-N-18 Mod 1 was then superseded in the same year by the **SS-N-18 Mod 3** which has a larger number of lower-yield MIRVs and the same range.

In 1985 the **SS-N-23** entered service aboard the 'Delta IV'. This is a fifth generation, three-stage liquid-propellant SLBM with a MIRV warhead package of the type that first appeared on the SS-N-18 Mod 3. It is probable that the SS-N-23 will be retrofitted to

the 14 'Delta III' class boats.

Specification
SS-N-8
Type: submarine-launched ballistic missile
Dimensions: length 12.9 m (42.3 ft); diameter 1.65 m (5 ft 5 in)
Launch weight: 30000 kg (66,000 lb)
Performance: range (Mod 1) 7800 km (4,845 miles) or (Mod 2) 9100 km (5,655 miles); CEP (Mod 1) 1410 m (1,540 yards) or (Mod 2) 1550 m (1,695 yards)
Warhead: one 800-kiloton re-entry vehicle
Propulsion: liquid-propellant rocket
Guidance: stellar-inertial

Specification
SS-N-18
Type: submarine-launched ballistic missile
Dimensions: length 13.6 m (44.6 ft); diameter 1.8 m (5 ft 10.9 in)
Launch weight: 34000 kg (74,956 lb)

Performance: range (Mods 1 and 3) 6500 km (4,040 miles) or (Mod 2) 8000 km (4,970 miles); CEP (Mods 1 and 3) 1410 m (1,540 yards) or (Mod 2) 1550 m (1,695 yards)
Warhead: three 200-kiloton yield MIRVs in Mod 1, one 450-kiloton RV in Mod 2 or seven 100-kiloton MIRVs in Mod 3
Propulsion: liquid-propellant rocket
Guidance: stellar-inertial

Specification
SS-N-23
Type: submarine-launched ballistic missile
Dimensions: length 14.1 m (46.3 ft); diameter 2 m (6.7 ft)
Launch weight: 40000 kg (88,000 lb)
Performance: range 8300 km (5,190 miles); CEP 900 m (984 yards)
Warhead: Ten 100 kiloton MIRVs
Propulsion: liquid propellant rocket
Guidance: stellar-inertial

'Delta III' class SSBN

Specification
'Delta' classes

Displacement: 8,750 tons surfaced and 10,000 tons dived for Delta I, 9,750 tons surfaced and 11,000 tons dived for Delta II/III, 10,100 tons surfaced and 11,600 tons dived for Delta IV

Dimensions: length 136.5 m (447.8 ft) for Delta I, 152.7 m (501 ft) for Delta II/III and 156.5 (516.7 ft) for Delta IV, beam 12.0 m (39.4 ft), draught 8.7 m (28.5 ft)

Propulsion: two pressurized water cooled reactors powering four steam turbines driving two shafts with five-bladed (Delta IV seven-bladed) propellers

Speed: 20 kts surfaced and 26 kts (Delta I), 25 kts (Delta II), 24 kts (Delta III) or 23.5 kts (Delta IV) dived

Diving depth: 400 m (1,315 ft) operational and 600 m (1.970 ft) maximum

Armament: 12 (Delta I) or 16 (Delta II) launch tubes for 12 (Delta I) or 16 (Delta II) SS-N-8 submarine-launched ballistic missiles, or 16 launch tubes (Delta III) for 16 SS-N-18 Submarine-launched ballistic missiles or 16 launch tubes (Delta IV) for 16 SS-N-23 submarine-launched ballistic missiles, and six 533 mm (21 in) bow tubes for a maximum of 12 533 mm (21 in) weapons though the normal load is eight 533 mm (21 in) ASW/anti-ship torpedoes and six 406 mm (16 in) ASW torpedoes

Electronics: one 'Snoop Tray' surface search radar, one low frequency bow sonar, one medium frequency torpedo fire-control sonar, one low frequency towed sonar array (Delta IV only), VHF/SHF/UHF communications, one VLF towed communications buoy, one ELF floating antenna, one 'Cod Eye' navigation system, one 'Pert Spring' satellite navigation system, one 'Park Lamp' direction finder, one 'Brick Group' ESM suite

Complement: 130 (Delta I), 140 (Delta II/III) and 150 (Delta IV)

Above: Construction of the 'Delta III' class peaked at Severodvinsk at the rate of two units per year. The hatches in the aft part of the raised rear decking are believed to cover towed very low frequency communications buoys, whilst just forward of the rudder can be seen the top of a submarine rescue buoy marker.

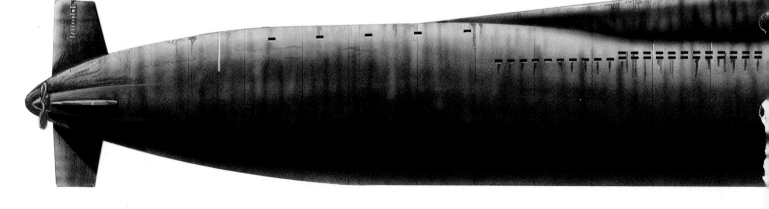

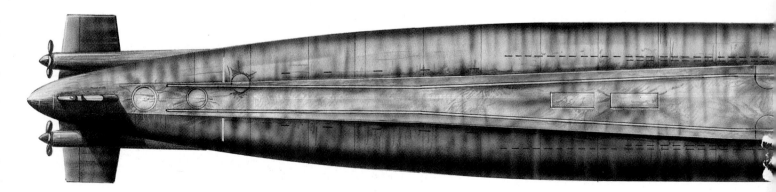

16

Soviet `Delta III´class Ballistic Missile Submarine

Below: For many years the world's largest underwater vessel, the 'Delta III' class of ballistic missile submarine is a mainstay of current Soviet strategic capability. A total of 14 were built at Severodvinsk, with the class being replaced on the stocks by the 'Delta IV' derivative, armed with SS-N-23 missiles. At present the 'Delta III' class is armed with 16 SS-N-18 MIRV missiles, each with several low-yield warheads. The SS-N-18 has a range of up to 8000 km (almost 5,000 miles).

'Benjamin Franklin' and 'Lafayette' class SSBNs

Although actually two classes, the 12 'Benjamin Franklin' class and 19 'Lafayette' class submarines are very similar in appearance. The main difference is that the former were built with quieter machinery outfits. All have diesel-electric stand-by propulsion, snort masts and an auxiliary propeller. As built, the first eight 'Lafayettes' carried 16 single 800-kiloton yield warhead 2775-km (1,725-mile) range Polaris A2 SLBMs, the rest receiving the Polaris A3 fitted with three 200-kiloton yield MRVs. Of the Polaris A2 boats four (SSBN620 and SSBN622-625) were rearmed with the Polaris A3 during refuelling overhauls in 1968-70. In August of the latter year SSBN627 became the first of the Poseidon C3 SLBM conversions, whilst between September 1978 and December 1982 12 units were further converted to carry and fire the Trident I C4 SLBM. The remaining units serve with the Atlantic Fleet, several being forward-deployed to a submarine tender located at Holy Loch on the River Clyde in Scotland. Several units with Poseidon missiles have been reassigned to the theatre nuclear role in support of NATO. Each American SSBN is assigned two crews designated Blue and Gold, one manning the vessel during a 70-day patrol and helping during the following 32-day minor overhaul before the other crew takes the vessel out on patrol. Every six years each boat undergoes a complete overhaul and reactor refuelling that lasts about 22-23 months. The individual submarines that comprise the two classes are the USS *Lafayette* (SSBN616), USS *Alexander Hamilton* (SSBN617), USS *John Adams* (SSBN620), USS *James Monroe* (SSBN622), USS *Woodrow Wilson* (SSBN624), USS *Henry Clay* (SSBN625), USS *Daniel Webster* (SSBN626), USS *James Madison* (SSBN627), USS *Tecumseh* (SSBN628), USS *Daniel Boone* (SSBN629), USS *John C. Calhoun* (SSBN630), USS *Ulysses S. Grant* (SSBN631), USS *Von Steuben* (SSBN632), USS *Casimir Pulaski* (SSBN633), USS *Stonewall Jackson* (SSBN634), USS *Nathaniel Greene* (SSBN636), USS *Benjamin Franklin* (SSBN640), USS *Simon Bolivar* (SSBN641), USS *Kamehameha* (SSBN642), USS *George Bancroft* (SSBN643), USS *Lewis and Clark* (SSBN644), USS *James K. Polk* (SSBN645), USS *George C. Marshall* (SSBN654), USS *Henry L. Stimson* (SSBN655), USS *George Washington Carver* (SSBN656), USS *Francis Scott Key* (SSBN657), USS *Mariano G. Vallejo* (SSBN658) and USS *Will Rogers* (SSBN659). Those from SSBN640 onwards, are of the 'Benjamin Franklin' subclass. In line with the SALT-II agreement limits, the 'Lafayette' class boat USS *Sam Rayburn* (SSBN 635) was deactivated, followed in 1986 by the USS *Nathan Hale* (SSBN 623) and the USS *Andrew Jackson* (SSBN 619). As the Trident armed 'Ohio' class enters service, more will follow.

Specification
'Lafayette' and 'Benjamin Franklin' classes
Displacement: 7,250 tons surfaced and 8,250 tons dived
Dimensions: length 129.5 m (425.0 ft); beam 10.1 m (33.0 ft); draught 9.6 m (31.5 ft)
Propulsion: one S5W pressurized water-cooled reactor powering two steam turbines driving one shaft
Speed: 28 kts surfaced and 25 kts dived
Diving depth: 350 m (1,150 ft) operational and 465 m (1,525 ft) maximum
Armament: 16 launch tubes for 16 Trident I C4 (SSBNs 627, 629, 630, 632-634, 640, 641, 643, 655, 657 and 658) or for 16 Poseidon C3 (remainder) submarine-launched ballistic missiles, and four 533-mm (21-in) bow tubes for 12 Mk 48 ASW/anti-ship torpedoes
Electronics: one BPS-11A or BPS-15 surface-search radar, one ESM system, one BQR-7 sonar, one BQR-15 towed-array sonar, one BQR-19 sonar, one BQR-21 sonar, one BQS-4 sonar, and extensive communications and navigation systems
Complement: 142 ('Lafaytte') or 159 ('Benjamin Franklin')

Left: The C4 Trident I-equipped 'Benjamin Franklin' class vessel USS Mariano G. Vallejo (SSBN658).

Below: The last 12 units built to the 'Lafayette' SSBN design were officially designated the 'Benjamin Franklin' class because they were completed with quieter propulsion machinery. Of these vessels, six have been converted to carry the C4 Trident I SLBM in place of the C3 Poseidon.

Lockheed UGM-73A Poseidon C3 SLBM

By 1964 two follow-on designs to the Polaris were under review. One subsequently evolved into the **Lockheed UGM-73A Poseidon C3** SLBM which could use the launch tubes of the existing fleet of SSBNs. Ultimately 31 out of the original 41 SSBNs built were refitted to carry the Poseidon, although some were later fitted to carry the Trident I. The Poseidon C3 entered operational service in 1970 after initial flight tests in 1968. The missile introduced the concept of MIRVing to American SLBMs. Up to a maximum of 14 Mk 3 independently targeted RVs (each with a yield of 40 kilotons) can be carried over a range of 4000 km (2,485 miles), but with the normal loading of 10 MIRVs the range is increased to 5200 km (3,230 miles). Penetration aids to confuse defence systems are also carried. The two-stage solid-propellant missiles are targeted mainly against soft military and industrial targets such as airfields, storage depots, and above-ground command and control facilities. A total of 619 operational missiles was bought, and 256 of these plus their 2,560 associated warheads are still afloat on the remaining 16 Poseidon-equipped SSBNs. Two or three Poseidon vessels are always assigned to the NATO high command for the theatre nuclear role in Europe and the Mediterranean. The Poseidon will eventually be replaced by the Trident II.

A C3 Poseidon SLBM just after launch. One problem for an SSBN commander is that he would prefer all his SLBMs to be launched in one go and not in several groups because each firing points to his location.

The USS John C. Calhoun *(SSBN630) enters the US Navy's forward deployment SSBN base at Holy Loch on the River Clyde in Scotland after the 1,000th American ballistic missile submarine patrol.*

Lockheed UGM-73A Poseidon C3 SLBM (continued)

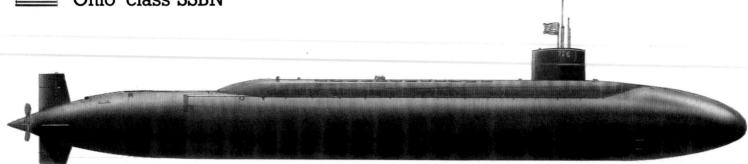

Specification
Poseidon C3
Type: submarine-launched ballistic missile
Dimensions: length 10.4 m (34.1 ft); diameter 1.9 m (6 ft 2 in)
Launch weight: 29030 kg (64,000 lb)
Performance: range 4000-5200 km (2,485-3,230 miles) depending on the number of MIRVs carried; CEP 553 m (605 yards)

Warhead: between 10 and 14 MIRVs each with a 40-kiloton weapon
Propulsion: solid-propellant rocket
Guidance: inertial

Still in service aboard 16 'Lafayette/ Benjamin Franklin' class SSBNs, the C3 Poseidon can carry up to 14

relatively low-yield warheads to attack independent targets.

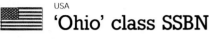

USA
'Ohio' class SSBN

Destined to become the mainstay of the American SSBN fleet in the next decade and after, the 'Ohio' class will eventually carry the D-5 Trident II SLBM that will allow these submarines to operate in patrol zones close to the American coasts, where they can be protected more easily.

Designed in the early 1970s as the follow-on SSBN to the 'Benjamin Franklin' and 'Lafayette' classes, the lead ship of the **'Ohio' class**, the USS **Ohio** (SSBN726) was contracted to the Electric Boat Division of the General Dynamics Corporation in July 1974. As the result of an unfortunate series of problems both in Washington, DC, and at the shipyard, the lead vessel did not run her first sea trials until June 1981, and was not finally commissioned until November of that year, three years

late. Since then further delays have occurred in the programme but the rate of production is now beginning to get back on schedule.

Each submarine is expected to have a 12-month reactor refuelling refit every nine years and will work a patrol period of 70 days with the next 25 days spent alongside a tender or jetty readying for the next patrol. Because of their longer-range Trident missiles, the 'Ohio' class boats have patrol areas in the remoter parts of the world's

oceans, making effective Soviet ASW measures against them virtually impossible for the foreseeable future, especially as the boats are acoustically very quiet.

At present eight 'Ohios' are in commission: the *Ohio*, USS **Michigan** (SSBN727), USS **Florida** (SSBN728), USS **Georgia** (SSBN729), USS **Henry M. Jackson** (SSBN730), USS **Alabama** (SSBN731), USS **Alaska** (SSBN732) and USS **Nevada** (SSBN733). Five more are building and at least another 11 are

projected. The first eight are based in the Pacific at Bangor, Washington, whilst the remainder will go to the Atlantic Fleet at Kings Bay, Georgia, to replace Poseidon boats. From SSBN734 onwards the 'Ohios' will carry the Trident II missile in their 20 launch tubes whilst the others will be refitted at the first available opportunity.

Specification
'Ohio' class
Displacement: 16,764 tons surfaced and 18,750 tons dived
Dimensions: length 170.7 m (560.0 ft); beam 12.8 m (42.0 ft); draught 10.8 m (35.5 ft)
Propulsion: one S8G pressurized water-cooled natural-circulation reactor powering a turbo-reduction drive to one shaft
Speed: 20 kts surfaced and 24 kts dived
Diving depth: 300 m (985 ft) operational and 500 m (1,640 ft) maximum
Armament: 24 launch tubes for 24 Trident I C4 submarine-launched ballistic missiles, and four 533-mm (21-in) bow tubes for an unknown number of Mk 48 ASW/anti-ship torpedoes
Electronics: one BPS-15A surface-search radar, one WLR-8(V) ESM system, one BQQ-6 sonar, one BQS-13 sonar, one BQS-15 sonar, one BQR-19 sonar, one BQR-23 towed-array sonar, and extensive communications and navigation systems
Complement: 171

The USS Ohio *(SSBN726) under way. This class represents the latest in American technology, and is designed to defeat all foreseeable ASW threats that the Soviets are known to possess or believed to be capable of developing.*

Above: Missile submarines rely on secrecy for their own protection, the latest sonars being used to evade any hostile tactical confrontation.

Below: Although much better off than crewmen aboard conventional submarines, those on long submerged SSBN patrols can still find life tedious.

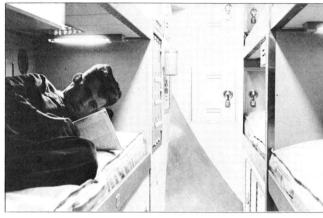

Above: The immense size of the 'Ohio' class can be gauged from this internal view of the C4 Trident I missile tube compartment. Any

maintenance on the missiles whilst in their tubes is performed here, as are the continual checks to see if they are still functional.

Below: The primary offensive station aboard any SSBN is the missile fire control panel. Should the unthinkable occur, the men in these

positions would have the awesome responsibility of exercising the final option, and potentially causing destruction on an unparalleled scale.

'Resolution' class SSBN

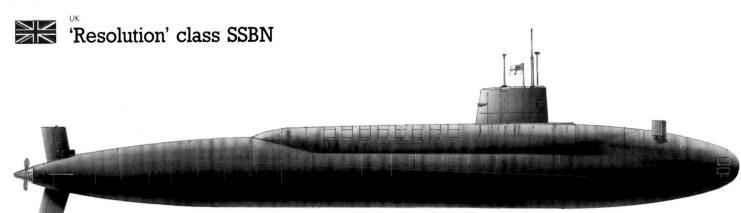

Although constructed in the United Kingdom, the four 'Resolution' class SSBNs have a considerable amount of their internal systems based on American components that were used in the 'Lafayette' class.

Officially stated in February 1963 was the British government's intention to order four or five **'Resolution' class** Polaris missile-equipped 7,000-ton nuclear-powered submarines that would take over the nuclear deterrent role from the Royal Air Force's V-bomber force from 1968 onwards. The first two pairs of boats were ordered in May 1963 from Vickers Shipbuilding Ltd, Barrow-in-Furness, and Cammell Laird & Co. Ltd, Birkenhead; the option on a fifth unit was cancelled in February 1965. With characteristics very similar to the American 'Lafayettes' the lead ship HMS *Resolution* (S22) was launched in September 1966 and commissioned in October of the following year. The second vessel, HMS *Repulse* (S23), followed in September 1968, with the third, HMS *Renown* (S24), and fourth, HMS *Revenge* (S27), commissioning in November 1968 and December 1969 respectively. Early in 1968 the *Resolution* sailed to Florida in the United States for missile launch trials, making the UK's first successful Polaris launch on 15 February. Four months later she sailed on her first deterrent patrol. As in French and American SSBNs, two crews (Port and Starboard) are used to maximize the time spent at sea, each patrol lasting around three months. When not aboard the crews take leave and undergo refresher training at the 10th Submarine Squadron base at Faslane on the Clyde. According to current plans the Polaris boats are to be replaced on a one-for-one basis from 1994 onwards by four 15,000 ton 'Vanguard' class Trident II missile-carrying submarines. All four boats have recently undergone conversions during normal overhauls to carry the Polaris A3TK variant fitted with the Chevaline MRV warhead system.

Specification
'Resolution' class
Displacement: 7,500 tons surfaced and 8,400 tons dived
Dimensions: length 129.5 m (425.0 ft); beam 10.1 m (33.0 ft); draught 9.1 m (30.0 ft)
Propulsion: one pressurized water-cooled reactor powering two steam turbines driving one shaft
Speed: 20 kts surfaced and 25 kts dived

Diving depth: 350 m (1,150 ft) operational and 465 m (1,525 ft) maximum
Armament: 16 launch tubes for 16 Polaris A3TK submarine-launched ballistic missiles, and six 533-mm (21-in) bow tubes for 18 Mk 24 Tigerfish ASW/anti-ship torpedoes
Electronics: one Type 1007 surface-search radar, one type 2001 bow sonar, one Type 2007 sonar, one Type 2023 retractable towed-array sonar,

HMS Revenge (S27). In 1983 she became the second of Britain's Polaris submarines to operate with the upgraded Polaris A3TK Chevaline system designed to penetrate Soviet ABM defences around Moscow.

one Type 2019 intercept sonar, one ESM suite, and an extensive communications outfit
Complement: 154

Lockheed UGM-27C Polaris A3 SLBM

Now the sole user of the US-designed **Lockheed UGM-27C Polaris A3** SLBM, the Royal Navy has recently had its stockpile of Polaris missiles re-engined so that it can continue as the UK's nuclear deterrent force. The British buy of the missile was, according to US Congressional records, 102 with another 31 purchased later to make up attrition. These were equipped with three British-designed and -built 200-kiloton yield MRVs for use against area targets such as cities and oilfields: the effect of a single high-yield warhead falls off rapidly with distance from the point of impact, whereas several smaller-yield weapons

around the target perimeter cause significantly more damage. However, as a result of Soviet developments in ABM defences it was decided in the early 1970s that countermeasures would have to be built into the Polaris system. The result was the **Polaris A3TK Chevaline** project, which had its roots in a cancelled US warhead programme called Antelope. Chevaline involves the replacement of the 200-kiloton MRVs with three 60-kiloton weapons hardened against EMP and fast radiation, as well as the modification of the carrier bus to present defending radar systems with a confusingly large number of credible threats at the same

Now used only by the United Kingdom, the Polaris A3 SLBM has undergone a rocket-motor replacement programme.

time, with the result that the incoming warhead picture is swamped. Although not specified, these modifications are believed to include the fitting of chaff penetration aids and the carriage of about a dozen decoys. Both the warheads and decoys are carried in the Manoeuvrable Penetration Aid Carrier (PAC) bus. The first boat to be retrofitted was HMS *Renown* in 1982, followed by HMS *Resolution* (1984), HMS *Repulse* (1986) and HMS *Re-*

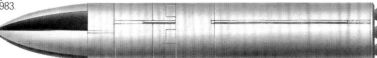

venge (1988). The first Chevaline patrol was carried out by *Renown* in 1983.

Specification
Polaris A3TK
Type: submarine-launched ballistic missile

Equipping the 'R' class submarines of the Royal Navy, the Polaris A3 is the last model of the pioneering SLBM to remain operational.

Dimensions: length 9.8 m (32.2 ft); diameter 1.4 m (4 ft 6 in)
Launch weight: 15876 kg (35,000 lb)
Performance: range 4748 km (2,950 miles); CEP 930 m (1,017 yards)
Warhead: three 60-kiloton yield MRVs plus up to a dozen decoys and chaff penetration aids
Propulsion: solid-propellant rocket
Guidance: inertial

USA
Lockheed UGM-96A Trident I C4 SLBM

The purpose of the **Lockheed UGM-96A Trident I C4** missile development programme was essentially to increase the range of American SLBMs to allow the use of larger and remoter patrol areas. A three-stage solid-propellant missile, the Trident I was flight tested in 1977, becoming operational two years later aboard the SSBN conversions of the 'Benjamin Franklin' and 'Lafayette' classes. The first two stages of the missile are essentially the same as those fitted to the earlier Poseidon C3 SLBM, but the third stage is fitted with stellar-inertial guidance to give the required accuracy over the longer range. The first eight 'Ohio' class SSBNs are being fitted to carry the Trident I, but these will eventually be retrofitted to carry the yet longer-ranged Trident II in the early 1990s. Rapid onboard targeting to another pre-planned target co-ordinates package is possible, but a far lengthier operation is required if the system has to be fed new target co-ordinates from an external source. As increased range was considered to be more important than accuracy improvement, a CEP comparable with that of the Poseidon was accepted. The use of higher-yield warheads, however, allows more hardened military and industrial targets to be engaged on a satisfactory basis than was possible with the earlier missile, and as such it is believed that one Trident-equipped submarine will have its re-entry vehicles assigned to NATO for use in the theatre nuclear role. A total of 740 missiles is to be procured, with eight MIRVs per missile. Eventually, in the next century, the American SSBN force consist only of 'Ohio' class boats with Trident II missiles.

Specification
Trident I C4
Type: submarine-launched ballistic missile
Dimensions: length 10.4 m (34.1 ft); diameter 1.9 m (6 ft 2.8 in)

Launch weight: 31751 kg (70,000 lb)
Performance: range 6808 km (4,230 miles); CEP 549 m (600 yards)
Warhead: eight MIRVs each with a 100-kiloton weapon
Propulsion: solid-propellant rocket
Guidance: stellar-inertial

At enormous cost, the Trident programme will provide the seaborne element of the US strategic deterrent for the foreseeable future. Trident I employs the 7400-km (4,600-mile) ranged C4 missile, which will eventually be replaced by the D5.

Fitted to 12 of the 'Lafayette/Benjamin Franklin' class SSBNs and the new 'Ohios', the C-4 Trident 1 SLBM proves the nearest American equivalent to the long-range Soviet SLBMs but with more accurate payloads of MIRV warheads.

USA
Lockheed Trident II D5 SLBM

The **Lockheed Trident II D5** is the result of an improved accuracy programme for American SLBMs begun in Fiscal Year 1975. Scheduled for operational deployment on 'Ohio' class SSBNs from the ninth vessel onwards in December 1989, the Trident II will be more accurate and have the ability to carry a greater number of larger-yield warheads than its predecessor, the Trident I. The accuracy will be sufficient to make feasible the targeting of Soviet hardened underground missile silos and command bunkers. This will be the first time ever that American sea-based strategic forces will have had the capability to attack any Soviet target type. In addition to the Trident II the programme is aimed at increasing the number of warhead vehicles available to something like the total at the height of the Poseidon programme, but with greater megatonnage to match Soviet increases. A minimum of 857 missiles will be procured for 25 or more 'Ohio' class submarines.

A further batch of around 100 (to be serviced in the USA) will be procured by the UK, as in 1982 it was decided that this missile would be adopted for the new 'V' class submarines that are to replace the Polaris boats in the mid-1990s. The British missiles will differ in that they will carry only eight lower-yield MIRVs designed and built by the Atomic Weapons Research Establishment and Royal Ordnance Factories. This lower number of lighter warheads will allow the missiles to be fired over even longer ranges than the US versions. The first test firing of a Trident II round took place in January 1987 at Cape Canaveral.

Specification
Trident II D5
Type: submarine-launched ballistic missile
Dimensions: length 13.96 m (45.8 ft); diameter 1.89 m (6 ft 2.4 in)
Launch weight: 57153 kg (126,000 lb)
Performance: range 7400-11100 km (4,600-6,900 miles) depending load; CEP 92.5 m (101 yards)
Warhead: up to 14 MIRVs with 150kt warheads or 7 MARVs with 300kt yield warheads
Propulsion: solid-propellant rocket
Guidance: stellar-inertial

Modern Missile Submarines

The Royal Navy will put Trident to sea in the 1990s. The 'Vanguard' class submarines will be smaller than the American 'Ohios', with 16 missiles rather than 24.

Chinese SLBM programme

Design of an indigenous SLBM began in China during the late 1960s by a design team located at the Suang-Chengzi missile test centre. The two-stage solid-propellant missile which resulted was given the Western designation **CSS-N-2**, and was initially tested aboard the sole locally-assembled but Soviet-designed Type 200 'Golf' class conventionally-powered SSB. Fitted with two 10.6-m (34.78-ft) by 2.4-m (7.87-ft) missile tubes, the 'Golf' boat undertook its first trial launch in the early 1980s. Although at least one of the Type 07 'Han' class SSNs was also modified during construction to carry six CSS-N-2 tubes, a number of problems were encountered during the missile's protracted development, which resulted in only a limited production run being undertaken between 1975 and 1984.

Many of the faults were corrected in the following two-stage solid-propellant **CSS-N-3**, which was first test fired in October 1982 from its carrying platform, the 12-tube Type 09 'Xia' class SSBN, two or three of which are now in service. These are to be supplemented in the late 1980s by the first of six Type 09 'Xia (Mod)' class SSBNs, which are fitted with 14 tubes for the definitive two-stage solid-propellant **CSS-N-4** (Chinese designation Julang-1, JL-1 or Great Wave-1) which is due to become the standard SLBM for new-construction SSBNs until the mid-1990s.

Specification
CSS-N-2
Dimensions: length 10.0 m (32.81 ft); diameter 1.5 m (4.92 ft)
Weight: 14000 kg (30,864 lb)
Warhead: 1-megaton thermonuclear
Range: 2700 km (1,678 miles)
CEP: 2800 m (3,060 yards)
Guidance: inertial

Specification
CSS-N-4
Dimensions: length 12.8 m (41.99 ft); diameter 2.3 m (7.55 ft)
Weight: 20000 kg (44,092 lb)
Warhead: 1-megaton thermonuclear
Range: 3200 km (1,988 miles)

Built from designs supplied by the USSR, the 'Golf' class ballistic missile submarine has been the basis of Chinese SLBM development.

CEP: 1850 m (2,025 yards)
Guidance: inertial

Nuclear Attack Submarines

At this moment, beneath the surface of the ocean, a potentially deadly game of cat and mouse is being played between Soviet and NATO submariners. The prime tool of their trade is the modern nuclear attack and hunter-killer submarine, packed with weaponry and sensors and capable of operating at greater speeds and depths than ever before.

USS Jacksonville *is one of the 'Los Angeles' class attack submarines that are destined to serve with the US Navy into the 21st century as the primary underwater ASW platform. They carry Mk 48 torpedoes, Harpoon and Tomahawk SSMs.*

The development of the modern nuclear attack submarine started around the same time, in the late 1940s, in both the United States and the Soviet Union. Since then the two countries have developed their own characteristic designs, with the United States concentrating on the ASW-orientated boat (SSN) armed with torpedo tube-launched weapons, whilst the Soviets have also developed these craft and others (SSGN) specifically designed to carry large anti-ship cruise missiles. However, since the development of the Sub-Harpoon and Tomahawk underwater-launched missile systems for anti-ship and land attack roles, the American boats are gradually assuming a multi-mission capability.

The Soviets are also expected to move in this direction when their SS-NX-21 torpedo tube-launched nuclear cruise missile enters service later in the decade, although they will still be building the specialist cruise missile-carrying boats such as the 'Oscar' class, the underwater equivalent to the 'Kirov' class battle-cruisers. Currently the Soviets have five nuclear-powered attack submarine classes under construction: the 'Charlie III' SSGN, 'Oscar' SSGN, 'Alpha I' SSN, 'Victor III' SSN and, the newest, the 'Alpha II' SSN. In comparison the Americans, British and French have in construction only one SSN class apiece. The Soviets add between four and six boats of these five types to their fleet per year, with each class usually undergoing periodic updates to its systems and armament during its lifetime. The French and British boats are primarily for ASW work, whilst recently confirmed reports indicate that the People's Republic of China has six or so nuclear-powered attack boats in service. The first was built in 1973-4, and is 100 m (328 ft) long with an Albacore type hull for fast underwater speeds. Known as the 'Han' class, this model is expected to proliferate over the next few years. Other nations, including Argentina, Brazil and Canada are known to be interested in acquiring nuclear submarines.

The main advantages of the nuclear attack submarine are its ability to remain submerged for virtually unlimited periods, its deep-diving capability, the sophisticated long-range sensor systems that it carries, and the high power output of its reactor that can be translated into very high underwater speeds. All of these can be utilized to the full in modern submarine warfare. In the ocean environment in which these hunter-killer submarines spend most of their lives, there is nothing in the marine world that can match them for guile and potential destructiveness.

The Royal Navy's 'Swiftsure' class submarine HMS Sovereign *on the surface amidst ice-floes during her 1976 visit to the North Pole. As the ice cap is a relatively safe place to operate a ballistic missile boat, more and more anti-submarine patrols are spent in Arctic waters.*

'Valiant' and 'Churchill' class SSNs

Essentially an enlarged 'Dreadnought' class design with all-British reactor plant and systems, HMS *Valiant* (S 102) was ordered in August 1960 as the lead boat of the **'Valiant' class** and completed in July 1966, a year later than planned because of the priority accorded to the British Polaris programme. Her sistership HMS *Warspite* (S 103) was followed by three others built to a modified design as **'Churchill' class** boats. These three are HMS *Churchill* (S 46), HMS *Conqueror* (S 48) and HMS *Courageous* (S 50), and are believed to be slightly quieter in service, having benefited from the experience gained in operating the earlier boats. All are fitted with the Type 2001 long-range active/passive LF sonar mounted in the 'chin' position, though the three boats will be retrofitted with the Type 2020 set as a replacement during future overhauls. It is also reported that the five boats can be fitted with a LF clip-on towed array since identified as the Type 2024 sonar system. Other sonars identified with the craft are the Type 2007 long-range passive set and the joint Anglo-Dutch-French Type 2019 Passive/Active Range and Intercept Sonar (PARIS). A Type 197 passive ranging sonar for detecting sonar transmissions is also carried. When the boats were built the main armament comprised the pre-World War II Mk 8 anti-ship torpedo, the 1950s technology wire-guided Mk 23 ASW torpedo and World War II Mk 5 ground and Mk 6 moored mines. Since then the armament has been modernized to include the Mk 8, the Mk 24 Tigerfish wire-guided dual-role torpedo, the Sub-Harpoon anti-ship missile and the new Stonefish and Sea Urchin ground mines. It was the *Chur-*

chill that tested the Sub-Harpoon for the Royal Navy. During the 1982 Falklands war the *Conqueror, Courageous* and *Valiant* were deployed to the Maritime Exclusion Zone, the first sinking the Argentinian cruiser *General Belgrano* on 2 May 1982. All five vessels are due to remain in service until the mid- to late-1990s, and are increasingly being employed in the anti-surface ship role as quieter boats enter service.

Specification
'Valiant' and 'Churchill' classes
Displacement: 4,400 tons surfaced and 4,900 tons dived
Dimensions: length 86.9 m (285 ft 0 in); beam 10.1 m (33 ft 3 in); draught 8.2 m (27 ft 0 in)
Machinery: one pressurized-water reactor powering two steam turbines driving one shaft
Speed: 20 kts surfaced and 29 kts dived
Diving depth: 300 m (985 ft) operational and 500 m (1,640 ft) maximum
Torpedo tubes: six 533-mm (21-in) bow
Basic load: a mix of 32 Mk 8 and Mk 24 Tigerfish 533-mm (21-in) torpedoes or 64 Mk 5, Stonefish or Sea Urchin ground mines; this is being changed to 26 533-mm (21-in) torpedoes and six Sub-Harpoon anti-ship missiles
Missiles: none
Electronics: one Type 1007 surface-search radar, one Type 2001 sonar, one Type 2024 towed sonar, one Type 2007 sonar, one Type 2019 sonar, one Type 197 sonar, one direction-finding antenna, one ESM system, one DCB torpedo fire-control system, and one underwater telephone
Complement: 116

Essentially an enlarged version of the 'Dreadnought' design, HMS Valiant was built at the same time as the Polaris boats with an all-British PWR1 reactor plant and associated control systems.

Below: Destined to remain in service until the mid to late 1990s, the five 'Valiant' and 'Churchill' class vessels are undergoing modernization refits as they come in for overhauls.

'Swiftsure' class SSN

In 1971 the first of the UK's **'Swiftsure' class** second-generation SSNs was launched at Vickers Shipyard at Barrow-in-Furness. Called HMS *Swiftsure* (S 126), the boat introduced a shorter and fuller hull-form than that of the 'Valiant' class in order to give a greater internal volume and a stronger pressure hull. Hence it can operate at greater depths and speeds than the previous class. The fin is smaller and the

retractable diving planes are located below the water line. The *Swiftsure* was followed by five sister ships, HMS *Sovereign* (S 108), HMS *Superb* (S 109), HMS *Sceptre* (S 104), HMS *Spartan* (S 105) and HMS *Splendid* (S 106); the class is currently used both in the ASW screening role for task forces, and in the independent anti-ship and ASW roles because of the quieter machinery used. The sonar fit is the

Quieter than their predecessors, the 'Swiftsure' class have proved to be excellent ASW platforms in service. The sonar fit is being upgraded and will eventually include the Type 2046 towed array as successor to the Type 2024. To match the detection ranges of the sonars all Royal Navy submarines will carry the Marconi Spearfish heavyweight torpedo.

same as in the 'Valiant' class, but all will have the Type 2020 fitted as the Type 2001 replacement during normal refits. The armament is reduced by one tube and seven torpedoes, but this reduction is balanced by the fact that it takes only 15 seconds to reload individual tubes. Emergency power is provided by the same 112-cell electric battery and associated diesel generator and electric motor as fitted in the 'Valiant' and 'Churchill' classes. In 1976 the *Sovereign* demonstrated the Royal Navy's ability to conduct ASW operations under the ice pack when she undertook a trip to the North Pole, the operational aspects being combined with a successful scientific voyage. The *Spartan* and *Splendid* were both involved in the Falklands war.

Specification
'Swiftsure' class
Displacement: 4,200 tons surfaced and 4,500 tons dived
Dimensions: length 82.9 m (272 ft 0 in); beam 9.8 m (32 ft 3 in); draught 8.2 m (27 ft 0 in)
Machinery: one pressurized-water reactor powering two steam turbines driving one shaft

Speed: 20 kts surfaced and 30 kts dived
Diving depth: 400 m (1,315 ft) operational and 600 m (1,970 ft) maximum
Torpedo tubes: five 533-mm (21-in) bow
Basic load: 20 Mk 8 or Mk 24 Tigerfish 533-mm (21-in) torpedoes plus five Sub-Harpoon anti-ship missiles, or 50 Mk 5, Stonefish or Sea Urchin mines
Missiles: none
Electronics: one Type 1006 surface-search radar, one Type 2001 sonar, one Type 2024 towed sonar, one Type 2007 sonar, one Type 2019 sonar, one Type 197 sonar, one ESM system, one DCB torpedo and missile fire-control system, and one underwater telephone
Complement: 116

To improve underwater performance, HMS Swiftsure *was introduced into service with a shorter and fuller hull form. This gives greater internal volume and a stronger pressure hull than earlier boats.*

UK
'Trafalgar' class SSN

Essentially an improved 'Swiftsure' design, the **'Trafalgar' class** constitutes the third generation of British SSNs to be built at Vickers Shipyard in Barrow-in-Furness. The lead boat, HMS *Trafalgar* (S 107), was launched in 1981 and commissioned into the Royal Navy in March 1983, serving with the 'Swiftsure' class boats at the Devonport naval base. A class total of seven is expected with HMS *Trafalgar*. HMS *Turbulent* (S87), HMS *Tireless* (S88), HMS *Torbay* (S90) in service and HMS *Trenchant* (S91), HMS *Talent* (S92) and HMS *Triumph* (S93) under construction. The major improvements over the 'Swiftsure' class include several features to reduce the underwater radiated noise. These comprise a new reactor system, a pump-jet propulsion system rather than a conventional propeller and the covering of the pressure hull and outer surfaces with anechoic tiles to give the same type of protection as afforded by the Soviet 'Clusterguard' coating in reducing noise. The *Trafalgar* is the first boat to be fitted with the Type 2020 sonar, and is being used as the development test platform for the system. According to other reports there has also been an internal compartment rearrangement to rationalize and centralize the operations, sound and ESM/radar rooms.

The remaining systems, the armament and the sonars are the same as fitted to the 'Swiftsure' class boats, although a thermal imagery periscope is now carried as part of the search and attack periscope fit, and Type 197 sonar is no longer carried. The succeeding class is under consideration at the moment, and has been given the tentative designation **SSN20**. It will be powered by a variant of the PWR2 reactor being used in the 'Vanguard' class Trident missile submarines.

Specification
'Trafalgar' class
Displacement: 4,700 tons surfaced and 5,302 tons dived
Dimensions: length 85.4 m (280 ft 3 in); beam 9.8 m (32 ft 3 in); draught 8.2 m (27 ft 0 in)

Right: Similar in many respects to the 'Swiftsure' class, HMS Trafalgar *is the first Royal Navy submarine to be covered with anechoic tiles that reduced underwater radiated noise.*

Below: With HMS Illustrious *in the background, HMS* Trafalgar *enters Devonport Naval Base to tie up at the 2nd Submarine Squadron berth.*

Machinery: one pressurized-water reactor powering two steam turbines with pump-jet propulsion
Speed: 20 kts surfaced and 29 kts dived
Diving depth: 400 m (1,315 ft) operational and 600 m (1,970 ft) maximum
Torpedo tubes: five 533-mm (21-in) bow
Basic load: 20 Mk 8 and Mk 24 Tigerfish 533-mm (21-in) torpedoes and five

Sub-Harpoon anti-ship missiles, or 50 Mk 5, Stonefish or Sea Urchin mines
Missiles: none
Electronics: one Type 1007 surface-search radar, one Type 2020 sonar, one Type 2026 towed sonar, one Type 2007 sonar, one Type 2019 sonar, one Type 2047 sonar analysis set, one ESM system, and one DCB torpedo and missile fire-control system
Complement: 130

'Skipjack' class SSN

Although built in the late 1950s, the five **'Skipjack' class** boats currently in service are still considered to be frontline operational boats and were, until the advent of the 'Los Angeles' class, the fastest submarines available to the US Navy. A sixth boat, the USS *Scorpion* (SSN 589, whose original hull was used in the construction of the first American SSBN, the USS *George Washington*), was lost in May 1968 south west of the Azores whilst en route from the Mediterranean to Norfolk, Virginia, with all 99 men aboard. The class is notable for being the first to use the S5W reactor design, which was subsequently used in all nuclear submarine classes built in the United States up to the 'Glenard P. Lipscomb' class. The 'Skipjack' class also introduced the classic teardrop hull shape, and as such acted as the model for the British 'Dreadnought' and 'Valiant/Churchill' classes, the long rearward taper of the hull forcing the designers to dispense with stern torpedo tubes and adopt a single-shaft propulsion arrangement. The diving planes were also relocated to the fin to increase underwater manoeuvrability, a feature which the British did not copy. All the engine room fittings except the reactor and steam turbines are duplicated to minimize breakdown possibilities. At present all five boats (USS *Skipjack*, USS *Scamp*, USS *Sculpin*, USS *Shark* and USS *Snook* serve in the Atlantic Fleet. However, as a result of their age the 'Skipjack' class boats might well be relegated as training craft and high-

USS Shark *at its maximum surface speed of 18 kts. With an underwater speed of 30 kts, the five remaining 'Skipjack' class vessels are still considered to be front-line submarines.*

speed underwater ASW targets in place of the old SSBNs now being used in that role.

Specification
'Skipjack' class
Displacement: 3,075 tons surfaced and 3,515 tons dived
Dimensions: length 76.7 m (251 ft 9 in); beam 9.6 m (31 ft 6 in); draught 8.5 m (27 ft 10 in)
Machinery: one Westinghouse S5W pressurized-water reactor powering two steam turbines driving one shaft
Speed: 18 kts surfaced and 30 kts dived
Diving depth: 300 m (985 ft) operational and 500 m (1,640 ft) maximum
Torpedo tubes: six 533-mm (21-in) bow
Basic load: 24 Mk 48 533-mm (21-in) dual-role torpedoes, or 48 Mk 57 moored mines
Missiles: none
Electronics: one surface-search radar, one modified BQS-4 sonar suite, one Mk 101 torpedo fire-control system, and one underwater telephone
Complement: 106-114

Below: Compared with more modern US attack submarines, the 'Skipjack' class is limited in its armament and sonar, having only Mk 48 torpedoes and a modified BQS-4 sonar system. No ASROC ASW missiles or towed sonar array are carried as the expense of retrofitting them was too great.

'Thresher' class (later 'Permit' class) SSN

The first of the SSNs in the US Navy with a deep-diving capability, advanced sonars mounted in the optimum bow position, amidships angled torpedo tubes with the SUBROC ASW missile, and a high degree of machinery-quieting, the **'Thresher' class** is still an important part of US attack capability. The lead boat of this class, the USS *Thresher* (SSN 593), was lost with all 129 people on board during diving trials off the coast of New England on 10 April 1963, mid-way through the building period 1960-6. The class was then renamed the **'Permit' class** after the second ship. As a result of the lessons learnt from the enquiry following the *Thresher*'s loss, the last three of the class were modified during construction with SUBSAFE features, heavier machinery and taller sail structures, essentially to act as the prototypes for the follow-on 'Sturgeon' class. In addition USS *Jack* (SSN 605) was built to a different design with two propellers on one shaft and a contra-rotating turbine without reduction gear to test a new method of reducing machinery-operating noises. This was unsuccessful, however, and the vessel was refitted with standard machinery. During

the normal refit programme the original Mk 113 torpedo fire-control system and the BQQ-2 sonar suite are to be replaced with the all digital Mk 117 FCS and the BQQ-5 sonar suite with clip-on towed sonar array facilities. All will also be fitted to carry and fire the Sub-Harpoon and Tomahawk missiles. The SUBROC will be replaced by a new stand-off ASW missile in the early 1990's, with the choice of either a nuclear depth bomb or an ASW torpedo as the payload. At present eight 'Permit' class boats (USS *Permit*, USS *Plunger*, USS *Barb*, USS *Pollack*, USS *Haddo*, USS *Guardfish*, USS *Flasher* and USS *Haddock*) serve in the Pacific and five (USS *Jack*, USS *Tinosa*, USS *Dace*, USS *Greenling* and USS *Gato*) in the Atlantic.

Specification
'Permit' class
Displacement: 3,750 tons surfaced and 4,311 tons dived, except *Jack* 3,800 tons surfaced and 4,470 tons dived, and *Flasher, Greenling* and *Gato* 3,800 tons surfaced and 4,642 tons dived
Dimensions: length 84.9 m (278 ft 6 in) except *Jack* 90.7 m (297 ft 5 in) and *Flasher, Greenling* and *Gato* 89.1 m

(292 ft 3 in); beam 9.6 m (31 ft 8 in); draught 8.8 m (28 ft 10 in)
Machinery: one Westinghouse S5W pressurized-water reactor powering two steam turbines driving one shaft
Speed: 18 kts surface and 27 kts dived, except *Jack, Flasher, Greenling* and *Gato* 18 kts surfaced and 26 kts dived

The first US Navy SSN class with a deep diving capability, advanced sonars, amidships torpedo tubes, and machinery quieting systems was the 'Permit' class. USS Plunger *is seen here off the coast of Hawaii during her first fleet deployment in 1963.*

USS Barb executes a high speed turn on the surface. Underwater, the submarine would be 'flown' using controls similar to those found aboard aircraft in order to exploit its maximum manoeuvrability.

The 'Permit' class submarines are being upgraded with new sonars and weapon control systems in order that they might operate as first-line units into the 1990s to supplement the 'Los Angeles' class.

Diving depth: 400 m (1,315 ft) operational and 600 m (1,970 ft) maximum
Torpedo tubes: four 533-mm (21-in) amidships
Basic load: 17 Mk 48 533-mm (21-in) torpedoes and six SUBROC anti-submarine missiles (being modified to 15 Mk 48 torpedoes, four SUBROC missiles and four Sub-Harpoon anti-ship missiles), or 46 Mk 57, Mk 60 or Mk 67 mines: in the late 1980s the load will comprise 11 Mk 48 torpedoes, four

Sub-Harpoon missiles, eight Tomahawk cruise missiles
Missiles: none, but see above
Electronics: one BPS-11 surface-search radar, one BQQ-2 or BQQ-5 sonar suite (the latter with towed array), one Mk 113 or Mk 117 torpedo fire-control system, one WSC-3 satellite communications system, one ESM system, and one underwater telephone
Complement: 134-141

USA
'Sturgeon' class SSN

Essentially an enlarged and improved 'Thresher/Permit' design with additional quieting features and electronic systems, the **'Sturgeon' class** SSNs built between 1965 and 1974 were the largest class of nuclear-powered warships built anywhere until the advent of the 'Los Angeles' class boats. Like the previous class they are intended primarily for ASW, and employ the standard American SSN amidships torpedo battery aft of the fin, with two tubes firing diagonally outwards from the hull on each side. This allows a larger torpedo handling room than in bow-battery boats, and facilitates fast access, weapon choice and reloading of the tubes. The last nine of the class were lengthened to accommodate more electronic equipment. What is not widely known, however, is that these are the boats used in one of the most closely guarded and classified naval intelligence programmes currently in operation. Codenamed 'Holy Stone', the programme was initiated in the late 1960s and involves the use of these submarines in highly specialized intelligence-gathering missions close to the coasts of nations unfriendly towards the United States. The additional intelligence-gathering equipment is located in special compartments and is operated by National Security Agency personnel specifically carried for the task. During these operations several collisions with other underwater and surface craft have occurred, resulting sometimes in damage to the US boats involved; and on one occasion at least a 'Holy Stone' submarine was accidentally grounded for several hours during a mission within the territorial waters of the Soviet Far East. As in the case of the 'Thresher/Permit' class, the boats are being retrofitted with the Mk 117 FCS and BQQ-5 sonar suite, and will carry both the Sub-Harpoon and Tomahawk. The USS **Hawkbill**, USS **Pintado** and USS **William H. Bates** have also been converted to carry a DSRV (deep-submergence rescue vehicle) aft for launch and recovery underwater during SUBSMASH rescue operations.

Of the 22 'Sturgeon' class SSNs operational with the Atlantic Fleet, it is thought that the 'standard' boats are the USS **Sturgeon**, USS **Whale**, USS **Grayling**, USS **Sunfish**, USS **Pargo**, USS **Ray**, USS **Lapon**, USS **Hammerhead**, USS **Sea Devil**, USS **Bergall**, USS

Spadefish, USS **Seahorse**, USS **Finback**, USS **Flying Fish**, USS **Trepang**, USS **Bluefish**, USS **Sand Lance** and USS **Billfish**, while the 'Holy Stone' boats are probably the USS **Archerfish**, USS **Silversides**, USS **Batfish** and USS **L. Mendel Rivers**. The Pacific Fleet's 15 'Sturgeon' class boats are the 'standard' USS **Tautog**, USS **Pogy**, USS **Aspro**, USS **Queenfish**, USS **Puffer**, USS **Gurnard**, USS **Guitarro**, USS **Hawkbill**, USS **Pintado** and USS **Drum**, and the 'Holy Stone' USS **William H. Bates**, USS **Tunny**, USS **Parche** and USS **Richard B. Russell**. The former 'Holy Stone' unit USS **Cavalla** has been given the secondary role of special forces troop transport and has been equipped with a deck mounted cylindrical chamber aft (a 'DDS' or Dry Deck Shelter) to carry swimmer delivery vehicles for UDTs (Underwater Demolition Teams) and SEAL naval special warfare units.

Specification
'Sturgeon' class
Displacement: 4,266 tons surfaced and 4,777 tons dived
Dimensions: length 89.0 m (292 ft 3 in) except *Archerfish, Silversides,*

William H. Bates, Batfish, Tunny, Parche, Cavalla, L. Mendel Rivers and *Richard B. Russell* 92.1 m (302 ft 2 in); beam 9.65 m (31 ft 8 in); draught 8.9 m (29 ft 3 in)
Machinery: one Westinghouse S5W pressurized-water reactor powered two steam turbines driving one shaft
Speed: 18 kts surfaced and 26 kts dived
Diving depth: 400 m (1,315 ft) operation and 600 m (1,970 ft) maximum
Torpedo tubes: four 533-mm (21-in)
Basic load: in the late 1980s the load will comprise 11 Mk 48 torpedoes, four Sub-Harpoon missiles, and eight Tomahawk cruise missiles
Electronics: one BPS-15 surface-search radar, one BQQ-2 or BQQ-5 sonar suite (the latter with towed array), one Mk 113 or Mk 117 torpedo fire-control system, one ESM suite, one WSC-3 satellite communication system, and one underwater telephone
Complement: 121-141

Left: USS Ray (SSN653) carries a BQR-7 passive bow conformal sonar array (effective at 30-100 nm against a snorkling submarine, and 10-50 nm against a cavitating target), and a BQS-6 active spherical bow array that can operate in bottom-bounce and convergence-zone modes.

Right and below: USS Sturgeon (SSN637). The clean external lines have no unnecessary protuberances that could cause cavitation and hence radiated noise. Sturgeon is armed with the 10 kt yield SUBROC ASW missile and any orders to fire this weapon have to be cleared by the President of the USA, as it is considered to be a theatre tactical nuclear weapon.

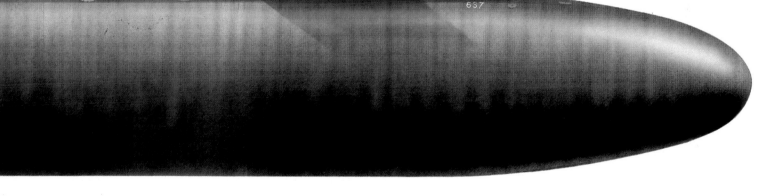

'Narwhal' and 'Glenard P. Lipscomb' class SSNs

USA

These two single-ship classes are test-beds for major new submarine technology. The USS **Narwhal** (SSN 671) was constructed in 1966-7 to evaluate the natural-circulation S5G nuclear reactor plant. This uses natural convection rather than several circulator pumps, with their associated electrical and control equipment, for heat transfer operations via the reactor coolant to the steam generators, thus effectively reducing at slow speeds one of the major sources of self-generated radiated machinery noise within ordinary nuclear-powered submarines. In all other respects the boat is similar to a 'Sturgeon' and will be retrofitted with new equipment and missiles in the course of a regular refit.

In contrast the USS **Glenard P. Lipscomb** (SSN 685) was constructed in 1971-3 to a much larger design to evaluate a turbine-electric drive propulsion plant. This eliminates the noisy reduction gear of the standard steam turbine plant and introduces a number of new and quieter machinery systems into the boat. However, because the system is much larger and heavier than the normal plant, a penalty has had to be paid in terms of underwater speed in comparison with that of contemporary American SSN classes. The *Lipscomb* is being used in an ongoing project designed to allow an actual at-sea evaluation of noise reduction techniques as a counter to ASW measures. Several of the quieting techniques which do not result in an underwater speed loss have already been incorporated in the 'Los Angeles' class. At present the two submarines operate in the Atlantic as fully operational units.

Specification
USS *Narwhal*
Displacement: 4,450 tons surfaced and 5,350 tons dived
Dimensions: length 95.9 m (314 ft 8 in); beam 11.6 m (38 ft 0 in); draught 7.9 m (25 ft 11 in)
Machinery: one General Electric S5G pressurized-water reactor powering two steam turbines driving one shaft
Speed: 18 kts surfaced and 26 kts dived
Diving depth: 400 m (1,315 ft)

operational and 600 m (1,970 ft) maximum
Torpedo tubes: four 533-mm (21-in) amidships
Basic load: 17 Mk 48 533-mm (21-in) torpedoes and six SUBROC anti-submarine missiles (being modified to 15 Mk 48 torpedoes, four SUBROC missiles and four Sub-Harpoon anti-ship missiles), or 46 Mk 57, Mk 60 or Mk 67 mines; in the late 1980s the load will comprise 11 Mk 48 torpedoes, four Sub-Harpoon missiles and eight Tomahawk cruise missiles
Missiles: none, but see above
Electronics: one BPS-11 surface-search radar, one BQQ-2 or BQQ-5 sonar suite (the latter with towed array), one Mk 113 or Mk 117 torpedo

fire-control system, one WSC-3 satellite communications system, one ESM system, and one underwater telephone
Complement: 141

Specification
USS *Glenard P. Lipscomb*
Displacement: 5,800 tons surfaced and 6,840 tons dived
Dimensions: length 111.3 m (365 ft 0 in); beam 9.7 m (31 ft 9 in); draught 9.5 m (31 ft 0 in)
Machinery: one Westinghouse S5Wa pressurized-water reactor powering two steam turbines driving one shaft
Speed: 18 kts surfaced and 24 kts dived

USS Narwhal *(SSN671) is the testbed for the natural-circulation S5G nuclear reactor plant. The S5G uses natural convection rather than circulator pumps for heat transfer to the steam turbines in order to reduce the self-generated noise levels at low speeds.*

Diving depth: 400 m (1,315 ft) operational and 600 m (1,970 ft) maximum
Torpedo tubes: four 533-mm (21-in) amidships
Basic load: as for *Narwhal*
Missiles: none
Electronics: as for *Narwhal*
Complement: 141

'Los Angeles' class SSN

USA

Destined to comprise the largest number of nuclear-powered warships built to one design, the **'Los Angeles' class** couples the speed advantage of the elderly 'Skipjack' class with the sonar and weapons capability of the 'Permit/ Sturgeon' classes. The significant increase in size is mainly the result of doubling installed power available by the fitting of a new reactor design, the S6G, which is reportedly based on the D2G reactor fitted in the 'Bainbridge' and 'Truxtun' class nuclear-powered cruisers. Reactor refuelling will take place every 10-13 years. Few other improvements have been made apart

from a slight increase in the weapon stowage space and in the addition of various underwater quieting aspects. The boats, built on a continuing basis since 1974, are fitted with the BQQ-5 sonar suite with a spherical long-range active/passive bow array, three passive target-ranging hydrophone arrays on each side of the hull, a conformal long-range passive array and a clip-on (later to be a retractable system) towed long-range passive low-frequency array. Because of the limited weapon stowage problems on all US submarines, from the 34th boat onwards 12 vertical launch tubes for

Tomahawk cruise missiles will be fitted in the empty free-flooding space between the pressure hull and the bow sonar complex. The earlier ships will each carry eight Tomahawks as part of their normal weapons outfit, to the detriment of the number of ASW weapons that can be carried. Already

in operational service, the class has proved to be an exceptionally good ASW platform, although on one occasion on the first out-of-area 'Alpha' deployment the Soviet boat was easily able to outrun a trailing 'Los Angeles' class boat off Iceland just by using its superior underwater speed. Against

With over 60 boats planned, the 'Los Angeles' design will be the most numerous nuclear-powered warship class, as well as being the most expensive SSN type.

more conventional Soviet nuclear-powered boats the success rate of detection and tracking is quite high, the BQQ-5 system on one occasion acquiring and holding contact with two Soviet 'Victor' class SSNs for an extended time. The high underwater speed of the 'Los Angeles' class boats allows them to be the first American SSN units to be capable of providing an effective underwater escort capability for American carrier battle groups. Previous SSNs were too slow for most of the missions assigned to such escorts. Currently 12 of the boats serve in the Pacific whilst another 22 are assigned to the Atlantic Fleet. It is estimated that another 13 will be in commission before the end of 1989. At least 20 more have been ordered or are planned for construction into the 1990s.

The names of the class so far are USS *Los Angeles*, USS *Baton Rouge*, USS *Philadelphia*, USS *Memphis*, USS *Omaha*, USS *Cincinnati*, USS *Groton*, USS *Birmingham*, USS *New York City*, USS *Indianapolis*, USS *Bremerton*, USS *Jacksonville*, USS *Dallas*, USS *La Jolla*, USS *Phoenix*, USS *Boston*, USS *Baltimore*, USS *City of Corpus Christi*, USS *Albuquerque*, USS *Portsmouth*, USS *Minneapolis-St Paul*, USS *Hyman G. Rickover*, USS *San Francisco*, USS *Atlanta*, USS *Houston*, USS *Norfolk*, USS *Buffalo*, USS *Salt Lake City*, USS *Olympia*, USS *Honolulu*, USS *Providence*, USS *Pittsburgh*, USS *Chicago*, USS *Key West*, USS *Oklahoma City*, USS *Louisville*, USS *Helena*, USS *Newport News*, USS *San Juan* and USS *Springfield* with the remaining units as

yet un-named. All units will carry the new Sea Lance stand-off ASW weapon when it enters service in the 1990s.

Specification
'Los Angeles' class
Displacement: 6,000 tons surfaced and 6,900 tons dived
Dimensions: length 109.7 m (360 ft 0 in); beam 10.1 m (33 ft 0 in); draught 9.85 m (32 ft 4 in)
Machinery: one General Electric S6G pressurized-water reactor powering two steam turbines driving one shaft
Speed: 18 kts surfaced and 31 kts dived
Diving depth: 450 m (1,475 ft)

operational and 750 m (2,460 ft) maximum
Torpedo tubes: four 533-mm (21-in) amidships
Basic load: 26 533-mm (21-in) weapons (Mk 48 torpedoes, Sub-Harpoon anti-ship missiles and Tomahawk cruise missiles) or 52 Mk 57, Mk 60 or Mk 67 mines
Missiles: (from 34th boat onwards) 15 Tomahawk cruise missiles
Electronics: one BPS-15 surface-search radar, one modified BQQ-5 sonar suite with towed array, one Mk 113 (first 13 units) or Mk 117 (later units, and to be retrofitted in first 13) torpedo fire control system, one WSC-3

USS Birmingham *(SSN695) shows off an emergency surfacing drill during her sea trials. Note the large volumes of water pouring from her sail and the sail-mounted diving planes. A normal surfacing is achieved gradually by selective blowing of ballast tanks.*

satellite communications system, one WLR-8(V)2 ESM system, one WLR-12 ESM system, one BRD-7 direction finder, and one underwater telephone
Complement: 142

The nuclear powered attack submarine USS San Francisco (SSN-711) runs on the surface during sea trials.

 USA
'Seawolf' class SSN

The **'Seawolf' class** will offer significant improvements over the preceding 'Los Angeles' class in terms of speed, quietness, diving depth, weapons load and sonar capabilities and will attempt to maintain an American lead over Soviet submarine technology. Although the specifications are not yet fixed it will be shorter than the 'Los Angeles' but will displace more when dived. Power will be provided by an advanced pressurized water cooled reactor that will drive a pump jet propulsion system. The boat will also be fitted with bow mounted retractable hydroplanes and six stern fins to improve manoeuvrability at the lower speed ranges. A

small wedge at the base of the forward edge of the fin will improve the hydrodynamic flow underwater. A totally new conformal sonar array will be fitted together with the Submarine Advanced Combat System (SUBACS) that is an integrated sonar/weapons control unit. The torpedo compartment will revert to the traditional bow position with the number of tubes doubled to eight for Mk 48 ADCAP torpedoes, Sea Lance ASW missiles. Sub-Harpoon anti-ship missiles and Tomahawk land attack and anti-ship cruise missiles.

The design is specifically configured to fight under the Arctic ice cap where the newer generation 'De-

lta IV' and 'Typhoon' class SSBNs of the Soviet navy spend most of their time. The first unit, USS *Seawolf*, is expected to be ordered under the Fiscal Year 1989 shipbuilding programme for delivery in 1994-5.

Specification (provisional)
'Seawolf' class
Displacement: 7,770 tons surfaced, 9,150 tons dived
Dimensions: length 99.4 m (326 ft 1 in), beam 12.2 m (40 ft), draught 10.9 m (35 ft 9 in)

Propulsion: one pressurized water cooled reactor powering two steam turbines driving a pump jet propulsion system
Speed: 20 kts surfaced, 34-35 kts dived
Diving depth: 550 m (1,805 ft) operational, 850 m (2,789 ft) maximum
Torpedo tubes: eight 533-mm (21-in) bow
Basic load: 36-40 533-mm (21-in) calibre weapons
Missiles: see text
Electronics: one conformal wide aperture passive sonar array, one SUBACS integrated sonar/weapons control suite, one ESM suite
Complement: 149

'Rubis' class SSN

In 1964 the French authorized the design of a 4,000-ton SSN. This was cancelled in 1968, however, just as construction was due to start. A new and smaller submarine design was then initiated, based on the hull form and overall layout of the conventional 'Agosta' class and with basically the same fire-control, torpedo-launching and sonar detection systems. The resulting 'SNA72' class built at Cherbourg is the smallest SSN type in service with any navy, and was made possible by the French development of a small 48-megawatt integrated reactor-heat exchanger system driving two turbo-alternators and a main electric motor. The increased hull depth has allowed the typical three-deck layout of larger SSNs to be used for the areas forward and immediately aft of the fin. The forward diving planes of the Agostas have been relocated to the fin to improve underwater manoeuvrability.

At present two squadrons of these SSNs are planned by the French navy, one based at Brest to cover the SSBN base and the other at Toulon. The first five boats of the SSN programme will be built to the basic 'SNA72' design. The first, *Rubis* (S601), entered service in 1983 after an extensive trials programme that started in 1981. She was followed by *Saphir* (S602) in 1984 and *Casabianca* (S603) in 1987, with *Emeraude* to commission in 1988. S605 was laid down in 1984 for commissioning in 1990. A further five boats will be built to a new design, the first, (S606), to be laid down in 1988. All will carry versions of the F17 and L5 torpedoes and, from 1985, the underwater-launched encapsulated SM.39 Exocet anti-ship missile.

Specification
Rubis (S601)
Displacement: 2,385 tons surfaced and 2,670 tons dived
Dimensions: length 72.1 m (236 ft 6.5 in); beam 7.6 m (24 ft 11 in); draught 6.4 m (21 ft 0 in)
Machinery: one 48-mW pressurized-water reactor (PWR) powering two turbo-alternators driving one shaft
Speed: 18 kts surfaced and 25 kts dived
Diving depth: 300 m (985 ft) operational and 500 m (1,640 ft) maximum
Torpedo tubes: four 550-mm (21.65-in), all bow
Basic load: 14 F17 wire-guided anti-ship and L5 mod.3 active/passive ASW torpedoes, or 28 TSM3510 ground mines; from 1985 will be 10 F17/L5 mod.3 and four SM.39 mines
Electronics: one DRUA 33 surface-search radar, one DSUV 22 passive sonar, one DUUA 2B active/passive sonar, one ARUR ESM system, one SADE combat data system, one DUUX 2 passive ranging sonar and one TUUM underwater telephone
Complement: 66

Currently the smallest of the world's front-line SSNs, the 'Rubis' class is powered by a French-developed and built 48 mW integrated reactor-heat exchanger system that fits well into what is essentially a heavily modified conventional 'Agosta' class submarine design.

'Echo' class SSN and 'Echo II' class SSGN

The five **'Echo' class** SSNs were originally built at Komsomolsk in the Soviet Far East between 1960-2 as **'Echo I' class** SSGNs. Armed with six tubes for the SS-N-3C 'Shaddock' strategic cruise missile, they lacked the fire-control and guidance radars of the later **'Echo II' class**. As the Soviet SSBN force was built up so the need for these boats diminished, and they were converted to anti-ship attack SSNs between 1969 and 1974. The conversion involved the removal of the 'Shaddock' tubes, the plating over and streamlining of the hull to reduce the underwater noise caused by the tube system, and modification of the sonar systems to the standard carried by the 'November' class SSNs. All were then deployed with the Pacific Fleet, although one suffered some damage in an internal fire and had to be towed back to its base near Vladivostok for major repairs.

The follow-on 'Echo II' class was built both at Severodvinsk (the lead yard, with 18 vessels built) and Komsomolsk (with 11 vessels built) between 1962 and 1967 as the Soviet Navy's primary anti-carrier missile submarines. They carry eight SS-N-3A 'Shaddock' anti-ship cruise missiles mounted in pairs above the pressure hull, and for firing have to surface and elevate the pairs to about 25-30°. The forward section of the sail structure then rotates through 180° to expose the two 'Front' series missile-guidance radars. The firing in pairs of all eight missiles probably takes around 30 minutes, and the submarine then has to remain on the surface until the missile mid-course correction and final target-selection commands have been sent unless guidance can be passed over to a third party such as a naval air force Tupolev Tu-142 'Bear-D' fitted with the appropriate command guidance system. From the mid-1970s the 'Echo II' class boats have gradually been converted during routine overhauls to carry the longer-range and much faster SS-N-12 'Sandbox' anti-ship cruise missile in place of the 'Shaddocks'. The conversions can be distinguished by the fitting of bulges to each side of the sail and at the forward end of the mis-

Above: A Soviet 'Echo II' SSGN. A total of 29 of these vessels are in service, armed with SS-N-12 'Sandbox' or SS-N-3C 'Shaddock' anti-ship cruise missiles. Their major disadvantage is that they have to surface to fire and guide their missiles.

Below: The forward part of the 'Echo II' sail structure rotates through 180° to expose 'Front Piece' and 'Front Door' missile guidance radar antennae before firing. The many holes and hull protuberances make for a very noisy boat under water.

sile tubes abreast the bridge. The 28 'Echo II' boats are split evenly between the Pacific and Northern Fleets, with one unit of the latter normally to be found in the Mediterranean with a 'Juliett' class SSG. The 29th Echo II unit is used for secondary purposes, having been withdrawn from front-line service in the early 1980s.

Specification
'Echo' class
Displacement: 4,500 tons surfaced and 5,500 tons dived
Dimensions: length 110.0 m (360 ft 11 in); beam 9.0 m (29 ft 6 in); draught 7.5 m (24 ft 7 in)
Machinery: one pressurized-water reactor powering two steam turbines driving two four-blade propellers
Speed: 20 kts surfaced and 28 kts dived
Diving depth: 300 m (985 ft) operational and 500 m (1,640 ft) maximum
Torpedo tubes: six 533-mm (21-in) bow and two 406-mm (16-in) stern

Basic load: 20 533-mm (21-in) torpedoes (16 anti-ship or anti-submarine HE and four anti-ship 15-kiloton nuclear) and two 406-mm (16-in) anti-ship torpedoes
Missiles: none
Electronics: one 'Snoop Tray' surface-search radar, one Hercules sonar, one Feniks sonar, one 'Stop Light' ESM system and one underwater telephone
Complement: 90

Specification
'Echo II' class
Displacement: 5,000 tons surfaced and 6,000 tons dived
Dimensions: length 115.0 m (377 ft 4 in); beam 9.0 m (29 ft 6 in); draught 7.5 m (24 ft 7 in)
Machinery: as for 'Echo' class
Speed: 20 kts surfaced and 25 kts dived
Diving depth: as for 'Echo' class
Torpedo tubes: as for 'Echo' class
Basic load: as for 'Echo' class
Missiles: eight SS-N-3A 'Shaddock' (four with 1000-kg/2,250-lb HE and four

with 350-kiloton nuclear warheads) or (in 10-12 converted boats) eight SS-N-12 'Sandbox' (four with 1000-kg/2,205-lb HE and four with 350-kiloton nuclear warheads)
Electronics: as for 'Echo' class, but with the addition of one 'Front Door' and one 'Front Piece' missile-guidance radar
Complement: 100

On 28 August 1976 an 'Echo II' class vessel collided with USS Voge, a 'Garcia' class frigate, in the Ionian sea. The 'Echo II' suffered severe hull lacerations and sail damage, and was patched up by a 'Prut' class submarine salvage vessel before sailing back to port for repairs.

USST
'Charlie I' and 'Charlie II' class SSGNs

Designated PLARK by the Soviets the first **'Charlie I' class** SSGN was launched at the inland shipyard at Gorki in 1967. Over the next five years a further 10 were completed there, with two banks of four missile tubes angled upwards on each side of the hull external to the pressure hull to give the class a distinctive blunt nose appearance. The tubes have large outer doors and are designed to carry the short range SS-N-7 submerged-launch anti-ship missile for the pop-up surprise attack on high-value surface targets such as a carrier. From 1972 to 1980 at Gorki an improved **'Charlie II' class** design was built with a 9-m (29.5-ft) hull insertion in the hull forward of the fin for the electronics and launch systems necessary for targeting and firing the SS-N-15 and SS-N-16 weapons. The six 'Charlie II' class boats also carry the longer-range SS-N-9 anti-ship missile in place of the SS-N-7. In both classes, once the missiles have been fired the boat has to be reloaded back at port, although the secondary torpedo armament and sonar systems allow each boat to be used as a useful anti-ship and ASW platform if required in the interim. In mid-1983, a 'Charlie I' of the Pacific Fleet was lost with all hands off Petropavlovsk, the boat subsequently being salvaged. At full strength, the Pacific Fleet now has three 'Charlie Is' and two 'Charlie IIs' while the Northern Fleet has eight and four respectively.

Specification
'Charlie I' class
Displacement: 4,000 tons surfaced and 5,000 tons dived

Dimensions: length 93.9 m (308 ft 1 in); beam 10.0 m (32 ft 7 in); draught 7.8 m (25 ft 7 in)
Machinery: one pressurized-water reactor powering two steam turbines driving one five-blade main propeller and two two-blade quiet propellers
Speed: 20 kts surfaced and 27 kts dived
Diving depth: 400 m (1,315 ft) operational and 600 m (1,970 ft) maximum
Torpedo tubes: six 533-mm (21-in), two with 406-mm (16-in) liners, all bow
Basic load: maximum of 12 533-mm (21-in) torpedoes, but normally a mixture of four 533-mm (21-in) anti-ship or anti-submarine HE, six 406-mm (16-in) anti-submarine HE and two 533-mm (21-in) anti-ship 15-kiloton nuclear torpedoes plus two SS-N-15 15-kiloton anti-submarine missiles, or a total of 24 AMD-1000 ground mines
Missiles: eight SS-N-7 (four with 500-kg/1,102-lb HE and four with 200-kiloton nuclear warheads)
Electronics: one 'Snoop Tray' surface-search radar, one low-frequency bow sonar, one medium-frequency missile and torpedo fire-control sonar, one 'Brick Spit' and one 'Brick Pulp' passive intercept and threat-warning ESM system, one 'Park Lamp' direction-finding antenna, VHF and UHF communications, and one underwater telephone
Complement: 100

Specification
'Charlie II' class
Displacement: 4,500 tons surfaced and 5,500 tons dived

Dimensions: length 102.9 m (337 ft 7 in); beam 10.0 m (32 ft 10 in); draught 7.8 m (25 ft 7 in)
Machinery: as for 'Charlie I' class
Speed: 20 kts surfaced and 26 kts dived
Diving depth: as for 'Charlie I' class
Torpedo tubes: as for 'Charlie I' class but with the addition of two 650-mm (25.6 in) in the bows for SS-N-16
Basic load: as for 'Charlie I' class but with two SS-N-16 anti-submarine missiles
Missiles: eight SS-N-9 'Siren' (four with 500-kg/1,102-lb HE and four with 200-kiloton nuclear warheads)

A 'Charlie I' class SSGN. This sub-class carries the SS-N-7 J-band active radar homing anti-ship missile in two banks of four missile tubes, angled upwards either side of the bow external to the pressure hull.

Electronics: as for 'Charlie I' class but with the addition of one VLF towed communications buoy and one ELF floating communications antenna
Complement: 110

A total of 20 'Charlie' class SSGNs have been built in three sub-classes since 1967 at the Gorki shipyard. Primarily used for surprise pop-up missile attacks on high-value surface targets such as carriers, the 'Charlie' SSGNs also have a useful secondary ASW capability.

'Papa' and 'Oscar' class SSGNs

In 1970 the Soviet shipyard at Severodvinsk launched a single unit of what came to be known in NATO circles as the **'Papa' class**. The 'Papa' class boat was considerably larger and carried two more missile tubes (for an unidentified type of missile) than the contemporary 'Charlie' class SSGNs, and was for many years a puzzle to Western intelligence services. However, the answer appeared in 1980 at the same shipyard when the first of the even larger **'Oscar' class** of SSGN was launched; the 'Papa' class unit had been the prototype for advanced SSGN concepts with a considerably changed powerplant and revised screw arrangement. The missile system had been to test the underwater-launched version of the SS-N-9 'Siren' for the subsequent 'Charlie II' series of SSGN. The 'Oscar' design introduced yet further improvements, with two 12-round banks of submerged-launch long-range SS-N-19 anti-ship missile tubes set in elevation at an angle of 40° and external to the main pressure hull on each side of the fin. Assessed as the underwater equivalents to the battlecruiser 'Kirov' by several authoritative sources, the boats of the 'Oscar' class

are believed to be designed to operate in conjunction with surface battle groups built around those ships. Both types of SSGN are designated as PLARK (*podvonaya lodka atomnaya raketnaya krylataya*, or nuclear-powered cruise missile submarine) by the Soviets, and operate with the Soviet Northern Fleet from the Kola peninsula. Three 'Oscar' class boats are now in service, a fourth is building and at least six more are projected.

Specification
'Papa' class
Displacement: 6,100 tons surfaced and 7,000 tons dived
Dimensions: length 109.0 m (357 ft 7 in); beam 11.5 m (37 ft 9 in); draught 7.6 m (24 ft 11 in)
Machinery: one pressurized-water reactor powering two steam turbines driving two shafts with five bladed propellors
Speed: 20 kts surfaced and 39 kts dived
Diving depth: 400 m (1,315 ft) operational and 600 m (1,970 ft) maximum
Torpedo tubes: six 533-mm (21-in), two with 406-mm (16-in) liners, all bow

Basic load: maximum of 12 533-mm (21-in) torpedoes, but normally a mixture comprising four 533-mm (21-in) anti-ship or anti-submarine HE, six 406-mm (16-in) anti-submarine HE and two 533-mm (21-in) anti-ship 15-kiloton nuclear torpedoes plus two SS-N-15 15-kiloton anti-submarine missiles, or a total of 24 AMD-1000 ground mines
Missiles: 10 SS-N-9 'Siren' (six with 500-kg/1,102-lb HE and four with 200-kiloton nuclear warheads)
Electronics: one 'Snoop Tray' surface-search radar, one low-frequency bow sonar, one medium-frequency torpedo and missile fire-control sonar, one 'Brick Spit' and one 'Brick Pulp' passive intercept and threat-warning ESM system, VHF/UHF communications, one 'Park Lamp' direction-finding antenna, and one underwater telephone
Complement: 110

Specification
'Oscar' class
Displacement: 10,000 tons surfaced and 14,000 tons dived
Dimensions: length 143.0 m (469 ft 2 in); beam 18.3 m (60 ft 0 in); draught

11.0 m (36 ft 1 in)
Machinery: two pressurized-water reactors powering two steam turbines driving two shafts with seven-bladed propellors
Speed: 20 kts surfaced and 35 kts dived
Diving depth: 500 m (1,640 ft) operational and 830 m (2,725 ft) maximum
Torpedo tubes: six 533-mm (21-in), two with 406-mm (16-in) liners and two 650-mm (25.6-in), all bow
Basic load: maximum of 24 533-mm (21-in) and 650-mm (25.6 in) torpedoes, SS-N-15 and SS-N-16 ASW missiles or a total of 48 AMD-1000 ground mines
Missiles: 24 SS-N-19 (18 with 1000-kg/2,205-lb HE and six with 500-kiloton nuclear warheads)
Electronics: as for 'Papa' class except one new-type 'Snoop' series surface-search radar, one VLF towed communications buoy, one ELF floating communications antenna and from the second unit onwards one LF towed array sonar
Complement: 130

'November' class SSN

Built as the Soviets' first nuclear-powered submarine design from 1958 to 1963 at Severodvinsk, the 14-vessel **'November' class** was designed for the anti-ship rather than anti-submarine roles. Armed with nuclear torpedoes, the task of these boats was and still is to attack carrier battle groups in the hope of getting a clear shot at the carrier itself. The hull form, elderly reactor design and the many free flood holes in the casing make this type very noisy underwater. They are also considered to be, together with the 'Echo I' SSGN and 'Hotel' SSBN classes based on the 'November' design, something of a radiation hazard to their crews because of design defects and poor shielding. It is known that several specialist hospitals have been set up in the Soviet Union to treat the radiation casualties from these boats, and it is reported that they acquired the nickname 'widow-makers' amongst Soviet submarine crews. In April 1970 a 'November' class boat was lost south west of the United Kingdom after an internal fire, the surviving crew being taken off before the boat sank, and there have also been numerous incidents of the three classes suffering machinery breakdowns whilst on operational patrol. At least one 'November' and two 'Hotel' class boats have been scrapped in recent years, while several other 'November' class units have been retired to reserve status. Retractable hydroplanes are carried just aft of the bow sonar systems, and two 406-mm (16-in) anti-escort torpedo tubes are fitted aft. The remaining 'November' class boats are distributed eight to the Northern Fleet

(probably some in reserve) and four to the Pacific Fleet.

Specification
'November' class
Displacement: 4,200 tons surfaced and 5,000 tons dived
Dimensions: length 109.7 m (359 ft 11 in); beam 9.1 m (29 ft 10 in); draught 6.7 m (22 ft 0 in)
Machinery: one pressurized-water reactor powering two steam turbines driving two four- or six-bladed propellors
Speed: 20 kts surfaced and 30 kts dived
Diving depth: 300 m (985 ft) operational and 500 m (1,640 ft) maximum
Torpedo tubes: eight 533-mm (21-in) bow and two 406-mm (16-in) stern
Basic load: maximum of 24 533-mm (21-

in) torpedoes, normally a mixture of 18 533-mm (21-in) anti-ship or anti-submarine and six 533-mm (21-in) anti-ship 15-kiloton nuclear torpedoes, plus two 406-mm (16-in) anti-ship torpedoes
Missiles: none
Electronics: one 'Snoop Tray' surface-search radar, one 'Stop Light' ESM system, one medium-frequency Hercules bow sonar, one medium-frequency Feniks bow sonar, VHF/UHF communications and one underwater telephone
Complement: 86

The 'November' class SSN, the 'Echo' class SSN, 'Echo II' class SSGN and the 'Hotel II' class SSBN are characterized in Soviet navy service by the number of breakdowns they have suffered on operational patrol. The 'November' class boat seen here subsequently sank in April 1970.

Nicknamed 'widow makers' in Soviet naval service because of poor reactor shielding, the 'November' class is expected to be retired rapidly over the next few years as more modern and much safer submarines enter service. Their primary armament is 15 kt yield 533-mm (21-in) anti-ship nuclear torpedoes.

'Victor I', 'Victor II' and 'Victor III' class SSNs

The **'Victor I' class** is designated by the Soviets as a PLA (*podvodaya lodka atomnaya*, or nuclear-powered submarine), and together with the contemporary 'Charlie I' SSGN and 'Yankee' SSBN classes formed the second generation of Soviet nuclear submarines. The 'Victor' and 'Charlie' class boats were the first Soviet submarines built to the teardrop hull design for high underwater speeds. The first 'Victor' was completed in 1967 at the Admiralty Shipyard, Leningrad, where the last of 16 units was completed in 1974. The 'Victor I' boats are the fastest pressurized-water reactor-powered SSNs afloat, even with the advent of the American 'Los Angeles' class. The enriched uranium fuelled reactor is of the same type as installed in both the 'Charlie' and 'Yankee' class vessels. In 1972, the first of the improved **'Victor II' class** was built at the Gorki shipyard, being produced in alternate years to the 'Charlie II' SSGN design. Five were built there, whilst another two were apparently constructed at the Admiralty Shipyard in 1975 as an interim measure whilst the first of the more complex **'Victor III' class** units were being laid down. Initially called the **'Uniform' class** by NATO, the 'Victor II' class is marked by a 6.1 m (20 ft) extension inserted into the hull forward of the sail for what is believed to be the original test fire-control and launch equipment for the SS-N-15/16 ASW missiles.

In 1976 the first of the 'Victor III' units was launched at the Admiralty Shipyard, and this class has subsequently been built there at the rate of one per year. In 1978 the Komsomolsk yard joined the production team, building two boats per year after the end of 'Delta I' class production. A total of 21 'Victor IIIs' have been built, with production at the Admiralty shipyard stopping in 1982 (replaced on the slips by the 'Sierra' class) and continuing at Komsomolsk until 1985, where the replacement design is thought to be the 'Akula'. The improvement over the 'Victor II' represented by the 'Victor III' class is a 3 m (9 ft 10 in) hull extension forward of the fin and a pod mounted atop the upper rudder for what is thought to be the first Soviet submarine-mounted towed sonar array. The extension probably provides the extra volume for the additional electronic equipment required to process the data from the array. All three classes are coated with the 'Clusterguard' anechoic coating developed to reduce the effectiveness of active sonar systems on NATO ships, submarines and ASW torpedoes. It is also known that there is a decrease in radiated noise levels as the design was improved, the 'Victor III' class being described officially in US Navy circles as the equivalent to the USS 'Sturgeon' class SSN in quietness. They also have bow hydroplanes that retract into the hull at high underwater speeds or when a boat is on the surface.

Like all boats after the 'Hotel' SSBN, 'Echo' SSGN and 'November' SSN classes, the 'Victor' class boats have had two of their 533-mm (21-in) tubes fitted with 406-mm (16-in) ASW torpedo liners for self-defence use. Two of these weapons are carried in the place of every 533-mm (21-in) reload offloaded. 'Victors' are used by the Pacific and Northern Fleets. There are thought to be three 'Victor Is', two 'Victor IIs' and 11 'Victor IIIs' in the former, and thirteen 'Victor Is', five 'Victor IIs' and ten 'Victor IIIs' in the North.

Specification
'Victor I' class
Displacement: 4,300 tons surfaced and 5,300 tons dived
Dimensions: length 93.9 m (308 ft 1 in); beam 10.0 m (32 ft 10 in); draught 7.3 m (23 ft 11 in)
Machinery: one pressurized-water reactor powering two steam turbines driving one five-blade propeller and two two-blade propellers
Speed: 20 kts surfaced and 32 kts dived
Diving depth: 400 m (1,315 ft) operational and 600 m (1,970 ft) maximum
Torpedo tubes: six 533-mm (21-in), two with 406-mm (16-in) liners, all bow
Basic load: maximum of 18 533-mm (21-in) torpedoes, but normally a mixture of eight 533-mm (21-in) anti-ship or anti-submarine, 10 406-mm (16-in) anti-submarine and two 533-mm (21-in) anti-ship 15-kiloton nuclear torpedoes plus two SS-N-15 anti-submarine 15-kiloton missiles, or a total of 36 AMD-1000 ground mines
Missiles: none
Electronics: one 'Snoop Tray' surface-search radar, one low-frequency bow sonar, one medium-frequency missile and torpedo fire-control sonar, one 'Brick Spit' and one 'Brick Pulp' passive intercept and threat-warning ESM system, VHF/UHF communications one 'Park Lamp' direction-finding antenna and one underwater telephone
Complement: 100

Specification
'Victor II' class
Displacement: 4,700 tons surfaced and 5,700 tons dived
Dimensions: length 100.0 m (328 ft 10 in); beam 10.0 m (32 ft 10 in); draught 7.3 m (23 ft 11 in)
Machinery: as for 'Victor I' class
Speed: 20 kts surfaced and 31 kts dived
Diving depth: as for 'Victor I' class
Torpedo tubes: as for 'Victor I' class plus two 650-mm (25.6-in) bow
Basic load: as for 'Victor I' class but with two SS-N-16 anti-submarine
Missiles: none
Electronics: as for 'Victor I' class plus one towed VLF communications buoy and one floating ELF communications antenna

A Soviet 'Victor I' class SSN in the Malacca Straits during 1974. The large number of personnel seen on the sail structure are sunbathing.

Complement: 100

Specification
'Victor III' class
Displacement: 5,000 tons surfaced and 6,300 tons dived
Dimensions: length 104 m (341 ft 2 in); beam 10.0 m (32 ft 10 in); draught 7.3 m (23 ft 11 in)
Machinery: as for 'Victor I' but driving either two tandem four bladed propellors oriented 22.5° apart or one seven bladed propellor plus two bladed propellors
Speed: 20 kts surfaced and 30 kts dived
Electronics: as for 'Victor II' but with one LF retractable towed sonar array and one 'Pert Spring' SATNAV system (being retrofitted in 'Victor I' and 'Victor II')
Complement: 115

Above: A windfall for Western naval intelligence, this Soviet 'Victor III' class SSN got into difficulties off the North Carolina coast in November 1983. The vessel had to be towed to Cuba for repairs after becoming enmeshed in the towed sonar array of a US Navy frigate.

Below: A Soviet 'Victor III' class vessel. The pod on the top of the upper rudder is for a towed sonar array, the first such installation on a Soviet submarine. To match the sonar's long range, the class carries both SS-N-15 and 16 ASW missiles.

USSR
'Alpha' class SSN

The prototype of what is the world's fastest and deepest diving operational submarine, the **'Alpha' class**, was launched at the Sudomekh shipyard, Leningrad in 1970-1 and underwent a series of trials with both the Baltic and Northern fleets. Major problems were encountered with both the powerplant and the hull, and the vessel was subsequently cut up for analysis in 1974, then scrapped. The reason for the problems were discovered by Western intelligence to be that the hull was suffering a severe cracking problem as it was constructed from a titanium alloy, a very difficult material to weld successfully, and that the reactor was of a very advanced type using a liquid-metal (lead-bismuth) coolant as the heat exchange medium between the reactor and the secondary steam turbine systems. This is similar to a type of reactor plant that the Americans had already tested and discarded as being too complex for submarine propulsion. However, by the mid-1970s solutions had been found to the problems, and the class entered slow series production at Sudomekh. A second production line started at Severodvinsk in the late 1970s to give a combined total of six completed by mid-1983 when production ceased. The new propulsion plant endows the class with a confirmed underwater speed of 45 kts, which is sufficient to outrun most, if not all, of the current western ASW torpe-

does and attack submarines. The Soviets have described the 'Alpha' class as an underwater 'interceptor' type with a considerable amount of automation on the machinery side. The titanium alloy hull allows a very deep operational submergence whilst also considerably reducing the magnetic anomaly signature, as the only ferrous materials are in the fittings inside the hull itself. The underwater signature in terms of noise is said to be similar to other contemporary Soviet SSNs at low speeds. The boat is also coated with the 'Clusterguard' anechoic coating to reduce the efficiency of enemy active sonar transmissions. Each of the class shows minor variations, possibly due to different systems being tested for later classes. All the 'Alpha' class boats serve with the Northern Fleet.

Specification
'Alpha' class
Displacement: 2,800 tons surfaced and 3,680 tons dived
Dimensions: length 81.0 m (265 ft 9 in); beam 9.5 m (31 ft 2 in); draught 8.0 m (26 ft 3 in)
Machinery: one liquid-metal reactor powering two steam turbines driving one seven-blade propeller
Speed: 20 kts surfaced and 45 kts dived
Diving depth: 700 m (2,297 ft) operational and 1160 m (3,805 ft) maximum

Torpedo tubes: six 533-mm (21-in), two with 406-mm (16-in) liners, all bow
Basic load: maximum of 18 533-mm (21-in) torpedoes, but normally a mixture of eight 533-mm (21-in) anti-ship or anti-submarine, 10 406-mm (16-in) anti-submarine and two 533-mm (21-in) anti-ship 15-kiloton nuclear torpedoes plus two SS-N-15 anti-submarine 15-kiloton missiles, or a total of 36 AMD-1000 ground mines
Missiles: none
Electronics: one unidentified surface-search radar, one 'Park Lamp' direction-finding antenna, one unidentified third-generation ESM system, one low-frequency bow sonar, one missile and torpedo fire-control sonar (probably medium-frequency) and one underwater telephone
Complement: 45

An early shot of a Soviet 'Alpha I' class SSN, which has demonstrated an underwater speed of 45 kts. The 'Alpha' class uses a highly automated liquid-metal-cooled reactor plant to achieve this speed.

The 'Alpha I' class introduced a titanium alloy hull into Soviet navy service. This is a notoriously difficult material to weld, and at least one 'Alpha' has been photographed by US reconnaissance satellites in dry dock with damage caused by hull cracking.

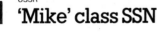

USSR
'Mike' class SSN

Construction of the first **'Mike' class** unit began at Severodvinsk in 1982 with the hull being launched in June 1983. Initial sea trials began late in the following year. The 'Mike' design appears to use the 'Alpha' class technology in that the hull is made from titanium and to enhance the power output the two nuclear reactors fitted use liquid lead-bismuth metal as the primary coolant medium. An assignment of the SSGN designation to the 'Mike' class might well be more appropriate as no rudder mounted sonar pod is fitted, which suggests that the armament is biased more towards attacking

surface targets than other submarines. The high underwater speed also supports this supposition as the boat can easily manoeuvre around an American surface action or carrier battle group's defences to attain the best launch position for its missiles. For such a mission the armament may therefore be an anti-ship attack optimized variant of the SS-N-21 cruise missile fired from vertical launch tubes in the hull and backed up by the anti-ship versions of 533mm (21 in) and 650mm (25.6 in) torpedoes with either HE or nuclear warheads. Retractable bow hydroplanes are fitted and the hull is covered with

the 'Clusterguard' anechoic coating. The sole 'Mike' is still undergoing trials with the Northern Fleet although the Americans believe it may well be series produced in the near future.

Specification (provisional)
'Mike' class
Displacement: 5,280 tons surfaced, 6,290 tons dived
Dimensions: length 110m (360.9 ft), beam 12.4m (40.7 ft), draught 9m (29.5 ft)
Propulsion: two liquid metal cooled reactors powering two steam turbines driving one shaft with a seven blade

propeller
Speed: 20 kts surfaced, 38-40 kts dived
Diving depth: 800 m (2,625 ft) operational, 1200 m (3,937 ft) maximum
Torpedo tubes: six 533-mm (21-in) and two 650-mm (25.6-in) bow
Basic load: 24 533-mm (21-in) and 650-mm (25.6-in) torpedoes, SS-N-15 and SS-N-16 ASW missiles
Missiles: 24-36 SS-N-21 anti-ship cruise missiles
Electronics: not known
Complement: 100

'Sierra' class SSN

The first 'Sierra' class unit was launched at Gorki in July 1983 and was then transported via the Soviet inland waterway system to Severodvinsk for fitting out, achieving trials status in late 1984. The design is faster, quieter, deeper diving and is fitted with a new low frequency sonar suite when compared to the earlier 'Victor' class series. Although it is possible that the 'Sierra' design represents an 'Alpha' follow-on class using similar titanium hull technology with a more conventional nuclear propulsion plant, the underwater tonnage and American sources indicate it is steel. Although still on trials during 1986, American intelligence sources suggested that series construction was due to start that year with the possibility that the Admiralty shipyard Leningrad had joined the construction programme. It differs primarily from the contemporary 'Akula' design in having a blunter and shorter sail with no towed communications buoy abaft. 'Clusterguard' anechoic coating is used on the hull surface with retractable hydroplanes fitted forward. Over the rudder is a 9m (29.5ft) long, 2.5m (8.2ft) diameter pod that houses a low frequency towed sonar array. The 'Sierra' operates with the Northern Fleet and is believed to be primarily an ASW platform with a secondary anti-ship role.

Specification (provisional)
'Sierra' class
Displacement: 6,765 tons surfaced, 8,060 tons dived
Dimensions: length 110m (360.9ft), beam 12.4m (40.7ft), draught 7.5m

(24.6ft)
Propulsion: two pressurized water cooled reactors powering two steam turbines driving one shaft with a seven-blade propeller
Speed: 20kts surfaced, 36kts dived
Diving depth: operational 550m (1,805ft), maximum 910m (2,986ft)
Torpedo tubes: six 533-mm (21-in) and two 650-mm (25.6-in) bow
Basic load: 24 533-mm (21-in) and 650-mm (25.6-in) torpedoes, SS-N-15 and SS-N-16 ASW missiles, SS-N-21 cruise missiles
Electronics: one 'Snoop Pair' surface search radar, one low frequency bow sonar, one low frequency fire control sonar, one low frequency towed sonar array, UHF/SHF/VHF communications, one 'Park Lamp' direction finder, one unidentified ESM suite, one 'Pert Spring' satellite navigation system and one underwater telephone
Complement: 120

An aerial view of a Soviet 'Sierra' class submarine under way, taken by a maritime patrol aircraft of the Royal Norwegian Air Force. The first of the class was launched in 1983.

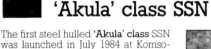

'Akula' class SSN

The first steel hulled 'Akula' class SSN was launched in July 1984 at Komsomolsk as the follow-on to the 'Victor III' units built there. The major identifying features are a longer, more streamlined fin than that of the contemporary 'Sierra' class and a broader hull than the earlier 'Victor' series indicating the use of a sound isolated (rafted) propulsion plant to significantly decrease radiated noise levels. 'Clusterguard' anechoic coating is used on the hull surface and the usual retractable hydroplanes are located forward. A towed sonar array pod similar to that fitted on the 'Sierra' and 'Victor III' classes is positioned over the rudder. Abaft the sail is a housing in the hull casing for a towed communications buoy.

Although stated to be still on first-of-class trials with the Soviet Pacific Fleet, in 1986 American intelligence sources indicated that series production was due to begin at Komsomolsk that year as a standard SSN class replacement for the 'Victor III' design. At least one and possibly two further hulls were launched. A final class total of between 16-20 units is expected.

Specification (provisional)
'Akula' class
Displacement: 6,600 tons surfaced, 7,860 tons dived
Dimensions: length 107.5m (352.7ft), beam 12.4m (40.7ft), draught 7.5m (24.6ft)
Propulsion: two pressurized water cooled reactors powering two steam turbines driving one shaft with a seven-blade propeller

Speed: 20kts surfaced, 35kts dived
Diving depth: operational 550m (1,805ft), maximum 910m (2,986ft)
Torpedo tubes: six 533-mm (21-in) and two 650-mm (25.6-in) bow
Basic load: 24 533-mm (21-in) and 650-mm (25.6-in) torpedoes, SS-N-15 and SS-N-16 ASW missiles, SS-N-21

cruise missiles
Missiles: see above
Electronics: one 'Snoop Pair' surface search radar, one low frequency bow sonar, one low frequency fire control sonar, one low frequency towed sonar array, UHF/VHF/SHF communications, one 'Park Lamp' direction finder, one

An 'Akula' class submarine moves through northern waters. It is a follow-on design to the 'Victor' class.

unidentified ESM suite, one 'Pert Spring' satellite system, one underwater telephone
Complement: 120

Modern Diesel Submarines

Since the end of World War I it has been recognized that the submarine has the potential for waging true strategic war. With the advent of nuclear power it seemed that the old-fashioned diesel-powered vessel had had its day – but this has not proved to be the case.

The Colombian navy submarine Pijao (SS28) was commissioned in 1975 and is of the West German 'Type 209' 56-m (183.7-ft) design. Armed with eight bow torpedo tubes and six reloads, she has a maximum underwater speed of 22 kts.

For most nations today the diesel-powered submarine provides a cost-effective solution to the problem of sea denial by undersea craft. Only the very large and rich nations can afford the nuclear powerplants required to give the submarine relatively unlimited endurance to perform its designated tasks. However, the diesel designs do have the significant advantage of being extremely quiet and when operating in the silent running state are virtually undetectable. Thus the smaller naval powers can, if necessary, use such vessels to effect considerable influence on the peacetime affairs in those maritime areas which interest them, and in times of conflict use their defensive and offensive capabilities to create a real threat to opposing forces.

The reality of the latter is no idle threat, as the 1982 Falklands war showed when the Argentine navy used a single Type 209 submarine to harass the much larger and better equipped British task force. The boat in question, the *San Luis*, made three abortive attacks with wire-guided ASW and anti-ship torpedoes, and caused the Royal Navy to maintain its ASW defensive tactics and airborne patrols for around three months or so, as its intelligence on the whereabouts of the Argentine submarine force was limited, to say the least.

Before this the only other time that a submarine force played a part in a major war after World War II was during the 1971 Indo-Pakistan War: the Pakistani navy had the ex-American World War II 'Tench' class submarine *Ghazi* sunk by Indian forces during a minelaying operation off the major naval base at Vishakhapatnam. In exchange for this loss, Pakistan's 'Daphné' class boat *Hangor* sank the Indian navy frigate *Khukri* in a torpedo attack, the first sinking gained in this fashion since World War II.

The most successful Western export submarine of the post-war period is the West German 'Type 209', which has been sold to navies in all parts of the world. The Peruvian Casma (S31), on her trials in the North Sea, is shown with a West German navy Westland Sea King SAR helicopter overhead.

'Agosta' class

Designed by the French Directorate of Naval Construction as very quiet but high performance ocean-going SSKs, the **'Agosta' class** boats are each armed with four bow torpedo tubes that are equipped with a rapid-reload pneumatic ramming system that can launch weapons with the minimum of noise signature. The tubes are of a completely new design which allows the submarine to fire its weapons at all speeds and at any depth down to its maximum operational limit.

The four boats in service with the French navy as its last conventionally powered submarines are the **Agosta** (S620), **Beveziers** (S621), **La Praya** (S622) and **Ouessant** (S623). All were authorized in the 1970-5 naval programme as the follow-on class to the 'Daphnés'. One, *La Praya*, has since been refitted with a removable swimmer delivery vehicle container aft of the sail to replace similar facilities that were available aboard the now-deleted submarine *Narval*. The Spanish navy built locally four 'Agostas' in the early 1980s, namely the **Galerna** (S71), **Siroco** (S72), **Mistral** (S73) and **Tramontana** (S74) using French electronics and L5, F17 and E18 torpedoes. Pakistan purchased in mid-1978 two units (built originally for South Africa but embargoed) as the **Hashmat** (S135) and **Hurmat** S136). Pakistan is known to be interested in acquiring a further two 'Agostas', and an order is believed to have been placed in 1983, with Spain. All the French units have been equipped with the subsurface-launched SM.39 version of the Exocet anti-ship missile, while the Pakistan navy has turned to the USA for the Sub-Harpoon missile. Spain is still deciding

between the two systems. The four French submarines are due to be deleted in the period 2002-3.

Specification
'Agosta' class
Displacement: 1,490 tons surfaced and 1,740 tons dived
Dimensions: length 67.6 m (221.8 ft); beam 6.8 m (22.3 ft); draught 5.4 m (17.7 ft)
Propulsion: two diesels delivering 3430 kW (4,600 hp) with one electric motor driving one shaft
Speed: 12.5 kts surfaced and 17.5 kts

dived (20.5 knots burst speed for five minutes)
Diving depth: 350 m (1,148 ft) operational and 700 m (2,297 ft) maximum
Torpedo tubes: four 550-mm (21.7-in) with 533-mm (21-in) liners
Basic load: 23 550-mm (21.7-in) or 533-mm (21-in) anti-submarine and anti-ship torpedoes, or 40 influence ground mines
Missiles: SM.39 Exocet underwater-to-surface anti-ship missiles
Electronics: one DRUA 33 surface-search radar, one DUUA 2A sonar, one

Agosta (S620) is lead ship of the last class of conventionally-powered submarines to be built for the French navy. All will be fitted to fire the SM-39 Exocet submerged launched anti-ship missile in the next few years.

DUUA 1D sonar, one DUUX 2A sonar, one DUUA 2D sonar, one DSUV 22 sonar, one ARUR ESM system, one ARUD ESM system, and one torpedo fire-control/action information system
Complement: 54

'Daphné' class

In 1952 plans were requested from STCAN for a second-class ocean-going submarine to complement the larger 'Narval' class. Designated the **'Daphné' class**, the boats were purposely designed with reduced speed in order to achieve a greater diving depth and heavier armament than was possible with the contemporary 'Aréthuse' design of conventionally-powered hunter-killer submarines. To reduce the crew's workload the main armament was contained in 12 externally-mounted torpedo tubes (eight forward and four aft), which eliminated the need for a torpedo room and reloads. Further crew reductions were made possible by adopting a modular replacement system for onboard maintenance. The design uses the double-hull construction technique with the accommodation spaces split evenly fore and aft of the sail, below which is the operations and attack centre.

A total of 11 units was built for the French navy. The **Daphné** (S641), **Diane** (S642), **Doris** (S643), **Eurydicé** (S644), **Flore** (S645), **Galatée** (S646),

Minérve (S647), **Junon** (S648), **Vénus** (S649), **Psyché** (S650) and **Sirène** (S651) entered service between 1964 and 1970. Of these two were lost (the *Minérve* in 1968 and the *Eurydicé* in 1970) with all hands while operating in the western Mediterranean. The remaining boats all underwent an electronics and weapons modernization from 1970 onwards. The first unit to be paid off was *Galatée* in 1986, with *Diane* and *Doris* following in 1987, *Daphné*, *Junon* and *Flore* in 1988, *Vénus* in 1989, *Psyché* in 1996 and *Sirène* in 1997. Besides those for the French navy, a further 10 were built for export. Portugal received the **Albacore** (S163), **Barracuda** (S164), **Cachalote** (S165) and **Delfin** (S166), of which S165 was sold to Pakistan in 1975 as the **Ghazi**

Below: Once the 'Daphné' class units wear out they will not be replaced, as the French navy will concentrate on building only nuclear attack submarines for the future.

Above: Lead ship of the class, the Daphné (S641), runs on the surface with her diesels. Of the nine remaining units of the class, only the Daphné has not undergone a full mid-life modernization which changes the shape of the bow area by adding a larger sonar dome.

'Daphné' class (continued)

(S134). Pakistan also has the **Hangor** (S131), **Shushuk** (S132) and **Mangro** (S133). South Africa operates the **Maria Van Riebeeck** (S97), **Emily Hobhouse** (S98) and **Johanna Van der Merwe** (S99) which are being modernized with locally built sonar and combat systems. A further four, the **Delfin** (S61), **Tonina** (S62), **Marsopa** (S63) and **Narval** (S64) were built under licence in Spain and have undergone a modernization similar to

that applied to the French boats. In 1971 the Pakistani submarine *Hangor* sank the Indian navy frigate *Khukri* during the Indo-Pakistan War: this was the first submarine attack since World War II.

Specification
'Daphné' class
Displacement: 869 tons surfaced and 1,043 tons dived
Dimensions: length 57.8 m (189.6 ft);

beam 6.8 m (22.3 ft); draught 4.6 m (15.1 ft)
Propulsion: two diesels delivering 1825 kW (2,448 hp) with two electric motors driving two shafts
Speed: 13.5 kts surfaced and 16 kts dived
Diving depth: 300 m (984 ft) operational and 575 m (1,886 ft) maximum
Torpedo tubes: 12 550-mm (21.7-in) located as eight in the bows and four in

the stern
Basic load: 12 550-mm (21.7-in) anti-submarine and anti-ship torpedoes, or 24 ground influence mines
Electronics: one Calypso II surface-search radar, one DUUX 2 sonar, one DSUV 2 sonar, one DUUA 1 sonar, one DUUA 2B sonar, and one torpedo fire-control/action information system
Complement: 45

UK 'Oberon' class

Built in the late 1950s to the mid-1960s as the follow-on design to the 'Porpoise' class, the **'Oberon' class** was outwardly identical with its predecessor while internally there are a number of differences. These include the sound-proofing of all the equipment for silent running and the use of a higher-grade steel for the hull to allow a greater maximum diving depth. A total of 13 units was commissioned into the Royal Navy between 1960 and 1967. They were HMS **Oberon** (S09), **Odin** (S10), **Orpheus** (S11), **Olympus** (S12), **Osiris** (S13), **Onslaught** (S14), **Otter** (S15), **Oracle** (S16), **Ocelot** (S17), **Otus** (S18), **Opossum** (S19), **Opportune** (S20) and **Onyx** (S21). The *Oberon* was modified with a deeper casing to house equipment for the initial training of personnel for the nuclear submarine fleet but was paid off in 1986 for disposal with the *Orpheus*. The remainder, starting with HMS *Opossum* in 1984, have received a new Type 2051 sonar in place of the old Type 187, new Manta ESM equipment, new DCH fire-control equipment, and the ability to mount the Type 2046 'clip-on' towed passive so-

nar array. The *Olympus* has also been fitted with a special five-man lock-out diving chamber in its forecasing for covert operations, and for training by the Special Boat Squadron and Special Air Service. The *Onyx* served in the South Atlantic during the Falklands war on periscope beach reconnaissance operations and for landing special forces, and while performing these duties she rammed a rock, which caused a live torpedo to become stuck in one of her bow tubes. This weapon had to be removed in dry dock after she had returned to Portsmouth. The two shortened 533-mm (21-in) stern tubes that were used for Mk 20S anti-escort torpedoes have been converted to carry additional stores such as extra stocks of beer.

The 'Oberon' design has also been sold to several foreign navies. Chile bought the **O'Brien** (22) and **Hyatt** (23); Brazil the **Humaita** (S20), **Tonelero** (S21) and **Riachuelo** (S22); Canada the

Ojibwa (72), **Onondaga** (73) and **Okanagan** (74); and Australia the **Oxley** (S57), **Otway** (S59), **Onslow** (S60), **Orion** (S61), **Otama** (S62) and **Ovens** (S70). The Canadian boats have received SOUP (Submarine Operational Update Project) modernizations, being extensively refitted with new fire-control systems, BQG Micropuffs ranging sonar, improved EW systems and enhanced weaponry in the shape of Mk 48 Mod 4 torpedos and Sub-Harpoon underwater-launched anti-ship missiles. The Australian boats have been modified to a similar high standard, with Sperry Micropuffs ranging sonar, Krupp Atlas attack sonar, AFCS fire-control system, and similar armament to the Canadian boats. They have also been fitted with the Karrawarra towed passive sonar array.

Specification
'Oberon' class
Displacement: 2,030 tons surfaced and

2,410 tons dived
Dimensions: length 90.0 m (295.25 ft); beam 8.1 m (26.5 ft); draught 5.5 m (18.0 ft)
Propulsion: two diesels delivering 5488 kW (7,360 hp) with two electric motors driving two shafts
Speed: 12 kts surfaced and 17.5 kts dived
Diving depth: 200 m (656 ft) operational and 340 m (1,115 ft) maximum
Torpedo tubes: eight 533-mm (21-in) located as six in the bows and two short in the stern
Basic load: 22 533-mm (21-in) anti-submarine and anti-ship torpedoes; British boats carry only 18 torpedoes
Electronics: one Type 1006 surface-search radar, one Type 2051 sonar, one Type 2007 sonar, one Type 186 sonar, one torpedo fire-control/action information system, and one ESM system
Complement: 69

Although somewhat long in the tooth, the 'Oberon' class are still considered to be amongst the quietest conventional submarines ever built and will serve on into the 1990s as training boats.

In a scene from the 1970s, ten 'Oberons' and 'Porpoises' are seen alongside at HMS Dolphin, the Gosport submarine base.

To meet a requirement for a new conventional submarine class for the Royal Navy, Vickers Shipbuilding and Engineering Ltd has developed the **'Type 2400'** or **'Upholder' class**. As with most new submarine classes, the emphasis has been placed on standardization and automation to reduce crew numbers. The first of the class HMS *Upholder* (S40) was ordered in 1983, launched in 1986 for commissioning in 1988. Three more boats, HMS *Unseen* (S41), HMS *Ursula* and HMS *Unicorn* were ordered in 1986. A class total of 12 units is envisaged at present to replace most of the earlier 'Oberon' class vessels. Also included in the design are several advanced noise-reduction features that will reduce the radiated noise levels below those generated even by the very quiet 'Oberon' class. There will also be a reduction in the short time required to

recharge the batteries to ensure the absolute minimum exposure time of any part of the masts above the water. The armament fit includes a new positive discharge and fully automated weapon-handling system which avoids the stability problems that arise at torpedo launch and the limitations that are sometimes made on the platform's speed and manoeuvrability. The weapons carried will include the heavyweight Tigerfish electric and the Spearfish thermal-powered dual-role wire-guided torpedoes, as well as the American Sub-Harpoon anti-ship missile. As part of the sensor fit a towed-array sonar will be carried, as will the Type 2040 active/passive bow sonar based on the French Thomson-CSF Argonaute set. The fifth and subsequent boats will be of a stretched (3,000 tons surfaced) design with increased endurance. All boats will have

five-man lock-out diving chambers for use by special forces on clandestine operations.

Specification
'Upholder' class
Displacement: 2,126 tons surfaced and 2,362 tons dived
Dimensions: length 70.3 m (230.6 ft); beam 7.6 m (25.0 ft); draught 5.4 m (17.7 ft)
Propulsion: two diesels with one electric motor driving one shaft
Speed: 12 kts surfaced and 20 kts dived

Diving depth: 300 m (984 ft) operational and 500 m (1,640 ft) maximum
Torpedo tubes: six 533-mm (21-in) bow
Basic load: 18 533-mm (21-in) anti-submarine and anti-ship torpedoes, or 36 influence ground mines
Missiles: Sub-Harpoon underwater-to-surface anti-ship missiles
Electronics: one Type 1007 surface-search radar, one Type 2040 bow sonar, one Micropuffs ranging sonar, one Type 2024 towed-array sonar, one Type 2019 sonar, one DCC torpedo fire-control/action information system, and one Porpoise ESM system
Complement: 44

The first vessel of the new 'Upholder' conventional submarine class has been ordered and is expected to enter service in the late 1980s armed with the new Spearfish torpedo and Sub-Harpoon anti-ship missiles.

USA
Guppy Fleet Submarine Conversions

Following World War II the US Navy had a large number of conventional oceangoing fleet submarines in service which had effectively been rendered obsolete by the German 'Type XXI' design. In order to modernize these boats and to train post-war ASW forces **Project GUPPY (Greater Underwater Propulsive Power)** was initiated. This involved increasing the battery capacity of the boats at the cost of four reload torpedoes, some freshwater tanks and the deck gun magazines. The superstructures were streamlined, all guns removed and a Snorkel fitted in all bar the two **'Guppy I'** prototypes. A total of two 'Guppy I' and 24 **'Guppy II'** conversions were made between 1947 and 1951. However, because of the high costs involved less extensive modification packages were developed for other conversions. These resulted in 10 **'Guppy IA'** (completed 1951-2). 16 **'Guppy IIA'** (completed 1952-4) and four **'Guppy IB'** (completed 1953-4 for export). These proved to be still too expensive, so a minimum conversion refit based on a 1947 trials conversion and involving the streamlining of the sail and the addition of a Snorkel was started under the title **Fleet Snorkel Program**. A total of 18 further conversions of this type was undertaken between 1951 and 1954.

Finally as part of the Fleet Rehabilitation and Modernization (FRAM) plan nine of the 'Guppy II' units were rebuilt during 1959-63 as **'Guppy III'** units with an additional 4.6 m (15 ft) insert added between the forward battery compartment and control room for new sonar equipment. A new lengthened plastic sail similar to those used on nuclear submarines was fitted and the control room beneath was extended to accommodate the latest

technology fire control electronic consoles which allowed the boats to carry and fire the Mk 45 ASTOR nuclear tipped ASW torpedo. However, as the US Navy had decided on an all nuclear submarine force the 'Guppies' became surplus to requirements and most were transferred abroad to other navies as part of the various American naval aid programmes. One unit, the Argentine navy 'Guppy II' *Santa Fé* (S11), was used as a special forces swimmer transport during the invasion of the Falklands in 1982, and while on another transport mission was damaged, beached and captured following attacks by Fleet Air Arm helicopters during the recapture of South Georgia. By late 1986 Brazil (two 'Guppy II' and two 'Guppy III'), Greece (one

'Guppy IIA' and one 'Guppy III'), Peru (two 'Guppy IA'), Taiwan (two 'Guppy II'), Turkey (one 'Guppy IA', seven 'Guppy IIA' and two 'Guppy III') and Venezuela (one 'Guppy II') had submarines of the type still in service.

Specification
'Guppy III' class
Displacement: 1,975 tons surfaced, 2,540 tons dived
Dimensions: length 99.5 m (326.4 ft); beam 8.2 m (26.9 ft), draught 5.2 m (17.1 ft)
Propulsion: four diesels delivering 4847 kW (6,500 hp) with two electric motors driving two shafts
Speed: 17.2 kts surfaced, 14.5 kts dived
Diving depth: 120 m (400 ft)

The Argentine submarine Santa Fé is seen at South Georgia after being disabled by the British. 'Guppies' introduced many of the world's smaller navies to submarine operations and a number remain in service.

operational, 300 m (984 ft) maximum
Torpedo tubes: ten 533-mm (21-in) as six in the bow and four in the stern
Basic load: 28 533-mm (21-in) and/or 482.6-mm (19-in) anti-ship and anti-submarine torpedoes or 40 influence ground mines
Electronics: one SS-2A surface search radar, one BQG-4 PUFFS passive ranging sonar, one BQR2B passive sonar, one underwater telephone
Complement: 86-95

'Type 206' and 'Type 209' classes

Israel ordered three of the 'Type 640' variant from Vickers in Barrow, all being commissioned in 1977. They were originally to be fitted with the SLAM anti-aircraft missile system in the fin.

Studies began in 1962 by IKL for a follow-on development of the 'Type 205' design. The new **'Type 206' class**, built of high-tensile non-magnetic steel, was to be used for coastal operations and had to conform with treaty limitations on the maximum tonnage allowed to West Germany. New safety devices for the crew were fitted, and the armament fit allowed for the carriage of wire-guided torpedoes. After final design approval had been given, construction planning took place in 1966-8, and the first orders (for an eventual total of 18 units) were placed in the following year. By 1975 all the vessels, *U13* to *U30* (S192-199 and S170-179), were in service. Since then the class has been given extra armament in the form of two external GRP containers to carry a total of 24 ground mines in addition to their normal torpedo armament. From 1988 onwards 12 of the class are to be modernized with new electronics and torpedoes to form the **'Type 206A' class**.

In the mid-1960s IKL also designed a new class of submarine for the export market that became the **'Type 209' class** in 1967. Designed specifically for the ocean-going role, the 'Type 209' can, because of its relatively short length, operate successfully in coastal waters. The 'Type 209' and its variants have proved so popular that over 40 have been built or ordered to date by a number of foreign navies. Six variants have appeared to date, the original **54.3m 'Type 1100'** (displacing 960 tons surfaced and 1,105 tons submerged) only being built for the original export order for four boats for Greece. Four of the **56m 'Type 1200'** were also delivered to Greece. These 980 ton boats (1,185 tons dived) proved popular, being ordered by Argentina (two boats), Colombia (two boats), Peru (six boats) and Turkey (12 boats, most built with W. German assistance). The **59.5m 'Type 1300'** (1,000 tons surfaced and 1,285 tons dived) has been acquired by Ecuador (two boats), Indonesia (two boats, with four more units, possibly larger, projected) and Venezuela (two boats). The **61.4m 'Type 1400'** displace 1,400 tons surfaced and 1,600 tons submerged, and have been built for Chile (two boats) and Brazil (two boats with three more projected). The **Type 1500** is a 64.4m (211.3ft) design ordered by India. These 1,660 ton (1,850 ton dived) boats have a central pressure bulkhead and an IKL developed rescue system based around a flotation chamber built

into the deck casing forward of the sail. Finally, the **Type 640** coastal variant resembles the original German 'Type 205/206' design. These 45m boats displace 420 tons on the surface and 600 tons underwater, and three are in service with Israel. Each country can choose its own equipment fit and crew complement level according to the amount of money it is willing to spend.

During the 1982 Falklands war the Argentine Type 209 submarine *San Luis* made three unsuccessful torpedo attacks on vessels of the British task force, but because of her presence tied up considerable British ship and aircraft resources in trying to find her.

Specification
'Type 206' class
Displacement: 450 tons surfaced and 500 tons dived
Dimensions: length 48.6 m (159.4 ft); beam 4.6 m (15.1 ft); draught 4.5 m (14.8 ft)
Propulsion: two diesels delivering 895 kW (1,200 hp) with one electric motor driving one shaft
Speed: 10 kts surfaced and 17 kts dived
Diving depth: 150 m (492 ft)

operational and 250 m (820 ft) maximum
Torpedo tubes: eight 533-mm (21-in) bow
Basic load: eight 533-mm (21-in) anti-submarine or anti-ship wire-guided torpedoes, or 16 influence ground mines, plus another 24 mines in external containers
Electronics: one Calypso surface-search radar, one low-frequency bow sonar, one high-frequency attack sonar, one WM-8 torpedo fire-control/action information system, and one ESM system
Complement: 22

Specification
56-m 'Type 209' class
Displacement: 980 tons surfaced and 1,185 tons dived
Dimensions: length 56.0 m (183.7 ft); beam 6.2 m (20.3 ft); draught 5.5 m (18.0 ft)
Propulsion: four diesels delivering 1790 kW (2,400 hp) with one electric

The Greek navy 'Type 209' Amphitrite (S117) was part of the second batch of four procured. The first batch was the first export order placed for the design, and they were delivered in the period 1971-2, with the second group following in 1979-80 (built to the larger 56-m/183.7-ft length).

motor driving one shaft
Speed: 10 kts surfaced and 22 kts dived
Diving depth: 300 m (984 ft) operational and 500 m (1,640 ft) maximum
Torpedo tubes: eight 533-mm (21-in) bow
Basic load: 14 533-mm (21-in) anti-submarine and anti-ship wire-guided torpedoes, or 28 influence ground mines
Electronics: one surface-search radar, one low-frequency bow sonar, one passive intercept sonar, one torpedo fire-control/action information system, and one ESM system
Complement: 31-35

The Peruvian navy has taken delivery of a total of six 'Type 209' submarines in three batches between 1975 and 1983. The Casma (S31) carries a total of 14 American NT-37C dual anti-ship/ASW torpedoes as her main armament in preference to the normal West German weapons sold with the vessels.

'Type 207' and 'Type 210' classes

In July 1959 Norway ordered from West Germany 15 'Kobben' or 'Type 207' class submarines under a 50 per cent funding agreement with the United States. Based on the West German navy's 'Type 205' coastal design, but with a stronger hull for deeper diving and locally produced electronics, the first, *Kinn* (S316), was commissioned in 1964. Prior to this between 1962 and 1964 the West German navy lent the *U4* under the name *Kobben* (S310) for training purposes. The other 14 boats commissioned between 1964 and 1967 were *Kaura* (S315), *Kya* (S317), *Kobben* (S318), *Kunna* (S319), *Ula* (S300), *Utsira* (S301), *Utstein* (S302), *Utvaer* (S303), *Uthaug* (S304), *Sklinna* (S305), *Skolpen* (S306), *Stadt* (S307), *Stord* (S308) and *Svenner* (S309). The *Svenner* is equipped as an officers training boat and as such is one metre (3.3 ft) longer than the other boats and has a second periscope. In 1982 the oldest unit, *Kinn*, was stricken from service and a long term replacement programme for the 'Type 207s' initiated.

Known as the 'Type 210' class an order for six was placed in West Germany that year. To back them up six of the 'Type 207s' are to be completely modernized whilst three others, the *Utvaer, Uthaug* and *Stadt*, are also to be modernized locally but then transferred to the Royal Danish navy to solve that country's problems in updating its submarine fleet. In order not to conflict with any of the names of the 'Type 210' or 'Ula' class as they are now known for the present 'Type 207' *Ula* is to be renamed *Kinn* (S316) in March 1987 whilst the *Utstein* will be renamed *Stadt* (S307) late in 1989. The first 'Type 210', *Ula* (S300), was laid down in 1987 and is due to enter service in 1990 with the other five, *Uredd* (S305), *Utvaer* (S303), *Uthaug* (S304), *Utstein* (S302) and *Utsira* (S301) following at six monthly intervals.

Specification
'Type 207' class
Displacement: 370 tons surfaced, 482 tons dived (*Svenner* 485 tons)

Dimensions: length 45.4 m (148.9 ft), *Svenner* 46.4 m (152.2 ft), beam 4.6 m (15.1 ft), draught 4.3 m (14.1 ft)
Propulsion: two diesels delivering 895 kW (1,200 hp) with one electric motor driving a single shaft
Speed: 13.5 kts surfaced, 17 kts dived
Diving depth: 190 m (623 ft) operational, 380 m (1,246 ft) maximum
Torpedo tubes: eight 533-mm (21-in) bow
Basic load: eight wire guided 533-mm (21-in) Tp.61 anti-ship and/or 482.6-mm (19-in) NT37C anti-submarine torpedoes or 16 influence ground mines
Electronics: one Calypso surface search radar, one KAE passive sonar, one KAE active sonar, one MSI-70U torpedo fire control/action information system, one ESM system, one underwater telephone
Complement: 17 (*Svenner* 18)

Specification
'Type 210' class
Displacement: 1,040 tons surfaced, 1,300 tons dived
Dimensions: length 59 m (193.6 ft), beam 5.4 m (17.7 ft), draught 4.6 m (15.1 ft)
Propulsion: two diesels developing 1,880 kW (2,520 hp) with one electric motor driving a single shaft
Speed: 11 kts surfaced, 23 kts dived
Diving depth: 250 m (820 ft) operational, 500 m (1,640 ft) maximum
Torpedo tubes: eight 533-mm (21-in) bow
Basic load: 14 533-mm (21-in) Seal 3 (DM2A3) wire guided dual anti-ship/anti-submarine torpedoes or 28 influence ground mines
Electronics: one Type 1007 surface search radar, one KAE CSU83 sonar, one MSI-9OU torpedo fire control/action information system, one ESM system, one underwater telephone
Complement: 18-20

Uthaug (S304) was launched in 1965. Partially funded by the USA, the Type 207s make up the bulk of Norway's submarine strength.

'Type 211' and 'Type 212' classes

The replacement for the six elderly 'Type 205' class submarines used as hunter-killers in the North Sea and the Norwegian Sea and eventually the six unmodernized 'Type 206' used in the Baltic will be the 'Type 211' class. The first six units are due to be in service between 1990 and 1993 replacing older boats one-for-one, with the remaining six commissioning in 1994-6. In practically all respects they will be the same as the Royal Norwegian navy's 'Type 210' class and will use the same MSI-9OU fire control suite and Krupp-

Atlas CSU83 sonar system.

As the follow-on derivative of the class the West German navy will build at least six 'Type 212' class units in the late 1990s. These will have a fuel cell propulsion system to make them independent of atmospheric oxygen and be fitted to fire Seal 3 (DM2A3) wire-guided dual anti-ship/anti-submarine heavyweight torpedoes, Sub-Harpoon anti-ship missiles and a lightweight surface-to-air missile system for defence against ASW helicopters in the Baltic Sea region.

Specification
'Type 211' class
Displacement: 1,040 tons surfaced, 1,450 tons dived
Dimensions: length 59 m (193.6 ft), beam 5.4 m (17.7 ft), draught 4.6 m (15.1 ft)
Propulsion: two diesels developing 1,880 kW (2,520 hp) with one electric motor driving one shaft
Speed: 11 kts surfaced, 23 kts dived
Diving depth: 250 m (820 ft) operational, 500 m (1,640 ft) maximum
Torpedo tubes: eight 533-mm (21-in) bow

Basic load: 14 533-mm (21-in) Seal 3 (DM2A3) wire-guided dual anti-ship/anti-submarine torpedoes or 28 influence ground mines
Electronics: one surface search radar, one KAE CSU83 sonar, one MSI-90U torpedo fire control/action information system, one ESM system, one underwater telephone
Complement: 20

'Santa Cruz' class

The long range HY80 steel hulled 'Santa Cruz' or 'TR1700' class was designed by the West German firm of Thyssen Noordseewerk to meet Argentine navy requirements. The first two units, ordered in 1977, *Santa Cruz* (S33) and *San Juan* (S34) were built at Emden and commissioned into the Argentine navy in 1984 and 1985 respectively. The third, *Santiago del Esturo* (S43), was laid down in the Argentine Astilleros Domecq Garcia shipyard at Tandanor in 1983 using West German technical assistance and components and was by 1986 in the final stages of fitting out. The fourth and fifth units were in the initial stages of construction there whilst only limited work had started on the sixth due to funding problems.

The major subsystems of the design have been supplied by companies from six countries, emphasizing redundancy of equipment and good habitability for routine patrols of up to 70 days in duration. A high underwater dash speed for short periods is said to be equivalent to the top speed of second generation nuclear attack submarines and increases the craft's ability to achieve favourable firing positions against fast surface craft. A main battery of six 533mm (21 in) bow torpedo tubes is carried which allows up to two wire-guided torpedoes to be fired and guided at the same time.

On the *Santa Cruz*'s delivery voyage in December 1984 she set a new re-cord for the distance travelled continuously submerged by a conventional submarine of 12839 km (7,978 miles). Twelve months later the *San Juan* equalled the record but took two days less in covering the distance. This means that the Argentine navy now has the means to effectively interdict Britain's sea lines of communications to the Falklands and South Georgia.

Specification
'Santa Cruz' class
Displacement: 2,150 tons surfaced, 3,364 tons dived
Dimensions: length 66 m (216.5 ft), beam 7.3 m (23.9 ft), draught 6.5 m (21.3 ft)
Propulsion: four diesels delivering 5,010 kW (6,720 hp) with one electric motor driving a single shaft
Speed: 15 kts surfaced, 28 kts (burst) dived
Diving depth: 270 m (886 ft) operational, 540 m (1,772 ft) maximum
Torpedo tubes: six 533-mm (21-in) bow
Basic load: 22 533-mm (21-in) SST4 anti-ship and SUT dual anti-ship/anti-submarine torpedoes or 44 influence ground mines
Electronics: one SMA surface search radar, one KAE CSU3 low frequency bow sonar, one DUUX5 passive ranging sonar, one SINBADS torpedo fire control/action information system, one underwater telephone
Complement: 30-32

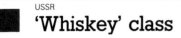
'Whiskey' class

Essentially a modified version of the German World War II 'Type XXI' design, the Soviets built between 1949 and 1957 at the Baltic, Gorki, Nikolayev and Komsomolsk shipyards a total of 236 'Whiskey' class submarines using prefabricated sections. They were built in four distinct versions, 'Whiskey I', 'Whiskey II', 'Whiskey III' and 'Whiskey IV', with the I, II and III series being fitted with gun armaments. All of these have now been converted to the definitive 'Whiskey V' configuration with no guns and a streamlined sail. Some have also been fitted with a deck mounted lock-out diving chamber for use by Special Forces combat swimmers, with several units so fitted apparently being used during intrusions into the coastal waters of Sweden and Norway.

In 1957 one unit was converted to the 'Whiskey Single Cylinder' launcher configuration for a single 'Shaddock' SS-N-3C strategic cruise missile. This was followed by five 'Whiskey Twin Cylinder' conversions for two SS-N-3C in 1959-61 and six 'Whiskey Long Bin' with four SS-N-3C missiles in a rebuilt sail in 1959-62. Finally six boats were converted into submarine air defence radar pickets around 1960-1 as the 'Whiskey Canvas Bag' class. Two others were converted to fishery research submarines. By 1985 all these conversions had been retired from service.

A total of 42 standard units were transferred abroad to Albania (four, one non-operational), Bulgaria (two, now deleted), China (five, followed by 16 locally built with most now in reserve), Cuba (one, non-operational), Egypt (eight, with two returned to the Soviets and two non-operational), Indonesia (14, all deleted), North Korea (four) and Poland (four, being deleted in favour of Kilo class units). Of the remainder the Soviets have around 50 remaining in active service with all four fleets with another 65 in the operational reserve category.

Specification
'Whiskey' class
Displacement: 1,050 tons surfaced, 1,350 tons dived
Dimensions: length 76 m (249.3 ft), beam 6.5 m (21.3 ft), draught 4.9 m (16.1 ft)
Propulsion: two diesels developing 2983 kW (4,000 hp) with two electric motors driving two shafts

In 1981 a 'Whiskey' class boat was left high and dry in a restricted Swedish military area, proving beyond doubt that the Soviet Baltic Fleet conducts clandestine operations in Swedish waters.

This 'Whiskey Canvas Bag' is one of a number of the class converted to air-defence radar pickets in the 1960s.

Speed: 17 kts surfaced, 13.5 kts dived
Diving depth: 200 m (656 ft) operational, 340 m (1,115 ft) maximum
Torpedo tubes: six 533-m (21-in) as four in the bow and two in the stern
Basic load: 12 533-mm (21-in) anti-ship/anti-submarine torpedoes (including nuclear warhead armed) or 24 influence ground mines
Electronics: one 'Snoop Plate' surface search radar, one 'Tamir' sonar, one passive sonar, one 'Stop Light' ECM system, one underwater telephone
Complement: 50

'Romeo' class

Although it was the Soviets who built the first **'Romeo' class** submarines in 1958 at Gorky, as an improvement on their 'Whiskey' design, the construction coincided with the successful introduction of nuclear propulsion into Soviet submarines, so only 20 were actually completed out of the 560 boats originally planned.

However, the design was passed to the Chinese as part of the development of their weapons production industry, and the class has been built in China since 1962, the first boats being completed at the Jiangnan (Shanghai) shipyard under the local designation **'Type 033'**. Three further shipyards, located at Guangzhou (Canton), Wuzhang and Huludao, then joined the programme to give a maximum yearly production rate of nine units during the early 1970s. Production was completed in 1984 with a total of 98 built for the Chinese navy, and a further 11 were exported, to Egypt (four) and North Korea (seven, with another 10 built locally with Chinese assistance). In February 1985 the North Koreans lost one of their 'Romeos' with all hands in the Yellow Sea.

Only five Soviet boats remain operational, two with the Northern Fleet and three with the Pacific Fleet. Six were transferred to Egypt in 1966-8, three to Bulgaria in 1972-3 and 1985, two were loaned to Algeria in 1982-3 for a five year period as training boats before the acquisition of more modern craft, and two were given to Syria late in 1985. In physical appearance both the Chinese and Soviet 'Romeos' are essentially identical except that the Soviet boats tend to have extra sonar installations around the bow.

Specification
'Romeo' class
Displacement: 1,330 tons surfaced and 1,700 tons dived
Dimensions: length 77.0 m (252.6 ft); beam 6.7 m (22.0 ft); draught 4.9 m (16.1 ft)

Propulsion: two diesels delivering 2983 kW (4,000 hp) with two electric motors driving two shafts
Speed: 6 kts surfaced and 13 kts dived
Diving depth: 300 m (984 ft) operational and 500 m (1,640 ft) maximum
Torpedo tubes: eight 533-mm (21-in) located as six in the bows and two at the stern
Basic load: 18 533-mm (21-in) anti-ship

or anti-submarine torpedoes, or 36 AMD-1000 influence ground mines
Electronics: one 'Snoop Plate' surface-search radar, one medium-frequency Feniks bow sonar, one high-frequency Herkules bow sonar, and one 'Stop Light' ECM system
Complement: 60

With only a few 'Romeo' class units left in service, the Soviet navy has transferred six to Egypt, two to Bulgaria and two to Algeria. The latter are on loan and are being used to train Algerian naval personnel in submarine operations prior to transfer of more modern units such as the export 'Foxtrot'.

The Chinese have adopted the Soviet 'Romeo' class as their main submarine production type. China has managed to export the design to Egypt and North Korea.

USSR

'Foxtrot' class

Built in the periods 1958-68 (45 units) and 1971-4 (17 units) at Sudomekh for the Soviet Union, the **'Foxtrot' class** remained in production at a slow rate for export, the last boat being launched in 1984. The class has proved to be the most successful of the post-war Soviet conventional submarine designs, a total of 62 entering service with the Soviet navy. Two were subsequently struck off as a result of damage sustained in accidents, one of them apparently caused by a collision with the Italian liner *Angelino Lauro* in the Bay of Naples on 10 January 1970, after which the unit was seen later at a Soviet naval anchorage off Morocco with 8 m (26.2 ft) of its bow missing. Three Soviet navy fleet areas operate 'Foxtrots', and the Mediterranean and Indi-

an Ocean squadrons regularly have units attached to them as part of their subsurface forces. There are thought to be 28 'Foxtrots' with the Northern Fleet, five with the Baltic Fleet and 27 in the Pacific. Fifteen of the Northern and Pacific boats are apparently in operational reserve.

The first foreign recipient of the type was India, which took eight brand new boats between 1968 and 1975. India was followed by Libya (with six units received between 1976 and 1983) and by Cuba (three boats handed over between 1979 and 1984). These differ from the standard Soviet units only in having export-grade electronic and weapon fits, although the Indian navy units are very close to the Soviet vessels.

Like all Soviet conventional and nuclear submarine classes, the 'Foxtrots' are fitted to carry the standard Soviet 15-kiloton yield anti-ship torpedo as part of its weapons load, but liners for 400-mm (15.7-in) ASW torpedoes have apparently not been fitted (contrary to several reports). The Soviet 'Foxtrots' were built in three distinct subclasses that differ only in the propulsion plant. The last group is thought to have served as prototypes for the follow-on 'Tango' design. The submerged non-snorkelling endurance of the class is estimated at around 5 to 7 days at very low (2-3 kts) speeds.

Specification
'Foxtrot' class
Displacement: 1,950 tons surfaced and 2,500 tons dived
Dimensions: length 91.5 m (300.2 ft); beam 8.0 m (26.25 ft); draught 6.1 m

(20.0 ft)
Propulsion: three diesels delivering 4474 kW (6,000 hp) with three electric motors driving three shafts
Speed: 18 kts surfaced and 16 kts dived
Diving depth: 300 m (984 ft) operational and 500 m (1,640 ft) maximum
Torpedo tubes: 10 533-mm (21-in) located as six at the bows and four at the stern
Basic load: 22 533-mm (21-in) anti-ship and anti-submarine torpedoes, or 44 AMD-1000 influence ground mines
Electronics: one 'Snoop Tray' surface-search radar, one medium-frequency Feniks sonar, one high-frequency Herkules sonar, one torpedo fire-control/action information system, and one 'Stop Light' ECM system
Complement: 80

A crew member of a 'Foxtrot' class patrol submarine prepares to dive into the Atlantic to retrieve a sonobuoy dropped by a NATO maritime patrol aircraft. Captured NATO surveillance equipment is of obvious value to the Soviet submarine service in the endless cat-and-mouse game between them and Western ASW forces. Armed with six 533-mm (21-in) torpedoes in the bow and four torpedoes in the stern, a 'Foxtrot' is capable of 18 kts on the surface and 16 kts submerged.

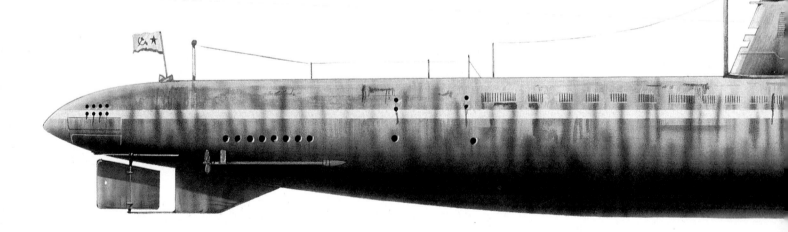

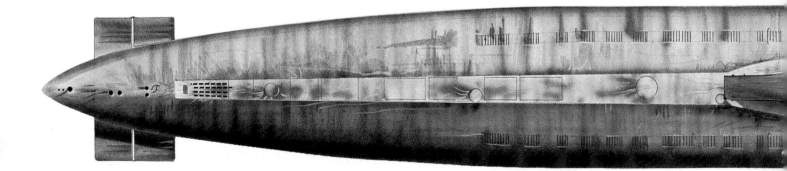

`Foxtrot´ Class Diesel-Electric Patrol Submarine

A total of 62 'Foxtrot' class units were built from the late 1950s onwards in several subgroups. Of the total, two have been written off due to accidents whilst some of the older units which are in their 25th year are believed to have entered the reserve fleet to be reactivated only in the case of general war.

'Tango' class

Built as the Soviet navy's interim long-range successor to the 'Foxtrot' class in the Black Sea and Northern Fleet areas, the first unit of the **'Tango' class** was completed at Gorky in 1972. Between then and 1982 a total of 18 units were constructed in two slightly different versions, the later type being several metres longer than the first in order to accommodate the fire-control systems necessary for launching the torpedo tube-launched SS-N-15, the Soviet equivalent of the American Subroc underwater-launched ASW missile with a nuclear warhead. The bow sonar installations appear to be the same as those fitted to the later classes of contemporary Soviet nuclear attack submarines, while the propulsion plant is almost certainly the same as was tested on the last subgroup of the 'Foxtrot' design. The battery capacity is said to be much higher than in any preceding Soviet conventional submarine class as a result of the increased pressure hull volume, this allowing an underwater endurance in excess of a week before snorkelling is required. Coupled with the new armament and sensor fit, this would appear to make the 'Tangos' ideal for use in 'ambush' operations against Western nuclear submarines at natural 'chokepoints'. Soviet deployment is thought to be 15 units with the Northern Fleet and three with the Black Sea Fleet. The Northern Fleet apparently deploys one or two of its boats to the Mediterranean at any one time.

Specification
'Tango' class
Displacement: 3,000 tons surfaced and 3,700 tons dived
Dimensions: length 92.0 m (301.8 ft); beam 9.0 m (29.5 ft); draught 7.0 m (23.0 ft)
Propulsion: three diesels delivering 4474 kW (6,000 hp) with two electric motors driving two shafts
Speed: 16 kts surfaced and 15.5 kts dived
Diving depth: 300 m (984 ft) operational and 500 m (1,640 ft) maximum
Torpedo tubes: eight 533-mm (21-in) located as six in the bows and two at the stern
Basic load: 18 533-mm (21-in) anti-submarine and anti-ship torpedoes, or 36 AMD-1000 influence ground mines
Missiles: two SS-N-15 underwater-to-underwater anti-submarine missiles
Electronics: one 'Snoop Tray' surface-search radar, one low-frequency bow sonar, one medium-frequency torpedo and missile fire-control sonar, one torpedo fire-control/action information system, and one 'Brick Group' ESM system
Complement: 60

Evolved from the 'Foxtrot' class, the 'Tango' class long-range patrol submarine has been in service since the early 1970s. The example seen here was photographed off the US coast during the Soviet navy's 24th deployment to the Caribbean, in transit to Havana during late December 1984.

Production of the 'Tango' class is now believed to be ended at the Gorky shipyard. The design appears to be an improved 'Foxtrot' but with the sensors and SS-N-15 ASW missiles of the third generation nuclear vessels.

The later 'Tango' class units were apparently built to a slightly longer length in order to accommodate all the systems associated with the ASW missile fire-control and targetting functions.

First seen at the July 1973 Sevastopol Naval Review in the Black Sea was the 'Tango' class prototype with the characteristic raised forecasing hump. The submarine to the front of the 'Tango' in the line is a 'Whiskey Twin Cylinder' cruise missile boat, which is used for training.

'Kilo' class

The 'Kilo' class submarines are the probable replacements for the 'Whiskey' and early 'Foxtrot' class units in the Soviet Navy, and as such are classed as medium-range vessels. Built at the river shipyard of Komsomolsk in the Soviet Far East, the first unit was launched in early 1980. By 1982, construction had also started at the Gorki shipyard, while export production commenced in 1985 at Sudomekh. As of 1987 some 16 'Kilos' had been built, with 12 with the Soviet Navy, two with the Polish Navy and two (out of six ordered) with the Indian Navy. The shorter hull form, more advanced than the other contemporary Soviet conventional submarine designs, is more typical of Western teardrop-shaped designs, but is well suited to the enclosed waters off the Soviet Pacific coastlines and islands. In August 1983 the first operational 'Kilo' went to the vast Vietnamese naval base at Cam Ranh Bay for the testing of its weapons systems under tropical conditions, and in the following year the first sighting of a 'Kilo' in the Indian Ocean was disclosed by the Royal Australian Navy: the presence of the 'Kilo' class in that area is thought to be due to the replacement of the normal pair of 'Foxtrot' class submarines as an operational necessity, the new boats having far more sophisticated sonar systems. Seven out of the first 12 boats have gone to the Pacific Fleet, with three and two to the Black Sea and Baltic Fleets respectively.

Medium-range boats, the 'Kilo' class have been entering service with the Soviet Pacific Fleet since 1980. This boat was seen in transit to the Indian Ocean from the important Soviet base at Cam Ranh Bay in Vietnam, where it is thought to have replaced one of two much less capable 'Foxtrot' class boats.

Specification
'Kilo' class
Displacement: 2,455 tons surfaced and 3,143 tons dived
Dimensions: length 69.0 m (226.4 ft); beam 9.0 m (29.5 ft); draught 7.0 m (23.0 ft)
Propulsion: three diesels with three electric motors driving one shaft
Speed: 15 kts surfaced and 24 kts submerged
Diving depth: 450 m (1,476 ft) and 650 m (2,133 ft) maximum
Torpedo tubes: six 533-mm (21-in) bow
Basic load: 12 533-mm (21-in) anti-submarine and anti-ship torpedoes, or 24 AMD-1000 influence ground mines, or a small number of 'rising mines'
Electronics: one 'Snoop Tray' surface-search radar, one low-frequency bow sonar, one low-frequency torpedo fire-control sonar, one torpedo fire-control/action information system, and one 'Brick Group' ESM system
Complement: 45-50

Like all modern Soviet boats, the 'Kilo' class has a covering of 'Clusterguard' anechoic noise-reduction tiles. The Soviets are building this class at an increasing rate both for their own use and for export.

Below: Built at three shipyards, the 'Kilo' class is the first new operational diesel-electric powered design to be built for a number of years by the Soviets. It is believed that they have specialized mine-laying equipment as part of their armament.

'Juliett' class

Launched at Gorki between 1961 and 1968 the 16 units of the 'Juliett' class were built as the conventionally powered equivalents of the 'Echo II' SSGN. Probably based on a considerably modified 'Foxtrot' hull the 'Julietts' are fitted with two pairs of elevating missile tubes for SS-N-3A 'Shaddock' anti-ship missiles. The fairly low sail, massive casing and the numerous free flood holes characterize this class. Current Soviet deployment is believed to be six with the Northern Fleet (with one detached to the Mediterranean at any one time), four with the Baltic Fleet, three with the Black Sea Fleet and three with the Pacific Fleet. A number of units have undergone modifications to carry additional electronics in a bulge on the port side of the sail. It is believed that this is associated with the Soviet satellite missile targetting network so that the maximum effective stand-off range of the 'Shaddock' can be achieved in order to improve the submarine's survivability, as it has to remain surfaced once a missile is launched in order to guide it.

Specification
'Juliett' class
Displacement: 3,000 tons surfaced, 3,750 tons dived
Dimensions: length 86.7 m (284.4 ft), beam 10.1 m (33.1 ft), draught 7 m (22.9 ft)
Propulsion: three diesels delivering 4,474 kW (6,000 hp) with two electric motors driving two shafts
Speed: 16 kts surfaced, 12 kts dived
Diving depth: 300 m (984 ft) operational, 500 m (1,640 ft) maximum

Torpedo tubes: six 533-mm (21-in) bow
Basic load: estimated 12 533-mm (21-in) anti-ship and anti-submarine torpedoes or 24 AMD-1000 influence ground mines
Electronics: one 'Snoop Slab' surface search radar, one 'Front Piece' and one 'Front Door' SS-N-3A fire control radars, one high frequency 'Hercules'

bow sonar, one medium frequency torpedo fire control radar, one 'Stop Light' ESM system, one underwater telephone
Complement: 80-90

'Juliett' class conventionally powered cruise missile submarines suffer the handicap common to older Soviet boats of this type, in that they must remain surfaced in order to fire their missiles. This makes them very vulnerable to a Carrier Battle Group's defences.

'Näcken' class

Ordered at the end of 1972 from Kockums the three **'Type A14'** or **'Näcken'** class submarines, the **Näcken** (Näk), **Najad** (Nad) and **Neptune** (Nep), entered service in 1980-1. They have X-configuration stern planes and two hydroplanes fitted to the sail. They were the first Swedish submarines to be fitted with an integrated Ericsson IDPS action-information and torpedo fire control system, an updated version of which (the IPS-17) is being fitted to the later 'Vastergötland' class and a simplified variant, the IBS-A17, to the 'Sjöormen' class during their mid life refits. The systems also monitor engine status parameters so as to reduce engineering personnel numbers. The boats have two decks and utilize a tear-drop hull shape. Only a single periscope is carried.

In 1986 one of the class was taken in hand by Kockums for the trial installation of a Stirling closed cycle auxiliary diesel propulsion engine in a 6 m (19.7 ft) long hull extension. Apart from not requiring any atmospheric oxygen for running as it uses liquid oxygen, the Sterling engine also has a much lower acoustic signature than conventional diesels. It is expected that the test unit will be used to either propel the boat during underwater operations at speeds of up to 5 kts on direct drive or, depending upon circumstances, to keep the battery charge continuously high in order to increase the submerged cruise radius by up to 500 per cent without the need to snort. All

accommodation space is forward of the control room that lies beneath the sail whilst the machinery spaces are located from amidships aft. A special externally mounted mine girdle is being developed by Kockums for this and the other Swedish submarine classes.

Specification
'Näcken' class
Displacement: 1,030 tons surfaced, 1,125 tons dived
Dimensions: length 49.5 m (162.4 ft), beam 5.7 m (18.7 ft), draught 5.5 m (18 ft)
Propulsion: one diesel developing 1,342 kW (1,800 hp) with one electric motor driving a single shaft
Speed: 12 kts surfaced, 20 kts dived
Diving depth: 300 m (984 ft) operational, 500 m (1,640 ft) maximum
Torpedo tubes: six 533-mm (21-in) and two 400-mm (15.7-in) bow
Basic load: eight Type 61 533-mm (21-in) wire-guided anti-ship torpedoes or 16 influence ground mines plus four Type 42 anti-submarine wire-guided torpedoes.
Electronics: one surface search radar, one KAE CSU3 low frequency bow sonar, one IDPS torpedo fire control/action information system, one ESM system and one underwater telephone
Complement: 19

Näcken is the name ship of a class of three submarines notable for their high degree of automation and manoeuvrability.

SWEDEN
'Sjöormen' class

The first of the modern type of submarines for the Swedish navy was the 'Sjöormen' class designed in the early 1960s by Kockums, Malmö and built by that company (three units) and Karlskrona Varvet (two units). The class comprises the **Sjöormen** (Sör), **Sjölejonet** (Sle), **Sjöhunden** (Shu), **Sjöbjörnen** (Sbj) and **Sjöhästen** (Shä). With an 'Albacore' type hull for speed and a twin-deck arrangement the class is extensively used in the relatively shallow Baltic, where its excellent manoeuvrability and silent-running capabilities greatly aid the Swedish navy's ASW operations. The control surface and hydroplane arrangements are the same as those fitted to the later Swedish submarine classes, and it is these together with the hull design that allows the optimum manoeuvrability characteristics to be used throughout the speed range, though they are more noticeable at the lower end. All were modernized in 1984-5 with new Ericsson IBS-A17 combat data/fire control systems. They are due to be replaced by the A19 class from the mid 1990s onwards. These are similar to the A-17s but will incorporate a fully integrated combat system, more extensive sensors and even quieter machinery to allow the boats to be used on offensive ASW patrols.

Specification
'Sjöormen' class
Displacement: 1,125 tons surfaced and 1,400 tons dived
Dimensions: length 51.0 m (167.3 ft); beam 6.1 m (20.0 ft); draught 5.8 m (19.0 ft)
Propulsion: four diesels delivering 2,100 hp (1566 kW) with one electric motor driving one shaft
Speed: 15 kts surfaced and 20 kts dived
Diving depth: 150 m (492 ft) operational and 250 m (820 ft)

maximum
Torpedo tubes: four 533-mm (21-in) bow and two 400-mm (15.75-in) bow
Basic load: eight Type 61 533-mm (21-in) anti-ship wire-guided torpedoes or 16 influence ground mines, plus four Type 42 anti-submarine wire-guided torpedoes
Electronics: one Terma surface-search radar, one KAE CSU3 low-frequency sonar, one IBS-A17 torpedo fire-control/action information system, and one ESM system
Complement: 18

The Sjölejonet (Sle) of the 'Sjöormen' class runs on the surface in the submarine's major operating area of the Baltic. In such a region speed and manoeuvrability is of greater importance than diving depth, since much of the sea is relatively shallow.

The Sjöbjörnen (Sbj) shows the sail-mounted hydroplanes which increase the vessel's underwater manoeuvring capabilities. The class can, at medium speeds submerged, out-turn most of the West's and Warsaw Pact ASW vessels likely to be encountered in the Baltic.

The five vessels of the 'Sjöormen' class are designated the Type-A11B by their builders. Fitted with X-configuration stern planes for increased manoeuvrability, they carry four 533-mm (21-in) and two 400-mm (15.7-in) calibre torpedo tubes for anti-ship and ASW torpedoes respectively.

Sjöormen cutaway drawing key

1 Screw
2 Single shaft
3 X-configuration fin
4 Electric propulsion motor
5 Diesel generating set
6 Central monitoring station
7 Outer casing
8 Aft escape hatch with coupling for rescue craft
9 Crew quarters
10 Washroom

11 Battery room
12 Control room
13 Batteries
14 Torpedo loading hatch
15 Watertight communication hatch
16 Fuel tank
17 Keel
18 Ballast tank
19 Pump
20 Conning tower

21 Snorkel
22 Omnidirectional antenna
23 Directional antenna
24 Observation periscope
25 Attack periscope
26 Bridge fin with hoisting equipment
27 Access trunk
28 CIC
29 Radio room
30 Torpedo store

31 Periscope wells
32 Watertight bulkheads
33 Torpedo room
34 Torpedo tubes
35 Trim tank
36 Forward escape/access hatch
37 Compressed air store
38 Bow tube covers

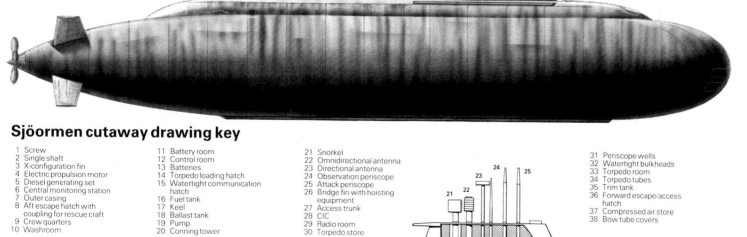

'Vastergötland' class

Designed by Kockums, Malmö under a 1978 contract, the four vessels of the **'A-17'** or **'Vastergötland' class** were ordered in 1981. The bows and sterns were built by the Karlskrona, Varvet shipyard and the mid-bodies and final assembly by Kockums. The *Vastergötland* (Vgd), *Hälsingland* (Hgd), *Södermanland* (Söd) and *Östergotland* (Ögd) are all due to enter service in the period 1987-9. The internal arrangement of the two main watertight compartments allows sufficient space for six spare berths for trainee submariners. Each compartment is also provided with its own set of fittings for deep-diving rescue vessels such as the Swedish URF. The control surfaces

are arranged in an X-configuration that is connected in pairs to two separate hydraulic systems and, until fairly recently, was a purely Swedish submarine design feature. Only two of the control surfaces are used at any one time for manoeuvring, thus providing a high measure of redundancy except in the case of a direct hit right aft by a torpedo. Two hydroplanes are also fitted to the sail and are connected to a common control shaft. The torpedo tubes are arranged in the unique Swedish arrangement of the six long 533-mm (21-in) tubes over the three short 400-mm (15.75-in) tubes. Each tube set has its own reload compartment. The larger tubes can also be

used for influence ground mines in place of the torpedo load. The class may also be fitted in the sail with four vertical launch tubes for the underwater launched anti-ship missile variant of the Bofors RBS 15 missile.

Specification
'Vastergötland' class
Displacement: 1,070 tons surfaced and 1,140 tons dived
Dimensions: length 48.5 m (159.1 ft); beam 6.1 m (20.0 ft); draught 6.1 m (20.0 ft)
Propulsion: two diesels delivering 1611 kW (2,160 hp) with one electric motor driving one shaft

Speed: 12 kts surfaced and 20 kts dived
Diving depth: 300 m (984 ft) operational and 500 m (1,640 ft) maximum
Torpedo tubes: six 533-mm (21-in) bow and three 400-mm (15.75-in) bow
Basic load: 12 Type 61 533-mm (21-in) anti-ship wire-guided torpedoes or 24 24 influence ground mines, plus six Type 42 anti-submarine wire-guided torpedoes
Electronics: one PEAB/Terma surface-search radar, one KAE CSU83 Low-frequency sonar, one IPS-17 torpedo fire-control/action information system and one ARGD ESM system
Complement: 20

'Zwaardvis' and 'Zeeleeuw' classes

Based on the US Navy's teardrop hulled conventional submarine 'Barbel' class, the *Zwaardvis* (S801) and *Tijgerhaai* (S807) of the **'Zwaardvis' class** were ordered in the mid-1960s. Because of the requirement to use indigenous Dutch equipment wherever possible, the design was modified. These modifications included the placement of all noise-producing machinery on a false deck with spring suspension for silent running. The two units entered service with the Dutch navy in 1972.

At the same time the need began to arise to start the design of a new class to replace the elderly 'Dolfijn' and 'Potvis' classes. The new design evolved as the **'Walrus' class**, and was based on the 'Zwaardvis' hull form with similar dimensions and silhouette but with more automation, a smaller crew, more modern electronics, X-configuration control surfaces and the French MAREI high-tensile steel hull material that allows a 50 per cent increase in maximum diving depth. The first unit, the *Walrus* (S802), was laid down in 1979 for commissioning in 1986 and the second, *Zeeleeuw* (S803), a year later for service entry in 1987. However, in August 1986 the *Walrus* suffered a serious fire (enough to make the hull glow white-hot) while in the final stages of construction. As a result, she may be scrapped before ever putting to sea. The class was later renamed the **'Zeeleeuw' class**. A further pair, *Dolfyn* (S808) and *Bruinvis* (S810) were due to be laid down in 1986, and a final pair in 1991. In 1981, Taiwan ordered two 'Improved Zwaardvis' boats, which were laid down in 1986 as the 'Hai Lung' ('Sea Dragon') class. The two boats are *Hai Lung* and *Hai Hu*.

Specification
'Zwaardvis' class
Displacement: 2,350 tons surfaced and 2,640 tons dived
Dimensions: length 66.0 m (216.5 ft); beam 8.4 m (27.6 ft); draught 7.1 m (23.3 ft)
Propulsion: three diesels delivering

The Zwaardvis (S806) runs at speed on the surface. Based on the American 'Barbel' class with a teardrop hull, she uses a large proportion of Dutch-designed and -built equipment internally and has all noise-producing machinery mounted on a spring-suspended false deck.

3132 kW (4,200 hp) with one electric motor driving one shaft
Speed: 13 kts surfaced and 20 kts dived
Diving depth: 300 m (984 ft) operational and 500 m (1,640 ft) maximum
Torpedo tubes: six 533-mm (21-in) bow
Complement: 67

Specification
'Walrus' class
Displacement: 2,390 tons surfaced and 2,740 tons dived
Dimensions: length 67.7 m (222.1 ft); beam 8.4 m (27.6 ft); draught 6.6 m (21.7 ft)

Propulsion: three diesels delivering 4101 kW (5,500 hp) with one electric motor driving one shaft
Speed: 13 kts surfaced and 20 kts dived
Diving depth: 350 m (1.148 ft) operational and 700 m (2,297 ft) maximum
Torpedo tubes: four 533-mm (21-in) bow

Basic load: 20 Mk 48 dual-role wire-guided torpedoes and Sub Harpoon anti-ship missiles, or 40 influence ground mines
Electronics: one Type 1001 surface-search radar, one Octopus bow sonar, one Type 2024 towed-array sonar, one Gipsy III torpedo fire-control system, one SEWACO VIII action information system, and one ESM system
Complement: 49

Ordered in the late 1970s, the two 'Walrus' class submarines are much improved versions of the 'Zwaardvis' design, with more modern electronics, greater automation and a smaller crew.

ITALY
'Enrico Toti' class

As the first indigenously-built Italian submarine design since World War II, the 'Enrico Toti' class had a chequered start as the actual plans had to be recast several times. With reasonable capabilities and performance, the four units are the *Attilio Bagnolini* (S505), *Enrico Toti* (S506), *Enrico Dandolo* (S513) and *Lazzaro Mocenigo* (S514), which entered service in 1968-9 for use in the notoriously difficult ASW conditions encountered in the central and eastern Mediterranean regions. For these operations the boats' relatively small size and minimum sonar cross-section stands them in good stead. The main armament carried is the Whitehead Motofides A184 533-mm (21-in) wire-guided torpedo. This is a dual ASW/anti-ship weapon with an active/passive acoustic-homing head that features enhanced ECCM to counter decoys launched or towed by a target. With a launch weight of 1265 kg (2,789 lb), a large HE warhead and a range in the order of 25 km (15.53 miles), the electrically-powered A184 can be used by the 'Enrico Totis' in 'ambush' situations at natural 'choke-points' to attack much larger opponents such as Soviet SSNs or SSGNs.

Specification
'Enrico Toti' class
Displacement: 524 tons surfaced and 591 tons dived
Dimensions: length 46.2 m (151.6 ft); beam 4.7 m (15.4 ft); draught 4.0 m (13.1 ft)
Propulsion: two diesels delivering 1641 kW (2,200 hp) with one electric motor driving one shaft
Speed: 14 kts surfaced and 15 kts dived
Diving depth: 180 m (591 ft) operational and 300 m (984 ft)

maximum
Torpedo tubes: four 533-mm (21-in) bow
Basic load: six A184 dual-role wire-guided torpedoes, or 12 ground influence mines
Electronics: one 3RM20/SMG surface-search radar, one IPD44 sonar, one MD64 sonar, one torpedo fire-control/action system, and one ESM system
Complement: 26

Third of the 'Enrico Toti' class was the Enrico Dandolo (S513) which shows off the characteristic JP-64 active sonar system housing on the

bow in this view. The crew for this relatively small class is four officers and 22 other ratings.

The 'Enrico Toti' class was designed specifically for the shallow water areas found around the Italian coastline. Armed with four bow torpedo tubes for the wire-guided A184 heavyweight torpedo, the four vessels have a top speed of 20 kts submerged for a short time, but can sustain 15 kts for one hour.

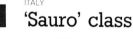

ITALY
'Sauro' class

During the early 1970s it rapidly became apparent to the Italian navy that a new submarine design was required for defence against amphibious landings and for ASW and anti-shipping tasks in the local area. The result was the Italcantieri design for the 'Sauro' class, whose first two units were the *Nazario Sauro* (S518) and *Carlo Fecia di Cossato* (S519), which entered service in 1980 and 1979 respectively following major problems with their batteries. A further two units, the *Leonardo da Vinci* (S520) and the *Guglielmo Marconi* (S521) were then ordered, and these commissioned into service in 1981 and 1982. The class has a single pressure hull with external ballast tanks at the bow and stern and a buoyancy tank in the sail. The pressure hull is made from the US-developed HY80 high-tensile steel, which allows a deeper diving capability than on the previous 'Enrico Toti' design. The main armament is the Whitehead Motofides A184 dual-role

wire-guided torpedo, but these can be replaced by several types of Italian ground mines if required. In February 1983 a third pair of improved 'Sauro' class units was ordered from Italcantieri for commissioning in 1987-88. Known as the *Salvatore Pelosi* (S522) and *Giuliano Prini* (S523) they are 1,476 tons surfaced and 1,662 tons dived. The length is increased to 64.4 m (211.2 ft).

Specification
'Sauro' class
Displacement: 1,456 tons surfaced and 1,631 tons dived
Dimensions: length 63.9 m (209.6 ft); beam 6.8 m (22.3 ft); draught 5.7 m

The Leonardo da Vinci (S520) is launched, in October 1979. The seven-bladed propeller used on the craft is noticeable, and is typical of the improvements made to submarines since the war.

'Sauro' class (continued)

(18.7 ft)
Propulsion: three diesels delivering 2394 kW (3,210 hp) with one electric motor driving one shaft
Speed: 11 kts surfaced and 20 kts dived
Diving depth: 250 m (820 ft) operational and 410 m (1,345 ft) maximum
Torpedo tubes: six 533-mm (21-in) bow
Basic load: 12 A184 dual-role wire-guided torpedoes, or 24 ground influence mines
Electronics: one MM/BPS704 surface-

The Nazario Sauro (S518). A third pair of this type was authorized in the 1983 budget, with longer torpedo tubes to accommodate the American Sub-Harpoon anti-ship missile. Future naval plans will include a fourth pair of even larger 'Sauros' if funding permits.

search radar, one IPD70 sonar, one Velox M5 sonar, one torpedo fire-control/action information system, and one ESM system
Complement: 45

JAPAN

'Yuushio' class

The 'Yuushio' class is the mainstay of a projected 15-boat submarine fleet that will eventually be armed with the American Sub-Harpoon anti-ship missile. All the classes incorporate Japanese-built equipment, weapons and electronics into their designs.

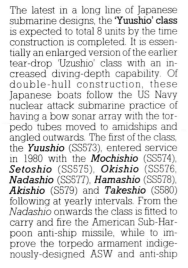

The latest in a long line of Japanese submarine designs, the **'Yuushio' class** is expected to total 8 units by the time construction is completed. It is essentially an enlarged version of the earlier tear-drop 'Uzushio' class with an increased diving-depth capability. Of double-hull construction, these Japanese boats follow the US Navy nuclear attack submarine practice of having a bow sonar array with the torpedo tubes moved to amidships and angled outwards. The first of the class, the *Yuushio* (SS573), entered service in 1980 with the *Mochishio* (SS574), *Setoshio* (SS575), *Okishio* (SS576), *Nadashio* (SS577), *Hamashio* (SS578), *Akishio* (S579) and *Takeshio* (S580) following at yearly intervals. From the *Nadashio* onwards the class is fitted to carry and fire the American Sub-Harpoon anti-ship missile, while to improve the torpedo armament indigenously-designed ASW and anti-ship

The 'Yuushio' class was based on the earlier 'Uzushio' design, of which the Isoshio was the third unit. With a double-hull teardrop shape, the 'Uzushios' introduced the angled amidships torpedo tubes into service in the early 1970s.

torpedoes are about to enter production for the submarine service. The electronics carried are of the latest designs, and are known to include several licence-built American systems. A new design of submarine is currently in the initial design phase as the follow-on class for construction in the 1990s.

Specification
'Yuushio' class
Displacement: 2,200 tons surfaced and 2,730 tons dived
Dimensions: length 76.0 m (249.3 ft); beam 9.9 m (32.5 ft); draught 7.5 m (24.6 ft)
Propulsion: two diesels delivering 2535 kW (3,400 hp) with one electric motor driving one shaft
Speed: 12 kts surfaced and 20 kts dived
Diving depth: 300 m (984 ft) operational and 500 m (1,640 ft) maximum
Torpedo tubes: six 533-mm (21-in) amidships
Basic load: 18 anti-submarine and anti-ship torpedoes
Electronics: one ZPS-4 surface-search radar, one ZQQ-4 bow sonar, and one SQS-36(J) sonar
Complement: 75

The Yuushio (SS573) is equipped with automatic three-dimensional controls, remote engine control and a ZYQ-1 digital information processing system within its high-tensile steel teardrop hull structure. A new 2400-tonne type is projected to follow the 'Yuushio' class.

Modern Aircraft Carriers

The aircraft-carrier has developed rapidly since World War II. Extremely expensive but flexible in operation, the carrier has become the most visible sign of power projection throughout the world, from the Falklands to the Lebanon and Grenada.

The first of Britain's ASW carriers heads an ASW task group. At the bow can be seen the twin area defence Sea Dart SAM launcher, together with the white dome of the newly-installed Phalanx 20-mm close-in weapon system.

Since World War II the aircraft-carrier has evolved from a relatively simple 'carrier of aircraft' into a highly complex and integrated weapons system which has the potential to fight and survive in nuclear war as well as constituting an especially important political tool in the field of world politics. Such carriers (as part of carrier battle groups) are regularly used by the United States as political and military fire brigade units, moved to high-tension areas which are of politico-economic interest to the USA. The most recent examples of this policy are the deployments off both the Pacific and Atlantic coasts of Nicaragua, off the Lebanon, outside the Persian Gulf and in the Caribbean off Grenada.

In the late 1980s most NATO countries find the cost of building and operating fixed-wing conventional aircraft-carriers to be prohibitive and have consequently withdrawn the few that they had from use. In the case of the United Kingdom such carriers were replaced by ships configured to carry the revolutionary V/STOL BAe Sea Harrier fighter. However, even though these ships performed magnificently during the Falklands war the aircraft they carry are limited in operational capabilities and numbers. It must be said that had there been present a fixed-wing carrier with an air group of McDonnell Douglas Phantoms, BAe Buccaneers and Fairey Gannet AEW aircraft in addition to Sea Harriers, then the defensive air war and counter-air operations against Port Stanley airport would have been considerably more successful than they were and the actual number of Royal Navy warships and auxiliaries lost or damaged would have been lower. The main point is that although V/STOL aircraft do provide a significant improvement (in terms of operational constraints removed from the the carrier during flight operations), it should have been realized in the relevant defence and political circles that such a combination is in fact complementary to the conventional carrier and not a replacement for it. For instance, the presence of the long-range Phantom and Buccaneer would have created serious defence problems for the Argentinian high command as these aircraft would easily have been capable of attacking the Argentinian air bases from which the strikes against the task force were launched, something which the Sea Harriers would have found very difficult to do. In addition the Buccaneers with a suitable anti-ship missile would have created an Exocet-type threat in reverse to the Argentinian navy, whilst the presence of airborne early warning and fighter-control aircraft would have resulted in a much more effective air defence for the task force. It is interesting to note that the US Navy has already conducted successful trials with US Marine Corps AV-8s as part of an air group with fixed-wing aircraft, whilst it will probably be the Soviets who will actually operate both carrier types within a single carrier group when their first nuclear-powered fixed-wing carrier is commissioned in the late 1980s. They already operate VTOL-equipped ships in the form of their hybrid cruiser-carrier 'Kiev' class.

For those smaller countries that still have carriers in service the current choice has mostly been to refit them to last until the 1990s while studying long-term replacement plans. Only France has committed itself to fixed-wing operations into the 21st century by planning two nuclear-powered replacements for the 'Clemenceau' class, whilst Spain and India have leaned towards V/STOL aircraft. In the case of the largest operator, the USA, heavy investment in nuclear-powered vessels has resulted in the fixed-wing option with any suggestion of V/STOL carriers quickly discarded on the grounds of such carriers' lack of multi-role capability. The US Marine Corps thus remains the major operator of V/STOL aircraft in that country.

An increasingly common sight on the world's oceans, this Soviet carrier group includes Kiev, a 'Kresta' class ASW cruiser, a 'Kashin' class SAM destroyer, and a fast support vessel.

'Kiev' class

Planning for a class of hybrid cruiser-carriers probably started in the Soviet Union in the early 1960s, when the need was seen for a small number of ships suitable for carrying interceptor aircraft capable of providing the air defence necessary for Soviet submarine-hunting forces and submarines operating in hostile sea areas. Although the 'Moskva' class of helicopter-cruisers was meant to be in series production, with a total of 12 planned, the units of the class could operate only ASW helicopters, and so did not meet the new requirement. Thus the yard building the 'Moskva' class, Black Sea Shipyard No. 444 at Nikolayev, was switched to building the new design after only two 'Moskva' class ships had been completed. The first of the new four-ship class, the *Kiev*, was laid down in September 1970, launched in December 1972 and commissioned in October 1976 after extensive trials. The second ship, the *Minsk*, followed in December 1972, was launched in August 1975 and commissioned in July 1979. The third ship, the *Novorossiysk* (to a modified design) was laid down in September 1975, launched in December 1978 and entered service in June 1983. The final vessel, the *Baku*, was laid down in January 1979, launched in April 1982 and entered service in 1986.

The *Kiev* and her sisterships are basically the same in physical appearance but differ in equipment fits. All have seven take-off and landing spots marked on their angled flightdecks on the port side: six (marked with the letter C and the numbers 1 to 6) are for helicopters, whilst the Yakovlev Yak-36MP 'Forger-A' VTOL fighters take off from position 6 and land on the 189-m (620-ft) long, 20.7-m (68-ft) wide asbestos tile-coated flightdeck near position 5 on a specially designated spot, marked with an E on the *Kiev* and an M on the *Minsk* and *Novorossiysk*. Each of the first two ships have seven deck lifts, a 7-m (23-ft) square unit for cargo on the port side of the island forward, a 19.2 m (63 ft) by 10.35 m (34 ft) unit for helicopters close to the island midpoint, an 18.5 m (60 ft 8 in) by 4.7 m (15 ft 5 in) unit aft of the island for the 'Forgers', three 6.5 m (21 ft 4 in) by 1.5 m (5 ft) weapons lifts in line astern next to the helicopter lift, and a similarly-sized personnel lift on the port side. The third ship does not have the cargo lift and has only two ammunition lifts. In addition she has a test area for running up the 'Forger' engines on the starboard side of the flight deck. The air wing for the 'Kiev' class comprises 13 Yak-38s (including one 'Forger-B' unarmed conversion trainer), 18 Kamov Ka-25 'Hormone-A' ASW helicopters, three 'Hormone-B' midcourse missile-guidance correction/target designator/ELINT helicopters and one 'Hormone-C' SAR plane-guard helicopter.

All have been seen with a number of Kamov Ka-27 'Helix' helicopters in place of 'Hormones'. All the embarked aircraft can be carried in the hangar. The *Novorossiysk* is fitted with space for the new SA-N-9 SAM vertical launch system in place of the SA-N-4 'Gecko' bin launchers carried by her sisters. On the electronics side the *Novorossiysk* does not carry the characteristic 'Side Globe' ESM domes on each side of the island susperstructure, but has instead two as yet unidentified radars and four 'Bell Crown' electro-optical targeting systems that were first seen on the nuclear-powered battle-cruiser *Kirov*. According to current thought it is believed that there will be two 'Kievs' each with the Pacific and Northern Fleets for surface action/ASW group command and control roles. Preliminary reports indicate that *Baku* has a number of configurational changes compared to the other three ships, with more modern radars, additional SS-N-12 launchers and possible redistribution of the SA-N-9 launcher bins.

Specification
Displacement: 36,000 tons standard, 44,000 tons full load
Dimensions: length 275 m (902 ft 3 in); beam 50 m (164 ft) including flightdeck and sponsons; draught 9.5 m (31 ft 2 in)
Machinery: four-shaft geared steam turbines delivering 180,000 shp (134225 kW)
Speed: 32 kts
Armament: four twin SS-N-12 'Sandbox' SSM launchers (16 missiles), two twin SA-N-3 'Goblet' area-defence SAM launchers (72 missiles), two twin SA-N-4 'Gecko' short-range SAM launchers (36 missiles, *Kiev* and *Minsk*) or 12 8-round vertical launchers for SA-N-9 short range SAMs (*Novorossiysk* and *Baku*), two twin 76-mm DP gun mounts,

eight ADG6-30 30-mm CIWS, two twelve barrel RBU6000 ASW rocket launchers, one twin SUW-N-1 dual-purpose ASW launcher (with 20 FRAS-1 and 14 SS-N-14 'Silex' missiles), and two quintuple 533-mm (21-in) torpedo tubes
Electronics: one 'Top Knot' TACAN system, one 'Top Sail' and one 'Top Steer' 3D radar, one 'Don Kay' and two 'Palm Frond' navigation and surface-search radars (three 'Palm Frond' and two 'Strut Pair' in *Novorossiysk*), one 'Bob Tail' radio sextant system, two 'Punch Bowl' satellite navigation systems, one 'Trap Door' SS-N-12 guidance radar, two 'Head Light' SA-N-3 guidance radars, two 'Pop Group' SA-N-4 guidance radars (*Kiev* and *Minsk*), two 'Owl Screech' 76-mm fire-control radars, four 'Bass Tilt' CIWS fire-control radars, large ESM suites including 'Side Globe', 'Rum Tub', 'Top Hat' and 'Bell' series, systems, two twin barrel chaff launchers, one low-frequency bow sonar, and one medium-frequency variable-depth towed array sonar
Complement: 1,200 excluding air wing

Kiev seen during a Soviet Fleet exercise in 1978 south of Iceland.

Below: Deployed on several occasions to the Mediterranean, Kiev uses her Yak-36MP 'Forger-A' VTOL fighters as maritime patrol aircraft interceptors under strict GCI conditions.

Below: Destined to be a class of four, there are already several variations in the 'Kiev' ships as to weapon and electronic fits. The third and fourth units will probably carry the new SA-N-8 vertical launch SAM system as soon as this has finished trials.

USSR

'Kremlin' class

In 1977 the then Commander of the Soviet Navy, the near legendary Admiral Gorshkov, acknowledged the fact that long lead items for a nuclear powered aircraft carrier had been ordered. In January 1983 the first unit of what has provisionally been called the **'Kremlin'** class was laid down in two sections at the Black Sea shipyard, Nikolayev, with the launching and mating of the two halves taking place in mid-1985. The vessel is due to start trials in 1989 and is expected to be fully operational as part of the Soviet nuclear powered carrier battle group by 1994. A second unit was laid down in the vacated docks in late 1985 and is due to be launched in 1989. The carrier air group is expected to total around 65-75 planes, including 40-50 conventional fixed wing fighters, attack aircraft and/or V/STOL fighter-bombers with approximately 25 ASW, AEW and utility helicopters. Trials utilizing a full scale 297 m (974 ft) long concrete flight deck with catapult, angled section, barriers, arrester wires and bow located ski-jump have been underway since 1980 at the Black Sea naval air fleet base at Saki in the Crimea. Aircraft types seen operating off the 'deck' include the Mikoyan-Gurevich MiG-23 'Flogger', and MiG-29 'Fulcrum', and the Sukhoi Su-25 'Frogfoot' and Su-27 'Flanker'. A final total of four CVNs may be in service by the year 2010 with two serving in the Pacific and two with the Northern Fleets. It is possible that one of the latter may well

be detached for operations in the Mediterranean or off West Africa whilst one of the former will forward deploy to the Indian Ocean/Arabian Gulf/Persian Gulf region to offset the presence of US Navy Carrier Battle Groups there.

Specification
'Kremlin' class
Displacement: 60,000 tons standard, 75,000 tons full load
Dimensions: length 300 m (984 ft) beam 38 ft (125 ft), draught 11 m (36 ft), flight deck width 73.1 m (240 ft)
Propulsion: four shaft steam turbines (two nuclear reactors) delivering 149 140 kW (200,000 hp)
Speed: 34 kts
Aircraft: 65-75
Armament: several vertical launch SAM systems (probably SA-N-9), one/two DP guns, eight ADG630 six-barrel 30-mm CIWS
Electronics: not known
Complement: 2,000 plus 1,500 air group

This US Department of Defense impression of the new Soviet carrier fitting out at Nikolayev shows the bow mounted ski-jump. The name Leonid Brezhnev has been assigned to the vessel, but of course it may well put to sea under an entirely different name depending upon the internal political situation within the USSR at the time.

INDIA

Vikrant

Formerly the British 'Glory' class carrier HMS *Hercules* that had been laid up in an incomplete state since May 1946, the **Vikrant** (as she was renamed) was purchased by India in January 1957, and taken in hand by the Belfast shipyard Harland & Wolff in April 1957 for completion with a single hangar, two electrically-operated aircraft lifts, an angled flight deck and steam catapult. She was also partially fitted with an air conditioning system for tropical service, and commissioned in March 1961. During the 1971 Indo-Pakistan War the *Vikrant* operated a mixed air group of 16 Hawker/Armstrong Whitworth Sea Hawk fighter-bombers and four Breguet Alizé ASW aircraft off East Pakistan (now called Bangladesh), the elderly Sea Hawks attacking many coastal ports, airfields and small craft in a successful operation to prevent the movement of Pakistani men and supplies during Indian army operations to 'liberate' that country. In January 1979 the *Vikrant* commenced a major refit that ended in January 1982 to enable her to operate BAe Sea Harrier FRS.Mk 1 aircraft. Included in the refit was the fitting of new boilers and engines, the provision of new Dutch radars and the fitting of a new operations control system. Interestingly enough, it was reported that the steam catapult had been retained in order that the carrier still operate the Alizé ASW aircraft, a number of which were refurbished at the same time. The new air group complement consisted of six Sea Harriers, six Alizés, and three Alouette IIIs. Sea Kings can be carried on deck although they cannot be accommodated in the hangar. In the mid-1980s, a ski-jump was

added, which meant that the Alizés had to be landed. Up to 12 Sea Harriers can now be carried. Under present plans the Indian naval air arm is undergoing a major modernization and expansion programme, and studies are being made on *Vikrant*'s eventual replacement. A projected in service date of the early to mid-1990s is assumed.

Specification
Displacement: 15,700 tons standard, 19,500 tons full load
Dimensions: length 213.4 m (700 ft); beam 24.4 m (80 ft); draught 7.3 m (24 ft); flightdeck width 39.0 m (128 ft)
Machinery: two-shaft geared steam turbines delivering 40,000 shp (29,830 kW)
Speed: 24.5 kts
Armament: seven single 40-mm AA
Aircraft: see text
Electronics: one LW-05 air-search radar, one ZW-06 surface-search radar, one LW-10 tactical search radar, one LW-11 tactical search radar, one Type 963 carrier controlled approach radar and one IPN 10 combat data system
Complement: 1,075 (including air group) in peace, 1,345 (including air group) in war

Used extensively in the 1971 Indo-Pakistan war, INS Vikrant was the major Indian Navy unit responsible for the blockade of East Pakistan. Her air group of Breguet Alizé ASW aircraft and Sea Hawk fighter-bombers sank a number of Pakistani naval and merchant craft.

 *Virat*

The original post-war HMS *Hermes* was the sixth vessel of the 'Centaur' class, but in October 1945 she was cancelled and the name given to the *Elephant* of the same class. As very little work had been done on this hull the vessel was able to benefit from a complete redesign and was thus commissioned in November 1959 with a 6½° angled flightdeck, a deck-edge aircraft lift as one of the two lifts fitted, and a 3D radar system. In 1964-6 the new HMS *Hermes* was refitted with two quadruple Seacat SAM systems in place of her original AA armament of five twin 40-mm Bofors mountings, and access to the seaward side of the island was constructed. In 1971 in a further refit the Type 984 3D radar was replaced by a Type 965 'bedstead' system, and a comprehensive deck landing light system was fitted after the ship had been paid off for conversion to a commando assault carrier, as she could operate only a 28-aircraft group of de Havilland Sea Vixen, Blackburn Buccaneer and Fairey Gannet fixed-wing aircraft but not the modern McDonnell Douglas Phantoms. By 1977 *Hermes* was again in refit to become an ASW carrier, though she retained the Commando carrying ability. As such she carried nine Westland Sea King ASW and four Wessex HU.Mk 5 utility helicopters. In 1980 the *Hermes*

began her third major conversion to change her role yet again, this involving a strengthening of the flight deck and the provision of a 7½° ski-jump ramp overhanging the bow to allow the operation of five BAe Sea Harriers in place of the Wessexes. In 1982, because of her more extensive communications fit and greater aircraft-carrying ability, the *Hermes* was made the flagship of the task force sent to recover the Falklands. During this operation she initially operated an air group of 12 Sea Harriers, nine Sea King HAS.Mk 5s and nine Sea King HC.Mk 4s. However, as the campaign progressed this became 15 Sea Harriers, six Harrier GR.3s, five ASW Sea Kings, three Sea King HC4s and one Westland Lynx equipped for Exocet decoy operations). Following her success in the Falklands the *Hermes* was refitted at the end of 1983 and became a training ship in harbour because she was too 'labour intensive' and not converted to use Dieso (the Royal Navy's current fuel type). Like the 'Invincibles' the *Hermes* carried nuclear depth bombs for her helicopters and tactical gravity bombs for the Sea Harriers.

In May 1986, she was purchased by the Indian Navy to form the nucleus of a second carrier group. Renamed *INS*

Virat she received an extensive refit before being handed over in November 1986. Her new air group will be a mix of Sea Harriers, Sea Kings and Alouette IIIs.

Specification
Displacement: 23,900 tons standard, 28,700 tons full load
Dimensions: length 226.9 m (744 ft 4 in); beam 27.4 m (90 ft); draught 8.7 m (28 ft 6 in); flightdeck width 48.8 m (160 ft)
Machinery: two-shaft geared steam turbine delivering 76,000 shp (56675 kW)
Speed: 28 kts
Armament: two quadruple Seacat SAM launchers (estimated 40 missiles carried)

HMS Hermes *with her goalkeeper, a Type 22 frigate, steaming in heavy weather. The Type 22 provides the necessary close-in anti-aircraft and anti-missile defence with the Sea Wolf SAM system that the carrier lacks;* Hermes *had two Seacat launchers.*

Aircraft: maximum 30
Electronics: one Type 965 air-search radar, one Type 993 surface-search radar, one Type 1006 navigation radar, two GWS22 Seacat guidance systems, one TACAN system, one Type 184 sonar, several passive and active ECM systems, two Corvus chaff launchers
Complement: 1,350 including air group

The Virat *is India's second carrier, whose primary offensive power (just as in her last days as HMS* Hermes) *will be projected by a force of British Aerospace Sea Harriers. Over 20 can be operated in an emergency, at the expense of ASW helicopters.*

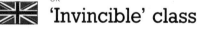

 UK 'Invincible' class

The demise of the British fixed-wing aircraft-carrier, when the CVA01 fleet carrier replacement programme was cancelled in 1966, resulted in the issue during the following year of a Staff Requirement for a 12,500-ton command cruiser equipped with six Westland Sea King ASW helicopters. A redesign of this basic concept to give more deck space (and the results from several operational analysis studies) showed that a nine-helicopter air group was much more effective. These new specifications resulted in a design draft which became known as the 19,500-ton 'through deck cruiser' (TDC) design, the term TDC being used for what was essentially a light carrier design because of the political sensitivity with which politicians viewed the possibility of a carrier resurrection at the time. Despite this the designers showed initiative in allow-

HMS Invincible *with several Sea Harriers on the flight deck. The slant of the forward ski-jump can readily be seen; this enables the V/STOL fighters to take off with larger fuel and ordnance loads than they could normally carry, a factor which was very useful during the Falklands war.*

ing sufficient space and facilities to be incorporated from the outset for a naval version of the RAF's V/STOL fighter programme that might surface. The designers were duly awarded for such foresight in May 1975 when it was announced officially that the TDC would carry the BAe Sea Harrier. Thus the first of the class, HMS *Invincible* (R05), which had been laid down in July 1973 at the Vickers shipyard at Barrow-in-Furness, was not delayed during building. In May 1976 the second ship, HMS *Illustrious* (R06), was ordered, and in December 1978 the third, HMS *Indomitable*, was contracted. However, as a result of public disquiet caused by the paying off of the last fixed-wing carrier, HMS *Ark Royal*, the Admiralty decided to change the name of the third to HMS *Ark Royal* in order to placate public opinion. The ships were commissioned in July 1980, June 1982 and November 1985.

The ships of the class are the largest gas turbine-powered warships in the world, with virtually every piece of equipment below decks, including the engine modules, suitable for maintenance by exchange. During building both the *Invincible* and the *Illustrious* were fitted with 7° ski-jump ramps, whilst the *Ark Royal* has a 12° ramp. In February 1982 in what can only be classed as one of the classic defence disaster statements of all time, it was announced that the *Invincible* was to be sold to Australia as a helicopter carrier to replace the *Melbourne* so that only two carriers would remain in British service. However, this deal was cancelled after the Falklands cam-

paign, to the relief of the naval high command, as it was realized by the government that three carriers ought to be available to ensure two in service at any one time. During Operation 'Corporate' the *Invincible* started with an air group of eight Sea Harriers and 11 Sea King HAS.Mk 5 ASW helicopters. However, as a result of losses and replacements this was modified to a group of 10 Sea Harriers, 11 ASW Sea Kings and one Lynx helicopter configured for Exocet decoy duties. One of the problems was that most of the extra aircraft had to be accommodated on the deck as there was insufficient rooom for them in the hangar. The *Illustrious* was hurried through to completion in time to relieve the *Invincible* after the war, and she went south with eight (later 10) Sea Harriers, nine ASW Sea Kings and two AEW Sea King conversions. She and her sistership were also fitted with two American 20-mm Phalanx Gatling gun CIWS for anti-missile defence and two single 20-mm AA guns to improve on the previous non-existent close-in air defences. *Ark Royal* entered service with three Phalanx CIWS. By 1986, the normal air group was six Sea Harriers (up from the original five), nine ASW Sea Kings and three AEW Sea Kings. All three carriers carry nuclear weapons for their air groups. According to official sources the Sea Kings can carry US nuclear depth bombs, and the Sea Harriers are believed to be able to carry tactical nuclear gravity bombs. If this is correct then the former are probably the same type as carried by RAF BAe Nimrods, almost certainly

the 227-kg (500-lb) American B57 type with a 10-kt yield. The tactical bombs, according to one British source, are variable-yield weapons (between 1 and 70 kt), British designed and built, and known by the codename Green Parrot. It was also implied by the same source that in the 1-kt yield version the bomb could be used as an anti-submarine weapon by the Sea Kings. Such an idea is highly likely as the more modern Green Parrot would logically be suited both to complement the greater-yield weapon on the bigger ASW aircraft and helicopters, and to become the nuclear armament said to be carried by the lighter ASW helicopters such as the Lynx and Westland Wasp. In addition the lower-yield (by a factor of 10) weapon would be particularly useful in combat scenarios where the use of the higher-yield weapon would cause considerable operational problems to friendly units such as submarines.

In 1986 *Invincible* started a long refit to modify her electronics, weapons and air group facilities. She will have a new 12° 'Ski-jump', three Goalkeeper 30-mm CIWS, increased accommodation for 1,400 crew, Type 2016 sonar, Type 996 3D radar, 50 per cent extra air weapon stowage and an air group of eight Sea Harrier FRS Mk 1 or 2, nine Sea King HAS Mk 5 or 6 (eventually to be replaced by nine EH.101 ASW helicopters) and three AEW Mk 2 Sea Kings. She is due to recommission in 1988/9. She will be followed by *Illustrious*, which will undergo a similar refit. *Ark Royal* already has a 12° ramp and is fitted for EH.101 helicopters.

Although more flexible in operations than fixed-wing carriers, 'Invincible' class ships suffer from inadequate numbers of fighters and have no fixed wing AEW aircraft.

Specification
Displacement: 16,000 tons standard, 19,500 tons full load
Dimensions: length 206.6 m (677 ft); beam 27.5 m (90 ft); draught 7.3 m (24 ft); flightdeck width 31.9 m (105 ft)
Machinery: two-shaft gas turbine (4 Rolls-Royce Olympus TM3B) delivering 112,000 shp (83520 kW)
Speed: 28 kts
Armament: one twin GWD30 Sea Dart area-defence SAM launcher (22 missiles), two 20-mm Phalanx CIWS and two single 20-mm AA
Aircraft: see text
Electronics: one Type 1022 air-search radar, one Type 002R air search radar, two Type 909 Sea Dart guidance radars, two Type 1006 navigation and helicopter direction radars, one Type 184 or Type 2016 bow-mounted sonar, one Type 762 echo sounder, one Type 2008 underwater telephone, one ADAWS 5 action information data-processing system, one UAA1 Abbey Hill ESM suite, two Corvus chaff launchers
Complement: 1,000 plus 320 air group (with provision for a Marine Commando in extreme circumstances)

HMS Invincible *steams through the waters of the South Atlantic in the early stages of the campaign to retake the Falklands Islands.*

Minas Gerais

A sistership of the Argentinian *Veinticinco de Mayo*, the ex-*Vengeance* started life in the Royal Navy in 1945. Three years later she was fitted out for an experimental cruise to the Arctic and was then lent to the Royal Australian Navy in 1953. She was returned to the Royal Navy in 1955 and was purchased by Brazil in December 1956 as the *Minas Gerais* (A11). She was transferred to the Netherlands, where she was comprehensively refitted between 1957 and 1960 with new weapons, a 13365-kg (29,465-lb) capacity steam catapult, an 8½° angled flight deck, a mirror sight deck landing system, a new island superstructure, new US radars and two centreline aircraft elevators. The hangar is 135.6 m (445 ft) long by 15.8 m (52 ft) wide and 5.3 m (17 ft 6 in) high. In 1976-81 the carrier underwent another refit to allow her to operate through to the 1990s. A data link system was installed so that the carrier can co-operate with the 'Niteroi' class of frigates in service with the Brazilian navy, and the obsolete American SPS-12 radar was re-

placed with a modern SPS-40B two dimensional air-search system. The role of the *Minas Gerais* throughout her service with the Brazilian navy has been anti-submarine warfare with an air group (since the late 1970s) of six to eight Grumman S-2E Trackers of the Brazilian air force (the Brazilian navy is not allowed to operate fixed-wing aircraft) plus four to six navy Sikorsky SH-3D/H Sea King ASW helicopters, three Aérospatiale AS.350 Ecureuils and two Bell 206 JetRanger utility helicopters. It is reported that when the *Minas Gerais* is eventually paid off the Brazilians will replace her with two carriers capable of operating a mixed air group of V/STOL fighter/strike aircraft and ASW helicopters.

Specification
Displacement: 15,890 tons standard, 19,890 tons full load
Dimensions: length 211.8 m (695 ft); beam 24.4 m (80 ft); draught 7.5 m (24.5 ft); flightdeck width 37.0 m (121.4 ft)

Machinery: two-shaft geared steam turbines delivering 40,000 shp (29830 kW)
Speed: 25.3 kts
Armament: two quadruple 40-mm AA, and one twin 40-mm AA
Aircraft: see text
Electronics: one SPS-40B air-search radar, one SPS-4 surface-search radar, one SPS-8A air control radar, one Raytheon 1402 navigation radar and

A recent view of Minas Gerais with four S-2E Trackers, four SH-3D Sea Kings, two Lynx and an Ecureil ranged on the flight deck. A more modern V/STOL carrier design is currently under study to replace her in the early 1990s.

two SPG-34 fire-control radars
Complement: 1,000 plus 300 air group

'Clemenceau' class

The *Clemenceau* (R98) was the first carrier designed as such to be completed in France. Built in the late 1950s and commissioned in November 1961, she incorporated all the advances made in carrier design during the early 1950s, namely a fully angled flight deck, mirror landing sight and a fully comprehensive set of air-search, tracking and air-control radars. The flight deck is 165.5 m (543 ft) in length and 29.5 m (96 ft 9 in) in width, and is angled at 8° to the ship's centreline. Two aircraft lifts, each rated at 20364 kg (44,895 lb) are provided, one abaft the island on the deck edge and the other offset to starboard and just forward of the island. Two steam catapults are fitted, one on the port side of the bow and the other on the angled flight deck. The hangar has a usable volume of 152 m (499 ft) by 24 m (78 ft 9 in) by 7 m (23 ft). The fuel capacity of the *Clemenceau* is 1200 m³ of JP5 aircraft fuel and 400 m³ of AVGAS whilst her sistership, the *Foch* (R99, commissioned in July 1963), carries 1800 m³ and 109 m³ respectively. During the period September 1977 to November 1978 the *Clemenceau* underwent a major refit, the *Foch* following between July 1980 and August 1981. During these refits both ships were converted to operate the Dassault-Breguet Super Etendard strike fighter, for which they carry AN52 15-kt tactical nuclear gravity bombs in their magazines. They also received SENIT 2 automated tactical information-processing systems as part of their command, control and communication suites. Following the refits the two carriers' air groups now each comprise 16 Super Etendard strike fighters, three Dassault-Breguet Etendard IVP photographic reconnaissance fighters, 10 Vought F-8E Crusader interceptors

and seven Breguet Alizé ASW aircraft, plus two Aérospatiale Super Frelon ASW and two Aérospatiale Alouette III utility helicopters. The carriers can also act, if required, as helicopter carriers with an air group of 30-40 helicopters depending upon the types embarked. During the Lebanon crisis of 1983 France used one of the carriers in support of her peace-keeping force, Super Etendards being used to attack several gun positions that had engaged French troops. Under current planning the *Clemenceau* is to be paid off in 1995 and the *Foch* in 1998. Their replacements will be two nuclear-powered carriers.

Specification
Displacement: 22,000 tons standard, 32,185 tons full load (*Clemenceau*) or 32,780 tons full load (*Foch*)
Dimensions: length 265 m (869 ft 5 in); beam 31.7 m (104 ft) with bulges; draught 8.6 m (28 ft 3 in)
Machinery: two-shaft geared steam turbines delivering 126,000 shp (93960 kW)
Speed: 33 kts
Armament: two octuple Crotale EDIR SAM launchers (36 missiles), four 100-mm (3.9-in) DP guns
Aircraft: see text
Electronics: one DRBV 23B air search radar, one DRBV 15 surface and low altitude search radar, two DRBI 10 height finding radars, two DRBC 32C fire control radars, one Decca 1226 navigation radar, one NRBA 51 aircraft landing aid, one SRN 6 TACAN system, one SENIT 2 combat information system, one ARBR 16 ECM system, one ARBX 10B ECM system, two Dagaie decoy launchers, two Sagaie decoy launchers, one SQS 503 sonar

Above: Seen entering Nice, Clemenceau and her sister provided air support to the French contingent in Lebanon in 1983.

Left: The 'Clemenceau' class were the first French vessels to be designed from the outset as aircraft carriers, incorporating all the design lessons learned in the 1950s.

After recent modification the two 'Clemenceau' class carriers will serve on until the 1990s. Their replacements will be two nuclear-powered vessels.

The first of two *Porte Avions Nucléaire* (PAN, nuclear-powered aircraft carrier), the *'Richelieu'*, was officially ordered in February 1986 as the long term replacement for the *Clemenceau* and is due to enter service in 1996. Based on the hull design of the conventional carriers the *'Richelieu'* class will be better protected. The new design will have the island moved farther forward to a position ahead of the two 19m by 12.5m (62.3ft by 41ft) 40-ton starboard deck edge aircraft lifts to permit greater utilization of the flight deck. The two reactors fitted will be of the same type as used in the *SNLE Nouvelle Génération* ballistic missile submarines. Provision for the fitting of a ski ramp for V/STOL aircraft will be made. A second vessel will be ordered in 1990 to replace the *Foch* around the turn of the century.

The flight deck will be fitted with two American C13 steam catapults, one on the 8½° angled deck and the other on the port side of the bow to allow aircraft to be launched and recovered simultaneously. The air group will initially comprise up to 43 McDonnell Douglas F/A-18-sized conventional fixed wing aircraft (including some for AEW duties) and two Aérospatiale Super Puma helicopters. In early 1987 a mid-life refit programme was revealed for the period 1991-4 for 50 of the 60 or so remaining Super Etendards in the Aéronavale inventory so that they will be effective into the 21st century. The aircraft will be modified to carry the ASMP nuclear armed strike and ANS anti-ship conventional warhead missiles, have new avionics fitted and their Thomson-CSF Agave radar replaced by the ESD Anemone set of greater capability.

Specification
'Richelieu' class
Displacement: 35,500 tons standard, 39,680 tons full load
Dimensions: length 261.5m (857.9ft), beam 31.8m (104.3ft), draught 8.5m (27.9ft), flight deck width 61m (200.1ft)
Machinery: two shaft geared turbines (two K15 nuclear reactors) delivering 59880kW (80,300hp)
Speed: 28kts
Aircraft: see text
Armament: seven octuple vertical launch SAN 90 launchers (56 missiles), two/three sextuple SADRAL point defence SAM launchers (60-90 missiles)
Electronics: one DRBJ 11B 30 radar, one DRBV 27 air search radar, one DRBV 15C air/surface search radar, two Decca navigation radars, one SAN 90 fire control radar, one ARBR-17 ECM system, one ARB-33 ECM system, four Sagaie decoy launchers, one SENIT 6 action information system, one DUBV 10 infra-red detection and fire control system, one TACAN system, one Syracuse II satellite communications system
Complement: 1,150 plus 550 air group (maximum 1850)

Veinticinco de Mayo

The *Veinticinco de Mayo* (25 May) was originally a 'Colossus' class carrier purchased from the UK by the Dutch and commissioned into the Royal Netherlands navy on 28 May 1948. In April 1968 the ship suffered a serious boiler room fire, and was subsequently judged to be uneconomical to repair. In the following October Argentina bought the vessel, which was refitted and commissioned into the Argentinian navy in the Netherlands. She sailed for Argentina on 1 September 1969. The vessel is fitted with a modified Ferranti CAAIS data-processing system and Plessey Super CAAIS console displays. This system allows the ship to control her carrier-based aircraft and to communicate via data links with the two Type 42 destroyers of the Argentinian navy and their ASAWS 4 action information systems. Her modified superstructure differs considerably from those of other ex-British carriers in service with other navies. In 1980-1 she underwent a further refit to increase the strength of the flightdeck and add extra deck space to allow three extra aircraft to be parked in readiness for the Dassault-Breguet Super Etendards that Argentina was acquiring. Luckily for the UK none of these strike aircraft had qualified to land on the carrier by the time of the Falklands war, and the carrier's air group consisted of eight McDonnell Douglas A-4Q Skyhawks, six Grumman S-2E Trackers and four Sikorsky SH-3D Sea Kings. The *Veinticinco de Mayo* played a major part in the initial landings on the Falklands and was ready to launch a strike against the British task force on 2 May 1982 when fate intervened in the form of poor flying conditions. The subsequent sinking of the *Belgrano* then forced the Argentine carrier to retire to the relative safety of Argentina's coastal waters, where she played no further part in the proceedings and landed her air group for land-based operations. After the Argentine loss of the Falklands the remaining Super Etendards were delivered. These were rapidly deck-qualified, but persistent problems have resulted in their partial replacement by the older Skyhawks. Typically, the air group now consists of four A-4Q Skyhawks, four Super Etendards, three S-2E Trackers and four SH-3D Sea Kings. The *25° de Mayo* was to be replaced in the early 1990s, but at the moment funds are unlikely to be available.

Specification
Displacement: 15,892 tons standard, 19,896 tons full load
Dimensions: length 211.3 m (693 ft 3 in); beam 24.4 m (80 ft 0 in); draught 7.6 m (25 ft 0 in); flight deck width 42.2 m (138 ft 5 in)
Machinery: two-shaft geared steam turbines delivering 40,000 shp (29830 kW)
Speed: 24.25 kts
Armament: nine single 40-mm AA
Aircraft: see text
Electronics: one LW-01 air-search radar, one LW-02 air-search radar, one SGR-109 height-finder radar, one DA-02 target-indicator radar, one ZW-01 navigation/surface-search radar, one URN-20 TACAN system, and one CAAIS action information system
Complement: 1,000 plus 500 air group

The main target for the British SSN force during the Falklands was Veinticinco de Mayo, *the flagship of the original task force that invaded the islands. The sinking of the* Belgrano *caused her to return to port without taking part in a battle.*

Dédalo and Príncipe de Asturias

The **Dédalo** (R01) is an ex-US 'Independence' class carrier built during World War II that ended her days in the US Navy as an aviation transport. She was reactivated and modernized as a carrier at the Philadelphia Naval Shipyard before being transferred to Spain on a five-year loan from 30 August 1967. In December 1975 the *Dédalo* was purchased outright and now acts as the Spanish navy's fleet flagship. Her flight deck is 166.1 m (545 ft) long and 32.9 m (108 ft) wide, and the hangar can accommodate 18 Sikorsky Sea King type helicopters with another six on the flight deck. The *Dédalo's* normal air wing comprises four air groups with at least one with eight BAe Matador V/STOL fighters, one with four SH-3D/G Sea King ASW helicopters, one with four Agusta (Bell) AB.212 ASW anti-submarine and electronic warfare helicopters, and one of four helicopters as required by the mission assigned to the carrier (these could, for example, be four Bell AH-1G Cobra attack helicopters to support an amphibious landing). A maximum of seven four-aircraft groups can be handled aboard.

Originally intended to replace the *Dédalo*, the Spanish ordered on 29 June 1977 a gas turbine-powered vessel based on the final design variant of the abortive US Navy's Sea Control Ship. Named **Príncipe de Asturias** (R11), the new ship has a flightdeck measuring 175 m (574 ft) in length and 30 m (98 ft 6 in) in width, fitted with a 12° ski-jump ramp blended into the bow. Two aircraft lifts are fitted, one of them at the extreme stern. For the *Príncipe de Asturias'* air wing Spain has ordered the McDonnell Douglas AV-8B Harrier II V/STOL fighter and the Sikorsky SH-60B Seahawk ASW helicopter. The complement of aircraft and helicopters will be 20, made up of six to eight AV-8Bs and 12-14 SH-60s and SH-3 Sea Kings (some of the latter being fitted for AEW). A fully digital

command and control system is fitted with a LINK 11 intership data transmission terminal. It is expected that a second vessel of this type will be ordered eventually to replace the *Dédalo*. The *Príncipe de Asturias* entered service in 1987.

Specification
Dédalo
Displacement: 13,000 tons standard, 16,416 tons full load
Dimensions: length 189.9 m (623 ft); beam 21.8 m (71 ft 6 in); draught 7.9 m (25 ft 11 in)
Machinery: four-shaft geared steam turbines delivering 100,000 shp (74570 kW)
Speed: 24 kts
Aircraft: see text
Armament: one quadruple 40-mm AA, and nine twin 40-mm AA
Electronics: one SPS-8 3D radar, one SPS-6 air-search radar, one SPS-40 air-search radar, one SPS-10 surface-search and tactical radar, two Mk 29 fire-control systems, two Mk 28 fire-control systems, two navigation radars, one URN-22 TACAN system, one WLR-1 electronic countermeasures system
Complement: 1,112 without air group

Specification
Príncipe de Asturias
Displacement: 15,150 tons full load
Dimensions: length 195.1 m (640 ft); beam 24.4 m (80 ft); draught 9.1 m (29 ft 10 in)
Machinery: one-shaft gas turbine (two GE LM 2500) delivering 46,400 shp (34600 kW)
Speed: 26 kts
Aircraft: see text
Armament: four Meroka 20-mm CIWS
Electronics: one SPS-55 surface-search radar, one SPS-52 3D radar, four PVS-2 Meroka fire-control radars, one SPN-35A air control radar, one URN-25 TACAN system, four Mk 36 Super RBOC chaff launchers, and one

Above: The elderly Spanish carrier Dédalo *was converted from an ex-US World War II carrier of the 'Independence' class.*

Nettunel ESM system
Complement: 790 without air group

Below: As USS Cabot, Dédalo *survived a kamikaze attack during the Battle of Leyte Gulf. Spanning naval generations, she is today one of the few ships to operate V/STOL aircraft on a regular basis.*

Giuseppe Garibaldi

Essentially designed as a gas turbine-powered carrier for helicopters the **Giuseppe Garibaldi** (C551) also incorporates features suiting her for the carriage and operation of V/STOL fighters. The flight deck is 173.8 m (570 ft 2 in) long and 21 m (68 ft 11 in) wide, and is fitted with a 6° ski-jump ramp. The hangar is 110 m (360 ft 11 in) long, 15 m (49 ft 3 in) wide and 6 m (19 ft 8 in) high, and is built to accommodate 12 Agusta (Sikorsky) Sea King ASW helicopters, or 10 V/STOL aircraft and one Sea King, although the available height will permit the embarkation of heavy-lift Meridionali (Boeing Vertol) CH-47 Chinook helicopters if required. Two aircraft lifts are fitted (one forward and one abaft the island), and there are six marked flightdeck spaces for helicopter operations. The *Giuseppe Garibaldi* was designed specifically to provide ASW support for naval task forces and merchant convoys, and as such is fitted with full flagship facilities plus command, control and communication systems for both naval and air operations. In emergencies she can also carry up to 600 troops for short periods. The extensive weaponry fitted also allows her to operate as an

independent surface unit. To permit helicopter operations in heavy weather she has been fitted out with two pairs of fin stabilizers, and her aircraft maintenance facilities are sufficient not only to service her own air group but also the light ASW helicopters of any escorting warships. Although a law dating back to the days of Mussolini placed *all* fixed-wing aircraft under the control of the Air Force, a 'gentleman's agreement' between the heads of the Italian Navy and Air Force means that the *Garibaldi* will receive her complement of V/STOL fighters. *Giuseppe Garibaldi* was commissioned in September 1985 as Flagship of the Italian Fleet, and if funds ever permit she will be joined by a sister ship (tentatively named the *Giuseppe Mazzini*).

Specification
Displacement: 10,100 tons standard, 13,139 full load
Dimensions: length 179 m (587 ft 3 in); beam 30.4 m (99 ft 9 in); draught 6.7 m (22 ft)
Machinery: two-shaft gas turbine (four Fiat/GE LM2500) delivering 80,000 hp (59655 kW)
Speed: 30 kts
Aircraft: 16 SH-3D Sea Kings (or

EH.101 when in service), or one helicopter and up to 10 V/STOL fighters (either Sea Harrier or AV-8B)
Armament: four twin Teseo Otomot Mk 2 SSM launchers with eight missiles, two octuple Albatros short-range SAM systems (90 missiles), three twin 40-mm Dardo CIWS, two triple 325-mm (12.75-in) ASW torpedo tubes for Mk 46 torpedoes
Electronics: one RAN 3L 3D radar, one RAT 20S air-search radar, one RAN 10S air-search radar, one SPS 702 surface-search radar, three RTN 20X Dardo CIWS tracking radars, two RTN 30X Albatros fire-control radars, one SPN 749(V) navigation radar, one SPN 703 helicopter control radar, one TACAN system, one IPN 10 data-processing system, various passive ESM systems, two SCLAR chaff launchers and one DE 1160 sonar
Complement: 550 normal, 825 maximum including air group

The first Italian aircraft-carrier to actually see service, the Giuseppe Garibaldi *is designed to carry V/STOL fighters, although her air group will consist of Sea King ASW helicopters for the foreseeable future as the Italian navy is short of funds.*

'Midway' class

Originally two of a class of three, the USS *Midway* and USS *Coral Sea* (CV41 and CV43, commissioned in September 1945 and October 1947) were the largest US carriers to be constructed during World War II and the only ones capable, in unmodified form, of operating the post-war generation of heavy nuclear-armed attack aircraft. All three eventually underwent modernization programmes which, because they occurred over a long time span, differed considerably in detail. Only the *Midway* and *Coral Sea* remain in service, the former being attached to the Pacific Fleet and homeported in Yokosuka, Japan, and the latter serving as a front-line carrier on the strength of the Atlantic Fleet. The third vessel, the USS *Franklin D. Roosevelt*, was struck off in 1977, her name subsequently being assigned to a new 'Nimitz' class carrier. Because of their smaller size the 'Midway' class carry the McDonnell Douglas F/A-18 Hornet in place of the Grumman F-14A Tomcat, and do not embark the Lockheed S-3A Viking. A typical air group consists of 48 F/A-18 Hornets, 10 A-6E Intruders, 4 KA-6D tankers, 4 EA-6B Prowlers, four E-2C Hawkeyes and 6 SH-3H Sea Kings (although more tankers might be carried at the expense of Intruders because of the Hornet's limited endurance). Both ships are fitted with three deck-edge aircraft elevators, but while the *Midway* has only two steam catapults the *Coral Sea* has three. A total of 1,210 tons of aviation ordnance and 4.49 million litres (1.186 million US gal) of JP5 aircraft fuel are carried for the air wing. Current planning calls for *Coral Sea* to serve until 1995, and *Midway* until 1998 (by which time she will have completed half a century in the active fleet) being replaced by the 'Im-

Midway and Coral Sea were the last two carriers to take the F-4 Phantom to sea, as they could not handle the larger F-14 Tomcat. The F-4 has now been replaced in service by the McDonnell Douglas F/4A-18 Hornet.

proved Nimitz' class carriers CVN74 and CVN75. In spite of their age, the two carriers are still potent weapons, especially with the F/A-18 Hornet, *Coral Sea* has been very active in the Mediterranean, being involved in both Libyan incidents in March and April 1986.

Specification
Displacement: *Midway* 51,000 tons standard, 64,000 tons full load; *Coral Sea* 52,500 tons standard, 63,800 tons full load
Dimensions: length 298.4 m (979 ft); beam 36.9 m (121 ft); draught 10.8 m (35.3 ft); flightdeck width 72.5 m (238 ft)
Machinery: four-shaft geared steam turbines delivering 212,000 shp (158090 kW)
Speed: 30.6 kts
Aircraft: see text
Armament: two octuple Sea Sparrow SAM launchers (no reloads) in *Midway* only, three 20-mm Phalanx CIWS in both
Electronics: (*Midway*) one LN-66 navigation radar, one SPS-65V air/surface-search radar, one SPS-43C air-search radar, one SPS-49 air-search radar, one SPS-48C 3D radar, one SPN035A, two SPN-42 and one SPN-44 aircraft landing aids, two Mk 115 fire-control radars, one URN-29 TACAN system, one SLQ-29 ESM suite, four Mk

36 Super RBOC chaff launchers
Electronics: (*Coral Sea*) one LN-66 navigation radar, one SPS-10 surface-search and navigation radar, one SPS-43C air-search radar, one SPS-30 air-search radar, one SPN-43A aircraft

landing aid, one URN-25 TACAN system, one SLQ-29 ESM suite, four Mk 36 Super RBOC chaff launchers
Complement: *Midway* 2,615 plus 1,800 air group; *Coral Sea* 2,710 plus 1,800 air group

Below: Because of their smaller size, the two 'Midway' class ships have to operate with reduced air groups. These contain no ASW aircraft and use the McDonnell Douglas F/A-18 Hornet as their main interceptor and strike aircraft in place of the larger and much heavier Grumman F-14 Tomcat.

A Marine Corps Hornet traps aboard Coral Sea during the US Sixth Fleet's confrontation with Lybia. Aircraft from the old carrier were heavily involved in the actions in the Spring of 1986.

'Forrestal' class

The four ships of the 'Forrestal' class were originally conceived as smaller versions of the ill-fated strategic carrier design, the USS **United States**, with four aircraft catapults and a flush flight-deck with no island. However, following a complete redesign they were actually completed as the first carriers designed and built specifically for jet aircraft operations with a conventional island and an angled flight deck to allow the four catapults to be retained. The ships are the USS **Forrestal**, USS **Saratoga**, USS **Ranger** and USS **Independence** (CV 59-62) commissioned in October 1955, April 1956, August 1957 and January 1959 respectively. Their aviation ordnance load is 1,650 tons; and 2.84 million litres (750,000 US gal) of AVGAS aviation fuel, 2.99 million litres (789,000 US gal) of JP5 aviation fuel are carried for the air wing embarked. The air group is similar to those of the larger, later carriers and comprises 24 F-14 Tomcats, 10 A-6E Intruders, 24 A-7E Corsair IIs, 4 KA-6D tankers, 4 EA-6B Prowlers, 4 E-2C Hawkeyes, 10 S-3A Vikings and 6 SH-3H Sea Kings. *Ranger* has a modified group of 24 F-14, 22 A-6/KA-6, 5 EA-6, 5 E-2, 10 S-3, and 6 SH-3H. As the F/A-18 Hornet gets introduced, the standard air group will have 20 Tomcats, 20 Hornets, 20 A-6s (including KA-6s and in the future A-6Fs), 5 Hawkeyes, 5 Prowlers, 10 Vikings and 6 Sea Kings. The low endurance of the otherwise excellent Hornet means that each carrier is likely to be assigned additional tankers, at the expense of Intruders and Vikings. The ships have four elevators to service the flight deck, and each of the class is the subject of a 28-month SLEP (Service Life Extension Program) refit, which will increase their service lives from 30 to at least 45 years. During the Grenada landings of November 1983, *Independence* provided the air cover and strike support to the US Marine Corps and US Army Ranger assaults whilst maintaining ASW cover against any possible incursions by the two Cuban 'Foxtrot' class conventional attack submarines. Following this, the *Independence* joined the *John F. Kennedy* off the coast of the Lebanon. On 4 December 1983, her A-6Es and A-7s were used to attack positions in the Chouf mountains in support of the US Marine peacekeeping force in Beirut. In March 1986, *Ranger* was prominent in the Gulf of Sidra, her aircraft destroying several Libyan SAM sites and, in company with planes from *Coral Sea*, sinking a Nanuchka II missile armed corvette. To rectify some of the deficiencies encountered in combat operations, the SLEP refits will improve the habitability, add Kev-

Saratoga and Independence *are seen in the Mediterranean in the heart of a Carrier Task Force. Two such carriers can project enormous strike power, matched by few of the world's air forces.*

lar armour to enclose the vital machinery and electronics spaces, improve the NTDS fitted, add TFCC facility and replace the catapults. The radar outfit will also be upgraded and the air-defence armament strengthened with the addition of the Phalanx 'Gatling' gun for anti-missile use. *Forrestal, Saratoga* and *Independence* have undergone SLEP and operate with the Atlantic Fleet. *Ranger*, with the Pacific Fleet, is not due to start her SLEP until 1993 (after *Kitty Hawk* and *Constellation*).

Specification
Displacement: (first two) 59,060 tons standard, 75,900 tons full load; (second two) 60,000 tons standard, 79,300 tons full load
Dimensions: length (first) 331 m (1,086 ft), (second) 324 m (1,063 ft), (third) 326.4 m (1,071 ft) and (fourth) 326.1 m (1,070 ft); beam 39.5 m (129 ft 6 in); draught 11.3 m (37 ft); flightdeck width 76.8 m (252 ft)
Machinery: four-shaft geared steam turbines delivering 260,000 shp (193880 kW) in *Forrestal* and 280,000 shp (208795 kW) in others
Speed: 33 kts (*Forrestal*) or 34 kts (others)
Aircraft: see text
Armament: three octuple Sea Sparrow SAM launchers (no reloads), three 20-mm Phalanx CIWS.
Electronics: one LN-66 navigation radar, one SPS-10 surface-search radar, one SPS-48C 3D radar, one SPS-58 low-level air-search (except *Ranger*), two SPN-42 and one SPN-43A aircraft landing aids, two Mk 91 fire-control radars (three in first two), one URN-25 TACAN system, one SLQ-29 ESM suite and three Mk 36 Super RBOC chaff launchers
Complement: 2,790 plus 2,150 air group

Seen here in 1975, USS Independence *was used to provide the air cover for the Grenada landings. She has also seen extensive combat service in the Vietnam war off both the North and South coasts.*

Forming a class of four, the 'Forrestal' ships will soon have their F-4 Phantoms exchanged for the more capable F-14 Tomcat. They will also operate the new F-18A Hornet multi-role fighter.

'Kitty Hawk', 'America' and 'John F. Kennedy' classes

Built to an improved 'Forrestal' class design these four carriers in reality constitute three sub-classes that are easily distinguished from their predecessors by the fact that their island superstructures are set farther aft. In addition two of their four aircraft elevators are forward of the island, the 'Forrestals' having only one in this location. A lattice radar mast is also carried abaft the island. The USS **America** (CV 66, commissioned in January 1965) is very similar to the first two ships (USS **Kitty Hawk** (CV 63) and USS **Constellation** (CV 64), commissioned in April 1961 and October 1961), and was built in preference to an austere-version nuclear-powered carrier. She is, however, the only US carrier of postwar construction to be fitted with a sonar system. The last unit, the USS **John F. Kennedy** (CV 67), was built to a revised design incorporating an underwater protection system developed originally for the nuclear car-

rier programme, and was commissioned in September 1968. All have four steam catapults and carry some 2,150 tons of aviation ordnance plus about 7.38 million litres (1.95 million US gal) of aviation fuel for their air groups. Current air groups consist of 24 F-14 Tomcats (which can carry TARPS reconnaissance pods, 12 A-6E Intruders, 24 A-7E Corsair IIs (20 on *America*), 4 KA-6D (5 on *America*), 4 E-2C, 10 S-3A, and 6 SH-3H. As the F/A-18 Hornet enters service, the air groups will be the same as those of the 'Forrestal' class. The 'Kitty Hawks' are fitted with comprehensive command, control and electronic equipment. SLEP refits are scheduled to start in 1988 for *Kitty Hawk*, 1990 for *Constellation*, 1996 for *America* and 1999 for *John F. Kennedy*. In December 1983 A-6Es from the *John F. Kennedy*, in company with aircraft from the USS *Independence*, bombed Druze positions in the Lebanon in support of the Multi-National Force in

Beirut. In March and April, 1986, *America's* air group was involved in the Gulf of Sidra incidents and in the attack on Libya. On 24 March, two of her A-6Es sank a Libyan 'Combattante II' missile armed Fast Attack Craft using air-launched Harpoon anti-ship missiles.

Specification
'Kitty Hawk', 'America' and 'John F. Kennedy' classes
Displacement: first two 60,100 tons standard, 80,800 tons full load; third 60,300 tons standard, 81,500 tons full load; fourth 61,000 tons standard, 82,561 tons full load
Dimensions: length (first two) 318.8 m (1,046 ft), (third) 319.3 m (1,047 ft 6 in) and (fourth) 320.7 m (1,052 ft); beam 39.6 m (130 ft); draught (first three) 11.3 m (37 ft) or (fourth) 10.9 m (35 ft 11 in)
Machinery: four-shaft geared steam turbines delivering 280,000 shp

(208795 kW)
Speed: 33.6 kts
Aircraft: see text
Armament: three octuple Sea Sparrow SAM launchers (no reloads), three 20-mm Phalanx CIWS
Electronics: one SPS-10F navigation radar, one SPS-43A air-search radar (SPS-49 in CV-67), one SPS-48C 3D radar, one SPN-35A, two SPN-42 and one SPN-43A (no SPN-43 in CV-67) aircraft landing aids, one URN-20 TACAN system, three Mk 91 fire-control radars, one SLQ-29 ESM suite, four Mk 36 Super RBOC chaff launchers (*America* only), one SQS-23 sonar
Complement: 2,900 plus 2,500 air group

Above: USS Constellation *and the guided missile cruiser* Leahy *undergo underway replenishment in the South China Sea from the fast combat support ship* Niagara Falls *whilst part of Carrier Task Force 77.7 during a deployment in 1979.*

Below: Essentially built to a improved 'Forrestal' design, these carriers carry an air group similar in size and composition to the 'Nimitz' class but with less fuel and ordnance due to the necessity of carrying their own bunkerage.

Enterprise

The world's first nuclear-powered aircraft-carrier, the *Enterprise* (CVN 65) was laid down in 1958 and commissioned in November 1961 as what was then the largest warship ever built. Since exceeded in size by the 'Nimitz' class ships, the *Enterprise* was built to a modified 'Forrestal' class design with her larger dimensions dictated by the powerplant of eight A2W pressurized-water enriched uranium fuelled nuclear reactors. The high cost of her construction prevented five other vessels in the naval building programme from being built. From January 1979 to March 1982 the *Enterprise* underwent an extensive refit which included the rebuilding of her island superstructure and the fitting of new radar systems and mast to replace the characteristic ECM dome and billboard radar antenna that had been used since she was built. The *Enterprise* is equipped with four steam catapults, four deck-edge aircraft elevators and carries 2,520 tons of aviation ordnance plus 10.3 million litres (2.72 million US gal) of aircraft fuel, sufficient for 12 days of sustained air operations before replenishment. Like that of other US carriers the *Enterprise's* ordnance includes 10-kT B61, 20-kT, B57, 100-kT B61, 330-kT B61 and 900-kT B61 tactical nuclear gravity bombs, 10-kT B57 depth bombs, while 1.4MT B43 and 1.1-MT B83 strategic bombs can be carried as and when required. The air group is similar in size and configuration to that carried by the 'Nimitz' class carriers, and the

The first nuclear-powered aircraft carrier, USS Enterprise, *is seen here on sea trials after the major drydocking that included the rebuilding of her island superstructure and the replacement of her old ECM and radar systems.*

Enterprise is fitted with the same ASCAC, NTDS and Tactical Flag Command Center (TFCC) facilities. In addition to her OE-82 satellite system she also carries two British SCOT satellite communications antenna units for use with British fleet units and NATO. These two systems were fitted in 1976. The *Enterprise* is currently deployed with the Pacific Fleet and is due for her SLEP refit between 1993 and 1995 when a third Sea Sparrow and Mk 23 TAS radar are to be fitted. It is estimated that she will be eventually paid off in about 2010.

Specification
Displacement: 75,700 tons standard, 89,600 tons full load
Dimensions: length 335.9 m (1,102 ft); beam 40.5 m (133 ft); draught 10.9 m (35 ft 9 in); flightdeck width 76.8 m (252 ft)

Machinery: four-shaft geared steam turbines (eight A2W nuclear reactors) delivering 280,000 shp (208795 kW)
Speed: 32 kts
Aircraft: see 'Nimitz' class
Armament: two octuple Sea Sparrow SAM launchers (no reloads), three 20-mm Phalanx CIWS, three single 20-mm AA guns
Electronics: one SPS-48C 3D radar, one SPS-49 air-search radar, one SPS-65 air/surface-search radar, one SPS-

58 low-level air-search radar, one SPS-10 surface-search and navigation radar, one each SPN-35A, SPN-41, SPN-42 and SPN-44 aircraft landing aids, one URN-25 TACAN system, two Mk 91 fire-control radars, one SLQ-29 ESM suite, four Mk 36 Super RBOC chaff launchers
Complement: 2,734 plus 2,627 air group

The use of nuclear power as the propulsion plant allows USS Enterprise *to carry sufficient aircraft fuel and ordnance for 12 days of sustained air operations before having to undergo underway replenishment.*

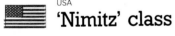

'Nimitz' class

The first three **'Nimitz' class** carriers were originally designed as replacements for the elderly 'Midway' class carriers. They differ from the earlier nuclear-powered USS *Enterprise* in having a new two-reactor powerplant design in two separate compartments with ordnance magazines between and forward of them. This increases the internal space available to allow some 2,570 tons of aviation weapons and 10.6 million litres (2.8 million US gal) of aircraft fuel to be carried. These totals are sufficient for 16 days of continuous flight operations before the stocks have to be replenished. The class has been fitted with an ASW Clasdo protection arrangement as carried by the USS *John F. Kennedy*, and is laid out with the same general arrangement and electronic fit as the 'JFK'.

Under the present multi-mission designations of the USN carrier force the class has been fitted with an ASW Classification and Analysis Center (ASCAC) for data sharing of subsurface operations between the carrier, her escorts, their airborne ASW aircraft and supporting long-range maritime ASW and patrol aircraft. The ships also have the Naval Tactical Data System (NTDS) with intership and aircraft data links 11 and 14, and are fitted with the OE-82 satellite communications outfit. A Tactical Flag Command Center has also been fitted for use by the fleet command officers normally

embarked. Four deck-edge aircraft elevators are available, two forward and one aft of the island on the starboard side and one aft on the port side. The hangar is 7.8 m (25 ft 7 in) high, and like those of other US carriers can accommodate at most only 40-50 per cent of the aircraft embarked at any one time, the remainder being spotted on the flightdeck in aircraft parks. The angled flight deck is 237.7 m (780 ft) long and is fitted with three arrester wires and an arrester net for recovering aircraft. Four steam catapults are carried, two on the bow launch position and two on the angled flightdeck. A typical 'Nimitz' class air group comprises two squadrons of Grumman F-14A interceptors, two squadrons of Vought A-7E Corsair light attack aircraft and one squadron of Grumman A-6E Intruder all-weather attack aircraft, plus Grumman KA-6D Intruder tankers, Grumman E-2C Hawkeye airborne early warning, Grumman EA-6B Prowler electronic countermeasures, Lockheed S-3A Viking ASW and Sikorsky SH-3H Sea King ASW units. There are also facilities for a Grumman C-2A Greyhound carrier on-board delivery aircraft. By the end of Fiscal Year 1988, the typical 'Nimitz' class air group will have incorporated the McDonnell Douglas F/A-18 Hornet and the composition will be similar to that of the other large US Navy carriers with 20 F-14 Tomcats (improved F-14D

from 1990), 20 Hornets (including up to four of the reconnaissance model currently being developed), 20 A-6E or A-6F Intruders (including a number of KA-6D tankers), five Hawkeyes, five Prowlers, 10 Vikings and six Sea Kings making a total of 86 aircraft. The core life of the A4W reactors fitted is under normal usage expected to provide a cruising distance of some 1.29 million to 1.61 million km (800,000 to one million miles) and last for 13 or so years before the cores have to be replaced. Although the class is relatively new, it is planned for the 'Nimitz' class to undergo Service Life Extension Program (SLEP) refits during the first decade of the next century in order to extend their service life by 15 years into the 2020s. The first of the class, USS **Nimitz** (CVN 68) was commissioned in May 1975 and is currently assigned to the Pacific Fleet after a decade in the Atlantic and the Mediterranean. The USS **Carl Vinson** (CVN 70, commissioned in 1982) is also Pacific based. The USS **Dwight D. Eisenhower** (CVN 69, commissioned October 1977) is currently with the Atlantic Fleet, recently joined by the first of the 'Improved Nimitz' class the '*Theodore Roosevelt*'.

USS Nimitz *prepares to launch four aircraft during operations in the late 1970s. An air group of almost 90 powerful warplanes make the modern nuclear powered aircraft carrier a frighteningly potent fighting machine.*

Specification

Displacement: 81,600 tons standard, 91,487 tons full load (except *Nimitz*, 90,944 tons)
Dimensions: length 332.8 m (1,092 ft); beam 40.8 m (134 ft); draught 11.3 m (37 ft); flightdeck width 76.8 m (252 ft)
Machinery: four-shaft geared steam turbines driven by two A4W/A1G nuclear reactors delivering 280,000 shp (208795 kW)
Speed: 35 kts
Aircraft: 24 F-14A Tomcat, 24 A-7E Corsair II, 10 A-6E Intruder, 4 KA-6D Intruder, 4 EA-6B Prowler, 4 E-2C Hawkeye, 10 S-3A Viking, 6 SH-3H Sea King and provision for one C-2A COD aircraft (from the late 1980s 20 F-14, 20 F/A-18, 20 A-6E/F, 5 EA-6B, 5 E-2C, 10 S-3A/B and 6 SH-3H)
Armament: three octuple Sea Sparrow SAM launchers (no reloads) three Phalanx 20-mm CIWS (four on CVN 70)
Electronics: one SPS-48B 3D radar, one SPS-43A (SPS-49 in CVN 69, 70) air-search radar, one SPS-10F (SPS-67 in CVN 69) surface-search radar, one LN-66 navigation radar, one SPN-41, two SPN-42, one SPN-43A and one SPN-44 aircraft landing aids, one URN-25 TACAN system, three Mk 115 (Mk 91 in CVN 70) fire-control radars, one Mk 23 TAS fire-control radar, one SLQ-29 ESM suite and four Mk 36 Super RBOC chaff launchers
Complement: 3,660 plus 2,626 air group

The ant-like figures of the crew manning the side and superstructure of USS Nimitz *amply demonstrate the enormous size of the modern nuclear powered aircraft carrier.*

 USA
'Improved Nimitz' class

In 1981 the first of at least five **'Improved Nimitz'** class aircraft carriers was ordered after much delay and discussion both within the US Congress and the Pentagon. These vessels will have Kevlar armour over their vital areas, and approximately the same aviation payload as the previous 'Nimitz's' of some 14,909 tons (including 1,954 tons of ordnance and around 9,000 tons of aviation fuel). The first unit, *USS Theodore Roosevelt* (CVN71) was commissioned into the Atlantic Fleet in October 1986. The second, *USS Abraham Lincoln* (CVN72), is due to commission in late 1989 or early 1990 whilst the third, *USS George Washington* (CVN73), is due some 20 months later. Orders for two more units have also been placed and these are expected to enter service in 1995 and 1998 respectively to replace the by then 45-year-old *USS Forrestal* and *Saratoga*. All five vessels will have the new carrier air group make-up of 20 Grumman A-6E/F, five EA-6B, five E-2C and 20 F-14; 10 Lockheed S-3A; 20 McDonnell Douglas F/A-18; and six Sikorsky SH-3H.

Specification
'Improved Nimitz' class
Displacement: 81,600 tons standard, 96,836 tons full load
Dimensions: length 332.8 m (1,092 ft), beam 40.8 m (134 ft), draught 11.7 m (38.4 ft), flight deck width 78.3 m (257 ft)
Machinery: four-shaft geared turbines

(two A4W/A1G nuclear reactors) delivering 280,000 hp (208795 kW)
Speed: 35 kts
Aircraft: see text
Armament: three octuple Sea Sparrow SAM launchers (no reloads) and four 20-mm Phalanx CIWS
Electronics: one SPS48E 30 radar, one

SPS49 air search radar, one SPS67 surface search radar, one SPS65 air/surface search radar, one LN66 navigation radar, one SPS64 navigation radar, one SPN41, one SPS43A, one SPN44, one SPN45 (CVN 72 and 73 one SPN46) aircraft landing aids, one URN25 TACAN system, three Mk 91

USS Theodore Roosevelt *(CVN-71) is seen under way during sea trials off Virginia in October 1986.*

fire control radars, one SLQ29 ESM system, one WLR1H ECM system, four Mk 36 Super RBOC chaff launchers
Complement: 3,408 plus 2,878 air group

`Nimitz´ class nuclear powered aircraft carrier

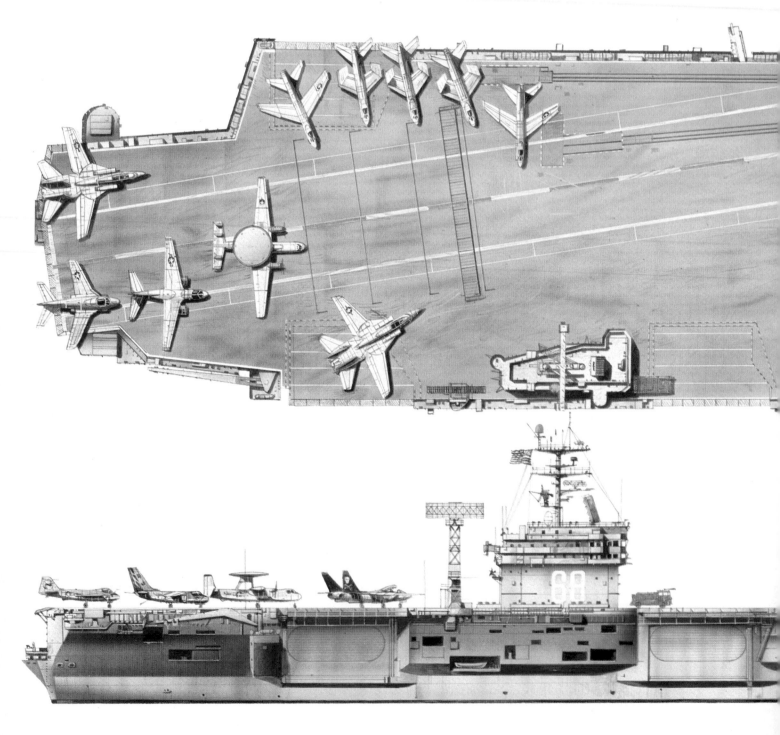

Built to survive in a nuclear war environment, USS
Nimitz is well capable of delivering its own nuclear
strike; it carries 100 or more nuclear weapons in its
magazines for tasks ranging from destroying a
nuclear submarine to devastating a large city. Its
aircraft can attack in all weathers at all altitudes
over long distances, and as such make Nimitz a
priority target.

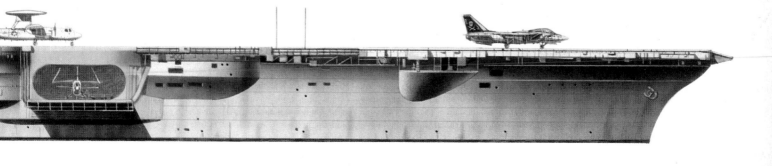

Modern Cruisers

The modern cruiser is a luxury item in the world's navies because of its immense cost. Only the two great superpowers still build them, and they have done away with all gun armament, replacing it with powerful surface-to-air and surface-to-surface missile systems more suitable for modern warfare.

A Soviet navy 'Kara' class Large Anti-Submarine Ship (BPK). These serve only with the Black Sea and Pacific fleets, where they have a command capability. The extremely heavy weapon and sensor fit is characteristic of Soviet practice, and contrasts strongly with the almost stark appearance of their American contemporaries.

Since World War II the cruiser has evolved into an expensive SAM-armed warship capable of operating in the highest-threat areas as a vital part of a task force unit. In the US Navy the cruiser has become both conventionally- and nuclear-powered, and is tasked primarily with the area SAM defence of fast carrier battle groups. In the Soviet navy only the 'Sverdlov' class of conventional gun cruisers remains, the other vessels classified by NATO as cruisers being purpose-built and anti-ship (RKR) or anti-submarine (BPK and PKR) warfare vessels. The traditional fire-support gun cruisers in most other navies have been paid off, sold or converted to hybrid helicopter carriers or SAM ships as the rush for missile-armed ships in the 1960s gained momentum. Most of the conversions have now been scrapped, but several of the older, ex-European gun ships still serve in South American waters under the Chilean and Peruvian flags.

The Soviets with their 'Kirov' class nuclear-powered vessel have introduced the nearest thing to the obsolete battle-cruiser category currently in service. In order to match this, and to beef up American surface fleet firepower capabilities in naval gunfire support and anti-ship warfare, the US Navy has started a reactivation and modification programme for their mothballed 'Iowa' class battleships which were last seen in action when the USS *New Jersey* served as a floating battery off Vietnam during 1968-9. With an armament of Harpoon and Tomahawk SSMs the 'Iowa' class ships will be the most powerful combatants afloat.

It is also salutary to note that had the UK had available either HMS *Tiger* or HMS *Blake* (the hybrid helicopter carrier conversions with a twin 152-mm/6-in automatic turret forward) for the Falklands campaign then the job of keeping Port Stanley airfield under naval and air bombardment to prevent Argentine air operations there might have been considerably easier than it was, and the heavier HE shells would also have caused greater damage to Argentine positions ashore. The Americans have also learnt this lesson as the *New Jersey* was used in 1983/4 off Lebanon to hit inland anti-aircraft positions with her 406-mm (16-in) main armament so as to limit the risks to American aircraft without hazarding personnel in air-defence suppression strikes.

This photograph of six US nuclear-powered cruisers steaming together is a rare sight. Normally operating in pairs to provide air cover to nuclear carriers, they were involved in Exercise 'READEX I-81' in the Caribbean on 26 February 1981.

'Long Beach' class

The first US surface warship to have nuclear power, the USS *Long Beach* (CGN 9) was to have originally been frigate-sized but grew rapidly during design to the dimensions of a heavy cruiser. As built she had two twin long-range Talos SAM missile systems (with 52 missiles), two Terrier medium-range SAM systems (with 120 missiles) and what was then the revolutionary SPS-32/33 fixed-array air-search radar system with an early version of the NTDS data system. During the Vietnam War the *Long Beach* used her Talos missiles to attack MiGs on seven occasions during 1967-8 whilst they flew deep within North Vietnamese territory, shooting down two (in May and June 1968) at ranges of more than 120 km (75 miles). As a result of experiences in the Vietnam War the *Long Beach* had a conventional SPS-12 air-search radar fitted in 1968 to supplement the fixed arrays, and an integral IFF and digital Talos fire-control system were added in 1970. By 1979 the Talos system was becoming obsolete, so the launchers and radars were removed, two quadruple Harpoon SSM launchers being added. In the following year the inadequate fixed-array systems were removed and replaced by SPS-48 and SPS-49 radars, the original planar array panels being replaced on the superstructure by armour plate. Standard SM-2ER SAMs, fitted in 1981, have replaced Terrier in service. *Long Beach* has also had two armoured box launchers for Tomahawk cruise missiles (Harpoons being relocated along the superstructure to make room) added in 1985 along with Kevlar armour and a Tactical Flag Command Center. Two 20-mm Phalanx CIWS have also been added atop the stern. No helicopter is carried, though there is a pad. *Long Beach* currently serves with the US Pacific Fleet.

Specification
'Long Beach' class
Displacement: 15,540 tons standard and 17,525 tons full load
Dimensions: length 219.8 m (721.2 ft); beam 22.3 m (73.2 ft); draught 9.5 m (31.2 ft)
Propulsion: two Westinghouse C1W pressurized-water cooled reactors powering geared steam turbines delivering 80,000 shp (59655 kW) to two shafts
Speed: 36 kts
Complement: 1,160 plus flag accommodation of 70
Aircraft: none
Armament: two quadruple Tomahawk SSM launchers with eight missiles, two quadruple Harpoon SSM launchers with eight missiles, two twin Standard SM2-ER SAM launchers with 120 missiles, one octuple ASROC ASW launcher with 20 missiles, two 127-mm (5-in) DP guns, two 20-mm Phalanx CIWS mountings and two triple 324-mm (12.75-in) Mk 32 torpedo tube mountings with six Mk 46 torpedoes
Electronics: one SPS-48C 3D radar, one SPS-67 surface-search radar, one SPS-49B air-search radar, four SPG-55C Standard fire-control radars, two SPG-49 gun fire-control radars, two Mk 35 fire-control radars, two VPS-2 fire-control radars, one LN66 navigation radar, one URN-20 TACAN system, one NTDS, one OE 82 satellite communications system, one SLQ 32(V)3 ESM suite, four Mk 36 super RBOC chaff launchers, and one SQQ-23 PAIR sonar.

USS Long Beach *(CGN9) was the first US surface warship to have nuclear power. During the Vietnam War in 1967-8 her long range Talos SAM systems engaged North Vietnamese MiGs on seven occasions.*

'Leahy' and 'Bainbridge' classes

The **'Leahy' class** was the first American warship design with the SAM missile as primary armament, with two twin 76-mm (3-in) guns added almost as an afterthought. The SAM launchers are two twin Mk 10 Terrier launchers fore and aft, the former being protected in heavy seas by the knuckling of the hull (a feature previously unseen in US ships). The ASW outfit was limited as the ships' primary mission is anti-air warfare defence. The nine ships are the USS *Leahy* (CG 16), USS *Harry E. Yarnell* (CG 17), USS *Worden* (CG 18), USS *Dale* (CG 19), USS *Richmond K. Turner* (CG 20), USS *Gridley* (CG 21), USS *England* (CG 22), USS *Halsey* (CG 23) and USS *Reeves* (CG 24), all commissioned between 1962 and 1964 and in their careers these have all undergone extensive modernization, an NTDS data system being fitted, the missile fire-control systems being upgraded for the Standard SM1-ER (later SM2-ER) missile, two quadru-

The lead ship of the class, USS Leahy *(CG 16). In the latter part of the Vietnam war her sister ship, USS* Worden, *was hit accidently by Shrike ARMs (Anti-Radiation Missiles) fired from US Navy planes. The missiles destroyed her fighting capability without damaging her sailing abilities.*

ple Harpoon launchers being fitted, and the 76-mm (3-in) mountings being replaced by two 20-mm Phalanx CIWS mountings.

At the same time as the 'Leahy' class cruisers were built a single nuclear-powered variant was also constructed in the form of the USS *Bainbridge* (CGN 25). She is essentially similar, but larger in dimensions and tonnage to accommodate the nuclear powerplant. Three of the 'Leahy' class cruisers plus the *Bainbridge* serve with the Atlantic Fleet whilst the remainder are with the Pacific Fleet.

Specification
'Leahy' class
Displacement: 6,670 tons standard and 8,203 tons full load
Dimensions: length 162.5 m (533.0 ft); beam 16.7 m (54.8 ft); draught 7.6 m (24.9 ft)

Propulsion: geared steam turbines delivering 85,000 shp (63385 kW) to two shafts
Speed: 32.7 kts
Complement: 513
Aircraft: none embarked, though a helicopter platform is provided
Armament: two quadruple Harpoon SSM launchers with eight missiles, two twin Standard SM2-ER SAM launchers with 80 missiles, one octuple ASROC ASW launcher with eight missiles, two 20-mm Phalanx CIWS mountings, four single 12.7 mm (0.50 in) MG, and two 324-mm (12.75-in) Mk 32 ASW torpedo tube mountings with 12 Mk 46 torpedoes
Electronics: one SPS-48A 3D radar, one SPS-49(V)3 air-search radar (SPS-37 in CG 20 and 24), one SPS-10F or SPS-67 surface-search radar, four SPG-55B Standard fire-control radars, one

LN 66 (CG 17-21 and 23) or CRP-1900D (CG 16) or CRP-2900 (CG 22 and 24) navigation radar, two VPS-2 fire-control radars, one URN-20 or SRN-6 TACAN, one SLQ-32(V)2 ESM suite (plus in CG 21, 23 and 24 one WLR-1 ECM and one WLR-3 ECM system), four Mk 36 Super RBOC chaff launchers, one OE82 satellite communication system, and one SQS-23B PAIR sonar

Specification
'Bainbridge' class
Displacement: 7,804 tons standard and 9,100 tons full load
Dimensions: length 172.2 m (565.0 ft); beam 17.6 m (57.75 ft); draught 7.7 m (25.25 ft)
Propulsion: two General Electric D2G pressurized-water cooled reactors powering geared steam turbines

The nuclear-powered cruiser USS Bainbridge (CGN25) executes a high-speed turn to port. Bainbridge is essentially similar to the 'Leahy' class cruisers, but has larger dimensions and tonnage to accommodate the two D2G pressurized-water cooled reactors that give her a 38 kts speed.

delivering 60,000 shp (44740 kW) to two shafts
Speed: 38 kts
Complement: 566 plus 18 Flag Group
Aircraft: none embarked, though a helicopter platform is provided
Armament: two quadruple Harpoon SSM launchers with eight missiles, two twin Standard SM2-ER SAM launchers with 80 missiles, one octuple ASROC ASW launcher with eight missiles, two 20-mm Phalanx CIWS mountings, and two 324-mm (12.75-in) Mk 32 ASW torpedo tube mountings with 12 Mk 46 torpedoes
Electronics: one SPS-48C 3D radar, one SPS-49 air-search radar, one SPS-67 surface-search radar, four SPG-55D Standard fire-control radars, one LN66 navigation radar, two VPS-2 fire-control radars, one URN-25 TACAN, one SLQ-32(V)2 ESM suite, one WLR-1 ECM system, four Mk 36 Super RBOC chaff launchers, one OE 92 satellite communication system, and one SQS-23 PAIR sonar

The 'Leahy' class cruiser USS Harry E. Yarnell (CG17). The primary mission of these ships is anti-air warfare, for which they carry two twin Standard SM2-ER SAM launchers that can engage targets out to over 140 km (87.5 miles) at altitudes up to 24390 m (80000 ft).

'Belknap' and 'Truxtun' classes

The **'Belknap' class** suffered a very long and tortuous development history even by American standards, being redesigned on a number of occasions as the costs gradually increased. The design eventually stabilized as a single-ended missile ship with facilities for the DASH ASW drone anti-submarine helicopter hangar and a single 127-mm (5-in) DP gun at the other end. The nine ships are the USS **Belknap** (CG 26), USS **Josephus Daniels** (CG 27), USS **Wainwright** (CG 28), USS **Jouett** (CG 29), USS **Horne** (CG 30), USS **Sterett** (CG 31), USS **William H. Standley** (CG 32), USS **Fox** (CG 33) and USS **Biddle** (CG 34). Since completion between 1964 and 1967 the class has been used as trials ships for a number of new systems: for example, the *Wainwright* was the test ship for the first NTDS data system integrated into a fire-control system and for the Standard SM2-ER missile, whilst the *Fox* evaluated the Tomahawk cruise missile box-launcher arrangement. On 22 November 1975 the *Belknap* suffered very severe fire damage following collision with the carrier USS *John F. Kennedy* in the Mediterranean, and had to be towed back to the USA for rebuilding. Before that time several of the *Belknap*'s sister ships had accumulated great combat experience in the Vietnam War both as combat air patrol fighter-guidance controllers and as air-defence ships. The 1972 North Vietnamese invasion of South Vietnam and the subsequent American bombing, mining and naval bombardment of North Vietnam coastal areas resulted in two air attacks on the American fleet that involved 'Belknap' class ships. The first, on 19 April 1972, saw the *Sterret* fighting off a combined air and surface attack on a gunfire support group, her Terrier missiles destroying a 'Styx' SSM (the first occasion on which a SAM was used to destroy an anti-ship cruise missile in combat) and two MiGs (one at 9-km/5.6-mile range and the other at 27.5-km/17-mile range). Later, on 19 July, the *Biddle* engaged an incoming raid of five MiGs attempting a night attack on Task Force 77 off the North

Vietnamese coast, her Terriers shooting down two MiGs at about 32 km (20 miles) and driving the rest off. As had occurred with the 'Leahy' class, a larger and nuclear-powered version of the 'Belknap' class ships was constructed, the USS *Truxtun* (CGN 35), basically similar in weapon and electronic fits. Four of the class serve with the Atlantic Fleet and five plus the *Truxtun* in the Pacific. USS *Belknap* has been rebuilt as flagship of the 6th Fleet in the Mediterranean, with additional command facilities in place of her hangar. The USS *Wainwright, Horne* and *Sterett* are to be fitted with the 18-man Tactical Flag Command Center.

Specification
'Belknap' class
Displacement: 6,570 tons standard and 8,200 tons full load (CG 27, CG 28 and CG 29) or 8,065 tons full load (others)
Dimensions: length 166.7 m (547.0 ft); beam 16.7 m (54.8 ft); draught 8.8 m (28.8 ft)
Propulsion: geared steam turbines delivering 85,000 shp (63385 kW) to two shafts
Speed: 32.5 kts
Complement: 511 (CG 26) or 492 (others)
Aircraft: one Kaman SH-2D Seasprite multi-role helicopter
Armament: two quadruple Harpoon SSM launchers with eight missiles, one twin Standard SM2-ER/ASROC SAM/ASW launcher with 40 Standard and 20 ASROC missiles, one 127-mm (5-in) DP gun, two 20-mm Phalanx CIWS mountings, and two triple 324-mm (12.75-in) Mk 32 ASW torpedo tube mountings with 12 Mk 46 torpedoes
Electronics: one SPS-48E 3D radar, one SPS-49(V)3 (CGs 26, 27, 28 and 30)

or SPS-43 (CG 29) or SPS-40 (CGs 31-34) air-search radar, one SPS-67 surface-search radar, one LN66 navigation radar, two SPG-55D Standard fire-control radars, one SPG-53A 127-mm (5-in) gun fire-control radar, two VPS-2 fire-control radars, one URN-25 or SRN-6 TACAN, one NTDS, one SLQ-32(V)2 ESM suite, four Mk 36 Super RBOC chaff launchers and one SQS-26BX sonar (SQS-53C in CG 26 and SQS-27AXR in CG 27)

Specification
'Truxtun' class
Displacement: 8,200 tons standard and 9,127 tons full load
Dimensions: length 171.9 m (564.0 ft); beam 17.7 m (58.0 ft); draught 9.5 m (31.2 ft)
Propulsion: two General Electric D2G pressurized-water cooled reactors powering geared steam turbines delivering 60,000 shp (44740 kW) to two shafts
Speed: 38 kts

The sole nuclear powered version of the 'Belknap' class is USS Truxtun *(CGN35).*

Complement: 568 plus 18 flag group
Aircraft: one Kaman SH-2D Seasprite multi-role helicopter
Armament: two quadruple Harpoon SSM launchers with eight missiles, one twin Standard SM2-ER/ASROC SAM/ASW launcher with 40 Standard and 20 ASROC missiles, one 127-mm (5-in) DP gun, two 20-mm Phalanx CIWS mountings, and two triple 324-mm (12.75-in) Mk 32 ASW torpedo tube mountings with 12 Mk 46 torpedoes
Electronics: one SPS-48C3D radar, one SPS-40D air-search radar, one SPS-67 surface-search radar, one LN66 navigation radar, two SPG-55C Standard fire-control radars, one SPG-53F 127-mm (5-in) gun fire-control radar, two VPS-2 fire-control radars, one URN-25 TACAN, one NTDS, one SLQ-32(V)3 ESM suite, one WLR-1 ECM system, four Mk 36 Super RBOC chaff launchers, one OE 82 satellite communications system, and one SQS-26BX sonar

USS Belknap *(CG26) had to be rebuilt following a devastating fire that followed a collision with the carrier USS* John F. Kennedy *in 1975. During the Vietnam war USS* Biddle *and USS* Sterett *of this class shot down four MiGs and a Styx SSM in two separate incidents off the North Vietnamese coast.*

'California' class

Intended originally to have been a five-ship nuclear-powered guided-missile frigate version of the ill-fated Fiscal Year 1966 conventionally-powered guided-missile destroyer design, the **'California' class** was cut back to only two vessels, the USS *California* (CGN 36) and USS *South Carolina* (CGN 37), the money for the others going towards the follow-on 'Virginia' class. The 'California' class ships were commissioned in 1974 and 1975, and were the first to have the improved D2G reactor systems with three times the core life of the original plant fitted in the USS *Bainbridge* and USS *Truxtun*. A helicopter landing pad is provided, but no hangar or maintenance facilities are fitted. Two torpedo tubes for the Mk 48 heavyweight ASW torpedo were also fitted in the transom, but these were discarded together with the original heavy Mk 42 127-mm (5-in) gun mounts, the latter being replaced by a pair of Mk 45 lightweight 127-mm (5-in) mountings. Under modernization plans two Phalanx CIWS mountings will be fitted, together with Kevlar plastic armour and Tomahawk SSM. The *California* serves in the Pacific and the *South Dakota* with the Atlantic fleet, as escorts to nuclear powered aircraft carriers.

The main SAM battery comprises two single-rail Mk 13 launchers with SPG-51D digital fire-control radars; the missile is the Standard SM1-MR. Harpoon SSM launchers have already been fitted, and the main ASW armament is provided by a reloadable eight-round Mk 16 ASROC launcher. The Standard SM2-MR will be carried as and when the launcher and fire-control systems are converted for it.

Specification
'California' class (as modified)
Displacement: 9,561 tons standard and 11,100 tons full load (CGN 36) or 10,473 tons full load (CGN 37)
Dimensions: length 181.7 m (596.0 ft); beam 18.6 m (61.0 ft); draught 9.6 m (31.5 ft)
Propulsion: two General Electric D2G pressurized-water cooled rectors powering geared steam turbines delivering 60,000 shp (44740 kW) to two shafts
Speed: 39 kts
Complement: 530-584
Aircraft: none embarked, though a helicopter platform is provided
Armament: two quadruple Tomahawk SSM launchers with eight missiles, two quadruple Harpoon SSM launchers with eight missiles, two single Standard SM2-MR SAM launchers with 80 missiles, one octuple ASROC ASW launcher with 24 missiles, two 127-mm (5-in) DP guns, two 20-mm Phalanx CIWS mountings, and four single 324-mm (12.75-in) Mk 32 ASW torpedo tubes with 16 Mk 46 torpedoes
Electronics: one SPS-48A 3D radar, one SPS-49 air-search radar, one SPS-67 surface-search radar, four SPG-51D Standard fire-control radars, one SPQ-9A fire-control radar, one SPG-60 127-mm (5-in) fire-control radars, two VPS-2 fire-control radars, one URN-25 TACAN, one SLQ-32(V)3 ESM suite, one NTDS equipment, four Mk 36 Super RBOC chaff launcher, one SQS-26CX sonar, and one OE 82 satellite communications system

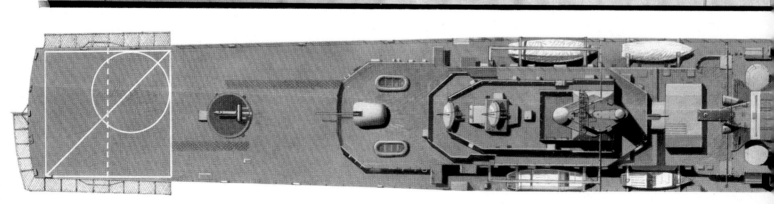

Above: A 'California' class vessel with her charge, the aircraft carrier USS Nimitz. Acting in the 'goalkeeper' role, it is her duty to eliminate any threats that have leaked through the carrier task group's outer defence zone.

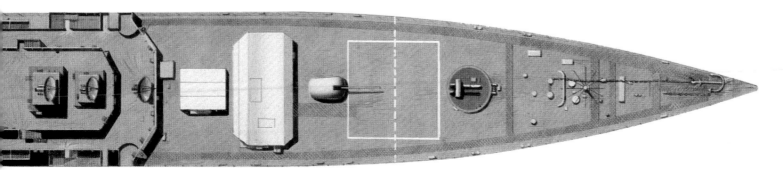

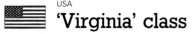

'Virginia' class

Initially intended as nuclear counterparts of the 'Spruance' class guided-missile destroyer design, the USS *Virginia'* (CGN 38), USS *Texas* (CGN 39), USS *Mississippi* (CGN 40) and USS *Arkansas* (CGN 41) eventually evolved into a slightly improved 'California' sub-class derivative, the 'Virginia' class. Like most guided-missile fornia' sub-class derivative, the '**Virginia' class**. Like most guided-missile guided-missile cruisers (CGN) during 1975, the ships commissioning between 1976 and 1980. A fifth unit was projected but not funded by the US Congress. Compared with the 'California' class ships they are some 3.35 m (11 ft) shorter, are fitted with two Mk 26 launcher systems for Standard SM1-ER SAMs, ASROC ASW missiles and, if required, Harpoon SSMs. They also had a hangar with telescoping hatch cover beneath the fantail flight deck and this leaked badly in heavy weather; the helicopter carried was the Kaman SH-2D Seasprite. The SQR-19 tactical towed sonar array will not be fitted because of the ships' inherently noisy reactor machinery systems.

The normal role of the 'Virginia' class ships is deployment in pairs to act as fast area-defence SAM escorts to nuclear-powered aircraft-carriers. Currently one pair is assigned each to the Atlantic and Pacific Fleets. All four ships have had two Phalanx CIWS mountings fitted, the SAM system adapted to fire Standard SM2-ER missiles, Kevlar plastic armour fitted in vulnerable command and machinery spaces, and eight Tomahawk cruise missiles in launcher boxes added to supplement the Harpoon SSMs already carried. The quadruple Harpoon launchers have replaced the helicopter facility on the fantail.

In the late 1970s, four units of a modified Virginia design were ordered which were to incorporate the then new AEGIS system. They were cancelled when it was decided that the conventionally powered 'Ticonderoga' class would get the system to sea much more quickly and economically.

Specification
'Virginia' class (as modified)
Displacement: 10,400 tons standard and 11,300 tons full load
Dimensions: length 177.3 m (581.7 ft); beam 19.2 m (63.0 ft); draught 9.5 m (31.2 ft)
Propulsion: two General Electric D2G pressurized-water cooled reactors powering geared steam turbines

Above: Last of the 'Virginia' class to be completed was USS Arkansas (CGN41). The 'Virginias' are smaller than the 'Californias' but have a much improved layout, including the provision of a hangar below decks for two LAMPS ASW helicopters.

delivering 70,000 shp (52,200 kW) to two shafts
Speed: 40 kts
Complement: 528-562
Aircraft: one Kaman SH-2D Seasprite multi-role helicopter (a second can be carried in emergencies)
Armament: two quadruple Harpoon SSM launchers with eight missiles, two quadruple Tomahawk SSM launchers with eight missiles, two twin Standard SM2-ER/ASROC SAM/ASW launchers with 50 Standard, 20 ASROC and two test missiles, two 127-mm (5-in) DP guns, two 20-mm Phalanx CIWS mountings, and two triple 324-mm (12.75-in) Mk 32 ASW torpedo tube mountings with 14 Mk 46 torpedoes
Electronics: one SPS-55 surface-search radar, one SPS-40B air-search radar, one SPS-48C 3D radar, two SPG-51D Standard fire-control radars, one

SPQ-9A fire-control system. one SPG-60D gun fire-control system, one URN-20 and SRN-15 TACAN (one URN-25 in CGN 41), one SLQ-32(V)3 ESM suite, four Mk 36 Super RBOC chaff launchers, one NTDS equipment, one OE 82 satellite communications system, and one SQS-53A sonar

USS Texas (CGN39) on constructor's trials. The fantail flight deck and rear Mk 26 SAM launcher are clearly seen. The 127 mm (5 in) gun mount is of the Mk 45 dual-purpose type, firing 31.8 kg (70-lb) rounds in the surface bombardment and anti-aircraft roles.

'Ticonderoga' class

Evolved as a minimum-cost AEGIS SAM area-defence platform for construction in large numbers, the '**Ticonderoga' class** is based on the hull of the largest existing destroyer design available, the 'Spruance' class. The original force level to be constructed was 28, but this was increased by the Reagan administration to 30 and then cut to 27 as only five SPY-1 radar systems can be constructed each year. The basic 'Spruance' class hull and machinery layout is used, but the larger displacement has resulted in a reduction in speed. Some criticism of the amount of topweight carried was reported as a result of experience with the lead ship, USS *Ticonderoga* (CG

47), which was commissioned in 1983, but in service the ships have proved to be the most capable air-defence platforms yet built. Other units in service are the USS *Yorktown* (CG 48), *Vincennes* (CG 49), *Valley Forge* (CG 50), *Thomas S. Gates* (CG 51), *Bunker Hill* (CG 52), *Mobile Bay* (CG 53), *Antietam* (CG 54), *Leyte Gulf* (CG 55) and *San Jacinto* (CG 56), with three more building and more on order. The class is distributed roughly equally between Atlantic and Pacific fleets. The heart of the ship is its computerized AEGIS area-defence system, which has two

The first of the AEGIS-equipped cruisers, USS Ticonderoga (CG 47).

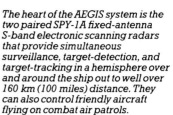

The heart of the AEGIS system is the two paired SPY-1A fixed-antenna S-band electronic scanning radars that provide simultaneous surveillance, target-detection, and target-tracking in a hemisphere over and around the ship out to well over 160 km (100 miles) distance. They can also control friendly aircraft flying on combat air patrols.

paired SPY-1A fixed-antenna electronic scanning radars that can control friendly aircraft as well as providing simultaneous surveillance, target-detection and target-tracking in a hemisphere over and around the ship. The missiles used are Standard SM2-ERs on two twin Mk 26 launchers, which can deal with saturation attacks by high-performance aircraft in combination with low-level and high-level air, surface and sub-surface launched anti-ship missiles in very heavy ECM environments. From the *Bunker Hill* on-

wards the two Mk 26 launchers and their magazines have been replaced by two Mk 41 vertical launchers for a total of 122 Harpoon, Standard, ASW and Tomahawk missiles instead of the 104 carried at present. Although new, the class has already seen action, with USS *Ticonderoga* giving bombardment assistance to the US Marine contingent in the Lebanon in 1983. More recently, USS *Yorktown* sank a Libyan 'Commbattante IIG' Fast Attack Craft during the night of 24/25 March 1986. The confrontation with Colonel Gad-

daffi was also the combat debut of the Harpoon missile, two of which did the job.

Specification
'Ticonderoga' class
Displacement: 7,260 tons light; CG 47-51 9,530 tons (except CG 49 9,400 tons) and CG 52 onwards 9,500 tons full load
Dimensions: length 172.8 m (566,8 ft); beam 16.8 m (55 ft); draught 9.5 m (31 ft)
Propulsion: four General Electric LM 2500 gas turbines delivering 80,000 shp (59655 kW) to two shafts
Speed: 32 kts
Complement: 362-395
Aircraft: two Kaman SH-2D Seasprite or Sikorsky SH-60B Seahawk multi-role helicopters
Armament: two quadruple Harpoon SSM launchers with 8 missiles, two twin dual purpose Standard SM2-MR/ASROC launchers with 68 Standard SAM and 20 ASROC ASW missiles,

Left: USS Bunker Hill *(CG 52) makes the first launch of a missile from the Mk 41 Vertical Launching System. This is the first of its type for the US Navy, though the Soviets have used such systems for several years.*

(replaced from CG 52 by two Mk 41 vertical launchers with a mix of 122 missiles selected from Standard SAM, Harpoon or Tomahawk SSM, and vertical launch ASROC ASW), two 127-mm (5-in) DP guns, two 20-mm Phalanx CIWS mountings, and two triple 324-mm (12.75-in) Mk 32 ASW torpedo launchers with 36 Mk 46 torpedoes
Electronics: two paired SPY-1A (or from CG 59 SPY-1B) AEGIS radar arrays, one SPS-49 air-search radar, one SPS-55 surface-search radar, one SPQ-9A gun fire-control radar, four SPG-62 Standard fire-control radars, two VPS-2 fire-control radars, one SLQ-32 ESM suite, four Mk 36 Super RBOC chaff launchers, one NAVSAT system, one OE 82 satellite communications system, one URN 25 TACAN system, one SQS-53A sonar (CG 47-55), one SQR-19 tactical towed-array sonar (CG 54 and 55 only), one SQQ-89 sonar (from CG 56 onwards)

Below: Based on the hull of the large 'Spruance' class destroyer but packed with electronics, computers and radar systems, USS Ticonderoga *and her sisters are the most capable air defence vessels in the world.*

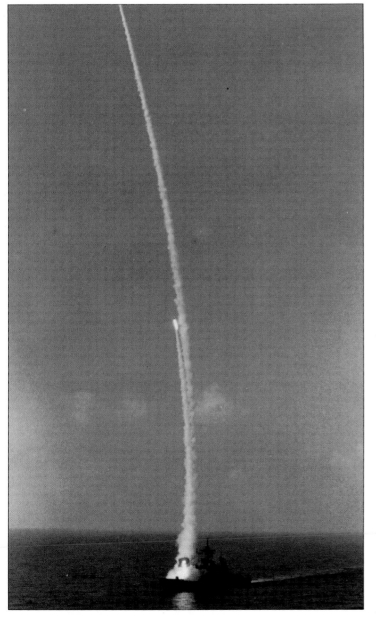

'Iowa' class

Although constructed (1940-4) during World War II as the largest examples of their type ever built apart from the Japanese *Yamato* and *Musashi*, the US battleships of the 'Iowa' class, USS *Iowa* (BB 61), USS *New Jersey* (BB 62), USS *Missouri* (BB 63) and USS *Wisconsin* (BB 64), saw considerable service after the war on various duties. In the immediate post-war period three were mothballed, whilst the *Missouri* served as a training ship. However, the Korean War (1950-3) saw all four again in active service for use as naval gunfire support vessels off the North and South Korean coastlines. They then reverted to reserve status during 1954-8 and were again mothballed. On 6 April 1967 the *New Jersey* began her second reactivation refit for active service off South Vietnam and the North Vietnamese panhandle region as a floating battery. During this deployment she spent 120 days on the 'gun line', firing 5,688 406-mm (16-in) rounds and 14,891 127-mm (5-in) rounds at targets; she then fell foul of economy cuts in 1969, when she decommissioned for her third period of mothballing.

By the 1970s the four battleships were considered as little more than relics from a bygone age, but in 1980 the need to augment the US surface combat fleet and match new Soviet warship classes resulted in the US Congress authorizing funds to reactivate the battleship force. After much heated debate the initial vessel chosen, the *New Jersey*, recommissioned after modernization on 27 December 1982, beginning her first operational deployment with the Pacific Fleet in March 1983. By the end of that year she had served as part of the task forces deployed off the Nicaraguan coasts and, in December off Lebanon, had used her main armament to bombard Syrian AA positions that had fired on US Navy reconnaissance aircraft that were supporting the US Marine Corps units ashore. Eventually all four ships are to be in fleet service to operate with battle groups in the highest-threat areas with or without organic air cover and to provide US amphibious units with much-needed heavy gun fire support.

The initial modernization programme included the upgrading of the electronics, conversion of the propulsion plant to burn Navy distillate fuel, the fitting of a Combat Engagement Center, and the addition of new weapons systems at the expense of four twin 127-mm (5-in) mountings. The fantail was also reshaped to accommodate up to three Kaman SH-2D Seasprite ASW helicopters in open stowage with a fourth on the helicopter landing pad located there. The main battery of 406-mm (16-in) guns fires both 862-kg

(1,900-lb) HE and 1225-kg (2,700-lb) AP shells out to 38000 m (41,560 yards) and 36750 m (40,190 yards) respectively. During the early 1950s a tactical nuclear shell, the Mk 23 'Katie' with a W23 warhead, was developed. The shell was subsequently retired from the nuclear weapons stockpile in October 1962, and it is believed that none were actually taken to sea although the ships' magazines were due to carry 10 of these shells within the 406-mm (16-in) inventory.

The four battleships will become the centres of Surface Action Groups, probably two each assigned to the Atlantic and Pacific Fleets. As a result of the Lebanon experience, Iowa was fitted with five Israeli Mazlat Pioneer recoverable RPVs, together with their control system. With a maximum video transmission range of 200 km (125 miles) and a service ceiling of 4572 m (15,000 ft) the RPV will be used for real-time targetting and reconnaissance duties. All four of the class are scheduled to receive the system.

Specification
'Iowa' class
Displacement: 45,000 tons standard and 57,353 tons full load
Dimensions: length 270.4 m (887.2 ft) except BB 62 270.5 m (887.6 ft); beam

33.0 m (108.2 ft); draught 11.6 m (38 ft)
Propulsion: geared steam turbines delivering 212,000 shp (158090 kW) to four shafts
Speed: 32.5 kts, except BB 63 27.5 kts as a result of a grounding accident
Complement: 1,526-1,545
Aircraft: two or four Kaman SH-2D Seasprite multi-role helicopters on the fantail landing pad
Armament: eight quadruple Tomahawk SSM launchers with 32 missiles, four quadruple Harpoon SSM launchers with 16 missiles, three triple 406-mm (16-in) guns, six twin 127-mm (5-in) DP guns, and four 20-mm Phalanx CIWS mountings
Electronics: one SPS-67 surface-search radar (SPS-10F in BB-61), one

Above: The first of the reactivated battleships is USS New Jersey (BB62). Her 406-mm (16-in) main guns have been fired in anger, giving much needed artillery support to the beleaguered US Marine Corps force located near Lebanon's international airport at Beirut.

SPS-49 air-search radar, one LN66 navigation radar, four VPS-2 fire-control radars, two Mk 38 gun fire-control systems, four Mk 37 gun fire-control systems, one Mk 40 gun director, one SLQ-32(V)3 ESM suite, eight Mk 36 Super RBOC chaff launchers, one WRN5A NAVSAT system, and one OE 82 satellite communications system

Below: Although considered for many years to be relics from a bygone age, the four 'Iowa' class battleships will become the most powerful surface combatants afloat following refitting with new weapons systems and electronics. They will serve on into the 1990s.

'Sverdlov' class

Destined originally to be a 24-ship programme in Stalin's post-war Soviet navy plan, the 'Sverdlov' class finally consisted of 20 hulls laid down, of which only 17 were launched; three of these latter were never completed and were laid up in the Neva river at Leningrad for a number of years before being scrapped. The remaining 14 were completed during the period 1951-5 in two slightly different forms, but all were essentially an improved version of the pre-war designed but post-war completed 'Chapayev' cruiser class. One, the *Ordzhonikidze*, was transferred to Indonesia in 1962 as the *Irian* (and scrapped in 1972 in Taiwan following a chronic spares problem), whilst in the late 1950s the *Dzerzhinsky* was converted into an experimental SAM cruiser with a navalized version of the Soviet army's SA-2 'Guideline' fitted in place of the X 152-mm (6-in) gun turret. This proved to be unsuccessful in service and by 1979 it had been discarded for scrapping. The *Admiral Nakhimov* was also converted around the same time to a trials ship for the SS-N-1 'Scrubber' anti-ship missile system, but was subsequently scrapped in 1961 without ever having left Soviet waters. Of the remaining ships two (the *Admiral Senyavin* and *Zhdanov*) were converted to the KU (*Korabl' Upravleuiye*, or command ship) role in 1971-2; the former serves as the Pacific Fleet flagship for special deployments and the latter with the Black Sea Fleet for the same purposes. The other nine are conventional cruisers (Soviet designation KR, *Kreyser*). *Aleksandr Suvorov*, *Dmitri Pozharsky* and *Admiral Lazarev* are with the Pacific Fleet, the latter in reserve, while *Aleksandr Nevsky* and *Murmansk* serve the Northern Fleet. *Oktyabrskaya Revolutsiya* is active in the Baltic, where the name ship *Sverdlov* is in reserve. The remaining pair, *Admiral Ushakov* and *Mikhail Kutuzov*, are with the Black Sea Fleet. Three (the *Yshakov*, the *Suvorov* and the *Oktyabrskaya Revolutsiya*) underwent refits in 1977-9 that included the extension of the bridge superstructure aft, the fitting of eight twin 30-mm AA guns with four 'Drum Tilt' fire-control radars, and the removal of the 'Egg Cup' 100-mm (3.9-in) fire-control radars from the main turrets. The prim-

ary use for these vessels now lies with their main and secondary armaments for the support of Soviet and Warsaw Pact army units and Naval Infantry in amphibious assaults and ground attacks on NATO and other Western targets. This capability is unmatched in all NATO navies other than the American, which has the reactivated 'Iowa' class battleships with an even heavier armament. Some of the unimproved units are used for cadet and gunnery training.

Specification
'Sverdlov' class
Displacement: 12,900 tons standard and 17,000 tons full load
Dimensions: length 210.0 m (689.0 ft); beam 22.0 m (72.2 ft); draught 7.2 m (23.6 ft)
Propulsion: geared steam turbines delivering 110,000 shp (82025 kW) to two shafts
Speed: 32.5 kts
Complement: 1,010
Aircraft: one Kamov Ka-25 'Hormone-C' utility helicopter (in *Admiral Senyavin* only)

Armament: one twin SA-N-4 'Gecko' SAM launcher with 18 missiles (in *Admiral Senyavin* and *Zhdanov* only), four triple 152-mm (6-in) DP guns (three triple mountings in *Zhadanov*, and two triple mountings in *Admiral Senyavin*), six twin 100-mm (3.9-in) DP guns, 16 twin 37-mm AA guns (14 twin mounting in 1977-9 modifications, and eight twin mountings in the *Admiral Senyavin* and *Zhdanov*), four twin 30-mm AA (in *Zhdanov* only, while the *Admiral Senyavin* and 1977-9 modifications have eight twin mountings), and up to 200 mines (none in *Admiral Senyavin* and *Zhdanov*)
Electronics: (*Admiral Senyavin* and *Zhdanov*) one 'Top Trough' air-search radar, one 'Pop Group' SA-N-4 fire-control radar, one 'Sun Visor' 152-mm (6-in) fire-control radar, two 'Top Bow' 152-mm (6-in) fire-control radars, four 'Drum Tilt' 30-mm fire-control radars (only two in *Zhdanov*), and six 'Egg Cup' gun fire-control radars
Electronics: (others) one 'Big Net' or 'Top Trough' air-search radar, one 'High Sieve' or 'Low Sieve' air search radar, one 'Knife Rest' air-search radar

(in some ships only), one 'Slim Net' air-search radar, one 'Don-2' or 'Neptune' navigation radar, two 'Sun Visor' gun fire-control radars, two 'Top Bow' 152-mm (6-in) fire-control radars, eight 'Egg Cup' gun fire-control radars, and two 'Watch Dog' ECM systems

The experimental SAM missile cruiser Dzerzhinsky, *fitted with a navalized version of the Soviet army's SA-2 'Guideline' missile, which proved unsuccessful in service. The vessel was placed in the reserve category with the Black Sea Fleet in the late 1970s, eventually to be scrapped.*

Below: Sverdlov, *seen here in the English Channel in the 1970s, displays the fine, pre-war Italian influenced lines of the class. The heavy gun battery's main use today is in amphibious fire support.*

'Kynda'class

Launched at the Zhdanov Shipyard in Leningrad between 1961 and 1964, in a programme that was curtailed after only four ships had been built, the 'Kynda' class cruisers *Grozny, Admiral Fokin, Admiral Golovko* and *Varyag* were the first ships in the Soviet navy to introduce a pyramid superstructure supporting the type's numerous radar and ESM systems. Classed as RKR units by the Soviets, these are dedicated anti-surface ship warfare vessels tasked with countering the American carriers. For this role the main armament comprises two trainable four-round launcher banks of SS-N-3B 'Shaddock' cruise missiles, one reload for each tube located within magazines in the superstructure immediately behind each launcher unit. The reloading operation is a slow and difficult process, however, requiring a relatively calm sea. The ships have no organic air component other than a simple helicopter landing pad aft, and thus have to rely on third-party targeting sources such as naval air force Tupolev Tu-95 'Bear-D' aircraft for over-the-horizon missile engagements.

Propulsion is provided by a set of pressure-fired geared steam turbines that exhaust through large twin funnels. The air-defence armament is limited to a single SA-N-1 'Goa' twin launcher forward and two 76-mm (3-in) DP gun turrets aft, whilst the ASW armament is limited to a pair of RBU 6000 ASW rocket-launchers and two triple ASW torpedo tube banks. The RBU 6000 fires a 75-kg (165-lb) HE projectile with optional depth or magnetic proximity fusing. The 12 barrels are fired in a paired sequence after the launcher has been trained in azimuth and elevation by a dedicated fire-control console. The launcher is reloaded automatically when it is trained to the vertical, the magazine being directly beneath the launcher. The 533-mm (21-in) torpedoes are

acoustic-homing types optimized for the ASW role. The *Grozny* is with the Baltic Fleet, the *Admiral Golovko* in the Black Sea and the other two are with the Pacific Fleet. All of the 'Kyndas' have been modernized in refits which included the upgrading of their SS-N-3B missiles.

Specification
'Kynda' class
Displacement: 4,400 tons standard and 5,600 tons full load
Dimensions: length 141.7 m (464.9 ft); beam 16.0 m (52.5 ft); draught 5.3 m (17.4 ft)
Propulsion: geared steam turbines delivering 100,000 shp (74570 kW) to two shafts

Speed: 35 kts
Complement: 375
Aircraft: none embarked, though a helicopter platform is provided
Armament: two quadruple SS-N-3B 'Shaddock' SSM launchers with 16 missiles, one twin SA-N-1 'Goa' SAM launcher with 16 missiles, two twin 76-mm (3-in) DP guns, four 30-mm ADG6-30 CIWS mountings (in *Varyag* only), two 12-barrel RBU 6000 ASW rocket-launchers, and two triple 533-mm (21-in) ASW torpedo tube mountings
Electronics: one 'Head Net-A' and one 'Head Net-C' air-search radars (in *Admiral Fokin* only) or two 'Head Net-C' air-search radars (remainder), two 'Plinth Net' fire-control radars, two 'Don-2' navigation radars, one 'Owl

One of the Soviet Pacific Fleet's two 'Kynda' class rocket cruisers (RKR), with a Lockheed P-3B Orion maritime patrol aircraft in attendance. The 'Kyndas' have to rely on third-party over-the-horizon targeting data to effectively use their main armament.

Screech' 76-mm (3-in) fire-control radar, one 'Peel Group' SAM fire-control radar, two 'Scoop Pair' SSM fire-control radars, two 'Bass Tilt' CIWS fire-control radars (in all but *Admiral Fokin*), one each 'Bell Clout', 'Bell Slam' and 'Bell Tap' ECM systems, four 'Top Hat' ECM systems, two 'High Pole-B' IFF antennae and one high-frequency hull sonar

---

'Kresta I' and 'Kresta II' classes

Built at the Zhadanov Shipyard in Leningrad, the first **'Kresta I' class** BPK (later changed by the Soviets to RKR) was completed in 1967. Only four ships were built (**Admiral Zozulya, Vladivostok, Vitse-Admiral Drozd** and **Sevastopol**, commissioned 1967-9), and it is likely that they were an interim design between the anti-ship 'Kynda' and the ASW 'Kresta II' classes. The 'Kresta I' class ships are larger than the former class with a different hull form, half the SS-N-3B 'Shaddock' SSM battery (but with no reloads) and increased anti-air warfare capabilities. The ships were also the first Soviet surface combatants to have a helicopter hangar, for a single Kamov Ka-25 'Hormone-B' missile-targeting helicopter. Two of the ships have since undergone additions to their superstructure, the *Vitse-Admiral Drozd* also having

two 'Bass Tilt' fire-control radars and four 30-mm CIWS fitted. The SA-N-1 'Goa' SAM systems carried in this class have a secondary anti-ship capability, with an alternate 10-kiloton yield nuclear warhead in place of the usual 60-kg (132-lb) HE type.

Following the last 'Kresta I' on the slipway came the first of 10 'Kresta II' BPK hulls (the **Kronshtadt, Admiral Isakov, Admiral Nakhimov, Admiral Makarov, Marshal Voroshilov,** **Admiral Oktyabrisky, Admiral Isachenkov, Vasily Chapayev** and **Admiral Yumashev**), all commissioned between 1970 and 1978. These are similar in design but have significantly different SAM, ASW and electronic outfits. The 'Shaddock' launchers were replaced by two quadruple SS-N-14 'Silex' ASW missile-launcher boxes (although the first mis-

siles were not actually carried for several years, hence the incorrect NATO designation of the SS-N-10 anti-ship missile assigned to these launchers), whilst the SA-N-1 SAM system was replaced by the SA-N-3 'Goblet' system. For operation in heavy weather fin stabilizers were fitted. The same hangar arrangement was adopted, but with a Kamov Ka-25 'Hormone-A' ASW

A Soviet 'Kresta II' class BPK, armed with SS-N-14 'Silex' ASW missiles in two quadruple launcher boxes either side of the bridge. The class also has a useful anti-ship capability in its 'Silexes' and SA-N-3 'Goblet' SAM missiles. The latter can be fitted with a 25 kt nuclear warhead in place of its HE warhead.

helicopter. At present the Soviet Northern Fleet has two 'Kresta I' and six 'Kresta II' cruisers, the Baltic Fleet one 'Kresta II' cruiser, and the Pacific Fleet two 'Kresta I' and three 'Kresta II' cruisers.

Specification
'Kresta I' class
Displacement: 6,000 standard and 7,600 tons full load
Dimensions: length 155.5 m (510.2 ft); beam 17.0 m (55.75 m) draught 6.0 m (19.7 ft)
Propulsion: geared steam turbines delivering 100,000 shp (74570 kW) to two shafts ·
Speed: 34 kts
Complement: 380
Aircraft: one Kamov Ka-25 'Hormone-B' missile-guidance helicopter
Armament: two twin SS-N-3B 'Shaddock' SSM launchers, two SA-N-1 'Goa' SAM launchers, two twin 57-mm DP guns, four 30-mm ADG6-30 CIWS mountings (in *Vitse-Admiral Drozd* only), two 12-barrel RBU 6000 ASW rocket-launchers, two six-barrel RBU 1000 ASW rocket-launchers, and two quintuple 533-mm (21-in) ASW torpedo tube mountings
Electronics: one 'Big Net' air-search radar, one 'Head Net' 3D radar, two 'Peel Group' SAM fire-control radars, two 'Muff Cob' 57-mm fire-control radars, two 'Bass Tilt' CIWS fire-control radars (in *Vitse-Admiral Drozd* only), two 'Plinth Net' fire-control radar, two 'Don-2' navigation radars, one 'Scoop Pair' SSM-guidance radar, one 'Side Globe' ESM suite, two 'High Pole-B' IFF systems, one 'Bell Clout', two 'Bell Tap' and two 'Bell Slam' ECM systems, and one medium frequency hull sonar

Specification
'Kresta II' class
Displacement: 6,200 standard and 7,700 tons full load
Dimensions: length 158.5 m (520.0 ft); beam 17.0 m (55.75 m) draught 6.0 m (19.7 ft)
Propulsion: geared steam turbines delivering 100,000 shp (74570 kW) to two shafts
Speed: 34 kts
Complement: 400
Aircraft: one Kamov Ka-25 'Hormone-A' ASW helicopter
Armament: two quadruple SS-N-14

'Silex' ASW launchers with eight missiles, two twin SA-N-3 'Goblet' SAM launchers with 48 missiles, two twin 57-mm DP guns, four 30-mm ADG6-30 CIWS mounting, two 12-barrel RBU 6000 ASW rocket-launchers, two six-barrel RBU 1000 ASW rocket-launchers, and two quintuple 533-mm (21-in) ASW torpedo tube mountings
Electronics: one 'Head Net-C' 3D radar, one 'Top Sail' 3D radar, two 'Head Light' SAM fire-control radars, two 'Muff Cob' 57-mm fire-control radars, two 'Bass Tilt' CIWS fire-control radars (except *Kronshtadt, Admiral*

The anti-ship RKR 'Kresta I' class carries two twin launchers for the SS-N-3B 'Shaddock' SSM either side of the bridge.

Isakov, Admiral Nakhimov and *Admiral Makarov*, which have optical directors only), one 'Don-2' and two 'Don-Kay' navigation radars, one 'Side Globe' ESM suite, one 'Bell Clout', two 'Bell Tap' and two 'Bell Slam' ECM systems, one 'High Pole-A' and one 'High Pole-B' IFF system, two twin barrel chaff launchers, and one medium-frequency bow sonar

---

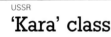
USSR
'Kara' class

Built at the 61 Kommuna, Nikolayev North Shipyard between 1971 and 1977, the seven units of the **'Kara' class** (***Nikolayev, Ochakov, Kerch, Azov, Petropavlovsk, Tashkent*** and ***Tallinn***) are rated by the Soviets as BPKs (*Bolshoy Protivolodochnyy Korabl'*, or large anti-submarine ship). They are an enlarged COGAG gas turbine-powered refinement of the steam-powered 'Kresta II' design with improved anti-air warfare and ASW warfare systems, commissioned between 1973 and 1980 for service in the Mediterranean and Pacific Fleet theatres of operations. They also have extensive command and control facilities and can act as hunter-killer task group leaders. The SA-N-3 'Goblet' and SS-N-14 'Silex' ASW missiles carried have secondary anti-ship capabilities, the former missile having a 25-kiloton nuclear warhead available in place of the normal 150-kg (331-lb) HE type. All Soviet ships with dual-capable weapon systems have at least 25 per cent of their missiles equipped

with nuclear warheads whilst at sea. The 'Kara' class design's large superstructure is dominated by a single low gas turbine exhaust funnel. On the ship's stern is a helicopter landing pad with a hangar partially recessed below the flight deck, and to stow the Kamov Ka-25 'Hormone-A' ASW helicopter the hangar roof hatch and doors have to be opened before the helicopter is pushed in and then lowered to the deck via an elevator. The fourth ship completed, the **Azov**, was the trials ship for the new generation SA-N-6 vertical SAM and 'Top Dome' fire-control radar in the Black Sea after her aft SA-N-3 'Goblet' and 'Headlight' fire-control radar combination had been replaced by the new systems.

At present four 'Kara' class ships are with the Black Sea Fleet (including the

Fitted to act as ASW hunter-killer task group leaders, the 'Kara' class are essentially COGAG gas-turbine-powered refinements of the 'Kresta II' design, with considerably improved defensive anti-air warfare systems.

A total of seven 'Kara' class were built at the 61 Kommuna, Nikolayev North Shipyard. One, the Azov, acted as trials vessel for the SA-N-6 vertical launch SAM system in the Black Sea, where she has remained since being built.

Azov which stays there), and the remaining three are in the Pacific Fleet. The Black Sea vessels (except *Azov*) regularly deploy to the Mediterranean squadron.

Specification
'Kara' class
Displacement: 8,200 tons standard and 9,700 tons full load
Dimensions: length 173.0 m (567.6 ft); beam 18.6 m (61.0 ft); draught 6.7 m (22.0 ft)
Propulsion: COGAG gas turbine arrangement delivering 120,000 shp (89485 kW) to two shafts
Speed: 34 kts
Complement: 525
Aircraft: one Kamov Ka-25 'Hormone-A' anti-submarine helicopter
Armament: two twin SA-N-3 'Goblet' SAM launchers with 72 missiles (except in *Azov* which has only one SA-N-3 system plus one SA-N-6 SAM system), two twin SA-N-4 'Gecko' SAM launchers with 36 missiles, two quadruple SS-N-14 'Silex' ASW launchers with eight missiles, two twin 76-mm (3-in) DP guns, four 30-mm ADG6-30 CIWS mountings, two 12-barrel RBU 6000 ASW rocket-launchers, two (none in *Petropavlovsk*) RBU 1000 ASW rocket-launchers, and two quintuple 533-mm (21-in) ASW torpedo tube mountings.
Electronics: one 'Top Sail' 3D radar, one 'Head Net-C' 3D radar, two 'Pop Group' SA-N-4 fire-control radars, two 'Head Light' SA-N-3 fire-control radars (except in *Azov*, which has one 'Head Light' plus one 'Top Dome' SA-N-6 fire-control radar), two 'Owl Screech' 76-mm (3-in) fire-control radars, two 'Bass Tilt' CIWS fire-control radars, two 'Don Kay' navigation radars, one 'Don-2' or 'Palm Frond' navigation radar, one 'Side Globe' ESM suite, two 'Bell Clout', two 'Bell Slam', and two 'Bell Tap' ECM systems or four 'Rum Tub' ECM systems, two 'Square Head' IFF systems (*Nikolayev* only), one 'Salt Pot' IFF system, two twin chaff launchers, two 'Round House', TACAN (*Petropavlovsk* only), one low frequency bow sonar and one medium frequency variable-depth sonar.

'Kirov' class

In December 1977 at the Baltic Shipyard in Leningrad the Soviet Union launched the largest warship built by any nation since World War II except for aircraft-carriers. Commissioned into Soviet fleet service in 1980, the *Kirov* was assigned the RKR (*Raketnyy Kreyser*, or missile cruiser) designation by the Soviets and a CGN designation by the Americans. However, in appearance and firepower the *Kirov* is more akin to the obsolete battlecruiser category. Her powerplant is unique in being a combined nuclear and steam propulsion system with two reactors coupled to oil-fired boilers that superheat the steam produced in the reactor plant to increase the power output available during high-speed running. The massive superstructure has most of the weapons systems located forward of it, the after end thus being available for machinery and a below-decks helicopter hangar. Up to five Kamov Ka-25 'Hormone' or Ka-27 'Helix' helicopters can be accommodated in the hangar, with access to the flight deck by a deck lift. The helicopters are a mix of the ASW and missile-guidance/ELINT variants, the latter providing target data for the main battery of 20 SS-N-19 Mach-2.5 anti-ship missiles.

The area-defence SAM is the vertical launch SA-N-6 system, which has 12 below-decks eight-round rotary launchers forward of the SS-N-19 bins. The SA-N-6 is some 7 m (23 ft) long with a 10/100-km (6.2/62-mile) range envelope, and can engage sea-skimming Cruise missiles if required. The maximum target engagement height is around 30000 m (98,425 ft), and with the two 'Top Dome' missile-control radars up to 12 missiles can be controlled at any one time. Close-in air defence is handled by a mix of SA-N-4 'Gecko' missiles, 30-mm CIWS mountings and 100-mm (3.9-in) DP guns.

The ASW armament is unique in being based on a reloadable twin SS-N-14 'Silex' ASW missile-launcher with associated variable-depth low-frequency sonar aft and a low-frequency bow sonar. The usual ASW rocket-launchers and 533-mm (21-in) ASW torpedoes complement the SS-N-14 system.

The *Kirov* is fitted with an extensive command, control and communications outfit, suiting the ship to act as a task group command escort to the future nuclear-powered carrier or to operate on its own. In late 1983 the second 'Kirov' class ship was completed. Called the *Frunze*, it differs from the *Kirov* in a number of ways. It has a single twin 130-mm (5.12-in) gun mount in place of the two 100-mm singles, lacks the SS-N-14 ASW system forward and has eight SA-N-9 vertical launch bins in its place, and has a different electronic outfit. *Kirov* is with the Northern Fleet, while *Frunze* serves with the Pacific Fleet. A third unit is expected to be in commission by 1988/9. These impressive vessels normally carry three Kamov 'Hormone' or 'Helix' helicopters for ASW, mid-course targeting and utility purposes.

Frunze is seen being shadowed by a US Navy P-3C Orion soon after commissioning. The most obvious difference from Kirov *is the single stern gun turret, although there are a number of other changes.*

The Soviet warship Kirov, *built in the late 1970s, is the closest thing to a modern version of the battlecruiser. She carries the heaviest armament seen to date on a Soviet surface combatant, and more of the class are under construction at the Baltic shipyard, Leningrad.*

Specification
'Kirov' class
Displacement: 24,000 tons standard and 28,000 tons full load
Dimensions: length 248.0 m (813.65 ft); beam 28.0 m (91.86 ft); draught 8.8 m (28.87 ft)
Propulsion: two pressurized-water cooled reactors with combined superheating boilers delivering 150,000 shp (111855 kW) to two shafts
Speed: 36 kts
Complement: 900
Aircraft: five Kamov Ka-25 'Hormone' or Ka-27 'Helix' anti-submarine and missile-guidance helicopters
Armament: 20 SS-N-19 SSM launchers each with one missile, 12 SA-N-6 SAM launchers with 96 missiles, two twin SA-N-4 'Gecko' SAM launchers with 36 missiles, 16 SA-N-9 systems (in eight vertical launch bins) with c. 128 missiles, two 100-mm (3.9in) guns (Kirov) or one twin 130-mm (5.12 in) DP gun (Frunze), eight 30-mm ADG6-30

CIWS mounts, one twin SS-N-14 'Silex' ASW launcher with 16 missiles (Kirov only), one 12-barrel RBU 6000 ASW rocket-launcher, two six-barrel RBU 1000 ASW rocket-launchers, and two quintuple 533-mm (21-in) torpedo tube mounts
Electronics: one 'Top Pair' 3D radar, one 'Top Steer' 3D radar, two 'Top Dome' SA-N-6 fire-control radars, two 'Pop Group' SA-N-4 fire-control radars, three 'Palm Frond' navigation radars, one 'Kite Screech' fire-control radar, two 'Eye Bowl' SS-N-14 fire-control radars (Kirov ony), four 'Bass Tilt' CIWS fire-control radars, one 'Side Globe' ESM suite (Kirov only), 10 'Bell' series ECM systems, four 'Rum Tub' ECM systems (Kirov only), one 'Fly Screen' helicopter landing aid, two 'Punch Bowl' satellite communication systems, two 'Big Ball' satellite communication systems (Frunze only), four 'Tin Man' optronic fire-control systems, two 'Bob Tail' navigation aids, one 'Salt Pot' IFF

system, two twin barrel chaff/flare launchers, one low-frequency bow sonar, and one low-frequency variable-depth sonar

The towering superstructure of the **Frunze** *displays the multiplicity of electronic systems so typical of Soviet warship designs.* **Frunze** *and* **Kirov,** *being larger and more heavily armed than almost any other ship, necessarily have more radar and fire-control than anything else afloat.*

'Moskva' class

Classified by the Soviets as PKRs (*Protivolodochnyy Kreyser*, or anti-submarine cruiser), the two **'Moskva' class** ships are in fact hybrid helicopter carriers and missile cruisers, and were developed to counter the Western strategic missile submarines in the regional seas adjacent to the Soviet Union. However, by the time the first two vessels, the **Moskva** and the **Leningrad**, had been completed at the Nikolayev South Shipyard in 1967 and 1968, it was found that they were incapable of coping with both the numbers of submarines and their capabilities, so the programme was terminated. The 'Moskva' class ships are deployed primarily to the Mediterranean as part of the Soviet 5th Eskadara. They have also on occasion appeared in the North Atlantic, North Sea, Baltic and Indian Ocean as part of deployed task forces or on transit. They are poor sea boats in heavy weather.

In appearance the two ships are missile cruisers forward with extensive anti-air warfare and ASW systems located step-wise on the forward superstructure arrangement, which then ends abruptly in a large steam turbine exhaust stack and main radar mast assembly. A 15-m (49.2-ft) long hangar suitable for two helicopters side by side is located within this structure between the stack uptakes. The after end of the ship is taken up by an 86 m (282.2 ft) by 34 m (111.5 ft) flight deck with four mesh-covered helicopter take-off and landing spots marked out with the numbers 1 to 4. A fifth spot, marked with the letter P, is located centrally. Two 16.5 m (54.1 ft) by 4.5 m (14.8 ft) aircraft lifts serve the flight deck from the 65 m (213.25 ft) by 24 m (78.75 ft) hangar deck below. The hangar space can accommodate a maximum of 18 Kamov Ka-25 'Hormone-A' ASW helicopters, although 14 is the number usually carried. The Leningrad has been seen with two Mil Mi-14 'Haze-B' helicopters stowed on her flight deck for minesweeping duties when she assisted in the clearing of the southern end of the Suez Canal zone following the Yom Kippur War of 1973.

The quintuple 533-mm (21-in) ASW torpedo tubes originally carried behind the accommodation ladders in the ship's sides have been removed. The ASW armament relies on two 6000-m (6,500-yard) range 250-mm (9.84-in) calibre automatically reloaded rocket-launchers and a twin SU-W-N1 unguided ballistic missile-launcher firing the 30-km (18.6-mile) range FRAS-1 (Free Rocket Anti-Submarine) rocket fitted with a 15-kiloton nuclear depth bomb as the warhead. The target data for the FRAS-1 is generated by the low-frequency bow sonar and medium-frequency variable-depth sonar carried. The 'Hormone-A' helicopters provide the ASW screen at medium ranges (between 55 and 74 km/34 and 46 miles from the ship) using dipping sonar, sonobuoys, 450-mm (17.7-in) ASW torpedoes, and conventional and nuclear depth bombs. However, these helicopters do not have a night sonar-dipping capability such as that possessed by the later Ka-27 'Helix-A'. The 'Moskva' class ships are fitted to serve as command ships for ASW hunter-killer groups with maritime patrol ASW aircraft in support.

Specification
'Moskva' class
Displacement: 14,500 tons standard and 17,500 tons full load
Dimensions: length 189.0 m (620.1 ft); beam 26.0 m (85.3 ft); draught 7.7 m (25.25 ft)
Propulsion: geared steam turbines delivering 100,000 shp (74570 kW) to two shafts
Speed: 30 kts
Complement: 850
Aircraft: 18 Kamov Ka-25 'Hormone-A' anti-submarine helicopters

Armament: eight twin SA-N-3 'Goblet' SAM launchers with 48 missiles, two twin 57-mm DP guns, one twin SU-W-N1 ASW launcher with 20 FRAS-1 rockets, and two 12-barrel RBU 6000 ASW rocket-launchers
Electronics: one 'Top Sail' 3D radar, one 'Head Net-C' 3D radar, two 'Head Light' SAM fire-control radars, two 'Muff Cob' 57-mm fire-control radars, three 'Don-2' navigation radars, one 'Side Globe' ESM suite, two 'Bell Clout' ECM systems, two 'Bell Slam' ECM systems, two 'Bell Tap' and two 'Top Hat' ECM systems, two twin-barrel flare chaff launchers, one low-frequency hull sonar, and one medium-frequency variable-depth sonar

Below: The 'Moskva' class have full command and control facilities to co-ordinate both hunter-killer task groups and maritime patrol aircraft, including their own ASW helicopters, to 'sanitize' areas of ocean.

Above: the PKR **Moskva** *is a hybrid helicopter-carrier and missile cruiser designed originally to counter the Western SSBNs in seas close to the Soviet homeland. An air group of 14 Kamov Ka-25 'Hormone-A' helicopters is normally carried, which work in four aircraft flights to form medium range ASW screens.*

847

'Slava' class

In 1983 the first of the 'Kara' follow-on design, the '**Slava**' class (or 'Krasina' class as it was originally known) RKR missile cruiser, was seen outside the Black Sea Fleet area in the Mediterranean. The lead ship, *Slava*, was laid down at the same Nikolayev shipyard in 1978, launched in 1979 and completed in 1983 after an extensive trials programme during 1982 in the Black Sea. Since then two more units have been commissioned into service but their names are not yet known. A fourth unit is still under construction. The class has a long forecastle, a continuous maindeck and a short stern section at a level slightly lower than that of the main deck. The transom is of the broad and raking type. Surprisingly, for a new design the equipment fit is conservative, unlike other recent Soviet types. The hangar floor is one half-deck below the flight-deck which is accessed via an inclined ramp with the helicopter being moved around by a deck mounted haulage system. Monitoring of the *Slava* during fleet operations indicates that she and her sisters are intended to serve as flagships, with their primary combat role being that of leading surface battle groups targetted against NATO's carriers and sea lines of communications in the Atlantic and Pacific Oceans.

Specification
'Slava' class
Displacement: 10,500 tons standard, 12,500 tons full load

Dimensions: length 187 m (613.5 ft), beam 20.3 m (66.6 ft), draught 8 m (26.2 ft)
Propulsion: COGAG gas turbine arrangement delivering 92467 kW (124,000 hp) to two shafts
Speed: 34 kts
Aircraft: one Kamov Ka-25 'Hormone B' missile targetting/ELINT helicopter
Armament: eight twin SS-N-12 'Sandbox' SSM launchers (no reloads), eight SA-N-6 SAM launchers with 64 missiles, two twin SA-N-4 'Gecko' SAM launchers with 36 missiles, one twin 130-mm (5.12-in) OP gun, six 30-mm ADG6-30 CIWS mountings, two 12 barrel RBU6000 ASW rocket

launchers, two quintuple 533mm (21 in) ASW torpedo tubes
Electronics: one 'Top Pair' 3D radar, one 'Top Steer' 3D radar, one 'Top Dome' SA-N-6 fire-control radar, two 'Pop Group' SA-N-4 fire-control radars, one 'Front Door' SS-N-12 missile guidance radar, three 'Palm Frond' navigation radars, one 'Kite Screech' 130-mm (5.12-in) fire-control radar, three 'Bass Tilt' CIWS fire-control radars, four 'Tee Plinth' optronic fire control systems, one 'Side Globe' ESM

The Soviet missile cruiser Slava is seen at anchor off Solum, Libya in a photograph taken by a Sea King helicopter from HMS Illustrious. *This powerful ship is designed to lead surface action groups against NATO carriers and western sea lines of communication.*

suite, four 'Rum Tub' ECM systems, several 'Bell' series ECM systems, two twin chaff launchers, one medium frequency bow sonar, one low frequency variable depth sonar
Complement: 720

'Almirante Grau' class

In 1973 Peru bought from the Netherlands navy the cruiser *de Ruyter* which dated originally from World War II. Commissioned into the Peruvian navy in May of that year as the *Almirante Grau* (pennant number 81) she was returned to the Netherlands in 1985 for an extensive 2½ year modernization that involved the reconditioning of her mechanical and electrical systems, the fitting of six to eight MM38 Exocet launcher-containers, replacement of the radars and fire control systems and the adding of one CSEE Sagaie and two Dagaie chaff/decoy launcher units.

Three years after buying the *de Ruyter* Peru bought her sister ship, the Terrier SAM equipped *de Zeven Pro-*

vincien. Due to American pressure the missile system had to be removed and returned to the United States Navy but it was replaced by a 20.4×16.5 m (66.9×54.1 ft) hangar and a 35×17 m (114.8×55.8 ft) flight deck for three Agusta-Sikorsky SH-3D Sea King helicopters fitted to fire AM39 Exocet air launched anti-ship missiles. A secondary landing spot is located on the hangar roof. Renamed the *Aguirre* (84) she entered service on 31 October 1977. She was returned to Holland in mid-1986 for a major overhaul of her propulsion plant. Both ships are expected to serve on well into the 1990's.

Aguirre was the Dutch cruiser de Zeven Provincien before being acquired by Peru in 1976. She can operate up to three Exocet capable Agusta-Sikorsky SH-3D Sea Kings in place of the long range Terrier SAMs fitted while in service with the Netherlands.

Specification
'Almirante Grau' class
Displacement: *Almirante Grau* 9,529 tons standard, 11,850 tons full load; *Aguirre* 9,850 tons standard, 12,250 tons full load
Dimensions: length 187.3 m (614.5 ft), Aguirre 185.7 m (609.3 ft), beam 17.3 m (56.8 ft), draught 6.7 m (22 ft)
Propulsion: geared steam turbines delivering 63385 kW (85,000 hp) to two shafts
Speed: 32 kts
Aircraft: *Aguirre* only three Agusta-Sikorsky SH-3D Sea King ASW/anti-ship helicopters

Armament: *Almirante Grau* (before modernization): four twin 152-mm (6-in) DP guns, six single 40-mm AA guns, two depth charge racks. *Aguirre:* two twin 152-mm (6-in) DP guns, three twin 57-mm AA guns, four single 40mm AA guns, two depth charge racks
Electronics: *Almirante Grau* (before modernization): one LW01 air search radar, one LW02 air search radar, one ZW01 surface search radar, one VIO1 height finder radar, one DA02 air/surface search radar, two M25 152-mm (6-in) gun fire control radars, four M44 AA fire control radars, one ESM suite, one CWC10W hull sonar. *Aguirre:* one LW02 air search radar, one ZW01 surface search radar, one DA02 air/surface search radar, one ZW03 surface search radar, one M25 152-mm (6-in) gun fire control radar, four M44 AA fire control radars, one ESM suite, one CWC10W hull sonar
Complement: *Almirante Grau* 953, *Aguirre* 856

'Colbert' class

A development of the pre-war 'De Grasse' design, the post-war Brest-built **Colbert** (C 611) was commissioned in 1959, and incorporated a number of modifications such as an increase in beam, different armour protection and a shortened transom stern that improved her stability and allowed for a helicopter landing pad to be carried aft.

From April 1970 until October 1972 the *Colbert* underwent a major refit to equip her with the Masurca area-defence SAM system for fleet-defence duties. As a result of financial restraints the original refit plan had to be modified to include the retention of some of her original AA armament. The bridge structure was rebuilt and air-conditioning was installed throughout. In order to cope with the increased power requirements thus needed, the electrical generator system was uprated to give a 5000-kW output. A modernized electronics suite was also installed, and a SENIT-1 action information system was fitted in the operations room to enable the *Colbert* to act as a flagship for the French Mediterranean fleet, a role in which she has served since the end of the 1970 refit. From August 1981 to November 1982 she underwent a second major refit to extend her operational life to 1997. During this a satellite communications system was fitted and improvements made to extend the range of the Masurca Mk 2 Mod 3 semi-active hom-

ing missiles beyond their normal 60 km (37 miles); the altitude engagement limits of the missile are between 30 and 22500 m (100 and 73,820 ft).

Specification
'Colbert' class
Displacement: 8,500 tons standard and 11,300 tons full load
Dimensions: length 180.0 m (590.55 ft); beam 20.2 m (66.27 ft); draught 7.9 m (25.9 ft)
Propulsion: geared steam turbines delivering 86,000 shp (64130 kW) to two shafts

Speed: 31.5 kts
Complement: 562
Aircraft: none embarked, though a helicopter platform is provided
Armament: four MM.38 Exocet SSM launchers with four missiles, one twin Masurca SAM launcher with 48 missiles, two 100-mm (3.9-in) DP guns and six twin 57-mm AA guns
Electronics: one DRBV 23C air-search radar, one DRBI 10D height-finder radar, one DRBV 50 surface/air-search radar, one DRBN 32 navigation radar, one DRBV 20C air-search radar, two DRBR 51 SAM fire-control radars, one

Serving as the flagship of the French Mediterranean Fleet, the Colbert *recently underwent a refit to extend her operational life past the year 1995.*

DRBR 32C gun fire-control radar, two DRBC 31 100-mm gun fire-control radars, one URN-20 TACAN, one SENIT-1 action information system, one Syracuse satellite communication system, one ARBB 31 ECM system, one ARBB 32 ECM system, one ARBR 10F ECM system and two Syllex chaff launchers.

'Vittorio Veneto' class

Originally to have been a third 'Andrea Doria' class ship, the **Vittorio Veneto** (C 550) was radically altered in design on several occasions when it was realized that these earlier ships were too small. The *Vittorio Veneto* is thus half as large again as an 'Andrea Doria', with a raised 40 m (131.2 ft) by 18.5 m (60.7 ft) flight deck aft with a two-decks deep 27.5 m (90.2 ft) by 15.3 m (50.2 ft) hangar below it. This allows up to nine AB.204As or AB.212ASW or six SH-3D Sea King ASW helicopters to be carried, although the two 18 m (59.1 ft) by 5.3 m (17.4 ft) aircraft lifts preclude the Sea Kings from being struck down into the hangar. The normal complement is six AB.212 ASWs. The extra space forward allows the fitting of an American Mk 20 Aster SAM/ASW launcher system in place of the Mk 10 used on the 'Andrea Doria' class. The new launcher has three rotary drums loaded with 40 SAMs and 20 ASROC ASW missiles so that the operations centre can choose the missile type to be fired

according to the nature of the threat detected. During her latest refit (1981-3) the *Veneto* was modified to fire the Standard SM1-ER SAM. She also had fitted four Teseo launchers for Otomat SSMs, and two Dardo close-in weapon system mountings with three twin 40-mm Breda gun turrets. The *Veneto*, which was originally commissioned in 1969, was used as the Italian navy's flagship, but she has now handed this role over to the carrier *Giuseppe Garibaldi.*

Specification
'Vittorio Veneto' class
Displacement: 7,500 tons standard and 8,870 tons full load
Dimensions: length 179.6 m (589.25 ft); beam 19.4 m (63.6 ft); draught 6.0 m (19.7 ft)
Propulsion: geared steam turbines delivering 73,000 shp (54435 kW) to two shafts
Speed: 30.5 kts
Complement: 565

Aircraft: nine Agusta (Bell) AB.212ASW or six Agusta (Sikorsky) SH-3D Sea King anti-submarine and anti-ship helicopters
Armament: one twin Standard SM1-ER/ASROC SAM6 ASW launcher with 40 Standard and 20 ASROC missiles, four Teseo SSM launchers with four Otomat Mk 2 missiles, eight 76-mm (3-in) DP guns, three twin 40-mm Dardo CIWS mountings, and two triple 324-mm (12.75-in) ASW torpedo tube mountings for Mk 44 and Mk 46 torpedoes
Electronics: one SPS-52C 3D radar, one RAN-20X air-search radar, one SPS-702 surface-search radar, two SPG 55C SAM fire-control radars, two RTN20X Dardo fire-control radars, three RTN10X Argo 76-mm fire-control radars, three RM7 navigation radars, one URN-20 TACAN, one Abbey Hill passive ESM suite, two SCLAR flare/chaff launchers, and one SQS-23G sonar

Above: The Vittorio Veneto *(C 550) was the Italian navy's flagship until replaced in the role by the carrier Guiseppe Garibaldi. The* Veneto *operates up to nine AB.212ASW or six SH-3D Sea King ASW helicopters from her flight deck.*

Originally to have been a third 'Andrea Doria' class hybrid cruiser/ helicopter carrier, the Vittorio Veneto *was radically altered in design when it became apparent to the Italian navy that the earlier ships were much too small for their assigned tasks.*

Modern Destroyers

The modern destroyer would hardly be recognizable to one familiar with the classic gun- and torpedo-armed vessels of World War II. Even the term 'destroyer' is somewhat loose, covering as it does vessels ranging from the small, gun-armed 'Kotlin' class of the Soviet navy up to the Soviet 'Sovremenny' and American 'Spruance' and 'Kidd' classes, each as large as light cruisers of the 1940s.

Since World War II the destroyer has evolved from a torpedo-armed, all-gun surface warfare vessel into a specialist anti-air or anti-submarine warfare ship capable either of independent operations for a short time or of operating as an escort in a task force. The losses suffered by the Navy's destroyers during the Falklands conflict proved to NATO that the UK's minimally armed warships, which had been thus constructed to satisfy the monetary constraints imposed by the Treasury for political reasons, were extremely vulnerable in a conventional war, let alone the nuclear scenarios proposed for the North Atlantic theatre of operations. Unfortunately the mistakes inherent in the destroyers' design will be around for a few more years yet until the ships are scrapped. Short-term plans to rectify some of the faults (such as the inadequate numbers of close-range defence weapons) are already being implemented, but are no real substitute for well designed ships as seen in other navies. For instance, the Soviets are building specialist classes for both the ASW and surface ship warfare roles, whilst the Americans, with their 'Spruance' class, have managed to produce the most capable ASW destroyer yet built. Modifying this design for the anti-air warfare role has produced the 'Kidd' class ships, which are the most powerfully armed general-purpose destroyers in the world. The new 'Arleigh Burke' design will

Conceived as an escort to the cancelled British 'CVA-01' carrier, HMS Bristol was the first vessel to be armed with the Sea Dart missile system. The cancellation of the carrier, and cost constraints, meant that her successors would be the much smaller and less capable 'Type 42' class.

take excellence even further up the scale. The French in the meantime have followed their own way to take the 'Spruance' and 'Kidd' concept yet further in producing a single hull design and then fitting it out (even to the engine fit) to suit the role assigned to it. The 'Type C70' which has resulted from this policy will be the mainstay of the French destroyer force for a considerable number of years to come. Other navies have tended to follow the USA in either buying new-build ships from that source or taking American technology and building it into their own designs. Very few have bought new-build British ships, but instead have tended to rely on getting such units as second-hand items as they are discarded from the Royal Navy.

The first post-war US destroyer design, the 'Forrest Sherman' class, dates from the mid-1950s. Originally gun-armed destroyers, four were converted to guided missile configuration in the mid-1960s. USS Somers was the last of the class to be modified, recommissioning in 1968.

'Haruna' and 'Shirane' classes

The **'Haruna' class** and follow-on improved **'Shirane' class** are the only destroyer-sized ships in the world which can carry and operate three large Sea King ASW helicopters. Both ship classes were built with strong ASW armaments and are weaker than most Western designs in both anti-air and anti-surface warfare systems, although they are to be modernized within the next few years with systems such as the Harpoon SSM and the 20-mm Phalanx CIWS to help rectify these shortcomings. The 'Haruna' class, *Haruna* (DDH141) and *Hiei* (DDH142), have continuous superstructures with their single combined radar mast and funnel (known as a 'mack') offset to port to allow space for the third helicopter in the hangar. The later 'Shirane' class units, *Shirane* (DDH143) and *Kurama* (DDH144) have a broken superstructure with two 'macks', one offset to port atop the main superstructure forward and the other atop the detached hangar aft. For landing the helicopters in most weather conditions they are fitted with the Canadian Bear Trap hauldown system, whilst to reduce their underwater radiated noise levels from the main propulsion machinery they adopted the 'Masker' bubble-generating system: this forms a continuous curtain of minute air bubbles over the parts of the hull beneath the machinery spaces with the bubbles acting as a sound-damping layer. Two quadruple Harpoon SSM launchers are to be fitted in the future.

Hiei (DDH 142) executes a turn to port at high speed.

Specification
'Haruna' class
Displacement: 4,700 tons standard and 6,400 tons full load
Dimensions: length 153.0 m (502 ft); beam 17.5 m (57 ft 5 in); draught 5.1 m (16 ft 9 in)
Machinery: geared steam turbines delivering 70,000 shp (52,200 kW) to two shafts
Speed: 32 kts
Aircraft: three Mitsubishi-Sikorsky SH-3 Sea King ASW helicopters
Armament: one octuple Sea Sparrow SAM launcher, two single 127-mm (5-in) DP guns, two 20-mm Phalanx CIWS, one octuple ASROC ASW missile launcher (16 missiles), and two triple 324-mm (12.75-in) Type 68 ASW torpedo tubes (6 Mk 46 torpedoes)
Electronics: one SPS-52B 3D radar, one OPS-17 surface-search radar, two Type 72 gun fire-control radars, one WM-25 missile fire-control radar, two VPS-2 fire-control radars, one ORN6 TACAN, one OLR9 ECM system, one OQS-3 hull sonar, and one SQS-35(J) variable-depth sonar
Complement: 340

Specification
'Shirane' class
Displacement: 5,200 tons standard and 6,800 tons full load
Dimensions: length 158.8 m (521 ft);

beam 17.5 m (57 ft 5 in); draught 5.3 m (17 ft 5 in)
Machinery: geared steam turbines delivering 70,000 shp (52200 kW) to two shafts
Speed: 32 kts
Aircraft: as 'Haruna' class
Armament: one octuple Sea Sparrow SAM launcher with 24 missiles, two single 127-mm (5-in) DP guns, two 20-mm Phalanx CIWS, one Octuple ASROC ASW missile launcher with 16 missiles and two triple 324-mm (12.75-

in) Type 68 torpedo mounts with 6 Mk 46 torpedoes
Electronics: one OPS-12 3D radar, one OPS-28 surface-search radar, one OPS-22 navigation radar, one WM-25 missile fire-control radar, two Type 72 gun fire-control radars, two VPS-2 fire control radars, one URN-25 TACAN, one NOLQ 1 ECM system, one OLR-9B ECM system, one OQS-101 hull sonar, one SQR-18A towed-array sonar, and one SQS-35(J) variable-depth sonar
Complement: 370

The 'Haruna' class and the follow-on 'Shirane' design are the only destroyer-size ships in the world to carry three large ASW helicopters as part of their armament. Although very capable ASW platforms, they are very weak in anti-air and surface ship weapons.

'Tachikaze', 'Takatsuki' and 'Hatsuyuki' classes

In order of building, the **'Takatsuki' class** was the first of these three classes to be constructed. Comprising the *Takatsuki* (DD164), *Kikuzuki* (DD165), *Mochizuki* (DD166) and *Nagatsuki* (DD167), the class has a typical American appearance in having two single 127-mm (5-in) guns and an ASROC ASW missile launcher. They originally carried and operated the American ASW DASH system for which they carried a hangar aft for three QH-50 drones. Although DASH was unsuccessful in American service, it proved successful in the Japanese navy, and was retired from service with this class only in 1977. The four ships have undergone major refits both to enhance their already formidable ASW armament and to improve their weak anti-air and anti-surface armaments.

During the early 1970s the Japanese Maritime Self-Defense Force needed to improve its medium-range area-defence SAM capabilities and thus laid down the three **'Tachikaze' class** ships at three-yearly intervals from

1973. These vessels are the *Tachikaze* (DDG168), *Asakaze* (DDG169) and *Sawakaze* (DDG170) and commissioned in 1976, 1979 and 1982 respectively. They each carry a single-rail Mk 13 launcher for the Standard SM-1MR missile. No helicopter facilities are provided, and the ASW armament is confined to ASROC missiles and Mk 46 self-defence torpedoes. In order to save on construction costs the class adopted the propulsion plant and machinery of the 'Haruna' class of helicopter-carrying ASW destroyers.

The **'Hatsuyuki' class** was ordered in the mid-1970s as a gas turbine-powered multi-purpose design with a balanced anti-air, anti-ship and anti-submarine sensor and armament fit from the outset. An aluminium-alloy superstructure is used. All 12 of the class, namely the *Hatsuyuki* (DD122), *Shirayuki* (DD123), *Mineyuki* (DD124), *Sawayuki* (DD125), *Hamayuki* (DD126), *Isoyuki* (DD127), *Haruyuki* (DD128), *Yamayuki* (DD129), *Matsuyuki* (DD130), *Setoyuki* (DD131), *Asayuki* (DD132), and *Shimayuki*

(DD133) were in service by early 1987. A slightly larger **'Improved Hatsuyuki'** class of eight units with steel superstructure is due for the late 1980s.

Designed to enhance the Japanese Maritime Self-Defence Force's anti-aircraft defences, the guided-missile destroyer Tachikaze (DDG 168) and her two sisters carry a single-rail Mk 13 Standard MR-1 SAM system aft to provide area defence.

Specification
'Takatsuki' class
Displacement: 3,200 tons standard and 4,500 tons full load
Dimensions: length 136.0 m (446 ft 2 in); beam 13.4 m (44 ft); draught 4.4 m (14 ft 5 in)
Machinery: geared steam turbines delivering 60,000 shp (44740 kW) to two shafts
Speed: 32 kts
Armament: two quadruple Harpoon SSM launchers (no reloads), one octuple Sea Sparrow SAM launcher with 16 missiles, one single 127-mm (5-in) DP gun, one 20-mm Phalanx CIWS mount (DD164-165), one octuple ASROC ASW missile launcher (no reloads), one Type 71 375-mm (14.76-in) Bofors ASW rocket launcher (36 rockets), and two triple Type 68 324-mm (12.75-in) ASW torpedo tubes (6 Mk 46 torpedoes)
Electronics: one OPS-11B air-search radar, one OPS-17 surface-search radar, two Mk 56 fire-control radars (Type 72 in DD167), one VPS-2 fire-control radar (DD164-165 only), one NOLR-6C ECM system, two Mk 36 Super RBOC chaff launchers, one OQS-3 hull sonar, one SQS-35(J) variable-depth sonar (DD166-167 only) and one SQR-18A towed-array sonar (DD164-165 only)
Complement: 270

Specification
'Tachikaze' class
Displacement: (DD168-169) 3,850 tons standard and 4,800 tons full load; (DD170) 3,950 tons standard and 4,800 tons full load
Dimensions: length 143.0 m (469 ft 2 in); beam 14.3 m (46 ft 11 in); draught 4.6 m (15 ft 1 in)
Machinery: geared steam turbines delivering 70,000 shp (52200 kW) to two shafts
Speed: 32 kts
Armament: two quadruple Harpoon SSM launchers (no reloads, in DD170 only), one single-rail Mk 13 Standard SM-1MR launcher (40 missiles), two single 127-mm (5-in) DP guns, one 20-mm Phalanx CIWS mounting (being fitted), one octuple ASROC ASW missile launcher (16 missiles), and two triple Type 68 324-mm (12.75-in) ASW torpedo tubes (6 Mk 46 torpedoes)
Electronics: one SPS-52B 3D radar, one OPS-11B (OPS-28 in DD170) air-search radar, one OPS-17 surface-search radar, two SPG-51C Standard fire-control radars, two Type 72 gun fire-control radars, two SATCOMM communications systems, one OLT-3 ESM suite, four Mk 36 Super RBOC chaff launchers, and one OQS-3 (OQS-4 in DD170) hull sonar
Complement: 277

Specification
'Hatsuyuki' class
Displacement: 2,950 tons standard and 3,700 tons full load (DD122-128) or 3,050 tons standard and 3,800 tons full load (DD129-133)
Dimensions: length 131.7 m (432 ft 1 in); beam 13.7 m (45 ft); draught 4.3 m (14 ft 2 in)
Machinery: two Rolls-Royce Olympus TM3B gas turbines delivering 45,000 shp (33555 kW) and two Rolls-Royce Tyne RM1C gas turbines delivering 10,680 shp (7965 kW) in a COGOG arrangement to two shafts
Speed: 30 kts
Aircraft: one Mitsubishi-Sikorsky SH-3 Sea King ASW helicopter
Armament: two quadruple Harpoon SSM launchers (no reloads), one octuple Sea Sparrow SAM launcher with 16 missiles, one single 76-mm (3-in) DP gun, two 20-mm Phalanx CIWS mountings, one octuple ASROC ASW missile launcher (16 missiles), and two triple Type 68 324-mm (12.75-in) ASW torpedo tubes (6 Mk 46 torpedoes)
Electronics: one OPS-14B air-search radar, one OPS-18 surface-search radar, one FCS2 missile fire-control radar, one GFCS2 gun fire-control radar, two VPS-2 fire-control radars, one NOLR-6C ECM system, one OLT-4 ECM system, one URN-25 TACAN system, one OQS-4 hull sonar and one SQR-19 towed array sonar system
Complement: 195 (200 from DD 129 onwards)

ITALY

'Audace' and 'Animoso' classes

Essentially an enlarged version of the 'Impavido' class hull design with greatly improved armament and an increased freeboard, the **Audace** (D551) and **Ardito** (D550) have proved to be excellent ships in terms of habitability and seaworthiness, so much so that two further units of an **'Improved Audace' class** design were ordered in March 1986. **Animoso** (D560) and **Ardimentoso** (D561) are due to commission in 1991, when they will replace the two 'Impavido' class destroyers Impavido and Intrepido. In terms of capabilities the two **'Audace' class** units improve on the 'Andrea Doria' class of helicopter carriers in almost every respect save the number of helicopters carried. They are to receive the Otomat Mk 2 SSM system in the near future, and are relatively rare in NATO service in having four stern-mounted 533-mm (21-in) torpedo tubes for dual-role long-range wire-guided active/passive acoustic-homing A184 torpedoes as well as self-defence 324-mm (12.75-in) tubes for American Mk 46 ASW torpedoes. The Whitehead A184 is a dual-role 1300-kg (2866-lb) weapon with a range of around 14 km (8.7 miles). The two embarked ASW helicopters carry both Mk 44 and Mk 46 torpedoes, American Mk 54 depth bombs, dipping sonar and sonobuoys for use against sub-surface targets, and the French AS.12 missile for use against surface targets. The helicopters are also being provided with the capability to give mid-course guidance for the Otomat missiles during 'over-the-horizon' missile engagements.

Specification
'Audace' class
Displacement: 3,950 tons standard and 4,559 tons full load
Dimensions: length 136.6 m (448 ft); beam 14.23 m (46 ft 8 in); draught 4.6 m (15 ft)
Machinery: geared steam turbines delivering 73,000 shp (54435 kW) to two shafts
Speed: 33 kts
Aircraft: two Agusta-Bell AB.212ASW helicopters or one Agusta-Sikorsky SH-3D Sea King ASW helicopter
Armament: one single-rail Mk 13 Standard SM-1MR SAM launcher (40 missiles), two single 127-mm (5-in) DP guns, four single 76-mm (3-in) AA guns, two triple 324-mm (12.75-in) ILAS-3 ASW torpedo tubes (12 Mk 46 torpedoes), and two twin 533-mm (21-in) torpedo tubes (12 A184 torpedoes)
Electronics: one SPS-52 3D radar, one RAN20S air-search radar, one SPQ2 air- and surface-search radar, two SPG-51B Standard fire-control radars, one 3RM20 navigation radar, one ESM suite, two 20-barrel SCLAR chaff and IR decoy launchers, and one CWE610 hull sonar
Complement: 381

The 'Audace' class, by use of modern lightweight weapon systems and the mounting of a Mk 13 SAM launcher atop the hangar, has greater capabilities in almost every respect (save the number of helicopters carried) than the 'Andrea Doria' class.

The Audace (D551) uses an enlarged version of the 'Impavido' class hull design with increased freeboard. A vastly improved armament fit includes a hangar and flight deck suitable for operating either two Agusta-Bell AB.212ASW or one Agusta-Sikorsky SH-3D Sea King ASW helicopters.

Specification (provisional)
'Animoso' class
Displacement: 4,500 tons standard and 5,250 tons full load
Dimensions: length 137 m (449.5 ft); beam 15 m (49.2 ft); draught 5 m (16.4 ft)
Machinery: two Fiat/GE LM 2500 gas turbines delivering 55,000 shp (41013 kW) and two GMT BL230-20 DVM diesels delivering 12,500 bhp (9321 kW) in a CODOG arrangement to two shafts
Speed: 32 knots
Aircraft: two Agusta-Sikorsky ASH-3D Sea King or EH.101 medium ASW helicopters
Armament: Four single Otomat Mk 2 SSM launchers, one single rail Mk 13 SAM launcher with 40 Standard SM-1MR missiles, two octuple Albatros SAM launchers with 48 missiles, one single 127-mm (5-in) DP gun, three single 76-mm (3-in) DP guns, three twin 40-mm DARDO CIWS, two triple ILAS-3 324-mm (12.75-in) torpedo tubes with 24 Mk 46 torpedoes
Electronics: one SPS-52C 3D radar, one RAN-20S air-search radar, one surface-search radar, one navigation radar, two RTN-30X Albatros fire-control radars, two SPG-51D Standard fire-control radars, three RTN-20X DARDO fire-control radars, one ESM suite, two 20-barrel SCLAR chaff and I-R decoy launchers, one DE-1164 bow sonar and one variable depth sonar
Complement: 350

The graceful lines so typical of Italian ship design are apparent as the 'Audace' class guided-missile destroyer Ardito *cuts through the waves.*

'Luda' class

Construction of the most numerous class of surface combatants built in China since World War II, the **'Luda' class** destroyers, began in 1966 at the Luda shipyard. The first unit, **No. 105**, was launched in 1970 and completed the following year. This was followed by three further vessels (**Nos 106, 108 and 109**) completed there in 1972-5, one (**No. 107**) completed at the Guang-zhou shipyard in 1974 and two (**Nos 110 and 111**) completed at the Zhonghua shipyard in 1975-6. Further building was then held up due to the political upheavals in the Chinese armed forces caused by the attempted coup and subsequent death of the defence minister Lian Biao whilst trying to flee to the Soviet Union in the early seventies. In 1977 the first unit (**No. 131**) of the second series was laid down at Zhon-ghua, launched in 1979 and completed in 1980. This was followed by one other (**No. 132**) completed there in 1981 and six more (**Nos 160-165**) completed at Guangzhou between 1982 and 1985. Based on the Soviet 'Kotlin' destroyer design they are in fact larger with a flat transom type stern. All have been equipped for underway replenish-ment and tend to differ from each other in equipment detail. A number have been used on Chinese navy out of area task force deployments. Plans to mod-ernize eight units (with British electro-nics and container-launched Sea Dart SAMs) fell through in 1983 due to finan-cial problems, although it is now be-lieved that several are going to be re-

built with a hangar and flight deck aft for a lightweight ASW helicopter, new electronics, a 20-mm Phalanx CIWS and two triple ILAS-3 324-mm (12.75-in) ASW torpedo tubes for Mk46 tor-pedoes.

Specification
'Luda' class
Displacement: 3,250 tons standard, 3,960 tons full load
Dimensions: length 131 m (429.8 ft), beam 12.7 m (41.7 ft), draught 4.8 m (15.7 ft)
Machinery: geared steam turbines delivering 60,000 hp (44742 kW) to two shafts
Speed: 32 kts
Aircraft: none
Armament: two triple container-launchers for Feilong-1 (FL-1) anti-ship missiles, two twin 130-mm (5.12-in) DP guns, four twin 37-mm AA guns (Nos 105, 108 and 132 twin 57-mm AA), two twin 25-mm AA, two 12 barrel 250-mm FQF2500 ASW rocket-launchers with 120 rockets, four BMB-2 depth charge throwers and two depth charge racks (with total of 48 depth charges), up to 60-80 mines according to type
Electronics: one 'Bean Sticks' air search radar ('Pea Sticks' in 107, 131 and 162), one 'Eye Shield' surface search radar, one Type 756 or 'Fin Curve' navigation radar, one 'Square Tie' missile fire control radar, one 'Sun Visor B' (on 105, 108, 131, 161 and 162 only) 130-mm (5.12-in) fire control radar, two 'Rice Lamp' 57-mm AA fire

control radars (on 103, 108 and 132 only), two 'Watch Dog' ECM systems, one RW23 ESM system, one Pegas 2M hull sonar, three 'Square Head' and one 'High Pole' A IFF systems
Complement: 350

In common with many older Chinese weapon systems, the 'Luda' class destroyers are a modified development of a Soviet design of the 1950s. The 'Ludas' are enlarged versions of the Soviet 'Kotlin'.

FRAM destroyer conversions

By 1958 it had become apparent to the US Navy that the large numbers of World War II vintage destroyers it had in service were beginning to wear out. In order to extend their useful lives by eight years or so the **Fleet Rehabilitation and Modernization (FRAM) I** programme was initiated in the early sixties for 77 **'Gearing'** class destroyers. Essentially this involved rebuilding the ships to an ASW configuration, virtually eliminating all anti-aircraft warfare capability. All the major systems were rehabilitated, DASH ASW drones and an ASROC launcher with a magazine were added, as were two triple Mk 32 324 mm (12.75 in) ASW torpedo tubes and a long range SQS-23 sonar.

At the same time as the FRAM Is were underway a more limited five year life extension programme called **FRAM II** was implemented for 32 of the **'Allen M. Sumner'** class destroyers and 16 more 'Gearings'. In the case of the 'Sumners' this involved the retention of the three twin 127 mm (5 in) gun mounts, the fitting of a new bridge and ECM equipment, the upgrading and relocation of the SQS-4 sonar and the fitting of an SQS-35 variable depth sonar and two triple Mk 32 ASW torpedo tubes. The longer range ASROC launcher could not be fitted due to its weight and the lack of space, so the DASH drone system and a pair of Mk 25 533 mm (21 in) torpedo tubes for Mk 37 ASW torpedoes were fitted instead.

The heavy operational requirements of the Vietnam War strained US Navy resources, however, and many old vessels soldiered on long past their planned retirement dates. Most FRAM destroyers were retained into the seventies, with some even going on to the early 1980s as part of the US Navy Reserve (until they were transferred

abroad). By early 1987 the following navies still had FRAM destroyers in service: Brazil (two 'Gearing FRAM I', four 'Allen M. Sumner FRAM II'), Chile (two 'Allen M. Sumner FRAM II'), Ecuador (one 'Gearing FRAM I'), Greece (one 'Allen M. Sumner' FRAM II, one 'Gearing FRAM II', six 'Gearing FRAM I'), Iran (two 'Allen M. Sumner FRAM II'), South Korea (two 'Allen M. Sumner FRAM II', two 'Gearing FRAM II', five 'Gearing FRAM II', two 'Gearing FRAM I'), Mexico (two 'Gearing FRAM I'), Pakistan (six 'Gearing FRAM I'), Spain (five 'Gearing FRAM I'), Taiwan (two 'Allen M. Sumner FRAM II', 12 'Gearing FRAM I', two 'Gearing FRAM II') and Turkey (one 'Allen M. Sumner FRAM II', one 'Gearing FRAM II', seven 'Gearing FRAM I'). Most of these have been modernized again with new systems and several countries have fitted SSM launchers.

On 22 July 1974 the Turkish 'FRAM II Gearing', the *Kocatepe* (DD354), was sunk by Turkish Air Force jets in mistake for an identical Greek navy destroyer trying to interfere with the amphibious landings being undertaken on Cyprus. She was subsequently replaced by a further 'FRAM II' taking the same name and pennant number in an attempt to disguise the loss. In 1982 two of three Argentine 'Sumner FRAM IIs' (all now deleted), the *Hippo Bouchard* and *Piedra Buena*, were accompanying the cruiser *General Belgrano* when she was sunk by HM Submarine *Conqueror*. The *Hippo Bouchard* was apparently hit midships by a dud Mk 8 torpedo during the attack.

Specification
South Korean 'Gearing FRAM I'
Names: *Taejon* (DD919), *Kwang Ju* (DD921), *Kang Won* (DD922), *Kyong Ki* (DD923), *Jeon Ju* (DD924)

The Rio Grande do Norte (formerly USS Strong) was sold to Brazil in 1973. She is equipped with one Westland Wasp ASW helicopter.

Displacement: 2,425 tons standard, 3,500 tons full load
Dimensions: length 119.0 m (390.4 ft), beam 12.6 m (41.3 ft), draught 6.4 m (21 ft)
Machinery: geared steam turbines delivering 60,000 hp (44742 kW) to two shafts
Speed: 32.5 kts
Aircraft: one Aérospatiale Alouette III ASW helicopter
Armament: 919, 921, 922: two twin Harpoon SSM launchers with four missiles, two twin 127 mm (5 in) DP guns, one twin 40 mm AA gun, one 20 mm Vulcan Gatling CIWS (except 921), two triple 324 mm (12.75 in) Mk 32 ASW torpedo tubes (six Mk 46 torpedoes). 923, 925: two twin 127 mm (5 in) DP guns, one twin 40 mm AA gun, four single 20 mm AA guns, one 20 mm Vulcan Gatling CIWS, one octuple ASROC ASW missile launcher with 17 missiles, two triple 324 mm (12.75 in)

ASW Mk 32 torpedo tubes (six Mk 46 torpedoes)
Electronics: one SPS40 (919 and 921) or SPS29 (remainder) air search radar, one SPS10 surface search radar, one SRN15 TACAN system, one WLR1 ESM system, two four barrel RBOC chaff launchers, one SQS23 hull sonar
Complement: 274-280

'Charles F. Adams' class

Guided-missile destroyers of the **'Charles F. Adams' class** are currently in service with the Australian navy in the form of HMAS **Perth** (D38), HMAS **Hobart** (D39) and HMAS **Brisbane** (D41) with the West German navy in the form of the **Lütjens** (D185), **Mölders** (D186) and **Rommel** (D187), and with the US Navy (23 ships). Each version differs from the others, the Australian ships having two single-rail Ikara ASW missile launchers amidships with 32 missiles in place of the ASROC launcher, and the German vessels having combined funnel and radar mast layout. They are excellent sea boats and are considered to be very capable

multi-purpose vessels. All 23 American ships were due to receive extensive midlife refits but due to massive cost increases this has had to be limited to three ships, the USS **Tattnall** (DDG 19), USS **Goldsborough** (DDG 20), USS **Benjamin Stoddart** (DDG 22), with the other 20 due for deletion from the late 1980s onwards. The 'Charles F. Adams' class was built to a revised 'Forrest Sherman/Hull' design to

One of the best of the earlier missile ship designs, the 'Charles F. Adams' class were at first equipped with a twin Mk 11 Tartar SAM system, as seen here on USS John King (DDG3).

accommodate either a single- or twin-rail Tartar SAM launcher system. Since completion some units have been fitted with a four-round ASROC reload magazine on the starboard side alongside the forward funnel. The modernized vessels will have a three-computer NTDS action data system, an integrated combat system, more modern sensors and countermeasures equipment, and the Standard SM-2MR missile. The ships which are not being modernized are the USS **Charles F. Adams** (DDG 2), USS **John King** (DDG 3), USS **Lawrence** (DDG 4), USS **Claude V. Ricketts** (DDG 5), USS **Barney** (DDG 6), USS **Henry B. Wilson**

(DDG 7), USS **Lynde McCormick** (DDG 8), USS **Towers** (DDG 9), USS **Sampson** (DDG 10), USS **Sellers** (DDG 11), USS **Robison** (DDG 12), USS **Hoel** (DDG 13), USS **Buchanan** (DDG 14), USS **Berkeley** (DDG 15), USS **Joseph Strauss** (DDG 16), USS **Conyngham** (DDG 17), USS **Semmes** (DDG 18), USS **Cochrane** (DDG 21) and USS **Waddell**

The last 10 'Charles F. Adams' class vessels, including USS Semmes (DDG 18), were equipped with the single-rail Mk 13 Tartar SAM launcher. It was this sub-class that attracted the attention of the Australian and West German navies.

(DDG 24). The vessels in the other two navies have already been modernized for service into the 1990s.

Specification
'Charles F. Adams' class (US Navy)
Displacement: 3,370 tons standard and 4,526 tons full load
Dimensions: length 133.2 m (437 ft); beam 14.3 m (47 ft); draught 6.1 m (20 ft)
Machinery: two geared steam turbines delivering 70,000 shp (52200 kW) to two shafts

Speed: 31.5 kts
Aircraft: none
Armament: one twin Mk 11 Tartar SAM/Harpoon SSM launcher (36 Tartar and 6 Harpoon, in DDG 2-14 only) or one single Mk 13 Tartar SAM/Harpoon SSM launcher (36 Tartar and 4 Harpoon, in DDG 15-24 only), two single 127-mm (5-in) DP guns, one octuple ASROC ASW missile launcher (4 reloads), and two triple Mk 32 324-mm (12.75-in) ASW torpedo tubes (6 Mk 46 torpedoes)
Electronics: one SPS-52B 3D radar

SPS-52C in DDGs 19, 20 and 22), one SPS-40B air-search radar (SPS-400 in DDGs 19, 20 and 22), one SPS-10F surface-search radar SPS-100 in DDGs, 19, 20 and 22), one LN 66 navigation radar in DDGs 19, 20 and 22 only, two SPG-51C Tartar fire-control radars, one SPG-53A 127-mm (5-in) gun fire-control radar (DDGs 19, 20 and 22 have one SPQ-9A fire-control radar, one SPG-60 fire-control radar, and two SPG-51D fire-control radars), one URN-25 TACAN, one SLQ-32(V)2 ESM system, four Mk 36 Super RBOC

chaff launchers, one OE 82 satellite communications system (DDGs 19, 20 and 22), one SQS-23A hull (DDG 2-19) or bow (DDG 20-24) sonar and one Fanfare torpedo decoy system
Complement: 339-354

USA

'Coontz' Class

The **'Coontz' class** were the first purpose designed missile-armed escorts. The first three to be built, USS *Farragut* (DDG 37, ex-DLG 6), *Luce* (DDG 38, ex-DLG 7) and *McDonough* (DDG 39, ex DLG-8) were actually intended to be gun-armed frigates (which is what the post-war US Navy called destroyer leaders, a classification later changed to either cruiser or guided missile destroyer). The reason that the class is usually known after its fourth ship, USS *Coontz* (DDG 40, ex-DLG 9) is that she was the first to be ordered as a missile frigate. The remaining ships in the class are USS *King* (DDG 41, ex-DLG 10), *Mahan* (DDG 42, ex-DLG 11), *Dahlgren* (DDG 43, ex DLG 12) *William V Pratt* (DDG 44, ex-DLG 13), *Dewey* (DDG 45, ex DLG-14) and *Preble* (DDG 46, ex-DLG 15). Intended to act as fast task force escorts, the class had little ASW detection equipment and no ASW weaponry. Although their main function was to remain air defence, the threat from an increasingly capable Soviet submarine force saw the design change to incorporate the then newly introduced ASROC, replacing one of the two forward 127-mm (5-in) guns. At the same time the sonar fit was upgraded.

The 'Coontz' class has an aluminium superstructure, reducing topweight and improving stability. Unfortunately, aluminium is vulnerable to fire, as was shown in the disastrous blaze aboard the cruiser *Belknap* after a collision in 1975. Nevertheless, the class has put in a considerable amount of useful service. *King* and *Mahan* were trials ships for the prototype NTDS (Naval Tactical Data System) in the early 1950s, while *Coontz* tested the Phalanx CIWS in 1973. *Mahan* was test ship for the operational trials of the long range Standard SM-2ER SAM, and in 1982 was the first ship to receive the NTU, or New Threat Upgrade system. This incorporates the SPS 48E 3D radar, SPS 49(V)5 search radar, SYS 2 computerized AIO (Action Information Organization) system, and Standard SM-2ER missiles. This is the fit planned for all larger surface combatants for the 1990s, by which time the 'Coontz' class will have been replaced by the 'DDG-51' class.

Specification
'Coontz' class
Displacement: 4,150/4,580 tons standard and 6,150 tons full load
Dimensions: length 156.2 m (512.5 ft); beam 16 m (52.5 ft); draught 7.1 m (23.4 ft)
Machinery: two geared steam turbines delivering 85,000 shp (63385 kW) to two shafts
Speed: 33 kts
Armament: two quadruple Harpoon SSM launchers with eight missiles, one twin Mk 10 SAM launcher with 40 Standard SM-2 ER missiles, one 127-

mm (5-in) DP gun, one ASROC octuple launcher with eight missiles (except *Farragut* with 16), two triple Mk 32 324-mm (12.75-in) torpedo tubes with 12 Mk 46 torpedoes
Electronics: one SPS-48C 3D radar, one SPS-49(V) air-search radar (SPS-29E in DDGs 37, 39 and 41), one SPS-10 surface-search radar, one SPG-53 fire-control radar, two SPG-55B missile fire-control radars, one LN-66 navigation radar in DDGs 37, 39, 40, 42 and 44 or one CRP-1500B (Pathfinder)

in DDGs 38 and 43, or one CRP (Pathfinder) in DDGs 41, 45 and 46, one URN-25 TACAN system, one SLQ-32(V) ESM system, four Mk 36 Super RBOC chaff launchers, one OE-82 satellite communication system, one SQS-23 hull mounted sonar and one Fanfare torpedo decoy system
Complement: 467

USS Farragut *is seen in the Atlantic. These large destroyers are highly capable vessels, with strong anti-aircraft armament.*

USS Farragut, *a 'Coontz' class destroyer, was originally classed as a frigate (as were the guided missile cruisers of the same vintage). While looking similar to the 'Charles F. Adams' class, USS* Farragut *is larger, and is almost as capable as a cruiser.*

USA

'Spruance' and 'Kidd' classes

Built as the replacements for the many 'Gearing (FRAM I)' class destroyers, the 31-strong **'Spruance' class** is the most capable ASW surface ship class yet built, so much so that construction of the class is to resume in the late 1980s to replace the 'Forrest Sherman' and 'Hull' classes in the early 1990s. Constructed by the modular assembly technique, whereby large sections of the hull are built in various parts of the shipyard then welded together on the slipway, these were the first large US warships to employ all gas-turbine propulsion. From 1985 through 1987, DDs 963, 964, 966, 990 and 991 are being fitted with a 32 cell Mk 41 vertical launch system. Initially, Tomahawk cruise missiles or a mixture of Tomahawk and vertical launch ASROC ASW missiles will be carried. Standard SM-2MR might also be fitted, for use when operating with a Carrier Battle Group and under the direct control of an AEGIS equipped ship. The active/passive SQS-53 low-frequency sonar carried in the large bow dome is capable of operating in both the short-range direct-path and the long-range bottom-bounce and convergence-zone modes, targets at long ranges being engaged by the ASW helicopters carried aboard. The current units of the 'Spruance' class are the USS *Spruance* (DD 963), USS *Paul F. Foster* (DD 964), USS *Kinkaid* (DD 965), USS *Hewitt* (DD 966), USS *Elliott* (DD 967), USS *Arthur W. Radford* (DD 968), USS *Peterson* (DD 969), USS *Caron* (DD 970), USS *David R. Ray* (DD 971), USS *Oldendorf* (DD 972), USS *John Young* (DD 973), USS *Comte de Grasse* (DD 974), USS *O'Brien* (DD 975), USS *Merrill* (DD 976), USS *Briscoe* (DD 977), USS *Stump* (DD 978), USS *Conolly* (DD 979), USS *Moosbrugger* (DD 980), USS *John Hancock* (DD 981), USS *Nicholson* (DD 982), USS *John Rodgers* (DD 983), USS *Leftwich* (DD 984), USS *Cushing* (DD 985), USS *Harry W. Hill* (DD 986), USS *O'Bannon* (DD 987), USS *Thorn* (DD 988), USS *Deyo* (DD 989), USS *Ingersoll* (DD 990), USS *Fife* (DD 991), USS *Fletcher* (DD 992), and USS *Hayler* (DD 997).

In 1974 the government of Iran ordered six SAM-equipped versions of the 'Spruances' for service in the Persian Gulf and Indian Ocean. However, following the revolution in that country two were cancelled in 1979 whilst the remaining four under construction were taken over by the US Navy as the **'Kidd' class**. These are the world's most powerfully armed general-purpose destroyers, and are unofficially known in the US Navy as

Lead ship of the 31-strong 'Spruance' class is USS Spruance *(DD963). She was the first large US warship to be fitted with an all-gas turbine propulsion system. The class was built by Ingalls Shipbuilding Corporation under the modular assembly technique, and has proved to be the best ASW destroyer type yet built.*

the **'Ayatollah' class**. The four ships were commissioned as the USS *Kidd* (DDG 993), USS *Callaghan* (DDG 994), USS *Scott* (DDG 995) and USS *Chandler* (DDG 996).

Specification
'Spruance' class
Displacement: 6,950 tons standard and 8,040 tons full load
Dimensions: length 171.7 m (563 ft 3 in); beam 16.8 m (55 ft 2 in); draught 8.8 m (29 ft)
Machinery: four General Electric LM2500 gas turbines delivering 80,000 shp (59655 kW) to two shafts
Speed: 32.5 kts
Aircraft: two Kaman SH-2D/F Seasprite LAMPS Mk I helicopter or one Sikorsky SH-3H Sea King ASW helicopter or two SH-60B Seahawk LAMPS Mk III helicopters

Armament: two quadruple Harpoon SSM launchers (no reloads), two quadruple Tomahawk SSM launchers (DDs 974, 976, 979, 983, 984, 985 and 989), one octuple Sea Sparrow SAM launcher (24 missiles), one octuple ASROC ASW missile launcher (24 missiles), two single 127-mm (5-in) DP guns, two 20-mm Phalanx CIWS mountings (being fitted), and two triple 324-mm (12.75-mm) Mk 32 ASW torpedo tubes (18 Mk 46 torpedoes)
Electronics: one SPS-40B air-search radar, one SPS-55 surface-search radar, one SPG-60 fire-control radar, one SPQ-9A fire-control radar, one Mk 91 Sea Sparrow fire-control system, one Mk 86 gun fire-control system, one Mk 116 ASW fire-control system, one SLQ-32(V)2 ESM suite, four Mk 36 Super RBOC chaff launchers, one SQS-53 bow sonar, one SQR-19 towed-array sonar, one OE-82 communications system, and one Fanfare torpedo decoy system
Complement: 296

Specification
'Kidd' class
Displacement: 7,250 tons standard and 9,574 tons full load

Dimensions: length 171.6 m (563 ft); beam 16.8 m (55 ft); draught 9.1 m (30 ft)
Machinery: as 'Spruance' class
Speed: 32 kts
Aircraft: one or two Kaman SH-2D/F Seasprite LAMPS Mk I or two Sikorsky SH-60B Seahawk LAMPS Mk III helicopters
Armament: two quadruple Harpoon SSM launchers (no reloads), two twin Mk 26 Standard SM-1ER SAM/ASROC ASW missile launchers (50 Standard, 16 ASROC and 2 test missiles), two single 127-mm (5-in) DP guns, two 20-mm Phalanx CIWS mountings, two triple 324-mm (12.75-in) Mk 32 ASW torpedo tubes (18 Mk 46 torpedoes)
Electronics: one SPS-48C 3D radar, one SPS-55 surface-search radar, two SPG-51D Standard fire-control radars, one SPG-60 fire-control radar, one SPQ-9A fire-control radar, two Mk 86 gun fire-control systems, two VPS-2 fire-control radars, one Mk 116 ASW fire-control system, one URN-25 TACAN, one OE-82 satellite communications system, one SLQ-32(V)2 ESM suite, four Mk 36 Super RBOC chaff launchers, one SQS-53A bow sonar, one SQR-19 towed-array sonar, and one Fanfare torpedo decoy system
Complement: 368

USS Comte de Grasse *(DD974). Although carrying the Kaman SH-2D LAMPS I ASW helicopter at present, the 'Spruances' will eventually carry the Sikorsky SH-3H Sea King or two Sikorsky SH-60B Seahawk LAMPS Mk III helicopters.*

USS Kinkaid *(DD 965) prepares for underway replenishing. Criticized at first for their large size and sparse weapon fit, the 'Spruance' class has received progressively upgraded equipment until they are now amongst the most capable ASW vessels afloat. Had they been smaller, they would not have been able to house the extra weaponry, sensors and control equipment necessary for this great improvement in capability.*

USA
'Arleigh Burke' class

Designed as the gas turbine-powered replacement for the 'Coontz' guided-missile destroyer class and the 'Leahy' and 'Belknap' classes of missile cruisers from the early 1990s, the **'Arleigh Burke' class** will be less capable than the contemporary 'Ticonderoga' class missile cruisers in the anti-air warfare role but will also have a secondary anti-surface ship role assigned to them. Apart from aluminium funnels each ship will be constructed from steel to prevent any recurrence of the USS *Belknap*'s fire damage when she collided with the carrier USS *John F. Kennedy*. Plastic Kevlar armour will be fitted over all vital machinery and operations room spaces whilst, surprisingly enough, the class will also be the first US warship class to be equipped fully for warfare in a nuclear, chemical or biological (NBC) environment with the crew confined in a citadel located within the hull and superstructure. The main sensors will be a pair of the reduced-capability SPY-1D AEGIS radars, with a laser designator fire-control system for the guidance of 127-mm (5-in) Deadeye shells fired from the single lightweight 127-mm (5-in) gun mount. The Mk 32 self-defence torpedo tubes will be the first to em-

The entire 'Arleigh Burke' ship, except for aluminium funnels, will be made of steel, and will be the first US warship class to have a collective protection system for defence against nuclear fallout and biological and chemical weapons, with the crew being encased in a citadel-type structure with double airlock doors.

ploy the Mk 50 Barracuda Advanced Lightweight Torpedo now under development. At least 29 vessels (DDG 51 onwards) are planned, although the final number will be subject to much Congressional debate as costs rise. USS *Arleigh Burke* (DDG 51) was laid down in 1985 for commissioning in 1989. One point of criticism already raised is that no hangar has been provided for a helicopter although a flight-deck for a Sikorsky SH-60B Seahawk ASW helicopter is part of the design.

Specification (provisional)
'Arleigh Burke' class
Displacement: 7,250 tons standard and 8,300 tons full load
Dimensions: length 142.1 m (466 ft); beam 18.3 m (60 ft); draught 7.6 m (25 ft)
Machinery: four General Electric LM2500 gas turbines delivering 100,000 shp (74570 kW) to two shafts
Speed: 32 kts
Aircraft: helicopter landing pad only
Armament: two quadruple Harpoon SSM launchers (no reloads), two vertical-launch missile systems (90 Standard SM-2MR SAM, ASROC ASW and Tomahawk SSM missiles), one 127-mm (5-in) DP gun, two 20-mm Phalanx CIWS mountings, and two triple 324-mm (12.75-in) Mk 32 ASW torpedo tubes (24 Mk 50 torpedoes)
Electronics: two SPY-1D paired AEGIS

radars, one SPS-67 surface-search radar, one SPS-64 navigation radar, three SPG-62 Standard fire-control radars, two VPS-2 fire-control radars, one laser designating 127-mm gun fire-control system, one SLQ-32(V)2 ESM suite, four Mk 36 Super RBOC chaff launchers, one SQQ-89 sonar suite comprising one SQS-53C bow sonar and one SQR-19 towed-array sonar
Complement: 303

Artist's impression of the new 'Arleigh Burke' (DDG51) class of destroyers. To be armed with vertical-launch SAM systems, they will use the AN/SPY-1D version of AEGIS, and are expected to supplement the 'Ticonderoga' class of missile cruisers in the anti-air warfare role as replacements for the 'Coontz/Leahy/Belknap' classes.

'Suffren' class

Originally classed as light cruisers, the **Suffren** (D602) and the **Duquesne** (D603) were reclassed as **'Suffren' class** destroyers. In actual fact they are guided-missile destroyers designed to give area anti-air warfare and ASW protection to the 'Clemenceau' class aircraft-carriers. Initial plans called for three ships to be built as a start, with more planned, but in practice only two were laid down. Built almost exclusively with French weapons and sensors, they were the first French naval vessels to be designed to carry SAM missiles, and with three pairs of gyro-controlled non-retractable stabilizers are very stable missile platforms. They are distinguishable in French service by the isolated tall central 'mack' and the distinctive DRBI 23 radome forward, the radome being unique to this class. In the mid-1970s both vessels underwent modifications to fit new weapons and to upgrade the area-defence SAM system to fire only the Masurca Mk 2 Model 3 semi-active radar homing missile. Both ships are now serving with the French Mediterranean Fleet as escorts to the carriers, being transferred there in 1975. The area-defence ASW missile carried is the Malafon, a 1500-kg (3,307-lb) 13-km (8.1-mile) range command-guided glider. This is launched with the aid of a double booster and has as payload a 30-kt 533-mm (21-in) L4 active/passive acoustic-homing ASW torpedo weighing 540 kg (1,190 lb) and having a range of around 5.5 km (3.4 miles). The vessels use the 35-kt 1000-kg (2,205-lb) L5 Model 4 ac-

tive/passive acoustic-homing torpedo in their self-defence tubes. These have a 150-kg (331-lb) HE warhead compared with the 104-kg (229-lb) warhead of the L4, and a range in the order of 7 km (4.35 miles).

Specification
'Suffren' class
Displacement: 5,090 tons standard and 6,090 tons full load
Dimensions: length 157.6 m (517 ft); beam 15.54 m (51 ft); draught 7.25 m (23 ft 9 in)
Machinery: geared steam turbines delivering 72,500 hp (54065 kW) to two shafts
Speed: 34 kts
Aircraft: none
Armament: four single MM.38 Exocet launchers (no reloads), one twin Masurca SAM launcher (48 missiles), two single 100-mm (3.9-in) DP guns, four single 20-mm AA guns, one single Malafon ASW missile launcher (13 missiles), and four single fixed ASW 533-mm (21-in) torpedo tubes (10 L5 torpedoes)
Electronics: one DRBI 23 air-search and target-designation radar, one DRBV 50 surface-search radar, two DRBR 51 Masurca fire-control radars, one combined DRBC 33 fire-control radar and Piranha III tv/laser optronic system, one DRBN 32 navigation radar, one URN-20 TACAN, one SENIT 1 action information system, one ARBB 31 ECM system, one ARBB 32 ECM system, two Sagaie and two Dagaie chaff/decoy launchers, one DUBV 23 hull sonar, and one DUBV 43 variable-depth sonar
Complement: 355

The two 'Suffren' class vessels are characterized in French navy service by the very distinctive radome covering the DRBI-23 3D radar system, which provides target data for the stern mounted twin-rail Masurca semi-active radar homing area defence SAM launcher. The main ASW defence is the amidships Malafon ASW missile launcher.

Above: Classed initially as a missile cruiser and then as a frégate, the Suffren (D602) was the first French warship designed from the outset to carry surface-to-air missiles in order to act as an ASW and anti-air warfare escort for the two French fixed-wing aircraft carriers, Clemenceau and Foch.

D 602

'Type C70' class

The **'Type C70' class** is designed to replace both the 'Type T47' and 'Type T53' class destroyers built in the 1950s, and as such is divided into two groups, one specifically for the ASW task and the other for anti-air warfare duties.

The seven **'Type C70/ASW'** vessels, the **George Leygues** (D640), **Dupleix** (D641), **Montcalm** (D642), **Jean de Vienne** (D643), **Primauguet** (D644), **La Motte-Picquet** (D645) plus one other as yet unnamed, incorporate many of the features employed in the three 'Type F67T' frigates but on a smaller displacement. The first four **'Type C70/1'** ships have the same hangar and facilities for the two embarked Westland Lynx helicopters, one of which is equipped for the localization, classification and attack of sub-surface targets with dipping sonar, Mk 44 and Mk 46 torpedoes, and 161-kg (355-lb) depth bombs, whilst the other is configured for the detection, identification

and attack of small lightly-defended surface targets with AS.12 wire-guided missiles. The last three ships form a separate sub-class (**'Type C70/2'**) and will incorporate several modifications to the basic design, including a longer-range anti-missile capable Crotale SAM system, a towed-array sonar and a raised bridge structure. No Malafon ASW missile system could be carried by either sub-class because of the space required for the gas-turbine propulsion system and its exhaust outlets.

The same hull is used for the **'Type C70/AA'** anti-air warfare version, but the armament and propulsion fits are completely different. Only two ships have been ordered for completion in 1988-90. These are the **Cassard** (D614) and **Jean Bart** (D615). The Mk 13 Standard missile launchers used will be refurbished units taken from 'Type T47' destroyers as they pay off for re-

placement by the 'Type C70s'. The single Aérospatiale SA 365F Dauphin helicopter carried by each ship will be used primarily in the anti-surface ship role with AS.15TT missiles, and will also be capable of providing mid-course guidance for over-the-horizon targeting of the MM.40 Exocets.

Specification
'Type C70/ASW' class
Displacement: 3,830 tons standard and 4,170 tons full load
Dimensions: length 139.0 m (456 ft); beam 14.0 m (45 ft 11 in); draught 5.7 m (18 ft 8 in)
Machinery: CODOG arrangement with two Rolls-Royce Olympus gas turbines delivering 52,000 shp (38775 kW) and two SEMT-Pielstick 16PA6 CV280 diesels delivering 10,400 shp (7755 kW) each to two shafts

Speed: 30 kts
Aircraft: two Westland Lynx anti-submarine and anti-ship helicopters
Armament: up to eight single MM.38 Exocet (MM.40 Exocet from *Montcalm* onwards) anti-ship missile launchers (no reloads), one octuple Crotale Naval SAM launcher (26 missiles), one single 100-mm (3.9-in) DP gun, two single 20-mm AA guns, and two single fixed 533-mm (21-in) ASW torpedo tubes (10 L5 torpedoes)
Electronics: one DRBV 26 air-search radar (not in D644-46), one DRBV 51C air- and surface-search radar (DRBV 51 in D644-46), one DRBC 32D fire-control radar (DRBD 32E in D644-46), two DRBN 32 navigation radars, one SENIT 4 action information system, one each ARBR 16, 11B, and one ARBR 32 ECM system (one ARBR 17 ECM system only in D644-46), one DIBV 10 Vampir IR optronic system, one Syracuse II satellite communications

'Type C70' class (continued)

'Type C70' class (continued)

Modern Destroyers

'Don 2' navigation radar, two 'Watch Dog' ECM systems, one 'Square Head' and one 'High Pole A' IFF system, and two MF hull-mounted sonars.
Complement: 280

Specification
'Kotlin' class
Displacement: 2,850 tons standard 3,500 tons full load
Dimensions: length 126.5 m (415 ft); beam 12.9 m (42.3 ft); draught 4.6 m (15.1 ft)
Machinery: four high-pressure boilers powering two geared steam turbines delivering 72,000 shp (53690 kW) to two shafts
Speed 36 kts
Armament: two 130-mm (5.1-in) twin, four 45-mm quad, two to six 25-mm twin gun mounts, six depth charge throwers and two depth charge racks

or two 16-barrelled RBU 2500 and two 6-barrelled RBU 600 ASW rocket launchers, 10 533-mm (21-in) torpedo tubes or five in RBU equipped ships, 'SAM Kotlins' have one SA-N-1 twin SAM launcher with 16 missiles, one 130-mm twin and one 45-mm quad gun mount, two 12-barrel RBU 6000 rocket launchers and five 533-mm torpedo tubes. Four ships have an additional four twin 30-mm gun mounts and two ships have 16-barrel RBU 2500 ASW rocket launchers in place of RBU 6000
Electronics: one 'Slim Net' search radar ('Head Net' in SAM ships) one 'Sun Visor B' and two (one in SAM ships) 'Egg Cup' 130-mm gun fire-control radars, one 'Peel Group' missile fire-control radar (SAM ships only), one 'Hawk Screech' 45-mm gun fire-control radar, one 'Drum Tilt' 30-mm gun fire-control radar (four SAM

ships only), one/two 'Don 2' or one 'Neptun' navigation radar (one 'Don 2' or 'Don Kay' in SAM ships), one 'High Pole B' IFF, one 'Square Head' IFF (not on SAM ships), two 'Watch Dog' ECM systems, one HF hull sonar (one ship modified to deploy a VDS or Variable Depth Sonar)
Complement: 300

Specification
'Kanin' class
Displacement: 3,700 tons standard and 4,750 tons full load
Dimensions: length 139 m (456 ft); beam 14.7 m (48.2 ft); draught 5 m (16.4 ft)
Machinery: four water-tube boilers powering two geared steam turbines delivering 85,000 shp (63385 kW) to two shafts
Speed: 35 kts

Aircraft: none, but helicopter platform fitted
Armament: one SA-N-1 twin SAM launcher with 16 missiles, two 57-mm quad and four 30-mm twin gun mounts, three 12-barrelled RBU 6000 ASW rocket launchers, and 10 533-mm torpedo tubes
Electronics: one 'Head Net C' search radar, one 'Peel Group' missile fire-control radar, one 'Hawk Screech' 57-mm gun fire-control radar, two 'Drum Tilt' 30-mm gun fire-control radars, two 'Don Kay' navigation radars, four 'Top Hat' and two 'Bell Squat' ECM systems, one 'High Pole B' IFF and one MF hull sonar
Complement: 350

USSR
'Kashin' and 'Kashin (Mod)' classes

Built as the world's first major class of warships powered by gas turbines, the 20-ship **'Kashin' class** was produced from 1963 onwards at the Zhdanov Shipyard, Leningrad (four units 1964-6), and at the 61 Kommuna (North) Shipyard, Hikolayev (16 units 1963-72). The last ship, *Sderzhanny*, was completed to a revised design subsequently designated **'Kashin (Mod)' class** by NATO. This involved lengthening the hull, modernizing the electronics and fitting four SS-N-2c 'Styx' SSM launchers, ADG6-30 CIWS mountings and a variable-depth sonar. Since the *Sderzhanny* was completed five other ships (the *Ognevoy, Slavny, Smely, Smyshlenny* and *Stroyny*) have undergone conversion to this configuration between 1973 and 1980. In 1974 the *Otvazhny* of the standard type foundered in the Black Sea following a catastrophic explosion and fire that lasted for five hours. Over 200 of her crew were killed, making this the worst peacetime naval disaster since World War II. In 1981 the *Provorny* re-entered service with the Black Sea Fleet following conversion to the trials ship for the SA-N-7 SAM system. Apart from the previously mentioned units the other units of this *bolshoy protivo-lodochny korabl'* (large ASW ship) type are the *Komsomolets Ukrainy, Krasny-Kavkaz, Krasny-Krim, Obraztsovy, Odarenny, Reshitelny, Skory, Smetlivy, Soobratzitelny, Sposobny, Steregushchy* and *Strogy*. Most are expected to serve into the 1990s, although a new missile-armed destroyer class is expected to enter service soon as their eventual replacements. Three further units, designated **'Kashin II'** by NATO, were built at Nikolayev in the late 1970s for India; named *Rajput* (D51), *Rana* (D52) and *Ranjit* (D53) these are considerably modified in comparison with the Soviet ships, having only a single 76-mm (3-

in) gun mount, four SS-N-2c 'Styx' SSM launchers in pairs on each side of the bridge, four twin 30-mm AA guns, and a helicopter flight deck and hangar aft for one Kamov Ka-25 'Hormone-A' ASW helicopter in place of the after 76-mm (3-in) gun mount. A further three ships were ordered by India in 1982, the first, *Danvir* being delivered in 1986.

Specification
'Kashin' class
Displacement: 3,750 tons standard and 4,500 tons full load
Dimensions: length 144.0 m (472 ft 5 in); beam 15.8 m (51 ft 10 in); draught 4.8 m (15 ft 9 in)
Machinery: four gas turbines delivering 96,000 shp (71585 kW) to two shafts
Speed: 36 kts
Aircraft: helicopter landing pad only
Armament: two twin SA-N-1 'Goa' SAM launchers (32 missiles) except *Provorny* one twin SA-N-7 single-rail SAM launcher (20 missiles), two twin 76-mm (3-in) DP guns, two 250-mm (9.84-in) RBU 6000 ASW rocket launchers, two 300-mm (11.8-in) RBU 1000 ASW rocket launchers, one quintuple 533-mm (21-in) ASW torpedo mount (except *Provorny* none), and 20-40 mines (according to type)
Electronics: (*Provorny*) one 'Head Net-C' 3D radar, one 'Top Steer' 3D radar, one 'Don 2' navigation radar, eight 'Front Dome' SA-N-7 fire-control radars, one 'High Pole-B' IFF system, two 'Owl Screech' 76-mm (3-in) fire-control radars, and one high-frequency hull sonar
Electronics: (remainder) one 'Big Net' air-search and one 'Head Net-C' 3D radars (eight ships), or two 'Head Net

Although construction of the 'Kashin' class has long since halted for the Soviet navy, the class in a heavily modified form has been reintroduced specifically for export to India.

A' air-search radars, (two ships), or two 'Head Net C' 3D radars (*Obraztsovy* and *Soobratzitelny*), two or three 'Don Kay' or 'Don 2' navigation radars, two 'Owl Screech' 76-mm (3-in) gun fire-control radars, two 'Watch Dog' ECM systems (*Obraztsovy* and *Soobratzitelny*) also have 'Guard Dog' ECM system, two 'High Pole-B' or 'Salt Pot' IFF systems, and one high-frequency hull sonar
Complement: 280

Specification
'Kashin (Mod)' class
Displacement: 3,950 tons standard and 4,650 tons full load
Dimensions: length 147.0 m (482 ft 3 in); beam 15.8 m (51 ft 10 in); draught 4.8 m (15 ft 9 in)
Machinery: as 'Kashin' class
Speed: 35 kts
Aircraft: helicopter landing pad only
Armament: four single SS-N-2c 'Styx' SSM launchers (no reloads), two twin SA-N-1 'Goa' SAM launchers (32

missiles), four 30-mm ADG6-30 CIWS mountings, two 250-mm (9.84-in) RBU6000 ASW rocket launchers, and one quintuple 533-mm (21-in) ASW torpedo tube mounting
Electronics: one 'Big Net' aft-search radar, one 'Head Net-C' 3D radar, two 'Don Kay' navigation radars, two 'Owl Screech' 76-mm (3-in) fire-control radars, two 'Bass Tilt' CIWS fire-control radars, two 'Peel Group' SA-N-1 fire-control radars, two 'Bell Shroud' and two 'Bell Squat' ECM systems, four 16-barrel chaff and IR decoy launchers, one 'High Pole B' IFF system, one medium-frequency hull sonar, and one low-frequency variable-depth sonar
Complement: 300

The 'Kashin' class first entered service in the early 1960s with the last of 20 units commissioning in 1972. Surprisingly, only six have undergone extensive modifications during that time to form the 'Kashin Mod' sub-class, whilst the others have undergone only normal refits.

'Udaloy' class

The 'Udaloy' class (Soviet designation *bolshoy protivolodochny korabl'*, or large ASW ship) was originally given the provisisonal NATO codename **Bal-Com 3**. The nine ships operational by 1987 (the *Udaloy, Vitse Admiral Kulakov, Marshal Vasilievsky, Admiral Zakorov, Admiral Spiridinov, Admiral Tributs, Marshal Shaposhnikov* and two vessels with as yet unknown names), are similar in concept to the American 'Spruance' class ASW destroyers, even to the use of gas turbine propulsion. The class is under construction at the Yantar Shipyard (Kaliningrad) and the Zhdanvo Shipyard (Leningrad) at a rate of about one completion per year. The class has four funnels in an arrangement similar to that of the 'Kashin' class missile destroyers, and carries two quadruple launchers for the SS-N-14 'Silex' missile as the main armament. A unique twin hangar system with associated helicopter flight deck is located aft for two Kamov Ka-27 'Helix-A' ASW helicopters. These carry dipping sonar, sonobuoys, a surface-search radar, nuclear or conventional depth charges, and 450-mm (17.7-in) ASW torpedoes for their anti-submarine role, and can be used in all-weather and night dipping sonar operations. It is probable that the 'Helix-A' also carries a targeting and

mid-course guidance unit for the 'Silex' missiles, so making it possible for the missile's 55-km (34.1-mile) maximum range to be exploited fully. If this is correct, the capability of the 'Udaloys' is considerably enhanced over that of other Soviet ASW ships, it being thought previously that only suitably equipped surface ships could guide the 'Silex'. The self-defence SAM carried is the vertical-launch SA-N-9 system.

Specification
'Udaloy' class
Displacement: 6,700 tons standard and 8,200 tons full load
Dimensions: length 162.0 m (531 ft 6 in); beam 19.3 m (63 ft 4 in); draught 6.2 m (20 ft 4 in)
Machinery: four gas turbines in a COGOG arrangement delivering 120,000 shp (89485 kW) to two shafts
Speed: 34 kts
Aircraft: two Kamov Ka-27 'Helix-A' ASW helicopters
Armament: two quadruple SS-N-14 'Silex' ASW missile launchers (no reloads), eight SA-N-9 SAM launchers (64 missiles), two single 100-mm (3.9-in) DP guns, four 30-mm ADG6-30

CIWS mountings, two 250-mm (9.84-in) RBU6000 ASW rocket launchers, two quadruple 533-mm (21-in) ASW torpedo tubes, and 30-50 mines (depending on type)
Electronics: two 'Strut Pair' air- and surface-search radars (first pair only, remainder mounting 'Top Plate/Top Mesh' 3D radar), three 'Palm Frond' navigation and helicopter-control radars, two 'Cross Swords' SA-N-9 missile fire-control radars, two 'Eye Bowl' SS-N-14 fire-control radars, one 'Kite Screech' 100-mm (3.9-in) fire-control radar, two 'Bass Tilt' CIWS fire-control radars, one 'Round House' TACAN, one 'Salt Pot A', one 'Salt Pot B' IFF system, one 'Fly Screen-B' aircraft landing aid, two 'Bell Shroud' and two 'Bell Squat' ECM systems, two twin-barrel chaff and IR decoy launchers, one low-frequency bow sonar, and one low-frequency variable-depth sonar
Complement: 300

Right: Fitted with eight launchers for a new vertical launch point defence SAM system plus the usual variety of Soviet ASW weapon systems, the 'Udaloy' class of ASW destroyer is well capable of taking care of itself in unfriendly waters whilst prosecuting a submarine contact.

Below: 'The Udaloy' class, according to the latest American intelligence reports, is being constructed at a very fast rate with up to nine units operational and another three either being built or fitted out at two different shipyards. This building of specialist surface ship classes follows the doctrine laid down by Admiral Gorshkov in the 1960s.

'Sovremenny' class

Known originally as **BalCom 2** (Baltic Combatant no. 2) by NATO, the **'Sovremenny' class** took over the construction slipway at the Zhdanov Shipyard, Leningrad, that had been used by the 'Kresta II' ASW cruiser class. Seven units, the *Sovremenny, Otchyanny, Otlichnny, Osmotritelny, Bezuprechny*, and two of unknown name were in service by 1987, with one new unit being commissioned per year. Designated by the Soviets as *eskadrenny minonosets* (destroyer), the class is devoted to surface strike warfare with a self-defence SAM system and a limited ASW capability. The propulsion plant is of the pressurized geared steam turbine type, and the design, derived from the 'Kresta' class cruiser, is the first Soviet warship type to be fitted with a telescoping helicopter hangar amidships next to the helicopter landing platform. The main armament comprises two quadruple SSM launchers for the new SS-N-22 (an improved and higher-speed version of the SS-N-9 'Siren') fitted with either a 500-kg (1,102-lb) HE or 200-kiloton nuclear warhead. Two twin 130-mm (5.12-in) fully automatic water-cooled gun mounts are also fitted fore and aft: controlled by a 'Kite Screech' H-band fire-control radar, these can engage surface targets out to 30,000-m (30,620-yard) range. The SAM system fitted is the SA-N-7, which uses two single-rail

launchers and six 'Front Dome' radar directors. The Mach 3 SA-N-7 is a navalized version of the Soviet army's solid-fuel SA-11 missile and will eventually replace the SA-N-1 'Goa' as the navy's medium-range SAM system. Target engagement altitudes are between 30 m (100 ft) and 14000 m (45,930 ft), with a minimum range of 3 km (1.86 miles) and a maximum range of 28 km (17.4 miles). According to some sources, the missile is a close copy of the US Navy's SM-1MR Standard SAM.

Specification
'Sovremenny' class
Displacement: 6,300 tons standard and 7,900 tons full load
Dimensions: length 155.6 m (510 ft 6 in); beam 17.3 m (56 ft 9 in); draught 6.5 m (21 ft 4 in)
Machinery: geared steam turbines delivering 100,000 shp (74570 kW) to two shafts
Speed: 34 kts
Aircraft: one Kamov Ka-25 'Hormone-B' missile-guidance/Elint helicopter
Armament: two quadruple SS-N-22 SSM launchers (no reloads), two single SA-N-7 SAM launchers (40 missiles), two twin 130-mm (5.12-in) DP guns, four 30-mm ADG6-30 CIWS mountings, two RBU1000 300-mm (11.8-in) ASW rocket launchers, two twin 533-mm (21-in) ASW torpedo tubes, and 30-50

The 'Sovremenny' class introduced a new fully-automatic water-cooled 130-mm (5.12-in) dual-purpose gun

mines (according to type)
Electronics: one 'Top Steer' 3D radar (Osmotritelny has one 'Top Steer/Top Plate' 3D radar), three 'Palm Frond' navigation and helicopter-control

into service, as well as a telescopic helicopter hangar forward of the landing pad.

radars, one 'Band Stand' SS-N-22 fire-control radar, two 'Bass Tilt' CIWS fire-control radars, one 'Kite Screech' 130-

Continued overleaf

The Modern Soviet Destroyer

Above: The latest class to be designated 'EM' (Eskadrenny Minonosets, or destroyer) is the 'Sovremenny' class. Although not carrying anti-ship torpedoes, its major weapon system is the supersonic sea-skimming SS-N-22 anti-ship cruise missile, which is backed up by two twin fully-automatic 130-mm (5.12-in) gun turrets capable of very high rates of fire.

mm (5.12-in) fire-control radar, six 'Front Dome' SA-N-7 fire-control radars, two 'Bell Shroud' and two 'Bell Squat' ECM systems, one 'Squeeze Box' optronic fire-control system, two twin-barrel chaff/IR decoy launchers, and one medium-frequency hull sonar
Complement: 380

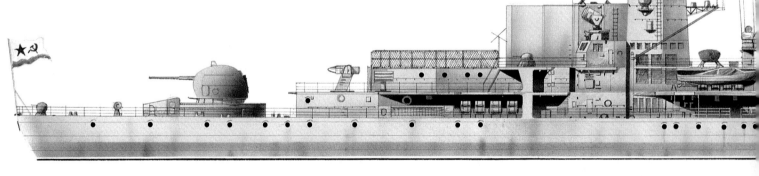

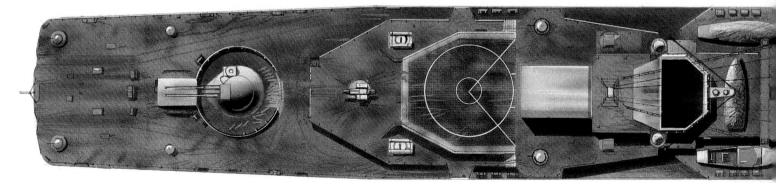

'Sovremenny' class destroyer

Above and below: Perhaps the most impressive of the new generation of
Soviet surface warships of destroyer size is the 'Sovremenny' class, built for
the surface strike role. Latest American intelligence reports indicate that at
least six are operational, with another three on the slipways being built or
fitted out. More are expected, with the production run at the Zhdanov
shipyard, Leningrad, likely to continue into the next decade to give a final total
of between 15 and 20 units for NATO to worry about.

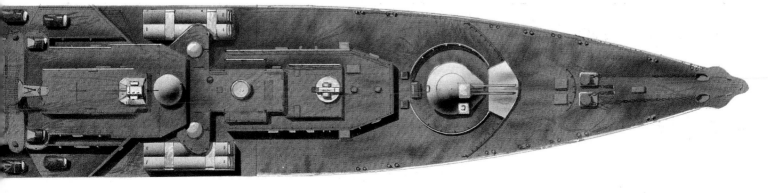

'Iroquois' class

Ordered in 1968 as anti-submarine destroyers, the four **'DDH 280' class** destroyers HMCS *Iroquois* (280), HMCS *Huron* (281), HMCS *Athabaskan* (282) and HMCS *Algonquin* (283) are a revised version of the eight Tartar SAM-equipped 'Tribal' class of general-purpose frigates cancelled in 1963. They have the same hull design, dimensions and basic characteristics as the 'Tribals' but have enhanced ASW features such as three sonars, a helicopter flight deck and twin hangar for two licence-built Sikorsky CH-124 Sea King ASW helicopters. The weapons and sensor fit is a mixed bag with an Italian 127-mm (5-in) OTO-Melara Compact gun, two four-rail launchers for the American Sea Sparrow SAM system that retract into a deckhouse in the forward part of the superstructure, Dutch and American electronics, and a British ASW mortar. The last is the ubiquitous triple-barrelled Mk 10 Limbo that fires 175-kg (385-lb) hydrostatic or proximity fused HE projectiles to a maximum range of 900 m (985 yards) and down to depth of 375 m (1,230 ft). The Sea Sparrow system uses a ship-launched version of the AIM-7E Sparrow air-to-air missile, and is reputed to be able to engage targets flying between 15 and 15240 m (50 and 50,000 ft) at ranges from 14.9 km (9.25 miles) to 22.2 km (13.86 miles) depending upon target height. For a new class of helicopter-carrying destroyers due shortly, the *Huron* tested a vertical-launch Sparrow system in 1982. For the embarked helicopters the ships carry both the active acoustic-homing 30 kt Mk 44 5.5 km (3.44-mile) range torpedo with a 34-kg (75-lb) HE warhead for use in shallow waters, and the active/passive acoustic-homing 45-kt 11-km (6.84-mile range) Mk 46 torpedo with a 43.5-kg (96-lb) HE warhead for deep-water work.

From 1986 through 1991, the four destroyers will undergo consecutive modernization under the Tribal Update and Modernization Plan (TRUMP). This involves replacing the 127-mm (5-in) gun with a 32 round Mk 41 vertical launch system for Standard SM-2MR SAMs, fitting a 76-mm DP gun in what is now the Sea Sparrow magazine area, and fitting a 20-mm Phalanx CIWS system with its associated VPS-2 fire-control radar. A DA.06 air/surface-search radar and a HSA STIR missile and gun fire-control system will be added, and the Mk 10 Limbo ASW

mortar and the Sea Sparrow SAM system are to be deleted. The WLR-1 ECM system and Corvus chaff launchers are to be replaced by the CANEWS system and two six-barrel Plessey Shield decoy launchers. The SHINPADS command and control is also expected to be fitted.

Specification
'Iroquois' class
Displacement: 3,551 tons standard and 4,700 tons full load
Dimensions: length 129.8 m (426 ft); beam 15.2 m (50 ft); draught 4.4 m (14 ft 6 in)
Machinery: two Pratt & Whitney FT4A gas turbines delivering 50,000 shp (37285 kW) and two Pratt & Whitney FT12AH3 cruising gas turbines

delivering 7,400 shp (5520 kW), both to two shafts
Speed: 29 kts
Aircraft: two Sikorsky CH-124 Sea King ASW helicopters
Armament: two quadruple Sea Sparrow SAM launchers (32 missiles), one single 127-mm (5-in) DP gun, one triple-barrel Mk 10 ASW mortar, and two triple Mk 32 324-mm (12.75-in) ASW torpedo tubes (12 Mk 46 torpedoes)
Electronics: one SPS-501 air-search radar, one SPQ2D surface-search and navigation radar, two WM-22 weapon-

The 'Iroquois' class destroyer HMCS Huron (281) launches a Sea Sparrow SAM missile from her starboard side missile rack just forward of the bridge. The design allows for the carriage and operation of two licence-built CH-124 Sea Kings.

control radar systems, one URN-25 TACAN, one WLR-1 ECM system, two Corvus chaff launchers, one SQS-505 bow sonar, one SQS-505 variable-depth sonar, and one SQS-501 target-classification hull sonar
Complement: 285

The Iroquois (280) was commissioned in July 1972 and with her three sister ships is destined to serve on into the late 1990s as the major ASW platforms of the Canadian Navy. A new class will supplement them from the late 1980s onwards to replace the older frigates now approaching the end of their operational lives.

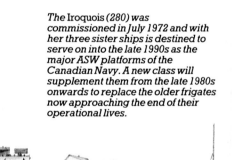

'Meko 360H2' class

Originally to have been a class of six, with four to have been built in Argentina, the **'Meko 360H2' class** design is based on the modularized systems concept whereby each of the weapons and sensor systems carried form a separate modular unit and can be interchanged with a replacement or newer system without the usual reconstruction that otherwise accompanies the modernization of a ship. The final

agreement signed with the West German firms of Thyssen Rheinstahl and Blohm und Voss in December 1978 was for four ships to be built in West Germany. All four, the **Almirante Brown** (D10), **La Argentina** (D11), **Heroina** (D5) and **Sarandi** (D13), commissioned in 1983-4. During the Falklands war the ships were under construction, and the British Rolls-Royce Olympus and Tyne gas turbines which

propel them were embargoed for a short time. Although usually classed as frigates, the Argentine Navy consider their Meko 360s as destroyers. The Nigerian frigate **Aradu**, a near sister, was ordered in November 1977 and was the first warship in the world to use extensive modular prefabrication and containerized weapons in building. She differs from the Argentine vessels in having Otomat Mk 2 SSMs, a single

helicopter and a combined diesel or gas turbine (CODOG) propulsion system. The Meko modular building technique has since been extended to smaller frigate designs.

Specification
'Meko 360H2' class
Displacement: 3,360 tons full load
Dimensions: length 125.9 m (413 ft

1 in); beam 14.0 m (46 ft); draught 5.8 m (19 ft)
Machinery: four Rolls-Royce gas turbines (two Olympus TM3B and two Tyne RM1C) in COGOG arrangement delivering 51,800 shp (38625 kW) to two shafts
Speed: 30.5 kts
Aircraft: two AB.212 with ten A244/S torpedoes
Armament: four twin MM.40 Exocet launcher (no reloads), one octuple Albatross SAM launcher (24 missiles),

Initially to have been a class of six, Argentina's order was subsequently changed to four 'Meko 360H2' destroyers to be built by Blohm und Voss at Hamburg and six 'Meko 140A16' class corvettes to be built by AFNE at Rio Santiago in Argentina.

one single 127-mm (5-in) DP gun, two twin 40-mm AA guns, and two triple 324-mm (12.75-in) ILAS-3 ASW torpedo tubes (18 Whitehead A244/S torpedoes)
Electronics: one DA-08A air- and surface-search radar, one ZW-06 navigation radar, one Decca 1226 navigation radar, one WM-25 fire-control system with STIR facilities, two HSA LIROD 40-mm optronic/radar fire-control systems, one AEG-Telefunken ECM suite, two 20-barrel SCLAR chaff and IR decoy launchers, and one Atlas 80 hull sonar
Complement: 198

Right: The first two of the 'Meko 360' destroyers, Almirante Brown (D10) and La Argentina (D11) undergo sea trials off West Germany. The commissioning of these vessels and their sister ships into the Argentine navy represents a significant increase in its capabilities that will tax the Royal Navy heavily in any future conflict that may break out over the Falkland Islands.

'County' class

The title 'destroyer' was applied to the 'County' class ships in order to obtain Treasury approval for their construction, but they are little short of guided-missile cruisers. Built around the British first-generation Seaslug beam-riding area-defence SAM system, the 'County' class was ordered in two batches. Three out of four Batch 1 ships have been deleted, (*Devonshire* sunk as a target, *Hampshire* scrapped, *Kent* hulked as an accommodation ship), whilst the *London* was sold to the Pakistan navy as the light cruiser *Babur* (C84) without the Seaslug system. The 'County Batch 2' ships *Fife, Glamorgan, Antrim* and *Norfolk* were modernized with Exocet missiles in place of one of their two 114-mm (4.5-in) gun mounts and carried the Seaslug Mk 2 SAM with limited SSM capability. All four ships were scheduled to remain in service until the late 1980s because of their extensive command and control facilities, which made them good flagships. HMS *Glamorgan* (D19) and HMS *Antrim* (D18) served with distinction in the Falklands war, the former surviving a direct hit from an MM.38 Exocet and the latter a hit from a bomb which failed to explode. As a result of the 1981 British defence cuts, however, the *Norfolk* had been sold to the Chilean navy as the missile destroyer *Prat* (11) whilst the *Fife* (D20) underwent a major refit which kept her out of the war. In February 1984 it was announced that the *Antrim* was to be decommissioned and sold to Chile as the *Almirante Cochrane* (12). The Chileans retain the vessels' Seaslug capabilities. *Glamorgan* was sold to

Chile in November 1986, where she was renamed *Latorre*. *Fife* will probably follow in 1987 after serving as the training ship for the Royal Naval College at Dartmouth. She has had her Seaslug launcher replaced by an accommodation deckhouse for her final Royal Navy commission.

Specification
'County Batch 2' class
Displacement: 6,200 tons standard and 6,800 tons full load
Dimensions: length 158.7 m (520 ft 6 in); beam 16.5 m (54 ft); draught 6.3 m (20 ft 6 in)
Machinery: COSAG arrangement with two geared steam turbines delivering 30,000 shp (22370 kW) and four G.6 gas turbines delivering 30,000 shp (22370 kW) to two shafts
Speed: 32.5 kts
Aircraft: one Westland Lynx HAS.Mk 2 or 3 ASW and surface strike helicopter
Armament: four single GWS Mk 50 MM.38 Exocet SSM launchers (no reloads), one twin Seaslug Mk 2 SAM launcher with 30 missiles (not in *Fife*), one twin 114-mm (4.5-in) DP gun, two quadruple GWS Mk 22 Sea Cat SAM launchers (32 missiles), two single 20-mm AA guns, and two triple 324-mm (12.75-in) STWS1 ASW torpedo tubes (12 Mk 46 torpedoes, only in *Fife* and *Glamorgan*)
Electronics: one Type 965M air-search radar, one Type 992Q air-search and target-designation radar, one Type 901 Seaslug fire-control radar, one

Type 278M height-finder radar, two Type 904 Sea Cat fire-control radars, one MRS3 114-mm (4.5-in) fire-control system, one Type 1006 navigation and helicopter-control radar, one ADAWS 1 action information system, one ESM suite, two Corvus chaff launchers, one Type 184 hull sonar, one Type 170B attack sonar, one Type 182 torpedo decoy system, and one Type 185 underwater telephone
Complement: 472

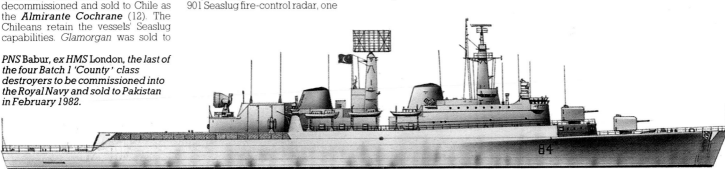

Above: HMS Glamorgan (D19) following a refit to repair the damage suffered during the Falklands war. Second of the four Batch 2 'County' class destroyers, she now carries a Westland Lynx HAS.Mk 2 helicopter in place of the original Westland Wessex HAS.Mk 3.

PNS Babur, ex HMS London, the last of the four Batch 1 'County' class destroyers to be commissioned into the Royal Navy and sold to Pakistan in February 1982.

'Type 82' and 'Type 42' classes

Used during the Falklands war, the solitary **'Type 82' class** destroyer HMS *Bristol* (D23) was originally to have been the lead ship of a class of four vessels designed for the ASW and area-defence SAM escorts to the 'CVA-01' class aircraft-carriers. With the demise of the carrier project in 1966 the class was cut back to one unit for specific deployment as a trials vessel for the new generation of weapons systems entering British service. The ship has a unique three-funnel configuration for her combined steam and gas turbine propulsion system, and superficially resembles a cleaned-up 'County' class destroyer. The main weapons systems are a twin GWS Mk 30 zero-length Sea Dart SAM launcher and an Ikara ASW missile launcher. The 549-kg (1,210-lb) semi-active radar homing ramjet-powered Sea Dart is an area-defence weapon with a maximum range of 65 km (40 miles) and engagement altitude limits of 30 m (100 ft) and 18290 m (60,000 ft). Although considered by many to be a white elephant, the *Bristol* is in fact a very valuable member of the Royal Navy's surface forces, having the necessary command and control facilities required to act as a flagship and the communications and data links necessary to act as a 'gateway' ship for other RN vessels to communicate through her with NATO ships possessing incompatible communications systems.

With the cancellation of the carriers, a Naval Staff Requirement was issued for a small fleet escort capable of providing area defence. This resulted in the **'Type 42' class** design, which suffered considerably during gestation from constraints that were placed on the dimensions by the Controller of the Navy as a result of Treasury pressure to minimize costs. As built, the ships lacked any significant close-range air-defence systems, had reduced endurance on full power output from their gas turbines (necessitating regular replenishments at sea on operations), and a short forecastle which resulted in a very wet forward section. The main armament comprised the Sea Dart system, but with only half the missile outfit of the *Bristol* and 1950s-technology main radars, which did not exactly enhance their air-defence capabilities. The class was subsequently built in three batches: the **'Type 42 Batch 1'** comprised HMS *Sheffield*, HMS *Birmingham* (D86), HMS *Cardiff* (D108), HMS *Coventry*, HMS *Newcastle* (D87) and HMS *Glasgow* (D88); the **'Type 42 Batch 2'** consisted of HMS *Exeter* (D89), HMS *Southampton* (D90), HMS *Nottingham* (D91) and HMS *Liverpool* (D92);

and the **'Type 42 Batch 3'** was made up of HMS *Manchester* (D95), HMS *Gloucester* (D96), HMS *York* (D98) and HMS *Edinburgh* (D97). The Batch 3 vessels were lengthened and broadened in an effort to remedy some of the problems encountered in the first two batches.

During the Falklands war four Batch 1 ships (*Sheffield*, *Cardiff*, *Coventry* and *Glasgow*) saw action, together with the *Exeter* from Batch 2. Of these the *Sheffield* was hit by an AM.39 Exocet on 4 May 1982 and later sank, the *Glasgow* narrowly missed being blown apart on 12 May by a bomb which passed through her hull amidships from one side to the other without exploding, whilst the *Coventry* sustained three bomb hits on 25 May and sank within forty-five minutes. The lack of any close-range air-defence systems was a significant factor in each case. On the credit side the ships' Sea Dart missiles are officially credited with eight aircraft shot down, secured by some 31 Sea Darts launched from the *Bristol* and the 'Type 42s'. The *Coventry* shot down two McDonnell Douglas A-4 Skyhawks and an Aérospatiale SA 330 Puma helicopter in the days before she was sunk, whilst the *Exeter* was the most successful with two Skyhawks, an English Electric Canberra and a Learjet 35A. Tragically, HMS *Cardiff* shot down a Royal Marines AH.1 Gazelle by mistake. The Argentines knew all about the 'Type 42' and its Sea Dart missile system because their navy had bought two ves-

sels of this class from the UK, namely the *Hercules* (D1) and the *Santissima Trinidad* (D2).

Following the war considerable modifications were made to the British 'Type 42s', with respect particularly to the armament. The Argentinian Navy is periodically reported as wanting to sell their two destroyers due to chronic spares problems.

Specification

'Type 82' class
Displacement: 6,100 tons standard and 7,100 tons full load
Dimensions: length 154.5 m (507 ft); beam 16.8 m (55 ft); draught 7.0 m (23 ft)
Machinery: COSAG arrangement with

HMS Bristol *was to have been one of a class of four cruiser-size carrier escorts, but the cancellation of the carrier project in 1966 meant that the other 'Type 82s' were not built.*

The first of the stretched 'Type 42s', HMS Manchester *(D95). These vessels are designed to remedy the shortcomings of the original class by restoring the length cut-off and increasing the beam slightly. However, as originally conceived they would have suffered from the same lack of armament as HMS* Sheffield.

HMS Nottingham *(D91), built with the Type 1022 radar in place of the outdated Type 965 that proved to be of limited value in the Falklands war. The main weakness of the original 'Type 42s' lies in the constraints placed on their dimensions by Treasury pressure during the design phase.*

two geared steam turbines delivering 30,000 shp (22370 kW) and two Rolls-Royce Olympus TM1A gas turbines delivering 30,000 shp (22370 kW) to two shafts
Speed: 28 kts
Aircraft: helicopter landing pad only
Armament: one twin GWS Mk 30 Sea Dart SAM launcher (40 missiles), one single 114-mm (4.5-in) DP gun, two twin 30-mm and four single 20-mm guns
Electronics: one Type 965M air-search radar, one Type 992Q air-search and target-designation radar, two Type 909 Sea Dart fire-control radars, one Type 1006 navigation and helicopter-control radar, one ADAWS 2 action information system, one Abbey Hill ESM suite, two Mk 36 Super RBOC and two Corvus chaff launchers, two SCOTT satellite communications systems, one OE 82 satellite communications system, one Type 184M medium-frequency hull sonar, one Type 162M classification sonar, one Type 182 torpedo decoy system, and one Type 185 underwater telephone
Complement: 397

Specification
'Type 42 Batch 1' and 'Type 42 Batch 2' classes
Displacement: 3,150 tons standard and 4,100 tons full load
Dimensions: length 125.6 m (412 ft); beam 14.3 m (47 ft); draught 5.8 m (19 ft)
Machinery: COGOG arrangement with two Rolls-Royce Olympus TM3B gas turbines delivering 56,000 shp (41760 kW) and two Rolls-Royce Tyne RM1A gas turbines delivering 8,500 shp (6340 kW) to two shafts
Speed: 30 kts
Aircraft: one Westland Lynx (HAS. Mk

2/3 ASW and surface strike helicopter
Armament: one twin GWS Mk 30 Sea Dart SAM launcher (20 missiles), one single 114-mm (4.5-in) DP gun, two twin 30-mm AA guns, four single 20-mm AA guns, four to six single 7.62-mm GPMG and two triple 324-mm (12.75-in) STWS 1 ASW torpedo tubes (12 Mk 46 or Sting Ray torpedoes)
Electronics: one Type 1022 air-search radar, one Type 996 air-search and target-designation radar, two Type 909 Sea Dart fire-control radars, one Type 1006 navigation and helicopter-control radar, one ADAWS 7 action information system, one UAA1 Abbey Hill ESM suite, two Corvus and two Mk 36 Super RBOC chaff launchers, two SCOTT satellite communications systems, one Type 184M medium-frequency hull sonar (Type 2016 in *Glasgow*), one Type 162M classification sonar, one Type 182 torpedo decoy system, and one Type 185 underwater telephone
Complement: 253-312

Specification
'Type 42 Batch 3' class
Displacement: 4,100 tons standard and 4,775 tons full load
Dimensions: length 141.1 m (462 ft 9 in); beam 14.9 m (49 ft); draught 5.8 m (19 ft)
Machinery: as 'Type 42 Batches 1 and 2'
Speed: 31.5 kts
Aircraft: as 'Type 42 Batches 1 and 2'
Armament: as 'Type 42 Batches 1 and 2' except 40 missiles for Sea Dart system, and the possibility of fitting Lightweight Sea Wolf SAM system in place of one Type 909 radar is being explored
Electronics: as 'Type 42 Batches 1 and 2' except one Type 1022 air-search radar, one ADAWS 8 action

information system, and one Type 2016 multi-frequency hull sonar
Complement: 301-312

Above: HMS Southampton *(D90) in June 1983. Since the Falklands war most 'Type 42s' have had additional close-range air defence guns fitted.*

Below: HMS Exeter *seen in 1983. All the 'Type 42s' had their AA weaponry increased considerably as a result of the Falkland conflict.*

Modern Western Frigates

Second of the 46-strong 'Knox' class, USS Roark (FF1053) typifies US frigate design. Although as large and capable as many destroyers, the class's single-shaft propulsion and lower speeds lead to it being classified as a frigate.

Over the centuries, the frigate has performed a wide variety of tasks, ranging from the classic 'eyes of the fleet' of Nelson's day to the suppression of the U-boat menace in the Battle of the Atlantic of World War II. Today, the name covers a wide variety of vessels.

The frigate has become the 'workhorse' of current Western navies. The term is applied to vessels ranging from the very expensive and highly specialized ASW ships of the Royal Navy's Type 22 design to what are essentially the cheap and reduced-capability 'Knox' and 'Oliver Hazard Perry' classes of the US Navy, which are used instead of specialized ASW and AAW destroyers and cruisers to escort convoys and groups of amphibious warships.

To counter the modern nuclear-powered submarine the frigate should have gas turbine propulsion and two shafts fitted with controllable-pitch propellers, both features of most western European designs. However, the Americans accept a lower maximum speed and only one shaft, which has lead to some criticism. Some European nations such as West Germany and the Netherlands have also got together to produce a standard frigate design for their navies, which in these countries has manifested itself as the 'Bremen' and 'Kortenaer' classes respectively. Further to help standardization, Greece has bought two of the Dutch ships and may build another three under licence. Of the two American designs ('Knox' and 'Oliver Hazard Perry') only Spain among the NATO countries has bought any, licence-building five and three respectively. However, in terms of exporting their designs it is the Italians who have now taken the lead with their 'Lupo' class, which has been sold to three

nations outside NATO in South America and the Middle East. The Italians themselves have taken four 'Lupos' and eight of the ASW 'Maestrale' class variant. France rates her frigates as *avisos* (sloops) and generally uses them on overseas patrols as a modern gunboat 'showing the flag'. The Japanese frigate is predominantly an ASW vessel for use in Japanese waters. In the Royal Navy the frigate was until the beginning of the 1970s primarily a general-purpose warship, as the 'Leander' class proved, but since then it has been either converted into or built as a specialist vessel to tackle either sub-surface, surface or anti-air warfare tasks. The latest British frigate design is the Type 23 'Daring' class, the first of which is still to be ordered after several years of planning.

For the long term a NATO standard frigate hull is under discussion, but like most alliance projects it is expected the outcome will probably be that consortium members will break up into groups and individuals, each going their own way.

HNLMS De Ruyter, a 'Tromp' class frigate of the Royal Netherlands navy, is accompanied by the 'Kortenaer' class frigate HNLMS Van Kinsbergen in the North Sea. The two 'Tromp' class vessels serve as flagships and carry a comprehensive weapon fit.

'Chikugo' class

Designed and built with structural features to reduce noise and vibration, the 'Chikugo' class ships are used primarily for coastal ASW missions around the Japanese home islands. To facilitate their use in this role they are gradually being equipped to carry and operate the SQS35(J) variable-depth sonar from an open well offset to starboard at the stern. They are also the smallest warships in the world to carry the octuple ASROC ASW missile-launcher system, though no reloads are carried; the amidships launcher is trained to the bearing and then elevated to fire a two-round salvo of the solid-fuel RUR-5A rockets with their Mk 46 parachute-retarded homing torpedo payloads out to a maximum range of 9.2 km (5.7 miles). The Japanese vessels do not carry the alternative payload of a 1-kiloton Mk 17 nuclear depth charge carried by American ships. The propulsion plant comprises either four Mitsubishi-Burmeister & Wain UEV30/40 (in DE 215, 217-219, 221, 223 and 225) or four Mitsui 28VBC-38 diesels (in the remainder). A Mk 51 fire-control

director with no radar controls the twin 40-mm mount aft. The hull-mounted OQS3 sonar is a licence-built version of the American SQS-23 set, a variant of which is used on the 'Spruance' class ASW destroyers. The 11 vessels in service are the *Chikugo* (DE215), *Ayase* (DE216), *Mikumo* (DE217), *Tokachi* (DE218), *Iwase* (DE219), *Chitose* (DE220), *Niyoda* (DE221), *Teshio* (DE222), *Yoshino* (DE223), *Kumano* (DE224) and *Noshiro* (DE225).

Specification
'Chikugo' class
Displacement: (DE215 and DE220) 1,480 tons standard, (DE216-DE219 and DE221) 1,470 tons standard or (DE222-DE225) 1,500 tons standard and 1,700-1,800 tons full load
Dimensions: length 93.1 m (305.5 ft); beam 10.8 m (35.5 ft); draught 3.5 m (11.5 ft)
Propulsion: four diesels delivering 16,000 hp (11931 kW) to two shafts
Speed: 25 kts
Armament: one twin 76-mm (3-in) Mk 33 DP gun, one twin 40-mm AA gun,

one octuple ASROC ASW missile launcher with eight missiles, and two triple 324-mm (12.75-in) Mk 68 ASW torpedo tubes with Mk 46 torpedoes
Aircraft: none
Electronics: one OPS-14 air-search radar, one OPS-16 surface-search radar, one GCFS-1B fire-control radar, one OPS-19 navigation radar, one NORL-5 ESM system, one OQS-3 hull sonar, and one SQS-35(J) variable-

Tokachi (DE218) pays a courtesy visit to Hawaii. As in all except the most recent Japanese designs, the 'Chikugo' class has significant ASW capability but little in the way of surface-to-surface or AAW equipment.

depth sonar (fitted in five units, to be fitted in rest)
Complement: 165

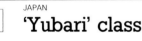

'Yubari' class

The **'Yubari' class** is basically an improved and enlarged variant of the 'Ishakiri' design authorized in 1977-8. The greater length and beam improved the seaworthiness and reduced the internal space constrictions of the earlier design. The original number of units to be built was three, but this was reduced by one when the Japanese government deleted funds from the naval budget in the early 1980s. A new 1,900-ton six-vessel class is to be constructed in the 1983-7 five-year plan.

Although not heavily armed and having no helicopter facilities in comparison with contemporary European designs, the 'Yubaris' are ideal for use in the waters around Japan, where they would operate under shore-based air cover. Most of the weapons, machinery and sensors have been built under licence from foreign manufacturers. The propulsion plant is a CODOG arrangement with a licence-built Kawasaki/Rolls-Royce Olympus TM3B gas turbine and a Mitsubishi 6DRV 35/44 diesel. Extensive automation of the machinery has reduced the crew total to below 100, which is extremely good for a warship of this size. The vessels which comprise the class are the *Yubari* (DE227) and *Yubetsu* (DE228).

Armament: two quadruple Harpoon surface-to-surface missile launchers with eight missiles, one 76-mm (3-in) DP gun, one 20-mm Phalanx CIWS (being fitted), one quadruple 375-mm (14.76-in) Bofors ASW rocket launcher with 48 rockets, and two triple 324-mm (12.75-in) Mk 68 ASW torpedo tubes with Mk 46 torpedoes

Aircraft: none
Electronics: one OPS-28 surface-search radar, one OPS-19 navigation radar, one GFCS-2 fire-control radar, one NOLQ-6 ESM system, one OLT-3 ECM jammer, two Mk 36 Super RBOC chaff launchers, and one OQS-4 hull sonar
Complement: 98

Smaller than the preceding 'Chikugo' class, the 'Yubari' class is highly automated, with a crew of under 100. Designed to operate under land-based air cover, the design has little AAW capability, although the Phalanx 20-mm close-in weapon system is being fitted.

Specification
'Yubari' class
Displacement: 1,470 tons standard and 1,690 tons full load
Dimensions: length 91.0 m (298.5 ft); beam 10.8 m (35.4 ft); draught 3.6 m (11.8 ft)
Propulsion: CODOG arrangement with one Rolls-Royce/Kawasaki Olympus TM3B gas turbine delivering 28,390 hp (21170 kW) and one Mitsubishi 6DRV diesel delivering 4,650 hp (3468 kW) to two shafts
Speed: 25 kts

Developed from the interim 'Ishakiri' design, Yubari and Yubetsu have been enlarged in both length and beam, the better to handle the armament mounted. Two quadruple Harpoon launchers give the class considerable anti-ship capability.

'Oslo' class

Based on the US 'Dealey' class destroyer escorts, the **'Oslo' class** frigates have a higher freeboard forward (to suit the sea conditions off Norway) and many European-built subsystems. They were built under the 1960 five-year naval plan, with half the cost borne by the USA. The class underwent modernization refits in the late 1970s, these including the fitting of Penguin Mk 2 SSMs, a NATO Sea Sparrow SAM launcher and Mk 32 ASW self-defence torpedo tubes. A replacement class is being designed for construction in the 1990s.

Currently the largest surface combatants in the Norwegian navy, the 'Oslos' provide the only major ASW force in the region. For this role they carry a forward-mounted sextuple rocket-launcher with a rapid reload capability for the 370 to 825-m (405 to 900-yard) range Terne III ASW rocket. This is a 120-kg (265-lb) weapon fitted with a combination depth and proximity Doppler fuse for its 6.1-m (20-ft) lethal radius 48-kg (105.8-lb) HE warhead; the target depth can be between 15 and 215 m (50 and 705 ft). Once fired the launcher is automatically trained to the vertical and reloaded within 40 seconds. The ships' SQS-36 sonar acts as the search unit whilst the Terne Mk 3 attack sonar is used for target range and depth determinations. For self defence the ships have the American 45-kt 11-km (6.8-mile) range Mk 46 acoustic-homing torpedo fired from the Mk 32 torpedo tubes. The five ships in service are the **Oslo** (F300), **Bergen** (F301), **Trondheim** (F302), **Stavanger** (F303) and **Narvik** (F304). Beginning in 1987 all five are to be modernized with the SQ5-36 sonar being replaced by a

The 'Oslo' class frigate Bergen (F301) *is seen firing a Penguin surface-to-surface missile.*

Thomson-CSF TSM2633 Spherion set, the after 76-mm (3-in) gun mount by a 40-mm AA mount, the addition of a variable depth sonar, and several decoy rocket launchers, and the upgrading of the electronics and accommodation areas.

Specification
'Oslo' class
Displacement: 1,450 tons standard and 1,850 tons full load
Dimensions: length 96.6 m (316.9 ft); beam 11.2 m (36.7 ft); draught 4.4 m (14.4 ft)

Propulsion: geared steam turbines delivering 20,000 hp (14914 kW) to one shaft
Speed: 25 kts

'Oslo' class frigates are a modification of the 'Dealey' class of destroyer escort (DE) built in the USA in the 1950s.

Armament: six single Penguin Mk 2 surface-to-surface missile launchers with six missiles, one octuple NATO Sea Sparrow surface-to-air missile launcher with 24 missiles, two twin 76-mm (3-in) Mk 33 DP guns, two single 20-mm AA guns, one sextuple Terne ASW rocket launcher, two triple 324-mm (12.75-in) Mk 32 ASW torpedo tubes with Mk 46 torpedoes, and one depth charge rack
Aircraft: none
Electronics: one DRBV 22 air- and surface-search radar, one WM-22 fire-control radar, one Decca 1226 navigation radar, one Mk 91 fire-control radar, one Terne Mk 3 attack sonar, and one SQS-36 hull sonar
Complement: 150

'Bremen' (Type 122) class

A Germanized modification of the gas turbine-powered Dutch 'Kortenaer' design, the eight-ship **'Bremen' class** has replaced the deleted 'Fletcher' (Type 119) class destroyers and the elderly 'Köln' (Type 120) class frigates. The hulls are mated with the propulsion plant in the building yards, and are then towed to Bremer Vulkan, where the weapon systems and electronics are fitted. The first order was placed in 1977, and the ship eventually commissioned in May 1982 after government approval has been given for the construction in 1976. The ships are fitted with fin stabilizers and the American Praerie/Masker bubble system on the hull and propellers to reduce radiated noise levels from the machinery spaces. A complete NBC defence citadel system is also fitted. Two of the new passive radar/infra-red terminal

Bremen (F207) is the first of a class of six frigates for the Bundesmarine. These general-purpose vessels carry their main anti-submarine punch in the two Lynx helicopters with which each ship is equipped.

homing 24-round RAM point-defence SAM launchers are to be installed atop the hangar in the near future. The ASW helicopters carried are Westland Lynx HAS.Mk 88s, which differ from Royal Navy machines in having an active Bendix DASQ-18 dunking sonar for use with the Mk 46 homing torpedoes and Mk 54 depth charges they carry. For flying in rough weather the ships are fitted with the Canadian Bear Trap landing system.

The eight ships are the **Bremen** (F207), **Niedersachsen** (F208), **Rhein-land-Pfalz** (F209), **Emden** (F210), **Köln** (F211), **Karlsruhe** (F212), in service and the **Augsberg** and **Lübeck** on

order for delivery in the late 1980s; plans call for them to remain in the front line into the 21st century.

Specification
'Bremen' class
Displacement: 2,930 tons standard and 3,780 tons full load
Dimensions: length 130.5 m (428.1 ft); beam 14.4 m (47.25 ft); draught 6.0 m (19.7 ft)
Propulsion: CODOG arrangement with two General Electric/FIAT LM2500 gas turbines delivering 51,600 hp (38478 kW) and two MTU 2OV TB92 diesels delivering 10,400 hp (7755 kW) to two shafts

Speed: 32 kts
Armament: two quadruple Harpoon surface-to-surface missile launchers with eight missiles, one octuple NATO Sea Sparrow surface-to-air missile launcher with 24 RIM-7M missiles, two 24-round RAM point-defence surface-to-air missile launchers with 48 missiles (being fitted), one 76-mm (3-in) DP gun, and four single Mk 32 324-mm (12.75-in) ASW torpedo tubes (eight Mk 46 torpedoes)
Aircraft: two Westland Lynx HAS.Mk 88 ASW helicopters with 16 Mk 46 ASW torpedoes
Electronics: one DA-08 air- and surface-search radar, one WM-25 fire-

control radar, one STIR fire-control radar, one 3RM20 navigation radar, one SATIR tactical data system, one FL1800S ESM intercept system, four Mk 36 Super RBOC chaff launchers, and one DSQS-21B(Z) bow sonar
Complement: 204 normal and 225 maximum

Developed from the Dutch 'Kortenaer' class of frigate, the 'Bremen' class has the same hull form and minor differences in armament. The major alteration is in the provision of diesel cruising engines in place of the turbines of the 'Kortenaer' class.

FRANCE
'D'Estienne d'Orves' (A-69) class

Designed for coastal ASW, the **'D'Es-tienne d'Orves' class** can also be used for scouting missions, training and for 'showing the flag' overseas, for which role a total of one officer and 17 men from the naval infantry can be accommodated. Since entering service in the mid-1970s the design has been sold to the Argentine navy, whose three ships the **Drummond** (P1), **Guerrico** (P2) and **Granville** (P3) saw service in the 1982 Falklands war. In this campaign the **Guerrico** suffered the ignominy of being damaged by shore fire from small arms and anti-tank rocket-launchers during the Argentine seizure of South Georgia on 3 April; this required her to be dry-docked for three days for repairs to the hull and armament.

Rated as *avisos* by the French, the first of the class was laid down at Lorient Naval Dockyard in 1972 and commissioned into service in 1976. Under present French navy plans the first three vessels built will be paid off in 1996, the other 14 units being decommissioned at regular intervals until 2004. All 17 vessels were built at Lorient, but at present ship a number of armament fits. Six vessels serve in the Mediterranean, eight in the Atlantic and three with the Channel squadron.

The class consists of the **D'Estienne d'Orves** (F781), **Amyot D'Inville** (F782), **Drogou** (F783), **Détroyat** (F784), **Jean Moulin** (F785), **Quartier**

The 'D'Estienne D'Orves' class are austere, simple vessels, designed with economy of operation very much in mind. Not suitable for deep water ASW, they are used around the coast, with secondary colonial patrol duties.

Maître Anquetil (F786), **Commandant de Pimodan** (F787), **Second Maître de Bihan** (F788), **Lieutenant de Vaisseau Le Henaff** (F789), **Lieutenant de Vais-seau Lavalle** (F790), **Commandant l'Herminier** (F791), **Premier Maître l'Her** (F792), **Commandant Blaison** (F793), **Enseigne de Vaisseau Jacoubet** (F794), **Commandant Ducuing** (F795), **Commandant Birot** (F796) and **Commandant Bouan** (F797).

Specification
'D'Estienne d'Orves' class
Displacement: 1,100 tons standard and 1,250 tons full load
Dimensions: length 80.0 m (262.5 ft); beam 10.3 m (33.8 ft); draught 5.3 m (17.4 ft)
Propulsion: two SEMT-Pielstick 12PC2 diesels delivering 11,000 hp (8203 kW) to two shafts; in F791 two SEMT-Pielstick 12PA6BTC diesels delivering 14,400 hp (10738 kW)
Speed: 24 kts
Armament: (F781, F783, F786 and F787) two single MM.38 Exocet surface-to-surface missile launchers with two missiles (to be replaced by MM.40 Exocet missiles), or (F792-F797) four single MM.40 Exocet

surface-to-surface missile launchers with four missiles, one 100-mm (3.9-in) DP gun, two single 20-mm AA guns, one sextuple 375-mm (14.76-in) Creusot Loire ASW rocket-launcher, and four single ASW torpedo launchers with four L3 or L5 torpedoes
Aircraft: none
Electronics: one DRBV 51A air- and surface-search radar, one DRBC 32E 100mm (3.9-in) gun-control radar, one DRBN 32 navigation radar, and one DUBA 25 hull sonar; all vessels are to be fitted with one ARBR 16 passive ESM system and two Dagaie decoy launchers
Complement: 105 plus 17 naval infantry on overseas deployments

Classed as an aviso, or coastal escort, Commandant Blaison is one of the most recent of the A-69 series to enter service. All the class have Exocet capacity, though the weapons are not always shipped.

Type 12 'Modified Leander' class

A total of 26 general-purpose 'Leander' class frigates were built for the Royal Navy in three sub-groups: eight 'Leander Batch 1', eight 'Leander Batch 2' and 10 broad-beam 'Leander Batch 3' ships. Since the first unit entered service in 1963 the class has undergone numerous refits and modernizations so that today it can actually be divided into six separate sub-classes. The five Batch 3 ships HMS *Andromeda* (F57), HMS *Hermione* (F58), HMS *Jupiter* (F60), HMS *Scylla* (F71) and HMS *Charybdis* (F75) have undergone conversion by the addition of a GWS25 Sea Wolf automatic point-defence missile system plus numerous new sensor systems to give the most capable of the sub-classes. The conversion of the remaining five Batch 3 units to this configuration was shelved because of the usual economic reasons. One of them, the ex-*Bacchante*, has since been sold to New Zealand as HMNZS *Wellington* (F69) to join an existing 'broad-beam' HMNZS *Canterbury* (F421) and the standard version HMNZS *Waikato* (F55). The remaining four units are HMS *Achilles* (F12), HMS *Diomede* (F16), HMS *Apollo* (F70) and HMS *Ariadne* (F72), which still retain their 114-mm (4.5-in) gun and Sea Cat SAM armament. The Batch 2 units were due to form a single Exocet-armed class, but this has now changed to three different types. The first comprises HMS *Cleopatra* (F28), HMS *Sirius* (F40), HMS *Phoebe* (F42) and HMS *Argonaut* (F56), and is known as the **Batch 2A** group. They have been fitted with the type 2031(I) general purpose surveillance and tactical towed-array sonar on the starboard side of the stern. The three **Batch 2B** vessels are HMS *Danae* (F47), HMS *Minerva* (F45) and HMS *Penelope* (F127) which are the remainder of the original Exocet conversion group with the twin Mk 6 114-mm (4.5-in) gun mount replaced by four MM.38 Exocet launchers and a third GWS22 Sea Cat SAM launcher. The last Batch 2 ship, HMS *Juno* (F52), had her Exocet conversion halted and is now converting to serve as the fleet's navigation training ship.

The eight Batch 1 vessels were con-

verted to ASW ships by the fitting of a GWS40 Ikara ASW missile installation in place of the gun mount. To compensate for the loss in AA capability a second GWS22 Sea Cat launcher was added aft atop the hangar. One vessel, the ex-*Dido* has been sold to New Zealand as HMNZS *Southland* (F104), whilst only two remain in RN service, namely HMS *Euryalus* (F15) and HMS *Arethusa* (F38). They are due to pay off in 1988 following the disposals of HMS *Ajax, Leander, Galatea, Naiad* and *Aurora*.

In addition to the vessels for the Royal Navy, a number of other nations have either purchased British-built 'Leanders' or constructed their own under licence. These latter include the Australian HMAS *Swan* (D50) and HMAS *Torrens* (D53), the Indian navy *Nilgiri* (F33), *Himgiri* (F34), *Udaygiri* (F35), *Dunagiri* (F36), *Taragiri* (F41) and *Vindhygiri* (F42), and the Dutch *Van Speijk* (F802), *Van Galen* (F803), *Tjerk Hiddes* (F804), *Van Nes* (F805), *Isaac Sweers* (F814) and *Evertsen* (F815). The former vessels are the Chilean *Condell* (06) and *Almirante Lynch* (07). In all cases the countries obtained 'Leanders' with better armament and sensor fits than Royal Navy vessels, apart from the latest Sea Wolf

conversions. The Dutch managed to double the surface-to-surface missile armament to eight by using the Harpoon.

In 1986, the Netherlands sold two of her 'Leanders', the *Tjerk Hiddes* and the *Van Spijk* to Indonesia, which also has an option on the *Van Galen* for 1987 and the *Van Nes* for 1988. The remaining two have been requested by Indonesia, but are unlikely to be released before 1992. All vessels have been or will be sold with a spares outfit, but not with helicopters. Weapons and electronics remain the same as when in Dutch service, except that the Indonesians will probably ship Westland Wasp Mk 1 helicopters. Three of the four Royal New Zealand Navy Leanders, namely HMNZS *Wellington, Canterbury* and *Southland* are having their Type 184 sonars replaced by Graseby Dynamics Type 750 sets. The Royal Navy are incorporating Type 750 technology into their own Type 184s producing the improved Type 184P, and the Indian Navy have had Type 750s installed in a number of units. During the mid-1970s, India evolved the basic Leander design into the longer and wider 'Godavari' class. Equipped with a mixture of western and Soviet systems, the *Godavari*

Completed in 1965, HMS Arethusa *was converted to carry an Ikara ASW rocket-launcher during a major refit completed in 1977. Eight of the original Batch 1 'Leander' class vessels have been altered in this way.*

(F20), the *Ganga* (F21), and the *Gomati* (F22) are each able to carry a pair of Westland Mk 42 Sea King ASW helicopters, notably enhancing ASW capability.

Specification
'Van Speijk' class
Displacement: 2,255 tons standard and 2,835 tons full load
Dimensions: length 113.4 m (372.0 ft); beam 12.5 m (41.0 ft); draught 4.2 m (13.8 ft)
Propulsion: as 'Leander' class
Speed: 28.5 kts
Armament: two quadruple Harpoon surface-to-surface missile launchers with eight missiles, two quadruple Sea Cat surface-to-air missile launchers with 32 missiles, one 76-mm (3-in) DP gun, and two triple 324-mm (12.75-in) Mk 32 ASW torpedo tubes with Mk 46 torpedoes

HMS Andromeda 'Leander' class frigate cutaway drawing key

1 Flagstaff
2 Variable depth sonar
3 Crane for sonar
4 Screw guard
5 Twin balanced rudder
6 Support
7 Twin screws
8 Shaft
9 Stores
10 Capstan
11 Three-barrel Mk 10 anti-submarine mortar
12 ASM local command post
13 Winch
14 Sonar and mortar control position
15 Mortar ammunition
16 Flight deck
17 Junior ratings' hall
18 Junior ratings' mess hall
19 Deck landing lights
20 Hangar
21 Aviation stores
22 Westland Lynx Mk II helicopter
23 Sea Cat director
24 Sea Cat missile launcher
25 Mainmast
26 Type 965 long-range air search radar and IFF
27 Receiving wireless aerials
28 Aft radar plotting room
29 Corvus chaff launcher
30 Air operation control room
31 Galley
32 Launch
33 Funnel casing
34 Funnel
35 Central control station
36 Boiler room
37 Boilers
38 Blower
39 Reserve feed tank
40 Engine room control panel
41 Diesel filling tank
42 Double bottom
43 Engine room
44 Wheel house
45 Stokers' mess
46 Wing tanks
47 Fuel

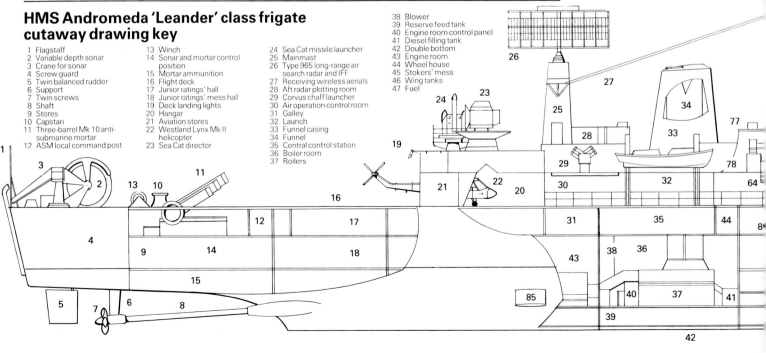

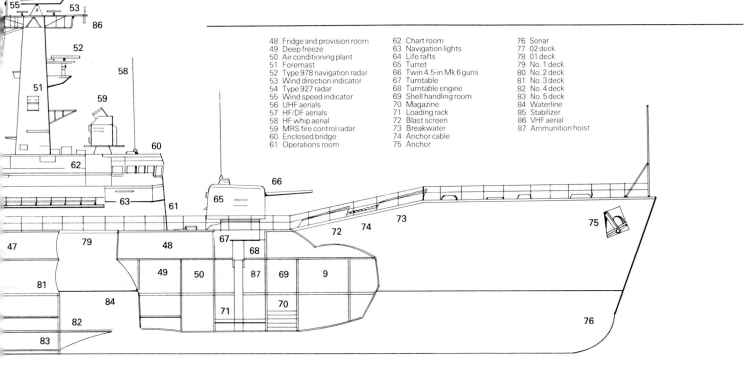

Below: After refitting, HMS Andromeda and the other four Batch 3 'Leanders' are the most powerful of the 'Leander' variants. The planned conversion of the other five Batch 3s has fallen victim to cuts in the defence budget.

Aircraft: one Westland SH-14B/C Lynx ASW helicopter
Electronics: one LW-03 air-search radar, one DA-05/2 target-indicator radar, one Decca TM1229C navigation radar, two WM-44 Sea Cat fire-control radars, one WM-45 gun fire-control radar, one SEWACO II data information system, one passive ESM system, two Corvus chaff launchers, one CWE610 hull sonar, and one SQR-18A towed-array sonar
Complement: 180

Specification
'Leander' class (RN Sea Wolf conversion)
Displacement: 2,500 tons standard and 2,962 tons full load
Dimensions: length 113.4 m (372.0 ft); beam 13.1 m (43.0 ft); draught 4.5 m (14.8 ft)
Propulsion: geared steam turbines delivering 30,000 hp (22371 kW) to two shafts

Speed: 27 kts
Armament: four single MM.38 Exocet surface-to-surface missile launchers with four missiles, one sextuple GWS25 Sea Wolf surface-to-air missile launcher with 30 missiles, two single 20-mm AA guns, and two triple 324-mm (12.75-in) STWS1 ASW torpedo tubes with Mk 46 and Stingray torpedoes
Aircraft: one Westland Lynx HAS.Mk 2 ASW helicopter
Electronics: one Type 967/978 air- and surface-search radar, one Type 910 Sea Wolf fire-control radar, one Type 1006 navigation radar, one CAAIS combat data system, one UAA-1 ESM system, two Corvus chaff launchers, one Type 2016 hull sonar, and one Type 2008 underwater telephone
Complement: 260

From the 17th 'Leander' the design was amended by increasing the beam. HMS Andromeda was the first of five broad-beamed 'Leanders' to be fitted with Sea Wolf and Exocet missiles, re-commissioning in 1980.

Specification
'Godavairi' class
Displacement: 3,500 tons standard, 4,100 tons full load
Dimensions: length 126.4 m (414.7 ft); beam 14.5 m (47.6 ft); draught 4.5 m (14.8 ft)
Propulsion: as 'Leander' class
Speed: 27 knots
Armament: four single container launchers for SS-N-2C 'Styx' SSMs, one twin SA-N-4 'Gecko' SAM launcher with 18 missiles, one twin SAM launcher with 18 missiles, one twin 57-mm AK725 AA gun, two twin AK230 30-mm AA guns, two triple 324-mm

(12.75-in) NST-ASW torpedo tube launchers with A244/S torpedos
Aircraft: two Westland Mk 42 Sea King ASW helicopters
Electronics: one 'Head Net C' air-search radar, one LW02 air-search radar, one LW06 air/surface-search radar, one 'Pop Group' SA-N-4 fire-control radar, one 'Muff Cob' fire-control radar, one 'Drum Tilt' fire-control radar, one Selenia CAIS combat data system, one SATNAV system, one Selenia ESM suite, one Type 750 hull-mounted sonar
Complement: 330 (30 officers, 300 men)

No.		No.		No.	
48	Fridge and provision room	62	Chart room	76	Sonar
49	Deep freeze	63	Navigation lights	77	02 deck
50	Air conditioning plant	64	Life rafts	78	01 deck
51	Foremast	65	Turret	79	No. 1 deck
52	Type 978 navigation radar	66	Twin 4.5-in Mk 6 guns	80	No. 2 deck
53	Wind direction indicator	67	Turntable	81	No. 3 deck
54	Type 927 radar	68	Turntable engine	82	No. 4 deck
55	Wind speed indicator	69	Shell handling room	83	No. 5 deck
56	UHF aerials	70	Magazine	84	Waterline
57	HF/DF aerials	71	Loading rack	85	Stabilizer
58	HF whip aerial	72	Blast screen	86	VHF aerial
59	MRS fire control radar	73	Breakwater	87	Ammunition hoist
60	Enclosed bridge	74	Anchor cable		
61	Operations room	75	Anchor		

Type 22 'Broadsword' class

UK

Originally to have been a class of 26 to follow the 'Leanders' the **Type 22** or **'Broadsword' class** design was conceived as an ASW ship for use in the Greenland-Iceland-UK gap against modern high-performance nuclear submarines. However, as has happened to most modern British naval programmes, the 'chop' fell during defence cuts and the procurement schedule has been changed somewhat. The original four **'Broadsword Batch 1'** vessels ordered were HMS **Broadsword** (F88), HMS **Battleaxe** (F89), HMS **Brilliant** (F90) and HMS **Brazen** (F91). Although rated as frigates, these are in fact larger than the contemporary Type 42 destroyers, and were designated frigates for purely political reasons. The hull, with greater freeboard than that of the destroyers is an improved Type 12 design for use in rough weather without a significant reduction in speed.

Unfortunately, because of design shortcomings they cannot be fitted with the definitive Type 2031(Z) towed-array sonar at the stern, so a lengthened **'Broadsword Batch 2'** ver-

sion had to be authorized. The six Batch 2s subsequently ordered to rectify the problem were HMS **Boxer** (F92), HMS **Beaver** (F93). HMS **Brave** (F94), HMS **London** (F95), HMS **Sheffield** (F96) and HMS **Coventry** (F97), and these will also differ amongst themselves as from the *Brave* onwards the propulsion plant will be two Rolls-Royce Spey SM1A and two Rolls-Royce Tyne RM1A gas turbines in a COGOG arrangement. HMS *Brave* is the first 'Type 22' to have the enlarged flight deck and hangar designed to take an helicopter of EH101 size.

Following the Falklands war, a **'Batch 3'** General Purpose variant was ordered. These have the same basic hull as the 'Batch 2s' but with a changed weapon fit which includes a single 114-mm (4.5-in) DP gun, eight Harpoon SSMs, one 30-mm Goalkeeper CIWS (two were to be fitted but economic constraints meant that each ship's allocation was halved) and two single 30-mm RARDEN guns. The four 'Batch 3' ships are HMS **Cornwall** (F99), HMS **Cumberland** (F85), HMS **Campbell-**

town (F86), and HMS **Chatham** (F87). They are due to join the fleet from 1987 to 1990. All three sub-classes will receive Type 2050 Fleet Sonar in place of the Type 2016 currently in service.

During the Falklands war the *Brilliant* and *Broadsword* distinguished themselves in combat, the former being the first vessel to fire the Sea Wolf SAM in anger.

Specification
'Broadsword Batch 1' class
Displacement: 3,500 tons standard and 4,400 tons full load
Dimensions: length 131.1 m (430.0 ft); beam 14.8 m (48.5 ft); draught 6.1 m (19.9 ft)
Propulsion: COGOG arrangement with two Rolls-Royce Olympus TM3B gas turbines delivering 50,000 hp (37285 kW) and two Rolls-Royce Tyne RM1A gas turbines delivering 8,500 hp (6338 kW) to two shafts
Speed: 29 kts
Armament: four single MM.38 Exocet surface-to-surface missile launchers with four missiles, two sextuple GWS25 Sea Wolf surface-to-air missile

Batch 3 variants of the 'Broadsword' class will be highly capable ships, although the frigate description may seem odd for a vessel nearing 5000 tonnes and with significant air, surface and anti-submarine capabilities.

launchers with 60 missiles, two single 40-mm AA guns, two single 20-mm AA guns, and two triple 324-mm (12.75-in) STWS1 ASW torpedo tubes with Mk 46 and Sting Ray torpedoes
Aircraft: one or two Westland Lynx HAS.Mk 2/3 ASW/anti-ship helicopters
Electronics: one Type 967/968 air- and surface-search radar, two Type 910 Sea Wolf fire-control radars, one Type 1006 navigation radar, one CAAIS combat data system, one UAA-1 ESM

A high-speed turn is made by HMS Broadsword (F88), first of the Type 22 class. These vessels, with their twin Lynx helicopters, were designed to counter modern high-performance nuclear submarines, and to do so in the harsh seas north and west of the British Isles.

system, one SCOT satellite communication system, one SATNAV system, two Corvus and two Mk 36 Super RBOC Chaff launchers, one Type 2016 hull sonar (to be replaced by Type 2050) and one Type 2008 underwater telephone
Complement: 223 normal and 248 maximum

Specification
'Broadsword Batch 2' class
Displacement: 4,200 tons standard, 4,800 tons full load
Dimensions: length F92-F93 145m (475.7ft), F94-F97 146.5m (480.6ft); beam 14.8m (48.5ft) draught 6.1m (19.9ft)
Propulsion: F92 and F93 as Batch 1, F95-F97 COGAG arrangement, with two Rolls-Royce Spey gas turbines delivering 37,540hp (27993kW) and two Rolls-Royce Tyne RM1C gas turbines delivering 10,680hp

(7964kW) to two shafts. F94 has Speys and Tynes in COGOG for trials
Speed: 30 kts (F92, F93) or 29 kts (F94-F97)
Armament: four single MM38 Exocet GWS 50 SSM launchers, two sextuple GWS 25 Mod 0 (Mod 3 to be fitted) launchers with 60 missiles (F94-F97 have Mod 3 with 72 missiles), two single 40-mm AA guns (being replaced by 30-mm RARDEN), two triple 324-mm (12.75-in) ASW STWS-1 torpedo tubes for Mk 46 and Sting Ray torpedos
Aircraft: one or two Westland Lynx Mk 2/3 ASW/anti-ship helicopters or (F94-F97), one Westland Sea King HAS Mk 5/6 or EH101 ASW helicopter
Electronics: one Type 967/968 air/ surface-search radar, two type 910 (to be replaced by Type 911) Sea Wolf fire-control radars, one Type 1006 navigation radar, one CACS1 combat data system, one SCOT satellite

communication system, one SATNAV system, one UAA1 Abbey Hill ESM system, two Type 690 jammers, four Plessey Shield six-barrel decoy launchers, one Type 2016 or 2050 hull sonar, one Type 2008 underwater telephone, one Type 2031(Z) towed sonar array
Complement: 273 normal (320 maximum)

Specification
'Broadsword Batch 3' class
Displacement: 4,380 tons standard, 5,250 tons full load
Dimensions: length 148.1m (486ft); beam 14.8m (48.5ft); draught 6.4m (21ft)
Propulsion: as Batch 2, F95-F97
Speed: 30 kts
Armament: two quadruple Harpoon SSM launchers, two sextuple GWS 25 Mod 3 Sea Wolf SAM launchers with 72 missiles, one single 114-mm (4.5-in) DP

gun, one 30-mm Goalkeeper CIWS, two single 30-mm RARDEN AA guns, two triple 324-mm (12.75in) STWS-2 ASW torpedo tubes for Sting Ray torpedos
Aircraft: as Batch 2 F94-F97
Electronics: one Type 967/968 air/ surface-search radar, two Type 911 Sea Wolf fire-control radars, one Goalkeeper fire-control radar, one Type 1006 navigation radar, one CAC5 combat data system, one SCOT satellite communications system, one SATNAV system, one UAA1 Abbey Hill ESM suite, four Plessey Shield decoy launchers, two Mk 36 Super RBOC chaff launchers, one Type 2050 hull sonar, one type 2008 underwater telephone, one Type 2031(2) towed sonar array
Complement: 286 normal and 320 maximum

Modern Western Frigates

Type 23 'Duke' class

The **Type 23** or **'Duke' class** was originally to be a cheap one-for-one replacement design both for the 'Leander' class and the very expensive 'Type 22' class frigates. However, profiting from the lessons learned from the Falklands war and to meet more challenging operational requirements the design was radically altered, increasing costs dramatically. Thus it was not until 1984 that the first of class, **HMS Norfolk (F230)** was ordered for commissioning in 1989. Due to subsequent financial restraints on the Defence Budget the second of the class, **HMS Marlborough (F231)**, was not ordered until 1986 for commissioning in 1990. Two further units **HMS Argyll (F232)** and **HMS Lancaster (F233)** were ordered at the same time with a minimum of four more planned as funding permits.

The ship is fitted with a unique COD-LAG (Combined Diesel-Electric and Gas Turbine) propulsion plant for maximum sensitivity when towing the Type 2031(Z) sonar array at up to 10 knots. The array when fully deployed trails for over 1.6km (1 mile) behind the ship. To prosecute targets which can be detected at ranges of up to 200km (125 miles) a large Westland Sea King HAS.Mk 5/6 or EH 101 helicopter is carried. One hard learned Falklands

lesson meant that a medium gun for shore bombardment has had to be added to the design. The self defence weapon fit includes the first vertical launch GWS Mk 26 Sea Wolf system, a Goalkeeper 30mm CIWS and two single 30mm Rarden cannon. For operations with a Surface Action Group two quadruple container-launchers are fitted for the increased range Block 1C RGM88 Harpoon anti-ship missile. Targetting for the missiles will either be by ESM systems, the ship's helicopter or a third-party source. In comparison to the previous 'Type 22/ Type 42' classes the crew accommodation will be austere.

Specification
'Duke' class
Displacement: 3,500 tons standard, 3,850 tons full load
Dimensions: length 133m (436.2ft), beam 15m (49.2ft), draught 4.3m (14.1ft)
Propulsion: two Rolls-Royce Spey SM1A gas turbines with four Paxman Valenta 12RPM200A diesels and two electric motors developing 41,540hp (30976kW) total in CODLAG arrangement driving two shafts
Speed: 28kts (15kts on electric drive)
Armament: two quadruple Harpoon SSM container-launchers (no reloads),

one 32-round GWS Mk 26 Sea Wolf vertical launch SAM system (no reloads), one 114-mm (4.5-in) Mk 8 DP gun, one 30-mm Goalkeeper CIWS, two single 30-mm Rarden guns, two triple 324-mm (12.75-in) STWS-2 ASW torpedo tubes (for Mk 46 and Sting Ray torpedoes)
Aircraft: two Westland Lynx HAS.Mk 3/8 or one Westland Sea King HAS.Mk 6 or EH 101 helicopter(s)
Electronics: one Type 996 air search radar, one Type 1007 navigation radar; two Type 911 Sea Wolf fire control radars, one CACS4 combat

The 'Duke' class were intended as inexpensive frigates, but the lessons of the Falklands war meant the capability of the design has been changed dramatically.

information system, one UAF1 ESM system, one Decca Cygnus active ECM system, four Sea Gnat chaff launchers, one SCOT satellite communications system, one SATNAV system, one Type 2050 bow sonar, one Type 2031(Z) towed sonar
Complement: normal 157 maximum 177

Type 21 'Amazon' class

The **Type 21** or **'Amazon' class** general-purpose frigate was a private shipbuilder's design to replace the obsolete Type 41 or 'Leopard' and Type 61 or 'Salisbury' class frigates. Because of numerous bureaucratic problems, private and official ship designers were not brought together on the project, resulting in a class which handles well and is well liked by crews, but lacks sufficient 'growth' potential to take the new generation of sensor and weapon fits. Thus the vessels will not receive new equipment as such during their refit cycles. During the 1982 Falklands war HMS **Avenger** (F185), HMS **Ardent** (F184), HMS **Antelope** (F170), HMS **Arrow** (F173), and HMS **Alacrity** (F174) served in the main combat zone, whilst HMS **Active** (F171) and

HMS **Ambuscade** (F172) assisted in supporting operations and the occasional shore bombardment. Only the lead ship, HMS **Amazon** (F169), missed the war as she was in the Far East. On 21 May 1982 the *Ardent* was so badly damaged in bomb attacks that she sank, whilst two days later the *Antelope* caught fire and exploded when an unexploded bomb that was being defused detonated aboard her. After the war the remaining class members were found to have suffered severe hull cracking; indeed one unit, *Arrow*, had to limp precariously home from the Falklands to enter emergency refit. All have now been strengthened with steel inserts welded to the hull structure, but the future of the class remains uncertain at present.

Specification
'Amazon' class
Displacement: 2,850 tons standard and 3,350 tons full load
Dimensions: length 117.0m (384.0ft); beam 12.7m (41.7ft); draught 5.9m (19.5ft)
Propulsion: COGOG arrangement with two Rolls-Royce Olympus TM3B gas turbines delivering 50,000hp (37285kW) and two Rolls-Royce Tyne RM1A gas turbines delivering 8,500hp (6338kW) to two shafts
Speed: 32 kts
Armament: four single MM.38 Exocet surface-to-surface missile launchers with four missiles, one quadruple GWS24 Sea Cat surface-to-air missile launcher with 20 missiles, one 114-mm (4.5-in) DP gun, four single 20-mm AA

guns, and two triple 324-mm (12.75-in) STWS1 ASW torpedo tubes with Mk 46 and Sting Ray torpedoes
Aircraft: one Westland Lynx HAS.Mk 2 ASW helicopter
Electronics: one Type 1006 navigation radar, one Type 992Q air- and surface-search radar, two Tp.912 fire-control radars, one CAAIS combat data system, one UAA-1 ESM system (only in some), two Corvus chaff launchers, one Type 162M hull sonar, and one Type 184M hull sonar, one SCOT satellite communications system, one SATNAV system
Complement: 177 normal and 192 maximum

Type 21

Seen during the first bombardment of the runway at Port Stanley, the Type 21 made use of the fine sea-keeping qualities inherent in the design to provide a stable firing platform. Later events were tragically to reveal less fighting capacity, especially against large-scale air attack.

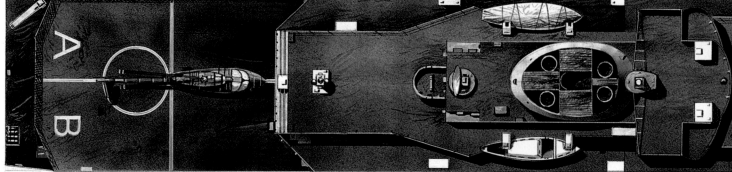

`Type 21´class frigate
HMS Amazon

Completed in May 1974, HMS Amazon was the only Type 21 not to
see action in the South Atlantic campaign. A bad fire aboard her in
1977 brought to light the dangers inherent in all aluminium
superstructures, but it was not until after the Falklands conflict that
the Royal Navy decided to revert to steel. After HMS Amazon and
Antelope, subsequent Type 21s were constructed with four MM.38
Exocet launchers which give them a powerful punch, but their
inability to take newer systems remains a major handicap.

F172

'Lupo' class

Built and designed by CN Riuniti naval shipbuilders, the four vessels of the **'Lupo' class** in the Italian navy are the **Lupo** (F564), **Sagittario** (F565), **Perseo** (F566) and **Orsa** (F567). These were designed primarily for the convoy escort role, with a capability for anti-surface warfare using SSMs if required. The hull is based on 14 watertight compartments and has fixed-fin stabilizers. To reduce the ship's complement the machinery plant has been highly automated and divided into four separate compartments housing the auxiliaries, gas turbine modules, reduction gearbox and the diesel alternator sets. A telescope hangar has also been fitted to accommodate a light ASW helicopter that can also double in the missile-armed surface strike role.

The 'Lupos' have proved very popular in Italian navy service, and the type has been exported to Venezuela, Peru and Iraq in a modified form that has a fixed-hangar structure and no reloads for the SAM launcher. The six Venezuelan ships are the **Mariscal Sucre** (F21), **Almirante Brion** (F22), **General Urdaneta** (F23), **General Soublette** (F24), **General Salom** (F25) and **Almirante José de Garcia** (F26). The four Peruvian ships are the **Meliton Carvajal** (F51), **Manuel Villaviciencio** (F52), **Montero** (F53) and the **Mariategui** (F54), all armed with octuple Aspide SAM systems. The four Iraqi units, (**Hittin, Thi Qar, Al Yarmook** and **Al Qadisyaa**) have been completed but are undelivered due to the Iran/Iraq War.

The main anti-ship weapon carried on the Italian ships is the Otomat Mk 2 Teseo missile, which has an Italian SMA active radar-homing seeker and a sea-skimming flight profile. To utilize the missile's over-the-horizon capabilities fully, the embarked helicopter is used for mid-course guidance. Export ships carry the less capable Otomat

Mk 1 missile that has a pop-up terminal attack manoeuvre.

Specification
'Lupo' class (Italian navy)
Displacement: 2,208 tons standard and 2,525 tons full load
Dimensions: length 113.2 m (371.3 ft); beam 11.3 m (37.1 ft); draught 3.7 m (12.1 ft)
Propulsion: CODOG arrangement with two General Electric/FIAT LM2500 gas turbines delivering 51,600 hp (38478 kW) and two GMT A230 diesels delivering 7,900 hp (5891 kW) to two shafts

Speed: 35 kts
Armament: eight single Otomat Mk 2 surface-to-surface missile launchers with eight missiles, one octuple NATO Sea Sparrow surface-to-air missile launcher with 24 missiles, one 127-mm (5-in) DP gun, two twin 40-mm Dardo CIWS, and two triple Mk 32 324-mm (12.75-in) ASW torpedo tubes with Mk 46 torpedoes
Aircraft: one Agusta-Bell AB.212ASW helicopter
Electronics: one RAN10S air- and surface-search radar, one SPQ2F surface-search radar, one RAN11/LX air- and surface-search radar, one

Perseo, *the third 'Lupo' class frigate to enter service with the Italian navy, is seen with her forward OTO-Melara 127-mm gun at high elevation.*

RTN10X fire-control radar, two RTN20X Dardo fire-control radars, one SPN703 navigation radar, one IPN10 command and control system, active and passive ESM systems, two SCLAR chaff launchers, and one DE1160B hull sonar
Complement: 186

'Maestrale' class

The **'Maestrale' class** is essentially a stretched version of the 'Lupo' design with less weapons and a greater emphasis on ASW. The increase in length and beam over the earlier 'Lupos' was to provide for a fixed hangar installation and a variable-depth sonar (VDS) housing at the stern. The improvements have resulted in better seaworthiness and habitability, plus the room required to carry and operate a second light helicopter. However, to compensate for this the class carries four less SSMs, and because of the extra tonnage has suffered a speed reduction of around 3 kts. The Raytheon VDS operates on the same frequencies as the hull sonar set and gives the vessels a valuable below-the-thermal-layer capability for use in the very difficult ASW conditions met in the Mediterranean. To enhance the ships' ASW operations further, the Agusta-Bell AB.212 helicopters carried are fitted with Bendix ASQ-13B active dunking sonars. The armament they carry is either the American Mk 46 homing torpedo or Mk 54 depth charge. It is also fitted with two fixed tubes for the 36-kt, 25-km (15.5-mile) range Whitehead Motofides A184 533-mm (21-in) wire-guided torpedo beneath the helicopter pad aft. The A184 can be used against surface and sub-

surface targets. A towed-array system that can use the existing VDS installation is currently under development. The helicopters can also carry AS.12 wire-guided anti-ship missiles.

The eight ships in service are the **Maestrale** (F570), **Grecale** (F571),

Libeccio (F572), **Scirocco** (F573), **Aliseo** (F574), **Euro** (F575), **Espero** (F576) and **Zeffiro** (F575).

Comparable to the Dutch 'Kortenaer' or German 'Bremen' classes, the 'Maestrale' class is somewhat faster. Largely a stretched version of the preceding 'Lupo' class, Maestrale and her seven sisterships possess enhanced ASW abilities.

Faster than most Western frigates (although slower than the 'Lupo' class), Maestrale is comprehensively equipped with modern ASW technology, including both a hull sonar and towed variable-depth sonar.

Specification
'Maestrale' class
Displacement: 3,040 tons standard and 3,200 tons full load
Dimensions: length 122.7 m (402.6 ft); beam 12.9 m (42.3 ft); draught 8.4 m (27.6 ft)
Propulsion: CODOG arrangement with two General Electric/FIAT LM2500 gas turbines delivering 51,600 hp (38478 kW) and two GMT B230 diesels delivering 10,146 hp (7566 kW) to two shafts
Speed: 32 kts
Armament: four single Otomat Mk 2 surface-to-surface missile launchers with four missiles, one octuple Albatros surface-to-air missile system with 24 Aspide missiles, one 127-mm (5-in) DP gun, two twin 40-mm Dardo CIWS, two single 533-mm (21-in) torpedo tubes for A184 torpedoes, and two triple 324-mm (12.75-in) ILAS-3 ASW torpedo tubs for Mk 46 lightweight torpedoes.
Aircraft: two Agusta-Bell AB.212 ASW helicopters
Electronics: one RAN10S air- and surface-search radar, one SPQ2F surface-search radar, one RTN30X Albatros acquisition radar, two RTN20X Dardo fire-control radars, one RTN10X fire-control radar, one SPN703 navigation radar, one IPN10 command and control system, active and passive ESM systems, two SCLAR D chaff launchers, one DE1160B hull sonar, and one DE1164 variable-depth sonar
Complement: 224

USA
'Garcia' and 'Brooke' classes

Designed in the late 1950s as replacements for World War II destroyers, the **'Garcia' class** ASW escort and **'Brooke' class** SAM ship were ordered by the US Navy to the extent of 10 and six units respectively. Further production of the latter ended during Fiscal Year 1963 because of their high cost and limited capability. Although they are relatively modern, there are no plans to modernize the ASW ships USS **Garcia** (FF1040), USS **Bradley** (FF1041), USS **Edward McDonnell** (FF1043), USS **Brumby** (FF1044), USS **Davidson** (FF1045), USS **Voge** (FF1047), USS **Sample** (FF1048), USS **Koelsch** (FF1049), USS **Albert David** (FF1050) and USS **O'Callahan** (FF1051) with new guns, Harpoon SSM and modern ESM equipment. Over the years the class has been used to test a number of prototype systems including the SQR-15 linear towed-array sonar which is now fitted to FF1040 and FF1043 in place of a LAMPS I ASW helicopter. An automated ASW tactical data system (TDS) is carried by FF1047 and FF1049, whilst from FF1047 onwards an ASROC reload magazine has been fitted within the superstructure.

The SAM ships USS **Brooke** (FFG1), USS **Ramsey** (FFG2), USS **Schofield** (FFG3), USS **Talbot** (FFG4), USS **Richard L. Page** (FFG5) and USS *Julius F. Furer* (FFG6) are identical to the 'Garcias' except that a single-rail Mk 22 launcher, originally for Tartar and now for Standard SM-1MR missiles, replaces the aft 127-mm (5-in) gun mount. From FFG4 onwards an ASROC reload magazine was also incorporated into the superstructure. The *Talbot* was used as the test ship for the weapons and sensor fit for the 'Oliver Hazard Perry' class, but has now been returned to normal appearance. The only planned modernization of the ships is the fitting of the SLQ-32(V)2 ESM suite to replace older systems.

Specification
'Garcia' class
Displacement: 2,620 tons standard and 3,560 tons full load
Dimensions: length 126.3 m (414.5 ft); beam 13.5 m (44.2 ft); draught 4.4m (14.5 ft)
Propulsion; geared steam turbines delivering 35,000 hp (26100 kW) to two shafts
Speed: 27.5 kts
Armament: two single 127-mm (5-in) DP guns, one octuple ASROC anti-submarine missile launcher with eight (first five ships) or 16 (other ships) missiles, and two triple 324-mm (12.75-in) Mk 32 ASW torpedo tubes with Mk 46 torpedoes
Aircraft: one Kaman SH-2F Seasprite LAMPS I helicopter (not in FF1040 and FF1043)
Electronics: one SPS-40 air-search radar, one SPS-10 surface-search radar, one SPG-35 fire-control radar, one LN66 navigation radar, one WLR-1 ECM system, one WLR-3 ECM system, one ULQ-6 ECM system, one SRN-15 TACAN (not in FF1040 and FF1043), one SQS-26 bow sonar, and (FF1040 and FF1043 only) one BQR-15 towed sonar
Complement: 247 except FF1040, FF1041, FF1043 and FF1044 239

Specification
'Brooke' class
Displacement: 2,643 tons standard and 3,426 tons full load
Dimensions: length 126.3 m (414.5 ft); beam 13.5 m (44.2 ft); draught 4.6 m (15.0 ft)
Propulsion: as 'Garcia' class
Speed: 27.2 kts
Armament: one single-rail Mk 22 Standard surface-to-air missile launcher with 16 SM-1MR missiles, one 127-mm (5-in) DP gun, one octuple ASROC anti-submarine missile launcher with eight (first three ships) or 16 (other ships) missiles, and two triple 324-mm (12.75-in) Mk 32 ASW torpedo tubes with Mk 46 torpedoes
Aircraft: one Kaman SH-2F Seasprite LAMPS I helicopter
Electronics: one SPS-52B 3D radar, one SPS-10F surface-search radar, one LN66 navigation radar, one SPG-51C Standard fire-control radar, one SPG-35 gun fire-control radar, one SRN-15 TACAN, one SLQ-32(V)2 ESM system, two Mk 36 Super RBOC chaff launchers, and one SQS-26 bow sonar
Complement: 248

USS Edward McDonnell (FF1043) of the 'Garcia' class plunges through a heavy sea. Unlike later US frigate classes, the 'Garcias' are ASW-dedicated, and have little or no modern anti-aircraft capability.

USS Brooke (FFG1) is name ship of a six-vessel class built to a modified 'Garcia' design. The difference lies in the fitting of a Mk 22 single-rail missile launcher in place of the aft 5-in (127-mm) gun. The standard SM-1MR missiles now carried give the class considerable anti-aircraft potential.

'Knox' class

The **'Knox' class** is similar to the 'Garcia' and 'Brooke' designs, but is slightly larger because of the use of non-pressure fired boilers, and was designed in the early 1960s. The first vessels entered US Navy service in 1969, the last units of the 46-strong class being delivered in 1974. They are specialized ASW ships and have been heavily criticized because of their single propeller and solitary 127-mm (5-in) gun armament.

A five-ship class based on the design but with a Mk 22 missile launcher for 16 Standard SM-1MR missiles, four to eight single Harpoon launchers and a Meroka 20-mm CIWS has been built in Spain for the Spanish navy. Built with American aid, the *Baleares* (F71), *Andalucia* (F72), *Cataluna* (F73), *Asturias* (F74) and *Extremadura* (F75) also carry two Mk 25 ASW torpedo tubes as well as the two triple Mk 32 systems, with a total of 22 Mk 44/46 and 19 Mk 37 ASW torpedoes.

From 1980 onwards the American 'Knoxes' were taken in hand to receive raised bulwarks and strakes forward to improve their seakeeping in heavy weather. Like the 'Garcia' class, numerous 'Knoxes' have been used over the years to test individual prototype weapon and sensor systems. A total of 32 (FF1052-1083) were equipped with an octuple Sea Sparrow launcher, but this will be replaced by a 20-mm Phalanx CIWS of the type due to be fitted to all 46 ships. The port pair of the four twin cells of the ASROC launcher have been retrofitted to fire Harpoon SSMs, whilst all vessels are also to be fitted to carry the SQR-18A TACTASS towed-array sonar. In 37 ships it will supplement a SQS-35A VDS system carried in a stern well. For helicopter operations an SRN-15 TACAN is carried and the SLQ-32(V)1 ESM system is being upgraded to the SLQ-32(V)2 configuration. To reduce

underwater radiated noise the Prairie/Masker bubble system has been used on the hull and propeller. The ASW TDS first evaluated in the 'Garcia' class is being installed as ships enter refit. By 1988 eight units will have been assigned to the Naval Reserve Force as replacements for old World War II destroyers. The class comprises the USS *Knox* (FF1052), USS *Roark* (FF1053), USS *Gray* (FF1054), USS *Hepburn* (FF1055), USS *Connole* (FF1056), USS *Rathburne* (FF1057), USS *Meyerkord* (FF1058), USS *W.S. Sims* (FF1059), USS *Lang* (FF1060), USS *Patterson* (FF1061), USS *Whipple* (FF1062), USS *Reasoner* (FF1063), USS *Lockwood* (FF1064), USS *Stein* (FF1065), USS *Marvin Shields* (FF1066), USS *Francis Hammond* (FF1067), USS *Vreeland* (FF1068), USS *Bagley* (FF1069), USS *Downes* (FF1070), USS *Badger* (FF1071), USS *Blakely* (FF1072), USS *Robert E. Peary* (FF1073), USS *Harold E. Holt* (FF1074), USS *Trippe* (FF1075), USS *Fanning* (FF1076), USS *Ouellet* (FF1077), USS

Joseph Hewes (FF1078), USS *Bowen* (FF1079), USS *Paul* (FF1080), USS *Aylwin* (FF1081), USS *Elmer Montgomery* (FF1082), USS *Cook* (FF1083), USS *McCandless* (FF1084), USS *Donald B. Beary* (FF1085), USS *Brewton* (FF1086), USS *Kirk* (FF1087), USS *Barbey* (FF1088), USS *Jesse L. Brown* (FF1089), USS *Ainsworth* (FF1090), USS *Miller* (FF1091), USS *Thomas C. Hart* (FF1092), USS *Capodanno* (FF1093), USS *Pharris* (FF1094), USS *Truett* (FF1095), USS *Valdez* (FF1096) and USS *Moinester* (FF1097).

Specification
'Knox' class
Displacement: 3,011 tons standard and 3,877 tons (FF1052-FF1077) or 4,250 tons (other ships) full load
Dimensions: length 133.5 m (438.0 ft); beam 14.3 m (46.8 ft); draught 4.6 m (15.0 ft)

USS Pharris *(FF1094) is seen during an exercise off the South American coast. The 46 'Knox' class vessels are dedicated to the ASW role and have recently undergone major refits to improve seakeeping.*

Propulsion: geared steam turbines delivering 35,000 hp (26 100 kW) to one shaft
Speed: 27 kts
Armament: one 127-mm (5-in) DP gun, one 20-mm Phalanx CIWS (being fitted), one octuple Sea Sparrow surface-to-air missile launcher with eight missiles (being replaced), one octuple ASROC anti-submarine and Harpoon surface-to-surface missile launcher with 12 ASROC and four Harpoon missiles, and two twin 324-mm (12.75-in) Mk 32 ASW torpedo tubes with 22 Mk 46 torpedoes
Aircraft: one Kaman SH-2F Seasprite LAMPS I helicopter
Electronics: one SPS-40B air-search radar, one SPS-67 surface-search radar, one SPG-53 fire-control radar, one LN66 navigation radar, one ASW tactical data system, one SRN-15 TACAN, one SQS-26C bow sonar, and one SQS-35 variable-depth sonar (in 37 ships); all are to have either SQR-18A sonar fitted to the VDS body or a SQR-18A(V)2 installation in non VDS ships
Complement: 283

USS Knox *(FF1052) was the first of its class. Evolved from the preceding 'Garcia' and 'Brooke' classes, the 'Knox' class vessels are to be fitted with Harpoon SSMs and the 20-mm Phalanx close-in weapon system (CIWS).*

'Oliver Hazard Perry' class

Destined to be numerically the largest warship class in the US Navy, the **'Oliver Hazard Perry' class** was designed for anti-air warfare with ASW and anti-surface warfare as its secondary roles. Because of cost considerations the first 26 will not be refitted to carry two LAMPS III ASW helicopters, but will retain the present two LAMPS I machines. The LAMPS facilities will include the Recovery Assistance, Security and Traversing (RAST) system which will allow the launch and recovery of the Sikorsky SH-60 Seahawk helicopters with the ship rolling through 28° and pitching up to 5°. All have aluminium alloy armour over

their magazine spaces and Kevlar plastic armour over vital electronics and communications facilities.

Four Australian FFG-7s (HMAS *Adelaide, Canberra, Sydney* and *Darwin*) are to be joined by HMAS *Melbourne* and another, built to a modified design, in the early 1990s. Spain built three units, the *Santa Maria* (F81), *Victoria* (F82), and *Numancia* (F83). A fourth has been ordered and a fifth is projected if funds permit.

The magazine for the single-rail Mk 13 SAM launcher can take only Standard and Harpoon missiles, so the shipboard ASW weapons are Mk 46 torpedoes and the LAMPS helicopters.

Sixteen of the US class have been assigned to the Naval Force Reserve as training ships along with several 'Knox' class ASW frigates. Under current planning the US Navy will not be ordering any new frigate construction as it has a surplus of such hulls. The class consists of the USS *Oliver Hazard Perry* (FFG7), USS *McInerney* (FFG8), USS *Wadsworth* (FFG9), USS *Duncan* (FFG10), USS *Clark* (FFG11), USS *George Philip* (FFG12), USS *Samuel Eliot Morison* (FFG13), USS *John H. Sides* (FFG14), USS *Estocin* (FFG15), USS *Clifton Sprague* (FFG16), USS *John A. Moore* (FFG19), USS *Antrim* (FFG20), USS *Flatley* (FFG21), USS

Fahrion (FFG22), USS *Lewis B. Puller* (FFG23), USS *Jack Williams* (FFG24), USS *Copeland* (FFG25), USS *Gallery* (FFG26), USS *Mahlon S. Tisdale* (FFG27), USS *Boone* (FFG28), USS *Stephen W. Groves* (FFG29), USS *Reid* (FFG30), USS *Stark* (FFG31), USS *John L. Hall* (FFG32), USS *Jarret* (FFG33), USS *Aubrey Fitch* (FFG34), USS *Underwood* (FFG36), USS *Crommelin* (FFG37), USS *Curts* (FFG38), USS *Doyle* (FFG39), USS *Halyburton* (FFG40), USS *McClusky* (FFG41), USS *Klakring* (FFG42), USS *Thach* (FFG43), USS *De Wert* (FFG45), USS *Rentz* (FFG46), USS *Nicholas* (FFG47), USS *Vandergrift* (FFG48), USS *Robert*

USS Oliver Hazard Perry *(FFG7) is the first of a class of 51 general-purpose vessels designed to escort merchant convoys or amphibious squadrons. ASW is handled by the two LAMPS helicopters embarked, and the class can also fire Harpoon and Standard missiles.*

G. Bradley (FFG49), USS *Taylor* (FFG50), USS *Gary* (FFG51), USS *Carr* (FFG52), USS *Hawes* (FFG53), USS *Ford* (FFG54), USS *Elrod* (FFG55), USS *Simpson* (FFG56), USS *Reuben James* (FFG57), USS *Samuel B. Roberts* (FFG58), USS *Kauffman* (FFG59), USS *Rodney M. Davis* (FFG60) and USS *Ingraham* (FFG61).

Specification
'Oliver Hazard Perry' class
Displacement: 2,769 tons standard and 3,658 tons full load; FFG 8, 36-61 3,010 tons standard, 3,900 tons full load
Dimensions: length 135.6 m (445.0 ft) in LAMPS I ships or 138.1 m (453.0 ft) in LAMPS III ships (FFG8, FFG36-FFG61); beam 13.7 m (45.0 ft); draught 4.5 m (14.8 ft)
Propulsion: two General Electric LM2500 gas turbines delivering 40,000 hp (29828 kW) to one shaft
Speed: 29 kts
Armament: one single-rail Mk 13 Standard/Harpoon missile launcher with 36 SM-1MR surface-to-air and four Harpoon surface-to-surface missiles, one 76-mm (3-in) DP gun, one 20-mm Phalanx CIWS, and two triple 324-mm (12.75-in) Mk 32 ASW torpedo tubes with 24 Mk 46 torpedoes

Aircraft: two Kaman SH-2F Seasprite LAMPS I or two Sikorsky SH-60B LAMPS III
Electronics: one SPS-49 air-search radar, one SPS-55 surface-search radar, one Mk 92 fire-control radar, one STIR fire-control radar, one URN-25 TACAN, one SLQ-32(V)2 ESM system, two Mk 36 Super RBOC chaff launchers, one SQS-56 hull sonar, and one SQR-19A or one SQR-18A towed sonar

USS Oliver Hazard Perry *is seen together with USS* Antrim *(FFG20) and USS* Jack Williams *(FFG24).*

Complement: 215

'Tromp' class

Although designated by the Dutch as frigates, the **'Tromp' class** vessels *Tromp* (F801) and *De Ruyter* (F802) are, by virtue of their armament and size, more akin to guided-missile destroyers. They are equipped with an admiral's cabin and supporting command and control facilities to serve as the flagships of the two Dutch navy ASW hunter-killer groups assigned to EASTLANT control during wartime. Fitted with fin stabilizers, they are excellent seaboats and weapons platforms in most types of weather. The propulsion is of the COGOG type with pairs of Rolls-Royce Olympus and Tyne gas turbines that have been downrated to improve gas generator life and ease of maintenance. A full NBC citadel defence is built into the hull.

The primary role assigned to the ships is the provision of area SAM defence against aircraft and missiles to the hunter-killer group or convoy it may be escorting. They also have a secondary ASW and anti-surface vessel role. The main armament is a single-rail Mk 13 Standard SM-1MR SAM launcher, backed up by an octuple NATO Sea Sparrow SAM launcher with a large reload magazine. The appearance of the vessels is characterized by the large plastic radome fitted over the forward SPS-01 3D radar. The *Tromp* is due to undergo a major updating programme for its sensor, weapon and command systems so she will last well into the 1990s whilst the De Ruyter's service life will be extended to only 1992.

Specification
'Tromp' class
Displacement: 3,665 tons standard and 4,308 tons full load
Dimensions: length 138.4 m (454.0 ft); beam 14.8 m (48.6 ft); draught 4.6 m (15.1 ft)
Propulsion: COGOG arrangement with two Rolls-Royce Olympus TM3B gas turbines delivering 50,000 hp (37285 kW) and two Rolls-Royce Tyne RM1C gas turbines delivering 8,200 hp (6115 kW) to two shafts
Speed: 30 kts
Armament: two quadruple Harpoon surface-to-surface missile launchers with eight missiles, one single-rail Mk 13 Standard surface-to-air missile launcher with 40 SM-1MR missiles, one octuple NATO Sea Sparrow surface-to-air missile launcher with 60 missiles, one twin 120-mm (4.72-in) Bofors DP gun, and two triple 324-mm (12.75-in) Mk 32 ASW torpedo tubes with Mk 46 torpedoes
Aircraft: one Westland SH-14B/C Lynx ASW helicopter
Electronics: one SPS-01/D radar, two Decca 1226 navigation radars, one WM-25 fire-control radar, two SPG-51C fire-control radars, one SEWACO I data information system, one Ramses ESM system, four Mk 36 Super RBOC chaff launchers, one Type 162 hull sonar, and one CWE610 hull sonar
Complement: 306

Replacing two cruisers in service with the Royal Netherlands navy, HNLMS Tromp *and* De Ruyter *are among the largest and most capable of frigates afloat. Weapons fitted include Harpoon, Standard and Sea Sparrow missiles.*

'Kortenaer' and 'Jacob van Heemskerck' classes

The **'Kortenaer'** or **'Standard' class** frigate design was authorized in the late 1960s as the replacement for the 12 ASW destroyers of the 'Holland' and 'Friesland' classes. The propulsion plant and machinery layout was taken from the 'Tromp' design, the power of the gas turbines being kept normal to give higher maximum and cruising speeds in order to permit operations against nuclear submarines. A single pair of fin stabilizers is fitted, and as far as possible internal systems have been automated to reduce crew numbers. Eight ships were ordered in 1974, and a further four in 1976. In 1982, however, two newly completed units were purchased by Greece as the *Elli* (F450) and *Limnos* (F451). These were replaced in the Dutch order by two vessels to be constructed to an air-defence variant design known as the **'Jacob van Heemskerck' class**. The two ships are the *Jacob van Heemskerck* (F812) and *Witte de With* (F813), and were planned to alternate as the flagship of the Dutch navy's third ASW hunter-killer group, assigned to NATO's Channel Command in wartime. The helicopter facility of the 'Kortenaers' has been replaced by a Mk 13 Standard SAM missile launcher. They entered service in 1986. The 10 vessels of the ASW class are the *Kortenaer* (F807), *Callenburgh* (F808), *Van Kingsbergen* (F809), *Banckert* (F810), *Piet Hein* (F811), *Abraham Crijnssen* (F816), *Philips van Almonde* (F823), *Bloys van Treslong* (F824), *Jacob van Brakel* (F825) and *Pieter*

HNLMS Banckert (F810) was the fourth 'Kortenaer' class frigate to enter service with the Royal Netherlands navy.

Florisz (F826). All are due to receive thorough systems and equipment updates from 1992 through to 1996.

Specification
'Kortenaer' class
Displacement: 3,050 tons standard and 3,786 tons full load
Dimensions: length 130.5 m (428.1 ft); beam 14.6 m (47.9 ft); draught 4.3 m (14.1 ft)
Propulsion: COGOG arrangement with two Rolls-Royce Olympus TM3B gas turbines delivering 51,600 hp (38478 kW) and two Rolls-Royce Tyne RM1C gas turbines delivering 9,800 hp (7308 kW) to two shafts
Speed: 30 kts
Armament: two quadruple Harpoon surface-to-surface missile launchers with eight missiles, one octuple NATO Sea Sparrow surface-to-air missile launcher with 24 missiles, one 76-mm (3-in) DP gun, one 30-mm Goalkeeper CIWS, and two twin 324-mm (12.75-in) Mk 32 ASW torpedo tubes with Mk 46 torpedoes
Aircraft: two Westland SH-14B/C Lynx ASW helicopters
Electronics: one LW-08 air-search radar, one ZW-06 navigation radar, one WM-25 fire-control radar, one STIR fire-control radar, one Goalkeeper fire-control radar, one SEWACO data information system,

one Sphinx or Ramses ESM system, two Mk 36 Super RBOC chaff launchers, and one SQS-505 bow sonar
Complement: 200

Specification
'Jacob van Heemskerck' class
As 'Kortenaer' class except
Displacement: 3,000 tons standard and 3,750 tons full load
Armament: one single-rail Mk 13 Standard SAM launcher with 40 SM-1MR in place of DP gun
Aircraft: none

Electronics: one DA-05 air/surface-search radar, one ZW-06 navigation radar, one STIR-18 fire-control radar, two STIR-24 fire-control radars, one Goalkeeper fire-control radar, one SEWACO II data information system, one Ramses ESM system, four Mk 36 Super RBOC chaff launchers, and one SQS-509 bow sonar.
Complement: 176 plus 20 flag staff

'Wielingen' (E-71) class

The **'Wielingen' class** is the first post-war warship type to be completely designed and built in Belgium. The programme was approved in June 1971, the final studies being completed in July 1973. The order for the first two ships was placed in October of that year, and the hulls were laid down in 1974. The remaining two were laid down in 1975, all four units commissioning into the Belgian navy in 1978.

Based at Zeebrugge, the four vessels are the largest surface warships in the Belgian navy and form its only seagoing escort ship element. They are fully air conditioned, and are fitted with Vosper fin stabilizers and a Westinghouse hull sonar. The armament and sensor fit is from a wide variety of NATO countries and was chosen to make the class as well-armed as possible for so compact a size. For economy a combined diesel or gas turbine (CODOG) machinery outfit was installed using a single Rolls-Royce TM3B Olympus gas turbine and two Cock-

erill CO-240V-12 diesels to drive two shafts fitted with controllable-pitch propellers. The four vessels built are the *Wielingen* (F910), *Westdiep* (F911), *Wandelaar* (F912) and *Westhinder* (F913), and these will remain in operational service until the early years of the next century.

Specification
'Wielingen' class
Displacement: 1,880 tons standard and 2,283 tons full load
Dimensions: length 106.4 m (349.1 ft); beam 12.3 m (40.4 ft); draught 5.6 m (18.4 ft)
Propulsion: CODOG arrangement with one Rolls-Royce Olympus TM3B gas turbine delivering 28,000 shp (20880 kW) and two diesels delivering 6,000 hp (4474 kW) to two shafts
Speed: 29 kts
Armament: four single MM.38 Exocet surface-to-surface missile launchers with four missiles, one octuple NATO

Sea Sparrow surface-to-air missile launcher with eight missiles, one 100-mm (3.9-in) DP gun, two single 20-mm AA guns (to be replaced by one 30-mm Goalkeeper CIWS), one sextuple 375-mm (14.76-in) Creusot Loire ASW rocket-launcher, and two single ASW torpedo catapults with 10 L5 torpedoes
Electronics: one DA-05 air- and

surface-search radar, one WM-25 fire-control radar, one TM1645/9X navigation radar, one SEWACO IV tactical data system, two Mk 36 Super RBOC chaff launchers, one SLQ-25 NIXIE ASW decoy system, one SQS-505A hull sonar, and one Elcos 1 ESM system
Complement: 160

Distinguished by their low superstructure and relatively massive funnel, the 'Wielingens' are the first post-war Belgian-designed and -built vessels. Gun armament includes a 100-mm dual purpose weapon, together with a Goalkeeper 30-mm CIWS soon to be installed.

Above: Wielingen has no helicopter facilities, but is well armed for a small ship. First of four vessels, Wielingen and her sisters provide Belgium's only ocean-going escort capability

Modern Frigates (Part 2)

Frigates today are ostensibly designed for anti-submarine warfare, and in major fleets are used in this role. In smaller nations, however, such vessels must serve a variety of purposes.

The Brazilian general-purpose frigate Constitução (F42) was built by Vosper Thornycroft in England as part of the six-ship 'Niteroi' class order. She is armed with four single launchers for the MM.38 Exocet as well as two single Mk 8 4.5-in (114-mm) DP guns and Sea Cat SAM systems.

Other than the Soviet Union and China, which each produce their own frigates, most non-Western nations tend to buy either off-the-shelf standard frigate designs in service with NATO navies or, if they can afford it, a vessel customized for their own particular requirements. One of the most recent examples of the latter is the Saudi Arabian order to France for four Type F2000 frigates. In terms of capabilities these vessels will be able to outperform most of the frigates in service with the NATO navies today. They are based on state-of-the-art electronics, and because of their sophistication may well cause some operating problems to their owner.

At the other end of the scale is the large missile corvette, or small light frigate depending on which view you take of the type. These are being bought by a number of navies as cheaper alternatives to more conventional frigates as replacements for World War II units that are now hopelessly out of date.

With its overall naval policy in mind, the Soviet Union subscribes to both philosophies, producing highly sophisticated designs for ASW operations and smaller, cheaper but still highly capable designs for surface strike missions. Surprisingly, it is only in recent years that the USSR has built a frigate-type class with an integral onboard ASW helicopter. In practically all Western nations, a frigate without its own helicopter is nowadays the exception.

Although China designs her own frigates she still has a long way to go before she catches up with either the West or the Soviet Union. Lacking modern technology sources, China has frigate classes that appear robust enough, but certainly do not match up in terms of electronics and armament subsystems, to the extent that the ASW weapons carried are still depth charges or based on 1950s-technology Soviet rocket-launchers. This is all expected to change in the course of the next decade.

A 'Jiangnan' class frigate of the People's Republic of China leads a mixed flotilla of 'Riga' class frigates and 'Huchwan' class torpedo-armed hydrofoils in a demonstration of China's rapidly-expanding naval power.

'Parchim' class

Previously known to NATO as the 'BAL-COM-4' class (Baltic Combatant No. 4) and to the technical press as the 'Koralle' class, the 'Parchim' class of light frigates is believed to be based on the Soviet 'Grisha' design with local modifications to suit its use by the East German navy. Built at the Peenewerft shipyard at Wolgast from the late 1970s onwards, the 'Parchims' have replaced the unsatisfactory 'Hai III' class of large patrol craft that was constructed in the mid to late 1960s. The new class is designed primarily for coastal ASW operations, but carries the heavy AA armament characteristic of Warsaw Pact naval units operating in the Baltic.

Eighteen ships are in service (the *Wismar, Parchim, Bad Doberan, Bützow, Perleberg, Lübz, Teterow, Purna, Waren, Gädebusch, Bergen, Güstrow, Ribnitz-Damgarten, Ludwigslust* and four others) while up to 12 of an enlarged 'Parchim II' class are likely to be built with the first being completed in 1987. The 77-m (252.6-ft) 'Parchim II' displaces 1,000 tons standard and has a revised armament fit (including a single 76-mm/3-in DP gun aft, an ADG-630 30-mm CIWS forward and two twin 533-mm/21-in torpedo tubes). A new radome covered air-search radar is thought to replace the older 'Strut Curve'.

Specification
'Parchim' class
Displacement: 960 tons standard and 1,200 tons full load
Dimensions: length 72.5 m (237.9 ft); beam 9.4 m (30.8 ft); draught 3.5 m (11.5 ft)
Propulsion: two diesels delivering 8948 kW (12,000 hp) to two shafts
Speed: 25 kts
Armament: two quadruple launchers for 32 SA-N-5 'Grail' SAMs, one twin 57-mm AA and one twin 30-mm AA guns, four single 406-mm (16-in) tubes for anti-submarine torpedoes, two 12-barrel RBU6000 250-mm (9.84-in) ASW rocket-launchers with 120 rockets, two

racks for 24 depth charges, and between 20 and 30 mines according to type
Aircraft: none
Electronics: one 'Strut Curve' air-search radar, one 'Muff Cob' fire-control radar, one TSR333 navigation radar, one 'High Pole-B' IFF, two 'Watch Dog' ECM systems, two 16-barrel chaff launchers, one medium-frequency hull-mounted sonar, and (in some on starboard side of the main superstructure) one high-frequency dipping sonar
Complement: 60

'Grisha' class

Built as a *malyy protivolodochnyy korabl'* (MPK, or small anti-submarine ship) between 1968 and 1974 the **'Grisha I' class** provided more specialized ASW capability than the earlier 'Mirka' and 'Petya' classes. Initial production ended after 15 had been produced, to be followed from 1974 at the Leninskaya yard by series production of 11 **'Grisha II'** *pogranichnyy storozhevoy korabl'* (PSKR, or border patrol ship) units for the Maritime Border Directorate of the KGB. These differed from the 'Grisha Is' in having a second twin 57-mm AA mount substituted for the SA-N-4 'Gecko' SAM launcher forward and in having no 'Pop Group' fire-control radar. From 1975 onwards to the present the **'Grisha III' class** has been the Soviet navy's production model. A 'Bass Tilt' gun fire-control radar (atop a small deckhouse to port on the aft superstructure) has replaced the 'Muff Cob' system on the earlier versions, whilst the space previously occupied by this radar has been taken up by a single 30-mm CIWS. To date, 32 'Grisha IIIs' have been built with production only now switching to the **'Grisha V' class** at Leninskaya. This has a single 76-mm gun aft, only one RBU 6000 (on the port side) and a 'Strut Pair' air-search radar in place of 'Strut Curve'. By early 1987 four 'Grisha Vs' were in service.

Specification
'Grisha' classes
Displacement: 950 tons standard and 1,200 tons full load
Dimensions: length 72.0 m (236.2 ft) beam 10.0 m (32.8 ft) draught 3.7 m (12.1 ft)
Propulsion: CODAG arrangement with one gas turbine and four diesels delivering power to two shafts
Speed: 30 kts
Armament: one twin launcher for 18 SA-N-4 'Gecko' SAMs, one twin 57-mm AA and ('Grisha III' only) one 30-mm AA CIWS gun, two 12-barrel RBU6000 250-mm (9.84-in) ASW rocket-launchers with 120 rockets, two twin 533-mm (21-in) tubes for anti-

submarine torpedoes, two rails for 12 depth charges, and between 20 and 30 mines according to type
Aircraft: none
Electronics: one 'Strut Curve' air-search radar, one 'Pop Group' SAM fire-control radar, one 'Muff Cob' or ('Grisha III' only) 'Bass Tilt' gun fire-control radar, two 'Watch Dog' ECM systems, one 'High Pole-B' IFF, one medium-frequency hull-mounted sonar, and one high-frequency dipping sonar
Complement: 80

Right: A 'Grisha I' unit in heavy weather shows that there is no bow sonar dome. There is a hull set and a dipping sonar which is housed in the deckhouse aft beneath the hump-shaped superstructure.

The 'Grisha II' class light frigate is used solely by the maritime element of the KGB for protecting Soviet territorial waters and to prevent people escaping to the West by boat.

Above: The 'Grisha II' retains the same ASW armament as the Soviet navy units, but has a second twin 57-mm gun forward in place of the SA-N-4 'Gecko' SAM launcher bin system.

'Riga' class

Built at the Kaliningrad, Nikolayev and Komsomolsk shipyards in the Soviet Union, the 64 units (including eight for export) of the **'Riga' class** were the design successors to the six slightly older 'Kola' class escorts. Always designated *storozhevoy korabl'* (SKR, or patrol ship) by the Soviets, the class has proved to be an excellent coastal-defence design and followed the Soviet practice in the 1950s of building flushdecked hulls with a sharply raised forecastle. Over the years the 'Rigas' have become one of the larger Soviet ship classes, and have been exported in some numbers. In all, 17 were transferred; two to Bulgaria, five to East Germany (of which one was burnt out in an accident soon after being taken over), two to Finland and eight to Indonesia. Most of these units have now been either scrapped or placed in reserve, and China built four further units in her shipyards from components supplied by the Soviets. At present the Soviet navy has some 34 'Rigas' in active service with another 14 in reserve. A small number of the operational vessels were modified during the 1970s, a twin 25-mm AA gun being added on each side of the funnel and a dipping sonar fitted abreast of the bridge. Before this, however, most units were fitted with two hand-loaded 16-barrel RBU2500 ASW rocket-launchers forward to replace the original ASW armament of a single MBU600 'Hedgehog' and four aft-mounted BMB-2 depth-charge throwers. One of the active units was also fitted with a taller stack cap and several 'Bell' series ECM systems, one high-frequency

Specification
'Riga' class
Displacement: 1,260 tons standard and 1,510 tons full load
Dimensions: length 91.5 m (300.2 ft); beam 10.1 m (33.1 ft); draught 3.2 m (10.5 ft)
Propulsion: geared steam turbines delivering power to two shafts
Speed: 28 kts

Armament: three single 100-mm (3.9-in) DP, two twin 37-mm AA and (some units) two twin 25-mm AA guns, two 16-barrel RBU2500 250-mm (9.84-in) ASW rocket-launchers with 160 rockets, two racks for 24 depth charges, and one twin or triple 533-mm (21-in) tube mounting for two or three anti-ship torpedoes
Aircraft: none

One of the most popular pastimes practised by the Soviets in warm climates is relaxing on deck away from their spartan living conditions, as the majority of the crew of this 'Riga' class frigate is doing.

Electronics: one 'Slim Net' air-search radar, one 'Sun Visor-B' fire-control radar, one 'Wasp Head' fire-control radar, one 'Don-2' or 'Neptune' navigation radar, one 'High Pole-B' IFF, two 'Square Head' IFF, two 'Watch Dog' ECM systems, and one high-frequency hull-mounted sonar
Complement: 175

Now obsolete, the 'Riga' class remains in service with the Soviet navy in relatively large numbers for second-line duties and as training vessels.

Seen during the 'Okean '70' exercise off the Philippines, this 'Riga' class frigate of the Pacific Fleet is still useful in that area because one of the potential adversaries is the similarly equipped navy of the People's Republic of China.

The two Finnish navy 'Riga' class frigates Hameenmaa and Uusimaa lead a group of patrol boats. In 1980 the latter was stricken to provide spares for her sister ship, which was redesignated as a minelayer.

'Petya' classes

The 18 units of the **'Petya I' class** were constructed at the Kaliningrad and Komsomolsk shipyards between 1961 and 1964. From the latter year until 1969 both shipyards switched to building a total of 27 **'Petya II' class** units, which differed from their predecessors in having an extra quintuple 406-mm (16-in) ASW torpedo tube mounting in place of the two aft ASW rocket-launchers. The two forward-mounted RBU2500 rocket-launchers were also exchanged for the RBU6000 system with automatic loading facilities. Both variants also had mine rails.

From 1973 onwards eight 'Petya I' vessels were modified to give the **'Petya I Mod' class.** The conversion involved the addition of a medium-frequency variable-depth sonar (VDS) system in a new raised stern deckhouse, which necessitated the removal of the mine rails. A further three units were then converted as trials vessels and given the same sub-group designation: one was fitted with a larger VDS system with no deckhouse at the stern; the second had a deckhouse installed abaft the stack (following the removal of the torpedo tubes) and fitted with a complex reel/winch installation that may be either a towed non-acoustic ASW sensor or a towed surface-ship sonar array; the third vessel had a small box-like structure built at the stern for a towed sensor deployed from a hole in the stern. In 1978 a single unit of the Petya II type was also converted to a trial vessel and given the title **'Petya II Mod' class.** The conversion was along the lines of the 'Petya I Mod' but with a slimmer VDS deckhouse which allowed retention of the minelaying capability.

In late 1986 the Soviet navy had a total of seven 'Petya I', 11 'Petya I Mod' including three trials vessels, 21 'Petya II' and one 'Petya II Mod' (for trials) in service with all four fleets. A further five 'Petya II' of the Soviet navy were transferred to Vietnam (three ships) and Ethiopia (two ships), whilst another 16 export ships were specifically built with a triple 533-mm (21-in) torpedo tube mounting and RBU2500 ASW rocket-launchers for the navies of India (12 ships), Vietnam (two ships) and Syria (two ships). The 'Petyas' are currently rated by the Soviets as *stororzhevoy korabl'* (SKR, or patrol ship).

Specification
'Petya' classes
Displacement: 950 tons standard and 1,150 tons or ('Petya II') 1,160 tons full load
Dimensions: length 81.8 m (268.4 ft) or ('Petya II') 82.5 m (270.7 ft); beam 9.1 m (29.9 ft); draught 2.9 m (9.5 ft)
Propulsion: CODAG arrangement with two diesels and two gas turbines delivering power to three shafts
Speed: 33 kts
Armament: two ('Petya I Mod' towed-array trials ship one) twin 76-mm (3-in) DP guns, four 16-barrel RBU 2500 250-mm (9.84-in) ASW rocket-launchers with 320 rockets or ('Petya II' and 'Petya II Mod' only) two 12-barrel RBU6000 250-mm (9.84-in) ASW rocket-launchers with 120 rockets or ('Petya I Mod' only) two 16-barrel RBU2500 launchers with 160 rockets, two ('Petya I Mod' only one) racks for 24 or 12 depth charges, one ('Petya II Mod' two and 'Petya I Mod' towed-array trials ship none) 533-mm (21-in) quintuple tube mounting for five or 10 anti-submarine torpedoes, and between 20 and 30 mines (none in 'Petya I Mod') according to type
Aircraft: none
Electronics: one 'Slim Net' or 'Strut Curve' air-search radar, one 'Hawk Screech' 76-mm gun fire-control radar, one 'Don-2' navigation radar, one 'High Pole-B' and (only in 'Petya I') two 'Square Head' IFF, two 'Watch Dog' ECM systems one high-frequency hull-mounted sonar, one high-frequency dipping sonar, and (in some, see text) one variable-depth sonar
Complement: 98

This unmodified member of the 'Petya I' class of light frigates is easily identified by the presence of the RBU2500 ASW rocket-launchers in front of the bridge and the lack of any stern superstructure for a variable-depth sonar system.

Above: One task sometimes undertaken by the 'Petyas' in the absence of any larger units is that of the 'Tattle-tale'; here a 'Petya II' shadows the carrier HMS Eagle in 1975 while the latter was on an exercise.

The 'Petya II' differs from the earlier 'Petya I' in having a heavier ASW armament in the form of RBU6000 automatic rocket-launchers and extra torpedo tubes.

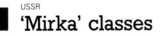

'Mirka' classes

Built between 1964 and 1965 at the Kaliningrad shipyard, the nine **'Mirka I' class** vessels were followed on the stocks during the latter half of 1965 and 1966 by nine **'Mirka II' class** units. They were constructed as a more specialized variation of the early 'Petya' design and were initially rated by the Soviets as *malyy protivolodochnyy korabl'* (MPK, or small anti-submarine ship). As with some other ASW-oriented ship classes, this was changed in 1978 to *stororzhevoy korabl'* (SKR, or patrol ship).

The various vessels of the two 'Mirka' classes serve only with the Soviet Baltic and Black Sea Fleets. The propulsion plant is similar in concept to the combined diesel and gas turbine plant of the 'Petyas', with a high maximum speed for use in attacks on submerged submarines. The basic difference in the two variants is that the 'Mirka IIs' lack the two aft 250-mm (9.84-in) RBU6000 ASW rocket-launchers of the

The 'Mirka I' and 'Mirka II' units of the Black Sea fleet are regularly deployed to the Mediterranean squadron to provide ASW protection to higher-value surface units and the many deep water anchorages that the Soviet navy has in the region.

'Mirka I' but have instead an additional quintuple ASW torpedo tube mounting for 406-mm (16-in) electric torpedoes fitted between the bridge and the mast. Also, the later 'Mirka II' units have a 'Strut Curve' air-search radar in place of the earlier ships' 'Slim Net' set. Almost all units of both classes have now been fitted with a dipping sonar either instead of the internal depth-charge rack in the port side of the stern (Mirka 1) or in a housing abaft the aft gun position. This is meant for use in areas like the Baltic where oceanographic conditions for ASW operations are notoriously difficult. The 'Mirka' series is expected to serve on into the early 1990s before replacement.

Specification
'Mirka' classes
Displacement: 950 tons standard and 1,150 tons full load
Dimensions: 82.4 m (270.3 ft); beam 9.1 m (29.9 ft); draught 3.0 m (9.8 ft)
Propulsion: CODAG arrangement with two diesels and two gas turbines delivering power to two shafts
Speed: 35 kts

Armament: two twin 76-mm (3-in) DP guns, four ('Mirka I') or two ('Mirka II') 12-barrel RBU6000 250-mm (9.84-in) ASW rocket-launchers with 240 or 120 rockets, and one ('Mirka I') or two ('Mirka II') 533-mm (21-in) quintuple tube mountings for five or 10 anti-submarine torpedoes
Aircraft: none

Electronics: one 'Slim Net' or (some 'Mirka II' only) 'Strut Curve' air-search radar, one 'Hawk Screech' 76-mm gun fire-control radar, one 'Don-2' navigation radar, two 'High Pole-B' IFF, two 'Square Head' IFF, two 'Watch Dog' ECM systems, one medium-frequency hull-mounted sonar, and (in most units) one high-frequency dipping sonar
Complement: 98

All the nine 'Mirka II' class frigates built have now been fitted with a new type of dipping sonar in place of the internal depth charge rack on the port side of the stern to improve their ASW capabilities in the Mediterranean and Baltic.

USSR
'Koni' class

Although constructed in the Soviet Union at the Zelenodolsk Shipyard on the Black Sea, the **'Koni' class** of *storozhevoy korabl'* (SKR, or patrol ship) is intended only for export, a mere one unit, the ***Timofey Ul'yantsev***, being retained by the Soviets as a crew training ship for the naval personnel from those countries which have bought vessels of this class. There are two distinct sub-classes, the **'Koni Type II' class** differing from the **'Koni Type I' class** in having the space between the funnel and the aft superstructure occupied by an extra deckhouse believed to contain air-conditioning units for use in tropical climates.

The countries which have taken delivery of 'Konis' include East Germany with four Type Is (***Rostock, Berlin***, and two others, pennant nos *143* and *144*), Yugoslavia with two Type Is (***Split*** and ***Koper***), Algeria with three Type IIs (***Raïs Kellik, Mourad Raïs*** and ***Raïs Torfo***), and Cuba with two Type IIs (***Mariel*** and one name not known). The Yugoslavs have modified their units to carry a pair of aft firing SS-N-2B 'Styx' container launchers on either side of the aft deckhouse. Libya has taken delivery of two Type IIs, one of which is called the ***El Haru***. These differ from other 'Konis' in having a narrow deckhouse projecting forwards from the bridge, only one RBU 6000 and two paired forward firing launchers at upper deck level for SS-N-2C 'Styx'. A 'Plank Shave' missile targeting radar has been added atop the bridge and two single 400-mm (15.75-in) ASW torpedo tubes have been added either side of the new deckhouse.

Specification
'Koni' class
Displacement: 1,700 tons standard and 1,900 tons full load
Dimensions: length 95.0 m (311.7 ft);

beam 12.8 m (42.0 ft); draught 4.2 m (13.8 ft)
Propulsion: CODAG arrangement with one diesel and two gas turbines delivering power to three shafts
Speed: 27 kts
Armament: one twin launcher for 18 SA-N-4 'Gecko' SAMs, two twin 76-mm

(3-in) DP and two twin 30-mm AA guns, two 12-barrel RBU6000 250-mm (9.84-in) ASW rocket-launchers with 120 rockets, two racks for 24 depth charges, and between 20 and 30 mines according to type
Aircraft: none
Electronics: one 'Strut Curve' air-

search radar, one 'Pop Group' SAM fire-control radar, one 'Hawk Screech' 76-mm fire-control radar, one 'Drum Tilt' 30-mm gun fire-control radar, one 'High Pole-B' IFF, two 'Watch Dog' ECM systems, and one medium-frequency hull-mounted sonar
Complement: 110

The Type I 'Koni' class frigate is built in the Soviet Union primarily for export. The Type II differs in having additional superstructure, which houses air conditioning systems for use in tropical climates.

The East German navy has four Type I 'Koni' class frigates, the Rostock *(141) and the* Berlin *(142). They differ slightly from other 'Koni' class units in having no chaff launchers, and carry East German-built TSR333 navigation radars in place of the more usual Don-2 sets.*

'Krivak' classes

In 1970 the first unit of the gas turbine-powered **'Krivak I' class** of *bol'shoy protivolodochnyy korabl'* (BPK, or large anti-submarine ship) entered service with the Soviet navy. Built at the Zhdanov Shipyard in Leningrad, the Kaliningrad Shipyard and the Kamish-Burun Shipyard in Kerch between 1970 and 1982, 21 units of this variant were constructed. In 1976 the **'Krivak II' class**, of which 11 were built at Kaliningrad between that year and 1981, was first seen. This differed from the previous class in having single 100-mm (3.9-in) guns substituted for the twin 76-mm (3-in) turrets of the earlier version, and a larger variable-depth sonar housing at the stern. Both classes were re-rated to *storozhevoy korabl'* (SKR, or patrol ship) status in the late 1970s, possibly in view of what some Western observers considered to be the type's deficiencies in terms of size and limited endurance for ASW operations in open waters.

The first unit of the **'Krivak III' class**, designed to remedy some of the probable defects, appeared in mid-1984. This has a helicopter hangar and flight deck in place of the aft gun turrets and SA-N-4 'Gecko' SAM launcher, and the forward quadruple SS-N-14 'Silex' ASW missile-launcher is replaced by a single 100-mm DP gun turret. The variable-depth sonar system is retained beneath the flight deck at the stern, whilst single 30-mm ADG630 CIWS are located on each side of the hangar. The other ASW armament of the 'Krivak I/II' classes and the forward SA-N-4 launcher is also retained. The electronic fit has been altered with the removal of some weapons, the two 'Eye Bowl' SS-N-14 fire-control radars and one of the 'Pop Group' SAM fire-control systems having been removed, and one 'Bass Tilt' fire-control radar having been added. Sonar, ECM and IFF systems have unchanged from earlier 'Krivaks', while full-load tonnage has increased to 3,900 tons. The 'Krivak III' is in slow series production at Kamish Burun for the KGB Maritime Border Guard. Two units are in service with the Soviet Pacific Fleet and at least two more are under construction. A replacement for the 'Krivak' class is due in the 1990s.

Specification
'Krivak' classes
Displacement: 3,000 tons standard and 3,700 tons ('Krivak I') or 3,800 tons ('Krivak II') full load
Dimensions: length 123.5 m (405.2 ft); beam 14.0 m (45.9 ft); draught 4.7 m (15.4 ft)
Propulsion: COGAG arrangement with

four gas turbines delivering power to two shafts
Speed: 32 kts
Armament: one quadruple launcher for SS-N-14 'Silex' anti-submarine missiles, two twin launchers for 36 SA-N-4 'Gecko' SAMs, two twin 76-mm (3-in) DP ('Krivak I') or two single 100-mm (3.9-in) DP ('Krivak II') guns, two 12-barrel RBU6000 250-mm (9.84-in) ASW rocket-launchers with 120 rockets, two quadruple 533-mm (21-in) tube mountings for anti-submarine

torpedoes, and between 20 and 40 mines according to type
Aircraft: none
Electronics: one 'Head Net-C' air-search radar, two 'Pop Group' SAM fire-control radars, two 'Eye Bowl' 'Silex' fire-control radars, one 'Owl Screech' ('Krivak I') or 'Kite Screech' ('Krivak II') gun fire-control radar, one 'Don Kay' or 'Palm Frond' navigation radar, two 'Bell Shroud' ECM systems, two 'Bell Squat' ECM systems, four 16-barrel chaff launchers, one 'High Pole-

The long rack of the bow with the anchor well forward betrays the presence of a large bow sonar dome for a medium frequency active sonar. For underlayer searching a variable-depth low-frequency sonar system is fitted aft.

B' or 'Salt Pot' IFF, one medium-frequency hull-mounted sonar, and one medium-frequency variable-depth sonar
Complement: 220

Right: A 'Krivak I' displays its major ASW weapons, with the massive quadruple SS-N-14 'Silex' launcher dwarfing the pair of horseshoe shaped RBU 6000 12-barrelled rocket launchers ahead of the bridge. Also visible are the starboard 533-mm (21-in) torpedo tubes.

Opposite page: A 'Krivak I' in the English Channel shows the typically Soviet multitude of electronic and sensor gear with which the class is equipped.

Above: The 'Krivak I' frigate Storozhevoy *is seen in the North Atlantic. A good gauge of the number of crew a Soviet warship carries can be obtained by counting the number of liferaft containers the vessel carries, and multiplying by 10 (the number of persons carried by each raft).*

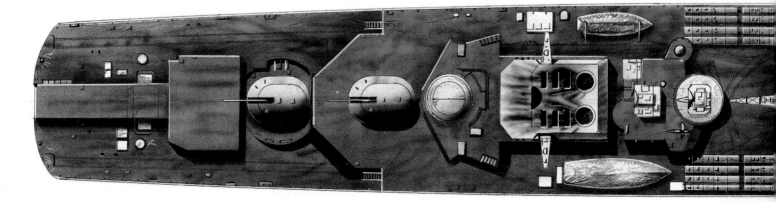

`Krivak 11´ class patrol ship

Below: The 11 'Krivak IIs' differ from their 21 predecessors in having single 100-mm guns in place of twin 76-mm weapons in the two aft turrets. Classified by the Soviets as a Storozhevoy Korabl (SKR, or patrol vessel), the 'Krivak' I or II is armed with a massive quadruple launcher for SS-N-14 ASW missiles; two twin launchers in pop-up mountings fore and aft for SA-N-4 air defence missiles; two RBU6000 ASW rocket-launchers behind the forward SAM mount; and eight 533-mm (21-in) torpedo tubes amidships.

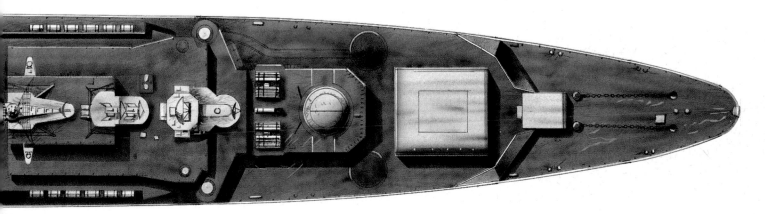

'Poti' class

Although slowly being phased out following the introduction of the 'Pauk' class the **'Poti'** class of *maly protivolodochny korabl* (MPK, or small anti-submarine ship) will still be in service for a number of years. A total of 70 were built between 1961-8 of which three (V31-33) were transferred to the Romanian navy in 1970 and three to the Bulgarian navy in 1975. Of the 64 used by the Soviet navy only 51 remain in service with the others either scrapped or placed in reserve. The 'Potis' were the first large gas turbine vessels built by the Soviets and remain their fastest surface ASW ships. The two propeller shafts are mounted in special thrust tubes which run the length of the poop, the gas turbines exhausting through ports above them in the transom. When not in use the ports are closed by sliding covers. The turbines also power air compressors which duct into the thrust tubes for additional propulsive power. The larger 'Mirka' MPK class uses a similar propulsion system.

The earliest units built had an open twin 57-mm AA gun mount, two 16 barrel RBU2500 203-mm (8-in) manually reloaded ASW rocket launchers with 96 rockets, and two single 400-mm (15.7-in) ASW torpedo tubes whilst the three Romanian craft had the same guns and ASW rocket launchers but two single 533-mm (21-in) ASW torpedo tubes in place of the 400-mm (15.7-in) mountings. All the later Soviet units and the Bulgarian craft had fully automatic twin AK725 57-mm AA guns and 250-mm (9.8-in) RBU 6000 ASW rocket launchers with 72 rockets and four 400-mm (15.7-in) ASW torpedo tubes installed.

Specification
'Poti' class
Displacement: 400 tons standard, 480 tons full load
Dimensions: length 59.4 m (194.9 ft), beam 7.9 m (25.9 ft) draught 2 m (6.6 ft)
Propulsion: two diesels and two gas turbines in CODAG arrangement delivering 48,000 hp (35794 kW) to two shafts
Speed: 38 kts

Armament: one twin 57-mm AK725 AA gun, four single 400-mm (15.7-in) ASW torpedo tubes (no reloads), two RBU 6000 ASW rocket launchers with 72 rockets.
Electronics: one 'Strut Curve' air search radar, one 'Spin Trough' navigation radar, one 'Muff Cob' fire control radar, one 'High Pole' B IFF system, two 'Watch Dog' ECM systems, one high frequency hull sonar, one side mounted medium frequency dipping sonar (of 'Hormone helicopter' type) in a number of units in Pacific and Baltic Fleet areas
Complement: 80

Above: The Poti *class were the first large gas-turbine powered vessels to be built for the Soviet Navy*

Below: The 38-knot 'Potis' remain the fastest Soviet ASW vessels.

'Pauk' class

In 1977 the first **'Pauk'** class *maly protivolodochny korabl* (MPK, or small anti-submarine ship) was laid down in the Baltic area for completion in 1979 as the long term replacement for the 'Poti' class. Now in series construction in the Baltic and Pacific Fleet areas the design shares the same hull form as the 'Tarantul' class missile corvettes but has had a 2 m (6.6 ft) extension added to the stern. This allows for a medium frequency dipping sonar housing, as carried by the 'Grisha I, III, V' class MPKs, for use in the difficult ASW environments of the northern Pacific and Baltic Sea. The propulsion plant has also been changed from the gas-turbines of the 'Tarantul' to an all diesel type. A comprehensive outfit of communications antennae indicates that the 'Pauks' operate under the control of a shore based or large BPK ASW command post. They have also been seen operating in conjunction with land based Mil Mi-14 'Haze A' ASW helicopters on area searches. A number, belonging to the Pacific Fleet, are believed to be operated by the KGB maritime border guard.

The only variation seen to date has occurred from the fourth unit onwards which has the pilothouse one half deck higher. By 1987 a total of 24 'Pauks' were in service with both the Baltic and Pacific Fleets whilst India is due to be the first export customer, having apparently ordered six, with the first two due for delivery in late 1987.

Specification
'Pauk' class
Displacement: 480 tons standard, 580 tons full load
Dimensions: length 58 m (190.3 ft), beam 10.5 m (34.4 ft), draught 2.5 m (8.2 ft)
Propulsion: four diesels delivering 14914 kW (20,000 hp) to two shafts
Speed: 34 kts
Armament: one quadruple SA-N-5 Grail SAM launcher with 16 missiles, one single 76-mm (3-in) DP gun, one 30-mm ADG6-30 CIWS, four single 400-mm (15.7-in) ASW torpedo tubes

(no reloads), two five barrel RBU1000 300-mm (11.8-in) ASW rocket launchers with 60 rockets, two depth charge racks with 12 depth charges
Electronics: one 'Plank Shave' air search radar, one 'Spin Trough' surface search/navigation radar, one 'Bass Tilt' fire control radar, several ECM systems, one medium frequency hull sonar, one medium frequency dipping sonar.
Complement: 60

The 'Pauk' class small anti-submarine ships are enlarged 'Tarantul' hulls designed to replace the 'Poti' class.

USSR
'Nanuchka' classes

Classed by the Soviets as a *malyy raketnyy korabl'* (MRK, or small rocket ship), the 17 units of the **'Nanuchka I' class** were built between 1969 and 1974 at Petrovsky, Leningrad with a modified variant, the **'Nanuchka II' class** being built there and on the Pacific at the Ulis yard, Vladivostok from 1977. Now in slow series construction (one per year) the 'Nanuchkas' are considered by Western observers to be coastal missile corvettes, although the fact they are very often seen quite far from home waters (on deployment to such areas as the North Sea, the Mediterranean and the Pacific) tends to put them more in the very light frigate category, especially when the firepower of the class is considered. The anti-ship missile carried is the Mach 0.9 SS-N-9 'Siren', which can be fitted to carry either a 500-kg (1,102-lb) HE or 200-kiloton nuclear warhead over a range of 110 km (68 miles). The SS-N-9 uses a dual active radar and infra-red terminal homing system, with third-party targeting and mid-course corrections to guide it in over the horizon engagements.

In 1977, the first of three **'Nanuchka II'** units was delivered to India. The *Vijay Durg* (K71), *Sindhu Durg* (K72) and the *Hos Durg* (K73) were designed for export, and differ from Soviet boats in having twin SS-N-2B/C 'Styx' missiles in place of the triple SS-N-9. As many as five more boats are being built or are on order for the Indian navy. Algeria has received four vessels from 1982, the *Raïs Hamidou* (801), the *Salah Raïs* (802), the *Raïs Ali* (803) and a fourth of the class delivered in 1987. Libya also took delivery of four 'Nanuchka IIs' in the 1980s, the *Ean Mara, Ean al Gazala, Ean Zara* and the *Ean Zaquit*. The *Ean Mara* was sunk and one of the others was seriously damaged if not sunk by US carrier aircraft on the night of 24/25 March 1986. Libya will probably obtain replacements from the USSR.

The 'Nanuchka I' class of small missile ship carries the SS-N-9 'Siren' anti-ship missile as its main armament.

A 'Nanuchka I' small missile ship underway. The export 'Nanuchka II' class differs mainly in carrying SS-N- 2B 'Styx' missile launchers, whilst the latest Soviet variant, the 'Nanuchka III', has a different gun armament.

Specification
'Nanuchka' classes
Displacement: 780 tons standard and 900 tons full load
Dimensions: length 59.3 m (194.6 ft); beam 12.6 m (41.3 ft); draught 2.4 m (7.9 ft)

Propulsion: three paired diesels delivering power to three shafts
Speed: 32 kts
Armament: two triple container-launchers for SS-N-9 'Siren' anti-ship missiles, one twin launcher for 18 SA-N-4 'Gecko' SAMs, one twin 57-mm AA gun or ('Nanuchka III' only) one 76-mm (3-in) DP and one 30-mm CIWS guns
Aircraft: none
Electronics: one 'Band Stand' air- and surface-search radar, one 'Peel Pair' surface-search and navigation radar, one 'Spar Stump' surface-search and navigation radar, two 'Fish Bowl' SAM fire-control radars, one 'Muff Cob' or ('Nanuchka III' only) 'Bass Tilt' fire-control radar, one 'High Pole-B' IFF, two passive ECM systems, and two 16-barrel chaff launchers
Complement: 70

USSR
'Tarantul' class

Built at Petrovsky, Leningrad, the first **'Tarantul I' class** unit was completed in 1978. Like the 'Nanuchka', the class is designated a *malyy raketnyy korabl'* (MRK, or small rocket ship), but only two units were retained by the Soviet navy. Other 'Tarantul Is' have been built at the Volodarsky shipyard at Rybinsk for export. They include two units, the *Gornik* (434) and the *Hutnik* (435) for the Polish navy (with six more deliveries expected), and four units for East Germany, the only known name being the *Albin Koebis* (772). India is thought to have ordered five for delivery during 1988 to 1990. In order to rectify some design shortcomings and to make the class suitable for Soviet use,

the **'Tarantul II'** entered production in 1981 at the Sreidniy Neva (Kolpino) shipyard, and at the original Petrovsky yard. By 1987 19 had been built with production running at about three units per year. One unit was completed in 1981 to the experimental **'Tarantul III'** design, with two twin over-and-under missile container-launchers for the long-range supersonic SS-N-22 derivative of the SS-N-9 'Siren' in place of the original SS-N-2C 'Styx' system.

The 'Tarantuls' deploy a modified version of the Soviet navy's small ship armament of a fully automatic 76-mm (3-in) DP gun, capable of 120 rounds per minute, and two 30-mm 6-barrel Gatling gun mounts that in the Soviet

navy have the designation AK-630 (the ADG630 designation often used being a NATO nickname).

Specification
'Tarantul' classes
Displacement: 480 tons standard and 580 tons full load
Dimensions: length 56.0 m (183.7 ft); beam 10.5 m (34.4 ft); draught 2.5 m (8.2 ft)
Propulsion: CODOG arrangement with two diesels and two gas turbines delivering power to two shafts
Speed: 36 kts

Armament: two twin container-launchers for SS-N-2C 'Styx' anti-ship missiles, one quadruple launcher for 16 SA-N-5 'Grail' SAMs, one 76-mm (3-in) DP and two 30-mm CIWS guns
Aircraft: none
Electronics: one 'Band Stand' air- and surface-search radar or 'Plank Shave' surface-search radar, one (not in early units) 'Light Bulb' targeting data system, one 'Spin Trough' navigation radar, one 'Bass Tilt' gun fire-control radar, one 'High Pole-B' IFF, one 'Square Head' IFF, four passive ECM systems, and two 16-barrel chaff launchers
Complement: 50

ITALY

'Esmeraldas' class

Although strictly speaking rated as missile corvettes rather than small light frigates, the units of the **'Esmeraldas' class** must, because of their multipurpose capabilities, be ranked with the latter. Ordered in 1978 from the Italian firm CNR del Tirreno, the design is based on the **'Wadi M'ragh (now 'Assad') class** for Libya but with more powerful diesel engines, the addition of a helicopter landing platform amidships and a SAM launcher aft of the bridge. All six units of the class, the **Esmeraldas** (CM11), **Manabi** (CM12), **Los Rios** (CM13), **El Oro** (CM14), **Galapagos** (CM15) and **Laja** (CM16) are in service with the Ecuadorean navy as the country's primary antiship surface strike force. The helicopter platform is used to operate one of the navy's three Aérospatiale Alouette III light helicopters in the surface-search and air-sea-rescue roles as circumstances dictate. The anti-ship missile system fitted is the 65-km (40.4-mile) range MM.40 Exocet, with two banks (each of three single container-launchers, firing outwards) located between the landing platform and the bridge. The SAM system fitted is the lightweight four-round launcher version of the Italian Albatros weapon system which uses the Aspide multi-role missile. Only self-defence ASW torpedo tubes are fitted, together with a hull-mounted sonar set, for sub-surface warfare operations.

Specifications
'Esmeraldas' class
Displacement: 620 tons standard and 685 tons full load
Dimensions: length 62.3 m (204.4 ft); beam 9.3 m (30.5 ft); draught 2.5 (8.2 ft)
Propulsion: four MTU diesels delivering 18195 kW (24,400 hp) to four shafts
Speed: 37 kts
Armament: six single container-launchers for MM.40 Exocet anti-ship missiles, one Albatros quadruple launcher for four Aspide SAMs, one 76-mm (3-in) DP and one twin 40-mm AA gun, and two triple 324-mm (12.76-in) ILAS-3 tube mountings for six

The Galapagos (CM15) is the fifth unit of the 'Esmeraldas' class, built in Italy for Ecuador. The quadruple Albatros SAM launcher behind the bridge superstructure and mast fires the multi-role Aspide missile.

Whitehead A244/S anti-submarine torpedoes
Aircraft: provision for one light helicopter on a landing pad
Electronics: one RAN10S air- and surface-search radar, one Orion 1OX fire-control radar, one Orion 2OX fire-control radar, one Decca TM1226 navigation radar, one IPN20 data information system, one Gamma ESM system, and one Diodon hull-mounted sonar
Complement: 51

Although more correctly classed as a missile corvette, the Ecuadorian navy's 'Esmeraldas' class has more firepower per ship than a number of light frigate classes. They are armed with six MM.40 Exocets, a quadruple Albatros SAM launcher, guns and torpedoes.

WEST GERMANY/ARGENTINA
'MEKO 140A16' class

As part of the Argentine navy's modernization plans, a contract was signed in October 1980 with the West German firm of Blohm und Voss for six **'MEKO 140A16' class** ships, to be built (to a light frigate design scaled down from the Meko 360 destroyer plan) under licence at the AFNE shipyard in Rio Santiago, Ensenada and known locally as the **'Espora' class**. The lead ship **Espora** (P4) together with the **Rosales** (P5), commissioned into the Argentine navy in 1985, but the **Spiro** (P6), the **Parker** (P7), the **Robinson** (P8) and the **Seaver** (P9) remain in various stages of completion for economic reasons. The first three differ from the last three units in initially having only a helicopter

landing platform amidships, whereas the others are being constructed with a telescopic hangar to allow the permanent carriage of a light helicopter. The earlier units will be retrofitted at the first available opportunity.

The Argentines are currently studying a plan whereby in order to cut military expenditure they might well have to sell off some of their new ships. Among the ships being considered are two 'Espora' class units. Even so, the 'Esporas' are replacing Argentina's obsolete ex-American destroyers of WWII vintage, and are particularly adapted to ASW and surface action. Such was the delay in construction that the completed vessels have been fitted with eight lightweight, long-

range MM.40 Exocet missiles in place of the four MM.38 originally intended. Although intended for coastal operations, the class could still form an effective surface threat in the South Atlantic against the Falklands or around Cape Horn against Chile.

Specification
'MEKO 140A16' class
Displacement: 1,470 tons standard and 1,700 tons full load
Dimensions: length 91.2 m (299.2 ft); beam 12.2 m (40.0 ft); draught 3.3 m (10.8 ft)

Propulsion: two diesels delivering 16853 kW (22,600 hp) to two shafts
Speed: 27 kts
Armament: eight single container-launchers for MM.40 Exocet anti-ship missiles, one 76-mm (3-in) DP and two twin 40-mm AA guns, two single 12.7-mm (0.5-in) machine-guns, and two triple 324-mm (12.76-in) tube mountings for 12 Whitehead A244/S anti-submarine torpedoes
Aircraft: one Aérospatiale Alouette III or Westland Lynx HAS.Mk 23 light helicopter
Electronics: one DA-05/2 air-search radar, one WM-28 fire-control radar, one Decca TM1226 navigation radar, two LIROD optronic fire-control systems, one Daisy automatic action information system, one RDC-2ABC ESM system, one RCM-2 ESM system, two Dagaie chaff launchers, and one KAE ADS-4 hull-mounted sonar
Complement: 93

As part of the Argentine navy's modernization programme in the 1970s, six West German 'MEKO 140' class light frigates were ordered to be licence-built in Argentina. All will eventually be fitted with a hangar facility.

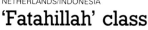

'Fatahillah' class

The **'Fatahillah' class** of Dutch-designed and -built light ASW frigate was ordered in August 1975 as the first major new-build warship type for the Indonesian navy since the acceptance of Soviet ships in the 1950s and 1960s. Classified locally as corvettes, the class numbers only three, the last unit, the *Nala* (363), differing from her two sisterships, the *Fatahillah* (361) and *Malahayati* (362), in having a new type of helicopter landing deck aft which folds around the MBB BO105 light helicopter carried to form a hangar structure; the other ships have no helicopter facilities at all. The armament and electronics fit was procured from a variety of NATO countries, whilst for service in the hot climates of the Far East the ships are fitted with air-conditioned living spaces. They also have a full nuclear-biological-chemical (NBC) warfare citadel, and have fin stabilizers and a combined diesel or gas turbine (CODOG) propulsion plant arrangement for 'quick-start' operations. The magazines fitted can carry a total of 400 120-mm (4.7-in), 3,000 40-mm rounds and 50 chaff rockets. The main radar fire-control system for the guns is backed by a single LIROD television/laser/infra-red optronic fire-control unit.

The anti-ship missile armament fitted to the 'Fatahillahs' is two pairs of container-launchers for the 42 km (26-mile) range MM.38 Exocet, and this primary armament allows the ships to operate as effective supports for the growing force of missile- and gun-armed attack units which are being procured for use among the myriad islands which make up the Indonesian republic.

Specification
'Fatahillah' class
Displacement: 1,160 tons standard and 1,450 tons full load
Dimensions: length 84.0 m (275.6 ft); beam 11.1 m (36.4 ft); draught 3.3 m (10.8 ft)
Propulsion; CODOG arrangement with one Rolls-Royce Olympus TM3B gas turbine delivering 16674 kW (22,360 shp) and two MTU diesels delivering 5966 kW (8,000 hp) to two shafts
Speed: 30 kts
Armament: four single container-launchers for MM.38 Exocet anti-ship missiles, one 120-mm (4.7-in) DP, one (two in *Nala*) 40-mm AA and two single 20-mm AA guns, one twin Bofors 375-

The Indonesian navy 'Fatahillah' class frigate Malhayti (362). The class is being joined by a number of missile and gun armed small surface craft for use among the myriad islands of the Indonesian Archipelago.

mm (14.76-in) ASW rocket-launcher with 54 rockets, and (except in *Nala*) two triple 324-mm (12.76-in) Mk 32 tube mountings for 12 Whitehead A244/S or Mk 44 anti-submarine torpedoes
Aircraft: (*Nala* only) one MBB BO105 light helicopter

Electronics: one DA-05 air- and surface-search radar, one Decca AC1229 navigation radar, one WM-28 fire-control radar, one LIROD optronic fire-control system, one Daisy automatic action information system, one SUSIE I ESM system, two Corvus chaff launchers, one T Mk 6 torpedo decoy system, and one PHS-32 hull-mounted sonar
Complement: 89

The Dutch-built 'Fatahillah' class for the Indonesian navy has proved a success in service. The general-purpose version armed with MM.38 Exocet missiles is shown here.

'Type F2000' class

Ordered from France in October 1980 as a major part of the 14,000 million franc Sawari weapons supply contract, the first of a total of four **'Type F2000' class** frigates was laid down in the Arsenal de Lorient shipyard in 1981 and launched in 1983 for commissioning in early 1985 as *Al Madinah* (702). This was followed by *Hofouf* (704), *Abha* (706) and *Taif* (708), all built at the CNIM shipyard at Seyne-sur-Mer from 1982 onwards and commissioned in late 1985 and 1986.

The class is a very complex design and uses much untried state-of-the-art electronics technology, and may well be too sophisticated for so young a navy as that of Saudi Arabia. The weapon systems are predominantly French in origin, although the surface-to-surface missiles are the Franco-Italian Otomat Mk 2 rather than the more usual member of the Exocet family, which indicates a long-range anti-ship strike role, especially as the Aérospatiale SA.365 Dauphin 2

embarked helicopter will be able to carry out targeting functions.

The presence of the class, in an area of particularly sensitive strategic importance to both major power blocs, will be of considerable interest to all the Arabian Gulf oil states, and the 'Type F2000s' will be matched only by Iraq's Italian 'Lupo' class frigates. A further two large frigates armed with an area-defence SAM system are under consideration, France proposing a 'Type F4000' design equipped with the American single-rail Mk 13

A 'Type F2000' frigate of the Saudi Arabian navy. The purchase of this sophisticated class from France is typical of oil-rich Arab nations buying weapons with more capacity than is necessary.

launcher for Standard SM-1MR missiles and container-launchers for Otomat SSMs. When the Saudis are going to order these vessels is not known at present.

Specification
'Type F2000' class
Displacement: 2,250 tons standard and 2,610 tons full load
Dimensions: length 115.0 m (377.3 ft); beam 12.5 m (41.0 ft); draught 4.7 m (15.4 ft)
Propulsion: four SEMT-Pielstick

diesels delivering 24235 kW (32,500 hp) to two shafts
Speed: 30 kts
Armament: eight single container-launchers for Otomat Mk 2 anti-ship missiles, one octuple Crotale EDIR SAM launcher, one 100-mm (3.9-in) DP and two twin 40-mm AA guns, two single 533-mm (21-in) tubes for F17P wire-guided anti-ship and anti-submarine torpedoes, and two single 324-mm (12.76-in) Mk 32 tubes for Mk 46 anti-submarine torpedoes
Aircraft: one Aérospatiale SA.365 Dauphin 2 light strike helicopter
Electronics: one DRBV 15 air- and surface-search radar, one Castor II fire-control radar, two Decca 1226 navigation radars, one DRBC 32E SAM fire-control radar, one TAVITAC action information system, one DR4000 ESM system, two Dagaie chaff launchers, one Diodon TSM2630 hull-mounted sonar, and one Sorel variable-depth sonar
Complement: 179

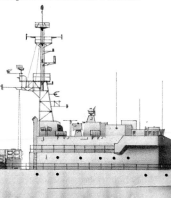

'Niteroi' class

Ordered in September 1970 from the English shipyard Vosper-Thornycroft in ASW and general-purpose versions, the **'Niteroi' class** ships were based on the company's Mk 10 frigate design and were constructed both in the UK and Brazil. The four ASW ships are the *Niteroi* (F40), *Defensor* (F41), *Independencia* (F44) and *União* (F45), and are fitted with the Branik missile-launcher system derived specifically for the Brazilians from the Australian Ikara ASW missile system. The two general-purpose units are the *Constituçâo* (F42) and *Liberal* (F43), and these are similar to the ASW ships though instead of the Branik system they have a second 114-mm (4.5-in) Mk 8 DP gun mount aft (in the place occupied by the Branik system in the ASW ships) and two pairs of container-launchers for MM.38 Exocet SSM missiles located between the bridge and the funnel. Fitted with a combined diesel or gas turbine (CODOG) propulsion plant, the design is considered to be exceptionally economical in terms of manpower when compared with previous warships of this size. A CAAIS action information system is fitted to allow co-ordinated surface-ship ASW and surface strike operations with other vessels of the Brazilian

navy, including the aircraft-carrier *Minas Gerais*. All ships eventually will have their Seacats replaced by Avibras FILA 20-mm AA gun systems, and during 1986-87 the Ikara units have had a pair of MM.38 Exocets fitted. A modified 'Niteroi', the *Brasil* is in service as a training ship with light AA armament and facilities for a pair of Westland Lynx HAS Mk 21 helicopters.

Specification
'Niteroi' class
Displacement: 3,200 tons standard and 3,800 tons full load
Dimensions: length 129.2 m (423.9 ft); beam 13.5 m (44.3 ft); draught 5.5 m (18.0 ft)
Propulsion: CODOG arrangement with two Rolls-Royce Olympus TM3B gas turbines delivering 41759 kW (56,000 shp) and four MTU diesels delivering 11752 kW (15,760 hp) to two shafts
Speed: 30.5 kts
Armament: (F40, F41, F44 and F45) one Branik ASW missile launcher with 10 Ikara missiles, two triple launchers for 60 Seacat SAMs, one 114-mm (4.5-in) DP and two single 40-mm AA guns, one twin Bofors 375-mm (14.76-in) ASW rocket-launcher with 54 rockets,

The 'Niteroi' class ASW vessel União *(F45) has a Branik missile launcher system aft which fires the Australian Mk 44/46 torpedo-equipped Ikara*

two triple 324-mm (12.76-in) STWS-1 tube mountings for six Mk 46 anti-submarine torpedoes, and one rail for five depth charges
Armament: (F42 and F43) four single MM.38 Exocet, two triple Seacat SAM launchers (60 missiles), two 114-mm (4.5-in) DP guns, two 40-mm AA guns, one twin Bofors 375-mm (14.76-in) ASW rocket-launcher with 54 rockets, two triple 324-mm (12.76-in) STWS-1 tube mountings for 12 Mk 46 anti-submarine torpedoes, and one rail for

ASW missile. The magazine carries a total of 10 such missiles, which are targeted by both the bow sonar and the VDS system.

five depth charges
Aircraft: one Westland Lynx HAS Mk 21 light helicopter
Electronics: one AWS 2 air-search radar, one ZW-06 surface-search radar, two RTN1OX fire-control radars, one Ikara tracking radar (not in F42 and F43), one CAAIS action information system, one RDL-2/3 ESM system, one EDO 610E hull-mounted sonar, and (not in F42 and F43) one EDO 700E variable depth sonar
Complement: 201

'Jiangnan' and 'Jianghu' classes

In the late 1950s the Chinese assembled in their Hutung shipyard at Shanghai four frigates of the Soviet 'Riga' class from components supplied by the USSR. Known locally as the **'Chengdu' class**, these ships were followed in 1965 by the laying down of the first hull of an indigenous enlarged and modified variant at the Jiangnan shipyard in Shanghai, resulting in the designation **'Jiangnan' class**. Four further units were completed at the Tung Lang shipyard, Guangzhou (Canton) between 1967 and 1969. Four of the class, together with the four 'Chengdu' class ships, serve with the Chinese navy's South Sea Fleet, whilst the 'Jiangnan' class lead ship serves with the East Sea Fleet. At least one of the 'Jiangnans' took part in the combat operations against South Vietnamese naval vessels during the January 1974 occupation of the Paracel Islands. Apart from being larger than the 'Chengdus', the 'Jiangnans' have the major differences of a diesel propulsion plant (instead of geared steam turbines) and that they have not been refitted to carry the Shanghou-Yihou 1 (the Chinese copy of the Soviet SS-N-2 'Styx') anti-ship cruise missile.

Following the political upheaval of the Cultural Revolution the first frigate design to emerge was the **'Jiangdong' class**, two units of which were constructed at the Hutung shipyard between 1970 and 1978. The long building and commissioning times were caused by the fact that the ships were due to carry the first Chinese-designed and -built naval SAM system.

This, the HQ-61 (western designation CSA-NX-2), is a short-range semi-active homing missile launched from twin-rail units fore and aft and it has only recently entered service after a very protracted development.

While the 'Jiangdongs' were under construction, a new design for greater anti-ship engagement capability was being formulated. The first three or four units of what became known as the **'Jianghu I' class** were laid down in 1973-4 at Hutung, launched in 1975 and commissioned in 1976. A second shipyard, the Jiangnan at Shanghai has joined the programme. To date, there are an estimated 17 units in commission with another three at the fitting-out stage and three more under construction. Apart from the 'Jianghu I' series (with a rounded stack for venting the diesel exhaust fumes from its propulsion plant), at least three of those built so far were constructed to the **'Jianghu II' class** design with a squared stack thought to be for a locally-designed and -built combined diesel or gas turbine (CODOG) powerplant. There are also two **'Jianghu III' class** which revert to the rounded stack of the first subclass but has twin 57-mm DP mounts (fore and aft) plus six twin 37-mm AA guns, four RBU 1200 ASW rocket launchers, four BMB-2 depth

charge throwers and two depth charge racks. Both units were sold to Egypt as the *Najim Az Zaffer* (951) and the *El Nasser* (956) in 1984 and 1985 respectively. In 1986, the first **'Jianghu IV' class** frigate commssioned. This is fitted with a hangar and flight deck aft for one Harbin Z-9 ASW helicopter (license built Aérospatiale Dauphin 2). This takes the place of the aft guns, depth charge racks, mine rails and one of the twin FL-1 SSM missile launchers. The gun armament is reduced to one twin 100-mm (3.9-in) turret and four twin 37-mm AA mounts. Further units are expected which may be equipped with a multi-cell launcher for the CY-1 ASW weapon. This is a torpedo carrying single stage ballistic anti-submarine rocket that is currently under development.

Specification
'Jianghu' classes
Displacement: 1,568 tons standard and 1,900 tons full load
Dimensions: length 103.2 m (338.6 ft); beam 10.2 m (33.5 ft); draught 3.1 m (10.2 ft)
Propulsion: ('Jianghu I' and 'Jianghu III') two diesels delivering power to two shafts
Propulsion: ('Jianghu II') probably a CODOG arrangement delivering power to two shafts
Speed: 26.5 kts for 'Jianghu I' and 'Jianghu III', and 30 kts for 'Jianghu II'
Armament: two twin container-launchers for Feilong-1 anti-ship missiles, two single (or twin in 'Jianghou III') 100-mm (3.9-in) DP and six twin 37-mm AA guns, two or four 5-barrel RBU1200 250-mm (9.84-in) ASW rocket-launchers with 50 or 100 rockets, two racks for 36 depth charges, and between 40 and 60 mines according to type
Aircraft: none
Electronics: one 'Eye Shield' air-search radar (being fitted), one 'Square Tie' missile fire-control radar, one 'Sun Visor-B' fire-control radar (in some), one 'Fin Curve' and/or one 'Don-2' navigation radar, one 'High Pole-B' IFF, one 'Yard Rake' IFF (being fitted), and one high-frequency hull-mounted sonar
Complement: 195

The People's Republic of China has built the 'Jianghu' frigate in three different versions. Still in production, the Egyptian navy has recently bought two 'Jianghu I' units with revised gun armaments.

Modern Patrol Craft

Fast, versatile and highly manoeuvrable, the patrol craft has now re-established itself as a potent asset in navies large and small. Equipped with the latest in a wide array of weaponry and technology, these small craft can very easily cause havoc against ships many times their size.

One of the forerunners of the US Navy's 'Pegasus' class of hydrofoils, the experimental vessel USS Tucumcari makes a high speed run in the English Channel off Plymouth.

For many years after World War II the torpedo attack craft remained the major threat in coastal forces. Armed with increasingly longer-ranged torpedoes as their primary anti-ship weapons and with heavy automatic guns, and powered by reliable diesel engines giving maximum speeds in excess of 45 kts at full power, the torpedo craft saw relatively little use in combat.

However, in the late 1950s the Soviet Union envisaged the capabilities of such craft increasing to a much greater extent if they were equipped with the then brand-new surface-to-surface anti-ship missile. The first such Soviet craft, the 'Komar' class, was a conversion of the 'P6' class motor torpedo boat. Unproven in combat until 1967, the missile-armed attack craft was neglected by most of the Western powers. Once the Egyptians sank the Israeli destroyer *Eilat*, however, this situation changed rapidly, and most NATO powers procured various types of such craft or converted torpedo boats or motor gunboats. The notable exception is the United Kingdom, which has consistently ignored the procurement of such vessels. Non-aligned and smaller nations saw the missile boat as the equalizer between themselves and the threat of the larger powers' navies, a missile boat carrying two or more missiles being capable of engaging and sinking much larger vessels such as a destroyer, this being conclusively proved in the 1971 Indo-Pakistan War, when a force of Indian 'Osa' class missile craft attacked the harbour at Karachi, sinking or damaging a number of Pakistani naval ships and foreign merchant ships, including the destroyer *Khaibar*, with SS-N-2A 'Styx' missiles. Surprisingly enough, battle involving missile boats on

both sides did not arise until the 1973 'Yom Kippur' War between the Arabs and Israelis, the latter proving that the well-equipped missile craft is a deadly weapon when handled by a well-trained crew. The next major test did not arise until the current Gulf War broke out between the Iranians and the Iraqis. Used by both sides, the missile craft has not proved as effective as in 1973 as both countries lack the expertise and tactical know-how required to use it properly. In recent years the surface-to-surface missile has been mated with hydrofoil designs, although this has not proved a total success except with the Soviets. The Iraelis have been particularly disappointed with their craft.

In the case of the riverine warfare craft, the French in Indo-China built up the first effective river combat force in the 1950s during their war there. When the Americans entered the ground war in the mid-1960s they had to relearn the lessons and ended up building their own riverine force, using modified LCM6 designs and specially-built craft. These proved themselves in combat and most were turned over to the South Vietnamese in the late 1960s and early 1970s as the Americans gradually withdrew their forces. The early 1900s concept of the river gunboat and monitor still lives in the areas of the world where big rivers are found; the oldest examples of river warfare craft afloat are still plying the great rivers of South America.

A US riverine monitor leads a group of Armoured Troop Carriers (ATCs) during an anti-guerrilla operation on one of the many navigable rivers in South Vietnam. Sometimes those rivers and canals provided the only ground-level axis to Viet Cong strongpoints in the Mekong delta.

NORWAY/SWEDEN
'Hauk' and 'Hugin' class fast attack craft (missile)

In 1975 the Norwegian navy ordered ten missile boats from the Bergens Mekanishe Verksteder shipyard and four from Westemarine, Mandal. The new design was based on the previous 'Snögg/Storm' class fast attack craft and given the class name of **'Hauk'**. All 14 units were commissioned into service between 1978-80 and now form a major component of the Norwegian navy's coastal defence missile boat force.

At the same time as the Norwegians ordered their boats the Swedish Navy placed an order at the same yards for 16 similar craft as part of a trade offset agreement. Known as the **'Hugin'** class, they were ordered after a three year evaluation of a prototype named the *Jägaren* which had been procured in 1972. Due to her age she has now been downrated to a fast attack craft-patrol and placed in the reserve category. The 16 production vessels were commissioned into service between 1978-82 and with the 'Spica' classes form the major part of the Swedish navy's defensive missile boat forces. Both navies have fitted their classes with the Penguin Mk 2 SSM as the main armament because it was designed to be used in the confines of coastlines with many small islands or deep, landlocked fjords.

Specification
'Hauk' class
Names: *Hauk, Ørn, Terne, Tjeld, Skarv, Teist, Jo, Lom, Stegg, Falk, Ravn, Gribb, Geir, Erle*
Displacement: 130 tons standard, 155 tons full load
Dimensions: length 36.6m (120ft), beam 6.3m (20.7ft), draught 1.7m (5.6ft)
Propulsion: two MTU diesels delivering 5473kW (7,340hp) to two shafts
Maximum speed: 35 kts
Armament: two/six single Penguin Mk 2 SSM container-launchers, one single 40-mm AA gun, one single 20-mm AA gun, two single 533-mm (21-in) torpedo tubes (for Tp613 wire-guided anti-ship torpedoes)
Electronics: two Decca 1226 navigation radars, one TVT-300 optronic fire control system, one Ericsson laser rangefinder, one SQ3D/SF hull sonar
Complement: 22

Specification
'Hugin' class
Names: *Jägaren, Hugin, Munin, Magne, Mode, Vale, Vider, Mjölner, Mysing, Kaparen, Väktaren, Snapphanen, Styrbjörn, Starkodder, Tordön, Tirfing*
Displacement: 120 tons standard, 150 tons full load
Dimensions: as 'Hauk' class
Propulsion: two diesels delivering 5639kW (7,200hp) to two shafts
Maximum speed: 36 kts
Armament: two/six Penguin Mk 2 (RB12) SSM container-launchers, one single 57-mm DP gun, four nine barrel ELMA ASW rocket launchers, up to a maximum of 24 mines or depth charges in lieu of missiles

Norway and Sweden have large numbers of Fast Attack Craft in Service, many of them being of the 'Hauk' or 'Hugin' classes. The 'Hauk' class boat Stegg is seen in Norwegian waters.

Electronics: one Scanter 009 navigation radar, one PEAB 9LV200 fire control radar, one EWS905 ECM system, one SQ3D/SF hull sonar
Complement: 22

SWEDEN
'Stockholm' and 'Göteborg' class fast attack craft (missile)

As a result of an increase in the numbers of incursions into Swedish coastal waters by mainly Eastern Bloc submarines the Swedish navy has been ordered to strengthen its ASW defensive capabilities. As part of this process a pair of **'Spica III'** or **'Stockholm' class** missile boats were ordered in 1981 to act as both fast attack craft squadron leaders and as coastal corvette type ASW platforms. The two units commissioned into service during 1985 with an armament that can be changed depending upon the tasks assigned to them. The RBS-15 SSM launchers are interchangeable with 533-mm (21-in) anti-ship torpedo tubes, 400-mm (15.7-in) ASW torpedo tubes and/or mine or depth charge rails. The 57mm remote-control gun mount by Bofors is also unique in that it can be manned for local control, a feature not found on the export version.

As a further strengthening of its forces the Swedish navy ordered the first four of an eventual six **'Göteborg'** or **'Spica IV'** class vessels in 1985 to replace the original 'Spica I' class. Due to be delivered from 1989 onwards they are essentially an expanded version of the 'Stockholms' and carry an enhanced armament which can include both Tp617 anti-ship and Tp43 series ASW torpedoes.

Both designs also carry four nine barrel 100-mm (3.9-in) calibre Elma ASW rocket launchers which fire 27.8-cm (10.9-in) long grenades, each weighing 4.35kg (9.6lb) to a range of about 250-300m (273-328 yards) in programmable salvoes of 9, 18, 27 or 36 rounds. The grenades are fitted with shaped charges that ensure the target's pressure hull is penetrated by the blast jet even if it is protected by an outer waterfilled ballast tank. The small charge is unlikely to sink the hostile submarine but the damage is likely to be sufficiently severe to force it to the surface.

Specification
'Stockholm' class
Names: *Stockholm, Malmo*
Displacement: 310 tons standard, 335 tons full load
Dimensions: length 50m (164ft), beam 7.5m (24.6ft), draught 1.9m (6.2ft)

Propulsion: one Allison 570KF gas turbine and two MTU diesels in CODAG arrangement delivering 8471kW (11,360hp) total to three shafts
Maximum speed: 33 kts
Armament: six (two twin and two single) or eight (four twin) RBS-15 SSM container-launchers, one single 57-mm DP gun, one single 40-mm AA gun, two single 533-mm (21-in) torpedo tubes (for Tp617 anti-ship wire-guided torpedoes), four nine barrel ELMA ASW rocket launchers, rails for 18 mines and/or depth charges (or no RBS-15 SSMs and up to six 533-mm (21-in) torpedo tubes or four 400-mm (15.7-in) ASW torpedo tubes)
Electronics: one navigation radar, one Sea Giraffe 50HC search radar, one PEAB 9LV200 fire control radar, one PEAB 9LV100 optronic fire control system, one EWS-90 ECM system, two Philax IR/chaff decoy launchers, one SS304 Spira hull sonar, one TSM 2642 Salmon variable depth sonar
Complement: 30

Specification
'Göteborg' class

Names: *'Göteborg, Gävla, Kalmar, Sundsvall, Helsingborg, Hämösund*
Displacement: 355 tons standard, 380 tons full load
Dimensions: length 57m (187ft), beam 8m (26.2ft), draught 2m (6.6ft)
Propulsion: three diesels driving three pumpjets
Maximum speed: 32 kts
Armament: four twin RBS-15 container-launchers, one single 57-mm DP gun, one single Trinity 40-mm AA gun, two single 533-mm (21-in) torpedo tubes (for wire-guided Tp617 anti-ship torpedoes), four nine barrel ELMA ASW rocket launchers, rails for 18 mines and/or depth charges. Four 533-mm (21-in) and four 400-mm (15.7-in) torpedo tubes can be carried in place of the RBS-15 launchers.
Electronics: one navigation radar, one PEAB Karin search radar, two PEAB 9LV200 fire control radars, one EWS905 ECM system, two Philax chaff/IR decoy launchers, one SS304 Spira hull sonar, one TSM 2642 Salmon variable depth sonar.
Complement: 30

'Spica' class fast attack craft (torpedo and missile)

Because of Sweden's close proximity to the Soviet Union and that nation's extensive Baltic Fleet, which includes large numbers of small combatants, the Swedish navy has gradually paid off most of its large surface combatants and replaced them by a surface fleet of fast torpedo and missile attack craft, the backbone formerly being provided by the **Spica I'** and **Spica II'** classes. The six 'Spica Is' were commissioned between 1966 and 1968, and are currently armed with a single 57-mm dual-purpose Bofors gun and six 533-mm (21-in) torpedo tubes for the Tp61 anti-ship wire-guided heavyweight torpedo. Each side of the bridge are rails for a total of four 103-mm and six 57-mm rocket flare launchers. If necessary the torpedo tubes can be replaced by mines. For fire-control purposes the 'Spica Is' have an M22 system with co-mounted radars in a single radome. In 1985, the 'Spica I' class boats *Sirius* and *Castor* were stricken whilst two more were placed in reserve a year later.

Between 1973 and 1976 a further 12 vessels were commissioned to the improved 'Spica II' design. These have an armament similar to the 'Spica I' but carry only eight 57-mm flare-launcher rails on each side of the forward gun turret. Their armament was modified from 1982 to 1985 with the addition of an LM Ericsson Giraffe low-level air-search radar and two RBS-15 SSM container launchers. Mines can be substituted for the missiles or torpedo tubes. Four Elma ASW harrassment rocket launchers have also been fitted as a result of foreign submarine incursions into Swedish waters. They are not designed to sink submarines but to force them to the surface. They have the earlier PEAB 9LV200 Mk 1 analog version of the digital fire-control system that is fitted to the later 'Hugin' class. Both the classes have to have the two foremost torpedo tubes swung out through several degrees before they can be fired.

Specification
'Spica I' class
Names: *Spica, Sirius, Capella, Castor, Vega* and *Virgo*
Displacement: 210 tons full load
Dimensions: length 42.7 m (140.1 ft);

Above: The 'Spica' classes form the backbone of the Swedish navy's fast attack craft forces. They are designed as multi-role vessels with the capability of switching armament fits to suit the assigned mission.

Right: A 'Spica II' class vessel carries four container-launcher boxes for the new Bofors RBS-15 surface-to-surface anti-ship missile. The 'Spica II' class were all converted to RBS-15 carriers by the end of 1984.

beam 7.1 m (23.3 ft); draught 2.6 m (8.5 ft)
Propulsion: three Rolls-Royce Proteus gas turbines delivering 12,720 hp (9485 kW) to three shafts
Maximum speed: 40 kts
Complement: 28
Armament: see text
Electronics: one Scanter 009 search radar and one HSA M22 fire-control system

Specification
'Spica II' class
Names: *Norrköping, Nynäshamn, Norrtälje, Varberg, Västeraås, Väster-*

vik, *Umeå, Piteå, Luleå, Halmstad, Strömstad* and *Ystad*
Displacement: 230 tons full load
Dimensions: length 43.6 m (143 ft); beam 7.1 m (23.3 ft); draught 2.4 m (7.9 ft)
Propulsion: three Rolls-Royce Proteus gas turbines delivering 12,900 hp

(9620 kW) to three shafts
Maximum speed: 40.5 kts
Armament: see text
Electronics: one Scanter 009 search radar and one PEAB 9LV200 Mk 1 fire-control system
Complement: 27

'Huchuan' and 'Shanghai' class fast attack craft (gun and torpedo)

For many years the Chinese navy relied on vessels given to it by the Soviet Union or on building basic copies of Soviet designs in their shipyards. In 1959 the first prototypes of what has become the major construction programme in the coastal forces build-up were seen. These were of the **'Shanghai' class** motor gunboats, which are

still constructed at the rate of 10 per year in several yards. A relatively unsophisticated design that has been built in five versions, the 'Shanghai' class now provide the bulk of the coastal patrol craft with 10 **'Shanghai I'** and over 330 **'Shanghai II', 'Shanghai III', 'Shanghai IV'** and **'Shanghai V'** craft in service. A large number have also

been exported to Albania (6), Angola (1), Bangladesh (8), Cameroon (2), Congo (3), Egypt (4), Guinea (6), Guinea-Bissau (2), N. Korea (8), Pakistan (12), Sri Lanka (7), Sierra Leone (3), Tanzania (7), and Vietnam (8). Romania also uses the 'Shanghai' class

The 'Huchuan I' class of torpedo-equipped hydrofoil as used by the People's Republic of China, which has some 140 in service.

(22 built locally in three variants). The last is particularly intriguing as Romania is a member of the Soviet Warsaw Pact alliance.

Around 1966 the first of an indigenously designed and built hydrofoil torpedo attack craft was seen. Constructed by the Hudung shipyard in Shanghai, this **'Huchuan' class** has subsequently been identified in two versions. The first, the **'Huchuan I'**, has a twin 14.5-mm (0.51-in) heavy machine-gun mounting amidships with a second twin mounting aft of it, whilst the bridge is placed forward of the torpedo tube mouths. The second, the **'Huchuan II'**, has the bridge placed father aft, in line with the tubes, and the amidships mounting moved to the forecastle. The all-metal hull has one pair of retractable foils forward. Some units have

been seen without foils. Construction ended in 1980. At present some 140 are in Chinese service, with numbers being exported to Albania (32), Pakistan (4), Tanzania (4) and Romania (3 plus 17+ as part of the local construction programme). The torpedoes carried are Chinese-built copies of Soviet 533-mm (21-in) anti-ship designs.

Specification
'Huchuan' class
Displacement: 39 tons
Dimensions: length 21.8 m (71.5 ft); beam 4.9 m (16.1 ft) or 7.5 m (24.6 ft) when foilborne; draught 1.0 m (3.3 ft) or 0.31 m (1.0 ft) when foilborne
Propulsion: three M50 diesels delivering 3,600 hp (2685 kW) to three shafts
Maximum speed: 54 kts
Complement: 12-15

Armament: two 533-mm (21-in) anti-ship torpedo tubes and two twin 12.7-mm (0.5-in) heavy machine-guns
Electronics: one 'Skin Head' radar

Specification
'Shanghai I' class
Displacement: 125 tons full load
Dimensions: length 35.1 m (115 ft); beam 5.5 m (18 ft); draught 1.7 m (5.5 ft)
Propulsion: four diesels delivering 4,220 hp (3148 kW) to four shafts
Maximum speed: 28 kts
Complement: 25
Armament: one twin 57-mm AA and one twin 37-mm guns, eight depth charges and up to 10 mines
Electronics: one 'Skin Head' radar and one hull-mounted sonar

Specification
'Shanghai II, III, IV and V' classes
Displacement: 155 tons full load
Dimensions: length 38.8 m (127.3 ft); beam 5.4 m (17.7 ft); draught 1.5 m (4.9 ft)
Propulsion: four diesels delivering 4,800 hp (3580 kW) to four shafts
Maximum speed: 30 kts
Complement: 38
Armament: (Type II) two twin 37-mm AA and two twin 25-mm AA guns; (Types III and IV) one twin 57-mm AA and one twin 25-mm AA guns; some boats carry a twin 82-mm recoilless rifle mounting in the bows, and all types carry eight depth charges and have provision for up to 10 mines
Electronics: one 'Pot Head' or 'Skin Head' radar and one hull-mounted or variable depth sonar

---

USA
'Pegasus' class patrol combatant hydrofoil (missile)

Hydrofoils were the only exception to the United States Navy's lack of interest in fast attack craft during the 1950s. The first such unit launched was the USS *High Point*, in 1962, for ASW trials work. Interest then shifted to fast gunboats during the mid-1960s, when the USS *Flagstaff* and USS *Tucumcari* were tested. The final shift was when it was decided to develop a missile-armed patrol hydrofoil (PHM) successor to the missile-armed 'Asheville' class patrol gunboat variant that had been used in the Mediterranean. The US Navy combined with West Germany and Italy on the project to make a NATO design. However, as costs rose only the USA, which planned 30 units, remained in the programme. The numbers to be built were cut back to six, and then, after only *Pegasus* (PHM1) had been launched in 1974, the Department of Defense decided in April 1977 to cancel the remaining five units. However, in August 1977 these five **'Pegasus' class** craft were reinstated in the building programme at the request of the Congress. By 1982 the last unit, USS *Gemini*, had been commissioned into service with the deliveries of the

craft from the builders (the Boeing Company in Seattle) running seven months late and 26 per cent over cost estimates. All six craft form a unit based at Key West, Florida, for tests and the evaluation of systems and tactics, and for surveillance duties in the Caribbean area. As the US Navy believes that the class requires too specialized a logistic support network for forward deployment to the Mediterranean and similar front line areas, the craft will only have a limited role within the fleet. No further missile or gunboat classes are planned at present.

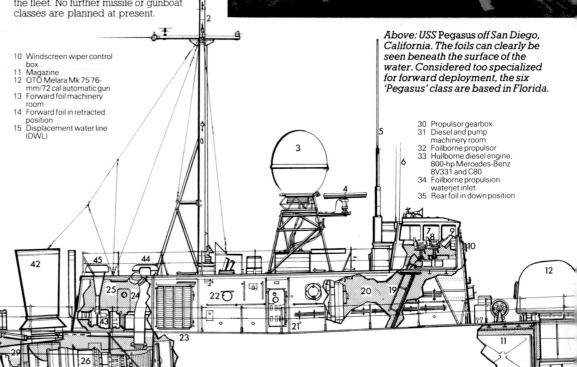

Above: USS Pegasus *off San Diego, California. The foils can clearly be seen beneath the surface of the water. Considered too specialized for forward deployment, the six* 'Pegasus' *class are based in Florida.*

USS *Taurus*

10 Windscreen wiper control box
11 Magazine
12 OTO Melara Mk 75 76-mm/72 cal automatic gun
13 Forward foil machinery room
14 Forward foil in retracted position
15 Displacement water line (DWL)

30 Propulsor gearbox
31 Diesel and pump machinery room
32 Foilborne propulsor
33 Hullborne diesel engine, 800-hp Mercedes-Benz 8V331 and C80
34 Foilborne propulsion waterjet inlet
35 Rear foil in down position

1 Masthead navigation lights
2 Main mast
3 Fire control antenna structure/dome
4 Radar
5 Radio mast
6 Radio antenna
7 Pilot house
8 Pilot's seat
9 Instrument panel

16 Forward foil in down position
17 Normal foilborne water line
18 Bow thruster
19 Companionway ladder
20 Communication room
21 Passageway

22 Electronics equipment room
23 Gas turbine air intake
24 Gas turbine machinery room door
25 Auxiliary machinery room no. 1

26 Marine gas turbine, General Electric LM 2500
27 Fuel tank (aft)
28 Gas turbine machinery room
29 Auxiliary machinery room no. 2

36 Hullborne water jet nozzle
37 SSPU no. 2 (Ship Service Power Unit)
38 Rear foil in retracted position
39 Auxiliary machinery room no. 3

The *Pegasus* itself is fitted with the Mk 94 fire-control system, which is the US designation for the Hollandse Signaalapparaten WM28 system; the remaining five craft are fitted with the Mk 92 Model 1 system, which is a modified WM28 built by the Sperry Company of the USA. The single 76-mm (3-in) Mk 75 licence-built OTO-Melara automatic gun carried has a total of 400 rounds in its ready-use magazine and main below-deck magazine. There is also additional space abaft the mast for mounting two single 20-mm Mk 20 AA guns if required. However, the main armament is a pair of quadruple Harpoon SSM container-launcher canister groupings fitted on the stern.

Specification
Names: *Pegasus, Hercules, Taurus, Aquilla, Aries* and *Gemini*
Displacement: 241 tons full load
Dimensions: hull length 44.3 m (145.3 ft), beam 8.6 m (28.2 ft) and draught 2.3 m (7.5 ft); foilborne length 40.5 m (132.9 ft) and beam 14.5 m (47.5 ft)
Propulsion: foilborne one General Electric gas turbine delivering 18,000 shp (13423 kW) to two waterjets, and hullborne two MTU diesels delivering 3,200 hp (2387 kW) to two waterjets
Maximum speed: 11 kts hullborne and 48 kts foilborne
Complement: 21-24
Armament: one 76-mm (3-in) Mk 75 dual-purpose gun and eight Harpoon SSMs in two quadruple launchers
Electronics: one SPS-63 search radar, one Mk 92 fire-control system (Mk 94 in *Pegasus*), one SLR-20 ECM system, two Mk 34 Super RBOC Chaff launchers, one OE 82 satellite communication system, one SSQ-87(V) Collision avoidance and tracking system

Right: USS Pegasus *in company with a USN VC-1 composite squadron Sikorsky SH-3G Sea King helicopter and McDonnell Douglas TA-4J Skyhawk two-seat operational attack trainer jet off Hawaii. It is envisaged that the 'Pegasus' class will have only a limited role within the US Fleet.*

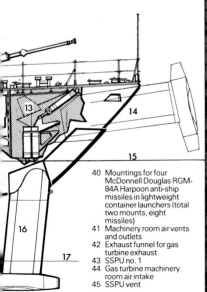

40 Mountings for four McDonnell Douglas RGM-84A Harpoon anti-ship missiles in lightweight container launchers (total two mounts, eight missiles)
41 Machinery room air vents and outlets
42 Exhaust funnel for gas turbine exhaust
43 SSPU no. 1
44 Gas turbine machinery room air intake
45 SSPU vent

'PCF', 'PBR' and 'PB' series patrol craft

The two principal coastal warfare craft used by the Americans in the Vietnam War were the **PCF** (or **'Swift' class**) and the **PBR** (or **Plastic**) type. The Patrol Craft, Fast design was adopted from that of a standard commercial work boat used for oil rig support work in the Gulf of Mexico. The 200 or so PCFs were all constructed by Sewart Seacraft of Berwick, Louisiana in 1965-6. The first 104 were of the **PCF Mk I** design, whilst the remainder (with less sheer, the pilot house located farther aft and a broken deck line) were built to the improved **PCF Mk II** design. Currently three Mk I and two Mk II craft remain in service with the US Navy. A total of 104 was transferred to South Vietnam in 1968-70, 12 to the Philippines in 1966, nine to Cambodia in 1972-3 and seven to Zaire. More were built for the Philippines, South Korea and Thailand, and a number were lost in the war.

The Patrol Boat, River, of which some 500 were constructed in **PBR Mk I** and **PBR Mk II** variants between 1966 and 1973, is smaller than the PCF, with a glassfibre-reinforced plastic hull, ceramic armour and an open-topped conning bridge. Propulsion and steering are by means of a waterjet system. For work in the narrow and shallow inland waterways of Vietnam the boats were designed with a draught of less than 1m (3.3ft). Less than 40 PBRs remain in service with the US Naval Reserve, most having been transferred to Vietnam, Cambodia and Thailand. The **'Seafox'** is a high-speed twin-engined GRP craft which has replaced the PBR in Special Forces service for the 1980s. With a three-man crew it can deliver a SEAL or UDT team and their equipment from off-shore support ships. Thirty-six were acquired during the expansion of the US Special Forces in the late 1980s.

The **Patrol Boat** was intended to succeed the PCF. Two **PB Mk I** and 17 **PB Mk III**, were ordered as the **Sea Spectre** class of multi-mission inshore warfare craft. Derived from a Gulf of Mexico oil-rig work boat, the Sea Spectre can carry a wide variety of weapons, including Penguin Mk 2 anti-ship missiles. Three stretched **Sea Spectre PB Mk IV** were ordered for use in the Panama Canal Zone.

The US Navy has requested funds for up to 19 **Special Warfare Craft (Medium)**, to be known as the **Sea Viking** class. These 150-ton, 35-knot craft are to be longer-ranged, more capable counterparts to the Seafox, and are intended for use by the new Unified Special Operations Command of the US Forces in the 1990s.

Above: A PB Mk III patrol craft under way. Known as the 'Sea Spectre' class, this design was derived from a Gulf of Mexico oil rig work boat.

The Seafox special warfare craft (light) is designed to carry a special forces team and its equipment ashore from a support ship at sea. 36 had been acquired by 1987/88.

Seen during the Vietnam war, this PCF is returning to base after a mission with a US Navy Underwater Demolition Team embarked. The armament has been modified to include a twin 12.7-mm (0.5-in) heavy machine-gun mounting.

A PBR Mk II craft on a high-speed patrol in the Long Tau river, South Vietnam. The PBR was especially useful in patrolling the rivers and canals to prevent movement of enemy forces and supplies.

Specification
PCF Mk I
Displacement: 19 tons full load
Dimensions: length 15.3 m (50.2 ft); beam 4.0 m (13.1 ft); draught 1.1 m (3.6 ft)
Propulsion: two General Motors diesels delivering 850 hp (634 kW) to two shafts
Maximum speed: 28 kts
Complement: 6
Armament: two single 12.7-mm (0.5 in) heavy machine-guns and one combined 81-mm mortar and 12.7-mm (0.5 in) heavy machine-gun mounting
Electronics: one LN66 navigation radar

Specification
PCF Mk II
Displacement: 19.2 tons full load
Dimensions: length 15.6 m (51.2 ft); beam 4.1 m (13.5 ft); draught 1.1 m (3.6 ft)
Propulsion: two General Motors diesels delivering 850 hp (634 kW) to two shafts
Maximum speed: 28 kts
Complement: 6
Armament: as for PCF Mk I
Electronics: one LN66 navigation radar

Specification
PBR Mk I
Displacement: 6.5 tons full load
Dimensions: length 9.5 m (31.2 ft); beam 3.2 m (10.5 ft); draught 0.6 m (2 ft)
Propulsion: two General Motors diesels delivering 430 hp (321 kW) to two pumpjets
Maximum speed: 25 kts
Complement: 4-5
Armament: one twin 12.7-mm (0.5-in) heavy machine-gun, one 7.62-mm (0.3-in) medium machine-gun and one 40-mm grenade-launcher
Electronics: one Raytheon 1900 search radar

Specification
PBR Mk II
Displacement: 8.9 tons full load
Dimensions: length 9.7 m (31.8 ft); beam 3.6 m (11.8 ft); draught 0.8 m (2.6 ft)
Propulsion: two General Motors diesels delivering 430 hp (321 kW) to two pumpjets
Maximum speed: 25 kts
Complement: 4-5
Armament: as for PBR Mk I plus one 60-mm mortar in some boats
Electronics: one Raytheon 1900 search radar

Specification
PB Mk I
Displacement: 36.3 tons full load
Dimensions: length 19.8 m (65 ft); beam 4.9 m (16.1 ft); draught 1.5 m (4.9 ft)
Propulsion: two General Motors diesels delivering power to two shafts
Maximum speed: 26 kts
Complement: 5
Armament: one 40-mm or two 25-mm guns, two 12.7-mm (0.5-in) machine guns
Electronics: one LN66 navigation radar

Specification
PB Mk III
Displacement: 41.3 tons full load
Dimensions: length 19.8 m (65 ft); beam 5.5 m (18 ft); draught 1.8 m (5.9 ft)
Propulsion: three General Motors diesels delivering 950 hp (709 kW) to three shafts
Maximum speed: 26 kts
Complement: 5
Armament: as PB Mk I
Electronics: one LN66 navigation radar

'Sparviero' class fast attack hydrofoil (missile)

Together with the United States Navy, Italy is unique among NATO navies in having missile-armed hydrofoils as part of its operational surface fleet. The prototype of the **'Sparviero' class** was based on the Boeing Tucumcari design and assessed in detail by the Alinavi Society, which was formed in 1964 by the Italian government's IRI, Carlo Rodriguez (a builder of commercial hydrofoils) of Messina and the US Boeing Company. Built between 1971 and 1974, the original craft was followed by six others between 1980 and 1983. They use the Boeing jetfoil system, with one foil forward and two aft.

Power for the foilborne mode comes from a gas turbine driving a waterjet system, whilst hullborne power comes from a single diesel. The hull is made entirely of aluminium, and it has been found that the craft have a relatively short range and limited armament for combat operations. However, the Italian navy is willing to accept this as Italy is surrounded by restricted waters ideal for such craft.

The six later vessels have a more modern surface search radar than the *Spaviero*, and all carry the later 150-km (93-mile) range Teseo Mk 2 SSM variant of the Otomat SSM, though use of this extra range capability requires a helicopter for mid-course guidance and targeting. The radar is fitted with an IFF interrogator unit, and the gun armament is a single OTO-Melara 76-mm (3-in) dual-purpose gun forward.

Specification
Names: *Sparviero, Nibbio, Falcone,* *Astore, Grifone, Gheppio* and *Condore*
Displacement: 62.5 tons full load
Dimensions: hull length 23.0 m (75.4 ft), beam 7.0 m (22.9 ft) and draught 1.6 m (5.2 ft); foilborne length 24.6 m (80.7 ft) and beam 12.1 m (39.7 ft)
Propulsion: CODOG (COmbined Diesel Or Gas turbine), foilborne one Rolls-Royce Proteus gas turbine delivering 4,500 hp (3357 kW) to waterjet, and hullborne one diesel delivering 180 hp (134 kW) to one shaft
Maximum speed: foilborne 50 kts and hullborne 8 kts
Armament: one 76-mm (3-in) dual-purpose gun and two Teseo Mk II SSMs
Electronics: one 3RM-7 radar, one RTN-10X fire-control radar and one NA10 fire-control system

The Italian hydrofoil Sparviero. *Italy is unique in European NATO navies in having missile-armed hydrofoils in Fleet service.*

'Ramadan' class fast attack craft (missile)

As a direct result of the break with the Soviet Union in the early 1970s, and to make good the war losses from the 1973 'Yom Kippur' War with Israel, Egypt turned to the British shipbuilders Vosper Thornycroft in 1977 with a £150 million contract to build a six-boat class of missile craft to complement its ageing missile craft force of seven 'Osa I', six 'Hegu' and six 'October' class craft (of which the last is a locally built variant of the 'Komar' with two Otomat SSMs). Vosper came up with a 52-m (170.6-ft) design that was subsequently designated the **'Ramadan' class** by the Egyptians. The first was launched in 1979 and the last in 1980, and all were in service by 1982. Capable of facing the Israeli missile craft classes on equal terms the boats have an opera-

tions room equipped with a Marconi Sapphire fire-control system with two radar and TV gun directors for the weapons aboard. Two alternative optical fire-control directors are also carried. The operations room is also fitted with a Ferranti CAAIS action information system. The main gun armament comprises a single Italian-built 76-mm (3-in) OTO-Melara dual-

purpose gun forward. The gun is effective up to 7000 m (7,655 yards) for anti-aircraft fire and to 15000 m (16,405 yards) in the surface-to-surface role. Turreted aft is a twin Breda 40-mm AA mounting, whilst the missile armament comprises four launcher-containers for Otomat Mk I SSMs. To back up the 'Ramadans' the older missile boats are gradually being put through modernization programmes.

Specification
Names: *Ramadan, Khyber, El Kadesseya, El Yarmouk, Hettein* and *Badr*
Displacement: 312 tons full load
Dimensions: length 52.0 m (170.6 ft); beam 7.6 m (25 ft); draught 2.0 m (6.6 ft)
Propulsion: four MTU diesels delivering 17,150 hp (12795 kW) to four shafts
Maximum speed: 40 kts
Complement: 40
Armament: see text
Electronics: one S820 radar, one S810 radar, two ST802 fire-control radars, one Sapphire fire-control system, one Cutlass ECM system, one Matilda ECM system, one Cygnus ECM system, two six-barrel Protean chaff launchers and one CAAIS action information system.

The Vosper Thornycroft-built Ramadan *missile boat, lead vessel of a six-vessel class that has given the Egyptian navy a quantum leap in its missile boat capabilities.*

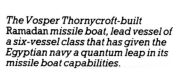

'Komar', 'Osa' and 'Matka' class fast attack craft (missile)

The **'Komar' class** of missile craft (Soviet designation RKA, or *raketnyy kater*) was built between 1959 and 1961. Heralding an entirely new concept in coastal forces, the first of the 'Komars' were converted from newly completed 'P6' motor torpedo boat hulls. About 100 were built of the wooden-hulled design. The 'Komar' carries one fixed forward-firing open-ended missile-launcher bin aimed at about 1.5° outboard and elevated at about 12°, on each side of the deck aft. The missiles carried are the specially designed SS-N-2A 'Styx', a liquid-fuel rocket-engined type with a solid-fuel jettisonable booster motor. The 6.3-m (20.66-ft) long SS-N-2A has fixed wings, and is fitted with an autopilot and an I-band active-radar terminal-homing seeker. The warhead is HE and weighs 500 kg (1,102 lb) and maximum range is 46 km (29 miles). To decrease the load placed on the bow of the modified 'P6' design, the single 25-mm mount and the bridge were moved aft. Wedge-shaped sponsons were also fitted at deck level aft as the missile installation was wider than the boat itself. Struts were fitted to protect the launchers from spray. No 'Komars' remain in service with the Soviet navy, but several still serve in other navies. The Chinese still build a steel-hulled variant, the **'Hegu' class** with two 25-20-mm AA mountings. A more obvious difference is the siting of the missile launchers farther aft, well clear of the bridge, and the use of a simple pole mast. The 'Komar' was the world's first missile boat to be used in action when in October 1967 two Egyptian boats sank the Israeli destroyer *Eilat*. In April 1972 a North Vietnamese 'Komar' launched a 'Styx' SSM at three American warships bombarding coastal targets in North Vietnam. The USS *Sterett*, a guided-missile cruiser, engaged the missile with a Terrier SAM and shot it down, this being the first time an anti-ship missile was destroyed by another missile in combat.

From 1961 onwards to 1966 the replacement for the 'Komars' was built, this being the steel-hulled **'Osa I' class.** The design carried four completely enclosed launcher bins for the SS-N-2A, two on each side of the superstructure and arranged so that the aft launchers, elevated to 15°, fire over the forward pair, elevated to 12°. From 1966 to 1970 the **'Osa II' class** was produced for the Soviet navy, and then subsequently for export. This version has four cylindrical launcher-containers for the SS-N-2B 'Styx', which differs from the SS-N-2A variant in having infra-red terminal homing and folding wings. The 'Osa' class has an NBC citadel for nuclear, biological and chemicl warfare environments. Many of the 'Osa II' craft have now been fitted with a quad-

ruple launcher for the SA-N-5 SAM system (the navalized version of the SA-7 'Grail' man-portable infra-red homing missile). Currently there are some 120 'Osa I' and 'Osa II' class craft in service with the four Soviet fleets. 'Osa I' has seen combat service with four navies: those of Egypt (1973), India (1971), Iraq (current Gulf War) and Syria (1973). The 'Osa II' has seen combat with Iraq. The type has been exported widely. The Chinese build their own variant, having received four 'Osa I' boats in 1961 to act as patterns. From 1962 the first of more than 125 **'Huangfeng' class** boats began entering service, initially armed with two twin 25-mm AA guns and four Feilung-1 (FL-1) SSMs. Latterly the 'Huangfengs' have been seen with two twin 30-mm, four FL-2 missiles and a locally produced fire-control radar.

In 1978 the first of the 'Osa' replacement class was seen. This is the **'Matka' class**, which utilizes the 'Osa' hull but has a hydrofoil system similar to that of the 'Turya' class of torpedo hydrofoil in order to improve seaworthiness. The missile armament is reduced to two single cylindrical container-launchers for the much improved SS-N-2C variant of the 'Styx', this having a 74-km (46-mile) range and the choice of either infra-red or active-radar termin-

al homing. The gun armament is considerably enhanced with a new model of single-barrel 76-mm (3-in) dual-purpose turret forward and an ADG6-30 Gatling-type close-in defence system aft. Although the design, which was built at the Izhora shipyard in Leningrad, was more seaworthy than the Osa, production was stopped after only 16 units in favour of the larger and more capable 'Tarantul' class of missile corvettes.

140 'Komars' remain in service with six navies, while more than 400 'Osas' are active in nearly 25.

Specification
'Komar' class
Displacement: 80 tons full load
Dimensions: length 26.8 m (87.9 ft); beam 6.4 m (21 ft); draught 1.8 m (5.9 ft)
Propulsion: four diesels delivering 4,800 hp (3580 kW) to four shafts
Maximum speed: 40 kts
Complement: 11
Armament: two SS-N-2A 'Styx' SSM launchers and one twin 25-mm AA gun
Electronics: one 'Square Tie' search radar, one 'High Pole-A' IFF and one 'Dead Duck' IFF

Specification
'Osa I' class
Displacement: 210 tons full load
Dimensions: length 39.0 m (128 ft); beam 7.7 m (25.3 ft); draught 1.8 m (5.9 ft)
Propulsion: three diesels delivering 12,000 hp (8950 kW) to three shafts
Maximum speed: 38 kts
Complement: 30
Armament: four SS-N-2A 'Styx' SSM launchers and two twin 30-mm AA guns
Electronics: one 'Square Tie' search radar, one 'High Pole-B' IFF, one 'Drum Tilt' fire-control radar and two 'Square Head' IFF interrogators

An Egyptian 'Osa I' missile boat. Most Egyptian Soviet-built missile boats have undergone refits with Western electronic equipment in place of the Soviet systems. They also carry SA-N-5 SAMs.

Specification
'Osa II' class
Displacement: 245 tons full load
Dimensions: 39.0 m (128 ft); beam 7.7 m (25.3 ft); draught 1.9 m (6.2 ft)
Propulsion: three diesels delivering 15,000 hp (11190 kW) to three shafts
Maximum speed: 40 kts
Complement: 30
Armament: four SS-N-2B 'Styx' SSM launchers, one quadruple SA-N-5 SAM launcher and two twin 30-mm AA guns
Electronics: as on 'Osa I' class

Specification
'Matka' class
Displacement: 260 tons full load
Dimensions: length 40.0 m (131.2 ft); beam 7.7 m (25.3 ft) for the hull and 12.0 m (39.4 ft) for the foil; hull draught 1.9 m (6.2 ft)
Propulsion: three diesels delivering 15,000 hp (11190 kW) to three shafts
Maximum speed: 42 kts
Complement: 30
Armament: two SS-N-2C 'Styx' SSM launchers, one 76-mm (3-in) dual-purpose gun and one ADG6-30 AA 'Gatling' gun
Electronics: one 'Cheese Cake' search radar, one 'Bass Tilt' fire-control radar, one 'High Pole-B' IFF and one 'Square Head' IFF interrogator

The 'Komar' class was the first small coastal craft to be armed with missiles. It is now out of service in the USSR but is used by several Soviet client states.

'P4', 'P6', 'Shershen', 'Mol' and 'Turya' class fast attack craft (torpedo)

The **'P4' class** was the second Soviet post-war torpedo boat class. Built with aluminium hulls from around 1952 to 1958, their small size restricted employment to inshore waters. Armed with two 457-mm (18-in) anti-ship torpedo tubes, a twin heavy machine-gun mounting and between four and eight depth charges, the 'P4' has long been struck from Soviet navy service, although it still can be found with other navies.

The successor to the 'P4' was the wooden-hull **'P6' class**, built from 1953 to 1960. This was the standard Soviet torpedo attack craft until the mid-1970s, over 500 hulls being constructed. The basic hulls were also converted to other types, such as the 'Komar' (about 100), the 'MO-VI' patrol craft (50), the 'P8' and 'P10' experimental torpedo attack craft (20) and as target and KGB border surveillance patrol craft. Large numbers were exported, whilst the last versions in Soviet service have now been retired.

North Korea has built a large number of steel-hulled P6 boats in four main variants. The 66 **'Cha-Ho' class** have 20-mm main guns, two twin 14.5-mm machine guns, and a 4-tube 20-mm (7.9-in) rocket launcher. The 38 **'Chong-Jin' class** boats have an additional 85-mm tank turret, and seven **'Chong-Ju' class** are improved and enlarged with an 11-tube 122-mm multiple rocket launcher. The **'Sinpo'** class are straight copies of the Chinese or Soviet supplied P6 with no torpedoes.

The largest conventional torpedo attack craft built was the **'Shershen' class** from 1962 to 1974. This design was based on a smaller version of the 'Osa I' hull with the same powerplant and four 533-mm (21-in) tubes for long-range anti-ship torpedoes instead of missiles. Fitted with an NBC citadel, the class is intended to work with the 'Osa' missile boats in mixed brigades of coastal craft. The **'Mol' class** is a modified version for export and based on the standard 'Osa' hull. These carry shorter-range torpedoes than those carried on Soviet navy torpedo craft. The Soviets built some 85 'Shershens' and seven 'Mols', but have only some 30 'Shershens' in service at present. These are slowly being phased out.

In 1971 the 'Shershen' was joined in production by the **'Turya' class** torpedo-armed fast attack hydrofoil. This has the 'Osa II' hull and machinery with a single foil system forward. The class is usually stated to be for anti-ship attacks, but the four 533-mm (21-in) torpedo tubes fitted actually carry acoustic-homing anti-submarine torpedoes. The vessels act as fast-reaction ASW units and work in conjunction with shore-based ASW helicopters and aircraft (and other small ASW surface units) for coastal defence. For these operations they carry a dipping sonar (of the type seen on the Kamov Ka-25

'Hormone-A' ASW helicopter) fitted to their transom. The sonar is particularly useful in the Baltic and Pacific areas for searching below thermal layers.

More than 100 P4s and over 300 P6s remain in use with 14 countries (the majority are operated by the Chinese Navy, although the North Koreans maintain 60 P6s alongside their locally built versions). Over 90 'Shershen' and 'Mol' class have been supplied to 14 navies, only ten remaining with the Soviet Navy. Thirty-one 'Turya' class hydrofoils were built for the Soviet Navy, with a further 17 exported to Cuba, Ethiopia, Kampuchea and Vietnam. These were delivered without sonar and fitted with 533-mm (21-in) torpedo tubes.

Specification
'P4' class
Displacement: 25 tons full load
Dimensions: length 22.0 m (72.2 ft); beam 4.7 m (15.4 ft); draught 1.5 m (4.9 ft)
Propulsion: two diesels delivering 2,400 hp (1790 kW) to two shafts
Maximum speed: 42 kts
Complement: 12
Armament: two 457-mm (18-in) anti-ship torpedo tubes, one twin 12.7- or 14.5-mm (0.5- or 0.57-in) heavy machine-gun and between four and eight depth charges
Electronics: one 'Skin Head' search radar, one 'High Pole-A' IFF and one 'Dead Duck' IFF

Specification
'P6' class
Displacement: 73 tons full load
Dimensions: length 26.0 m (85.3 ft); beam 6.0 m (19.7 ft); draught 1.5 m (4.9 ft)
Propulsion: four diesels delivering 5,800 hp (4325 kW) to four shafts
Maximum speed: 43 kts
Complement: 12
Armament: two 533-mm (21-in) anti-ship torpedo tubes, two twin 25-mm AA guns and eight depth charges
Electronics: one 'Pot Head' search radar, one 'High Pole-A' IFF and one 'Dead Duck' IFF

Specification
'Shershen' class
Displacement: 180 tons full load
Dimensions: length 34.0 m (111.5 ft); beam 7.2 m (23.6 ft); draught 1.5 m (4.9 ft)
Propulsion: three diesels delivering 12,000 hp (8950 kW) to three shafts
Maximum speed: 47 kts
Complement: 23
Armament: four 533-mm (21-in) anti-ship torpedo tubes, two twin 30-mm AA guns and 12 depth charges
Electronics: one 'Pot Drum' search radar, one 'Drum Tilt' fire-control radar, one 'High Pole-A' IFF and two 'Square Head' IFF interrogators

Specification
'Mol' class

The 'Turya' class hydrofoil. The 31 vessels in Soviet service have been given the designation torpedny kater (torpedo cutter).

Displacement: 220 tons full load
Dimensions: length 39.0 m (128 ft); beam 7.7 m (25.3 ft); draught 1.7 m (5.6 ft)
Propulsion: three diesels delivering 15,000 hp (11190 kW) to three shafts
Maximum speed: 36 kts
Complement: 25
Armament: four 533-mm (21-in) anti-ship torpedo tubes and two twin 30-mm AA guns
Electronics: one 'Pot Head' search radar, one 'Drum Tilt' fire-control radar, one 'High Pole-B' IFF and one 'Square Head' IFF interrogator

Specification
'Turya' class
Displacement: 240 tons full load
Dimensions: length 39.0 m (128 ft); beam 7.2 m (23.6 ft) over the hull and 12.0 m (39.4 ft) over the foil; draught 1.8 m (5.9 ft) without the foil
Propulsion: three diesels delivering 15,000 hp (11190 kW) to three shafts
Maximum speed: 42 kts
Complement: 30
Armament: four 533-mm (21-in) anti-submarine torpedo tubes, one twin 57-mm AA gun and one twin 25-mm AA gun
Electronics: one 'Pot Head' search radar, one 'Muff Cob' fire-control radar, one 'High Pole-A' IFF, one 'Square Head' IFF interrogator and one helicopter-type dipping sonar

A 'Shershen' class torpedo attack craft. Latest Intelligence reports indicate that only 10 now remain in Soviet navy service, being replaced by missile vessels and hydrofoils.

'Stenka', 'Zhuk' and 'Shmel' class patrol craft

Designated as a border patrol ship (PSKR, or *pogranichnyy storozhevoy korabl*)' by the Soviets, the **'Stenka' class** currently comprises the second largest coastal-force class in service, with some 100 vessels. These are primarily operated by the Maritime Border Guard Directorate of the KGB and are built at Leningrad. The design utilizes the 'Osa' hull with the same machinery outfit as the 'Osa I' but a modified superstructure and bridge that reflect the operational role. Although used for maritime patrol, the craft have a useful ASW outfit with four single torpedo tubes for the 400-mm (15.75-in) electric-powered acoustic-homing ASW torpedo and two depth-charge racks for a total of 12 charges. A dipping sonar of the type carried on the 'Turya' class of hydrofoil is also carried. Several of the boats have had the torpedo tubes removed to make space for a motor launch, presumably for close inshore patrol where the mother ship cannot go.

To support the 'Stenkas' in their KGB role the Soviets began to build a small coastal patrol boat from 1970 onwards. Known as the **'Zhuk' class** the design is still in production primarily for export. Some 30 or more are in service with the KGB and Soviet navy, whilst over 92 have been built for transfer to 19 other countries.

The Soviets also have a great tradition in riverine and inland waterway warfare. During World War II they developed a series of improvised armoured craft for use on the Danube, Volga, Amur and Ussuri river complexes and the many large lakes found in the Soviet Union. They continued this practice with post-war designs, of which the most recent, built between 1967 and 1974, is the **'Shmel' class**. The most distinctive feature of the 85-vessel class is the forward 76-mm (3-in) gun turret, which is similar to that of the PT-76 light amphibious tank with its co-axial 7.62-mm (0.3-in) machine-gun. Behind the turret is an armoured bridge and enclosed space fitted with bulkheads, a heavy machine-gun position and several firing slits for small arms and LMGs. A twin 25-mm AA mounting with light protection is on the after deck. On a number of boats between this and the battle position are mounted one or two 17-tube BM-14 140-mm (5.5-in) multiple rocket-launcher systems for shore bombardment. It is estimated that for short-distance raiding missions, a platoon of Naval Infantry or army special forces could be carried on three 'Shmels'.

In 1981 the first of the new **'Yaz' class** of river monitors was seen in the Amur Flotilla in the Far East. A large vessel of 400 tons and armed with two single 100-mm (3.9-in) guns it had been joined by 17 sisters by 1987. The smaller **'Piyavak'** and **'Vosh'** classes are also in series construction on the Pacific coast.

Specification
'Stenka' class
Displacement: 210 tons full load
Dimensions: length 39.5 m (129.6 ft); beam 7.7 m (25.3 ft); draught 1.8 m (5.9 ft)
Propulsion: three diesels delivering 12,000 hp (8950 kW) to three shafts
Maximum speed: 36 kts
Complement: 22
Armament: four 400-mm (15.75-in) anti-submarine torpedo tubes, two twin 30-mm AA guns and 12 depth charges on two racks
Electronics: one 'Pot Drum' search radar, one 'Drum Tilt' fire-control radar, one 'High Pole-B' IFF, two 'Square Head' IFF interrogators and one helicopter-type dipping sonar

Specification
'Zhuk' class
Displacement: 50 tons full load
Dimensions: length 22.9m (75.1 ft); beam 4.9 m (16.1 ft); draught 1.5 m (4.9 ft)
Propulsion: two diesels delivering 2,400 hp (1790 kW) to two shafts
Maximum speed: 30 kts
Complement: 17
Armament: one or two twin 14.5-mm (0.57-in) heavy machine-guns
Electronics: one 'Spin Trough' search radar

Specification
'Shmel' class
Displacement: 60 tons full load
Dimensions: length 28.3m (92.8 ft); beam 4.6 m (15.1 ft); draught 1.0 m (3.3 ft)
Propulsion: two diesels delivering 2,400 hp (1790 kW) to two shafts
Maximum speed: 22 kts
Armament: one 76-mm (3-in) gun in light tank turret, one twin 25-mm AA gun, one or two 17-tube 140-mm (5.5-in) rocket-launchers, plus provision for heavy and medium machine-guns, and for mines
Electronics: none

The 'Stenka' class of patrol craft is almost exclusively operated by the Maritime Border Guard Directorate of the KGB to help prevent 'escapes' from the USSR.

A 'Schmel' class riverine warfare craft seen on the River Danube at Vienna. The Soviet navy uses many such craft on its inland waterways and is building more.

'Combattante II' and 'Combattante III' class fast sttack craft (missile)

Surprisingly enough, the French navy has not adopted either the **'Combattante II' class** or the **'Combattante III' class** for its own use. The 'Combattante II' class is reported to be derived from a West German Lürssen design and, together with its larger version, has proved very popular with a number of navies. The hull is made of steel whilst the superstructure is made of light alloys. The versatility in the design allows the operator country to choose its own electronics and weapon fits, although the French tend to be a lot happier if its Thomson-CSF fire-control systems and radars with Aérospatiale MM38 or MM40 Exocet SSMs are selected. At present the following countries have the 'Combattante II' in service: Greece (four with MM38s), Iran (12 with Harpoon SSMs), Libya (10 with Otomat SSMs) and Malaysia (four with MM38s). The Iranian craft, known as the **'Kaman' class,** are seeing extensive service in the current Iranian-Iraqi Gulf War, at least two and a 1,135-ton frigate having been lost to AM39 Exocets air-launched from Aérospatiale Super Frelon helicopters flown by the Iraqi air force. The craft have apparently launched several Harpoons against Iraqi naval ships, with at least one 'Polnocny' LSM and several 'P6' MTBs being sunk by them.

Both the 'Combattante II' and the larger steel-hulled 'Combattante III' have excellent habitability, the latter being designed for longer endurance and to act as command ships for smaller craft. The 'Combattante III' has been adopted by Greece (four with MM38s plus six locally built with cheaper machinery, electronics and missile fit of Penguin Mk II SSMs), Nigeria (three with MM38s) and Tunisia (three with MM40s). Typical class characteristics are given in the accompanying specifications. The builder for both versions is CNM at Cherbourg. The Greek 'Combattante IIIs' of the first type differ from the rest in having two rearward-firing 533-mm (21-in) torpedo tubes. These carry the West German SST4 wire-guided anti-ship active/passive acoustic homing torpedo with a warhead of 260 kg (573 lb) and maximum range of about 20 km (12.4 miles).

Libya's 'Combattantes' were involved in the 1986 confrontation with the US Sixth Fleet. The *Waheed* was sunk with all hands on the evening of 24th March by four Grumman A-6E Intruders from USS *America* which attacked with Rockeye cluster bombs and a Harpoon missile. A second 'Combattante' was believed sunk by two ship-launched Harpoons fired from the AEGIS cruiser USS *Yorktown* in the small hours of the same night.

A Type I Greek navy 'Combattante III' class missile boat with four MM38 Exocet container-launchers, two 76-mm (3-in) guns and two torpedo tubes.

Specification
'Combattante II' or 'Kaman' class
Displacement: 275 tons full load
Dimensions: length 47.0 m (154.2 ft); beam 7.1 m (23.3 ft); draught 1.9 m (6.2 ft)
Propulsion: four MTU diesels delivering 14,400 hp (10740 kW) to four shafts
Maximum speed: 36 kts
Complement: 31
Armament: four single Harpoon SSM container-launchers, one 76-mm (3-in) dual-purpose gun and one 40-mm AA gun
Electronics: one WM28 radar fire-control system

Specification
'Combattante III' class (Greek version)
Displacement: 447 tons full load

Dimensions: length 56.15 m (184.2 ft); beam 8.0 m (26.2 ft); draught 2.5 m (8.2 ft)
Propulsion: (Type I) four MTU diesels delivering 18,000 hp (13425 kW) to four shafts; (Type II) four MTU diesels delivering 15,000 hp (11190 kW) to four shafts
Maximum speed: (Type I) 36.5 kts and (Type II) 32.5 kts
Complement: 42
Armament: (Type I) two single 76-mm (3-in) dual-purpose guns, two twin 30-mm AA guns, four single MM38 Exocet SSM launcher-containers and two 533-mm (21-in) torpedo tubes; (Type II) six Penguin Mk 2 SSM launcher-containers in place of Exocet
Electronics: (Type I) one Thomson-CSF fire-control system, one Castor radar, one Pollux radar and one Triton

radar; (Type II) one Thomson-CSF fire-control system, one Decca TM1226 radar and one D1280 radar

The first of the Type II Greek navy 'Combattante III' class, Simeoforos Kavaloudis, equipped with six container-launchers for the cheaper Penguin Mk II surface-to-surface missile system in place of Exocet.

WEST GERMANY

'Type 148' and 'Type 143' class fast attack craft (missile)

The steel hulled **'Type 148' class** missile boats were ordered in December 1970 as the replacements for 20 of the old 'Type 140/141 Jaguar' class torpedo attack craft. Twelve were built by the CMN shipyard at Cherbourg with the other eight built at the Lürssen shipyard, Vegesack. All, however, were fitted out at the French yard. The design is actually designated the **'Combattante II A4L'** which, ironically, was based on a Lürssen design. All 20 craft were commissioned into service between 1972 and 1975 and constitute the Third (first 10 boats) and Fifth (second 10 boats) Fast Patrol Boat squadrons based at Flensburg (with the tender *Rhein*) and Olpenitz (with the tender *Main*) respectively.

In 1972 an order was placed for the larger **'Type 143' class** to replace the remaining 10 'Jaguars'. Built by Lürssen (seven units) and Kröger, Rendsburg (three units) the class entered service in 1976-7. They are now due for their mid-life modernization refit to bring them up to the standard of the latest missile craft. After this they will be known as the **'Type 143B' class** and based together at Olpenitz will form, with the tender *Donau*, the Second Fast Patrol Boat squadron.

In mid-1976 a repeat order was placed for 'Type 143s' to replace the ten 'Type 142 Zobel' class torpedo attack craft. Known as the **'Type 143A'**, the new boats will have wooden planked hulls on steel frames like their predecessors and also the same main armament of Exocet anti-ship missiles. All commissioned during 1982-4 and they constitute the Seventh Fast Patrol Boat Squadron at Kiel with the tenders *Neckar* and *Elbe*. During the late eighties they will be fitted with a 21-round RIM114A SAM launcher aft. They all have mine rails in place of the aft firing torpedo tubes for wire-guided torpedoes as seen on the 'Type 143/143B class'.

S 143 A

Specification
'Type 148' class
Names: *Tiger, Iltis, Luchs, Marder, Leopard, Fuchs, Jaguar, Löwe, Wolf, Panther, Häher, Storch, Pelikan, Elster, Alk, Dommel, Weihe, Pinguin, Reiher, Kranich*
Displacement: 234 tons standard, 264 tons full load

Dimensions: length 47 m (154.2 ft), beam 7 m (23 ft), draught 2.7 m (8.9 ft)
Propulsion: four MTU diesels delivering 10738 kW (14,400 hp) to four shafts
Maximum speed: 35.8 kts
Armament: four single MM38 Exocet SSM container-launchers, one single 76-mm (3-in) DP gun, one single 40-mm AA gun (or eight ground influence mines in lieu of the 40-mm)
Electronics: one 3RM20 navigation radar, one Triton tracking radar, one Pollux fire control radar, one ECM system, one Palis data link transfer system
Complement: 30

Specification
'Type 143B' class
Names: *Albatros, Falke, Geier, Bussard, Sperber, Grief, Kondor, Seeadler, Habicht, Kormoran*

Displacement: 300 tons standard, 393 tons full load
Dimensions: length 57.7 m (189.3 ft), beam 7.6 m (24.9 ft), draught 2.6 m (8.5 ft)
Propulsion: four MTU diesels delivering 11931 kW (16,000 hp) to four shafts
Maximum speed: 32-36 kts (depending upon tonnage)
Armament: four single MM38 Exocet SSM container-launchers, two single 76-mm (3-in) DP guns, two single 533-mm (21-in) torpedo tubes (for wire-guided Seal anti-ship torpedoes)
Electronics: one 3RM20 navigation radar, one WM27 fire control system, one OGR7/3 optical fire control system, one ECM system
Complement: 34-40

Specification
'Type 143A' class

The 'Type 143A' class boat Puma is seen fitted with an early 21-cell launcher for the RIM-114A SAM.

Names: *Gepard, Puma, Hermelin, Nerz, Zobel, Frettchen, Dachs, Ozelot, Wiesel, Hyane*
Displacement: 300 tons standard, 391 tons full load
Dimensions: as Type 143B class
Propulsion: as Type 143B class
Maximum speed: as Type 143B class
Armament: four single MM38 Exocet SSM container-launchers, one single 76-mm (3-in) DP gun, one 21-round RIM-114A SAM launcher (being fitted), mine rails for up to 18 ground influence mines
Electronics: one 3RM20 navigation radar, one WM27 fire control system, one FL1800 ESM system, one AGIS action information system
Complement: as Type 143B class

Israeli fast attack craft

After the USSR (and hastened in its plans by the loss of the *Eilat* to an Egyptian missile attack in 1967) the Israeli navy was the first of the 'European' powers to realize the importance of the missile craft. The first class that Israel ordered was the **'Saar' class**, built by the French CMN shipyard in Cherbourg between 1967 and 1969 to a West German Lürssen design with steel hulls and light alloy superstructures. The first six units were originally built as the **'Saar I' class** with an all-gun armament of three single 40-mm AA guns. The second six were constructed as the **'Saar II' class** with a single 76-mm (3-in) OTO-Melara gun forward, two single 12.7-mm (0.5-in) heavy machine-guns and two triple mountings for the Gabriel Mk I SSM. Currently all the 'Saars' have been modified to carry new armament. Four of the original 'Saar I' have been modified as ASW units with EDO 780 variable-depth sonar aft and two to four Mk 32 tubes for 324-mm (12.75-in) Mk 46 45-kt, 11-km (6.8-mile) range active/passive acoustic-homing ASW torpedoes. The gun fit is one single 40-mm AA and two single 12.7-mm (0.5-in) heavy machine-guns. The remaining two units have been given an extra 40-mm gun aft plus one triple and two single launchers for Gabriel Mk I and Mk II missiles. They have been redesignated 'Saar II', while the original six 'Saar II' craft have been re-equipped with a pair of Harpoon SSM launchers in place of one of the triple Gabriel mountings and redesignated the **'Saar III' class**. The remaining Gabriel launcher has been equipped to fire Mk I and Mk II missiles.

For longer-range missions in the Mediterranean and the Red Sea Israel required a new boat, so the locally designed and built **'Reshef' (or 'Saar IV') class** of steel-hulled craft was produced. The first two of these, *Reshef* and *Keshet*, were involved in the 1973

Arab-Israeli war. These craft have air-conditioned quarters, a combat operations centre, and Italian- and Israeli-built ESM/ECM systems. A total of 10 was constructed (two subsequently being transferrd to Chile), whilst three others were built in Israel for South Africa. A further nine have been built under licence at Durban, where they are known as the 'Minister' class and are armed with Skorpioen SSMs (licence built Gabriel IIs). Currently, Israeli 'Reshefs' carry a mix of two or four Harpoon and four or six Gabriel Mk II or Mk III SSMs, one 76-mm (3-in) DP gun aft, one 20-mm Phalanx CIWS forward, plus two single 20-mm cannon and three twin 12.7-mm heavy machine-guns. Some craft have an EDO sonar fitted in addition to the usual electronic fit. In 1979, one boat (the *Tarshish*) carried a temporary helicopter platform aft to enable a Bell 206 to be used in Harpoon mid-course targeting trials.

One of the results of the *Tarshish* trials was the adoption of a hangar and helicopter platform in the succeeding **'Aliya' or 'Saar 4.5' class**. These larger boats act as flotilla leaders and are armed with four Gabriel launchers and a 20-mm Phalanx CIWS forward, four Harpoons amidships, two single 20-mm cannon and four single 12.5-mm MGs. The second pair of boats have dropped the helicopter in favour of two or four more Gabriel launchers and a 76-mm DP gun. Provision has been made for the fitting of a Barak short-range VLS missile system when it eventually enters service.

Other missile craft include the one-off *Dvora* (probably the smallest missile boat in the world) and three **'Flagstaff 2' class** hydrofoils (out of what was planned to be a class of twelve).

Below: Built as a private venture by Israel Aircraft Industries and based on the 'Dabur' class coastal patrol craft, the Dvora *is one of the smallest missile boats in the world.*

A 'Reshef' class vessel, used as the testbed for the IAI Barak short-range point-defence missile system. This will take the place of the SA-7 'Grail' and the Redeye shoulder-launched missiles currently used.

Specification
'Saar II and III' classes
Displacement: 250 tons full load
Dimensions: length 45.0 m (147.6 ft); beam 7.0 m (23 ft); draught 2.5 m (8.2 ft)
Propulsion: four Maybach (MTU) diesels delivering 14,000 hp (10440 kW) to four shafts
Maximum speed: 40 kts
Complement: 35-40
Armament: see text
Electronics: one Thomson-CSF Neptune TH-D1040 radar, one Selenia Orion RTN-10X radar, ECM equipment and EDO 780 variable-depth sonar

Specification
'Reshef' class
Displacement: 450 tons full load
Dimensions: length 58.1 m (190.6 ft);

beam 7.6 m (24.9 ft); draught 2.4 m (8 ft)
Propulsion: four Maybach (MTU) diesels delivering 14,000 hp (10440 kW) to four shafts
Maximum speed: 32 kts
Complement: 45
Armament: see text
Electronics: one Thomson-CSF Neptune TH-D1040 radar, one Selenia Orion RTN-10X radar, one Elta MN-53 ECM system, one 45-barrel chaff launcher (in some), four or six 24-barrel chaff launchers and four single decoy launchers.

Specification
'Alia' class
Displacement: 500 tons full load
Dimensions: length 61.7 m (202.4 ft); beam 7.6 m (24.9 ft); draught 2.4 m (7.9 ft)
Propulsion: four Maybach (MTU) diesels delivering 14,000 hp (10440 kW) to four shafts
Maximum speed: 31 kts
Complement: 53
Armament: see text
Electronics: as on the 'Reshef' class craft

A 'Saar' class boat at sea off the coast of Israel is seen in company with a torpedo armed 'Dabur' class patrol craft.

An Israeli 'Reshef' class missile boat. Equipped with a cocktail of missile types, the vessels of this class are amongst the most capable missile boats in service.

South American river warfare craft

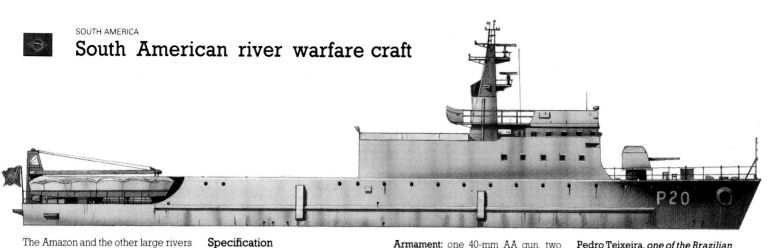

The Amazon and the other large rivers of South America provide one of the last havens for the river gunboat and its modern day counterparts. Brazil, Colombia, Peru and landlocked Paraguay all have such craft in service. The Brazilians have the largest fleet with five vessels (two 'Pedro Teixeira' class and three 'Roraima' class patrol ships) in the Amazon flotilla and one 'Thornycroft' type river monitor in the Matto Grosso flotilla. The latter dates from the 1930s. Colombia utilizes two 'Arauca' class patrol craft dating from the 1950s and a 'Baranquilla' class river gunboat built in 1930. Peru has four purpose-built (two 'Maranon' class and two 'Loreto' class) gunboats for use on the upper Amazon. Paraguay has two purpose-built 'Humaita' class river-defence ships, three 'Bouchard' class converted ex-Argentinian minesweepers, and a 1908-vintage converted tug for use on its internal river systems. Brazil has recently built a new 'Roraima' class unit for the Paraguayan navy. The *Itaipu* has a helicopter platform aft, but is otherwise similar to the Brazilian craft with the same armament.

The five Brazilian vessels belong to the Amazon flotilla and make up by far the most modern and capable river force in the continent. The two 'Pedro Teixeira' class have a helicopter platform and hanger for a Bell JetRanger, but the three 'Roraimas' each have a pair of LCVPs instead. The first of three 'Porto Esperanca' class vessels for the Matto Grosso flotilla will enter service in 1988, taking the place of the 50 year old *Parnaiba*. Midway between the 'Teixeira' and 'Roraima' classes, the new craft will have a helicopter platform and two LCVPs. Armament will comprise two single 127-m (5-in) guns and two 40-mm AA guns.

The Brazilian Parnaiba, *dating from 1937, is one of the oldest naval vessels serving anywhere in the world. Armed with one 76-mm (3-in) gun and 20-mm, 40-mm and 47-mm cannon,* Parnaiba *serves in the Matto Grosso.*

Specification
'Pedro Teixeira' class
Names: *Pedro Teixeira* and *Raposo Tavares*
Displacement: 700 tons full load
Dimensions: length 62.0 m (203.4 ft); beam 9.35 m (30.7 ft); draught 1.65 m (5.4 ft)
Propulsion: two diesels delivering 3,840 hp (2865 kW) to two shafts
Maximum speed: 16 kts
Complement: 78
Armament: one 40-mm AA gun, two single 81-mm mortars, six single 12.7-mm (0.5-in) heavy machine-guns, one helicopter and one LCVP
Electronics: two navigational radars
Built: 1972-3

Specification
'Thornycroft' type
Name: *Parnaiba*
Displacement: 720 tons full load
Dimensions: length 55.0 m (180.5 ft); beam 10.1 m (33.3 ft); draught 1.6 m (5.1 ft)
Propulsion: two Thornycroft triple-expansion steam engines delivering 1,300 hp (970 kW) to two shafts
Maximum speed: 12 kts
Complement: 90
Armament: one 76-mm (3-in) dual-purpose, two single 47-mm, two 40-mm AA and six single 20-mm AA guns
Electronics: none
Built: 1937

Specification
'Roraima' class
Names: *Roraima, Rondonia* and *Amapa*
Displacement: 365 tons full load
Dimensions: length 45.0 m (147.6 ft); beam 8.45 m (27.7 ft); draught 1.37 m (4.5 ft)
Propulsion: two diesels delivering 912 hp (680 kW) to two shafts
Maximum speed: 14.5 kts
Complement: 63

Armament: one 40-mm AA gun, two single 81-mm mortars, six single 12.7-mm (0.5-in) heavy machine-guns and two LCVPs
Electronics: three navigational radars
Built: 1975-6

Specification
'Arauca' class
Names: *Rio Hacha* and *Arauca*
Displacement: 184 tons full load
Dimensions: length 47.25 m (155 ft); beam 8.23 m (27 ft); draught 1.0 m (3.3 ft)
Propulsion: two Caterpillar diesels delivering 800 hp (597 kW) to two shafts
Maximum speed: 13 kts
Complement: 43
Armament: two single 76-mm (3-in) dual-purpose and four single 20-mm AA guns
Electronics: none
Built: 1955

Specification
'Baranquilla' class
Name: *Cartagena*
Displacement: 142 tons full load
Dimensions: length 41.9 m (137.5 ft); beam 7.16 m (23.5 ft); draught 0.8 m (2.6 ft)
Propulsion: two Gardner diesels delivering 600 hp (448 kW) to two shafts
Maximum speed: 15.5 kts
Complement: 39
Armament: two single 76-mm (3-in) and one 20-mm AA guns, and four single 7.7-mm (0.3-in) machine-guns
Electronics: none
Built: 1930

Specification
'Humaita' class
Names: *Paraguay* and *Humaita*
Displacement: 865 tons full load
Dimensions: length 70.15 m (230.2 ft); beam 10.7 m (35.1 ft); draught 1.65 m (5.4 ft)

Pedro Teixeira, one of the Brazilian vessels designed for use on the Amazon. It can carry a light Bell JetRanger helicopter and two armed LCVPs for use in the region. This large, corvette-sized vessel forms part of the Amazon Flotilla.

Propulsion: two Parsons geared steam turbines delivering 3,800 hp (2835 kW) to two shafts
Maximum speed: 17.5 kts
Complement: 86
Armament: two twin 120-mm (4.7-in), three single 76-mm (3-in) AA and two single 40-mm AA guns, plus six mines
Electronics: none
Built: 1931

Specification
'Maranon' class
Names: *Maranon* and *Ucayali*
Displacement: 365 tons full load
Dimensions: length 47.22 m (154.8 ft); beam 9.75 m (32 ft); draught 1.22 m (4 ft)
Propulsion: two British Polar diesels delivering 800 hp (597 kW) to two shafts
Maximum speed: 12 kts
Complement: 40
Armament: two single 76-mm (3-in) dual-purpose and two twin 20-mm AA guns
Electronics: none
Built: 1951

Specification
'Loreto' class
Names: *Amazonas* and *Loreto*
Displacement: 250 tons full load
Dimensions: length 46.7 m (153.2 ft); beam 6.7 m (22 ft); draught 1.2 m (4 ft)
Propulsion: two diesels delivering 750 hp (560 kW) to two shafts
Maximum speed: 15 kts
Complement: 25
Armament: two single 76-mm (3-in) dual-purpose, two single 40-mm AA and two single 20-mm AA guns
Electronics: none
Built: 1934

Amphibious Assault Ships

The 1982 conflict in the Falkland Islands has demonstrated that today, as in the Pacific operations or invasion of occupied Europe during World War II, the amphibious task force is still one of the most effective methods of projecting power over long distances.

In order to operate at the sustained 20-kt speed of modern US amphibious squadrons, the latest LSTs no longer have bow doors, and vehicles are unloaded over the pointed bow by means of a ramp.

Amphibious warfare ships have been in service since before Christ: the Romans, for example, used such vessels to transport elements of their legions in cross-Channel raids in the 1st century BC before their invasion of Britain in the 1st century AD. Since then the art and tactics of conducting amphibious assaults have been continually refined, World War II from 1939 to 1945 being a peak in the evolution. Particularly in their Pacific island-hopping campaigns, the Americans created new designs of ships and equipment for amphibious landings. The war also proved the idea of strategic landings, such as those conducted during the June 1944 D-Day assault on Normandy, in which whole armies and their resources were committed in an invasion to gain a specific strategic objective. When this war finished the lessons learnt were applied in the 1950s to the American landing at Inchon in the Korean War and to the Anglo-French landing at Suez in 1956. This latter landing saw the use of helicopters by the Royal Navy in the helicopter assault role.

The Americans digested the data from these conflicts and then produced the multi-role ship concept of the modern Landing Ship Dock (LSD), Amphibious Transport Dock (LPD) and Amphibious Helicopter Carrier (LPH), in which a single hull could combine the roles that were previously undertaken by several ships. The object was both to improve the amphibious force's capabilities and to decrease the number of vessels in a force. The Vietnam War allowed some validation of these designs and of the combat use of helicopters and resulted in the ultimate in very large multi-purpose ships, namely the 'Tarawa' class of LHA and the new amphibious assault dock (LHD) class that is under construction. Both these classes are virtually self-contained in practically all the equipment required to conduct a landing.

The most recent amphibious operations were conducted in 1982 as parts of the Falkland Islands war and the Israeli invasion of southern Lebanon. The former was a classic by the Royal Navy in terms of the projection of an amphibious assault force over 11250 km (7000 miles) and then the undertaking of the assault without the loss of any amphibious warfare vessel in an operational area only some 650 km (400 miles) from the enemy coast. The Israelis demonstrated that the Soviet operational tactic (supporting ground forces by landing battalion-sized and larger formations of mechanized infantry in the enemy's rear to seize specific objectives and to cut lines of communication and supply) works extremely well in practice.

One disadvantage of the amphibious assault is that it is relatively slow in its approach, although the Americans have solved this somewhat by the use of prepositioned merchant ships carrying the heavy equipment and supplies required, the US Marines to be kitted out with the equipment being flown into a friendly country near the scene of the conflict to marry up with it at a suitable port. The disadvantage of this is that friendly countries are required to give facilities, whereas the amphibious task force is virtually autonomous within the operational area. The latest addition to the amphibious warfare armoury is the Air Cushion Vehicle (ACV) to provide very rapid and relatively safe beach assault capabilities. The Soviet navy is the world's leading exponent of this tactic with some four types of ACV in service. The Americans are in the process of introducing this type into service over the next few years.

The amphibious assault ship HMS Fearless *and the V/STOL carrier HMS* Hermes *complete the transfers of assault units immediately prior to the British assault on the Falkland Islands.*

'Jeanne d'Arc' Class Helicopter Carrier

The single vessel of the **'Jeanne d'Arc'** class was laid down at Brest Naval Dockyard in 1960, launched in 1961 and commissioned in 1964. Although used in peacetime as a training ship for 192 officer cadets, *Jeanne d'Arc* (R97) can be rapidly converted for wartime use as an amphibious assault, anti-submarine warfare or troop transport vessel. The helicopter platform is 62 m (203.4 ft) wide and is connected to the hangar deck by a 12218 kg (26,935-lb) capacity elevator located at the after end of the flight deck. The deck is capable of flying-on two Aérospatiale SA 321 Super Frelon heavy-lift helicopters and can accommodate a further four parked. The hangar, with some internal modifications, can accommodate a further eight helicopters. At the aft end extensive machine, inspection and maintenance workshops are sited with weapon handling rooms and magazines for the armaments carried by the helicopters. In the commando-carrier or troop-transport role the ship has facilities for a 700-man infantry battalion with light equipment in her fully air-conditioned interior. France has a 9,230-man marine division and four naval commando assault units (including one reserve) available for use from its amphibious warfare ships.

A modular type action information and operations room with a SENIT-2 computerized tactical data handling system is fitted, together with a separate helicopter control bridge and a combined command and control centre for amphibious warfare operations. On each side of the funnel two LCVPs are normally carried. Under current plans she is due to pay off in 2004.

Specification:
Name: *Jeanne d'Arc*
Commissioned: 1 July 1964
Displacement: 12,365 tons full load
Dimensions: length 182 m (597.1 ft); beam 24 m (78.7 ft); draught 7.3 m (24 ft)
Propulsion: two geared steam turbines delivering 40,000 shp to two shafts
Speed: 26.5 kts
Complement: 627 (31 officers plus 596 enlisted men)
Troops: 700
Cargo: normal four Super Frelon, in wartime up to eight Super Frelon heavy-lift helicopters in hangar plus further six on deck; four LCVPs
Armament: four single 100 mm DP guns, six single MM.38 Exocet surface-to-surface missile launcher-containers
Electronics: one DRBV 22D air-search radar, one DRBV 50 surface-search radar, one DRBN 32 navigation radar, three DRBC 32A fire-control systems, one URN 6 TACAN, one SQS 503 sonar, two Syllex electronic countermeasures rocket-launchers, one SENIT-2 data system

Above: The French navy's helicopter carrier Jeanne d'Arc. Used as a training ship in peacetime, she can be rapidly converted in wartime to a commando ship, ASW helicopter carrier or troop transport.

Below: Commissioned in 1964, the Jeanne d'Arc is equipped to act as an amphibious command ship to transport a battalion of marines, or to operate up to 14 Super Frelon helicopters.

'Ouragan' Class Landing Ships Dock (TCD)

The **'Ouragan'** class of dock landing ship is used both for amphibious warfare and logistic transport by the French. They are fitted with a 120-m (397.7-ft) long well dock that has a stern gate measuring 14 m (45.9 ft) by 5.5 m (18 ft). The well dock can accommodate two 670-ton full load EDIC LCTs (carrying 11 light tanks, or 11 trucks or five LVTs) or 18 LCM6s (carrying 30 tons of cargo or vehicles). Above the well dock is a 24.2-m (79.4-ft) long six-section removable helicopter deck capable of operating one Aérospatiale Super Frelon heavy-lift helicopter or three Aérospatiale Alouette utility helicopters. If required, a 90-m (295.3-ft) long temporary deck can also be fitted to stow cargo or vehicles, but its use reduces the number of landing craft carried as half the well dock is taken up. If used with this extra deck as a logistic transport then the total cargo capacity of the vessel becomes some 1,500 tons. This can comprise either 18 Super Frelon or 80 Alouette helicopters, or 120 AMX-13 light tanks or 84 DUKW amphibious vehicles or 340 jeeps or 12 50-ton barges. There is a permanent helicopter deck for up to three Super Frelons or 10 Alouettes located next to the starboard bridge area. Two 35-ton capacity cranes handle the heavy equipment carried. Each of the two ships also has command and control facilities to operate as amphibious force flagships. They also carry an extensive range of repair and maintainance workshops to support the units embarked. Troop accommodation is provided for 349 men under normal conditions, although 470 can be carried for short distances. Three LCVPs are carried as deck cargo.

The *Orage* (L9022) is allotted to the French Pacific nuclear experimental centre as the logistic transport to and from France. It is also employed as the centre's floating headquarters, employing a modular facility within the well dock area. The *Ouragan* is due to pay off in 1990 and the *Orage* in 1993.

Specification:
Names: *Ouragan* (L9021) and *Orage* (L9022)
Commissioned: L9021 1 June 1965; L9022 1 April 1968
Displacement: 5,800 tons standard, 8,500 tons full load
Dimensions: length 149 m (488.9 ft); beam 23 m (75.4 ft); draught 5.4 m (17.7 ft)
Propulsion: two diesels delivering 8,600 hp to two shafts
Speed: 17 kts
Complement: 211 (10 officers plus 201 enlisted men)
Troops: 349 (14 officers plus 335 enlisted men) normal, or 470 overload
Cargo: 1,500 tons as logistic transport; two LCTs, or 18 LCMs plus 3 LCVP for amphibious operations
Armament: four single 40-mm AA guns, two 120-mm mortars (L9021 only)
Electronics: one DRBN 32 navigation radar, one SQS 17 sonar (L9021 only)

Used for both amphibious warfare and as a logistic transport, Ouragan is capable of deploying and supporting half a battalion of marines (349 men).

'Foudre' class landing ship dock (TCD)

The three **'Foudre' class** TCD (*Transport de Chalands de D'ebarquement*) are the replacements for the 'Ouragan' class and will be assigned to France's Rapid Reaction Force. They will be able to carry one third of a mechanized regiment, (typically 350 men) with six AMX-30 MBTs, 15 AMX-10RC armoured cars, eight VAB APCs, 30 trucks, 22 jeeps and 27 trailers, and the stores to support them. They will also be able to act as logistics support ships by carrying up to 1,800 tons of cargo when required. For the amphibious role they have extensive command and control facilities and a 30 bed sickbay with two operating rooms. The

$1,080\,m^2$ ($11,625\,ft^2$) helicopter landing platform amidships has two landing/take-off spots with a third positioned on the rolling well-dock cover. The 122 m (400.3 ft) long, 13.5 m (44.3 ft) wide well-dock itself can accommodate either two fully loaded CDIC (replacing the 650 ton EDIC LCT now in service), 10 CTM LCAs, one EDIC and four CTMs or one P400 'Super Patra' class patrol boat. A 60-ton elevator connects the cargo decks with the dock area. There are also side loading doors.

The first unit, *Foudre* (L9011), was laid down in 1986 and is due to commission in 1990, being joined by her sisters in 1992 and 1993 respectively.

Specification
'Foudre' class
Displacement: 9,300 tons standard, 11,800 tons full load
Dimensions: length 168 m (551.2 ft), beam 23 m (75.4 ft), draught 5.4 m (17.7 ft)
Propulsion: two diesels developing 14914 kW (20,000 hp) driving two shafts
Speed: 21 kts
Armament: two sextuple SADRAL point defence SAM systems with 60 missiles, one twin 40-mm AA gun, two single 20-mm AA guns, two single 12.7-mm and two single 7.5-mm machine-guns
Electronics: one Rodeo air search

radar, one Decca 2459 surface search radar, one Decca 1226 navigation radar, one optronic fire control system, one Syracuse II satellite communications system, one passive ESM system, two Sagaie decoy launchers
Complement: 210
Troops: 350 normal (475 in emergency)
Cargo: total of $1,360\,m^2$ ($14,639\,ft^2$) vehicle parking area, two CDIC or 10 CTM or one EDIC and four CTM in docking well, four Aérospatiale AS 332 Super Puma or two Aérospatiale SA 321 Super Frelon helicopters

---

'San Giorgio' class landing ship dock (LPD)

In order to support the 1,000-man San Marco marine battalion in amphibious warfare operations the Italian Navy ordered the first of the **'San Giorgio' class** landing ship dock in 1984. It was launched in February 1987 for commissioning in early 1988. The *San Giorgio* (L9892) can carry 400 fully equipped troops and has a hangar which can accommodate up to five Meridionali-Boeing Vertol CH-46C Chinooks. The forward hangar deck is taken up by a vehicle parking area for up to 36 VCC-1 APCs. A bow ramp enables the ship to beach itself for off-loading opera-

tions. A floodable well dock aft accommodates three loaded LCMs whilst three LCVPs are carried on davits (two to port, one to starboard) on the flight deck. As an alternative to the APCs and the LCMs the well deck and vehicle parking area can be used to transport 30 MBTs of an armoured regiment.

A second ship of the class, the *San Marco* (L9893), was due to be launched in June 1987 and this will be used by the Ministry of Civil Protection as a disaster relief vessel although she will be run by the navy. Both units can also

be used as ASW platforms with Agusta-Sikorsky SH-3D Sea King or EH 101 ASW helicopters embarked.

Specification
'San Giorgio' class
Displacement: 5,000 tons standard, 7,677 tons full load
Dimensions: length 133.3 m (437.3 ft), beam 20.5 m (67.3 ft), draught 5.3 m (17.4 ft)
Propulsion: two diesels developing 12528 kW (16,800 hp) driving two shafts
Speed: 21 kts
Armament: one 76-mm (3-in) DP gun,

two single 20 mm AA guns
Electronics: one RAN10S air search radar, one RTN30X fire control radar, one navigation radar, one ESM system, two 20-barrel SCLAR decoy launchers, one TACAN system, one SATNAV system
Complement: 170
Troops: 400
Cargo: 60 tons aviation fuel, normally one CH-47C or three SH-3D helicopters (maximum five CH-47C), 36 APCs, three LCM and three LCVP, $99\,m^3$ ($3,496\,ft^3$) refrigerated stores, $300\,m^3$ ($10,594\,ft^3$) dry stores

---

'Polnocny' class landing ship medium (LSM)

Designated by the Soviets as *srednyy desantnvy korabl'* (SDK, medium landing ship) the **'Polnocny'** LSM series were built between 1962 and 1973 by the Polnocny shipyard at Gdansk in Poland. A total of 64 are thought to have been completed for the Soviet navy with another 23 built for the Polish navy between 1964 and 1971. A further 20 have since been built for direct export. Of the 64 Soviet units only 40 remain in service (nine **Type C**, 24 **Type B** and seven **Type A**) with one Type A stricken and 23 other units transferred to the navies of Algeria, Angola, Cuba, Egypt, Ethiopia, India, Somalia, South Yemen, Syria and Vietnam. The Polish navy has 11 Type A, 11 Type B and one Type C in service for use by the 7th Lusatian Sea landing division of the Polish army. The export units were for India (eight Type C of which the last four have a helicopter landing platform forward), Iraq (four C with helicopter platform and 122-mm rocket launchers) and Libya (four C with helicopter platform). Of these Iraq has lost one in combat with Iranian naval forces during November 1980 and Libya lost one to fire in September 1978 during an amphibious landing exercise.

The main differences between the three sub-classes are in armament and that the 770-ton full load Type As have a convex bow form, the 800-ton full load Type Bs a concave bow-flare and the Type Cs are longer with additional troop accommodation facilities. All Soviet and Polish units have been fitted with up to four quadruple SA-N-5 'Grail' SAM launchers. Typical loads for the 73 m (239.5 ft) long Type A are four-five APCs, medium or light tanks, increasing to six-seven for the 74 m (242.8 ft) long Type Bs and eight-nine

in the Type Cs. Tank deck dimensions are 36.6×5.2 m (120×17 ft) for the 8.6 m (28.2 ft) beam 2 m (6.6 ft) draught Type A, 45.7×5.2 m (150×17 ft) for the similarly sized Type B and 53.3×6.7 m (175×22 ft) for the Type C. In the early eighties at least three of the Soviet Type Bs were converted for beach defence minefield clearance duties during amphibious assaults. They carry two small remote controlled motor boats on chutes at the stern to tow large line HE charges that are carried in side chutes.

Specification
'Polnocny' class (Type C)
Displacement: 700 tons standard, 1,150 tons full load
Dimensions: length 81.3 m (266.7 ft), beam 10.1 m (33.1 ft), draught 2.1 m (6.9 ft)
Propulsion: two diesels delivering 3729 kW (5,000 hp) to two shafts
Speed: 18 kts (19 kts Type A/B)
Armament: four quadruple SA-N-5 'Grail' SAM launchers with 32 missiles, two twin 30-mm AA guns, two 18-barrel 140-mm (5.5-in) rocket launchers (in

Designated as a Medium Landing Ship by the Soviets, the Polish built 'Polnocny' series provide a large proportion of the Warsaw Pact's amphibious lift capability in the Baltic.

Iraqi ships)
Electronics: one 'Spin Trough' navigation radar, one 'Drum Tilt' fire control radar, one 'Square Head' and one 'High Pole B' IFF systems
Complement: 40 (35 in Type A)
Troops: 180

'Ropucha' Class Landing Ships Tank

Designated *Bol'shoy Desantnyy Korabl'* (BDK) or large landing ship by the Soviets, the 'Ropucha' class has been in series production at the Polish Polnocny shipyard, Gdansk since 1975 for the Soviet navy. The class is designed for roll-on/roll-off operations with both bow and stern doors. The 630 m² (6,780 sq ft) vehicle deck stretches throughout the conventional LST-type hull. Two spaces for multiple rocket-launchers are provided forward. Some units have had four quadruple SA-N-5 'Grail' SAM launchers fitted to supplement the two twin 57-mm AA guns carried. The multi-level superstructure has been specially built to accommodate the 230 men of two Soviet Naval Infantry companies for extended periods. This, together with the capacity for carrying 24 AFVs or 450 tons of cargo, allows the Soviet navy to employ these ships on distant ocean operations. There are currently some 21 in service with the Soviet navy, whilst another was transferred to the People's Democratic Republic of Yemen in 1979. All those built have minor differences in appearance.

The 'Ropucha' Class can accommodate two companies (230 men) of Soviet Naval Infantry for extended periods, allowing the USSR naval assault capacity far from Soviet home waters.

Specification:
Displacement: 4,300 tons full load
Dimensions: length 113 m (371 ft) beam 14.5 m (47.6 ft); draught 3.6 m (11.8 ft)
Propulsion: four diesels delivering 7457 kW (10,000 hp) to two shafts
Speed: 18 knots
Complement: 90
Troops: 230
Cargo: 24 AFVs or 450 tons of stores
Armament: two twin 57-mm AA guns, and four quadruple SA-N-5 SAM launchers (32 missiles) on some units
Electronics: one 'Don-2' navigation radar, one 'Strut Curve' air-search radar, one 'Muff Cob' 57-mm gun fire-control radar, one 'High Pole-B' IFF system

Below: 'Ropucha'-class LST; all vessels of this class have minor differences in appearance. They have a higher troop-to-vehicle ratio than the earlier 'Alligator' class.

Above: A starboard view of a 'Ropucha'-class LST. Latest intelligence estimates credit the Soviets with 21 of these craft in service, with more building in Gdansk, Poland.

USSR

'Alligator' Class Landing Ships Tank

Designated *Bol'shoy Desantnyy Korabl'* (BDK) or large landing ship by the Soviets, the 14-ship 'Alligator' class was built at the Kaliningrad shipyard between 1964 and 1977. During this time the roll-on/roll-off bow and stern door design evolved to form four distinct sub-classes. The first two series are primarily for the transport role whilst the remaining two are primarily for the over-the-beach assault role. The latter two classes have a navalized split 40-round BM-21 122-mm rocket-launcher pedestal mount fitted for shore bombardment purposes. The deck crane equipment also varies within the variants: Type I has one 15-ton capacity and two 5-ton capacity cranes,

whilst Types II, III and IV have only one 15-ton capacity crane. The Type III also has a raised superstructure and a forward deckhouse for the rocket-launcher; the Type IV is similar to the Type III but with additional 25-mm AA guns.

The ships are designed to carry the equipment required by a Naval Infantry battalion landing team, although the ships can also accommodate a Naval Infantry company for long periods. The vehicle parking area includes the upper deck, and both the SA-9 'Gaskin' SAM mounted on the BRDM-2 and the tracked ZSU-23-4 AA gun system have been observed on this deck, operating in pairs to supplement the ship's nor-

mal AA armament. Most of the class are currently being fitted with two quadruple SA-N-5 'Grail' SAM close-range launcher systems. The Type IVs have in addition two 25-mm AA gun mountings on the centreline abaft the bridge superstructure. The class regularly operates off the coastline of West Africa, in the Mediterranean and the Indian Ocean.

Specification
Commissioned: 1966 to 1977
Displacement: 4,700 tons full load
Dimensions: length 114 m (374 ft); beam 15.5 m (50.8 ft); draught 4.5 m (14.7 ft)

Propulsion: two diesels delivering 6711 kW (9,000 bhp) to two shafts
Speed: 18 kts
Complement: 100
Troops: 120 normal, 300 overload
Cargo: typically 50 AFVs
Armament: one twin 57-mm AA gun, two twin 25-mm AA guns (Type IV only), one 40-round 122-mm rocket-launcher (Types III and IV), two quadruple SA-N-5 SAM launchers being fitted in most
Electronics: two 'Don Kay' or one 'Don-2' and one 'Spin Trough' navigation radars, one 'Muff Cob' 57-mm fire-control radar in some, one 'High Pole-B' IFF system

An 'Alligator'-class LST of the Soviet navy. Built in four sub-variants, the 14-ship class regularly operates off West Africa and in the Mediterranean and Indian Ocean.

'Ivan Rogov' Class Amphibious Transport Docks (LPD)

Given the Soviet designation *Bol'-shoy Desantnyy Korabl'* the name ship of the **'Ivan Rogov' class** was completed at the Kaliningrad yard in 1978 as the largest amphibious warfare vessel yet built for the Soviet Navy. A second unit, the *Aleksandr Nikolaev* was completed in 1983 with a third unit under construction with completion due by 1989. The vessel is capable of carrying a reinforced Naval Infantry battalion landing team with all its APCs and other vehicles plus 10 PT-76 light amphibious tanks. An alternative load is the tank battalion of the Soviet Naval Infantry regiment. The *Ivan Rogov* is unique in Soviet amphibious ship design as it has both a well dock and a helicopter flightdeck and hangar. This allows the ship to perform not only the traditional role of over-the-beach assault by use of bow doors and ramp, but also the stand-off assault role using a mixture of helicopters, landing craft, air cushion vehicles and amphibious vehicles.

The bow doors and internal ramp position provide access to a vehicle parking deck located in the lower forward part of the ship. Further vehicles can be accommodated in the midships area of the upper deck, access to this being by hydraulically operated ramps that lead from the bow doors and the docking well. The vehicle deck itself leads directly into the floodable well which is some 79 m (259.2 ft) long with a stern door some 13 m (42.6 ft) across. The well can accommodate up to three preloaded 'Lebed' class air-cushion vehicles (ACVs), or up to six 145-ton full load 'Ondontra' class LCMs (or two 'Lebeds' and one 'Ondontra').

Two helicopter landing spots are provided, one forward with its own flight control station, and one aft on a flight deck located above the well deck. This also has its own flight control station. Both spots have access to the massive block superstructure, the

forward pad by a ramp leading up to the hanger and the aft by a set of hangar doors. The hangar has sufficient space for up to five Kamov Ka-25 'Hormone-C' utility or the new Kamov Ka-27 'Helix-B' assault transport helicopters currently entering service with the Soviet navy. Accommodation for the embarked Naval Infantry units is located within the superstructure block itself. Vehicle and helicopter maintenance workshops are also located there. To starboard, immediately in front of the block is a tall deck house on top of which is mounted a navalized version of the Soviet army's 122-mm BM-21 rocket-launcher system. This uses two 20-round packs of launcher tubes, one to each side of a pedestal mounting that trains them in azimuth and elevation. The rockets are used to provide a saturation shore bombardment capability for the assault units. A twin 76-mm DP gun turret is located on the forecastle, whilst a twin rail pop-up SA-N-4 SAM launcher bin unit and four 30-mm CIWS Gatling guns are mounted on top of the main superstructure block to provide air defence. Extensive command, control and surveillance equipment is fitted for amphibious force flagship duties. The *Ivan Rogov* has served with the Baltic and Pacific fleets and it is thought likely that a total of four will be built, permitting one to serve with each of the four fleet commands.

Above: The first Soviet LPD, the Ivan Rogov. *Capable of transporting a reinforced Naval Infantry battalion, the ship also operates four or five 'Hormone-C' helicopters, several air cushion vehicles and an LCM.*

Right: The Ivan Rogov *has been given the Soviet designation* Bol'shoy Desantnyy Korabl' *(large landing ship). In 1982 the second ship of the class,* Aleksandr Nikolaev, *was completed at the naval shipyard in Kaliningrad.*

Specification:
Displacement: 13,000 tons full load
Dimensions: length 159 m (521.6 ft); beam 24.5 m (80.2 ft); draught 6.5 m (21.2 ft)
Propulsion: two gas turbines delivering 45,000 shp to two shafts
Speed: 26 kts
Complement: 250
Troops: 550
Cargo: typically 40-50 AFVs; two 'Lebed' class ACVs plus one 'Ondatra' class LCM or three 'Gus' class ACVs; five 'Hormone-C' helicopters
Armament: one twin SA-N-4 SAM launcher, one twin 76-mm DP gun, four 30-mm ADG6-30 AA guns, one 40-round 122-mm rocket-launcher
Electronics: two 'Don Kay' helicopter control and navigation radars, one

'Head Net-C' air-search radar, one 'Owl Screech' 76-mm gun fire-control radar, one 'Pop Group' SA-N-4 missile fire-control radar, two 'Bass Tilt' ADG6-30 fire-control radars, one 'High Pole-B' IFF system, two 'Bell Shroud' ECM, two 'Bell Squat' ECM and two chaff launchers. (*Aleksandr Nikolaev* has a slightly different electronic fit.)

The LPD Ivan Rogov.

'Frosch' Class Landing Ships Tank

The **'Frosch I'** class ships are similar but not identical to the Soviet 'Ropucha' class of LST. They are smaller, have a blunter bow shape and are fitted with a bow ramp and a much heavier armament (two twin 57-mm and two twin 30-mm). The 12-ship class was built between 1975 and 1979 to replace the obsolete 'Robbe' and 'Labo' classes of landing ships. The single vehicle deck is capable of transporting some 800 tons of cargo or up to 12 MBTs. There is no roll-on/roll-off capability due to the absence of stern vehicle ramps. Forward, on the empty deck space between the bridge and the forward twin 57-mm mounting, two 122-mm 40-round navalized split BM-21 pedestal rocket-launcher mountings have been fitted for saturation shore-bombardment purposes. The 'Frosch I'

may also be used for minelaying, the mines being laid through two stern hatches. The presence of a large number of radio antennae suggests that the vessels can also undertake amphibious operation command and control duties. In 1980 two additional units, designated **'Frosch II'**, were built at the same Peenewerft shipyard at Wolgast that built the 'Frosch I' ships. These differ from the original class in having a 5-ton capacity crane amidships and two large cargo hatches. No rocket-launchers or 30-mm AA guns are carried, although two twin 25-mm AA guns are mounted right forward to cover the beach during a landing. It is thought that these craft act as assault cargo ships during amphibious operations, possibly carrying munitions. The East Germans have one regiment of

Naval Infantry and two amphibious trained motor rifle regiments (believed to be the 28th and 29th of the 8th Motor Rifle Division) each of three motorized rifle battalions and a tank battalion to act in the amphibious assault role. The East Germans also operate with the Polish army's 7th Sea landing Division of three assault regiments and a tank battalion and a Soviet Naval Infantry Brigade during Warsaw Pact amphibious assault exercises in the Baltic.

Specification:
Displacement: 'Frosch I' 1,950 tons and 'Frosh II' 2,000 tons full load

Dimensions: length 91 m (298.4 ft); beam 11 m (36.1 ft); draught 2.8 m (9.2 ft)
Propulsion: two diesels powering two shafts
Speed: 16 kts
Complement: 40
Troops: normal 80, for limited time 160
Cargo: 12 MBTs, or 16 AFVs or 800 tons of stores
Armament: two twin 57-mm AA guns, two twin 30-mm AA guns (or two twin 25-mm AA guns in 'Frosch II'), two 40-barrel 122-mm rocket-launchers (none in 'Frosch II'), mine numbers vary according to type carried
Electronics: one 'Strut Curve' air-search radar, one 'Square Head' IFF system, one 'High Pole-B' IFF system, one 'Muff Cob' fire-control radar, one TSR333 navigation radar

'Sir Lancelot' and 'Sir Bedivere' Class Landing Ships Logistic (LSL)

The *Sir Lancelot* was ordered in 1963 as the prototype **'Sir Lancelot'** class ship of an eventual six-ship LST type design for the British army. The remaining five ships were built to a slightly modified design and called the **'Sir Bedivere'** class, all six ships being named after the knights of King Arthur's 'round table'. Since then Australia has built HMAS *Tobruk* to a modified 'Sir Bedivere' design. In 1970 the army ships passed to the control of the Royal Fleet Auxiliary (RFA), which mans them today. During the Falklands war all six ships were used, and both the *Sir Galahad* and *Sir Tristram* were severely damaged by Argentinian bombs at Bluff Cove, the former being subsequently towed out and sunk and the latter being towed back to the UK for repair after use as an accommodation ship at Port Stanley.

Built into the bow and stern are ramps and doors for a roll-on/roll-off capability and over-the-beach assault facility, whilst interior ramps connect the two cargo decks. Onboard are facilities for vehicle maintenance, and two Mexeflottes can be carried on the hull sides for use as pontoons to ferry troops and vehicles ashore. A helicopter landing platform is located at the stern, with a second pad available on the foredeck. No hangar or maintenance facilities are carried. A replacement for the *Sir Galahad* has been built and commissioned in 1987 with the same name. The new ship is similar in appearance to but quite appreciably larger than the older design, having a displacement of 8,451 tons at full load and a length of 140.5m (461ft). The beam of 19.5m (64ft) and draught of 4.3m (14.1ft) remain similar to those of the older vessels although the greater length allows for a more spacious flight deck with room to handle larger helicopters. The new *Sir Galahad* has two cranes of 25 ton and 20 ton capacity in addition to the single 20 ton and pair of 8.5 ton cranes used by the previous 'Sir Lancelots'. Extensive automation has seen the crew reduced from 69 to 52. The rebuilt *Sir Tristram* has had an 8.9m (29.2ft) insert added to the hull, increasing displacement by 120 tons, and has seen a complete reconstruction of the bridge. The longer flight deck allows the *Sir Tristram* to operate heavy-lift helicopters up to the size of the Boeing-Vertol HC.Mk 1 Chinook flown by the Royal Air Force. The only other LSL with this capability is the new *Sir Galahad*.

The Logistic Landing Ship Sir Percivale *unloads equipment into the wintery landscape of a Norwegian fiord.*

Specification

Displacement: 5,550 tons (*Sir Lancelot*) or 5,674 tons (*Sir Bedivere* class) or 5,794 tons (*Sir Tristram*) full load

Dimensions: length 125.1m (412.1ft) except *Sir Tristram* 134m (439.6ft); beam 18.2m (59.8ft); draught 18.2m (13ft)

Propulsion: two diesels delivering 9,400 bhp/7,010kW (9,520 bhp/ 7,100kW in *Sir Lancelot*) to two shafts

Speed: 17 knots

Complement: 69 (18 officers and 51 men)

Troops: 340 normal or 534 maximum

Cargo: 18 MBTs, 32 4-ton trucks, 90 tons of general cargo, 120 tons petrol, oil and lubricants, 30 tons of ammunition (*Sir Lancelot* carries only 16 MBTs and 25 trucks with the same cargo), two Mexefloats, three Wessex, Lynx or Gazelle helicopters or two Sea Kings

Armament: (wartime) two Mk 9 40-mm AA guns plus 7.62mm GPMGs, Javelin and Blowpipe man-portable surface-to-air missiles (when troops are being carried)

Electronics: two Type 1006 navigation radars, two Corvus chaff launchers, one MARISAT satellite communication system

Above: HMS Fearless *and the LSL* Sir Tristram *undergoing alongside refuelling at speed from one of the RFA's old 'Leaf'-class support ships.*

Below: The LSL Sir Bedivere *under air attack in 'Bomb Alley' (San Carlos Water) by an Argentine Dagger in May 1982.*

The 'Sir Lancelot' and 'Sir Bedivere' class of LSL. Manned by the RFA, the LSLs were heavily committed to the Falklands war. One, the Sir Galahad, *was lost whilst another, the* Sir Tristram, *suffered such severe damage that she had to be completely rebuilt.*

'Fearless' Class Amphibious Transport Dock (LPD)

The two British LPDs, *Fearless* and *Intrepid*, are under the command of Flag Officer Third Flotilla (FOF3) who is concerned with the larger warships of the Royal Navy and the naval air elements. The infamous 1981 Defence Review forecast the disposal of *Intrepid* (L11) in 1982 and of *Fearless* (L10) in 1984, but sanity finally prevailed within the Ministry of Defence in February 1982, and it was decided that both ships would continue in service, their worth later being proved during the Falkland Islands war, since without them there could not have been an assault landing to recapture the islands.

The **'Fearless'** class ships are tasked to provide amphibious assault lift capabilities using an onboard naval assault group/brigade headquarters unit with a fully equipped assault operations room from which the force commanders can mount and control all the air, sea and land force assets required for the operation. The ships also carry an amphibious detachment that consists of an assault squadron subdivided into a landing craft (LC) squadron with four LCUs (ex-LCM9s) and four LCVPs, an amphibious beach unit (ABU) with its own Land Rover and a Centurion Beach Armoured Recovery Vehicle (BARV) to attend to stranded vehicles and landing craft, and a vehicle deck party (VDP) for marshalling vehicles for embarkation on the landing craft. An LCU can carry either one Chieftain or two Centurion MBTs, or four 4-ton trucks or eight Land Rovers and trailers, or 100 tons of cargo, or 250 troops as its payload. The LCVP carries either 35 troops or two Land Rovers.

A 50.29-m (165-ft) by 22.86-m (75-ft) flight deck is built over the well deck and is capable of operating most NATO helicopter types or, if required, BAe Sea Harrier VTOL fighter aircraft. Three vehicle decks are provided, in the form of one for tracked vehicles such as tanks or self-propelled guns, one for wheeled trucks, and a half-deck that is reserved for Land Rover vehicles and trailers. The overload troop capacity is sufficient for a light infantry battalion or Royal Marine Commando with an attached artillery battery. Further light vehicle stowage space can be obtained by using the helicopter flight deck. The vessels can also act as training ships, in which 150 midshipmen and naval cadets can be embarked for nine-week courses.

In 1985 *Fearless* was placed in reserve while *Intrepid* alternates between being a training ship and an assault ship. A decision to replace these ageing vessels has been consistently deferred, although all parties involved agree that they need to be if Britain is to retain an effective amphibious capability. If they are to be replaced in the 1990s, design of their successors should by now be under way, but even by the general election of June 1987 no final decision had been made.

The amphibious assault ship HMS Fearless *under attack by an Argentine Dagger in San Carlos Water. The camouflaged aircraft can be seen passing just in front of the mainmast and almost at bridge level.*

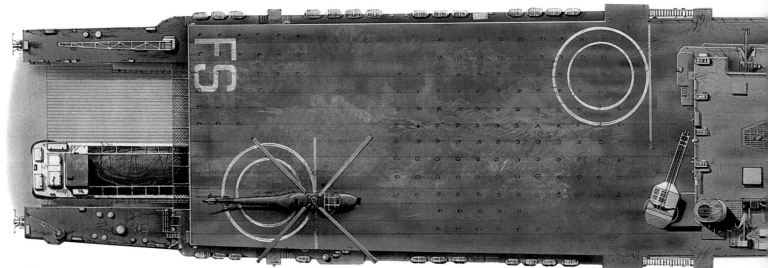

Specification:

Displacement: 12,210 tons full load
Dimensions: length 158.5 m (520 ft); beam 24.4 m (80 ft); draught 6.2 m (20.5 ft)
Propulsion: two geared steam turbines delivering 22,000 shp to two shafts
Speed: 21 kts
Complement: 617 (37 officers, 500 ratings and 80 Royal Marines)
Troops: 330 normal, 500 overload and 670 maximum
Cargo: maximum 20 MBT, one BARV, 45 4-ton trucks with 50 tons of stores, or up to 2,100 tons of stores; four LCUs and four LCVPs; five Westland Wessex HU.Mk 5 or four Westland Sea King HC.Mk 4 plus three Aérospatiale Gazelle or Westland Lynx helicopters

Armament: four GWS20 quadruple Sea Cat SAM launchers (only two in *Intrepid*), two Mk 9 40-mm AA guns (*Fearless*) or two twin 30-mm and two single 20-mm (*Intrepid*), large numbers of 7.62-mm GPMGs and Blowpipe hand-held surface-to-air missiles (when carrying combat troops).
Electronics: one Type 978 navigation radar, one type 994 air- and surface-search radar, one SCOT satellite communications system, one ESM system with a pair of Corvus chaff-launchers, one CAAIS operations room command and contol system

Right and below: Each of the four LCUs carried in the well deck of HMS Fearless can carry two MBTs or up to 250 troops. The LCVPs slung on the superstructure can each carry 35 troops or two Land Rovers. Air defence is provided by four quadruple Sea Cat launchers.

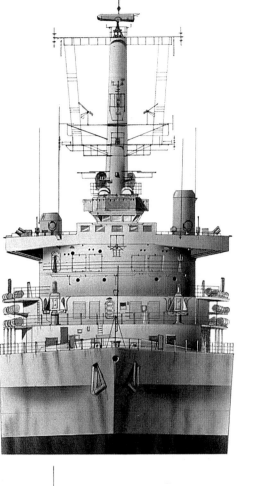

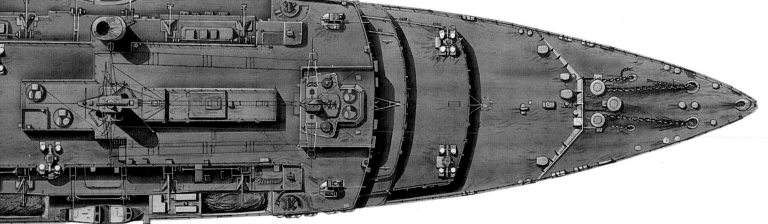

'Wasp' class multi-purpose amphibious assault ship (LHD)

Based on the older and slightly smaller 'Tarawa' class assault ship, the 40,000 ton **'Wasp' class** LHD will be the largest and most capable amphibious warfare vessel yet built. In addition to their assault roles, the 'Wasps' have been designed as Sea Control Ships, being able to convert to their secondary role as V/STOL carriers by changing their embarked air groups. The usual air group would comprise six McDonnell-Douglas/BAe AV-8B Harrier IIs and 30 or more helicopters including Boeing Vertol CH-46 Sea Knights, CH-53E Super Stallions, Bell UH-1s and AH-1 Cobras. Maximum helicopter load will be 42 Sea Knights. As Sea Control Ships the normal load will be 20 AV-8Bs and six Sikorsky SH-60F ASW helicopters.

Beneath the flight deck are two half length hangar decks connected by a 34-ton elevator amidships on the port side. There is another on the starboard side aft of the island. The single bay docking well in the stern is 15.2 m (50 ft) wide with a lowerable stern gate and can house up to three LCAC ACVs or 12 conventional LCM(6)s. The bridge is two decks lower than on the 'Tarawa' class and the command and control centre has been moved from the island into the hull for increased protection.

The US Navy's assault ships exist to land the US Marines. The 'Wasp' class has accommodation for a reinforced Marine Battalion of 1,800 men (and can carry over 2,000 in an emergency). There is over 2830 m³ (more than 100,000 ft³) of cargo space and over 1858 m² (20,000 ft²) of garage space for vehicles. Each ship in the class will have a 600 bed hospital with six oper-

ating theatres.

USS **Wasp** (LHD 1) was laid down in 1985 for completion in 1989 with USS **Essex** (LHD 2) due to enter service in 1991. Although the Navy would like 10 ships to replace the ageing 'Iwo Jima' LPH class one-for-one, only five have been planned for the moment.

Specification
'Wasp' class
Displacement: 28,233 tons light, 40,533 tons full load
Dimensions: length 257.3 m (844 ft); beam 32.3 m (106 ft); flight deck 42.7 m (140.1 ft); draught 8.0 m (26.1 ft)

Propulsion: geared steam turbines delivering 52199 kW (70,000 hp) to two shafts
Speed: 22 kts sustained, 24 kts maximum
Armament: two octuple Sea Sparrow SAM launchers with 16 missiles, three Phalanx 20-mm CIWS, eight or more 12.7-mm (0.5-in) machine-guns
Electronics: one SPS-52C 3D radar, one SPS-49(V)5 air-search radar, one SPS-67 surface search radar, one SPS-64 navigation radar, two Mk 23 TAS fire-control radars, one SPN-35A and one SPN-43B aircraft landing aids, one SLQ(V)3 ESM suite, four to eight Mk 36

The 'Wasp' class LHD is very similar to the earlier 'Tarawa' class but is even more capable. In the secondary Sea Control Ship role each ship could embark up to 20 V/STOL AV-8B aircraft.

Super RBOC chaff launchers, one OE82 satellite communication system
Complement: 1,080
Troops: 1,873 (over 2,000 in an emergency)
Cargo: total of 2127 m² (22,895 ft²) vehicle parking; 50 tons of vehicle fuel; 1,232 tons of JP-5 aviation fuel; 3087 m³ (109,016 ft³) palletized stores

---

'Whidbey Island' series landing ship dock (LSD)

Originally to have been a near repeat of the 'Anchorage' LSD design the **'Whidbey Island'** class had to be enlarged in order to carry four LCAC air-cushion vehicles in the 134.1 m (440 ft) by 15.2 m (50 ft) floodable docking well. The alternative loads to the LCACs are 21 LCM(6) or three LCU or 64 LVTP7A1 amphibious assault vehicles. The helicopter deck is raised clear of the docking well in order to ensure adequate ventilation for the gas turbine powered LCACs and has two landing spots for simultaneous use by helicopters as large as Sikorsky CH-53E Sea Stallions. No hangar is fitted but helicopter (and AV-8B) refuelling facilities are available. The additional deck cargo of one LCM(6), two LCPL Mk 12 and an LCVP Mk 7 is handled by two cranes (one of 60-ton and the other of 20-ton capacity). Three units are in service, the **Whidbey Island** (LSD41), **Germantown** (LSD42) and **Fort McHenry** (LSD43) with five more either building or on order for commissioning between 1988 and 1990.

The follow-on class is the **LSD49** 'Modified Whidbey Island' design, four of which (from an original requirement for six) have been requested for building from Fiscal Year 1988 onwards. These 16,000-ton full load units are essentially a cargo variant of the basic design and will only carry two LCAC with 1238 m² (13,330 ft²) of vehicle parking space and 1132.7 m³ (40,000 ft³) of palletized stores. The troop lift capacity remains the same.

Specification
'Whidbey Island' class
Displacement: 11,274 tons light, 15,726 tons full load
Dimensions: length 185.8 m (609.6 ft); beam 25.6 m (84 ft); draught 6.2 m (20.5 ft)
Propulsion: four diesels developing 31021 kW (41,600 hp) driving two shafts
Speed: 22 kts
Armament: two 20-mm Phalanx CIWS, two single 20-mm AA (25-mm from

LSD45 onwards), eight single 12.7-mm (0.5-in) machine-guns
Electronics: one SPS-49 air search radar, one SPS-67 surface search radar, one SPS-64 navigation radar, one URN-25 TACAN system, one SLQ-32(V)1 ESM system, four Mk 36 Super RBOC chaff launchers
Complement: 505
Troops: 504
Cargo: 90 tons JP-5 aviation fuel, helicopter landing pad, four LCAC or

Seen just after launch, USS Whidbey Island *is the first of a series of LSDs optimized for operations with the US Navy's LCAC (air-cushion landing craft).*

21 LCM(6) or three LCU or 64 LVTP7A1 plus one LCM(6), two LCPL Mk 12 and one LCVP Mk 7; 1214 m² (13,067.4 ft²) of vehicle parking area; 149 m³ (5,261.9 ft³) palletized stores

'Blue Ridge' Amphibious Command Ships (LCC)

The two **'Blue Ridge'** class integrated air, land and sea amphibious assault command ships are the first and only ships constructed by any nation solely for that role. A third ship of the class (designed at the outset for both amphibious and fleet command) was also programmed but was subsequently cancelled. In the late 1970s, as a result of the retirement of the elderly 'Cleveland' class flagship cruisers the two 'Blue Ridge' vessels also took on fleet flagship duties, the *Blue Ridge* herself becoming the flagship of the West Pacific 7th fleet and *Mount Whitney* the flagship of the Atlantic 2nd fleet.

The basic hull design and propulsion machinery is similar to that of the 'Iwo Jima' class LPHs, with the larger hangar area devoted to accommodation, offices and operations rooms required by the maximum possible 200 officers and 500 enlisted men of the embarked flag group. The ships have comprehensive satellite communications, command, control and intelligence analysis facilities fitted. These include the Amphibious Command Information System (ACIS); the Naval Intelligence Processing System (NIPS); the Naval Tactical Data System (NTDS) with its AN/UYK-20 and AN/UYK-7 digital computers to give an overall picture of the tactical underwater, surface and air warfare situations; Link 11 and Link 14 automatic data transmission systems to allow the exchange of tactical information with NTDS-equipped ships and Airborne Tactical Data System (ATDS)-equipped aircraft; extensive photographic laboratories and document publication facilities; and the satellite communications system with OE82 antenna, SSR-1 receiver and WSC-3 transceiver. Both ships have been fitted with Fleet Command Centers, protected by Kevlar armour.

The vessels each carry three LCPs, two LCVPs and one 10-m (32.8-ft) personnel launch in Welvin davits situated in prominent sponsons projecting from the ships' sides. A helicopter landing area is located at the stern but there are no hangar or maintenance facilities aboard. A small vehicle garage and elevator are provided. When necessary the ships operate two small utility helicopters as the ship's flight.

Specification:
Names: *Blue Ridge* (LCC19) and *Mount Whitney* (LCC20)
Commissioned: LCC19 14 November 1970 and LCC20 16 January 1971
Displacement: 19,290 tons full load
Dimensions: length 189 m (620 ft); beam 25 m (82 ft); draught 8.8 m (29 ft)
Propulsion: one geared steam turbine delivering 22,000 shp to one shaft
Speed: 23 kts maximum and 20 kts sustained

Complement: 775 (41 officers plus 734 enlisted men)
Flag Group: 700 (200 officers and 500 enlisted men) plus 150 marines.
Armament: two twin Mk 33 76-mm (3-in) AA, two 8-tube Mk 25 Sea Sparrow BPDMS launchers, two 20-mm Mk 16 Phalanx CIWS
Electronics: one SPS-48 3D-search radar, one SPS-10 surface-search radar, one SPS-40 air-search radar, two Mk 115 missile fire-control systems, two Mk 56 gun fire-control systems, two Mk 35 fire-control radars, four Mk 36 Super RBOC chaff launchers, one SLQ32(V)3 ESM system, one OE82 satellite communications system and one SRN6 TACAN

The nerve centre of an amphibious assault, the command ship USS Blue Ridge *(LCC19). The* Blue Ridge *also serves as the US 7th Fleet flagship and is homeported at Yokosuka, Japan.*

USS Blue Ridge *(LCC19). Fitted with a vast array of command, control and communications systems, the vessel is well suited for its additional role of Fleet flagship.*

'Iwo Jima' Class Amphibious Assault Ships Helicopter (LPH)

Ever since 1955, when the former escort carrier *Thetis Bay* was converted to a helicopter assault ship, the United States Navy has maintained a vertical airlift capability for the US Marine Corps. The **'Iwo Jima'** class ships were built to an improved World War II escort carrier design with accommodation for a US Marine infantry battalion landing team fore and aft of the centrally located box hangar. These vessels were the first in any navy to be designed specifically to carry and operate helicopters, and as such no catapult or arrester gear is fitted. The flight deck is able to operate or recover up to seven Boeing Vertol CH-46 Sea Knight or four Sikorsky CH-53 Sea Stallions simultaneously. The hangar deck, with a 6.1-m (20-ft) height clearance can accommodate 19 CH-46s or 11 CH-53s. The normal air group is a mixture of between 20 and 24 Sea Knights, four Sea Stallions and four Bell AH-1 Cobra attack or Bell UH-1 'Huey' utility helicopters. On LPH2, 3, 11 and 12 two foldable 22727-kg (50,100-lb) capacity deck-edge lifts are carried, whilst on LPH7, 9 and 10 the lifts have been reduced to 20000-kg (44,090-lb) capacity. Because (with the exception of LPH12 which has two LCVPs on davits) they do not carry landing craft, the ships are limited in the size of equipment they can carry for the embarked US Marines. Two small elevators carry palletized cargo from the cargo holds to the flight deck, whilst a small parking area for light vehicles and towed artillery pieces is also provided.

During 1972 to 1974 LPH9 operated as an interim sea control ship carrying BAe AV-8A Harrier VTOL fighters and Sikorsky SH-3 Sea King ASW helicopters. When converted back to an LPH

The 'Iwo Jima'-class LPH. This was the world's first ship class designed and constructed specifically to operate helicopters. Each LPH can carry a Marine battalion landing team with all its equipment, a reinforced helicopter squadron, and supporting personnel.

LPH9, USS Guam, carrying three Marine Corps AV-8A Harrier aircraft. In 1971 the Guam was modified to operate as an interim Sea Control Ship, carrying both Harriers and Sea King ASW helicopters.

she retained the Air Surface Classification and Analysis Centre (ASCAC) that was fitted for the experimental role. Several other LPHs have also operated as minesweeping headquarters boats, embarking US Navy RH-53 helicopter minesweeping units. These vessels cleared North Vietnamese ports in 1973 and the Suez Canal in 1974. All helicopter operations are controlled from a dedicated command and control centre located in the flight deck island. The 'Iwo Jima' class have extensive casualty handling facilities with a fully equipped 300 bed hospital. Currently USS *Iwo Jima* (LPH 2), USS *Guadalcanal* (LPH 7), USS *Guam* (LPH 9) and USS *Inchon* (LPH 12) serve with the Atlantic Fleet and USS *Okinawa* (LPH 3), USS *Tripoli* (LPH 10) and USS *New Orleans* (LPH 11) are in the Pacific. All are receiving limited service life extension (SLEP) refits but are to be replaced by the vastly more capable 'Wasp' class in the 1990s.

Specification
Displacement: 10,732-11,877 tons light, 18,000-18,825 tons full load

Dimensions: length 183.7 m (602.3 ft); beam 25.6 m (84 ft); draught 7.9 m (26 ft)
Propulsion: one geared steam turbine delivering 22,000 shp to one shaft
Speed: 23 kts maximum and 20 kts sustained
Complement: 754 (55 officers plus 699 enlisted men)
Troops: 2,090 (190 officers and 1,900 enlisted men)
Cargo: total 399.6-m^2 (4,300-sq ft) vehicle parking area; 24605 litres (6,500 US gal) MOGAS vehicle fuel; 1533090 litres (405,000 US gal) JPS Aviation fuel; 1059.8m^3 (37,425 cu ft) palletized stores
Armament: two twin Mk 33 76-mm (3-in) AA guns, two 8-tube Mk 25 Sea Sparrow BPDMS launchers; two 40-mm saluting guns; two 20-mm Mk 16 Phalanx CIWS
Electronics: one each SPS-10 surface-search, SPS-40 air-search, SPS-58 3D, LN-66 navigation radars, one SPN-43 aircraft landing aid, four Mk 36 Super RBOC chaff launchers, one SLQ 32(V)3 ESM system, one OE82 satellite communication system and one URN-25 TACAN system

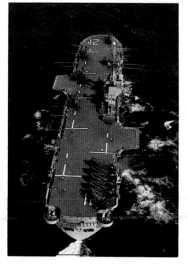

Based on an improved World War II escort carrier design, the 'Iwo Jima'-class vessels were the first to specifically accommodate helicopters. Here USS Inchon (LPH12) is shown with CH-46s on deck.

'Tarawa' Class General-Purpose Amphibious Assault Ships (LHA)

The 'Tarawa' class ships are the largest amphibious warfare ships yet constructed. They are intended to combine the capabilities of the LPH, the LPD, the LCC and the LKA in a single hull. The class was originally to have numbered nine, but as a result of the end of the Vietnam War and budgetary constraints the eventual number built was five. The Litton/Ingalls Pascagoula shipyard built them by means of its multi-ship construction technique between 1971 and 1979.

The ship's sides are vertical for some two-thirds of the length in order to maximize the internal space available for cargo. An 81.7 m (268 ft) long by 23.8 m (78 ft) wide hangar with a 6.1 m (20 ft) overhead is located above a similarly sized well deck set into the stern. The hangar is served by an 18182-kg (40,085-lb) capacity side lift to port and a larger 36364-kg (80,170-lb) capacity centreline lift at the stern. The docking well, vehicle deck, cargo holds and hangar deck are connected by a series of five elevators capable of carrying 1000-kg (2,205-lb) palletized loads. The three forward elevators serve the vehicle deck and use a conveyor belt system, whilst the aft two elevators (located at the other end of the belt) serve both the well deck, where an overhead cargo-carrying monorail system takes the pallets onto the landing craft, and the hangar deck. An angled ramp from the hangar deck leads to the flight deck to allow direct loading of helicopters.

Above: Lead ship of the LHA class, USS Tarawa, about to recover a Marine Corps V/STOL AV-8A Harrier during the 1980 Philippines 'Valiant Blitz' exercise.

Right: As a result of post-Vietnam budget restraints, only one more LHA was built after USS Nassau (LHA4), instead of the five planned.

Below: 'Tarawa'-class LHA.

Forward of the docking well (and connected to it and the flight deck by ramps) are the vehicle decks. These normally accommodate 160 tracked vehicles, artillery pieces and trucks together with 40 LVTP-7 amphibious assault personnel carriers. The well deck can accommodate up to four LCUs or two LCUs and three LCM8s or 17 LCM6s. The four LCUs and eight LVTP-7s can be launched simultaneously from the well deck. The vessels themselves normally carry two LCM6s and two LCPs stowed on deck for launch by a large deck crane. The aircraft hangar has the capacity for 30 Boeing Vertol CH-46 Sea Knight or 19 Sikorsky CH-53 Sea Stallion helicopters, although the normal air group embarked tends to be either 16 CH-46s, six CH-53s, four Bell AH-1 Sea-Cobra gunships and two Bell UH-1 utility or six CH-46s, nine CH-53s, four AH-1s and the two UH-1 helicopters. Both the BAe AV-8A Harrier and the Rockwell OV-10 Bronco fixed-wing aircraft have also been operated, the former being a VTOL close-support fighter and the latter a STOL observation/attack aircraft. A 464.5 m² (5,000 sq ft) training and acclimatization room is fitted for the 1,900-man reinforced US Marine battalion carried to exercise in a controlled environment. A 300-bed medical unit (with operating rooms, X-ray room, isolation ward, hospital ward, laboratories,

pharmacy, dentistry room, mortuary and medical store rooms) is also carried.

To act as an amphibious squadron flagship the LHA is fitted with the Tactical Amphibious Warfare Data System (TAWDS) to provide command and control over the group's aircraft, weapons, sensors and landing craft. The same satellite communications system and data links as fitted to the LCCs are carried. Two of the LHAs are assigned to the Atlantic fleets while the other three are with the Pacific fleets.

Specification

Displacement: 25,120 tons light, 39,300 tons full load
Dimensions: length 250 m (820 ft); beam 32.3 m (106 ft), flight deck width 36 m (118.4 ft); draught 7.9 m (26 ft)
Propulsion: two geared steam turbines delivering 70,000 shp to two shafts
Speed: 24 kts maximum and 22 kts sustained
Complement: 1,014 (94 officers plus 920 enlisted men)
Troops: 1,903 (172 officers plus 1,731 enlisted men)
Cargo: total of 3134-m² (33,735-sq ft) vehicle parking area; four LCUs or two LCUs and three LCM8s or 17 LCM6s plus two LCM6s and two LCPs; maximum 38 CH-46 sized helicopters; 37855 litres (10,000 US gal) of MOGAS

vehicle fuel; 378540 litres (100,000 US gal) of JP5 aviation fuel; 3311 m³ (116,925 cu ft) palletized stores
Armament: two single Mk 45 127-mm (5-in) DP guns, two 20-mm Mk 16 Phalanx CIWS, six single Mk 67 20-mm AA guns, two octuple Mk 25 Sea Sparrow SAM launchers.
Electronics: one each SPS-52B 3D, SPS-40B air-search, SPS-10F air-search, SPN-35 navigation and SPS-53 navigation radars, one Mk 86 gun fire-control system, two Mk 115 missile fire-control systems, one SPG-60 fire-control radar, one SPQ-9A fire-control radar, four Mk 36 Super RBOC chaff

LHA2 USS Saipan. The LHA class will be joined by up to 12 of the similar but slightly larger LHD class, the first five of which will augment the US Navy's current amphibious lift assets. The remaining seven will replace the LPHs from the late 1990s on a one-for-one basis.

launchers, with SLQ-32(V)3 ESM equipment, one WLR-1 ECM system, one OE82 satellite communication system, and one URN-25 TACAN system.

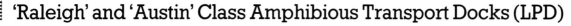

USA

'Raleigh' and 'Austin' Class Amphibious Transport Docks (LPD)

The LPD is a further development of the dock landing ship (LSD) with an increased troop and vehicle capacity at the expense of a reduction in the dock well size. The LPD essentially combines the troop-carrying of the APA with part of the cargo-carrying AKA, and the vehicle and landing craft capabilities of the LSD designs in one hull. Of the three-ship **'Raleigh'** class one has been converted to the Command Middle East Force (COMIDEASTFOR) flagship. This ship, USS *La Salle*, serves with the Indian Ocean task forces. The 'Raleigh' class ships have a stern docking well 51.2 m (168 ft) long and 15.2 m (50 ft) wide that can accommodate one LCU and three LCM6s, or four LCM8s, or 20 LVTP-7 amphibious vehicles or two Landing Craft Air Cushion. In addition, two LCM6s or four LCPLs are carried on the helicopter deck and lifted overboard by crane. The helicopter deck covers the landing craft well, but there are no onboard hangar or maintenance facilities. Up to six Boeing Vertol CH-46 helicopters can be operated for short times from the deck. An overhead monorail stores-transfer system is used to load the landing craft in the well deck from the forward cargo holds. Ramps connect the vehicle decks, docking well and flight deck, which can also be used to park additional vehicles if required. Side ports in the hull provide a roll-on/roll-off capability when docks are available.

The later **'Austin'** class ships are enlarged versions of the 'Raleigh' class. The docking well is the same size, but a 12-m (39.4-ft) extension has been inserted just forward of the well to increase the vehicle- and cargo-carrying capacities. A fixed flight deck is located above the well with two

landing spots. All except LPD4 are fitted with a variable 17.7 m (58 ft) to 19.5 m (64 ft) long, 5.8 m (19 ft) to 7.3 m (24 ft) wide hangar that can be extended to about 24.4 m (80 ft) long if required. Up to six CH-46s can be operated, although the hangar can accommodate only one utility helicopter. The LVTP-7 capacity is increased

Right: Similar to but larger than HMS Fearless, USS Shreveport (LPD12), can, like several of her sisters, act as an amphibious squadron flagship.

Below: The Austin class LPD USS Dubuque. From 1986 onwards this class, together with the 'Iwo Jima'-class LPHs, will undergo a service life extension programme (SLEP).

to 28 with alternative loads of one LCU and three LCM6s or nine LCM6s or four LCM8s. LPD7 to LPD13 are fitted with amphibious squadron flagship duties with an additional superstructure deck. Both classes have satellite communications systems of the type fitted to the LCCs. One 'Raleigh' and five 'Austin' class ships serve with the Atlantic fleets, whilst six 'Austin' class and the other 'Raleigh' serve in the Pacific fleets. The two 'Raleighs' are not scheduled for modernization, although all of the 'Austins' will receive SLEP refits by 1992 to extend their service lives by some 15 years.

Specification:
Displacement: LPD1/2 13,900 tons full load; LPD4/6 15,900 tons full load; LPD7/10 16,550 tons full load; LPD11/13 16,900 tons full load: LPD14/15 17,000 tons full load
Dimensions: (LPD1 and LPD2) length 159.1 m (521.8 ft); beam 30.5 m (100 ft); draught 6.7 m (22 ft); (LPD4 to LPD15) length 173.8 m (570 ft); beam 30.5 m (100 ft); draught 7 m (23 ft)
Propulsion: two geared steam turbines delivering 24,000 shp to two shafts
Speed: 21 kts maximum and 20 kts sustained
Complement: LPD1 413 (24 officers plus 389 enlisted men); LPD2 410 (23

officers plus 387 enlisted men); LPD4 to LPD15 410-447 (24-5 officers plus 386-442 enlisted men)
Flag group: LPD7 to LPD13 90
Troops: LPD1 to LPD6 930; LPD7 to LPD13 840; LPD14 and LPD15 930
Cargo: LPD4 to LPD15 (LPD1/2 figures are reduced slightly) total 1034.1-m² (11,130-sq ft) vehicle parking area; one LCU and three LCM6s or nine LCM6s or four LCM8s or 28 LVTP-7s; 616 m³ (21,750 cu ft) of palletized stores or 472 m³ (16,670 cu ft) of ammunition; 84545 litres (22,335 US gal) of MOGAS vehicle fuel; 368425 litres (97,328 US gal) of AVGAS aviation fuel; 17035 litres (4,500 US gal) of AV-LUB oil;

850095 litres (224,572 US gal) of JP5 aviation fuel
Armament: LPD1/2 three twin Mk 33 76-mm (3-in) AA guns, LPD4/15 two twin Mk 33 76-mm (3-in) AA guns; all to be fitted with two 20-mm Mk 16 Phalanx CIWS
Electronics: one SPS-10 surface-search radar, one SPS-40 air-search radar, one LN66 navigation radar, one URN-25 TACAN, four Mk 36 Super RBOC chaff launchers, one SLQ 32(V)1 ESM system, and one OE82 satellite communication system

---

'Newport' Class Landing Ships Tank (LST)

The **'Newport'** class represents the ultimate design in post-World War II LST design. The vessels use a pointed bow which allows them to sustain the speed of 20 kts required by American amphibious ships. There are both bow and stern ramps for unloading vehicles. The 34-ton aluminium bow ramp is 34.14 m (112 ft) long and can carry up to 75-ton loads. It is handled over the bow by two supporting derrick arms. The stern ramp has direct access to the tank deck to allow the unloading of LVTP-7s directly into the water. The stern ramps can also be mated to a landing craft or a pier for unloading purposes. Vehicles are driven onto the lower deck via a 75-ton capacity ramp or through a passage in the superstructure that leads to the helicopter deck aft. This has no hangar or helicopter maintenance facilities. Four pontoon causeway sections can be carried on the hull sides. These are handled by two derrick cranes located immediately aft of the two funnel intakes. The vehicle decks can alternatively be used for 500 tons of general cargo if required. Cargo space for ammunition, diesel fuel, MOGAS fuel and AVGAS supplies are also available. A total of nine ships are with the Atlantic fleets, and nine with the Pacific fleets. The remaining two are with the Naval Reserve Force, one in the Atlantic and one in the Pacific. An OE82 satellite

USS Newport *(LST1179) standing just offshore and in the process of lowering her bow ramp for vehicle disembarkation during a landing exercise.*

communications antenna and WSC-3 transceiver is fitted on all ships.

Specification:
Class: *Newport* plus 19 others
Commissioned: 1969-72
Displacement: 8342-8450 tons full load
Dimensions: length 159.2 m (522.3 ft); beam 21.2 m (69.5 ft); draught 5.3 m (17.5 ft)
Propulsion: six diesels delivering 16,500 bhp to two shafts
Speed: 20 kts sustained
Complement: 290 (18 officers plus 272 enlisted men
Troops: 431 (20 officers plus 211 enlisted men)
Cargo: total 1765-m² (19,000-sq ft) vehicle parking area for 25 LVTP-7s and 17 2½-ton trucks, or 21 M48/M60 MBTs and 17 2½-ton trucks, or 500 tons of general cargo; three LCVPs and one LCPL; 72.3 m³ (2,550 cu ft) ammunition; 508900 litres (134,438 US gal) of AVGAS aviation fuel; 27230 litres (7,194 US gal) of MOGAS vehicle fuel; 96150 litres (25,400 US gal) of diesel fuel
Armament: two twin Mk 33 76-mm (3-in) AA guns (to be replaced by two 20-mm Mk 16 Phalanx CIWS)

Electronics: one SPS-10 surface-search radar, one LN/66 navigation radar or CRP 3100 in LST 1188 and 1192-94, one Mk 36 Super RBOC chaff launcher, one OE82 satellite communication system

From above, USS Harlan County *(LST1196) displays the unusual lines of the 'Newport' class. Visible on the hull sides astern of the funnels are four detachable pontoon/causeway sections.*

'Cabildo', 'Thomaston' and 'Anchorage' Class Landing Ships Dock (LSD)

The LSD is a World War II design for carrying landing craft and heavy vehicles such as tanks. There are no **'Cabildo'** class LSDs still in service with the United States Navy, but three remain in service with other navies: the *Cheng Hai* with Taiwan, the *Nafkratoussa* as the HQ landing ship of the Greek navy and the *Galicia* with Spain. The 9,375-ton full load 'Cabildo' class can carry three LCUs or 18 LCM6s or 32 LVTP-5/7 amphibious carriers in its 103 m (338 ft) long, 13.3 m (43.66 ft) wide well deck. The class can also carry 1,347 tons of cargo, and 100 2½-ton trucks or 27 M48 MBTs or 11 helicopters as well. Troop accommodation is limited to 137 overnight or 500 for short day runs. The crew numbers 18 officers and 283 enlisted men. Maximum speed is 15.4 kts and the armament is a variable number of 40-mm AA guns. A helicopter platform is fitted over the well deck although no hangar or maintenance facilities are carried.

The **'Thomaston'** class was the first post-World War II LSD design, and stemmed from Korean War experiences. The docking well is 119.2 m (391 ft) long and 14.6 m (48 ft) wide, and can accommodate three LCUs or 19 LCM6s or nine LCM8s or 48 LVTP-7s. A vehicle-parking area forward of the dock can accommodate a further 30 LVTPs if required. The ship carries two LCVPs and two LCPLs in davits, but no palletized cargo is carried. The 'Thomaston' class ships are due to be relaced by the new 'Whidbey Island' class.

The **'Anchorage'** class is similar to the 'Thomaston' class, but the ships have a tripod mast to distinguish them.

USS Pensacola *(LSD38) off the coast of Massachusetts. 'Anchorage'-class LSDs were designed to incorporate lessons learned in World War II and Korea, and are similar to the 'Thomaston'-class LSDs.*

A removable helicopter landing platform is fitted over the major part of the docking well; the size of which has been increased to 131.1 m (430 ft) long by 15.2 m (50 ft) wide to accommodate three LCUs or 21 LCM6s or eight LCM8s or 50 LVTP-7s. The vessels also carry one or two LCM6s stowed on deck and one LCPL and one LCVP on davits. Troop capacity is also increased. Two 'Anchorage' class and one 'Thomaston' class ships serve with the Atlantic fleets whilst three 'Anchorage' and one 'Thomaston' class ships have the LCC satellite communications fit. Most of the 'Thomastons' have by now been decommissioned and passed to the National Defence Reserve Fleet where they will remain ready for emergency or wartime mobilization.

Specification:
Displacement: LSD28/31 and LSD35 11,270 tons full load; LSD32/34 12,150 tons full load; LSD36/40 13,700 tons full load

Dimensions: (LSD28 to LSD35) length 155.5 m (510 ft), beam 25.6 m (84 ft); draught 5.8 m (19 ft); (LSD36 to LSD40) length 168.6 m (553.3 ft); beam 25.6 m (84 ft); draught 6 m (20 ft)
Propulsion: two geared steam turbines delivering 24,000 shp to two shafts
Speed: 22.5 kts maximum and 20 kts sustained
Complement: LSD28/35 331-341 (18 officers plus 313-323 enlisted men), and LSD36/40 341-345 (18 officers plus 323-328 enlisted men)
Troops: LSD28/35 340, and LSD36/40 376
Cargo: LSD28/35 (LSD36/40 1115-m^2 (12,000-sq ft) vehicle parking area) total 975-m^2,(10,500-sq ft) vehicle parking area; three LCUs or 19 LCM6s or LCM8s or 48 LVTP-7s; 85 m^3 (3,000 cu ft) ammunition; 4540 litres (1,200 US gal) of AVGAS aviation or MOGAS vehicle fuel; 147650 litres (39,000 US gal) of diesel fuel
Armament: three twin Mk 33 76-mm (3-in) AA guns; two 20-mm Mk 16 Phalanx CIWS
Electronics: one SPS-10 surface-search radar, one SPS-6 (or SPS-40 in

LSD36/40) air-search radar, one Mk 36 Super RBOC Chaffroc system with associated ESM equipment

USS Anchorage (LSD36) *is very similar to the earlier and marginally smaller 'Thomaston' class of LSDs. She can accommodate three LCUs or up to 48 Marine LVTP-7 amphibians.*

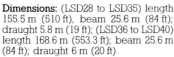

USA

'Charleston' Class Amphibious Cargo Ships (LKA)

The five **'Charleston' class** attack transports were briefly removed from the active list in the 1980s but *Charleston* and *St Louis* are back with the Atlantic and *Durham, Mobile* and *El Paso* are with the Pacific fleets. The LKA is designed to carry all the heavy equipment and supplies for the amphibious assault landing, and are the first to be designed specifically and built for the role. All previous ships of either the LKA or assault transport (LPA) types were either converted from or built to merchant ship designs. The class is fitted with a helicopter landing pad aft but no hangar or maintenance facilities are carried. Troop accommodation is limited to 226 but four LCM8s, four LCM6s, two LCVPs and two LCPs are normally carried as deck cargo. The landing craft and super heavy equipment are off-loaded by two 78.4-ton capacity heavy-lift cranes. There are also two 40-ton capacity booms and eight 15-ton capacity booms aboard. Cargo holds for palletized stores and ammunition are provided together with vehicle parking areas.

Originally designated Attack Cargo Ship (AKA), USS Durham was redesignated Amphibious Cargo Ship (LKA) in 1969. The five-vessel 'Charleston' class was the first class in the US Navy fitted with fully automated main propulsion plants.

Specification:
Names: *Charleston* (LKA113), *Durham* (LKA114), *Mobile* (LKA115), *St Louis* (LKA116) and *El Paso* (LKA117)
Commissioned: LKA113 19 December 1968, LKA114 24 May 1969, LKA115 29 September 1969, LKA116 22 November 1969 and LKA117 17 January 1970
Displacement: 20,700 tons full load
Dimensions: length 175.4 m (575.5 ft); beam 18.9 m (62 ft); draught 7.7 m (25.5 ft)
Propulsion: one steam turbine delivering 19,250 shp to one shaft
Speed: 20 kts sustained
Complement: 325 (24 officers and 301 enlisted men)
Troops: 226 (15 officers plus 211 enlisted men)
Cargo: not known
Armament: three twin Mk 33 76-mm

(3-in) AA guns; two 20-mm Mk 16 Phalanx CIWS to be fitted
Electronics: One LN/66 navigation radar, one SPS-10 surface-search

radar, four Mk 36 Super RBOC chaff launchers, one SLQ-32(V)1 ESM system, and one OE82 satellite navigation system

---

USA

Special Forces Transports

Since the deletion of the USS *Grayback* transport submarine in January 1984 the US Navy has made a special effort to increase its covert forces transportation resources as part of the American Armed Services Special Forces Expansion Program. Two former SSBNs of the 'Ethan Allen' class, the USS *Sam Houston* (SSN609) and the USS *John Marshall* (SSN611) were converted between 1983-5 as special mission submarines. Their duties include the transportation of frogmen and commandos whose wartime role is to infiltrate enemy coasts and harbours for reconnaissance and demolition purposes. The refits included the fitting of additional bunks and messing facilities for up to 85 Special Forces

personnel, the removal of some missile tubes and conversion of the others to air-locks, equipment stowage bins and Swimmer-Delivery Vehicle (SDV) garages. The latter can house varying numbers of two-man Mk9, four-man Mk7 and six-man Mk8 submersibles. The *Sam Houston* serves with the Pacific Fleet whilst the *John Marshall* is attached to the Atlantic Fleet. In addi-

A patrol boat at Subic Bay demonstrates one end of the US Navy's special forces delivery capability. The swimmers on the dinghy are shielded from the shore by the larger boat, and can be dropped off even at higher speed without arousing suspicion.

Amphibious assault ships

tion to these conversions a Pacific Fleet based SSN of the 'Sturgeon' class, USS **Cavalla** (SSN684), was converted in 1982 to carry an SDV Dry Deck Shelter stowage cylinder on the aft casing so she could act as a troop transport. The total US Navy requirement under the Special Forces plan is for seven submarines to have Special Forces capabilities by Fiscal Year 1992 and it is probable that other ex-SSBNs and SSNs will be converted over the next few years for this work.

For use by the US Navy's Special Boat Squadrons Special Boat Units (SBU), in direct support of the eventual six Sea-Air Land (SEAL) teams, there are a number of what are termed Special Warfare Craft (SWC). The fastest will be the 19 vessel **'Sea Viking SWC-Medium'** class currently under construction. These are rigid sidewall air cushion vehicles with flexible rubber seals at the bow and stern. All will be in service by Fiscal Year 1992 and they will be supported by 36 **'Seafox SWC-Light'** glass reinforced plastic hulled, 11.3-ton full load. 32kt craft. These are fitted with secure voice communications systems, an IFF system, night and low light vision equipment, and carry aft a five or six man rubber raft.

For use by US Navy Reserve SBU there are 22 mini **Armoured Troop Carriers (ATC)**. These 11m (36.1ft) long, 3.9m (12.8ft) shallow draught rectangular shaped vessels have aluminium hulls with ceramic armour and are fitted with a bow ramp. The crew totals two and the cargo can either be two tons of equipment or up to 15 Special Forces personnel. The armament can include up to four single 12.7-mm heavy machine-guns, a 40-mm Mk19 automatic grenade launcher and a

60-mm mortar plus the weapons of the passengers. An LN66 navigation radar can be fitted. Seven examples of a new **High Speed Boat** will also be in service by Fiscal Year 1992.

The largest vessels in use by the SBUs are three converted LCUs. Known as **Auxiliary Swimmer Delivery Vehicle (ASDV) 1-3** they support diving operations and have had their midship areas decked over and a light crane fitted aft. They also have a decompression chamber and operate with a crew of 13. Only small arms are carried.

Specification
'Ethan Allen' class SSN
Displacement: 6,930 tons surfaced, 7,880 tons full load
Dimensions: length 125m (410.1ft), beam 10m (32.8ft), draught 9m (29.5ft)
Propulsion: one SW5 pressurized water cooled reactor powering two steam turbines driving one shaft
Speed: 18kts surfaced, 25kts dived
Torpedo tubes: four 533mm (21in) bow
Basic load: eight Mk48 533-mm (21-in) dual anti-ship/ASW wire guided torpedoes
Electronics: one BPS-9 surface search radar, one active/passive BQS-4 sonar, one BQR-19 surface search sonar, one BQR-15 towed sonar array, one BQR-7 passive bow sonar, one underwater telephone, one satellite navigation system, one satellite communications system, one towed communications buoy
Complement: 124 (13 officers and 111 enlisted men)
Troops: 85 (10 officers and 75 enlisted men)
Cargo: unknown number SDVs

Specification
'Sea Viking SWC-Medium' class
Displacement: 83 tons light, 115 tons full load
Dimensions: length 23.9m (78.4ft), beam 10.7m (35.1ft), draught (on cushion) 0.6m (2ft), (on hull) 1.5m (4.9ft)
Propulsion: two diesels developing 2685kW (3,600hp) driving two shafts
Speed: 35kts
Armament: Stinger Post shoulder launched SAMs, two 25-mm Sea Vulcan

The missile tubes of an SSBN converted to special forces transport are large enough to hold swimmer delivery vehicles or to act as lockout chambers enabling divers to operate while submerged.

CIWS
Electronics: one SPS-64(V)9 navigation radar, one ARGO AR700 ESM system, two Mk36 Super RBOC chaff launchers
Complement: 9
Troops: 16

'Atsumi' and 'Miura' Class Landing Ships Tank

Although composed of several large and many smaller islands, Japan has relatively few amphibious assault ships, the reason being that such vessels tend to suggest an offensive rather than defensive naval role. Hence there is a distinct reluctance on the part of Japanese politicians rather than the Japanese Maritime Self-Defense Force to have a large number of such units available.

There are currently two main classes of amphibious warfare vessels in service, the **'Atsumi'** and the **'Miura'** class LSTs. Both are of conventional bow ramp assault-over-the-beach design. The 'Miura' class ships are slightly larger in tonnage and dimensions

and can carry more cargo. The 'Atsumi' class was built by Sasebo Heavy Industries and commissioned between 1972 and 1977, whilst the 'Miura' class was built by the Ishikawajima Harima shipyard of Tokyo and commissioned between 1975 and 1977. The 'Atsumi' class can carry 130 troops and 20 vehicles, together with two LCVPs in davits and a third on deck, amidships. The 'Miura' class ships can carry 190 troops and 1,800 tons of cargo or 10 type 74 MBTs plus two LCVPs in davits and two LCM6s on deck. The LCMs are handled by a travelling gantry with folding rails that extend over the ship's side to lower the craft into the water. Any ground forces embarked

would have to come from the Japanese Ground Self-Defense Force.

Specification:
Names: *Atsumi, Motobu* and *Nemuro; Miura, Ojika* and *Satsuma*
Commissioned: 'Atsumi' class 1972-7; 'Miura' class 1975-7
Displacement: 'Atsumi' 2,400 tons and 'Miura' 3,200 tons full load
Dimensions: 'Atsumi' class length 89m (291.9 ft); beam 13m (42.6 ft); draught 2.6m (8.5 ft); and 'Miura' class length 98m (321.4 ft); beam 14m (45.9 ft); draught 3m (9.8 ft)
Propulsion: two diesels delivering 4,400 hp to two shafts
Speed: 14 kts

Complement: 'Atsumi' 100 and 'Miura' 118
Troops: 'Atsumi' 130 and 'Miura' 190
Cargo: 'Atsumi' 20 vehicles and three LCVPs; 'Miura' 1,800 tons of stores or vehicles, or 10 MBTs, plus two LCVPs and two LCM6s
Armament: 'Atsumi' two twin '40-mm AA guns; 'Miura' one twin 76-mm (3-in) Mk33 AA gun, one twin 40-mm AA gun
Electronics: 'Atsumi' one OPS-9 radar; 'Miura' one OPS-14 radar, one OPS-16 radar, one GFCS1 fire-control system

In spite of her many islands, Japan does not maintain a significant amphibious warfare capability. The largest vessels, the 'Miura' class, can accommodate and land up to 190 troops at a time, together with up to 10 MBTs.

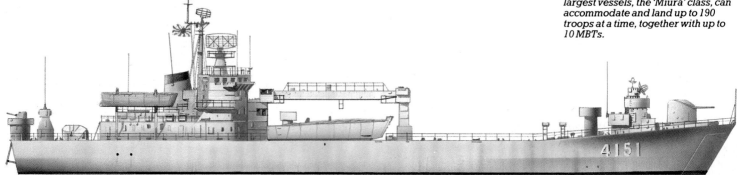

Modern Military Hovercraft

Modern sea warfare is hovering on the brink of a revolution as great as that sparked off by HMS Dreadnought in 1906. A British invention of the 1950s may well give the surface combatant of the year 2000 a performance undreamed of only a decade ago.

The only current hovercraft likely to see action are the SR.N6s and the BH.7 'Wellington' patrol craft of Iran, and the six SR.N6s of Iraq. The BH.7 was also the subject of some of the Royal Navy's Mine Countermeasures trials during which the air-cushion vehicle proved its suitability for the role.

Despite the fact that the hovercraft or ACV (Air-Cushion Vehicle) was a British invention more than 25 years ago, the lead in design and use of such craft has long since been lost by the UK to the USSR. With an operational fleet having at least six different classes, the Soviet navy has consistently demonstrated the craft's great versatility and viability as an assault vehicle, logistic transport and, it is believed, mine warfare vessel. In addition the USSR is actively exploring the two related areas of the Surface-Effect Ship (SES) and the Wing-In-Ground effect (WIG) aircraft for military applications.

Although the US Navy has realized the military potential of ACV and SES technology, so far it has limited its acquisition of the former to the LCAC landing craft plus a number of earlier trials craft, and of the latter to several SES prototypes and the new MCH 'Cardinal' class for mine countermeasures duties.

In Europe only France has shown a genuine interest in SES warships, whilst the Royal Navy has been forced to abandon hovercraft development (paying off its last ACV in the autumn of 1985) because of the lack of funds and lack of interest on the part of the MoD. Ironically, early in 1986

it was revealed that senior British ship designers and naval officers would be spending a month or so studying the US Navy's SES-200 trials during its eight-month demonstration visit to various European NATO navies.

In the Far East the People's Republic of China is also actively building ACV designs both for military purposes and research. Its Type 722 'Jing-sah' class is similar to a scaled-down British SR.N4 in appearance and is equal in most respects to any Western or Soviet design of similar type.

The Gulf War between Iraq and Iran, which is still being fought, has given ACVs their first extended use in a total-war situation, the only previous operational experience in a combat zone having been during the Vietnam War in the mid-1960s when the US Navy used three licence-built copies of the SR.N5 in the Mekong delta region.

A British Hovercraft AP1-88 demonstrates the air-cushion vehicle's ability to operate over terrain too thick to sail through, and too thin to drive over. It is estimated that 70 per cent of the world's beaches can be landed on by ACVs, as opposed to 17 per cent usable by conventional amphibious forces.

SR.N6 'Winchester' class air-cushion vehicle

UK

Designed originally as a fast ferry for operations in sheltered waters, the **BHC SR.N6 'Winchester' class** ACV has evolved into a number of variants over the years. Although extensively tested by the Royal Navy and British army all over the world, including the Falklands, the SR.N6 craft used were sold in 1982 following the demise of the Hovercraft Trials Unit. The basic **SR.N6 Mk 1** can accommodate either 38 passengers or 3 tons of supplies, and is in use with the Egyptian navy (one) and the Royal Saudi Arabian Frontier Force and Coast Guard (eight). This model was followed by the wholly military logistic support **SR.N6 Mk 2** and **SR.N6 Mk 3** variants, which feature a roof loading hatch and specially strengthened side decks for long loads weighing up to 0.5 ton; a roof-mounted armament of one 7.62- or 12.7-mm (0.3- or 0.5-in) machine-gun is carried for defensive purposes. The maximum payload is increased to 5 tons of supplies or between 20 and 30 fully armed troops. Only the Egyptian (two Mk 2s) and Iranian (two Mk 2s) navies have this type in service, though the former has had all three of its SR.N6s modified to carry six 500-kg (1,105-lb) ground mines if required. The Iranian navy also has six **SR.N6 Mk 4** variants in service. These are used for coastal defence duties and can carry either a 20-mm cannon or SS.12 wire-guided

missiles as alternatives to the more usual 7.62-mm medium machine-guns. The Iraqi customs service also uses the same hovercraft, but as the **SR.N6 Mk 6C** general-purpose model, with a larger cabin to accommodate up to 55 passengers or between 5 and 6 tons of supplies. Six are in use, and are known to have been used for combat duties in the Gulf War.

Saudi Arabia also has eight units of the **SR.N6 Mk 8** type in service. This is the latest of the military variants to be produced: it can carry up to 55 fully-equipped troops in the assault role, or have the same armament alternatives as the Mk 4 when used as a patrol craft. It differs from the earlier variants in having only a single propeller and the addition of two air conditioning units on the roof aft of the cockpit.

Specification
SR.N6 Mk 8
Dimensions: length 18.3 m (60.0 ft); beam 8.5 m (28.0 ft)
Propulsion: one 1,050-shp (785-kW) gas turbine driving one lift fan and one propeller
Weights: maximum 16.7 tons; payload see text
Speed: 50 kts
Electronics: one navigation radar

Above: SR.N6 'Winchester' is the military variant of the widely-used SR.N6 fast ferry. It can be used in the logistics role over swampy terrain or, as here, as a fast coastal patrol craft. It can be armed with 20-mm cannon or with short-range SSMs.

Left: The SR.N6 Mk 2/3 is a militarized version of the standard civil ferry, and unlike the later Mk 6 seen above is powered by a single propeller. This model was operated by the Royal Navy trials unit in locations as diverse as Hong Kong and the Falklands (ironically, practising amphibious landings!).

Variants of the SR.N6 are in service worldwide, involved in seismic survey, search and rescue, freight haulage, crash rescue and firefighting, amongst other tasks. The twin-propellered Mk 6 has a payload of between five and six tons of equipment or up to 55 passengers.

The immediate predecessor of the SR.N6 was the seven-ton SR.N5, developed in the early 1960s. The SR.N5 had the distinction of being the first air-cushion vehicle to go to war, serving with the US Navy and the US Army in Vietnam, and with the British army during the Indonesian confrontation.

BH7 'Wellington' class air-cushion vehicle

The **BHC BH7 'Wellington' class** was designed specifically for navy and military use, the **BH7 Mk 2** prototype serving with the Royal Navy (from 1970 to late 1985, when funds ran out) as an advanced-technology trials craft to evaluate hovercraft in the logistic support, fishery protection, ASW and MCM roles. This machine was followed on the production line by two **BH7 Mk 4** logistic support and four **BH7 Mk 5** combat versions for the Iranian navy. The former, armed with medium machine-guns on each side of the cabin, can carry loads such as 170 fully-armed troops, or 60 troops with three Land Rovers and trailers, or two light armoured vehicles, or up to 14 tons of supplies. The Mk 5s were designed for coastal defence duties, and have recesses on their side decks for two medium-range anti-ship SSMs (such as the MM.38 Exocet) plus the ability to carry a radar-controlled twin 30-mm turret on the foredeck in front of the centre cabin, which is used as the operations centre. Although not armed as such in Iranian service, the Mk 5s and the logistic Mk 4s have seen considerable combat service during the Gulf War.

In 1982 the Saudi Arabian navy ordered eight **BH7 Mk 5A** combat/logistic hovercraft, which are essentially similar to the Mk 5 but retain the bow door of the logistic model in order

Right: Seen here speeding past HMS Kent, the BH7 was evaluated by the Royal Navy from 1970 until 1985 in both combat and logistic support roles, but the funds for this important work ran out in 1985.

Below: The Mk 5 is capable of 58 kts and can carry four Exocet surface-to-surface missiles. The Iranians have made great use of their logistic support version, which can carry up to 170 fully-equipped troops.

to keep the load-carrying capability. However, instead of the 30-mm turret two single 20-mm cannon can be mounted on the roof positions previously used for machine-guns.

A follow-on version is the **BH7 Mk 20** multi-role craft, which is a stretched model with greater payload and the latest advances in skirt technology. To date no country has bought this variant.

Specification
BH7 Mk 5A
Dimensions: length 23.9 m (78.33 ft); beam 13.9 m (45.5 ft)
Propulsion: one 4,250-shp (3169-kW) gas turbine driving one lift fan and one propeller
Weights: maximum 55 tons; payload see text
Speed: 58 kts
Electronics: one navigation radar

Above: The latest variant of the BH7 'Wellington' is the Mk 20 Fast Attack Craft, which can carry an impressive weapon fit, in this case a pair of Rarden 30-mm cannon and four Sea Skua surface-to-surface missiles. Sea Cat SAMs or Exocet SSMs are alternative armaments.

Ekranoplan wing-in-ground effect machines

Since 1965 the Soviets have been experimenting in the Caspian Sea area with what has become known as the **Ekranoplan** or 'Caspian Sea Monster'. This machine has a potential speed of 300 kts (556 km/h; 346 mph) or more, and operates at a height of between 3.5 to 14 m (11.5 to 46 ft) above water, marshland or other such terrain. With a main hull like that of a wide-body airliner, the Ekranoplan can carry a payload of over 90 tons, or some 900 fully-equipped troops or Naval Infantry. Its propulsion system comprises eight marinized gas turbines mounted above a forward stub wing and two propulsion turbines aft installed at the base of a dihedral tailplane. The mode of operation is that all the engines are used to start the Ekranoplan moving whilst the machine is in contact with the water; the forward engines are

then directed downwards so that their exhausts create an air-cushion effect under the vehicle's main wing. The growing lift then raises the vehicle clear of the water so that the forward engines can be reorientated to direct their blast back over the upper surface of the wing to establish additional lift and so rapidly increase the forward motion until the cruising speed at which flight can be sustained is established. By flying in and out of this ground-effect cushion the Ekranoplan can clear shipping, shorelines and other obstructions as required. Such a capability is particularly useful to the Soviet navy for amphibious assault and logistic support duties as this type of vehicle effectively overcomes the problems of sea conditions, tidal currents, underwater obstacles, and defensive sea and land minefields by

flying over them.

A smaller **Turboprop Ekranoplan** has also been tested. Based on the 'sea monster' concept, this has improved aerodynamic shape and the rear-mounted gas turbines replaced by a single 15,000-shp (11184-kW) turboprop. The forward engines are also replaced by two internally-mounted gas turbines to provide the power augmentation for take-off and the initial lift. The new variant has also been used for amphibious assault trials with a swing-nose arrangement to allow for the carriage of vehicles and outsized loads. A missile attack variant (with two single underwing container-launchers for SS-N-22 anti-ship cruise missiles) has also been seen. According to American intelligence this type has entered slow series production as the *Orlan* class.

Specification (provisional)
Ekranoplan
Dimensions: span 40.0 m (131.23 ft); length 91.4 m (300.0 ft)
Propulsion: 10 gas turbines
Weights: maximum 307.4 tons; payload see text
Speed: 300 kts

Specification
Turboprop Ekranoplan
Dimensions: span 30.5 m (100.0 ft); length 60.9 m (200.0 ft)
Propulsion: one 15,000-shp (11184-kW) turboprop and two gas turbines
Weights: maximum 216 tons; payload 59 tons of cargo or 500 troops
Speed: 280 kts
Armament: see text

'Lebed' class air-cushion vehicle

The NATO reporting named **'Lebed' class** multi-duty surface-effect landing craft was first seen in prototype form in 1973 and entered series production in 1976-7. Used as amphibious initial assault landing and logistics-over-the-shore vehicles, 'Lebeds' are normally carried in pairs by the 'Ivan Rogov' class LPDs in their stern well docks. For an assault the 'Lebeds' would be preloaded before embarking. The design is an original Soviet one, and is thought to have been undertaken by the Soviet navy's High-Speed Ship Design Bureau in Leningrad. Twenty 'Lebeds' are in service with the Baltic, Black Sea and Pacific Fleets as well as aboard the LPDs. A bow ramp is provided for vehicle loading and unloading, whilst personnel can use doors located aft. Typical payloads include two PT-76 light amphibious tanks, two BTR-60/70/BMP-1/2 APCs, two loaded trucks up to a total weight of 34.38 tons, 120 Naval Infantry or some 40 tons of supplies.

In 1982 the prototype of the 'Lebed' successor, the **'Tsaplya' class**, was seen. This is now believed to be in series production on the construction line that was used for the 'Lebed' class.

A further design, called the **'Pelikan' class** is also undergoing trials.

Specification
'Lebed' class
Dimensions: length 24.8 m (81.4 ft); beam 10.8 m (35.4 ft)
Propulsion: three 3,600-shp (2684-kW) gas turbines driving four lift fans and two propellers
Weights: maximum 85 tons; payload see text
Speed: 70 kts (60/65 kts normal)

Armament: one ADMG6-30 six-barrel CIWS mounting on forward quarter of the starboard superstructure
Electronics: one navigation radar, and one 'High Pole-B' IFF system

The cockpit of the 'Lebed' is on the port side of the craft, balanced by a turret-mounted ADMG 30-mm remote-controlled Gatling-type cannon to the starboard. Typical payloads would include two PT-76 light tanks or two BMP infantry combat vehicles, or up to 40 tons of freight.

Mounted on the deck of a Soviet transport vessel, the 'Lebed' class of amphibious assault hovercraft is somewhat smaller than the American LCAC or the British Vosper VT2. The class has been designed to operate out of the docking wells of 'Ivan Rogov' class amphibious assault ships.

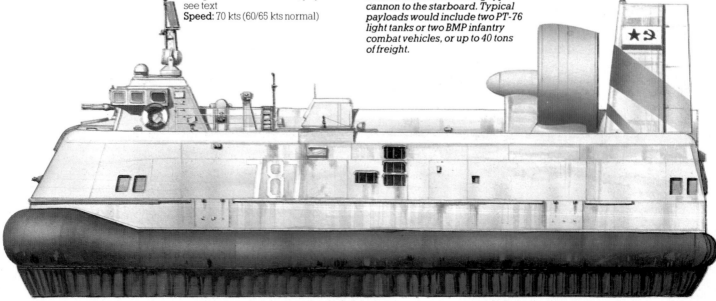

'Aist' class air-cushion vehicle

Built at the Leningrad Shipyards, the air-cushion vehicle known to NATO as the **'Aist' class** is the Soviets' first large ACV design, and while similar in general appearance to the British SR.N4 Mk 2 'Mountbatten' class is much heavier. The prototype was launched in 1970 and following extensive testing the class entered series production in 1975. Since then several variants have been built, these differing in fin height, overall length, superstructure detail and armament configuration. Some 20 'Aists' are in service at present, and more are being built. Used as an amphibious assault and logistic supply ACV, the 'Aist' can deliver Naval Infantry, armoured vehicles and supplies to beach-heads which can be well inland. Only two of the Soviet fleets (the Baltic and Black Sea Fleets) deploy the 'Aists', the former having its units extensively photographed by NATO aircraft and ships during Warsaw Pact landing exercises. Large bow and stern loading ramps provide through-ship opera-

tions, and typical payloads for the craft are two MBTs, four PT-76 light amphibious tanks and 50 Naval Infantry, three BTR-60/70/BMP-1/2 APCs and 100 Naval Infantry, four trucks and 100 Naval Infantry, 220 Naval Infantry or up to 50 or 60 tons of supplies.

Specification
'Aist' class
Dimensions: length 47.8 m (156.8 ft); beam 17.5 m (57.4 ft)
Propulsion: two 24,000-shp (17894-kW) gas turbines driving four lift fans and four propellers
Weights: maximum 270 tons; payload see text
Speed: 80 kts (60/65 kts normal)
Armament: two twin 30-mm turrets over the bow and two quadruple SA-N-5 'Grail' SAM launchers
Electronics: one 'Spin Trough' navigation radar, one 'Drum Tilt' fire-control radar, one 'High Pole-B' IFF system, one 'Square Head' IFF system, and two chaff launchers

Seen operating with Mil Mi-8 'Hip' helicopters off the Baltic coast of the German Democratic Republic, the Leningrad-built 'Aist' class large amphibious ACV is about the same size as the 'Mountbatten' class used on the English Channel, although giving the impression of being more rugged.

An 'Aist' class air-cushion vehicle on exercise in the Baltic delivers a PT-76 light amphibious tank of the Soviet Naval Infantry to the beach-head. These large machines give Soviet planners great flexibility during manoeuvres along the coasts of Northern Europe.

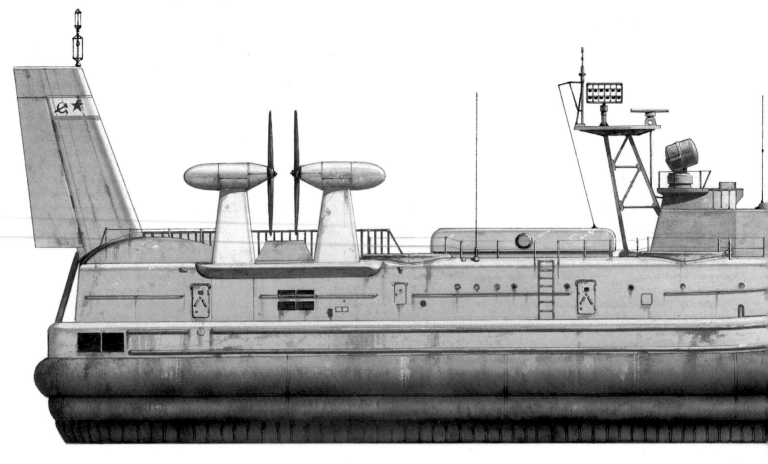

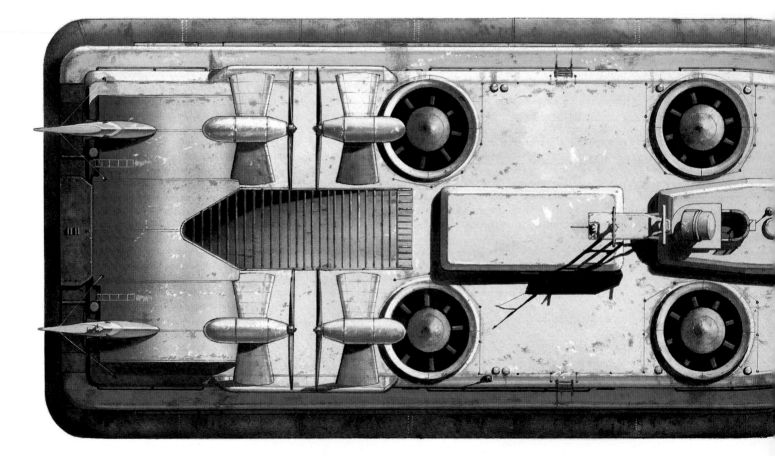

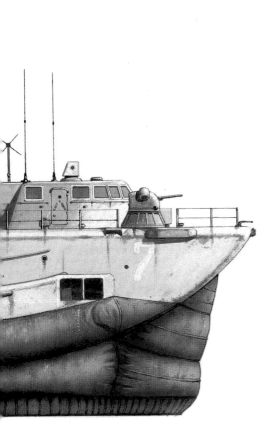

USSR 'Aist' Class
Large Naval Air-Cushion Vehicle

In service with the Black Sea and Baltic Fleets of the Soviet navy, the 'Aist' class has been in production since 1975 at a rate of approximately two completions per year. A typical load during operations on the Baltic would be two T-72 MBTs and two platoons (60 men) of a naval infantry company. Armament comprises two twin 30-mm DP turrets together with an associated 'Drum Tilt' AA fire control radar.

'Aist' class hovercraft are driven by twin marinized NK-12MV gas turbines originally developed by Kuznetsov to power the Tu-95 'Bear' bomber. Earlier models had the engine air intake at the mouth of a long dorsal tunnel, as seen here, but this was later eliminated.

'Gus' class air-cushion vehicle

Developed from the 50-seater 'Skate' class amphibious passenger ferry ACV, the **'Gus' class** logistic support ACV was tested in prototype form from 1969 onwards, series production of 36 craft taking place between 1970 and 1982 at a steady rate of two or three units per year. Deployed by all four Soviet fleets (the Northern, Baltic, Black Sea and Pacific), the 'Gus' can carry either a full Naval Infantry platoon of 25 men or several tons of supplies. It is used extensively for river patrol, special forces small-unit troop insertions, beach-head reconnaissance, and amphibious assault and logistic missions. For the last, the 'Ivan Rogov' class LPDs can each carry three 'Gus' class ACVs in place of the

two 'Lebed' class ACVs and one 'Ondatra' class LCM usually embarked. Some six or so of the 36 units were completed with two pilot positions and have been issued to the 'Gus' class ACV battalions of the fleets as operational conversion trainers. There has also been at least one further derivative of the design with twin ducted propellers, but this is believed not to have progressed beyond the prototype stage. It is likely that the long-term successor of the 'Gus' will be a much larger ACV whose first prototype is due soon.

Specification
'Gus' class
Dimensions: length 21.33 m (70.0 ft); beam 7.1 m (23.3 ft)
Propulsion: three 780-shp (582-kW) gas turbines driving one lift fan and two propellers
Weights: maximum 26.7 tons; payload see text
Speed: 60 kts (40 kts normal)
Armament: small arms and LMGs
Electronics: one navigation radar, and one 'High Pole-B' IFF system

The 'Gus' class logistic support ACV is roughly equivalent to the British SR.N6, although used by the Soviets in combat roles much more than those in the west. Used extensively by Soviet naval infantry on river patrol, small-unit insertions and assaults, the class serves with all Soviet fleets.

New Soviet air-cushion vehicles

During the 1980s four new Soviet naval ACV prototypes were sighted by NATO reconnaissance units. The first, named the **'Tsaplya' class** by NATO, is thought to be the successor to the 'Lebed' class which is about to end its production run. It is similar in size, configuration and performance to the British BH7 Mk 4 and incorporates a bow door and central load well. Designed for use aboard the 'Ivan Rogov' class LPDs and their successors, the craft can carry one PT-76 light amphibious tank and 80 Naval Infantry, 160 Naval Infantry, or some 25 tons of cargo. The second design, named the **'Utenok' class**, is slightly longer but smaller overall, and appears to be designed to carry one T-54/55/62/72/74 MBT as its primary payload. With two 'Utenoks' currently undergoing extensive testing along with the single 'Tsaplya', it is possible that both designs are actually complementary to one another with the aim that the 'Ivan Rogov' class LPDs will eventually have the ability to deliver MBTs beyond the water line of a beach-head rather than relying on the more conventional 'Ondatra' class LCM carried at present. If this assumption is correct, it is probable that the LPDs will be carrying mixed loads of 'Lebeds' and 'Utenoks', or 'Lebeds' and 'Tsaplya', or 'Tsaplya' and 'Utenoks' by the next decade, the actual mix depending upon the operation to be mounted. The third craft has been given the NATO reporting name **'Peli-**

kan'** and is believed to be broadly similar to the 'Tsalplaya' design. The fourth type, known as the **'Promornik' class** is the largest military air-cushion vehicle yet revealed. Designed and built at Leningrad, the first unit was seen taking part in amphibious exercises in the Baltic during 1986. The new class is estimated to be able to carry a payload of two MBTs, or four PT-76 light tanks plus a detachment of Soviet Naval Infantry. Like the earlier 'Aist' class the 'Promornik' design has a Roll-on/Roll-off hull, with large bow and stern doors and ramps. Three gas-turbine powered ducted fans at the stern propel the craft while four horizontally mounted hull fans provide lift. Armament includes a pair of Gatling type 30-mm CIWS and two quadruple SAM launchers, possibly for a naval variant of the SA-14 'Gremlin' man portable system known as the SA-N-8.

Specification (provisional)
'Tsaplya' class
Dimensions: length 24.0 m (78.75 ft; beam 14.0 m (45.9 ft)
Propulsion: not known
Weights: maximum 100 tons; payload see text
Speed: 65 kts
Armament: two 30-mm twin turrets
Electronics: one 'Spin Trough' navigation radar, and one 'High Pole-B' IFF system

Specification (provisional)
'Utenok' class
Dimensions: length 26.3 m (86.3 ft); beam 13.0 m (42.7 ft)
Propulsion: not known
Weights: maximum 80 tons; payload see text
Speed: 65 kts

Armament: two 30-mm twin turrets
Electronics: one 'Spin Trough' navigation radar, and one 'High Pole-B' IFF system

Specification (provisional)
'Promornik' class
Dimensions: length 56 m (183.7 ft); beam 22 m (72.2 ft)
Weights: maximum 350 tons; payload see text
Speed: 60 knots
Armament: two quadruple SAM launchers (possibly SA-N-8 Gremlin); two ADG6-30 CIWS
Electronics: one new air/surface search radar, one new navigation radar, one new fire control system, one IFF system

At 350 tons, the 'Promornik' class of air-cushion vehicles are the largest military hovercraft yet to enter service. The first example was seen on exercise in the Baltic in 1986 and demonstrate a continuing Soviet commitment to the surface skimmer for military use.

Bell Model 7467 LACV-30

The **LACV-30** (Lighter Air-Cushion Vehicle 30-short ton payload) is a stretched version of Bell Aerospace Textron's Voyageur civilian model. A total of 24 of these vehicles (company designation **Bell Model 7467**) is in the process of being delivered to replace the wheeled LARC-5 and LARC-15 (Lighter Amphibious Resupply Cargo 5 and 15-ton) models currently in service with the US Army's light and medium amphibian companies. The new craft will be used as high-speed amphibious vehicles for LOTS (Lighter-Over-The-Shore) operations where no port facilities exist. The LACV-30 can travel over water, land, snow, ice, marshes, swamps, low brush and other small obstacles or through 2.44-m (8-ft) high surf carrying a variety of containerized cargo, wheeled or tracked vehicles, heavy engineering plant or other supplies such as fuel and water containers. It can be carried fully assembled on a ship, be launched by the crew and be fully operational within a short time or, alternatively, it can be broken down into 15 sections for carriage by truck, rail or aircraft and then reassembled at its destination. In the simple drive-on/drive-off role using its bow ramp the craft can carry the maximum load of 30 tons with an endurance of 2 hours. If, however, it is used as a self-unloading platform for supplies via its swing crane in the bows the load is reduced to 26.5 tons though endurance remains the same. Other roles (such as medical evacuation, troop transport and water or fuel resupply) give greater endurance, times of between 5 and 9 hours being possible depending upon the actual payload figure.

Specification
LACV 30
Dimensions: length 23.32 m (76.5 ft); beam 11.18 m (36.7 ft)
Propulsion: two 1,800-shp (1342-kW) gas turbines driving two lift fans and two propellers
Weights: maximum 51.34 tons; payload see text
Speed: 33.5 kts (normal)
Armament: none
Electronics: one navigation radar

The Bell Aerospace Canada Textron Voyageur heavy-haulage ACV was developed in 1971, and was used as the basis for development of the US Army's LACV-30.

Below: The LACV-30 is much more efficient than previous LOTS (Lighter Over The Shore) systems, and will eventually replace the LARC-5 and LARC-15 amphibious vehicles currently in service. Secondary roles could include coastal, harbour and riverine patrol, search and rescue and fire control.

Below: Operable over an enormous variety of terrains from the Arctic to the tropics, the LACV-30 can ensure dry landing of the wide range of cargoes carried. These can include ISO containers, tracked and wheeled vehicles, engineering equipment, pallets and barrels, water, fuel, firefighting equipment or troops.

Above: The first of 30 LACV-30s was delivered to MERADCOM (the US Army's Mobility Equipment Research and Development Command) in 1981. Unlike the same company's LCAC, the LACV is not an assault craft but is designed to be used solely for the transportation of goods from ship to shore.

Landing Craft Air Cushion (LCAC)

The **Bell Aerospace Textron LCAC** is the definitive production version of the **JEFF(B)** amphibious assault landing craft that was tested alongside the Aerojet-General JEFF(A) prototype for over five years by the US Navy. Incorporating the best attributes of both, 107 LCACs were to have been built, but this has been cut to about 90, of which some 45 are to be based at the Little Creek Naval Amphibious Base, Virginia for the Atlantic Fleet and the remaining 45 at the US Marine Corps base at Camp Pendleton, California for the Pacific Fleet. The LCACs are being deployed in units of six to amphibious squadrons (PHIBRONS) and will be carried by the LHA, LPD, LHD and LSD classes (one, two, three and four craft respectively) to the disembarkation points. The open cargo deck is 168.06 m² (1,809 sq ft) in area and capable of accommodating 60 tons of cargo under normal conditions or up to 75 tons in the maximum overload state with a consequent decrease in per-formance. Typical loads include a 52-ton M60A1 MBT with five loaded jeeps, or a complete howitzer battery of six 105-mm/155-mm (4.13-in/6.1-in) guns and their loaded truck tractors and crews. The LCAC is fully skirted and can clear land obstacles up to 1.22 m (4 ft) high. Bow and stern ramps are fitted to allow ease of loading and un-loading. The first LCAC unit (ACU 5) was formed at Camp Pendleton in 1986.

Specification
LCAC
Dimensions: length 26.82 m (88.0 ft); beam 14.33 m (47.0 ft)
Propulsion: four 3,070-shp (2289-kW) gas turbines driving four lift fans and two propellers
Weights: maximum 170 tons; payload see text
Speed: 50 kts, or 40 kts with maximum payload
Armament: small arms
Electronics: one surface-search/navigation radar

The first production LCAC enters the well deck of USS Pensacola *(LSD 38) during the first underway mating of an LCAC and an LSD. The LCAC carries an M60 MBT, an M151 Jeep and an LAV-25 Light Armored Vehicle.*

Below: With a range of 300 nautical miles (approximately 550 km) at a speed of 35 kts, the LCAC can ferry large loads fast from vessels standing well out to sea and can carry those loads (more than 60 tons, which could include an MBT and light vehicles, or a full artillery battery) safely inland.

Above: Operating off the coast of Florida, the Bell Aerospace Textron AALC (Amphibious Assault Landing Craft) JEFF(B) approaches the docking well of the Landing Ship Dock USS Spiegel Grove. *The JEFF(B) formed the prototype for the US Navy's new LCAC.*

Right: JEFF(B) underway off the coast of Florida early in 1984, with a cargo including an M60 MBT and two 155-mm howitzers. The LCAC programme will give the US Navy the capacity to land at high speed US Marine units with their heavy equipment, while standing some distance off the coast.

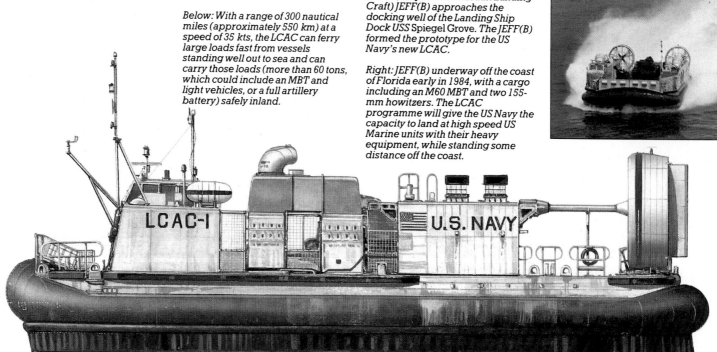

Bell SES-200 surface-effect test ship

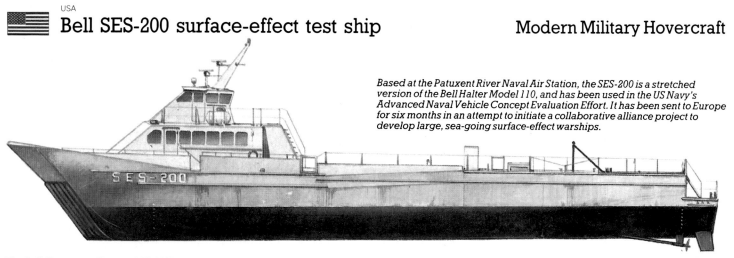

Based at the Patuxent River Naval Air Station, the SES-200 is a stretched version of the Bell Halter Model 110, and has been used in the US Navy's Advanced Naval Vehicle Concept Evaluation Effort. It has been sent to Europe for six months in an attempt to initiate a collaborative alliance project to develop large, sea-going surface-effect warships.

The **Bell Aerospace Textron SES-100B** was part of a long-term US Navy programme to develop large ocean-going ships with speeds of 80 kts or more for military uses. Stemming from research begun in 1960 and from the experimental 17-ton XR-1 which was completed in 1963 with a top speed of 34 kts, the 92-kt 100-ton 23.7-m (77.75-ft) SES-100B was launched in 1971 and used together with Aerojet-General's SES-100A 75-kt 110-ton 24.4-m (80-ft) long craft through the 1970s to test performance, stability and sea-keeping characteristics, structural loadings and the various operational tasks that a Surface-Effects Ship might undertake. In April 1976 the SES-100B travelling at 60 kts successfully fired a vertically-launched RIM-66B Standard SM-1MR air-defence missile against a surface target moored some 9.7 km (6 miles) away. The SES-100A was subsequently scrapped in 1982 after the evaluation had been finished, whilst the SES-100B was placed on static display at the David W. Taylor Naval Research and Development Center, Annapolis in the same year. The latest US Navy SES research vessel is the **Bell Halter SES-200 Model 730A** which was modified in 1982 from the **Bell Halter 110 Model 210A** demonstration SES after trials with the US Coast Guard as the USCG *Dorado* (WSES-1), the USCG then buying three units similar to the original. The main change involved a 15.24-m (50-ft) insert in the hull in order to increase the available fuel load and to allow the US Navy to assess the performance of a higher length-to-beam ratio. The aft decking was also strengthened to allow helicopter operations. The SES-200 was shipped to Europe in January 1986 for a six-month technical demonstration period for various NATO navies.

Specification
SES-200
Dimensions: length 48.77 m (160.0 ft); beam 11.88 m (39.0 ft); draught 1.7 to 2.6 m (5.5 to 8.5 ft)
Propulsion: two 1,600-hp (1193-kW) diesels driving two propellers and two 445-hp (332-kW) diesels driving two lift fans
Weights: maximum displacement 200 tons; payload see text
Speed: 32 kts
Armament: none
Aircraft: provision for one helicopter
Electronics: one Decca surface-search/navigation radar
Complement: 20 plus 3 technicians/scientists

The pioneer US Navy surface-effect vessel, SES-100B, is seen in April 1976 when she launched Standard SM-1MR surface-to-air missile while making a steady 60 kts. It was also the first vertical launch of the SM-1 from any ship. On 27 January 1980, SES-100B set a surface effect vessel speed record of 91.9 kts (170.25 km/105.8 miles) per hour.

Following the successful six-month trial of the BH 110, the US Coast Guard ordered three similar vessels for use out of Key West, Florida, in the war against drug-smuggling in the Caribbean and the Gulf of Mexico. Known as the 'Seabird' class, the three vessels are Seahawk (WSES-2), Shearwater (WSES-3) and Petrel (WSES-4).

Above: The original Bell-Halter BH 110 SES is seen before she was acquired for a joint US Navy/Coast Guard evaluation programme in 1980. After six months' Coast Guard appraisal she was handed to the Navy, where she was converted into the SES-200 by the addition of a 15.24-m (50-ft) hull extension.

Modern Mine Warfare Vessels

The 'Circé' class minehunters of the French navy use a remote control submarine to detect enemy mines and lay a demolition charge nearby. The submarine is then recalled and the charge detonated by an ultrasonic signal, destroying the mine.

Throughout the 20th century seamines have been of great importance in naval warfare. Without adequate mine countermeasures, ports can be blockaded, sea lanes disrupted and priceless warships destroyed at little cost to the enemy. Today it is a disturbing truth that most Western powers do not devote enough resources to mine countermeasures, while the Soviet Union has steadily increased its capacity.

Since World War II the leading Western nations (including the UK and USA) have tended somewhat to downgrade the importance of mine warfare and the mine countermeasures (MCM) techniques needed to counter it. Unfortunately their opinion is that a large fleet of small MCM vessels is labour-intensive, and in times of cash limitations the navies generally maintain what they consider to be their most important combat assets, namely carriers, submarines and the larger surface combatants. Under most circumstances this would be acceptable, but in this instance the principal mining threat to Europe and the North American continents comes from the USSR, a nation which has a total seamine inventory of considerably more than 400,000 weapons layable in all depths of water according to the intended target.

If one considers just the Royal Navy, then its projected fleet of some 40 to 50 'Hunt' class MCMVs, 'River' class fleet minesweepers and a new type of single-role minehunter would be hard pressed to keep open the required number of ports needed just to reinforce and resupply Europe,

let alone the naval bases and submarine transit routes as well. Similarly, the US neglect of its MCM fleet over the years and the pitifully small number of new vessels ordered, would make it impossible for the US Navy to keep open the ports from which the resupply convoys would sail, and all the home and foreign naval bases needed to sustain a maritime conflict.

In complete contrast the USSR has not only maintained its offensive capabilities but also its defensive forces, by continuously upgrading its MCM fleet with new designs at regular intervals. Although possibly these are not as good in quality as Western vessels, the large unit numbers more than make up for this.

The Tripartite minehunters are an unusual exercise in collaboration: Belgium provides most of the electronics, France the minehunting equipment, and the Netherlands the propulsion systems. This is Eridan, the first Tripartite to enter service with the French navy.

FRANCE
'Circé' class

The first of the **'Circé' class** minehunters were ordered in 1968, the five units were the **Cybèle** (M712), **Calliope** (M713), **Clio** (M714), **Circé** (M715) and **Ceres** (M716), these being commissioned into service during 1972-3. They are designed solely for the hunting and destruction of ground and moored mines laid to depths of about 60 m (197 ft). To locate the mines a DUBM 20 minehunting sonar is carried. Once located the mines are either destroyed by the six-strong detachment of divers (together with Gemini dinghies) or one of the two remote-controlled 6-kt PAP 104 submersibles. These weigh 700 kg (1,543 lb) are 2.7 m (8.9 ft) long and 1.1 m (3.6 ft) in diameter. Following the initial detection, they are lowered over the side aft by a large hydraulic winch mounted on the centreline. The PAP is then guided towards the contact via a 500-m (1640-ft) cable. Once in the mine's vicinity the TV camera in the nose is used for positive identification of the target as a mine and a 100-kg (220-lb) HE disposal charge is released next to it. The PAP is then guided back to the mother ship, recovered aboard and the charge detonated by an ultra-sonic signal. To aid in the plotting and classification processes involved during a hunt, an EVEC automatic plotting table is fitted in the

sonar and operations control room, which is located in the superstructure forward of the bridge. To reduce the magnetic and acoustic signatures of the vessels their hulls were constructed in a sandwich of wood and foam, the outer skin being covered by a thin film of GRP. The deckhead and superstructure are a composite of wood and glassfibre resin. All the propulsion systems can be operated from the bridge or a soundproofed

Circé was built in the early 1970s and is one of a class of five vessels that were constructed solely for the minehunting role. As such, they carry no normal minesweeping equipment such as sweeps.

deck. The class is due for deletion in the early 1990s.

Specification
'Circé' class
Displacement: 460 tons standard and 510 tons full load
Dimensions: length 50.9 m (167.0 ft); beam 8.9 m (29.2 ft); draught 3.4 m (11.2 ft)

Propulsion: one diesel delivering 1342 kW (1,800 hp) to one shaft, and an auxiliary 'active rudder' system for minehunting
Speed: 15 kts
Armament: one 20-mm AA gun
Electronics: one Decca 1229 navigation radar, one DUBM 20A minehunting sonar, and two PAP 104 mine-disposal systems
Complement: 48

The 'Circé' class are built with deckhead and superstructure of wood and glassfibre resins, and the hull is constructed as a sandwich of wood and foam to make magnetic and acoustic detection difficult.

BELGIUM/FRANCE/NETHERLANDS
Tripartite minehunter

A collaborative venture between the French, Belgian and Netherlands navies, the **Tripartite minehunter** design is gradually replacing the old ocean and coastal minesweepers built during the 1950s. Belgium is scheduled to get 10 units, the **Aster, Bellis, Crocus** and **Dianthus** (M915-918) being in service, the **Fuchsia, Iris, Lobelia, Myosotis, Narcis** and **Primula** (M919-924) completing or under construction. A follow-on order for another five is possible later. France has eight vessels in service, the **Eridan** (M641) being joined by **Cassiopée, Androméde, Pégase, Orion, Croix du Sud, Aigle** and **Lyre** (M642-648), Two more of the class, the **Persée** (M649) and the

Sagitaire (M650) are building. The Royal Netherlands Navy has ordered 15 of the class. Twelve ships, the **Alkmaar, Delfzijl, Dordrecht, Haarlem, Harlingen, Scheveningen, Maassluis, Makkum, Middelburg, Hellevoetsluis, Schiedam** and **Urk** (M850-861) have been completed with the remaining three, **Zierikzee, Vlaardingen** and **Willemstaad** (M862-864) commissioning by 1988. Two hulls have been sold to the Indonesian Navy for completion in 1987/88. These will differ from the tripartite craft in propulsion systems and equipment fit, reflecting the multiple roles they will be expected to fulfil in the waters of the East Indies. The design has the hull,

decks and partitions made out of some 180 tons of a glass weave/polyester resin (GRP) compound, and the propulsion system is essentially the same as that fitted to the French 'Circé' class of minehunters. A DUBM 21A minehunting sonar (smaller and more advanced than the DUBM 20A fitted to the 'Circés') is carried as a retractable hull system. The DUBM 21A can detect and

classify ground and moored mines down to a depth of 80 m (262 ft). The French 'Eridans' also have a position for a second sonar control centre on the upper deck aft to provide facilities for the DUBM 41 towed side-scan sonar system. All three classes also carry one light mechanical drag sweep to deal with conventional moored mines.

The Tripartite minehunters carry DUBM 21A minehunting sonar, an improved version of the DUBM 20A carried by the French 'Circé' class. This can detect and identify mines down to a depth of 80 m (262 ft).

The Tripartite Minehunter

Specification
'Eridan' class
Displacement: 510 tons standard and 544 tons full load
Dimensions: length 51.6 m (169.3 ft); beam 8.9 m (29.2 ft); draught 2.5 m (8.2 ft)
Propulsion: one diesel delivering 1417 kW (1,900 hp) to one shaft, and an auxiliary 'active rudder' system for minehunting
Speed: 15 kts
Armament: one 20-mm AA, and two 12.7-mm (0.5-in) machine-guns
Electronics: one Decca 1229 navigation radar, one Toran radio navigation system, one Syledis radio navigation system, one Decca Hi-fix navigation system, one DUBM 21A minehunting sonar, one DUBM 41B minehunting sonar (to be fitted), and two PAP 104 mine-disposal systems
Complement: 29 to 48 depending on assigned task

Above: Fifth of the Dutch 'Alkmaar' class is the Haarlingen. All the Tripartite class are fitted with French DUBM-21A minehunting sonar and two PAP-104 remote controlled mine disposal vehicles which carry high explosive charges.

Right: The Alkmaar and one of her sister ships are seen on an exercise. The latter is lowering one of her PAP-104 mine disposal vehicles over the side by hydraulic crane; guided by a cable link to the suspect mine, it can deposit the explosive charge beneath its belly as directed by its operator.

Below: The Eridan, with a maximum speed of 15 kts, could take days to reach an operational area. This is one of the penalties that modern mine countermeasures vessels have to put up with, because large propulsion plants for high speeds cause excessive magnetic signatures.

EAST GERMANY
'Kondor II' class

Classified as high-seas minesweepers by the East German navy, the **'Kondor II' class** units were built between 1971 and 1978 at the Peenewerft shipyard, Wolgast to replace the obsolete 'Habicht' and 'Krake' classes of minesweepers/minelayers. Twenty-four units (pennant numbers 311-316, 321-326, 331-336 and 341-346) currently serve in the minesweeping role, and six are now fitted with a large deckhouse abaft the main towed sweep reel for a Type 1-Ss/e magnetic minesweeping array. A further three (pennant numbers S321-323) are in use as training ships with the Walter Steffens Naval School, whilst another three (pennant numbers V381-383) serve as trials ships to test new minesweeping techniques and equipment. A further unit was extensively modified in 1978 to

serve as the hydrographic survey ship *Karl Friedrich Gauss* (D24), and the last unit was modified after launching with an enlarged superstructure to act as the state yacht *Ostseeland 1* (H04). Twenty of the earlier **'Kondor I' class** vessels, which were classed as coastal minesweepers, have been transferred to the Grenze Brigade Kuste (GBK, or coastal border guard) as patrol boats. However, they have retained their sweeping gear and would revert to the minesweeper role on the outbreak of hostilities. It seems that the 'Kondor II' class is equipped for moored, acoustic and magnetic minesweeping.

Specification
'Kondor II' class
Displacement: 310 tons standard and 400 tons full load
Dimensions: length 55.0 m (180.4 ft); beam 7.0 m (23.0 ft); draught 2.0 m (6.6 ft)
Propulsion: two diesels delivering

2983 kW (4,000 hp) to two shafts
Speed: 21 kts
Armament: two or three twin 25-mm AA guns
Electronics: one TSR33 navigation radar, and one small mine hunting sonar
Complement: 40

Twenty-four 'Kondor II' vessels serve in the minesweeping role in the East German navy, while three serve as training ships and another three are used to evaluate new mine countermeasure techniques and equipment.

USSR
'Vanya I' and 'Vanya II' classes

In series production from 1961 to 1973, the wooden-hulled **'Vanya I' class** was designated a *bazory tralschchik* (BT, or base minesweeper) design which could also double as a minehunter. A total of 65 'Vanya I' units remain in service with the Soviet navy, while six others were transferred to the Bulgarian navy and two to the Syrian navy in the early 1970s. One other unit was converted in 1974 to a pure minehunter configuration for research and development purposes, with its superstructure extended forward, a twin 25-mm AA gun added in place of the normal 30-mm mount, together with a lattice mast with 'Don Kay' navigation radar at the amidships break point and

two boats for divers on the quarterdeck.

The final six units were built to the **'Vanya II' class** design with an additional 1-m (3.3-ft) hull extension, a more extensive fantail work area and heavier davits aft, a 'Don Kay' navigation radar in place of the 'Don 2' system, and a larger diesel generator exhaust pipe amidships. This subvariant is used as the guidance ships for the unmanned 'Ilyusha' class of radio-controlled inshore minesweeper drones. The 'Ilyushas' displace some 85 tons full load and are 26.4 m (86.6 ft) long. They are believed to carry both normal sweep gear and a linear explosive mine-disposal system for laying

over the stern. For transit purposes they carry a crew of 10. Each 'Vanya II' can control up to three 'Ilyushas' during a sweep operation.

Specification
'Vanya' classes
Displacement: 200 tons standard and 245 tons ('Vanya I') or 260 tons ('Vanya II') full load
Dimensions: length 40.0 m (131.2 ft) for 'Vanya I' or 41.0 m (134.5 ft) for 'Vanya II'; beam 7.3 m (24.0 ft); draught 1.8 m (5.9 ft)
Propulsion: two diesels delivering 1641 kW (2,200 hp) to two shafts
Speed: 16 kts

Armament: one twin 30-mm AA gun, and between eight and 16 mines depending on type
Electronics: one 'Don 2' or 'Don Kay' navigation radar, one 'Dead Duck' IFF, one 'High Pole-B' IFF, and one minehunting sonar
Complement: 30

Designated a Bazory Tralshchik (base minesweeper) by the Soviets, the 'Vanya' class was in series construction from the early 1960s to the early 1970s. It is currently the most numerous of the coastal minesweeper forces, with 65 'Vanya', one 'Vanya Mod' and six 'Vanya IIs' in service in mid-1987.

'Yurka' class

The Soviet Union built 50 'Yurka' class sea-going minesweepers between 1962 and 1972. Their hulls are constructed from aluminium alloy and their equipment is similar to that fitted in Western vessels.

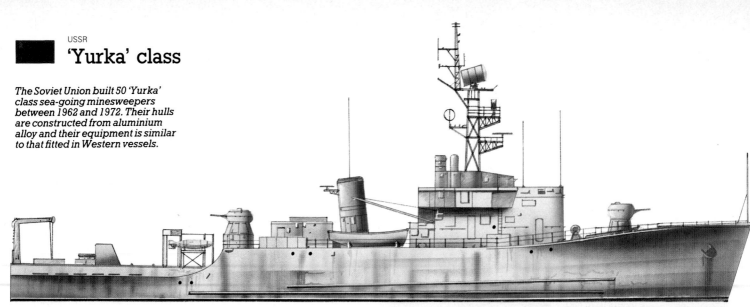

Built from 1963 to 1972, the aluminium alloy hull **'Yurka' class** was the smaller predecessor to the Natya design but without the latter's ASW weapons and stern ramp. Similarly designated *morskoy tralshchik* (MT, or seagoing minesweeper), the 'Yurkas' are fitted to sweep acoustic and magnetic mines only, with gear similar to that used by the West. A total of 50 units was completed, of which 45 standard units still serve in the Soviet navy, one other ex-Soviet unit being transferred to the Vietnamese navy in 1979. The remaining four were constructed to a more austere export configuration in the late 1960s for the Egyptian navy: they have no fire-control radar, and additional ship's side scuttles are provided for better air flow beneath decks for service in hot climates.

The broad funnel indicates that the diesel engines are in a side-by-side arrangement below decks, and aids the distinguishability from the 'Natyas'. Several units have now been retrofitted with the standard light forces AA armament update package of two quadruple SA-N-5 'Grail' SAM laun-chers with 16 reloads. The class also continues the Soviet tradition of fitting its MCM units with mine rails for defensive purposes in coastal and deep-sea anchorages. The minehunting sonar is a variant of the surface ship and submarine 'Tamir' high-frequency active set, modified to allow short-range classification of mine-like objects.

Specification
'Yurka' class
Displacement: 460 tons standard and 540 tons full load
Dimensions: length 52.0 m (170.6 ft); beam 8.8 m (28.9 ft); draught 2.6 m (8.5 ft)
Propulsion: two diesels delivering 2983 kW (4,000 hp) to two shafts
Speed: 19 kts
Armament: two twin 30-mm AA guns, and between 10 and 20 mines depending on type
Electronics: one or two 'Don 2' navigation radar, one 'Drum Tilt' AA fire-control radar, two 'Square Head' IFF, one 'High Pole-B' IFF, and one 'Tamir' minehunting sonar
Complement: 45-50

Above: The aluminium alloy-hulled 'Yurka' class of sea-going minesweepers is fitted for magnetic and acoustic sweeping operations. To improve their self-defence capabilities the class is currently being refitted with SA-N-5 'Grail' SAM launchers.

Below: The 'Yurka' classes' 'Drum Tilt' fire control radar is carried at the top of the mainmast above the IFF systems and the 'Don 2' navigation radar. Surprisingly for ocean-going minesweepers, this class does not have any ASW systems, which are fitted to earlier and later classes.

'Natya I' and 'Natya II' classes

First reported in 1971, the aluminium-hulled **'Natya I' class** is designated a *morskoy tralshchik* (MT, or seagoing minesweeper) by the Soviets and is the follow-on to the 'Yurka' design. The earliest units of the 34 Soviet navy 'Natya Is' built at Izhora and Khabarovsk in the period 1969-80 were fitted with two rigid davits aft, an arrangement changed in the later craft to articulated hydraulically operated davits to handle the sweep gear and towed MCM bodies over the stern ramp. The 'Natya Is' are also equipped with two five-barrel RBU1200 ASW rocket-launchers to facilitate the use of the class members as coastal ASW escorts. In addition most units have now been fitted with two quadruple SA-N-5 'Grail' SAM systems just abaft the lattice mast, while others have had a second navigation radar added atop the pilothouse.

In 1980 a single **'Natya II' class** variant was completed with a lengthened superstructure and the transom cut away amidships to take a 1.5-m (5-ft) sheath. This is believed to be a research and development minehunting vessel.

The 'Natya I' is still being produced in small quantities for the export mar-

The 'Natya I' usually operates in home waters, but on occasions vessels of this type have been deployed to the Mediterranean, Indian Ocean and West Africa, where in wartime their ASW armament of rocket launchers could come in handy for limited escort duties.

ket in the slightly less well equipped version. 21 have been built or are on order for India (12 by 1988), Libya (seven by 1985, with one more to come) and Syria (one with no MCM gear). Soviet units generally operate in home waters, but have been seen as far afield as the Indian Ocean and West Africa.

Specification
'Natya' classes
Displacement: 650 tons standard and 765 tons full load
Dimensions: length 61.0 m (200.1 ft); beam 10.0 m (32.8 ft); draught 3.5 m (11.5 ft)
Propulsion: two diesels delivering 3729 kW (5,000 hp) to two shafts
Speed: 18 kts
Armament: ('Natya I') in most units two quadruple SA-N-5 'Grail' SAM launchers with 16 missiles, two twin 30-mm AA and two twin 25-mm AA guns, two 250-mm (9.84-in) five-barrel RBU1200 ASW rocket-launchers with 50 rockets, and between 10 and 20 mines depending on type
Armament: ('Natya II') two quadruple SA-N-5 'Grail' SAM launchers with 16

'Natya I' class seagoing minesweepers occasionally double as intelligence gatherers if no specifically dedicated vessels are available. Here a 'Natya I' monitors the operations of the 'Leander' class frigate HMS Naiad.

missiles, and two twin 30-mm AA guns
Electronics: one or two 'Don 2' navigation radars, one 'Drum Tilt' AA fire-control radar, two 'Square Head' IFF, one 'High Pole-B' IFF, and one 'Tamir' minehunting sonar
Complement: 60

`Natya' Class Minesweeper

Built as a successor to the 'Yurka' class the 'Natya I' design of Morskoy
Tralshchik (seagoing minesweeper) is still in slow series production for
export. Latest intelligence reports estimate that the Soviets have 34 'Natya I'
and one 'Natya II' in service, whilst the Indian, Libyan and Syrian navies have
ten (plus two building), eight and one respectively.

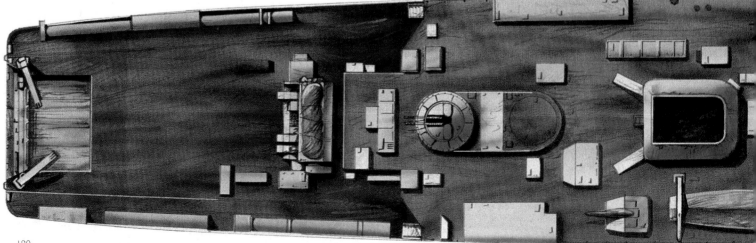

Below: The Soviet Union constructed 34 'Natya I' class minesweepers between 1969 and 1980, and although their minesweeping equipment might not be as effective as that of Western equivalents the sheer number of these ships will make up for any such deficiency. They are more heavily armed than many Western mine warfare vessels, mounting two quadruple SA-N-5 SAM launchers, two five-barrel RBU1200 ASW rocket launchers, and 25-mm and 30-mm AA guns.

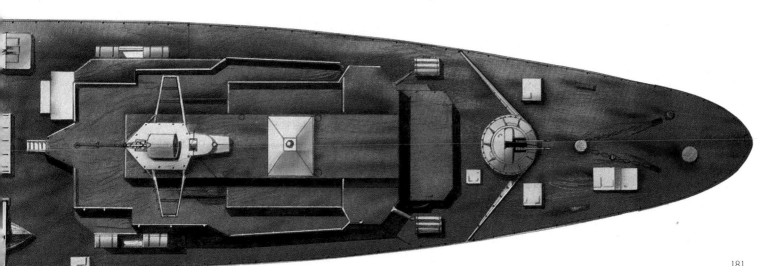

'Sonya' class

Built since 1972 and still in slow series production at the rate of some three or four per year, the **'Sonya' class** is designated a *bazory tralshchik* (BT, or base minesweeper) by the Soviets and is used in coastal areas and the approaches to the major naval and civil ports, much like the Royal Navy's 'Hunt' class MCMs. Some 57 are in service with the Soviet navy at present, with three further units transferred to Bulgaria and four to Cuba in the early 1980s.

The hull is of wood, but is sheathed with glassfibre to prevent attack by marine organisms. This hull arrangement was adopted after a three-ship prototype design, the **'Zhenya' class**, was tried with an all-GRP hull in the late 1960s. The experiment obviously did not work, possibly as a result of problems in working with such a large structure in GRP.

Several of the 'Sonyas' have now received a single quadruple SA-N-5 'Grail' SAM launcher abaft the ship's boat on the starboard side. The sweep gear appears to be of the standard type for mechanical, acoustic and magnetic mine operations, and is lifted in and out of the water by a hydraulically operated articulated davit on the stern. The elderly 25-mm gun mount aft is carried by the class for destroying swept floating mines as it is easier to use and more accurate for this work than the 30-mm turret forward.

'Sonya' class minesweepers are the broad equivalent of the Royal Navy's 'Hunt' class, being intended for operations in coastal areas and the approaches to major ports. They have a wooden hull sheathed with glassfibre.

Still in series production at three or four units per year, the 'Sonya' class of base minesweeper has also been exported to Bulgaria and Cuba in small numbers. There have been no conversions as yet to minesweeping R&D vessels, as in other classes.

Specification
'Sonya' class
Displacement: 380 tons standard and 450 tons full load
Dimensions: length 48.0 m (157.5 ft); beam 8.8 m (28.9 ft); draught 2.0 m (6.6 ft)
Propulsion: two diesels delivering 1790 kW (2,400 hp) to two shafts
Speed: 15 kts
Armament: one quadruple SA-N-5 'Grail' SAM launcher with eight missiles, and one twin 30-mm AA and one twin 25-mm AA gun
Electronics: one 'Spin Trough' search and navigation radar, two 'Square Head' IFF, one 'High Pole-B' IFF, and one minehunting sonar
Complement: 43

'Alesha' class

Designated *zagraditel' minnyy* (ZM, or minelayer) by the Soviets, the **'Alesha' class** (a NATO reporting name) can serve as minelayers, defensive netlayers, MCMV tenders and mine warfare command and control centres. The four sets of mine rail tracks fitted run from the amidships superstructure aft to a stern ramp arrangement that can also be used to haul large objects aboard. Two cranes are fitted forward, with another two amidships. On the second and third units of the class the forward cranes are replaced by two kingposts and booms. The only three 'Aleshas' are the **Pripiyat**, the **Suricot** and the **Vychegda**. All three units were completed between 1967-9 at an unnamed Black Sea shipyard.

The number of mines carried varies up to a maximum of 300 according to type, but it is known that apart from the conventional moored buoyant types such as the M08 contact and the KRAB influence mines the 'Aleshas' can also lay the MZ26 moored contact sweep obstructor and the AMD-500 and AMD-1000 ground influence mines. The main minelaying effort of the Soviet navy is concentrated into its bomber and maritime patrol aircraft, surface ships and conventional submarine fleet.

Specification
'Alesha' class
Displacement: 2,900 tons standard and 3,500 tons full load
Dimensions: length 98.0 m (321.5 ft); beam 13.5 m (44.3 ft); draught 5.4 m (17.7 ft)
Propulsion: four diesels delivering 5966 kW (8,000 hp) to two shafts
Speed: 17 kts
Armament: one quadruple 57-mm AA gun, and up to 300 mines
Electronics: one 'Don 2' navigation radar, one 'Strut Curve' air-search radar, one 'Muff-Cob' 57-mm fire-control radar, and one 'High Pole-B' IFF system
Complement: 190

NATO has alloted the reporting name 'Alesha' to this class of minelayers, built in the late 1960s in the Black Sea. They are able to carry up to 300 mines, ranging from moored to ground influence types.

Ton class
UK

During the Korean War it was realized that the Soviets had magnetic influence mines of the AMD type that were not affected by degaussing, thus making all steel hulled minesweepers obsolete. To counter this the Royal Navy built between 1952 and 1959 a massive 118 vessel coastal minesweeper class. The **'Ton' class** have an aluminium-framed, nylon-sheathed, double mahogany planked hull with most of the internal fittings and superstructure made out of non-magnetic materials. They are capable of open ocean transits and have served in most parts of the world, including the operations to clear the Suez canal in 1973 and the Red Sea in 1984. During the latter, one Royal Navy minehunter recovered a new type of Soviet influence ground mine intended for use from ships and

submarines. At present the Royal Navy has 13 (out of 16 converted between 1964-9) minehunters remaining in service (of which three belong to the Royal Navy Reserve 10th Minecountermeasures Squadron) and six minesweepers (of which two belong to the RNR and three to the Fisheries Protection Squadron). A total of 37 were transferred abroad, six to Argentina in 1968 (all still in service, two as minehunters), six to Australia in 1962 (one remaining as minehunter), one to Ghana in 1964 (deleted), three to Ireland in 1971 (one remaining), seven to Malaysia in 1960-8 (all deleted) and 10 to South Africa in 1958-9 (all still in service, two as minehunters and two as patrol boats). Those ships still in foreign service are now getting old, and are in dire need of replacement.

Several of the Royal Navy minehunters have had to have extensive refits in order to remain serviceable until their replacement 'Sandown' class vessels are commissioned.

In 1973 HMS *Wilton* (M1116) was commissioned to test the concept of the then projected 'Hunt' class MCMVs. All the machinery and fittings were taken from an old 'Ton' class vessel, but her hull was of glass-reinforced plastic, making her the world's first major GRP-hulled warship.

Specification
'Ton' class minehunter
Displacement: 370 tons standard, 425 tons full load
Dimensions: length 46.6 m (153 ft), beam 8.8 m (28.9 ft), draught 2.5 m (8.2 ft)

Propulsion: two diesels delivering 2237 kW (3,000 hp) to two shafts
Speed: 15 kts
Armament: one single 40 mm AA gun, one-two single 20 mm AA guns, one-three 7.62 mm GPMGs
Electronics: one Type 1006 navigation radar, one Type 193 hull mounted minehunting sonar (Type 193M in one unit), one six barrel Plessey Shield decoy launcher (in recently refitted units)
Complement: 38 (including clearance diving team)

'Ton' class minesweepers were used as patrol boats in Hong Kong for many years. They have recently been replaced by the much more capable 'Peacock' class.

'Sandown' class
UK

In 1985 *HMS Sandown* (M101), the first of what was hoped to be a 20 ship single role minehunter class (but which now for economic reasons will apparently be only 12 strong) was ordered from Vosper Thornycroft Ltd for commissioning in 1989. In 1987 tenders for four more units of this class were asked for. Designed as the replacement for the 'Ton' class minehunters, these GRP hulled vessels use an electric propulsion drive coupled with a bow thruster for low speed (up to 6 kts), quiet minehunting operations.

They are capable of mine clearance operations down to 200 m (656 ft) depth with a variety of disposal systems. They carry a mine clearance team of six divers for shallow water work, and two remote controlled Mine Disposal Systems Mk2 (which use improved PAP104 submersibles) for identification and disposal tasks in deep water. The sonar used is a Plessey Type 2093 high frequency set which uses a variable depth body that is lowered through the keel. This has search, depth finding, classification and route

survey modes of operation. All the fittings are as far as possible non-magnetic and the electric low speed drive is meant to be extremely quiet for use when hunting combination influence mines that are fitted with acoustic actuators as well as the more normal magnetic or pressure sensors.

Specification
'Sandown' class
Displacement: 400 tons standard, 492 tons full load
Dimensions: length 52.7 m (172.9 ft),

beam 10.5 m (34.4 ft), draught 2.1 m (6.9 ft)
Propulsion: two diesels delivering 2237 kW (3,000 hp) to two shafts; electric motors for low speed work
Speed: 13 kts
Armament: one single 20 mm AA gun
Electronics: one Type 1007 navigation radar, one Type 2093 variable depth minehunting hull sonar, two improved PAP104 mine disposal vehicles
Complement: 40

Modern Mine Warfare Vessels

STANAVFORCHAN (Standing Naval Force Channel) is a multi-national NATO minesweeping unit. In this picture, the 'Hunt' class minesweepers HMS Brocklesby (M33) and Ledbury (M30) are joined by the Dutch Ommen (M813), the Belgian Breydel (M906), the West German Weilheim (M1077) and another 'Dokkum' class vessel from the Netherlands.

'Hunt' class

At the same time that the first GRP-built minehunter, HMS *Wilton* (M1116), was being built on the lines of the 'Ton' class, work began on the new generation of mine-countermeasures vessels capable of undertaking both mine-sweeping and minehunting operations. The result was the **'Hunt' class**, named after various hunt meetings around the UK. They are the largest and most expensive GRP-hulled ships in the world, every effort having been made to minimize the ships' magnetic signatures and to cut radiated noise levels underwater, while maintaining a capability for deep-sea passages to any part of the world. Eleven are now in service with the Royal Navy, namely HMS *Brecon* (M29), *Ledbury* (M30), *Cattistock* (M31), *Cottesmore* (M32), *Brocklesbury* (M33), *Middleton* (M34), *Dulverton* (M35), *Bicester* (M36), *Chiddingfold* (M37), *Atherstone* (M38), *Hurworth* (M39) and *Berkeley* (M40). HMS *Quorn* (M41) is building for completion in 1988; the Navy would like more of the type but that will depend on future funding.

For minehunting the ships each carry a team of divers and two French-built PAP-104 unmanned submersible mine-disposal systems to go with a Type 193 minehunting sonar system. For conventional sweeping they have a Sperry Osborn TA6 acoustic system, an MM Mk 11 magnetic loop system and the M Mk 3 Mod 2 Oropesa wire sweep. All the hunting and sweeping manoeuvres are controlled by a mod-ified CAAIS action information data system in the operations room, using high-precision navigation aids. Both the *Brecon* and the *Ledbury* were used successfully after the 1982 Falklands war to sweep Argentine minefields that had been laid off Port Stanley. They were used in conjunction with a number of specially chartered commercial trawlers converted to the minesweeping role for the war.

Specification
'Hunt' class
Displacement: 625 tons standard and 725 tons full load
Dimensions: length 60.0 m (197.0 ft); beam 10.0 m (32.8 ft); draught 3.4 m (11.2 ft)
Propulsion: two diesels delivering 2834 kW (3,800 hp) to two shafts
Speed: 17 kts
Armament: one 40-mm Bofors AA gun
Electronics: one Type 1006 navigation radar, one CAAIS action information system, one Type 193 minehunting sonar, one Decca Mk 21 Hi-fix navigation system, and two PAP 104 mine-disposal systems
Complement: 45

The 'Hunt' class are the largest and most expensive GRP-hulled ships in the world, and have minimal acoustic and magnetic signatures. Ledbury *and* Brecon *swept up Argentine mines off Port Stanley in the Falklands.*

The 'Hunt' class mine countermeasures vessel Ledbury, *constructed from glass reinforced plastic (GRP), can dispose of mines in three ways: by conventional sweeping with cutter; by acoustic or magnetic sweeps; and by hunting with a sonar and then using clearance divers or mine disposal vehicles.*

'River' class

Based on a North Sea oilrig supply ship design, the **'River' class** of fleet mine-sweeper is gradually replacing the worn-out 'Ton' class coastal mine-sweepers assigned to the Royal Navy Reserve. There are twelve vessels in the class, HMS *Waveney* (M2003) being joined in service by HMS *Carron, Dovey, Helford, Humber, Blackwater, Itchen, Helmsdale, Orwell, Ribble, Spey* and *Arun* (M2004-M2014). The steel-hulled 'Rivers' were all built in the yards of Richards Ltd. at Lowestoft and Great Yarmouth and commissioned between 1984 and 1987.

All carry the BAJ-Vickers Mk 9 Extra-Deep Armed Team Sweep (EDATS) gear, with which two vessels work together, towing a sweep wire with special depth-keeping gear between them, that allows the cutting equipment to follow the contours of the sea-bed closely at very great depths. Explosive charges are attached at 91.4-m (300-ft) intervals to assist the mechanical cutters to break mooring chains.

The need for such a system has been generated by the Soviets' acquisition of rising mine and underwater electrical potential mine types, which can be laid in deep water on the continental shelf and rise regions for use against transitting dived nuclear submarines. The deep-sweep concept was originally tested in 1977-8, when the Royal Navy briefly chartered six commercial trawlers for the series of 'Highland Fling' minesweeping exercises off Scotland. Two more trawlers were then chartered for six years apiece late in 1978 to explore more fully the idea and develop it into the EDATS system. The two vessels were commissioned into the Royal Navy Reserve as HMS *Venturer* (M08) and *St David* (M07) and at the end of their commission in 1984 were returned to their owners.

Lead ship of the 'River' class minesweepers is the Waveney. *Steel-hulled, she is fitted with the EDATS sweep for the deep team sweeping role against Soviet deep water mines laid to catch British and American submarine traffic off the Scottish coasts.*

Specification
'River' class
Dimensions: length 47.5 m (156.0 ft); beam 10.5 m (34.5 ft); draught 3.1 m (10.3 ft)
Propulsion: two diesels delivering 2267 kW (3,040 hp) to two shafts
Speed: 14 kts
Armament: two 7.62-mm (0.3-in) machine-guns, and fitted for but not with one 40-mm Bofors AA gun
Electronics: two Decca RM1226 navigation radars, one Decca QM14 navigation system, one Decca Mk 6 Hi-fix navigation system, and one satellite navigation system
Complement: 30

The Dovey *was third of the 'River' class to be commissioned. In peacetime the class are allocated to the various RNR divisions, except for one which is being used for trial purposes to test new deep sweeping technology.*

DENMARK

'Fälster' class

Denmark has long been in a position to control access to the Baltic Sea, and the 'Fälster' class of minelayers stands ready to block the channels connecting the North Sea and the Baltic. The Møen *is fitted as a training ship and the* Sjaelland *as a depot vessel, but both can quickly revert to their designed role.*

Because of the strategic nature of Denmark's position across the entrance and exit to the Baltic Sea, the Danish navy has invested part of its defensive capabilities in minelayers. The largest of the three types currently in use is the NATO-designed 'Fälster' class of four ships. Named after Danish islands, the **Fälster** (N80), **Fyen** (N81), **Møen** (N82) and **Sjaelland** (N83) were ordered in 1960-1 and launched in 1962-3. They have a flushdecked steel hull with a raking stern through which four mine-laying tracks are run to lay the mines. There is also a near sistership, the **Nusret** (N110) launched in Denmark in 1964, serving with the Turkish navy as a minelayer. In peacetime the class is generally used on other duties, with the *Møen* converted to a midshipman training ship with specialist ECN gear aboard, and the *Sjaelland* converted in 1976 to act as a depot ship for Denmark's small fleet of conventional submarines and torpedo/missile boats. In wartime both units would revert to the minelaying role with only minimal internal change. All four have been refitted for service to the year 2000 and beyond, when they will be replaced by the 'Flex 2000' design.

Specification
'Fälster' class
Displacement: 1,800 tons standard and 1,900 tons full load
Dimensions: length 77.0 m (252.6 ft); beam 12.8 m (42.0 ft); draught 3.6 m (11.8 ft)
Propulsion: two diesels delivering 3579 kW (4,800 hp) to two shafts
Speed: 16.5 kts
Armament: two twin 76-mm (3-in) Mk 33 DP guns, and up to 400 mines
Electronics: one NWS2 navigation radar, one MWS1 tactical radar, one WM-46 fire-control system, one CWS2 air- and surface-search radar, two 57-mm multi-barrel chaff-rocket launchers, and (*Møen* only) one ECM system
Complement: 119

AUSTRALIA

'Bay' class

The **'Bay' class** of inshore minehunter is the first design of a totally new concept in mine countermeasures. The first two units, HMAS **Rushcutter** and **Shoalwater**, are in-service prototypes of a catamaran hull form with foam sandwich-filled fibreglass hulls that are 3 m (9.8 ft) in the beam and some 3 m (9.8 ft) apart. This arrangement provides greater stability, a larger deck working area, greater manoeuvrability at sweeping speeds, and a significant reduction in the magnetic/acoustic signatures by placing the heavier machinery above the waterline high up in the vessel. Each hull has a single propeller, and the victualling consists of pre-prepared foodstuffs. The sweep gear is fully containerized to allow for rapid removal or replacement. Four subsystems are located in the container aft of the bridge: the sonar, the tactical data information system, the precision navigation system and the mine disposal weapon-control unit. The last directs either of the two French-made PAP 104 unmanned wire-guided submersible vehicles carried on the aft working deck. The Royal Australian Navy plans to order a further four.

To support the force of six vessels which should be in use by 1991, the RAN will convert it's force of Sea King Mk 50 helicopters to tow a 360-kg (792-lb) minesweeping sled on a 240-m (787.4-ft) cable attached to the tail wheel yoke. Successful completion of trials in 1987 should mean that the American designed acoustic noise-maker sleds should be in operational service by 1990.

Specification
'Bay' class
Displacement: 100 tons standard and 170 tons full load
Dimensions: length 31.0 m (101.7 ft); beam 9.0 m (29.5 ft); draught 2.0 m (6.6 ft)
Propulsion: two diesels delivering 485 kW (650 hp) to two shafts
Speed: 10 kts
Armament: two 12.7-mm (0.5-in) machine-guns
Electronics: one navigation radar, one DSQS-11H minehunting sonar, and two PAP 104 mine-disposal systems
Complement: 14

The Royal Australian Navy is experimenting with a radically different minehunter design on a catamaran hull. This provides great stability, a large working area and much reduced magnetic and acoustic signatures.

ITALY
'Lerici' class

Modern Mine Warfare Vessels

The first four units of the 'Lerici' class of mine countermeasures vessels (MCMVs) were ordered in January 1978 under the Legge Navale plan from Intermarine at Sarzona. Delayed for a while because of a bridge they could not pass beneath until it was rebuilt, they are constructed of heavy GRP shock-resistant materials, and are equipped to carry two Italian MIN-77 mine-hunting submersibles, one smaller 'Pluto' remote-controlled submersible and six/seven trained divers. The sonar used is a licence-built version of the US 'Squeaky Fourteen' (SQQ-14) system, modified into a variable-depth set which is lowered from the keel forward of the bridge.

The 5-kt MIN system consists of a 1300-kg (2,866-lb) GRP vehicle fitted with a sonar and an underwater TV camera. For destruction of ground mines an 85-kg (187-lb) HE charge is carried, while moored mines are made buoyant by the cutting of their mooring chains with a small HE charge, for destruction by gunfire. Operations with the MIN are possible up to 250 m (820 ft) away from the mother ship at depths down to 150 m (492 ft), although 200 m (656 ft) is possible under certain circumstances.

Lerici, Sapri, Milazzo and *Vieste* (M5550/3) are the first four in service, to be followed by eight built to a slightly improved design (*Gaetta, Termoli, Alghero, Numana, Crotone, Viareggio* and two un-named, with pennant numbers M5554 to M5561) when fund-

ing permits. Malaysia has taken delivery of four vessels with French mine-hunting equipment (to replace some old British 'Ton' class sweepers) while Nigeria has taken delivery of two with Italian equipment and has an option on two more. With the failure of their 'Cardinal' class surface effect ship design, the US Navy has requested funds for 12 Lerici derivatives to be built in the USA as the **'MHC-1' class**. These will act as the inshore and coastal partners to the much larger 'Avenger' class, their primary task being to clear major US ports.

Specification
'Lerici' class
Displacement: 470 tons standard and 502 tons full load
Dimensions: length 50.0 m (164.0 ft); beam 9.6 m (31.5 ft); draught 2.6 m (8.5 ft)
Propulsion: one diesel delivering 1372 kW (1,840 hp) to one shaft
Speed: 15 kts
Armament: one 20-mm AA gun
Electronics: one SST7/DG navigation radar, various radio navigation systems, one SQQ-14 minehunting sonar, and one MIN-79 mine-disposal system
Complement: 40

Lerici is seen in service with the Italian navy. Built in the early 1980s, the GRP-hulled ship is the first of a probable 12 for the Italians, with another four built for the Malaysian navy and two for Nigeria.

The 'Lerici' class mine countermeasures vessels are equipped to carry the Italian MIN-77 minehunting submersible and six divers, who will use CAM mine destructor charges.

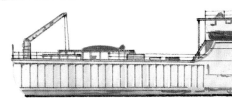

USA
'Avenger' class

To replace the ageing 'Aggressive' and 'Acme' class ocean minesweepers, the design of a new type of MCMV was begun in 1970. This eventually evolved into the **'Avenger' class**, of which 21 were originally planned to be built over the next 10-15 years. However, cutbacks, cost over-runs and an apparent lack of appreciation, not to say understanding of mine warfare in senior US naval and political circles has reduced the total to 14 with the first, USS *Avenger* (MCM1), commissioning in late 1986 with *Defender* (MCM2) and *Sentry* (MCM3) following soon after. Two more are due in 1988. The hull is of laminated oak, fir and cedar woods to take advantage of the materials' low magnetic signatures, while the superstructure is basically wood with a GRP covering to protect it from the elements.

A minehunting sonar is fitted for use in conjunction with two Honeywell remote-controlled SLQ-48 Mine Neutra-

lization System submersibles to sweep ground mines and deep-moored mines to a depth of 183 m (600 ft). The MNS vehicles are 3.8 m (12.5 ft) long, 0.9 m (3.0 ft) high and weigh 1136 kg (2,499 lb); 1524 m (5,000 ft) of control cable is carried for each 6-kt MNS. Later the class will be fitted with SQQ-32 variable-depth minehunting sonar as it becomes available. For conventional minesweeping tasks A Mk 4 and A Mk 6 acoustic sweeps, M Mk 5, M Mk 6 and M Mk 7 magnetic sweeps and an Oropesa No. 1 wire sweep are shipped. The two MNS vehicles are

controlled from an automated combat information centre which plots mine locations with the assistance of the SSN-2 precision navigation system and/or a Decca-Racal Hyper-Fix precision radio navigation aid. A satellite communications set is standard.

Specification
'Avenger' class
Displacement: 1,040 tons standard and 1,240 tons full load
Dimensions: length 68.3 m (224.0 ft); beam 11.9 m (39.0 ft); draught 3.5 m (11.4 ft)
Propulsion: four diesels delivering 1790 kW (2,400 hp) to two shafts
Speed: 14 kts
Armament: two 12.7-mm (0.5-in) machine-guns
Electronics: one SPS-55 surface-search radar, one SPS-56 navigation radar, one OE-82 satellite navigation system, one SQQ-30 minehunting sonar, and one MNS mine-disposal system
Complement: 72

The US Navy's lack of appreciation of the importance of mine warfare has become obvious, as only 14 'Avenger' class minesweepers have been ordered. This is utterly inadequate to deal with the Soviet minelaying forces.

Spyships

From the tranquil calm of a Mediterranean summer to the awesome force of an Atlantic winter, NATO mariners are accustomed to uninvited guests joining their exercises. Whether in small trawler-derived vessels or in large space research ships, the gathering of naval intelligence has become a major preoccupation of the Soviet navy, reciprocated to a certain extent by a number of other navies.

One requisite for any sailor aboard a Soviet AGI is not to suffer from sea-sickness, as this Moma demonstrates as she watches the warships HMS Tiger and the RFA Tidepool during the 1974 NATO exercise 'Northern Merger'.

Although this is the age of satellite-based reconnaissance systems, there is still a need for the intelligence-gathering ship to ply its trade off foreign shores. Such ships are now divided into two categories: the authentic 'spyship', or intelligence-gathering auxiliary (AGI) to give the type its correct name, which is covered with various aerials and antennae to gather signal and electronic intelligence data; and the more respectable civilian research vessels of the space event type, which although tasked with genuine peaceful missions are in fact engaged on occasion in obtaining useful information on foreign military missile tests.

In the Soviet Union there is no real distinction between the two categories as all military and civilian ships of whatever class are operated as part of the Soviet Ocean Surveillance System (SOSS), while the space event units also perform additional military tasks such as relaying communications. The Americans in contrast have lost interest in the AGI following the attack on the USS *Liberty* during the 1967 Arab-Israeli war and the seizing of the USS *Pueblo* by the North Koreans a few years later.

They now rely on this type of work to be performed by the Project Holystone nuclear submarines and by aircraft. However, they do remain interested in the research type vessel as shown by the recent conversion of the USNS *Observation Island* to carry the 'Cobra Judy' surveillance radar. One exception to this has been the building of the SURTASS-equipped ships of the 'Stalwart' class to complement the SOSUS network around the coasts of the USA.

Those other countries which operate these vessels (such as France, China and some of the Warsaw Pact nations) tend to use either one or other of the categories but not both. Surprisingly, of the NATO nations only West Germany uses AGIs, the others relying on warships, submarines and specially configured aircraft to do the job.

Originally converted from a tanker design, the USNS Redstone *first served as a tracking and communication vessel for the Apollo moon programme. She has since been assigned to the USAF Eastern Space Missile Center at Patrick AFB in Florida.*

'Henri Poincaré' class

The *Henri Poincaré* is the sole ship of her type and the flagship of Force M, the French naval test and measurement group, which takes measurements and conducts experiments as requested by the navy or any other organization, civil or military. The *Henri Poincaré's* chief mission is to monitor and measure the trajectory of the SSBS (IRBMs) and MSBS (SLBMs) fired from the experimental station at Landes (or from missile-carrying submarines) in order to compute their flight characteristics, especially in the re-entry and impact stages. During such tests the *Henri Poincaré* also acts as the range safety and command ship by assisting the flag officer-in-charge in controlling the naval and air elements in the test zone, particularly in the final descent and recovery phases.

The Henri Poincaré is the flagship of Group M, the French navy's test and measurement unit, and is responsible for monitoring the French SSBS and MSBS strategic missile tests so that parameters such as CEP and warhead characteristics can be determined.

Built originally as an Italian tanker, the *Henri Poincaré* was reconstructed at Brest between 1964 and 1967, a second major refit following between 1979 and 1980 to update her electronic systems. These include one Savoie and two Gascogne tracking radars, a fully automatic tracking station, celestial position-fixing equipment, a cine-camera-equipped theodolite, infrared tracking systems, Transit navigational and Syracuse satellite communications systems, meteorological and oceanographic equipment, a data collection and collation system, and hull-mounted sonar. For the vertical replenishment and communications tasks she has a hangar and flightdeck aft for either two Aérospatiale SA321 Super Frelon heavy-lift or up to five Aérospatiale Alouette III light com-munications/transport helicopters. It is expected that the *Henri Poincaré* will eventually be replaced in the mid- to late 1990s.

Specification
'Henri Poincaré' class.
Displacement: 19,500 tons standard and 24,000 tons full load
Dimensions: length 180.0 m (590.6 ft); beam 22.2 m (72.8 ft); draught 9.4 m (30.8 ft)
Propulsion: one geared steam turbine delivering 7457 kW (10,000 hp) to one shaft
Speed: 15 kts
Aircraft: two Aérospatiale SA321 Super Frelon or up to five Aérospatiale Alouette III helicopters
Armament: two single 20-mm AA guns
Electronics: one DRBV 22D air-search radar, navigation radars plus items mentioned in the text
Complement: 325

'Yuan Wang' class

First seen during the May 1980 ICBM test series in the central Pacific, the **'Yuan Wang' class** of satellite- and missile-tracking ships is an important part of China's space technology and missile-testing programme. The two vessels, the *Yuan Wang 1* and *Yuan Wang 2*, were built by the Jiangnan Shipyard at Shanghai and commissioned in 1979. For their tracking and monitoring duties they carry a large parabolic tracking antenna amidships, two log-

The Yuan Wang class was first observed during the 1980 Chinese ICBM tests in the central Pacific. They have a large helicopter landing platform aft, but no hangar for the French-built Aérospatiale SA321 Super Frelon heavylift helicopters normally embarked.

periodic HF antennae (fore and aft) shaped like 'fish-spines', two small missile-tracking radars and several precision theodolite optical tracking director stations. There are also several additional positions available for the later installation of equipment. For vertical replenishment and personnel transfer there is a large helicopter deck located aft, but this lacks hangar facilities. A helicopter type known to use the deck is the heavy-lift Aérospatiale SA321 Super Frelon. A bow thruster and retractable fin stabilizers are fitted for station-keeping and stability in rough seas.

To support these vessels the

Chinese Academy of Sciences also has a fleet of research ships sailing under the name **'Xiang Yang Hong'** (East is Red) and individual numbers. These vessels are capable of a wide variety of duties including general oceanographic, upper atmosphere, missile and satellite research, and also hydrometeorology. Further vessels of an **'Improved Yuan Wang' class** are expected to be built in the near future as the Chinese space programme gathers momentum towards the eventual launch of a manned spacecraft. Such vessels will then assume the communications relay role as well as the current tasks.

Specification
'Yuan Wang' class
Displacement: 17,100 tons standard and 21,000 tons full load
Dimensions: length 190.0 m (623.4 ft); beam 22.6 m (74.1 ft); draught 7.5 m (24.6 ft)
Propulsion: one diesel powering one shaft
Speed: 20 kts
Aircraft: helicopter landing deck only
Armament: none
Electronics: navigation radars plus items mentioned in the text
Complement: 300-400

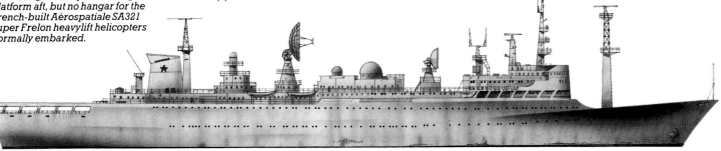

'Mod Kondor I' class

Two of a number of 'Kondor I' inshore minesweeper class conversions, the pair of **'Mod Kondor I' class** vessels produced between 1968 and 1970 are the *Komet* (D42) and *Meteor* (D43). These had their armament and minesweeping gear removed and various signal intelligence (Sigint) and electronic intelligence (Elint) antenna added, together with a deckhouse aft to accommodate the associated recording equipment. The vessels are used with a trawler-type unit, the *Hydrograph* (D41) of the Soviet 'Okean' design, to monitor NATO naval exercises in the Baltic, and regularly patrol

offshore near highly sensitive West German and Danish military installations to gather classified signal data and electronic order-of-battle information. They have also been known on a number of occasions to appear near neutral Swedish installations and warships on similar missions. Very often the trips near NATO bases are co-ordinated with East German air force intelligence-gathering missions by Mikoyan-Gurevich MiG-21 'Fishbed-H' visual and electronic reconnaissance fighters and Ilyushin Il-14 'Crate' Elint platforms; these simulate penetration flight profiles into NATO

airspace in order to trigger air-defence systems into revealing operating frequencies and procedures. The ships waiting offshore can thus record all the communications and signal traffic generated by the defending systems. The material gathered is then fed into the Soviet intelligence network for evaluation and comparison with existing data, and any deviations or new material are logged for future use in an all-out war.

Specification
'Mod Kondor I' class
Displacement: 245 tons standard and

320 tons full load
Dimensions: length 52.0 m (170.6 ft); beam 7.0 m (23.0 ft); draught 2.0 m (6.6 ft)
Propulsion: two diesels delivering 3729 kW (5,000 hp) to two shafts
Speed: 17 kts
Aircraft: none
Armament: SA-7 'Grail' SAMs, light machine-guns and small arms
Electronics: one TSR333 navigation radar plus various unidentified Elint and Sigint systems
Complement: 40

'Mod Kondor I' class (continued)

The East Germans converted two of their 'Kondor I' coastal minesweepers (shown here) into intelligence-gathering units by removing all the sweeping gear and armament, fitting various antennaè and making several small changes to the superstructure. The 'Kondor I' Elint ships work in conjunction with East German air force aircraft as required.

'Nawigator', 'Baltyk' and 'Piast' classes

The Polish navy uses two modified 'Moma' class survey ships, the Hydrograf and Nawigator, in the intelligence role in the Baltic to monitor West German, Danish and Norwegian naval exercises and shore installations for the Warsaw Pact.

The two vessels that comprise the 'Nawigator' class, namely the *Nawigator* (262) and *Hydrograf* (263), and the 'Piast' class salvage vessels are all based on the Soviet-designed 'Moma' class survey ships. 'Nawigator' and 'Piast' class vessels mount a conspicuous lattice mainmast, the 'Nawigators' being distinguished by the addition of two large radomes, one immediately aft of the bridge atop the main superstructure and the other atop the aft superstructure. The *Hydrograf* differs slightly from her sister in having a much longer forecastle that is one deck higher. Although no armament is openly carried at present, there are positions for four twin 25-mm AA guns, two forward and two aft. Both the masts are fitted with a variety of DF and signal-intercept antennae, but it is believed that no real-time analysis capability is carried. Thus all the data obtained have to be recorded for eventual analysis at a shore station fitted with the necessary equipment and computer systems. All the information received after processing is then fed into the Soviet intelligence network for future use.

There is a third vessel, the 1,200-ton 'B10' class *Baltyk* (264), a converted trawler which also serves in the AGI role with the Polish navy. Both the 'Nawigator' class units are quoted as navigational training ships, but like others are betrayed as to their real role by the enormous amount of electronic gear fitted.

Specification
'Nawigator' class
Displacement: 1,260 tons standard and 1,540 tons full load
Dimensions: length 67.0 m (219.8 ft); beam 10.5 m (34.4 ft); draught 4.0 m (13.1 ft)
Propulsion: two diesels delivering 2685 kW (3,600 hp) to two shafts
Speed: 17 kts
Aircraft: none

Armament: fitted for four twin 25-mm AA (not shipped), otherwise SA-7 'Grail' SAMs, machine-guns and small arms
Electronics: two RN231 navigation radars plus various unidentified Elint and Sigint systems
Complement: 60

Like the 'Nawigator' class of AGI, the 'Piast' class salvage vessel is based on the Soviet 'Moma' class survey ship. Note, however, the absence of radomes, the one lattice mast and the conspicuous diving bell together with its launching apparatus on the port side.

USSR
'Okean' class

Spyships

Built in East Germany from 1959 to the mid-1960s, the **'Okean' class** of 15 converted side trawlers is the largest and hence the most observed class of Soviet AGI. They are designated *gigrograficheskoye sudno* (GS, or survey ship) in the Soviet navy, and retain their trawler tripod mast forward and a pole mast well aft. These are festooned with the various aerials and antennae that characterize their role. It is vessels of this class (together with the eight larger trawler units of the 'Mayak' class and the four ex-whalers of the 'Mirnyy' class) that are regularly seen off the

Western nuclear submarine bases monitoring the coming and going of SSBNs in transit. There are many variations within the class. One modified subgroup of four (the **Linza, Lotlin, Reduktor** and **Zond**) has the port side superstructure enclosed and the starboard side open; these ships also have additional accommodation on the well-deck. The *Reduktor*, **Alidada, Barometr, Ampermetr** and **Gidrofon** have no installation for shoulder-launched SA-7 SAMs, while such has been added to the **Barograf, Deflektor, Ekholot, Krenometr**, *Linza, Lotlin,*

Repiter, Teodolit, Traverz and *Zond*. The *Barograf* also has two twin 14.5-mm (0.57-in) heavy machine-gun mountings to supplement the small arms carried by the crew. It is likely that the 'Okean' class will eventually be replaced by conversions of the **'Al'pinist' class** stern trawlers which are currently being built at the Leninskaya Kuznitsa Shipyard at Kiev and at the Volgograd Shipyard. At present there are four such units in service, with the former fish hold converted to allow extensive space for electronics and/or additional accommodation for specialist personnel.

Specification
'Okean' class
Displacement: 650 tons standard and 760 tons full load
Dimensions: length 51.0 m (167.3 ft); beam 8.8 m (28.9 ft); draught 3.7 m (12.1 ft)
Propulsion: one diesel delivering 403 kW (540 hp) to one shaft
Speed: 13 kts
Aircraft: none
Armament: see text
Electronics: one or two 'Don Kay' navigation radars, and various Elint and Sigint systems
Complement: 70

The Linza of the 'Okean' class shadows the amphibious warfare ship HMS Fearless. The 'Okeans' are the most numerous of the Soviet

AGIs, with the antenna outfits varying considerably between the units of the class so that they can perform different roles.

The 'Okean' class AGI Gidrofon. Most of the class have now been fitted with two positions for quadruple SA-N-5 'Grail' SAM launchers. The Barograf

has also been fitted with two twin 14.5-mm heavy machine-guns for use off such unfriendly areas as the African coast and China.

'Okean' class intelligence collection ships cutaway drawing key

1 Aft wheel
2 Searchlight
3 Derrick
4 Steering compartment
5 Rudder post
6 Rudder
7 Single screw
8 Bulkhead/framing
9 Single shaft
10 Auxiliary engine
11 Dynamo
12 Engine room
13 540-bhp diesel engine
14 Exhaust uptake
15 Double bottom
16 Fuel
17 Officers'/crew quarters
18 Funnel
19 Mainmast
20 Disc cone omnidirectional receiver antenna
21 Radar receiver
22 Direction-finding loop
23 Air search
24 Folded dipole for HF reception
25 Coaxial feeder to wire dipole antenna
26 Vertical rod antenna
27 Don 2 navigation radar
28 Radar receiver
29 Ventilator
30 Bridge
31 Deck light
32 Chart room
33 Navigation light
34 Radar room
35 Extended space for information processing
36 Waterline
37 Forward hold
38 Tripod foremast
39 Bow light
40 Direction-finding loop with earthplane
41 Raised foredeck
42 Hull guard
43 Anchor
44 Winch
45 Lifeboat

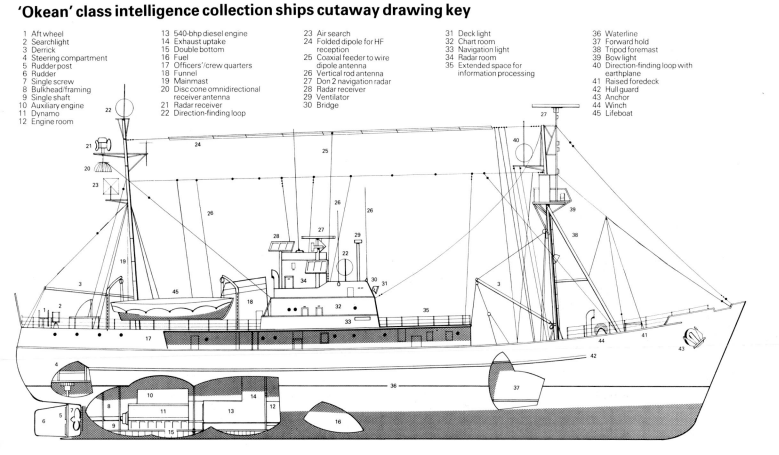

'Bal'zam' class

Designated by the Soviets as *sudno svyazyy* (SSV, or communications vessels) the **'Bal'zam'** class vessels are the first military ships purpose-built for intelligence collection and processing. Three are currently in service, with a fourth due to join the fleet soon following completion at the Kaliningrad Shipyard. The ships carry an array of intercept and direction-finding antennae that feed raw intelligence information into the onboard data analysis and processing equipment located within the extensive superstructure. The product can then be sent via the two satellite transmitting and receiving antennae located beneath the spherical radomes, either to.shore stations or to the flagships of surface action battle groups for immediate action. For the extended sea periods which they serve, the ships are equipped to refuel underway and to transfer solid cargo and personnel via constant-tension transfer rigs on each side of the aft mast. The class was also the first Soviet AGI type to be defensively armed, the lead ship appearing in service during 1980 with two quadruple SA-N-5 'Grail' SAM launchers and a 30-mm six-barrel ADG6-30 CIWS. However, no radar fire-control systems are fitted (presumably to prevent interference with the electronic equipment already carried) so the weapons instead use a re-

mote 'Kolonka' pedestal director. The 'Bal'zams' are now commonly seen at sea monitoring major NATO naval exercises in the North Atlantic, and also American carrier battle groups. One ship serves in the Northern fleet, the other two in the Pacific.

SSV 516 is the lead ship of a new class of very large AGIs given the NATO codename 'Bal'zam'. Armed with two quadruple SA-N-5 'Grail' SAM launchers and a 30-mm CIWS, the class also has elaborate at-sea underway replenishment facilities and real-time satellite transmitter and receiver installations beneath the two dome installations.

There are three 'Bal'zam' class AGIs in service with the Soviet navy at present, with a fourth unit building. Designated a Sudno Svyazyy (SSV or communications vessel) they are the world's best equipped intelligence-gathering ships.

Specification
'Bal'zam' class
Displacement: 4,000 tons standard and 5,000 tons full load
Dimensions: length 105.0 m (344.5 ft); beam 15.5 m (50.9 ft); draught 5.0 m (16.4 ft)
Propulsion: two diesels delivering 6711 kW (9,000 hp) to two shafts
Speed: 22 kts
Aircraft: none
Armament: two quadruple SA-N-5 'Grail' SAM launchers with 16 missiles, and one ADG6-30 30-mm CIWS
Electronics: two 'Don Kay' navigation radars, various Elint and Sigint systems, two satellite transmitter/receiver systems, and one real-time intelligence-analysis centre
Complement: 200

'Primor'ye' class

Although its units resemble small passenger liners in appearance, the **'Primor'ye'** class of AGI was the first commercially-based intelligence-gathering design to have an onboard analysis capability. Based on the hull of the highly successful 'Mayakovskyy' series of stern trawler-factory ships, the six vessels are the *Kavkaz* (SSV591), *Krym* (SSV590), *Primor'ye* (SSV465), *Zabaykalye* (SSV464), *Zakarpatye* and *Zaporozhye* (SSV501). They have a distinctive superstructure with box-like structures fore and aft (to house electronic processing equipment) and three main masts (for the associated aerials and antennae). Two of the units, the *Krym* and *Kavkaz*, have lost the forward mast but have retained the trawler kingpost aft, while all six vessels differ among themselves in minor details of superstructure and antennae outfits. Most have now been refitted with platforms to carry one or two quadruple SA-N-5 'Grail' SAM launchers for local air defence, the remainder in preparation with the Soviet army's shoulder-launched SAM-7 'Grail' SAM that had been issued to the

Soviet naval infantry.

The 'Primor'ye' class ships have often been seen off both coasts of the USA, especially during the missile tests held off Florida by British and American SSBNs. They also regularly accompany major NATO exercises and American aircraft-carriers, but do not have the modern real-time data transmission facilities possessed by the later 'Bal'zam' class.

Specification
'Primor'ye' class
Displacement: 2,600 tons standard and 3,700 tons full load
Dimensions: length 83.6 m (274.3 ft); beam 13.7 m (44.9 ft); draught 7.0 m (23.0 ft)
Propulsion: one diesel delivering 1491 kW (2,000 hp) to one shaft
Speed: 13 kts
Aircraft: none
Armament: one (SSV 590) or two (SSVs 464, 501 and 591) quadruple SA-N-5 'Grail' SAM launchers with eight or 16 missiles respectively (other ships to be fitted with launchers), machine-guns

The Zakarpatye of the 'Primor'ye' class shows the multitude of arrays and antennae that are required by an intelligence-gathering ship. Those

and small arms
Electronics: two 'Don Kay' or 'Don 2' navigation radars, various Elint and

on the foremast are primarily of the direction-finding type so as to pinpoint the origin of an electronic transmission.

Sigint systems, and one real-time intelligence-analysis centre
Complement: 160

The 'Primor'ye' class of AGI comprises six units, and is regularly seen attending NATO naval exercises and American space events and missile tests to gather electronic and photographic intelligence for use by Soviet designers on their own systems.

USSR
'India' class

Although said to be designed for the underwater-rescue role, with two small deep submergence recovery vessels (DSRVs) semi-recessed in wells on the deck abaft the sail structure, the two units of the **'India' class** diesel-electric submarine would in wartime or for certain clandestine intelligence-gathering operations probably operate with the Soviet navy's Spetsnaz special forces brigades to carry combat mini-subs and frogman units. The DSRVs normally carried are about 11 m (36.1 ft) long and are fitted out to lock onto the rescue hatches of submarines lying disabled on the seabed. For under-ice and covert operations direct access to and exit from the DRSVs in their wells is possible while the submarine is submerged. Although no torpedo armament is believed to be carried, the hull of the submarine has been designed for high surface speed operation in order to cut down on transit times to possible rescue areas. For operations in the extreme north, where ice-floes are likely to be encountered, the bow can be specially strengthened by the fitting of an ice guard. For convenience (and better underwater manoeuvring in certain circumstances) the hydroplanes are fitted on the sides of the sail.

Only two 'India' class boats are in service, one with the Northern Fleet and the other with the Pacific Fleet. The former may have been detached to the Baltic Fleet on occasions for use in the various incursions that have been made into Swedish territorial waters over the past few years. It is believed that on this type of operation the 'India' class submarine carries two modified versions of the Soviet army's

new IRM amphibious reconnaissance armoured engineer vehicle with diver lock-out facilities; this vehicle is capable of travelling along the seabed on tracks as well as using the more conventional swimming mode.

Specification
'India' class
Displacement: 3,900 tons surfaced and 4,800 tons dived
Dimensions: length 106.0 m (347.8 ft); beam 10.0 m (32.8 ft); draught not known
Propulsion: three diesels delivering 8948 kW (12,000 hp) to two electric motors powering two shafts
Speed: 15 kts surfaced and 12.5 kts dived
Diving depth: mother craft 300 m (984 ft) operational and 500 m (1,640 ft) maximum; DSRVs 1000 m (3,281 ft) operational
Armament: demolition charges, small arms etc

Photographed in transit from the Pacific to the Northern Fleet, this 'India' class boat has landed both DSRVs and has been fitted with a built-up bow to cope with the rough conditions of the northern coast.

Electronics: one 'Snoop Plate' surface-search radar, one ESM system, one medium-frequency bow sonar, several types of underwater telephone and homing systems
Complement: 70 crew plus 120 passengers/divers

The 'India' class rescue submarines are equipped to carry and operate two deep submergence rescue vessels, and are believed to operate in support of the naval Spetsnaz special operations brigades when not being used in their primary role. Of the two 'Indias' one is in the Northern Fleet and the other in the Pacific Fleet. ⸋

'Gagarin' class

The *Kosmonavt Yuriy Gagarin*, sole unit of the 'Gagarin' class, is a space control monitoring ship based at the Black Sea port of Odessa. She is the world's largest vessel fitted for scientific studies and is also the largest ship with turbo-electric propulsion. Originally a 'Sofiya' class steam tanker, she was adapted before final completion to fulfil the research role. Built at Leningrad by the Baltic Shipbuilding and Engineering Works, she was completed in 1971 and is engaged in research into the conditions in the upper atmosphere and the problems associated with long-range communication, as well as undertaking space control and spacecraft communications activities. For this work the ship is fitted with two 27-m (88.6-ft) diameter 'Ship Shell' and two 12.5-m (41-ft) diameter 'Ship 'Bowl' stabilized communications dish antennae, two 'Vee Tube' HF communications systems and four 'Quad Ring' yagi arrays. With all the antennae deployed forward, the vessel suffers a loss in speed of 2 kts. To maintain the ship on station during a particular task, bow and stern thrusters are fitted. The ship is capable of staying at sea for 120 consecutive days without resupply, and for her crew's comfort she has three swimming pools, a theatre and a sports hall. The ship is named after the first man to travel in Earth orbit, and who was subsequently killed in an air crash in the Soviet Union during 1968.

Specification
'Gagarin' class
Displacement: 37,500 tons standard and 45,000 tons full load
Dimensions: length 235.9 m (774.0 ft); beam 31.0 m (101.7 ft); draught 9.2 m (30.2 ft)
Propulsion: one geared steam turbine delivering 14168 kW (19,000 hp) to an electric drive turning one shaft
Speed: 17.5 kts
Aircraft: none
Armament: none
Electronics: two 'Don Kay' navigation radars plus items mentioned in the text
Complement: 160 crew plus 180 scientists/technicians

The 45,000-ton Kosmonavt Yuriy Gagarin *is the largest Soviet research vessel, adapted from the unfinished hull of a tanker. Her powerful communication and detection equipment enable Soviet space missions to be controlled far from convenient ground stations.*

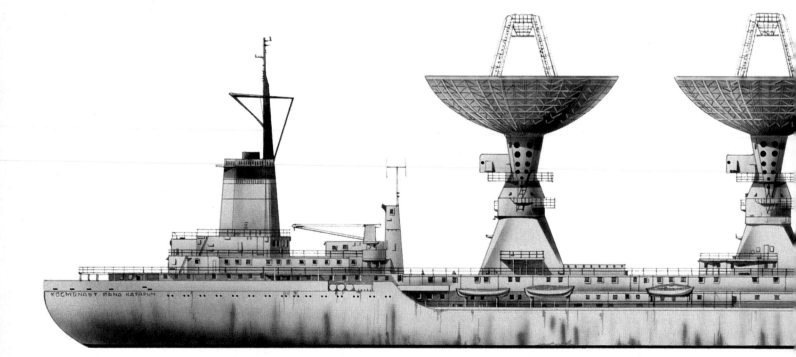

Kosmonavt Yuriy Gagarin

The Kosmonavt Yuriy Gagarin *is the largest of the Soviet space event ships and is subordinated to the Academy of Science for assignments. Adapted from a tanker hull whilst still on the stocks, she is homeported at Odessa in the Black Sea but operates in many parts of the world. The four huge dish antennae can act as brakes, and when in the correct orientation actually reduce the speed of the ship by up to two knots. For the crew's comfort on long voyages she has three swimming pools, a gymnasium and a 300-seat theatre aboard.*

'Converted Compass Island' class

The USNS *Observation Island* (T-AGM23) is a former ballistic missile trials ship that was modified as a **'Converted Compass Island' class** range instrumentation ship during 1979-81. This was specifically for the purpose of carrying SPQ-11 'Cobra Judy' phased-array missile-tracking radar aft to collect data on Soviet and Chinese ballistic missile tests. Operated for the USAF Eastern Space Missile Center in the Pacific area by the Military Sealift Command, she is painted white. Two large parabolic signal-collection antennae are fitted beneath the pair of geodesic radomes atop the bridge. An extensive communications fit, which includes satellite receivers and transmitters, allows for the real-time transmission of raw and analysed data to distant shore stations if required. During her original career as a missile trials ship she fired the first ship-launched Polaris missile at sea on 27 August 1959 and then, following a refit in 1969, the first Poseidon missile on 16 December 1969. The massive 'Cobra Judy' radar carried is very similar in operational aspects to the even larger land-based 'Cobra Dane' radar, the phased transmissions allowing the system to detect and track objects at a very fast rate. The installation aboard the *Observation Island* weighs about 250 tons, and the radar itself is located in a mechanically-rotated pyramid-like steel structure, with the data analysis and storage computers (plus the display consoles) in compartments on the decks beneath it. A refit in 1984 saw the addition of a new tracking radar.

Specification
'Converted Compass Island' class
Displacement: 13,060 tons light and 17,015 tons full load
Dimensions: length 171.9 m (564.0 ft); beam 23.2 m (76.0 ft); draught 7.6 m (25 ft)

Propulsion: geared steam turbines delivering 14355 kW (19,250 hp) to one shaft
Speed: 20 kts
Aircraft: none
Armament: none
Electronics: one Raytheon TM1650/9X navigation radar and one Raytheon TM1660/12S navigation radar, plus items mentioned in the text
Complement: 153

The large phased-array radar turret mounted on USNS Observation Island when working in concert with the similar system based on land in Alaska is capable of simultaneously tracking up to 200 missile targets.

USNS Observation Island is operated by MSC with a civilian crew and watches Soviet space and missile launches with her 'Cobra Judy' phased-array radar.

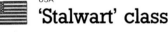

'Stalwart' class

The 26 vessels of the **'Stalwart' class** are to provide the gap-filling role for the American Sound Surveillance Under Sea (SOSUS) system in areas where there is no or only poor coverage. The sonar used by the 'Stalwarts' is the Surveillance Towed Array Sensor (AN/UQQ-2): this is a 1829-m (6,000-ft) long linear passive hydrophone array which is deployed over the ship's stern in a flexible, neutrally buoyant cable housing. The data picked up by the array is then instantaneously relayed to a shore monitoring station for processing and evaluation via a WSC-6 satellite communications link. The first seven ships are the USNS *Stalwart* (T-AGOS1), *Contender* (T-AGOS2), *Vindicator* (T-AGOS3), *Triumph* (T-AGOS4), *Assur-*

Unlike many ASW surveillance vessels, the 'Stalwart' class has no capacity for analysing data on board. Information picked up by the 1.8-km (1.1-mile) towed soner array is transmitted via satellite to a ground station for further processing and action.

ance (T-AGOS5), **Persistent** (T-AGOS6) and **Indomitable** (T-AGOS7), and all have been completed; the USNS **Prevail** (T-AGOS8), **Assertive** (T-AGOS9), **Invincible** (T-AGOS10), **Audacious** (T-AGOS11), **Bold** (T-AGOS12), **Adventurous** (T-AGOS13) and **Worthy** (T-AGOS14) are building whilst the remainder are on order or are planned. The last four units will be built on SWATH (semi-submerged catamaran) hulls to improve their operational capability under the worst of winter weather conditions at high latitudes. The ships are manned by Military Sealift Command civilian personnel, but carry a small six-man naval detachment to maintain the SURTASS and satellite communications link equipment. The class members are

expected to conduct 90-day patrols at a time, with a total of 300 days per year at sea on such patrols or on trials.

Specification
'Stalwart' class
Displacement: 1,650 tons light and 2,285 tons full load
Dimensions: length 68.3 m (224.0 ft); beam 13.1 m (43.0 ft); draught 4.6 m (15.1 ft)
Propulsion: four diesels delivering 2386 kW (3,200 hp) to electric drives turning two shafts
Speed: 11 kts
Aircraft: none
Armament: none
Electronics: two navigation radars plus items mentioned in the text
Complement: 30

The 'Stalwart' class is being used by the US Navy to carry and tow a long-range passive sonar system that is designed to help fill the gaps in the SOSUS underwater monitoring network around the coasts of the USA and fellow NATO nations.

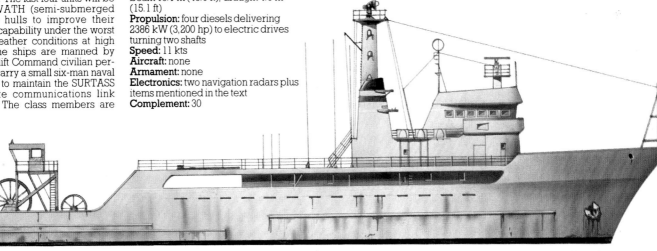

USA
'Converted Haskell' class

The USNS *Range Sentinel* (T-AGM22) is a **'Converted Haskell' class** attack transport developed for specific use as a range instrumentation ship, to monitor first the Poseidon and then the Trident I/II SLBM development programmes. Converted from October 1969 to October 1971, the *Range Sentinel* operates as a unit of the US Navy's Military Sealift Command (MSC) fleet. She is fitted with an SPQ-7 and three other radar tracking systems on a single-deck superstructure laid over the forward cargo hold area. Since commissioning for this role the *Range Sentinel* has had several electronic equipment updates, and these have resulted in changes of appearance over the years.

Converted from a former US Navy amphibious transport, the Range Sentinel *(T-AGM 22) now operates in support of SSBN missile firing in the Atlantic as a missile range instrumental vessel.*

Specification
'Converted Haskell' class
Displacement: 8,853 tons light and 12,170 tons full load
Dimensions: length 138.7 m (455.0 ft); beam 18.9 m (62.0 ft); draught 7.9 m (26.0 ft)
Propulsion: geared steam turbines delivering 6338 kW (8,500 hp) to one

shaft
Speed: 15.5 kts
Aircraft: none
Armament: none
Electronics: one Raytheon TM1650/9X navigation radar and one Raytheon TM1660/12S navigation radar, plus items mentioned in the text
Complement: 124

Originally commissioned in 1944, the converted attack transport Range Sentinel is based upon a 'Victory' ship hull, and is used in the SLBM test programmes. The forward radome has recently been lost following transfer from the Poseidon to the latest Trident range instrumentation ship.

'Vanguard' class

The USNS **Redstone** (T-AGM20) is the surviving range instrumentation member of the three-ship **'Vanguard'** class following the striking of the *Mercury* from the navy list and the conversion of the *Vanguard* into the US Navy's test ship for fleet ballistic missile guidance and ship navigation systems. Converted between 1964 and 1966 from a Type T2-SE-A2 tanker (by inserting a 22-m/72.2-ft extension amidships) to serve as the tracking and communications ship for the NASA Apollo lunar manned spaceflight programme, she now operates in support of the US Air Force's Eastern Space Missile Center at Patrick Air Force Base, Florida. To fulfil her current missions she is fitted with two large communications dish antennae and two tracking radars, plus a number of HF communications systems. To monitor upper-atmosphere conditions which might affect her work she has a high-altitude meteorological balloon hangar and launch platform located aft. Approximately 450 tons of electronic equipment are installed to support the radars and communications antennae; most of this is below decks in converted hold areas. The *Redstone* is to be replaced by a new range instrumentation ship (T-AGM24) which is to be converted from another naval unit under the FY87 programme. No further details have been released.

Specification
Displacement: 16,882 tons light and 24,710 tons full load
Dimensions: length 180.7 m (593.0 ft); beam 22.9 m (75.0 ft); draught 7.6 m (25.0 ft)
Propulsion: geared steam turbines delivering 6488 kW (8,700 hp) to an electric drive turning one shaft
Speed: 16 kts
Aircraft: none
Armament: none
Electronics: one Raytheon TM1650/9X navigation radar and one Raytheon TM1660/12S navigation radar, plus items mentioned in the text
Complement: 90 plus 108 scientists/technicians

Above: USNS Mercury *is the only one of the three converted 'Mission' class tankers to have been struck from the navy list. The vessels were named* after early US missile programmes, and were used during the manned space programme for tracking and communications relay tasks.

Above: USNS Redstone *operates in support of the Trident fleet ballistic missile programme, serving as a tracking and communication ship.*

She also has some upper atmosphere meteorology capability, essential for the analysis of missile performance.

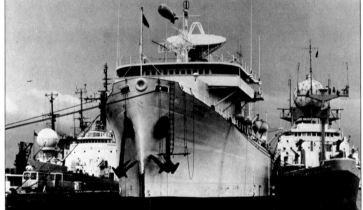

Above: The Vanguard *(T-AG 194) has taken part in a number of international upper atmosphere research exercises, including the GATE programme. Her sister ship* Redstone *(T-AGM20) now serves as the US Navy's navigation research ship, testing new systems.*

Below: Vanguard *(T-AG 194, formerly T-AGM19) supported the USAF missile-testing range in the Atlantic for a number of years, and is now temporarily laid up after conversion to ballistic missile guidance and ship navigation test ship in 1980.*

Modern Support Vessels

Resupply at sea is not a new concept, and many naval operations of World War II could not have taken place without it. Today, with the US Navy operating worldwide and as a result of conflict in the South Atlantic, the support ship is as important as ever.

The RFA Blue Rover *(A 270) takes part in a replenishment-at-sea (RAS) during the Falklands operation. The* Blue Rover *was the only one of her class to serve in the Total Exclusion Zone, and apart from RAS duties she supplied fuel and ammunition to the army from San Carlos Water between 1 June and 22 June.*

Modern auxiliary ships are usually divided into two broad categories: the underway replenishment (UNREP) ship designed to carry out the direct support of surface combat forces in the forward area of operations, and the fleet support ship which as its primary function provides maintenance and related services to naval forces at advanced bases and home ports with limited resources. To supplement these types in wartime, there would be a wide variety of merchant ships requisitioned to undertake specific tasks in direct support of fleet operations. A classic example of this last facet is the 1982 Falklands war when without the help of 50 merchant ships the Royal Navy could not have supported a task force, let alone have undertaken an amphibious assault of the magnitude required to recapture a number of islands 12875 km (8,000 miles) from its home ports. It should be noted, however, that most of the major sea powers in the world today can call on reserves of commercial shipping for such tasks, the Soviet navy having the unquestioning obedience of the immense Soviet merchant fleet, wherever it is found on the seas. However, since the Falklands war both the Royal Fleet Auxiliary and the British merchant marine have suffered cutbacks for economy reasons, and it is a moot point whether a task force support train of similar ilk could be formed again.

The US Navy in the meantime is gradually strengthening its support and UNREP force to be able to supply the 600-ship level projected in current construction plans. To meet the unique requirements of the carrier battle groups the US Navy has designed several specialist classes of UNREP ships that combine the capabilities of several older designs in one hull. Such ships form the basis of UNREP groups with their own escort ships and will be the linchpin of any future war at sea, for without constant resupply the warships will not fight effectively.

By contrast the expansion of Soviet naval power has not been matched by a corresponding increase in UNREP capability. Although support, salvage and engineering vessels are in service in some numbers, only the Berezina approaches US replenishment standards.

The Berezina *refuels a 'Kiev' class carrier and a guided missile cruiser. It is believed that the* Berezina *was constructed for the carrier support role, and may well be testing the concept for a new generation of replenishment vessels that will be built for the new Soviet fixed wing carrier under construction.*

'Protecteur' class replenishment fleet oiler

In design the 'Protecteur' class is an improvement on that of the prototype HMCS *Provider* (AOR 508). The two ships have been given the US AOR (replenishment fleet oiler) designation, and have four replenishment-at-sea stations, one elevator aft of the navigation bridge, two 15-ton capacity cranes on the aft deck, and a large helicopter hangar and flight deck at the stern. The cargo capacity is 12,000 tons of fuel oil, 600 tons of diesel, 400 tons of aviation fuel, 1,250 tons of munitions and 1,048 tons of dry cargo/spares and refrigerated provisions. The aircraft hangar/flight deck area can be used either for spare task group ASW helicopters or for military vehicles and bulk equipment for sealift operations. If required HMCS **Protecteur** (AOR 509) and HMCS **Preserver** (AOR 510) can also serve as limited-capacity amphibious assault transports with room for 50 or more troops serving in the commando role. Four LCVPs are carried as part of each ship's boat complement. The sole armament is a twin 76-mm (3-in) Mk 33 DP gun mount

The Canadian Navy replenishment ship HMCS Preserver *(AOR 510) is equipped to carry up to three licence-built Sikorsky SH-3 Sea King ASW helicopters. These can be used as spare aircraft by an ASW hunter-killer task group as well as being able to provide vertical replenishment of ammunition, dry stores and fuel to the ships of the group.*

located at the bow in the eyes of the ship. This positioning has proved to be precarious, mountings having been washed away on several occasions. The *Preserver* completed a mid-life refit in 1982, whilst her sister ship is due to undergo such a refit in the near future. Both ships were laid down in October 1967, and commissioned in August 1969 and July 1970 respectively.

Specification
'Protecteur' class
Type: replenishment fleet oiler
Displacement: 8,380 tons light and

24,700 tons full load
Dimensions: length 171.9 m (564 ft); beam 23.2 m (76 ft); draught 9.1 m (30 ft)
Propulsion: 1-shaft geared steam turbine delivering 21,000 shp (15660 kW)
Speed: 21 kts

Armament: one twin 76-mm (3-in) DP gun
Aircraft: three Sikorsky CH-124 Sea King helicopters
Electronics: one Decca TM969 navigation radar, one Sperry Mk 2 navigation radar, one URN-20 Tacan, one SQS-505 hull sonar
Complement: 227 + 57 passengers

Given the US Navy AOR designation, the 'Protecteur' class can carry diesel and aviation fuel in addition to fuel oil. Unusually, it also carries four LCVPs, and can accommodate up to 50 troops for commando operations.

'Durance' class underway replenishment tanker

Currently in production for several navies the 'Durance' class is named as a *Pétrolier Ravitailleur d'Escadre* (PRE) by the French Navy. There are two port and two starboard solid/liquid cargo underway replenishment positions, one on each beam having a heavy transfer capability. A stern refuelling position is also provided so that up to three ships may be simultaneously refuelled. Vertical replenishment (VERTREP) operations are carried out by the embarked light helicopter. The **Durance** (A 629) was commissioned in 1976. She can carry 7,500 tons of fuel oil, 1,500 tons of diesel, 500 tons of TR 5 aviation fuel, 130 tons of fresh water, 170 tons of victuals, 150 tons of munitions and 50 tons of naval stores. The **Meuse** (A 607) commissioned in 1980, followed by the **Var** (A 608) and the **Marne** (A 630) in 1983 and 1986. A fifth ship was ordered in 1986. The *Meuse* carries less fuel oil but twice as much diesel and aviation fuel as the earlier ship, other stores being the same The last three of the class have an extended bridge structure to accommodate the flag staff for a

Maritime Zone as well as a commando unit of 45 men (at the expense of some stores capacity). A modified version has been built for the Royal Australian Navy, HMAS **Success** (AOR 304) being commissioned in 1986. She carries 8,220 tons of fuel oil, 1,131 tons of aviation fuel, 170 tons of munitions, 259 tons fresh water, and 45 tons of spares. She can also carry one SH-60B Seahawk in her hangar. The RAN may order a second of the class if funds permit. Two further vessels, the **Boraida** and the

Yunbou were built in France for the Saudi Navy. They have a secondary role as training ships, for which accommodation for 55 Cadets has been provided.

Specification
'Durance' class
Type: underway replenishment tanker
Displacement: 7,600 tons light and 17,800 tons full load
Dimensions: length 157.3 m (516.1 ft); beam 21.2 m (69.5 ft); draught 10.3 m

(33.8 ft)
Propulsion: 2-shaft diesels delivering 20,000 shp (14,914 kW)
Speed: 19 kts
Armament: two 40-mm AA guns, except *Meuse* one 40-mm AA and two 20-mm AA guns
Aircraft: one Aérospatiale Alouette III helicopter
Electronics: one navigation radar, one SATCOMM communications system
Complement: 150 except *Var* and unnamed vessel 250

Launch picture of Durance, *taken in 1975. Commissioned in 1976,* Durance *was the first of a class of four for the French navy. Two have been built for Saudi Arabia, and two are under construction for the Royal Australian Navy.*

'Poolster' class fast combat support ship

Essentially a fast combat support ship design, the **Poolster** (A835) is also capable of taking part in anti-submarine warfare operations with a hunter-killer group by operating and supporting up to five ASW helicopters with weapons and other supplies. She was commissioned in 1964, and her cargo capacity is 10,300 tons, of which 8,000 tons is devoted to liquid fuel products with the rest comprising fresh water, munitions, fleet spares and other stores. If required she can also carry 300 marines for short distances as an assault transport. In the early 1970s an **'Improved Poolster' class** unit was built as the **Zuiderkruis** (A832) and commissioned in 1975. Like her predecessor she has two fuelling stations per side amidships and one constant tension sliding-stay solid cargo transfer point per side forward. Her cargo capacity is 9,000 tons of liquid fuel products, 400 tons of TR5 aviation fuel, 200 tons of fresh water, plus munitions, spare parts and other stores. Two more vessels of this modified design are planned for the late 1980s, one to replace the Poolster and the other to support the Dutch navy's third ASW group. Unusually for vessels of this type, the ships carry depth charges as part of their armament outfit.

Specification
'Poolster' class
Type: fast combat support ship
Displacement: 16,836 tons full load
Dimensions: length 169.6 m (556.4 ft); beam 20.3 m (66.6 ft); draught 8.2 m (26.9 ft)
Propulsion: 1-shaft geared steam turbines delivering 22,000 shp (16405 kW)
Speed: 21 kts
Armament: two single 40-mm AA guns, and two depth-charge racks
Aircraft: between one and five Westland SH-14 Lynx helicopters
Electronics: one Decca 2459 air-search radar, one Decca 1226 navigation radar, one passive ECM suite, one Corvus chaff launchers, one CWE-610 hull sonar
Complement: 200

Specification
'Improved Poolster' class
Type: fast combat support ship
Displacement: 17,357 tons full load
Dimensions: length 171.1 m (561.4 ft); beam 20.3 m (66.6 ft); draught 8.2 m (26.9 ft)
Propulsion: 1-shaft diesels delivering 21,000 shp (15660 kW)
Speed: 21 kts
Armament: two single 20-mm AA guns, one 30-mm Goalkeeper CIWS, and

two depth-charge racks
Aircraft: between one and five Westland SH-14 Lynx helicopters
Electronics: two Decca 1226 navigation radars, one passive ECM suite, two Corvus chaff launchers
Complement: 173

HNLMS Zuiderkruis, a 'Poolster' class fast combat support ship (A832) is unique in NATO navies in having an ASW armament of depth charges to go with a helicopter group of up to five Westland Lynx ASW helicopters. The stores she carries include lightweight torpedoes and conventional depth bombs for use by the helicopters.

Capable of carrying fresh water and various dry stores in addition to liquid fuel products, the 'Poolster' class can transfer stores by means of one sliding stay transfer point and two fuelling stations per side.

'Rhein' class depot ship

Originally totalling 13 vessels, the **'Rhein' class** of depot ships is subdivided into three groups: the **Type 401** for missile and torpedo attack craft, the **Type 402** for mine countermeasures vessels, and the **Type 403** for submarines. Each group differs in overall length, machinery fit and cargo capacity. At present the West German navy only has 10 of the class in service. The Type 401 units are the **Rhein** (A 55), **Elbe** (A 61), **Main** (A 63), **Neckar** (A 66), **Werra** (A 68) and **Donau** (A 69); the Type 402 ships are the **Saar** (A 65) and **Mosel** (A 67); and the Type 403 units are the **Lahn** (A 58) and **Lech** (A 56). The ships were all commissioned

in the first half of the 1960s. Two others, the **Cezayirli Gaza Hasan Paşa** (ex-Type 401 **Ruhr**) and the **Sokulla Mehmet Paşa** (ex-Type 402 **Iser**) were given to Turkey, whilst the third unit, the **Aegeon** (ex-Type 401 **Weser**) was transferred to Greece. The two Type 403 submarine tenders **Lech** and **Lahn** do not carry the two characteristic single 100-mm (3.9-in) guns of the rest of the class, which allow those units to operate in place of frigates, but instead have 200 tons of stores and spares, 200 tons of fuel and 40 spare torpedoes for their submarines. The **Neckar**, **Werra** and **Donau** can also function as training vessels if required. All 13 ships were

equipped with mine rails to serve as minelayers in wartime. The Type 401 is distinguishable from the Type 402 by having a single crane to port, whilst the latter units have two cranes side-by-side farther aft. Two of the Type 401 tenders are to undergo refits to support the new type 143A missile craft.

Specification
'Rhein' class
Type: depot ship
Displacement: Type 401 2,370 tons standard and 3,000 tons full load: Type 402 2,330 tons standard and 2,940 tons full load: and Type 403 2,400 tons standard and 2,956 tons full load

Dimensions: length 98.2 m (322.2 ft) for Type 401, 98.5 m (323.2 ft) for Type 402 and 98.6 m (323.5 ft) for Type 403; beam 11.83 m (38.8 ft); draught 5.2 m (17.1 ft)
Propulsion: 2-shaft diesels delivering 14,400 hp (10738 kW)
Speed: 20.5 kts
Armament: two single 100-mm (3.9-in) DP (except A 55 and A 56) and four single 40-mm AA guns (except two twin 40-mm AA in A 55 and A 56), plus provision for up to 70 mines according to type (Type 401 and 402 to get RAM point-defence missile system)
Electronics: one DA-02 air- and surface-search radar, two WM-45 fire-control radars, one Kelvin Hughes 14/9 navigation radar, one hull sonar
Complement: 153 except A 55 and A 56 114, A 61 and A 68 163, and A 65 and A 67 125

'Rhein' class depot ships are designed for operations in the restricted waters of the Baltic and German North Sea. Serving as depot ships of Fast Patrol Craft and diesel submarines, the armament fit enables the vessels to operate in place of frigates or as training ships.

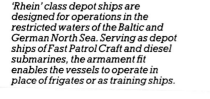

'Yellowstone' and 'Samuel Gompers' class destroyer tenders

The **'Samuel Gompers' class** ships were the US Navy's first destroyer tenders designed after World War II specifically to support surface combatants armed by guided missiles and with nuclear or gas turbine propulsion. The two ships are similar in layout to the 'L.Y. Spear' class submarine tenders, and were completed with a landing platform and hangar for ASW DASH drones. In the USS *Samuel Gompers* (AD 37) the hangar has been converted to a boat repair shop. The design was followed by the modified **'Yellowstone' class** of four ships, which offer the same facilities and, like the two earlier ships, can simultaneously service up to six ships moored alongside. Each of the 'Yellowstones' carries two 30-ton and two 3.5-ton capacity travelling cranes, whereas the units of the earlier class each have only the latter. The newer design also has the additional capability of carrying and overhauling spare LM2500 gas turbine engines for the 'Ticonderoga', 'Spruance', 'Kidd' and 'Oliver Hazard Perry' classes of surface combatants. Two further units of the 'Yellowstone' class are due to be ordered under current US Navy construction plans in order to meet the growth of the gas turbine-powered fleet.

The *Samuel Gompers* was commissioned in 1968, her sister ship USS **Puget Sound** (AD 38) commissioning during the following year. The four 'Yellowstone' class ships are the USS **Yellowstone** (AD 41), USS **Acadia** (AD 42), USS **Cape Cod** (AD 43) and USS **Shenandoah** (AD 44), commissioned at yearly intervals from 1980 to 1983.

Specification
'Samuel Gompers' class
Type: destroyer tender
Displacement: 13,600 tons light and 22,260 tons full load
Dimensions: length 196.5 m (644.7 ft); beam 25.9 m (85 ft); draught 9.1 m

(30 ft)
Propulsion: 1-shaft geared steam turbines delivering 20,000 shp (14914 kW)
Speed: 18 kts
Armament: four single 20-mm AA guns
Aircraft: provision for a helicopter on a landing pad
Electronics: one LN-66 navigation radar, one SPS-10 surface-search radar, one OE 82 satellite communication system
Complement: 1,276

Specification
'Yellowstone' class
Type: destroyer tender
Displacement: 13,280 tons light and 20,244 tons full load
Dimensions: length 192.6 m (631.9 ft); beam 25.5 m (83.6 ft); draught 7.3 m (24 ft)
Propulsion: 1-shaft geared steam turbines delivering 20,000 shp (14914 kW)
Speed: 20 kts
Armament: two single 40-mm AA and

The first US destroyer tender of post-World War II design was the USS Samuel Gompers (AD37). The two vessels of the class were followed by four of the 'Yellowstone' design.

two single 20-mm AA guns and two 40mm Mk 19 grenade launchers
Aircraft: none
Electronics: one LN-66 navigation radar, one SPS-10 surface-search radar, one OE82 system
Complement: 1,508

'Kilauea' class ammunition ship

The **'Kilauea' class** of ammunition ship (AE) is easily recognized by its superstructure arrangement forward of the aft helicopter deck. The eight ships, all commissioned between 1968 and 1972, are designed for the rapid underway transfer of missiles and other munitions to the units of a battle group by alongside replenishment or helicopter VERTREP. For the latter they have a hangar 15.24 m (50 ft) long and 4.72-5.33 m (15.5-17.5 ft) wide built into the aft superstructure for the two Boeing Vertol UH-46A/D Sea Knight helicopters embarked. These are the standard US Navy VERTREP helicopters, and can carry either 1361 kg (3,000 lb) of cargo internally or up to 4536 kg (10,000 lb)

Right: USS Kilauea (AE26) has now been transferred to the civilian-manned Military Sealift Command with the pennant number T-AE26. Another, the USS Butte (AE27), is to follow shortly after being disarmed.

Below: The 'Kilauea' class can carry about 6,500 tons of munitions and has facilities for the transport and servicing of nuclear missile warheads and aircraft bombs carried by carrier battle groups.

externally in a sling. All the vessels have fin stabilizers, and with the exception of the USNS *Kilauea* (T-AE26) have the Mk 36 Super RBOC chaff rocket launcher system fitted. In 1980 the *Kilauea* was transferred to the civilian-manned Military Sealift Command though no others followed. Each ship's capacity is assessed to be around 6,500 tons of munitions including facilities for the transport and servicing of nuclear weapons such as missile warheads and aircraft bombs for use by a carrier battle group. The other units of the class are the USS *Butte* (AE27), USS *Santa Barbara* (AE28), USS *Mount Hood* (AE29), USS *Flint* (AE32), USS *Shasta* (AE33), USS *Mount Baker* (AE34) and USS *Kiska* (AE35).

Specification
'Kilauea' class
Type: ammunition ship
Displacement: 9,369-13,688 tons light

and 18,088 tons full load, except AE26 and AE27 17,931 tons full load
Dimensions: length 171.9 m (564 ft); beam 24.7 m (81 ft); draught 9.1 m (30 ft)
Propulsion: 1-shaft geared steam turbine delivering 22,000 shp (16405 kW)
Speed: 21 kts
Armament: T-AE26 none, AE27-29 two twin 76-mm (3-in) AA guns, and AE32 to AE35 two 20-mm Phalanx CIWS mountings
Aircraft: two Boeing Vertol UH-46D Sea Knight helicopters
Electronics: one SPS-10 surface-search radar, one OE 82 system, one SLQ-32(V)1 ESM suite, one Mk 36 Super RBOC chaff launcher (except T-AE26)
Complement: T-AE26 188, and others between 401 and 444

USS *Mount Baker (AE34)*, a 'Kilauea' class ammunition supply ship, is replenishing the aircraft carrier USS Nimitz (CVN68) during a training exercise off Guantanamo. She carries a wide range of aviation ordnance stores in her cargo.

USA
'Mars' class combat stores ship

The **'Mars' class** of combat support ship (AFS) are large purpose-built underway replenishment vessels that combine the capabilities of the stores ship (AF), stores issue ship (AKS) and aviation stores ship (AVS) in one hull. They do not carry bulk petroleum products as do the AOE and AOR classes, and are fitted with four M-shaped cargo masts with constant-tension transfer rigs. The cargo capacity is 7,000 tons, of which 1,300 tons are refrigerated goods. The cargo is stored in five holds: two for spares, one for dry provisions, one for refrigerated goods and one for aviation spares. Some 25,000 types of spares are carried, and these are divided between 40,000 bins and racks which are managed by five data-processing machines. Cargo transfer between decks and the helicopter deck is handled by as many as 11 5.5-ton capacity hoists, and on-deck replenishment operations are monitored by closed-circuit television. VERTREP helicopter operations are possible from a hangar 14.25-15.5 m (46.75-51 ft) long and 4.88-7.0 m (16-23 ft) wide and located with the flight-deck at the aft end of the superstructure for the two Boeing Vertol UH-46A/D Sea Knight helicopters normally embarked. No more AFS type vessels are due to be procured until the 1990s as the US Navy has bought the three ex-RFA 'Ness' class vessels from the UK to forestall any shortfall in numbers. The units of the class, commissioned between 1963 and 1970, are the USS *Mars* (AFS1), USS *Sylvania* (AFS2), USS *Niagara Falls* (AFS3), USS *White Plains* (AFS4), USS *Concord* (AFS5), USS *San Diego* (AFS6), and USS *San Jose* (AFS7).

Specification
'Mars' class
Type: combat stores ship
Displacement: 9,200-9,400 tons light

and 15,900-18,663 tons full load
Dimensions: length 177.1 m (581 ft); beam 24.1 m (79 ft); draught 7.3 m (24 ft)
Propulsion: 1-shaft geared steam turbine delivering 22,000 shp (16405 kW)
Speed: 20 kts
Armament: two twin 76-mm (3-in) AA guns
Aircraft: two Boeing Vertol UH-46D Sea Knight helicopters
Electronics: one SPS-10 surface-search radar, one OE 82 system, one SLQ-32(V)1 ESM suite, two Mk 36 Super RBOC chaff launchers
Complement: 486

Right: The 'Mars' class combat support ship USS White Plains *(AFS4), with a Boeing Vertol UH-46D Sea Knight VERTREP helicopter of Helicopter Combat Support Squadron 3 on the flight deck aft. She is fitted with M frames and automatic tensioning devices to transfer the stores and spare parts that she carries to ships steaming alongside.*

One of the 'Sacramento' class fast replenishment ships steams in company with a 'Mars' class combat stores ship. An Underway Replenishment Group in wartime would consist of such ships together with several guided missile and ASW frigates that would act as the Group's escorts.

'Wichita' class replenishment fleet oiler

A smaller and less expensive derivative of the 'Sacramento' design, the **'Wichita' class** of replenishment fleet oiler (AOR) provides for the rapid replenishment at sea of surface combatant ships with petroleum, munitions and a limited amount of provisions and fleet freight. All except the USS **Roanoke** (AOR7) were completed between 1969 and 1976 without hangars flanking the stack, but these are now being retrofitted to all units to allow the embarkation of two Boeing Vertol UH-46A/D Sea Knight helicopters for VERTREP operations. The cargo capacity is 175,000 barrels of liquid fuels, 600 tons of munitions, 425 tons of dry stores and spares, and 150 tons of refrigerated goods. There are four constant-tension stations for liquid cargo and two for solid cargo transfer to port, with three and two respectively to starboard. Although relatively modern, the class will have to undergo a Service Life Extension Program refit cycle in the late 1980s to ensure the US Navy's replenishment-at-sea capabilities into the next century. The seven units of the class are the USS **Wichita** (AOR1), USS **Milwaukee** (AOR2), USS **Kansas City** (AOR3), USS **Savannah** (AOR4), USS **Wabash** (AOR5), USS **Kalamazoo** (AOR6) and the previously mentioned *Roanoke*.

USS Roanoke *(AOR7) differs from the previous six 'Wichitas' in that she was built with two hangars, one on each side of the stack, permitting the operation of Boeing Vertol UH-46 Sea Knight helicopters.*

Specification
'Wichita' class
Type: replenishment fleet oiler
Displacement: 12,500 tons light except AOR7 13,000 tons light and 38,100 tons full load
Dimensions: length 200.9 m (659 ft); beam 29.3 m (96.1 ft); draught 10.2 m (33.5 ft)
Propulsion: 2-shaft geared steam turbines delivering 32,000 shp (23862 kW)
Speed: 20 kts
Armament: one octuple Sea Sparrow

SAM launcher with eight missiles, and two 20-mm Phalanx CIWS mountings (both being fitted)
Aircraft: provision for two Boeing Vertol UH-46D Sea Knight helicopters being provided
Electronics: one SPS-10 surface-search radar, one LN-66 or SPS-53 navigation radar, one TAS Mk 23 fire-control radar, one SPS-58 air-search radar (in AOR 3 and 7), one OE82 satellite communication system, one

USS Kalamazoo *(AOR6) can carry more than 1,000 tons of cargo in addition to 175,000 barrels of oil. She is to be fitted with a hangar on each side of her stack to enable the operation of VERTREP helicopters.*

SLQ-32(V)3 ESM suite, four Mk 36 Super RBOC chaff launchers, one URN 25 TACAN (SRN 15 in AOR 2, 3 and 7)
Complement: 420-498

'Sacramento' class combat support ship

The **'Sacramento' class** of fast combat support ship (AOE) are the world's largest 'one-stop' underway replenishment ships. They are specifically tasked to provide a carrier battle group with the fuel, munitions and victuals it requires to continue sustained operations, combining the capabilities of the AF (store ship), AO (oiler), AE (ammunition ship) and AK (cargo ship) single-role replenishment ships in one hull design. The cargo capacity is 177,000 barrels of liquid fuels, 2,150 tons of munitions, 250 tons of dry stores, 250 tons of refrigerated stores, and 250 tons of fleet freight and spares. Because of their immense individual cost only four of a planned five ships were built, the smaller and less expensive 'Wichita' class AOR being developed to supplement them. A large helicopter flight deck and hangar are fitted aft for the two or three Boeing Vertol UH-46A/D Sea Knight VERTREP helicopters embarked. All four units are to undergo Service Life Extension Program refits (each lasting 18 months) from Fiscal Year 1984 onwards. The four units (commissioned in 1964, 1967, 1969 and 1970 respectively) are the USS **Sacramento** (AOE1), USS **Camden** (AOE2), USS **Seattle** (AOE3) and USS **Detroit** (AOE4). In a further move

to augment and increase the underway replenishment capability of the US Navy, the first of four new design **'AOE' 6** class oilers was ordered in 1986. The resulting total of 15 large replenishment ships will match the 15 carrier force planned for the 1990s.

Specification
'Sacramento' class
Type: fast combat support ship
Displacement: 19,000 tons light and 51,400 tons full load
Dimensions: length 241.6 m (792.6 ft);

beam 32.6 m (107 ft); draught 12.0 m (39.4 ft)
Propulsion: 2-shaft geared steam turbines delivering 100,000 shp (74,570 kW)
Speed: 28 kts
Armament: one octuple Sea Sparrow SAM launcher with eight missiles, and two 20-mm Phalanx CIWS mountings
Aircraft: between one and three Boeing Vertol UH-46D Sea Knight helicopters
Electronics: one SPS-10 surface-search radar, one SPS-40 air-search

radar, one LN 66 navigation radar, one TAS Mk 23 fire-control radar, one OE82 satellite commmunication system, one SLQ-32(V)3 ESM suite, one URN-25 TACAN, four Mk 36 Super RBOC chaff launchers
Complement: 600-615

The fast combat support ship USS Detroit *(AOE4). An idea of her size can be gauged from the fact that she dwarfs the 'Spruance' class destroyer USS* Peterson *(DD969), which is being replenished.*

'Cimarron' class fleet oiler

Originally to have been a class of 15 ships, the **'Cimarron' class** of fleet oilers (AO) was built to the extent of only five units because of their limited cargo capacity of 72,000 barrels of fuel oil and 48,000 barrels of JP5 aviation fuel. The cargo is sufficient to provide two complete refuellings of a fossil-fuelled aircraft-carrier battle group with six to eight accompanying escorts. Each 'Cimarron' has four constant-tension replenishment stations to port and three to starboard, and these can transfer up to 408000 litres (107,782 US gal) of fuel oil and 245000 litres (64,722 US gal) of JP5 per hour whilst underway at 15 kts. A helicopter VERTREP platform is fitted aft, but no helicopter hangar or support facilities are provided. All five are to be 'Jumboized' during FYs 1987-90. This involves lengthening the hull to 215.9 m (708.3 ft) which will increase full load tonnage to 37,866 tons and draught to 10.2 m (33.5 ft). Speed will drop to 19.5 knots, but an SLQ-32(V)1 ESM suite and four Mk 36 Super RBOC chaff launchers will be added. Maximum crew capacity is to rise to 235, and the greatly increased cargo spaces will hold 183,000 barrels of fuel oil and JP5 jet fuel, 401 m³ of feedwater, 397 m³ of fresh water, 205 m³ of dry stores and eight refrigerated store containers. The US Navy has a requirement for a further 19 fast oilers of this size, which should be met by the new **'T-AO 187' class** currently being built. The first of the class is the **Henry J. Kaiser** (T-AO 187).

Specification
'Cimarron' class
Type: fleet oiler
Displacement: 8,210 tons light and 26,110 tons full load
Dimensions: length 180.5 m (592.2 ft); beam 26.8 m (88 ft); draught 10.7 m (35 ft)
Propulsion: 1-shaft geared steam turbine delivering 24,000 shp (17897 kW)
Speed: 20 kts
Armament: two 20-mm Phalanx CIWS mountings
Aircraft: provision for one helicopter on a landing pad
Electronics: one LN-66 navigation radar, one SPS-10 surface-search radar, one SATCOMM system, one Mk 36 Super RBOC chaff launcher
Complement: 135

Right: Lead ship of the 'Cimarron' class oilers, the USS Cimarron.

Below: The 'Cimarron' class oiler USS Platte (AO 186) in the Gulf of Mexico.

'Berezina' class underway replenishment oiler

Completed in 1977 at the 61 Kommuna Shipyard in Leningrad, the **Berezina** is unique in the Soviet navy as its largest and most capable replenishment ship, and was designed from the outset to supply petroleum products, munitions, fresh water, stores and provisions. Surprisingly, only one unit has been built to date and this may indicate that she is a prototype (preceding a further class) built to gain operational experience by testing and evaluating the replenishment-at-sea concept for eventual use with the conventional fixed-wing aircraft-carrier force now under construction. The Berezina can transfer fuel simultaneously to ships on each beam amidships and astern, whilst special provision is made for replenishing submarines. Four 10-ton capacity cranes are carried for loading stores and servicing ships moored alongside. Solid-cargo transfer underway is accomplished by two sliding-stay constant-tension transfer rigs on each side. VERTREP operations are carried out by the two Kamov Ka-25 'Hormone-C' utility helicopters with loads being slung beneath them. The cargo capacity is estimated at 16,000 tons of petroleum products, 500 tons of fresh water and 3,000 tons of munitions, spares and victuals. The large crew carried is thought to include two or three spare crews for submarines. The Berezina has the Soviet designation *Voyennyy Transport* (VTR) or military transport.

Specification
'Berezina' class
Type: underway replenishment oiler
Displacement: 14,000 tons light and 36,000 tons full load
Dimensions: length 212.0 m (695.5 ft); beam 26.0 m (85.3 ft); draught 12.0 m (39.4 ft)
Propulsion: 2-shaft diesels delivering 54,000 shp (40268 kW)
Speed: 22 kts
Armament: one twin SA-N-4 'Gecko' SAM launcher with 18 missiles, two twin 57-mm AA and four 30-mm ADG6-30 AA guns, and two RBU 1000 anti-submarine rocket launchers
Aircraft: two Kamov Ka-25 'Hormone-C' helicopters
Electronics: two 'Don Kay' navigation radars, one 'Don-2' navigation radar, one 'Strut Curve' air-search radar, one 'Muff Cob' 57-mm fire-control radar, one 'Pop Group' SAM fire-control radar, two 'Bass Tilt' CIWS fire-control radars, one medium-frequency hull sonar, two 'High Pole-B', two 'Square Head' IFF systems and two chaff launchers
Complement: 600

The Berezina is now the only Soviet replenishment ship to carry armament with both surface-to-air missiles, AA guns and RBU multiple ASW rocket launchers. Two Kamov Ka-25 'Hormone-C' utility helicopters are also embarked for vertical replenishment operations of warships.

Berezina Underway Replenishment Oiler

The Berezina

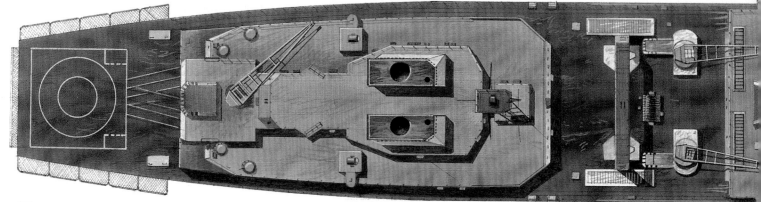

The only Soviet replenishment ship comparable to the US Navy's large AOR/AOE ships is the replenishment oiler Berezina, which can supply petroleum products, munitions, stores and fresh water to ships on either side and fuel to a ship astern. Armament is extremely heavy for a ship of this type, comprising a twin SA-N-4 SAM launcher, two twin 57-mm guns, four Gatling-type 30-mm close-in weapon systems, and two RBU 1000 ASW rocket launchers. If the two Kamov Ka-25 'Hormone' helicopter carried retain their ASW capacity, then Berezina has a considerable defence against hostile submarines.

'Boris Chilikin' class replenishment oiler

The **'Boris Chilikin' class** is the naval version of the 'Velikiy Oktyabr' merchant tanker design, which has been built for the Soviet merchant fleet and export. The class comprises the first Soviet navy purpose-built underway replenishment ships capable of supplying both liquid fuels and solids. The designed cargo capacity is 13,000 tons of diesel and fuel oil, 500 tons of fresh water, 400 tons of provisions, 400 tons of stores and spares, and 400 tons of munitions. The earlier units can supply the solids on constant-tension rigs to both sides forward, whilst the later units can supply them only to starboard, with liquids to port at the equivalent

stations. All six vessels were built at the Baltic shipyard, Leningrad (*Boris Chilikin, Boris Butoma, Dnestr, Genrikh Gasanov, Ivan Bubnov* and *Vladimir Kolyachitskiy*) and can supply liquids to each side amidships and astern. The first four ships were completed with two twin 57-mm AA mountings, a 'Muff Cob' fire-control radar and

One of the early 'Boris Chilikin' class replenishment oilers equipped with two twin 57-mm AA guns. The last two units completed were configured as merchant vessels without armament, but have the Soviet navy designation of Voyennyy Tanker (VT).

a 'Strut Curve' air-search radar. All these systems were subsequently removed, the last two units being completed in standard merchant ship configuration. The Soviet navy designation is *Voyennyy Tanker* (VT) or military tanker.

Specification
'Boris Chilikin' class
Type: replenishment oiler
Displacement: 8,750 tons light and 24,450 tons full load
Dimensions: length 162.2 m (532.2 ft); beam 21.4 m (70.2 ft); draught 11.5 m (37.7 ft)

Propulsion: 1-shaft diesel delivering 9,600 hp (7159 kW)
Speed: 16.5 kts
Armament: see text
Aircraft: none
Electronics: two 'Don Kay' navigation radars, one 'High Pole-B' IFF system, and see text
Complement: 150

The Boris Chilikin refuels two 'Kashin' class destroyers. The capacity to refuel warships under way increases the mobility of the Soviet navy and considerably reduces warship vulnerability during UNREP operations.

'Ugra' class submarine support ship

Built in the period 1963-72 at Nikolayev, the **'Ugra' class** is an enlarged version of the 'Don' class submarine tender design with a larger forward superstructure that stretches aft to a shorter funnel. Designated *Plavuchaya Baza* (PB, or floating base) by the Soviets, all are fitted with one 10-ton and two 6-ton capacity cranes. Since the ships were built many modifications have been made so that the class can now be divided into three sub groups. One unit, the **Ivan Kolyshkin**, has been fitted with a hangar for a single Kamov Ka-25 'Hormone-C' utility helicopter whilst the remainder only have a helicopter landing pad. Two ships, the **Volga** and **Ivan Kucherenko**, incorporate a larger aft lattice mast topped by a twin 'Vee Cone' communications antenna. The design allows for extensive engineering workshops and can provide logistic support for a submarine flotilla (of between eight and 12 boats that moor alongside) by providing diesel fuel,

An enlarged development of the 'Don' class, 'Ugra' class submarine support ships can provide base facilities for a flotilla of eight to 12 submarines. Two vessels serve as training ships.

Apart from being submarine depot ships, 'Ugra' class vessels can also serve as command and control ships for task groups and provide significant local defence for a replenishment area. Surprisingly, only one ship is fitted with a hangar whilst the others have to make do with a helicopter landing pad.

fresh water, provisions, spares, torpedo reloads and fresh crews. The 'Ugras' are also frequently used as Soviet navy task group flagships. The sixth unit was completed to a modified design and sold to the Indian navy as the **Amba** to support India's flotilla of 'Foxtrot' class submarines. Two further vessels, the **Gangut** and the **Borodino**, were configured whilst building to serve as training ships for naval officer cadets. The 'Ugra' class proper totals seven ships, comprising the three mentioned (*Ivan Kolyshkin, Ivan Kucherenko* and *Volga*), plus the **Ivan Vakhrameev**, the **Tobol**, and two units whose names are as yet unknown.

Specification
'Ugra' class
Type: submarine support ship
Displacement: 6,750 tons standard and 9,600 tons full load
Dimensions: length 145.0 m (475.7 ft); beam 17.7 m (58.1 ft); draught 6.4 m (21 ft)
Propulsion: 2-shaft diesels delivering 14,000 hp (10440 kW)
Speed: 17 kts
Armament: two quadruple SA-N-5 'Grail' SAM launchers with 16 missiles, and four twin 57-mm AA guns
Aircraft: provision for a helicopter on a landing pad, except *Ivan Kolyshkin* which has one Kamov Ka-25 'Hormone-C' light helicopter
Electronics: between one and three 'Don-2' navigation radars, one 'Strut Curve' air-search radar, two 'Muff Cob' 57-mm fire-control radars, four 'Watch Dog' ECM systems, one 'High Pole-A', one 'High Pole-B' IFF, and two 'Square Head' IFF
Complement: 450

The heavy AA armament of the 'Ugra' class submarine depot ships can be seen here with all four twin 57-mm guns at high elevation. To further enhance the close-range air defence of the ships two quadruple SA-N-5 'Grail' SAM launchers are also being fitted so that they can survive in forward operational areas.

'Lama' class missile support ship

Built in the period 1963-72 (with a seventh vessel added in 1979) the **'Lama' class** are missile transports which carry and service cruise missiles for surface ships and submarines. The engine room is sited aft to allow for a very spacious hangar arrangement amidships for stowage of the missiles. A set of hangar doors opens forwards to the point where a 12.2-m (40-ft) well deck with railway tracks is served by two 20-ton capacity travelling cranes that lift the missiles from the horizontal to the vessels being rearmed. For ships with low freeboards to come alongside mooring points are located along both hull sides. Only two of the class have been named, the rest having pennant numbers which change in the same fashion as major vessels. Two ships, including the **Veronezh**, service Soviet fast missile craft and have larger missile hangars and a smaller working deck. The remaining units, classed as *Plavuchaya Masterskaya* (PM, or floating workshop) and including the **General Ryabikov** handle the large Soviet force of cruise missile submarines.

Specification
'Lama' class
Type: missile support ship
Displacement: 4,500 tons standard and 6,000 tons full load

A modified 'Lama' class missile transport/tender with smaller cranes, enlarged superstructure and additional gun mount aft of the mast. She is tender to 'Nanuchka', 'Matka' and 'Osa' class missile craft, and carries and services SS-N-2 and SS-N-9 missiles for them.

Dimensions: length 112.8 m (370.1 ft); beam 14.9 m (48.9 ft); draught 4.4 m (14.4 ft)
Propulsion: 2-shaft diesels delivering 5,000 hp (3729 kW)
Speed: 14 kts
Armament: four quadruple SA-N-5 'Grail' SAM launchers with 32 missiles (*General Ryabikov* only), plus a gun armament that varies considerably, two ships having two quadruple 57-mm AA guns, one ship one quadruple 57-mm AA gun, two ships one twin 57-mm AA and one twin 25-mm AA guns, and one ship one twin 57-mm AA guns

Aircraft: none
Electronics: one 'Don-2' navigation radar, one 'Slim Net' or 'Strut Curve' air-search radar, one or two 'Hawk Screech' or 'Muff Cob' 57-mm fire-control radars, one 'High Pole-A' IFF, two 'Square Head' IFF
Complement: 250

PM 93 has a large hangar amidships to store and service the cruise-type missiles arming so many Soviet submarines and surface vessels. Armament comprises two quadruple 57-mm guns, one fore and one aft.

'OL' class large fleet tanker

Classified as large fleet tankers or AOF(L), the three **'OL' class** vessels are the **Olwen** (A122) commissioned in 1965, the **Olna** (A123) commissioned in 1966 and the **Olmeda** (A124) commissioned in 1965. All three are fully air conditioned and have specially strengthened hulls to operate in areas with pack ice conditions. They are operated by the Royal Fleet Auxiliary (RFA) with civilian crews for the underway replenishment of the fleet in both the alongside and the astern positions, with the added capability of VERTREP replenishment by helicopter. For this latter they have two hangars (one on each side of the funnel) and a large stern-sited flightdeck. The port-side hangar can accommodate up to two Westland Sea King sized helicopters whilst the starboard side hangar can either accommodate the same helicopter complement or be used as a vehicle garage. The ships provide training billets for naval helicopters as well as homes for detached flights of Sea King or Westland Wessex helicopters used in VERTREP. The cargo load is 18,400 tons fuel, 1,720 tons diesel, 130 tons of lubricant, 3,730 tons of AVCAT aircraft fuel and 280 tons of MOGAS vehicle fuel. During the 1982 Falklands war they were fitted with light AA guns and Corvus chaff rocket launchers. All three now carry satellite navigation and communication systems, and on combat duties restock their fuel cargoes from the RFA 'Leaf' class support tankers or tankers taken up from trade.

Specification
'OL' class
Type: large fleet tanker
Displacement: 10,890 tons light and 36,000 tons full load
Dimensions: length 197.5 m (648 ft); beam 25.6 m (84 ft); draught 11.1 m (36.5 ft)

Propulsion: 1-shaft geared steam turbines delivering 26,500 shp (19761 kW)
Speed: 19 kts
Armament: two single 20-mm AA guns
Aircraft: between one and four Westland Sea King HAS.Mk 5 or Westland Wessex HU.Mk 5 or Lynx HAS.Mk 2/3 helicopters
Electronics: one Kelvin Hughes 14/12 navigation radar, one Kelvin Hughes 14/16 navigation radar, one Type 1006 helicopter control radar, one MARISAT satellite communcation system, two Corvus chaff launchers
Complement: 87 excluding aircrew

Rough weather increases the turbulence between ships replenishing, seen here as a 'Type 21' class vessel is refuelled from an 'OL' class tanker.

UK 'Rover' class small fleet tanker

Designated small fleet tankers or AOF(S), the five 'Rover' class ships were designed to replenish frigate-sized warships on deployment with aviation fuel and Dieso, fresh water, lubricating oil, and limited dry cargo and refrigerated goods under all conditions whilst underway. There is no hangar, although a flight deck (for VERTREP transfer of dry stores and provisions by the helicopter of the ship undergoing replenishment-at-sea) is located aft. 6,600 tons of fuel can be carried plus water and dry goods. All five of the 'Rover' class are also capable of over-the-stern fuelling operations if required.

Normally one of the class is deployed to Portland on sea training duties in support of the Flag Officer Sea Training (FOST) in his operational training programme of Royal Navy and NATO warships. During the Falklands war only one of the class, the ***Blue Rover*** (A 270), served in the combat zone on replenishment-at-sea duties and supplying fuel and ammunition to the land forces ashore from San Carlos Water. The remaining four units are the ***Green Rover*** (A 268), ***Grey Rover*** (A 269), ***Gold Rover*** (A 271) and ***Black Rover*** (A 273), which bore the brunt of the RFA's operations in support of the Royal Navy and NATO ships nearer home. The ships were commissioned between 1969 and 1974.

Specification
'Rover' class
Type: small fleet tanker
Displacement: 4,700 tons light and 11,522 tons full load
Dimensions: length 140.6 m (461.3 ft); beam 19.2 m (63 ft); draught 7.3 m (24 ft)
Propulsion: 1-shaft diesels delivering 15,360 hp (11454 kW)
Speed: 19 kts
Aircraft: provision for one helicopter
Electronics: one Decca navigation radar, one MARISAT system, one SATNAV system, two Corvus chaff launchers.
Complement: 47

Seen passing through the Suez Canal, Gold Rover *is one of a class of small fleet tankers designed to deploy with and replenish destroyer- or frigate-sized vessels.*

Below: Gold Rover (A 271) *has a capacity of 6,600 tons of aviation and diesel fuel, lubricating oil, fresh water, and a small amount of dry and refrigerated stores. A helicopter pad is fitted permitting VERTREP, but there is no hangar for a permanent helicopter complement.*

A 271

'Fort' class fleet replenishment ship

The two **'Fort' class** fleet replenishment ships (AEFS) were ordered in November 1971 from Scott-Lithgow shipyard, Greenock, as the *Fort Grange* (A385) and *Fort Austin* (A386), and were commissioned in 1978 and 1979. They each have four holds with a volume of 12800 m³ (452,025 cu ft) for 3,500 tons of palletized munitions, provisions (including refrigerated goods) and stores. To handle the cargo the ships each have three 10-ton and three 5-ton capacity cranes, plus sliding-stay constant-tension transfer rigs on each side for use in alongside replenishment operations. For VERTREP operations a large flightdeck and hangar are available. The latter is usually reserved for the ship's own ASW helicopters, as she can act as a floating base for a task group's ASW helicopter force, for which she carries anti-submarine munitions. The hangar can accommodate up to four Westland Sea King helicopters in wartime, though only one is normally embarked in peacetime for VERTREP. The hangar roof may also be used to land helicopters if required.

A new RFA design has been laid down for commissioning in the 1990s. The *Fort Victoria* will combine AEFS supply capability with the AOF(L) oiling role in a single hull. The resulting large vessel will have similar capabilities to the US Navy's AOE fast combat support ship, as well as being able to maintain a task group's helicopter force while still being able to fly her own ASW helicopters. The first unit will be in service in 1990, and will carry 70,000 barrels of fuel, 5,000 m³ of munitions, 3,000 m³ of dry stores and 500 m³ of refrigerated stores. Full load displacement will be around 40,000 tons, length over 200m (more than 656 ft) and speed 20 knots. 120 RFA crew will be joined by up to 100 RN personnel. *Fort Victoria* will be well defended, with 32 vertical launch Sea Wolf GWS 26 launcher tubes, two 30-mm RARDEN cannon, chaff, infra-red decoys and towed ASW decoys. She will be able to operate up to six ASW helicopters such as the EH.101. There will also be facilities for Harrier and Sea Harrier V/STOL operations.

Right: Like most replenishment ships today the RFA Fort Austin (A386) can carry helicopters. She is seen here with two Westland HAS.Mk 2 Sea Kings occupying the two helicopter landing spots, the foremost of which is atop the main hangar. The helicopters can be used either for VERTREP or ASW duties, for which anti-submarine weapons are carried aboard.

Below: Fort Grange (A385) can store up to 3,500 tons of dry and refrigerated foods, stores and munitions on pallets in her four holds, and can handle cargo in both underway and vertical replenishment.

Specification
'Fort' class
Type: fleet replenishment ship
Displacement: 8,300 tons standard and 22,749 tons full load
Dimensions: length 183.9 m (603.3 ft); beam 24.1 m (79 ft); draught 8.6 m (28.2 ft)
Propulsion: 1-shaft diesel delivering 23,200 hp (17300 kW)
Speed: 22 kts
Armament: two single 20-mm AA guns
Aircraft: between one and four Westland Sea King HAS.Mk 5 or Wessex HU.Mk 5 helicopters navigation radar, one SCOT satcom system, one SATNAV system, two Corvus chaff launchers
Electronics: one Kelvin Hughes 21/16P navigation radar, one SCOT satcom system, one SATNAV system, two Corvus chaff launchers
Complement: 185 plus 40 Air group

Above: One of the 'Fort' class stores support ships closes alongside for an RAS operation. The constant tension transfer rig can clearly be seen with the stores or munitions shipped across in palletized form for greater efficiency in handling.

Below: RFA Fort Austin underway with HMS Hermes and the large fleet tanker RFA Olmeda. A new class of RFA for next decade will combine the roles of both support ships, with a capability similar to the American 'Sacramento' class.

Anti-ship Missiles

The anti-ship missile has in recent years become the weapon with which small nations are able to challenge the supremacy of the naval superpowers. The 1982 events in the South Atlantic have seen theory become practice to great effect.

A typical mobility kill hit. The damage caused would be sufficient to stop the ship dead in the water but not to sink it.

The role of the anti-ship missile is simply to prevent the target it hits from fulfilling its allotted role. The missile can do this in one of three ways: by causing a mobility kill, by effecting a weapon/sensor kill, or by sinking it. In the first case the idea is to deprive the enemy ship of its ability to move, either by destroying the engine facilities or by causing such damage that the ship is unable to move under its own power without the risk of sinking. In the second case the missile is targeted in such a way that it will explode either amongst the ship's external weapons and sensors such as radars (thereby destroying their ability to function) or actually within the ship's command, control and communications nerve centre (thus effectively paralysing the ship's fighting ability). In the third case the weight of the warhead is usually so great (above 500 kg/1,102 lb or so) that the resultant explosion causes such catastrophic damage that the ship has no hope of staying afloat. It is the USSR which subscribes to the last concept by fielding a huge variety of ship-, submarine- and air-launched anti-ship missiles that the West cannot match. However, where the West is ahead is in the numbers and types of weapons with which it fulfils the first two concepts. The recent Falkland Islands war

and the continuing battle in the Arabian Gulf between Iran and Iraq have proved a number of weapons in battle. These and the other conflicts in which anti-ship weapons have been employed have also proved to the world that the nation with a small navy and air force can stand up to others with larger forces on equal terms if it is equipped with anti-ship missiles, as it reduces the threat of 'gunboat diplomacy'. The mere threat of Iran closing the Gulf to oil tanker traffic is one such example; on the other side of the coin, however, a nation can enforce its will on a number of others by using the anti-ship missile as a political weapon.

Thus the advent of the anti-ship missile is not just that of a new weapon type but something considerably more. It is in this light that the lists of operator countries of the various types should be studied closely, especially with regard to the political stability of the areas in which the countries are to be found, as it is certain that these missiles will see a lot more use in the years to come.

The MBB Kormoran uses an active or passive radar-homing seeker mode to target itself on a point just above the waterline of its victim.

MBB Kormoran

Designed to meet a 1964 West German naval air arm (Marineflieger) requirement, the **MBB Kormoran** was originally based on a French Nord design, the **AS.34**, using the inertial guidance system from the defunct **AS.33** project. However, following the creation of the German MBB aerospace consortium, the missile became a major project with help from the French concern Aérospatiale. The weapon was given a new and more sophisticated guidance package, and the first flight trials were undertaken on 19 March 1970, the first production rounds being delivered in December 1977. By the middle of the following year MFG 2, equipped with Lockheed F-104G Starfighters, was fully operational with the missile at Eggbeck. Normally two missiles are carried under the wings of the F-104G, whilst the newly-introduced Panavia Tornados of the Marineflieger can carry four, although a maximum of eight is possible. The Kormoran is also operated by the Italian air force.

After release from the launch aircraft, two double-propellant SNPE Prades boost motors burn for about one second, then the main SNPE Eole IV sustainer motor cuts in to provide thrust for a further 100 seconds of powered flight. For the initial cruise phase of the mission a Stena/Bodenseewerk inertial guidance platform coupled with a modified TRT radio altimeter is used to hold the missile on course (using the cruciform rear fins) at a height of about 30 m (100 ft). Near the estimated target location the missile is commanded to descend to its wave-top attack altitude by the autopilot, and the Thomson-CSF two-axis radar, acting in either a pre-set active or passive mode, searches for, acquires and then locks on to the enemy vessel. The missile then strikes the target just above the waterline, the warhead (with 56 kg/123.5 lb of explosive, delay-action fuse and 16 radially-mounted charges) explodes deep within the hull to maximize the damage caused.

The **Kormoran Mk 2**, designed for production from 1988, has been considerably improved with a digital Thomson-CSF radar seeker, enhanced ECM resistance, longer range and a heavier and more destructive war-head.

Specification
Kormoran
Dimensions: length 4.40 m (14 ft 5.25 in); diameter 34.4 cm (1 ft 1.5 in); span 1.00 m (3 ft 3.4 in)
Weights: total round 600 kg (1,323 lb); warhead 165 kg (364 lb)
Performance: maximum speed Mach 0.95; range 37 km (23 miles)

Designed in the late 1960s, the first production rounds of the Kormoran were not delivered until 1977. A Mk 2 version is already under development for the West German navy to arm its Tornado strike aircraft in the mid-to-late 1990s.

The Kormoran Mk 1 is used by the Marineflieger and by Italian anti-shipping units. It is specifically designed to operate amongst the Baltic coastal islands, which would normally provide any potential enemy vessels with adequate radar cover.

OTO-Melara/Matra Otomat

Developed as a joint venture by OTO-Melara of Italy and Matra of France, the **Otomat** missile is powered by a Turboméca turbojet and is carried in a self-contained container-launcher unit. Two lateral jettisonable solid-propellant boosters are attached for the launch phase, boosting the missile to cruising speed. Initial target-location data is gained from either the launch platform's own sensors or external sources such as helicopters or other ships. The missile is then launched at an angle of up to 200° from the target's actual bearing, corrects its heading (with an autopilot controlling the cruciform rear fins) and climbs to its cruising altitude of 250 m (820 ft). At a predetermined point the missile then descends to 20 m (66 ft) above sea level and, when about 15 km (9.3 km) from the target's expected location, commences a search with its terminal active radar seeker. Once acquisition and lock-on are achieved, the missile descends to the final altitude of 10 m (33 ft) for the run in to the target. If the Italian SMA homing head is fitted then the missile stays as a sea skimmer until impact; if, however, the French Thomson-CSF 'col-vert' head is fitted, the missile undertakes a rapid climb to 175 m (574 ft) and then dives on to the target. In the Italian navy's **Otomat Mk II Teseo** version, a Marconi Italiano TG-2 command guidance system is fitted for mid-course guidance correction by airborne platforms. This allows targets to be engaged at ranges in excess of 180 km (112 miles). Both Matra and OTO-Melara have developed folding winged, tube launched models with the French **Otomat Compact** first firing in 1983 and the Italian **Otomat Mk 2** being announced in 1984. At least 850 missiles have been sold, and more than 80 ships have been fitted with Otomat. The navies operating the system include those of Algeria, Egypt, Iraq, Italy, Kenya, Kuwait, Libya, Nigeria, Peru, Saudi Arabia and Venezuela. A coast defence version of Otomat has been acquired by Egypt.

Italy is also proposing a supersonic successor to Otomat known as **Otomach 2**. Speed is indicated by the name, and the missile will incorporate new seeker technology. It will probably appear after 1990.

Designed to be used with an external target-designating source to get the maximum benefit from its range capabilities, the Otomat has yet to see combat service.

Specification
Otomat
Dimensions: length 4.82 m (15 ft 9.75 in); diameter 46.0 cm (1 ft 6.1 in); span 1.19 m (3 ft 10.85 in)
Weights: total round 770 kg (1,698 lb); warhead 210 kg (463 lb)
Performance: maximum speed Mach 0.9; range 60 km (37.3 miles) as a single missile or 80 km (50 miles) when fired in salvo

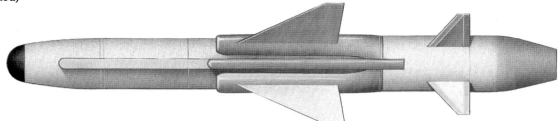

The Otomat is found in both coastal defence and shipborne versions.

ISRAEL
IAI Gabriel

Developed in the mid-1960s as the main armament for the 'Saar' class of missile craft, the **Israel Aircraft Industries Gabriel** has been proved to be one of the most successful anti-ship missiles ever used in combat. During the 1973 'Yom Kippur' war it was responsible for sinking a large number of Arab warships and neutral merchantmen. The missile is carried in a reinforced glassfibre container-launcher that can be mounted either in fixed single or in trainable triple cell units. Before launch the missile's guidance system is programmed with target data obtained from the launch platform's own sensors. The missile is then fired and, under control of its twin gyro system and radio altimeter (working on the cruciform rear fins), assumes a cruise flight profile to the target area. The initial part of this trajectory is flown at around 100 m (330 ft) with a programmed descent to 20 m (66 ft) for the major part. At a range of 1-2 km (1,095-2,190 yards) from the estimated target position the missile switches on its seeker, acquires the target and descends to one of the three pre-set terminal attack heights of between 1 and 3 m (3 and 10 ft) for the attack, the actual height being dependent on the sea state encountered. In the case of the **Gabriel Mk I** and **Gabriel Mk II**, terminal homing is carried out by a semi-active radar seeker that relies on target illumination by the I-band target designator radar of the launch platform, although a manual/optical control system and a command guidance with radar tracking mode are also available. In the **Gabriel Mk III** homing is by an I-band frequency-agile active radar system, which allows a fire-and-forget mode to be employed; the other two guidance options are also available for use. The Gabriel shipboard system is designed to permit the use of all three versions in a single ship, the different

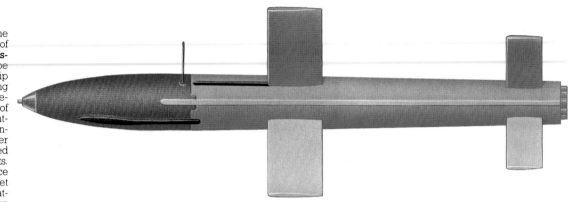

The Gabriel is available in three marks for shipboard use by Israel.

characteristics of each type allowing maximum flexibility in mission planning. The surface-launched Gabriel Mk I and Mk III are operated only by Israel, while the Gabriel Mk II is also used by Chile, Ecuador, Kenya, Singapore and Thailand.

In the early 1980s the Gabriel Mk III was developed into two air-launched variants for use by the Israeli air force on its McDonnell Douglas Phantom, McDonnell Douglas Skyhawk, IAI Kfir, General Dynamics Fighting Falcon and IAI Sea Scan aircraft. The **Gabriel Mk III A/S** version has a range of 40 km (25 miles), whilst the **Gabriel Mk III A/S ER** extended-range version has a lengthened sustainer motor within the existing body to give a range of 60 km (37.3 miles). Both have the same capabilities for fire-and-forget and fire-and-update launch modes as the

original Gabriel Mk III, but with 1.5 m, 2.5 m or 4 m (4.8 ft, 8.2 ft or 13.1 ft) selectable terminal attack heights. In 1985, the air-breathing, turbo-jet powered **Gabriel Mk IV** was announced. This version is 4.7 m (15.4 ft) long, 0.44 m (1.4 ft) in diameter and with a span of 1.6 m (5.2 ft). To make the most of a potential range of around 200 km (125 miles), mid-course guidance or a datalink for updating the advanced onboard inertial navigation system is essential. The Gabriel IV will be fitted with an active radar seeker for terminal homing when it enters service in the 1990s.

The Gabriel II is built under licence in South Africa, where it is known as the **Skorpioen**, and a Gabriel derived missile with local guidance is produced in Taiwan as the **Hsiung Feng** (Male Bee).

Specification
Gabriel Mk II
Dimensions: length 3.42 m (11 ft 2.65 in); diameter 34.00 cm (1 ft 1.4 in); span 1.34 m (4 ft 4.75 in)
Weights: total round 522 kg (1,151 lb); warhead 180 kg (397 lb)
Performance: maximum speed Mach 0.7; range 26 km (22.4 miles)

Specification
Gabriel Mk III A/S and Mk III A/S ER
Dimensions: length 3.84 m (12 ft 7.2 in); diameter 34.00 cm (1 ft 1.4 in); span 1.10 m (3 ft 7.3 in)
Weights: total round 558 kg (1,230 lb) for Mk III A/S and 600 kg (1,323 lb) for Mk III A/S ER; warhead 150 kg (33 lb)
Performance: maximum speed transonic; range 40 km (25 miles) for Mk III A/S and 60 km (37.3 miles) for Mk III A/S ER

Using a variety of command-guided and semi-active homing techniques, the Gabriel Mk I was used extensively in the 1973 Yom Kippur War by the Israeli navy, and sank a number of Syrian and Egyptian craft.

The air-launched Gabriel Mk III was developed from the active radar terminal homing ship-launched Mk III to give the Israeli air force a potent anti-ship capability.

Aérospatiale AS.12 and AS.15TT

The **SS.12** was originally developed by Nord as a multi-purpose weapon. The air-launched version of the SS.12, the **AS.12**, was first produced in 1960 for carriage by the French navy's Dassault Etendard and Aérospatiale Super Frélon aircraft. However, the missile soon became one of the main air-to-surface weapons carried by maritime patrol aircraft and ASW helicopters such as the Lockheed Neptune, Breguet Atlantic, Aérospatiale Alouette, Westland Wessex and Westland Wasp. The solid-propellant AS.12 used a basic command wire-guidance system to cruciform fins with optical tracking via a set of flares in the rear of the missile, the major disadvantage being that the aircraft has to remain within relatively close range of the target whilst the missile is under guidance, and is thus highly vulnerable to enemy defensive fire. During the 1982 Falklands war the Royal Navy fired a number of AS.12s from Wasp helicopters at the Argentinian submarine *Santa Fé* off South Georgia; these did some damage to the fin and pressure hull and helped prevent the boat from submerging. The AS.12 is being replaced in Royal Navy service by the Sea Skua. The SS.12 has also been used as an anti-ship weapon on fast attack craft. Countries operating the AS.12 include Argentina, Chile, France, Iran, Iraq, Kuwait, Turkey, the UK, and the United Arab Emirates.

The AS.12 may well be replaced in the French navy by the helicopter-launched solid-propellant command-guided **AS.15TT** (*tous temps*, or all-weather) missile. This relies on a radio link to cruciform rear fins for azimuth guidance, both the missile and target being tracked by the launch helicopter's Thomson-CSF Agrion 15 radar. The cruise height is between 3 and 5 m (10 and 16 ft) above the water, and is maintained by a radar altimeter. At around 300 m (330 yards) from the target the missile is commanded to descend to wave-top height in order to ensure a hit. The first complete test firing took place in October 1982, and Saudi Arabia has helped to pay for most of the development work. Both ship-launched and coastal-defence versions are also under development, and the only current customer is Saudi Arabia.

Saudi Arabia has helped pay for the development of the AS.15TT missile as part of a massive arms deal that they negotiated with France.

Above: A French navy Lynx helicopter fires a wire-guided AS.12 missile. A major disadvantage is that the Lynx has to stay within the defensive fire envelope of the target during guidance.

Specification
AS.12
Dimensions: length 1.87 m (6 ft 1.6 in); diameter 21.0 cm (8.25 in); span 65.0 cm (2 ft 1.6 in)
Weights: total round 76 kg (168 lb); warhead 28.4 kg (62.6 lb)
Performance: speed low subsonic; range 8 km (5 miles)

Specification
AS.15TT
Dimensions: length 2.16 m (7 ft 1 in); diameter 18.5 cm (7.3 in); span 56.4 cm (1 ft 10.2 in)
Weights: total round 96 kg (212 lb); warhead 29.7 kg (65.5 lb)
Performance: speed high subsonic; range 16 km (10 miles)

An SA.365F Dauphin 2 carrying a maximum load of four AS.15TTs. Being a command-guided weapon, the helicopter can use its search radar both to track the target and direct the missile, thus reducing its vulnerability to the target's defences.

Aérospatiale Exocet

Developed in the late 1960s to meet a French navy requirement, the **Aérospatiale Exocet** completed its first manufacturer's trials in mid-1972. In October of that year evaluation tests were undertaken by the French navy in conjunction with the Royal Navy and the West German Kriegsmarine. The results led to a missile improvement programme in 1973, the first production round being fired in the following year. Out of some 30 rounds fired the hit rate was 91 per cent. By late 1986 over 2,500 rounds of the various Exocet versions had been ordered by 31 customers.

The basic **MM.38** round is a two-stage solid-propellant missile fitted with four cruciform wings and four tail control surfaces. The missile is stored in a rectangular box-like container-launcher. Before firing the range and bearing of the target is determined by

The Exocet family is the most widely used of all Western anti-ship missiles.

the launch platform's own fire-control system and stored in the missile's guidance system. The missile is then launched towards the target, a low-altitude inertially-controlled profile being flown throughout the cruise phase. At around 10 km (6.2 miles) from the target's estimated location the ADAC active radar seeker is switched on and the target acquired by the missile; the seeker then locks on and the missile descends to one of three pre-set sea-skimming altitudes, chosen according to the sea state and the target damage required. MM.38 operators include Argentina, Belgium, Brazil, Brunei, Chile, Ecuador, France, W. Germany, Greece, Indonesia, S. Korea, Malaysia, Morocco, Nigeria, Oman, Peru, the Philippines, Thailand and the United Kingdom.

Improvements to the sustainer motor and container-launcher have resulted in the evolution of the larger **MM.40** variant. This has increased range, but also allows a larger number of rounds to be carried for the same space and weight occupied by the MM.38 system. Among operators of the MM.40 are Argentina, Bahrein, Brazil, Cameroon, Colombia, Ecuador, France, Kuwait, Malaysia, Morocco, Oman, Qatar, Tunisia and the UAE. The first variant to see action, however, was the air-launched **AM.39**. This version evolved from a modified MM.38 (called the **AM.38**) that incorporated a one-second ignition delay on the motor to allow the weapon to fall clear of the launch aircraft. The first AM.38 tests were conducted in April 1973. In 1977 the first test rounds of the shorter and lighter AM.39 were fired, before being sold to the French navy and for export to Abu Dhabi, Bahrein, Brazil, Egypt, Iraq, Kuwait, Pakistan, Peru, Qatar, Singapore and Thailand amongst other navies. The AM.39 was first used in anger from Iraqi Super Frelon helicopters in the Gulf War, sinking at least three Iranian warships and destroying or damaging a number of targets such as tankers and oil platforms. Argentina used both AM.39 and land based MM.38 versions in the Falklands, sinking HMS *Sheffield* and the container ship *Atlantic Conveyor* with missiles from Super Etendard fighters and severely damaging HMS *Glamorgan* from a jury-rigged shore battery. Iraq then leased five Etendards until Exocet capable Mirage F1 aircraft could be obtained from France. By 1987 well over 100 Exocets had been fired in the Gulf War, doing considerable damage (most notably against the American FFG-7 class frigate USS *Stark*, hit by two missiles in May 1987).

In the mid-1970s, the French navy had a requirement for a submarine-launched version of Exocet. The **SM.39** is encased in a 5.8 m (19 ft long) capsule which fits standard torpeo tubes. It can be launched from depths of 120 m (394 ft), the missile being released from the capsule at the surface. At no time does the missile rise higher than 40 m (131 ft) after launch, and it rapidly assumes the Exocet's sea-skimming profile. The SM.39 equips the growing French force of nuclear attack boats as well as the conventional submarines of the 'Agosta' class.

Specification
AM.38
Dimensions: length 5.21 m (17 ft 1.1 in); diameter 35.0 cm (1 ft 1.75 in); span

1.004 m (3 ft 3.5 in)
Weights: total round 750 kg (1,653 lb); warhead 165 kg (364 lb)
Performance: maximum speed Mach 0.93; range 42 km (26 miles)

Specification
AM.39

Dimensions: length 4.69 m (15 ft 4.65 in); diameter 35.0 cm (1 ft 1.75 in); span 1.004 m (3 ft 3.5 in)
Weights: total round 652 kg (1,437 lb); warhead 165 kg (364 lb)
Performance: maximum speed Mach 0.93; range 50-70 km (31-43.5 miles) depending on launch altitude

Specification
MM.40
Dimensions: length 5.78 m (18 ft 11.55 in); diameter 35.0 cm (1 ft

The AM-39 air-launched Exocet missile is fired from an Aérospatiale Super Frelon helicopter of the French navy. It is this combination that the Iraqi air force has recently used to sink three large Greek merchantmen off the Iranian coast.

1.75 in); span 1.135 m (3 ft 8.66 in)
Weights: total round 850 kg (1,874 lb); warhead 165 kg (364 lb)
Performance: maximum speed Mach 0.93; range 65 km (40.4 miles)

Left: An Exocet is launched from a Batch 2 'Leander' class frigate of the Royal Navy. Several of the Leanders have had their 114-mm (4.5-in) guns replaced by Exocets with an additional Seacat SAM launcher forward.

Above: Flown in by Argentine air force C-130 Hercules during May/June 1982, these container-launchers for MM.38 Exocets were removed from a warship and modified for launching from a trailer to act as an improvised coastal defence weapon for Port Stanley.

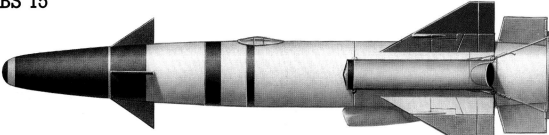

SWEDEN
Saab-Bofors RBS 15

The contract for the **RBS 15M** was awarded in July 1979 to the Saab-Bofors Missile Corporation. The missile will arm the 'Spica' and later classes of missile craft in place of the Norwegian Penguin Mk II. In August 1982 Saab-Bofors announced a development contract for the **RBS 15F** air launched version. This is to be used to arm the Royal Swedish air force's fleet of Saab Viggen attack aircraft and the new-generation Saab JAS 39 Gripen for anti-ship duties.

The RBS 15 is housed (with wings folded) in a container-launcher, and consists of three sections: the forward part contains the PEAB fully digital Ku-band frequency-agile pulsed active radar seeker and its associated microprocessor and electronics, the middle portion contains the FFV blast-fragmentation warhead with both delay-action and proximity fuses, and the aft section houses the Microturbo TRI-60 turbojet sustainer. The RBS 15 is also fitted with strap-on booster motors located on the launch-phase stabilizer fins; these boosters burn for about three seconds and are then jettisoned. The RBS 15F has no booster motors. The flight altitude is controlled throughout by a radio altimeter, and course by an autopilot working through the cruciform rear wings.

A typical launch runs as follows. The ship's active and passive sensors are continually used to update the missile's launch parameters on an automatic basis. Once a target has been detected a missile is fired, the boost motors accelerating it to its subsonic sustained flight speed whereupon they are jettisoned. At its maximum speed the missile turns towards the target's predicted location, flying either a high- or a low-altitude pre-set cruise phase depending upon the presence of obstacles (such as islands) or not. At the end of a high-altitude phase the missile drops to the low altitude, where it carries out its search and target-acquisition functions. Once a lock-on

has been achieved, then the final run-in to the target is flown at sea-skimming height. If no target is acquired the missile automatically self-destructs. The RBS 15 has been ordered by Finland as well as by the Swedish forces. The latest version of the RBS 15 is designed for coastal defence, and is currently being deployed along the Swedish coast. An underwater launched version is under tentative development for possible use from the 'Vastergötland' class of submarine in the 1990s.

Specification
Saab-Bofors RBS 15 and RBS 15F
Dimensions: length 4.35 m (14 ft 3.25 in); diameter 50.0 cm (1 ft 7.7 in); span 1.40 m (4 ft 7.1 in)
Weights: total round 780 kg (1,720 lb) for RBS 15 and 598 kg (1,318 lb) for RBS 15F; warhead 150 kg (330 lb) HE
Performance: maximum speed high subsonic; range 80-100 km (50-62.5 miles)

Right: An RBS 15 just after launch. The strap-on boosters are still in place and will be jettisoned after they burn out, when the propulsion is taken over by a turbojet sustainer.

Below: 'Spica' class missile boats will be the major launch platform for RBS 15 in its ship-launched guise.

The RBS 15 ship-launched anti-ship missile. An air-launched version is also under development.

British Aerospace Sea Eagle

The **P3T** was designed by British Aerospace to meet Air Staff Requirement 1226 issued in the early 1970s for an all-weather, night-capable, over-the-horizon range, fire-and-forget missile to replace the TV-guided AJ168 Martel missile. By 1977 the project had progressed to the definition phase with the launch trials taking place in November 1980. Full-scale development firings started in the following April, and in early 1982 a production contract was awarded for initial service deliveries in 1985. The **Sea Eagle**, as the missile is now called, arms the RAF's two remaining squadrons of Buccaneers (up to four missiles to each aircraft) and is also one of the weapons which the Sea Harrier has been cleared to carry. The Panavia Tornado is another potential carrier, and the missile may be sold to Saudi Arabia to arm their recently purchased strike aircraft. Sea Eagle has also been developed in zero speed launch versions for use from ships or helicopters, with two strap-on solid propellant boosters used at launch to bring the missile up to flight speed. The Indian navy has bought Sea Eagle to equip at least 20 Westland Sea King anti-shipping helicopters. Development of the ship-launched variant was stopped when the Royal Navy bought the American Harpoon system, but interest in coast defence missiles in the late 1980s has seen the restart of testing.

The airframe of the Sea Eagle is basically that of the Martel but fitted with an underbelly inlet for the Microturbo TRI-60 turbojet propulsion unit. Guidance is initially by an onboard autopilot with the target's last known position and speed stored in its microprocessor memory; the pre-set cruise-phase flight profile and altitude are maintained by the autopilot and a Plessey radar altimeter, working through cruciform rear fins, whilst the terminal target-acquisition phase is undertaken by a highly sophisticated Marconi Space and Defence Systems active radar seeker. This guidance package allows both salvo attacks on a single target with the missiles attacking from different directions, and the overflying of one target so that a second and more desirable target can be attacked.

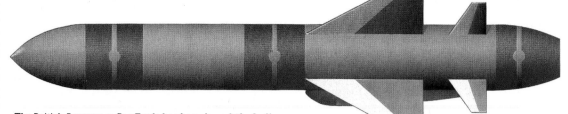

The British Aerospace Sea Eagle has been bought by India before it has actually entered service with the Royal Navy. India will operate it from a batch of new Westland Sea King helicopters.

Specification
BAe Sea Eagle
Dimensions: length 4.14 m (13 ft 7 in); diameter 40.0 cm (1 ft 3.75 in); span 1.20 m (3 ft 11.75 in)
Weights: total round 550-600 kg (1,213-1,323 lb); warhead 150-200 kg (331-441 lb)

Performance: maximum speed Mach 0.9+; range 50-100 km (31-62 miles)

Four test rounds on the wing pylons of a Hawker Siddeley S.Mk 2 Buccaneer. Two Sea Eagle-equipped Buccaneer squadrons will remain in service after the introduction of the Tornado to act as the main RAF anti-ship strike force in support of the Royal Navy.

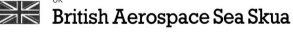
British Aerospace Sea Skua

Designed as the new-generation helicopter-launched anti-ship missile for use against small and agile missile-armed surface craft at ranges in excess of their missiles, the **British Aerospace Sea Skua** (formerly CL-834) has now replaced the obsolete Aérospatiale AS.12 wire-guided missile in Royal Navy service. Up to four Sea Skuas are carried by the RN's Westland Lynx, the target being illuminated by the helicopter's own frequency-agile I-band Ferranti Sea Spray surveillance and target-tracking radar to allow the semi-active homing seeker on the missile to pick up the reflected energy and so guide the weapon. The Sea Skua is treated as a round of ammunition and needs only minimal maintenance checks. The missile uses BAJ Vickers solid-propellant boost and sustainer motors when launched for powered flight. Its cruise height is preset to one of four sea-skimming altitudes according to the sea state encountered. Once the Sea Skua has been launched, its altitude is maintained by a British Aerospace-built TRT radio altimeter and an autopilot, working through the cruciform canard fins, until a position is reached near the target. Here a command instruction from the launch platform or from the missile's onboard guidance system orders the missile to climb to let the Marconi Space and Defence Systems semi-active radar homing head lock on.

The first trials using the complete

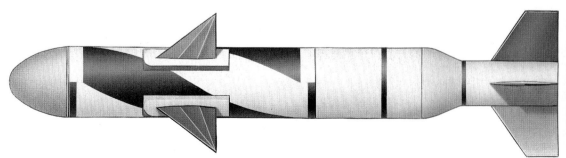

Treated as a round of ammunition, the Sea Skua missile was used in combat in the Falklands before it was actually declared operational. Sea Skua has been exported to Brazil, West Germany and Turkey.

guidance system were conducted in December 1979. However, the missile was committed to combat during the 1982 Falklands war before it was officially declared operational. The missile was fired on four occasions, and scored eight hits out of eight rounds launched, severely damaging several Argentinian navy vessels. The semi-armour-piercing warhead proved quite effective in penetrating the targets' hulls and superstructure.

The **Sea Skua SL** has been developed, and is intended for use from small craft, ACVs and coast defence batteries. BAe has also matched the missile to other helicopters as well as light aircraft. To date Sea Skuas have been exported to Brazil (for their navy Lynxes), West Germany (to arm Westland Sea Kings) and Turkey (to equip AB.212 ASW helicopters).

Specification
BAe Sea Skua
Dimensions: length 2.85 m (9 ft 4 in); diameter 22.2 cm (8.75 in); span 62.0 cm (2 ft 0.4 in)
Weights: total round 147 kg (325 lb); warhead 35 kg (77 lb)
Performance: maximum speed Mach 0.9+; range 20 km (12.4 miles)

The main carrier of the Sea Skua in Royal Navy service is the Westland Lynx. Up to four missiles can be carried, although a more normal load is two.

USA
McDonnell Douglas AGM-84A/RGM-84A Harpoon

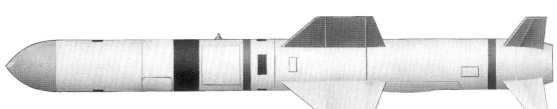

The Harpoon in its many forms will become the mainstay of the US Navy's anti-ship missile inventory until the end of the century.

In 1967, following the sinking of the Israeli destroyer *Eilat* by an SS-N-2 'Styx', the US Navy began to show serious interest in developing its own anti-ship missile. The result was a formal proposal that led to the **McDonnell Douglas Harpoon**, but an interim alternative was also sought. This became the **Fireflash** SSM, based on the BQM-34A Firebee target and reconnaissance drone. By late 1971, however, the Fireflash was dropped as it was rapidly becoming a serious competitor to Harpoon rather than just an interim weapon. In the meantime Harpoon had begun life in the Fiscal Year 1968 programme as a 92.5-km (57.5-mile) range anti-ship missile (designated **AGM-84A**) suitable for air launch. By 1970 Harpoon's capabilities had been extended to ship-launch applications (as the **RGM-84A**) and in January 1971 McDonnell Douglas was selected as the prime contractor. The final variant, the encapsulated torpedo tube-launched **UGM-84A** version for submerged launch from submarines, was started in 1972 and subsequently replaced the Submarine Tactical Missiles (STAM) programme that was cancelled in the following year.

The Harpoon development programme always emphasized simplicity and low technical risk. The missile, boosted by a solid-propellant rocket and sustained by a Teledyne CAE J402 turbojet, is usually fired in a pre-set Range and Bearing Launch (RBL) mode, turning on its Texas Instruments two-axis active-radar terminal only at the last moment to acquire the target without giving it time to instigate evasive measures. The frequency-agile radar can be set for large, medium or small acquisition windows that determine the range from the target at which the radar is activated. The smaller the window the more precise the initial target data must be, and the less the chance that the missile will be defeated by defensive ECM techniques in its terminal flight phase. Initial guidance in the flight is undertaken either by Lear Siegler or a Northrop three-axis strapdown altitude reference system with a Honeywell radar altimeter, working through cruciform rear fins. The alternative launch technique is the Bearing Only Launch (BOL) mode, in which the missile is fired on the target bearing and the radar is activated early in the flight, scanning 45° to each side of the missile's bearing to search for a target. If no target is acquired after a suitable time on the initial bearing, the missile switches to a pre-set search pattern. In either launch mode, once the target is detected and the seeker achieves a lock-on, the missile climbs rapidly in a pop-up manoeuvre and dives onto it. The newer Block IB and Block IC missiles now being built have a range increase of 23 per cent and a sea-skimming terminal attack profile. The latter was first adopted for the Royal Navy's Sub-Harpoon missiles. A Block II missile with a greater than 190-km (118-mile) range, variable flight profiles and improved ECM resistance is expected in the late 1980s for service in the 1990s.

It is reckoned that one Harpoon will destroy an 'Osa', 'Komar', 'Matka' or 'Nanuchka' class missile boat; two will disable a frigate; four will knock out a missile cruiser; and five will destroy a 'Kirov' class nuclear-powered battlecruiser or a 'Kiev' class carrier. The warhead is a 227-kg (500-lb) penetration-blast type fitted with time-delay contact and proximity fuses. On surface warships the Harpoon is either carried in its own cylindrical container-launcher or carried in the missile magazine of a Tartar/Standard SM-1 launcher. On some frigates two of the boxes in the ASROC ASW missile-launcher have been converted to fire the Harpoon. Aircraft normally carry two missiles under their wings. A new vertical-launch system for ships, capable of firing Harpoon among other missiles is in service with the latest US Navy warships.

Ship launched Harpoon is in service with Australia, Bahrein, Canada, Denmark, Egypt, West Germany, Greece, Iran, Israel, Japan, South Korea, the Netherlands, Pakistan, Portugal, Saudi Arabia, Spain, Turkey and the United Kingdom. Air launched Harpoon is in the inventories of Australia, Japan, Thailand and the UK, while Sub-Harpoon is used by Australia, Canada, Japan, Israel, the Netherlands, Pakistan and the UK. The US Navy uses all three types, and USAF B-52G Stratofortresses can carry up to 12 missiles each when on maritime strike missions. By 1986 close to 5,000 Harpoons had been delivered or were on order, and on the night of 24/25 March 1986 the missile saw its first combat use. A number of Libyan missile boats and corvettes in the Gulf of Sirte were destroyed or severely damaged by Harpoons fired from US Navy A-6 aircraft and the AEGIS cruiser USS *Yorktown*.

Harpoon in Operation

Guidance *Beneath the plastic radome in the nose of Harpoon an active radar antenna searches for targets. Immediately behind a bulkhead the solid state radar electronics are coupled with a radio altimeter unit (essential in a sea-skimming missile). Behind that, Harpoon has a three-axis inertial guidance and attitude reference system, together with a general-purpose digital computer, which can be fed target information from the onboard radar as well as from external radar or ESM sources. In the sub-launched system, these sources can include both periscope and sonar.*

Warhead *Harpoon is armed with a high explosive warhead of almost 277 kg (500 lb). Fitted with a time delayed contact fuse, the missile is designed to penetrate the target before exploding, thus causing the maximum possible damage, as well as increasing the potential for secondary explosions. Harpoon is also being considered as a potential nuclear warhead carrier.*

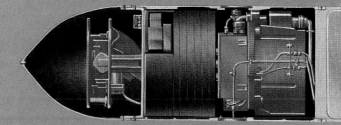

Specification
Dimensions: length 4.628 m (15.2 ft) for RGM-84 and UGM-84, 3.84 m (12.59 ft) for AGM-84; diameter 34.3 cm (13.5 in); span 91.4 cm (3 ft)
Weights: with booster 681 kg (1,498 lb) from canister, 680 kg (1,496 lb) from SAM launcher, 653 kg (1,437 lb) from ASROC launcher; AGM-84 without booster 526 kg (1,157 lb)
Warhead: 227 kg (500 lb) blast-fragmentation high-explosive
Performance: maximum speed Mach 0.85; range for early models 130 km (81 miles); range from Block 1B onwards 160 km (100 miles)

Below: Harpoon is seen fired from the ASROC launcher of the USS Lockwood.

Above: Harpoon is fired from the Mk 13 launcher of HMAS Canberra.

Sustainer *Harpoon is an air-breathing missile, with an air intake flush to the underside. The sealed fuel tank, containing about 45-kg (100 lb) of JP fuel, feeds a small 272-kg (600-lb) thrust jet engine. Also found in the sustainer section are the silver-zinc cells that provide power to the missile systems.*

Booster *Launching from ships or from submarines, Harpoon requires considerable power for a short time to reach cruising speed. The solid propellant rocket booster produces about 5443-kg (12000-lb) thrust for up to three seconds.*

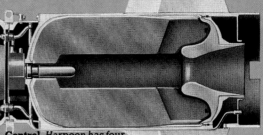

Control *Harpoon has four control fins in a cruciform arrangement.*

Above: A 'Knox' class frigate fires Harpoon from a combined Harpoon/ASROC launcher.

Above: F-18 Hornets will carry Harpoon for the US Navy into the 1990s.

Above: Damage caused by explosion of the Harpoon's penetration-blast warhead.

Below: Harpoon follows a sea-skimming path once a target has been located.

General Dynamics BGM-109 Tomahawk

In November 1972, when interest was already evident in an extended-range version of the Harpoon, the decision was taken to develop a tactical anti-ship version of the strategic Sea-Launched Cruise Missile (SLCM). For the SLCM programme two competitive designs were funded, the **General Dynamics ZBGM-109** and the LTV ZBGM-110, both suitable for torpedo-tube launching. After a fly-off the **BGM-109 Tomahawk** was chosen in 1977 for full-scale engineering development. The **BGM-109B Tactical Anti-Ship Missile (TASM)** looks very similar to the **BGM-109A Tactical Land Attack Missile-Nuclear (TLAM-N)** variant, but in place of a 200 kiloton thermonuclear device is the HE warhead originally fitted to the AGM-12C Bullpup-B to which has been added the active-radar terminal seeker used in the Harpoon. An inertial guidance unit is also fitted for control of the cruise phase by means of the cruciform rear fins, and the missile adopts the same pop-up and dive manoeuvre used by the Harpoon Block IA missiles. The missile can be fired from surface ships or from submarines and, after solid-propellant boost, cruises on a Teledyne turbojet. In the latter case the units of the 'Los Angeles' class of nuclear-powered attack submarines are to be fitted with a set of 12 vertical launch tubes in the space between the forward bow sonar sphere and the main pressure hull in order to conserve internal weapon space for ASW weapons. On surface ships Tomahawks will be carried in four-round armoured box launchers, or in the new vertical-launch system under development. The BGM-109B became operational aboard submarines late in 1982, whilst the first surface ships to be equipped will be operational in 1984. In order to make full use of the Tomahawk's over-the-horizon capabilities a long-range target-detection programme called 'Outlaw Shark' has been implemented to develop the techniques required.

The **BGM-109C Tactical Land Attack Missile-Conventional (TLAM-C)** is similar to the anti-ship version. Used from ships, submarines and aircraft, this variant is available with the same Bullpup derived HE warhead, or a newly developed cluster bomblet dispensing warhead for area targets. In it's first submarine-launched test in 1981 the inert warhead made a direct hit on a large building in Nevada, having been launched from a submarine off the coast of California 480 km (nearly 300 miles) away. At least 2,000 Tomahawks in various models are expected to be operational by 1989/90.

Specification
General Dynamics BGM-109 Tomahawk
Dimensions: length 6.40 m (21 ft 0 in); diameter 53.3 cm (1 ft 9 in); span 2.54 m (8 ft 4 in)
Weights: total round BGM-109A/B, 1200 kg (2,645 lb); BGM-109C, 1267 kg (2,794 lb)
Warhead: 200 kT yield W80 thermonuclear in BGM-109A or 454 kg (1,000 lb) high explosive in BGM-109B/C
Performance: maximum speed Mach 0.7; range 2590 km (1,609 miles) for BGM-109A, 460 km (286 miles) for BGM-109B/C

Adapted from the strategic sea-launched cruise missile, Tomahawk gives the US Navy long-range anti-ship capability.

Vertical launch systems mean great savings in space and complexity aboard ship. Here Tomahawk is launched vertically at the Pacific Missile Test Center at Point Magu, California.

Kongsberg Penguin

Development of the **Penguin Mk I** took place from 1961 to 1970 as a joint effort between the Royal Norwegian navy, the Norwegian Defence Research Establishment and A/S Kongsberg Vaapenfabrikk. The requirement called for an anti-invasion weapon system compatible with the concept of small- and medium-sized ships operating in coastal waters. The Penguin was also the first anti-ship missile to be developed in the Western world. In 1972 the Norwegian navy completed its tactical and operational evaluation, and the Penguin Mk 1 went into service with the 'Storm' and 'Snogg' class missile craft. In 1974 a new development programme was initiated by the NDRE and Kongsberg under contract from the Swedish and Norwegian navies for the development of an improved **Penguin Mk II** missile. Development was completed in 1979, and the missile entered production for both navies. Apart from the shipborne version there are also coastal-defence and helicopter-launched variants (with folding wings) of the Penguin Mk II. In 1980 Kongsberg was awarded a further contract to co-operate with the NDRE in the evolution of a **Penguin Mk III** version for use with the General Dynamics F-16 Fighting Falcon fighters of the Royal Norwegian air force. This version is now in advanced development and should enter service in 1988.

The ship-launched versions are carried in simple container-launcher boxes that weigh about 650 kg (1,433 lb) complete with missile. The box is located on a prepared deck mount that has an umbilical connection to the fire-control system. Once fitted the two-stage solid-propellant missile is ready for immediate launch. The Penguin employs inertial guidance for the cruise phase of its flight, initial target detection, acquisition and designation being carried out by the launch platform before the missile is fired. The missile is then launched on the target's bearing under control of its pre-programmed guidance system and cruciform canard fins. As soon as the missile enters the estimated target zone the infra-red seeker in the nose scans the area in front of the missile until the target is acquired, the seeker continuing to track the target while guiding the missile on an intercept course. The Penguin Mk III differs in having no booster motor and in the pulsed laser altimeter of the earlier versions being replaced by a radar altimeter. The warhead in all the versions is the Bullpup Mk 19 semi-armour-piercing model. Norway is a customer for all three Penguin models, other operators being Turkey for the Mk I, and Greece and Sweden for the Mk II.

The **Penguin Mk 2 Mod 7** is being developed for US Navy use from their Sikorsky SH-60B LAMPS III ASW helicopters, each of which will carry two missiles. The folding-winged Mod 7 has the seeker and warhead of the air-launched Mk III with the propulsion system from the Mk II. These missiles will provide the Seahawk with some defence against attacking surface vessels without degrading its ASW ability.

Right: A Penguin being launched from one of the Norwegian navy's five 'Oslo' class frigates.

Developed as the first Western anti-ship missile system, the Penguin has undergone considerable improvement over the years.

As Penguin is a 'fire-and-forget' system, it reduces helicopter exposure to the target and decreases vulnerability. The initial order for 272 missiles is enough to arm the LAMPS III aircraft carried aboard 35 'Oliver Hazard Perry' (FFG-7) class frigates and 20 'Spruance' (DD-963) class destroyers. The missile weighs 385 kg (849 lb) and has a range of more than 31 km (nearly 20 miles). Penguin has also been developed in static and mobile coastal defence variants.

Specification
Penguin Mk I and Mk II
Dimensions: length 2.96 m (9 ft 8.5 in); diameter 28.0 cm (11 in); span 1.40 m (4 ft 7.1 in)
Weights: total round 340 kg (750 lb); warhead 120 kg (264 lb)
Performance: maximum speed Mach 0.8; range 20 km (12.4 miles) for Mk I and 27 km (16.9 miles) for Mk II

Specification
Penguin Mk III
Dimensions: length 3.17 m (10 ft 4.8 in); diameter 28.0 cm (11 in); span 1.00 m (3 ft 3.4 in)
Weights: total round 360 kg (794 lb); warhead 120 kg (264 lb)
Performance: maximum speed Mach 0.9; range 40 km (25 miles) from a surface launch and 60 km (37.3 miles) from an air launch

Soviet ship- and submarine-launched anti-ship missiles

The Soviet Union first investigated the concept of anti-ship missiles in the early 1950s as the equalizer to the American threat of the aircraft-carrier and its nuclear-capable strike aircraft. The first Soviet ship-launched missile subsequently deployed was the relatively unsophisticated **SS-N-1 'Scrubber'**, which had a limited service life in the Soviet navy. It was not until 1959 that the first of the widely-deployed missiles, the **SS-N-2 'Styx'**, was introduced to service. This has been improved progressively over the years, and is still in production today both for the Soviet navy and for export. The 'Styx' was designed to give small craft a firepower equivalent to that of a single battleship salvo but with a higher hit probability. Powered by a liquid-fuel rocket motor and armed with a powerful conventional warhead, the missile has seen extensive combat service with the navies of Egypt, Syria, Iraq, Vietnam, India and China, sinking a number of warships and merchantmen. However, when faced with sophisticated ECM defences the missile has not proved to be very effective. There are three versions of the 'Styx', the **SS-N-2A** having I-Band active radar homing, the folding-winged **SS-N-2B** with radar or infra-red homing and the **SS-N-2C** with improved propulsion and guidance.

In 1960 the Soviets introduced the large **SS-N-3 'Shaddock'** into service as its prime anti-carrier missile both for surface ships and for surfaced submarines. This turbojet-powered missile was initially fielded with no terminal homing system (the **SS-N-3C**) and a large nuclear warhead for use as a strategic strike weapon. The **SS-N-3A** submarine-launched and the **SS-N-3B** ship-launched anti-ship variants soon followed into service. A third-party system is required for over-the-horizon targeting with these weapons. In the late 1970s an improved SS-N-3B was introduced into service using technology from the follow-on **SS-N-12 'Sandbox'**, the eventual successor to the 'Shaddock'. Introduced into service in 1973 on several modified 'Echo II' class nuclear-powered cruise-missile boats, the missile was subsequently deployed on the 'Kiev' class carriers and has most recently been seen on 'Slava' class cruisers. The 'Sandbox' uses a much improved 'Shaddock' propulsion system and is a surface-skimmer in its attack phase, unlike the 'Shaddock'.

With the advent of the 'Kirov' class nuclear-powered battle-cruiser and the 'Oscar' class nuclear-powered cruise-missile submarine, yet another new missile was introduced into service in the early 1980s. This is the **SS-N-19**, which is believed to be yet another improvement on the 'Shaddock/Sandbox' family with the probable addition of a home-on-jam capability.

The SS-N-3, SS-N-12 and SS-N-19 serve only with the Soviet navy, and the SS-N-2 'Styx' is operated by most Warsaw Pact and Soviet client states, in particular with the numerous users of 'Osa', 'Komar' and 'Nanuchka' class missile craft.

Seen here being launched from an 'Osa' class fast patrol craft, SS-N-2 'Styx' (known as P-15 to the Soviets) ushered in the age of the missile-armed patrol craft.

Specification
SS-N-2 'Styx'
Dimensions: length 6.30 m (20 ft 8 in); diameter 75.0 cm (2 ft 5.5 in); span 2.75 m (9 ft 0.25 in)
Weights: total round about 3000 kg (6,614 lb); warhead about 500 kg (1,102 lb)
Performance: maximum speed Mach 0.9; range 46 km (28.6 miles) for SS-N-2A and SS-N-2B, and 74 km (46 miles) for SS-N-2C

Specification
SS-N-3 'Shaddock'
Dimensions: length 10.2 m/33.5 ft (SS-N-3C 11.8 m/38.7 ft); diameter 86 cm (2 ft 9.85 in); span 5 m (16.4 ft)
Weights: 5400 kg/11,905 lb (SS-N-3C 5800 kg/12,786 lb); warhead about 1000 kg (2,205 lb) high explosive or 350 kiloton nuclear (SS-N-3C about 2300 kg/5,071 lb nuclear with 800 kiloton yield.
Performance: maximum speed Mach 1.4; maximum range with mid-course guidance 460 km/286 miles (SS-N-3C 740 km/460 miles)

Specification
SS-N-12
Dimensions: length 10.70 m (35 ft 1.25 in); diameter 86.0 cm (2 ft 9.85 in); span about 2.50 m (8 ft 2.4 in)
Weights: total round about 5,000 kg (11,023 lb); warhead 1000 kg (2,205 lb) high explosive or 350-kiloton nuclear
Performance: maximum speed Mach 2.5; range 560 km (348 miles)

Above: A 'Kynda' class cruiser armed with eight SS-N-3 'Shaddock' missiles. 'Shaddock' was the first missile to give the Soviet navy a blue-water anti-carrier capacity, and the 400-km (250-mile)-plus range missile arms many of the larger units of the Soviet fleet.

Below: A 'Kashin' Mod destroyer fitted to carry four of the launcher-containers for the SS-N-2C 'Styx', a longer-ranged variant of the original SS-N-2A.

SS-N-7, SS-N-9 'Siren' and SS-N-22

Introduced into service in 1968 and 1969 respectively, these two missiles have many components in common. Both are primarily anti-carrier weapons and are fitted with solid-fuel rocket engines. The SS-N-7 is used solely in the pop-up mode from submerged 'Charlie I' and 'Charlie II' class cruise missile submarines, whilst the longer SS-N-9 'Siren' is used from both large missile craft and the 'Papa' and later 'Charlie II' class nuclear-powered cruise-missile submarines. In the latter case it is underwater-launched. Both are sea skimmers in the final phase of their attacks, the SS-N-7 flying at around 30-m (100-ft) altitude for its cruise phase, while the 'Siren' flies at the higher altitude of 75 m (245 ft) during this phase because it requires the extra height for effective use of its dual active radar and infra-red terminal homing seeker. The SS-N-7 has only an active-radar terminal homing system. The major difference in the two missiles, however, is the fact that the 'Siren' can use a third-party targeting and mid-course correction aircraft (or helicopter) to guide it in over-the-horizon engagements, whereas the SS-N-7 has to rely on the target data generated by the launch submarine's own sonars before launch as its sole guidance help. Both missiles are considered to be high-threat priorities by the US Navy.

In the early 1980s an improved version of the 'Siren' was fielded by the Soviets. Given the NATO designation SS-N-22, this Mach 2.5 missile is carried by the 'Sovremenny' and 'Tarantul' classes. Range is around 150 km (93 miles) and it has a much improved electronics and propulsion system. Almost certainly a sea skimmer in operation, the missile is also thought to have a home-on-jam capability.

All three missile types are used exclusively by the Soviet navy.

Specification
SS-N-7
Dimensions: length 7 m (23 ft); diameter 55.0 cm (1 ft 9.66 in); span not known

Weights: total round about 2900 kg (6,390 lb); warhead 500 kg (1,102 lb) high explosive or 200-kiloton nuclear
Performance: maximum speed Mach 0.95; range 55 km (34 miles)

Specification
SS-N-9 'Siren'
Dimensions: length 8.8 m (28.9 ft); diameter 55.0 cm (1 ft 9.66 in); span about 2.50 m (8 ft 2.4 in)
Weights: total round about 3300 kg (7,275 lb); warhead 500 kg (1,102 lb) high explosive or 200-kiloton nuclear
Performance: maximum speed Mach 0.9; range 110 km (68 miles)

The SS-N-7 submerged-launched anti-ship missile is carried by the 11 boats of the 'Charlie I' class of SSGN. With a range of 55 km (34 miles), it will be used in pop-up surprise attacks on high-value NATO surface ship units such as attack carriers.

Soviet air-launched anti-ship missiles

The first Soviet air-launched anti-ship missile achieved operational status with the Soviet Naval air force in the late 1950s. Designated **AS-1 'Kennel'** by NATO, one such missile was carried under each wing of the Tupolev Tu-16 'Badger-B' bomber. Range was limited to about 80 km (50 miles) and the missile was a relatively unsophisticated beam-rider. The warhead was of conventional high explosive. Exported to Egypt and Indonesia, the missile is no longer in service with any of its users. In 1960 a new turbojet-powered missile was introduced into service, carried under the fuselage of the dedicated missile-carrying Tu-16 'Badger-C' bomber. Used only by the Soviet naval air force, the **AS-2 'Kipper'** is fitted with a conventional warhead and used solely as an anti-ship weapon. It has autopilot guidance with mid-course correction capability, and carries an active radar seeker suitable for use against large targets such as carriers. The missile remains in service today.

In the following year the Long-Range Air Force introduced into service the massive turbojet-powered aircraft-shaped **AS-3 'Kangaroo'** missile for strategic use. Designed for use against large area targets, the missile can also be used for attacks on groups of ships. Lacking any terminal guidance system, the AS-3 more than makes up for this by carrying an 800-kiloton thermonuclear warhead. A few missiles may remain in service with any Tu-95 'Bear B' still with the

AS-4 'Kitchen' arms the Tupolev Tu-26 'Backfire' bomber.

Soviet Air Force.

Although seen in early 1961, the **AS-4 'Kitchen'** was not actually deployed with the Tupolev Tu-22 'Blinder-B' until 1965. The missile is powered by a single-stage liquid-fuel rocket, and was the first Soviet air-launched missile of multi-purpose nature. Used by the Soviet navy and Long-Range Air Force, the missile is available in anti-radar, anti-ship and strategic forms with a variety of homing systems to suit its role: all have inertial guidance, with active, passive or no terminal homing. Evidence of a continuing development programme was seen with the deployment of the Tupolev Tu-22M (or Tu-26) 'Backfire-B' bomber with one missile in a recessed fuselage weapons bay or with one missile under each wing. Evaluation of available photographs and comparison with those under the 'Blinder' suggest that there are two different families of AS-4 missiles, one de-

The massive AS-3 is a relatively simple missile, lacking any terminal guidance system. It is the size of a small fighter, and carries an 800-kT warhead for use against area targets.

veloped for the 'Backfire' alone (the underfuselage single-round type being nuclear-armed, and the missiles under the wings being conventional-warhead anti-ship or anti-radiation variants). The US Navy believes that the AS-4 is most dangerous when launched at high altitude for a high-level flight profile and very steep terminal dive onto the target.

The replacement for the 'Kennel' was fielded in 1966, when the **AS-5 'Kelt'** was first seen under the wings of the Tu-16 'Badger-G' bomber. Powered by a single-stage liquid-fuelled rocket, the AS-5 is similar in appearance to the AS-1 and is fitted with a conventional warhead. The guidance system is considerably improved, and both active-radar and passive-radar homing versions were used in combat by the Egyptians dur-

ing the 1973 war against Israel. Out of 25 fired only five hit their targets, the rest being shot down by Israeli air-defence systems. The AS-5 is used by both the Soviet Naval Air Force and the Long-Range Air Force.

In 1970 the Soviet navy and Long-Range Air Force brought into service the **AS-6 'Kingfish'** missile to comple-

An AS-4 'Kitchen' derivative was developed for the Tu-22M 'Backfire' bomber. It is probable that this is the nuclear warhead armed version, although there are also conventional warhead-carrying variants for anti-ship and radar suppression missions.

ment the 'Kitchen'. The AS-6 is also a multi-role missile capable of the same roles as the AS-4 with the same types of guidance and homing. However, it is powered by a single-stage solid-propellant motor and is carried in pairs under the wings of the 'Backfire-B' Tupolev Tu-16 'Badger-C mod' and Tu-16 'Badger-G mod'. Like the 'Kitchen' it is considered a special threat by the US Navy. Both types are operated only by the USSR.

Specification
AS-2 'Kipper'
Dimensions: length 10.0 m (32 ft 9.7 in); diameter 90.0 cm (2 ft 11.4 in); span 4.90 m (16 ft 0.9 in)
Weights: total round 4200 kg (9,259 lb); warhead 1000 kg (2,205 lb)
Performance: maximum speed Mach 1.2; range 185 km (115 miles) from a high-altitude launch

Specification
AS-3 'Kangaroo'
Dimensions: length 14.90 m (48 ft 10.6 in); diameter 1.85 m (6 ft 0.8 in); span 9.15 m (30 ft 0.25 in)
Weights: total round 11000 kg (24,250 lb); warhead 2300 kg (5,071 lb) 800-kiloton thermonuclear
Performance: maximum speed Mach 1.8; range 650 km (405 miles) from a high-altitude launch

Specification
AS-5 'Kelt'
Dimensions: length 8.60 m (28 ft 2.6 in); diameter 90.0 cm (2 ft 11.4 in); span 4.60 m (15 ft 1.1 in)
Weights: total round 3000 kg (6,614 lb); warhead 1000 kg (2,205 lb)
Performance: maximum speed Mach 1.2; range 230 km (143 miles) from a high-altitude launch and 180 km (112 miles) from a low-altitude launch

Specification
AS-4 'Kitchen'
Dimensions: length 11.30 m (37 ft 0.9 in); diameter 90.0 cm (2 ft 11.4 in); span 3.00 m (9 ft 10 in)
Weights: total round 5900 kg (13,007 lb); warhead 1000 kg (2,205 lb) high explosive or 350-kiloton nuclear
Performance: maximum speed Mach 3.5; range 460 km (286 miles) from a high-altitude launch and 300 km (186 miles) from a low-altitude launch

Specification
AS-6 'Kingfish'
Dimensions: length 10.00 m (32 ft 9.7 in); diameter 90.0 cm (2 ft 11.4 in); span 2.50 m (8 ft 2.4 in)
Weights: total round 5000 kg (11,023 lb); warhead 1000 kg (2,205 lb) high explosive or 350-kiloton nuclear
Performance: maximum speed Mach 3; range 560 km (348 miles) from a high-altitude launch and 250 km (155 miles) from a low-altitude launch

AS-6 'Kingfish' is a multi-role missile capable of carrying a nuclear warhead or a ton of high explosive.

Above: AS-2 'Kipper' is used solely by Soviet naval aviation. Turbojet-powered, the missile has an active radar seeker suitable for use against large targets such as carriers, and has a range of 185 km (115 miles) from a high-altitude launch.

Right: AS-6 'Kingfish' is a Soviet missile of the 1970s, complementing the advanced AS-4 'Kitchen'. US sources consider 'Kingfish' would be used from high level, diving at Mach 3 onto the target.

Left: The AS-1 'Kennel' was the pioneering Soviet long-range ASM. The SSC-2B Samlet is a coastal version no longer used by the USSR but still in the inventories of nations such as Egypt and Cuba (although possibly inoperable)

Above: AS-5 'Kelt' appeared in the late 1960s as a replacement for 'Kennel'. Rocket-powered, the AS-5 appears similar to its predecessor but is much more capable. However, it was not successful when used by Egypt in 1973.

Modern Naval Artillery

The pre-eminence of the aircraft-carrier in the immediate post-war years and the rise of the guided missile seemed to signify the end of the naval gun as a major weapon system, but events of the last decade have shown the error of such a way of thinking and naval artillery has seen a revival.

Since the 1982 Falklands war and the troubles in Lebanon late in the following year, the terms Naval Gunfire Support (NGS) and Naval Gunfire Support Forward Observer (NGSFO) have begun to take on significant meanings in politico-military circles. In an age where defence money is difficult to find, it had become an easy option to say that a medium-calibre gun was obsolete aboard a naval warship which could be armed with longer-range 'all-singing, all-dancing' missile systems. Thus in the case of the Royal Navy it was decided that the new-generation 'Type 22 Batch 1/2/3' ASW frigates and the follow-on 'Type 23' class would no longer carry such a weapon. However, the Falklands war and the use to which such current naval guns were put forced a rapid rethink which has resulted in the 'Type 22 Batch 3' ships and the 'Type 23' or 'Duke' class being redesigned to incorporate the tried and trusted fully automatic 114-mm (4.5-in) Mk 8 gun.

It is interesting to contrast the original narrow-minded view of the British Ministry of Defence with its counterparts in the USSR and USA, which were then actively promoting the retention of big gun warships in their navies to perform NGS tasks amongst other things. Surprisingly, other European navies tended to follow the big powers' lead and tried

The Royal Navy found itself unexpectedly in action in the South Atlantic in 1982, with the supposedly outdated medium naval gun making an important contribution to the campaign to retake the Falklands. The 'Type 21' frigate HMS Active found herself on shore bombardment duty within days of arriving.

wherever possible to keep large-calibre guns in their warships. In addition both France and Italy have made a lucrative export trade out of selling their guns to other nations throughout the world. Of the guns sold by these two countries the most important is the Italian 76-mm (3-in) OTO-Melara Compact, which is used by some 35 different navies and has been used in combat on many occasions by the Israeli navy in both the shore-bombardment and anti-surface ship roles. However, the most famous gun by far is the immense American 406-mm (16-in) weapon of the 'Iowa' class battleships, which again fired in anger for a third time since World War II during the US Navy's involvement in the Lebanese tragedy.

For most of the last four and a half centuries, the primary aim of naval gunfire has been the destruction of enemy ships. World War II saw a considerable change in role, with the massive guns of the battleship providing awesome support to amphibious landings, a task still much in evidence today.

FRANCE

100-mm Model 1968-II gun

The 100-mm (3.9-in) **Model 1968-II** 55-calibre weapon is the latest version of a series of French 100-mm (3.94-in) guns which have the designations **Models 1953, 1964** and **1968-I.** Compared with these the Model 68-II is lighter and fully automatic, with the option of autonomous operation with a turret crew of only two. The barrel has a longer life than those of the previous guns because it is air-purged and water-cooled after each round has been fired. The gun can engage both air and surface targets, the former including sea-skimming anti-ship missiles. The round types fired include both a multi-purpose shell with either a time or proximity fuse, and a prefragmented shell with a proximity fuse. Apart from the

French navy, the Model 1968-II or its earlier variants serve with the navies of Belgium, Portugal, Argentina and Greece.

A 100-mm **Creusot-Loire Compact** variant (entirely automatic and possessing the same performance characteristics) has also been developed and sold to Saudi Arabia, Malaysia and the People's Republic of China. This has a weight of 13.5 tons, uses three rates of fire: 20 rpm, 45 rpm or 90 rpm using 1, 2, 3 or 6 round bursts.

Above: Admiral Charner, *a frigate of the 'Commandant Rivière' class, is fitted with the standard 100-mm gun turret fore and aft, although one of the aft turrets has been replaced by Exocet launchers.*

Specification
Model 1968-II
Calibre: 100 mm (3.94 in)
Weight: 22 tons
No. of barrels: one
Elevation: −15° to +80°
Muzzle velocity: 870 m (2,854 ft) per second

Projectile weight: 13.5 kg (29.8 lb)
Total round weight: 23.6 kg (52 lb)
Maximum rate of fire: 60 rpm
Maximum effective ranges: surface fire 15 km (9.3 miles), and anti-aircraft fire 8 km (5 miles)

Derived from the standard 100-mm weapon used by the French navy, the 100-mm Compact has been developed by Creusot-Loire and offered to several countries. Entirely automatic, it has a similar performance to the Model 1968-II, but an all-up weight of some 17 tons allows for installation on relatively small vessels. A feature of all the French turrets is the ability to replenish the magazine while firing is in progress.

Above: The Mediterranean-based aviso (frigate) Quartier Maitre Anquetil *of the 'A69' class is equipped with a single 100-mm dual-purpose gun in the Model 1968-II mounting. This version of the turret is a lightened and completely automatic derivation of the Models 1953, 1964 and 1968-I.*

Below: Second Maitre Le Bihan, based in the Channel, displays her bow-mounted 100-mm main armament. The gun has a rate of fire of 60 rounds per minute (which can be sustained) and is designed to engage both surface and aerial targets. Sea-skimming missiles can also be engaged.

5-in Gun Mounting Mk 42

The dual-purpose radar-controlled single **5-in Gun Mounting Mk 42** was adopted in the late 1950s and early 1960s as the successor to the semi-automatic twin 127-mm (5-in) 38-calibre Mk 32 and single 127-mm 54-calibre Mk 39 mountings of World War II and the immediate post-war years respectively. The Mk 42 is capable of a much higher rate of fire and is fitted with an automatic ammunition feed system with two 20-round ready-use drums. Driven by electro-hydraulic power units, the Mk 42 can be operated in local or automatic control. Crew for the **Mk 42 Mod 7/8** is 14, of whom four are actually on the mount. Over 150 guns of this type are at sea with the US Navy and the navies of Australia, Japan, Spain and West Germany. All bar a few of the US guns have been upgraded to the **Mk 42 Mod 10** standard by kit additions, this bringing the mount up to the same equipment fit as the lighter **Mk 42 Mod 9** variant which was constructed for the 'Knox' class frigates. This has solid-state electronics, a 10 per cent reduction in power requirements and a crew of only two on the mount, reducing the overall total to 12. The 127-mm gun barrel fitted to the Mk 42 mounts is designated the Mk 18. A semi-active laser-guided projectile, the Deadeye, is being procured for these and the later Mk 45 mountings. The round is 1.548 m (5.08 ft) long, weighs 47.4 kg (104.5 lb), and is similar in concept to the US Army's Copper-

Above: The radar guided 5-in Gun Mounting Mk 42 is in widespread use, over 150 units of various models being at sea with the US Navy and the navies of four Allied countries. The gun crew required to operate the system (14, with four in the turret itself) is almost half that of preceding twin-gun turrets.

Right: The single 5-in (127-mm) Mk 42 gun aboard a 'Forrest Sherman' class guided missile destroyer is engulfed by heavy seas. It should be remembered that naval guns have to function in all conditions.

head projectile for its 155-mm (6.1-in) howitzers.

Specification
Mounting Mk 42
Calibre: 127 mm (5 in)
No. of barrels: one
Weights: Mod 7/8 65.8 tons, Mod 9 57.65 tons and Mod 10 63.9 tons
Elevation: −5° to +80°
Muzzle velocity: 810 m (2,657 ft) per second
Projectile weight: 31.8 kg (70 lb)
Maximum rate of fire: 20 rpm
Maximum effective ranges: surface fire 23.8 km (14.8 miles), and anti-aircraft fire 14.8 km (9.2 miles)

The helicopter-carrying destroyer Shirane is armed with two single 5-in (127-mm) Mk 42 gun mountings. Altogether 11 vessels of the Japanese Maritime Self-Defence Force carry the Mk 42, with two more planned.

5-in Gun Mounting Mk 45

The lightweight radar-controlled single 5-in Gun Mounting Mk 45 utilizes a Mk 19 gun barrel and represents what is essentially a quantum leap for US naval medium gun technology. It was designed for fitting to new-build warships and is fully automatic in operation, with only six men required in the fixed-ammunition handling room to reload the single 20-round ready-use drum. The mount embodies all the improvements to 127-mm (5-in) gun mounts that have been developed over the last 40 years or so since the 127-mm 38-calibre gun was first introduced. In the **Mk 45 Mod 1** version now being produced the below-decks reloading arrangements have been modified to allow remote and rapid round selection between several

types of ammunition carried on the drum. The gun has already seen extensive combat use in the shore bombardment role during the US Navy's involvement in Lebanon, and has proved to be exceptionally reliable and easily maintained. The only export orders are for the Turkish 'Yavuz' class, but the type is the primary armament for most of the larger US Navy combatants. A **Product Improved Mk 45** using advanced controls and simpler systems is due to enter production in 1989 or 1990.

Specification
Mounting Mk 45
Calibre: 127 mm (5 in)
No. of barrels: one
Weight: 21.34 tons
Elevation: −5° to +65°
Projectile weight: 31.8 kg (70 lb)
Maximum rate of fire: 20 rpm
Maximum effective ranges: surface fire 23.8 km (14.8 miles), and anti-aircraft fire 14.8 km (9.2 miles)

Right: Built by the Northern Ordnance division of the FMC corporation, the single 5-in/54-calibre Gun Mounting Mk 45 is the most advanced of the turrets currently in service with the US Navy.

Below: One of the most important vessels to be commissioned in the last decade, USS Ticonderoga is equipped to command and control the air defences of a fleet. She is also equipped for surface action, with two Mk 45 mounts.

Above: The lean form of the 'California' class cruiser USS South Carolina cuts through the water. In common with all of the larger fighting ships of the US Navy built in the last 10 years, the 'Californias' are armed with Mk 45s, which are capable of firing 'Deadeye' laser guided projectiles.

Above: USS Texas of the 'Virginia' class is amongst the most potent cruisers afloat. With weaponry that includes Tomahawk, Harpoon, ASROC and Standard missiles, together with gun systems including Phalanx CIWS and two Mk 45 5-in (127-mm), the class has anti-air, anti-surface, and anti-submarine capability in no small measure.

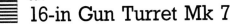

16-in Gun Turret Mk 7

Following the reactivation of the 'Iowa' class battleships the US Navy reintroduced to active service the largest-calibre naval guns in the world today. With nine radar directed **16-in Mk 7 Mod 0** guns in three 1,708-ton triple turrets, the 'Iowas' require a crew of 77 per mount alone plus an additional 30-36 men in the magazines. The ammunition fired is either High-Capacity High Explosive (HCHE) or Armour-Piercing (AP), the latter being capable of penetrating up to 9 m (29.5 ft) of reinforced concrete or 559 mm (22 in) of armour plate. Each battleship has a magazine load of 1,220 projectiles with a larger number of 49.9-kg (110-lb) full-

charge and 24-kg (52.8-lb) reduced-charge propellant bags. The length of each gun is 50 calibres, and the weight 108479 kg (239,156 lb) without its breech block. The guns can also be loaded, elevated and fired individually.

Since reactivation the USS *New Jersey* has used her guns in support of the Lebanese army and US Marines in and around Beirut, Lebanon, whilst during her previous Vietnam War activation the 406-mm gun proved one of the most accurate and deadly bombardment weapons of the whole war, hitting targets in direct support of ground troops and others which were

inland and heavily defended with respect to air attack. During the late 1950s a tactical nuclear round, the 15-kiloton yield Mk 23 'Katie', was developed for service and, although a number entered the active nuclear stockpile, it is thought that none were taken to sea. The 'Iowa's were equipped to carry 10 of these rounds in their magazines.

Specification
Turret Mk 7
Calibre: 406 mm (16 in)
No. of barrels: three
Weight: 1,708 tons
Elevation: −5° to +45°

Muzzle velocity: HCHE 762 m (2,500 ft) per second, and AP 579 m (1,900 ft) per second
Projectile weights: HCHE 862 kg (1,900 lb), and AP 1225 kg (2,700 lb)
Maximum rate of fire: 6 rpm
Maximum effective ranges: HCHE 38 km (23.6 miles), and AP 36.7 km (22.8 miles)

The need for powerful shore bombardment saw the re-activation of the class in both the Korean and Vietnam wars. New Jersey in 1968 was seen primarily as a gun platform, her 16-in (406-mm) guns being the only weapons manned.

Above: The most heavily-armoured US warships ever built, the 'Iowa' class was designed to withstand combat with the Japanese superbattleships Yamato *and* Musashi. *The main armament was also the most powerful available, in triple Mk 7 turrets.*

Below: The most recent activation has seen the 'Iowas' comprehensively refitted, and serving at the centre of surface action groups. The enormous main turrets are without parallel in today's navies, each barrel alone weighing over 100 tons.

Soviet naval rocket-launcher systems

For shore bombardment and defence suppression missions the Soviet navy has fitted some of its amphibious warfare vessels with modified versions of standard Soviet army multiple rocket-launcher systems. The oldest type used is an 18-tube 140-mm (5.51-in) launcher which is fitted amidships with blast shields in pairs on the 'Polnochny A/B/C' LSM classes. The rocket used is the spin-stabilized MF-14-0F, which weighs 39.6 kg (87.3 lb) and has an 18.8-kg (41.4-lb) HE-fragmentation warhead. The maximum range of the weapon is around 10 km (6.2 miles). It is believed that a smoke round can also be fired to screen an assault landing. The weapon has been exported aboard 'Polnochnys' to the navies of Algeria, Angola, Cuba, Egypt, Ethiopia, India, Iraq, Libya, Poland, Somalia, South Yemen, Syria and Vietnam.

In the late 1970s the Soviets introduced a new rocket-launcher aboard the 'Ivan Rogov' class LPD and the 'Alligator IV' class LST. Based on the 122-mm (4.8-in) BM-21, the naval system comprises a pedestal mount with two clusters of 20 loaded rocket tubes. Once fired, the empty tubes are discarded and the mount is automatically reloaded with two new pods from a below-deck magazine. Several of the East German's 'Frosch' class LSTs are also configured for this system. The standard rocket weighs some 77 kg (169.75 lb) and has a 19.4-kg (42.8-lb) HE-fragmentation warhead. Smoke and chemical rounds are available as options. The maximum range of the system is in the region of 20 km (12.4 miles), which allows the vessel to stand-off a fair distance to avoid return fire. In both cases the systems used can be fired individually, in multiples or complete salvoes.

Specification
122-mm launcher
Calibre: 122 mm (4.8 in)
No. of launcher tubes: 40 (two 20-round pods)
Weight of rocket: 77 kg (169.8 lb)
Types of rockets: HE, smoke, chemical
Reload time: 2-3 minutes
Maximum range: 20 km (12.4 miles)

Specification
140-mm launcher
Calibre: 140 mm (5.51 in)
No. of launcher tubes: 18
Weight of rocket: 39.6 kg (87.3 lb)
Types of rockets: HE, smoke
Reload time: 10 minutes
Maximum range: 10 km (6.2 miles)

Given previous Soviet practice in adapting naval systems for land use or vice versa, it should not be surprising to learn that the famous 'Katyusha' multiple rocket-launcher should appear on Soviet assault ships. On the Ivan Rogov, *the rockets are pedestal-mounted high in front of the bridge.*

76-mm guns

In the early 1960s the Soviet navy introduced into service on the 'Kynda' class missile cruisers a twin 76-mm 60-calibre rapid-firing dual-purpose gun mount which rapidly became the standard fit for a number of warship and auxiliary vessel classes. Now found on the 'Kiev' class aircraft-carriers, the 'Kara' and 'Kyunda' class missile cruisers, the 'Kashin' and 'Kildin' class destroyers, the 'Krivak I', 'Mirka' and 'Petya' class frigates and the 'Ivan Rogov' class amphibious warfare ships, the mount is usually associated with either an 'Owl Screech' or 'Hawk Screech' I-band fire-control radar. The system has also been exported to a number of Soviet client states on export version 'Kashin' class destroyers and 'Petya' and 'Koni' class frigates.

In the 1970s, the Soviets introduced a fully automatic single 76-mm, 60 calibre dual-purpose gun. Designed for smaller combatants such as the 'Grisha V', 'Tarantul', 'Nanuchka III', 'Pauk' and 'Matka' classes, the gun has been given the optional capacity of local

The 76-mm Dual Purpose gun fitted to the rear of the superstructure of the Soviet carrier 'Kiev' is seen in the anti-aircraft position in this picture taken in the Mediterranean by a Royal Air Force Nimrod maritime patrol aircraft.

on-mount control by a gun crew if required. Fire-control for aerial targets is by a 'Bass Tilt' H-band radar, whilst surface targets need the use of a local sighting system in conjunction with the ship's search radar.

Specification
76-mm L/60
Calibre: 76 mm (3 in)
No. of barrels: two
Elevation: 0° to +80°
Muzzle velocity: 900 m (2,953 ft) per second
Projectile weight: 16 kg (35.3 lb)
Maximum rate of fire: 90 rpm
Maximum effective ranges: surface fire 8 km (5 miles), and anti-aircraft fire 6 km (3.7 miles)

Specification
76-mm L/60
Calibre: 76 mm (3 in)
No. of barrels: one
Elevation: −5° to +85°
Muzzle velocity: 900 m (2,953 ft) per second
Projectile weight: 16 kg (35.3 lb)
Maximum rate of fire: 120 rpm
Maximum effective ranges: surface fire 10 km (6.2 miles), and anti-aircraft fire 7 km (4.3 miles)

First appearing on 'Kynda' class cruisers in the early 1960s, the twin 76-mm DP gun also appeared on the contemporary 'Kashin' class destroyers. Classes since carrying it include 'Kiev', 'Kara' and 'Krivak'.

100-mm and 130-mm guns

In the early 1970s the 'Krivak II' class missile frigates were seen to be armed with two new-pattern single 70-calibre 100-mm dual-purpose gun mounts aft. The barrel is water-cooled and the mounting is assessed by NATO as being fully automatic in operation, with fire-control by either a 'Kite Screech' radar or an on-mount optronic sighting system. The new gun was subsequently seen to be adopted for the 'Udaloy' class ASW destroyers, the 'Krivak III' class missile frigates and the lead ship of the nuclear-powered battle-cruisers, the *Kirov* herself.

The 100-mm (3.9-in) gun was followed in the mid-1970s by a brand new gun design mounted initially on the 'Sovremenny' destroyer class, and found to be a twin 130-mm 70-calibre dual-purpose gun mount. The barrels are also water-cooled to prolong life. The fitting of the barrels close together would seem to indicate that they share a common cradle system. The guns have a greater maximum range than the older 152-mm (6-in) Soviet guns (28 km/17.4 miles in comparison with 27 km/16.8 miles), and are now fitted as the main armament for the larger

Soviet surface combatants such as the 'Slava' class missile cruisers and the second nuclear-powered battle-cruiser, the *Frunze*. Fire-control is similar to that of the smaller 100-mm gun.

Specification
100-mm L/70
Calibre: 100 mm (3.94 in)
No. of barrels: one
Elevation: −5° to +80°
Muzzle velocity: 900 m (2,953 ft) per second
Maximum rate of fire: 80 rpm
Maximum effective ranges: surface fire 15 km (9.3 miles), and anti-aircraft fire 8 km (5 miles)

Specification
130-mm L/70
Calibre: 130 mm (5.12 in)
No. of barrels: two
Elevation: −5° to +80°
Muzzle velocity: 950 m (3,117 ft) per second
Maximum rate of fire: 130 rpm
Maximum effective ranges: surface fire 18 km (11.2 miles), and anti-aircraft fire 10 km (6.2 miles)

Above: Unlike earlier Soviet 100-mm guns, the new weapon that has appeared on later versions of the 'Krivak' class frigate is almost certainly fully automatic. The only other vessels so far thus equipped are the battlecruiser Kirov and the large ASW destroyer Udaloy.

Below: The powerful surface warfare armament of the 'Sovremenny' class destroyers is enhanced by the fitting of two twin 130-mm (5.12-in) automatic gun turrets. Also fitted to 'Slava' class cruisers, the weapon outranges the old 152-mm (6-in) gun aboard the 'Sverdlovs'.

152-mm triple gun mounting

The Soviet navy's 50-calibre **152-mm triple mounting** features the largest naval guns in service today with any navy save that of the USA. The guns are of a 1938 design, and are fitted on the unmodified 'Sverdlov' class cruisers in a conventional two forward and two aft turret arrangement. The barrels can be individually elevated, loaded and fired if required. The loading phase is believed to be semi-automatic in nature, each barrel having a maximum rate of fire of 10 rounds per minute, though a more practical rate is thought to be 4-5 rounds per minute. The guns also have a limited anti-aircraft capability using barrage fire. At the rear of each turret top is installed an 8-m (26.25-ft) long optical rangefinder, whilst for radar fire-control purposes the turrets usually mount an 'Egg Cup' E-band ranging only radar. An additional two 'Top Bow' fire-control radars for the guns are included as part of the ship's main electronic fit. Recently a tactical nuclear capability has been associated with these guns, possibly as a direct result of its naval gunfire support role in Warsaw Pact amphibious assault operations.

The only other country to use this gun was Indonesia, which had the weapon aboard a 'Sverdlov' class cruiser which has now been scrapped.

Specification
152-mm triple gun mounting
Calibre: 152 mm (5.98 in)
No. of barrels: three
Weight: not known
Elevation: $-5°$ to $+50°$
Muzzle velocity: 915 m (3,002 ft) per second
Projectile weight: 50 kg (110.2 lb)
Maximum rate of fire: 30 rpm
Effective ranges: surface fire 18 km (11.2 miles), and anti-aircraft fire 12 km (7.5 miles)

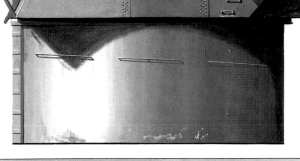

Right: The triple 152-mm gun mounting in service with the remaining 'Sverdlov' class cruisers of the Soviet Fleet are of the 1938 pattern, originally designed for the 'Chapayev' class. The 50-calibre guns are reported to have a maximum range of 27 km (16.8 miles), firing a projectile of some 50 kg (110 lb).

Right: This photograph dating from the 1970s contrasts the 'Sverdlovsk' class with the last British 6-in gun cruiser. The Soviet ship remains to all intents and purposes an unmodified World War II type, while HMS Blake bears little resemblance to any wartime forebears.

Below: Dzerzhinsky was altered in the early 1960s, being fitted with an SA-N-2 launcher in place of its X-turret. Presumably the conversion was not a great success, as no other 'Sverdlov' was so converted. Although potentially fine NGS ships, the 'Sverdlovs' remain vulnerable to modern weaponry and, since there is no sign of the Soviet navy updating their missile defences by the addition of close-in weapon systems, it may be that these large, impressive vessels are being retained as training ships and 'flag-showers'.

76-mm OTO Melara Compact gun

The 62-calibre **76-mm OTO Melara Compact** gun is now the most famous lightweight dual-purpose naval gun in the world. Developed from the 76-mm (3-in) **OTO Melara MMI** mount in the mid-1960s the gun first entered service in 1969 as a system intended for installation in ships of any size and class down to motor gunboats and hydrofoils. The fully automatic mounting consists of two parts, the shank and the turret assembly. The former is installed below deck and contains the 80-round rotating platform and hoist ammunition feed system to the gun in the turret above. This is covered by a watertight and NBC proof glassfibre shield. The only manpower required is in the main magazine, where ammunition handlers are needed to feed the drum in order to keep it loaded. The rate of fire is adjustable from a minimum of 10 to a maximum of 85 rounds per minute, although the **Super Rapid** variant increases the latter to 120 rounds per minute. The rate is adjusted on the operations room control console. Another option available is the ability to fit a stabilized line of sight local fire-control system if required.

The gun barrel is fitted with a muzzle brake and a fume extractor. Currently the gun is in service or on order with nearly 40 navies throughout the non-communist world and is under licence manufacture in the USA, Japan and in Spain. The Super Rapid version is in use with Italy, Denmark and Singa-

pore. Israel has used the weapon extensively in combat in anti-ship and in shore bombardment actions, possibly with new, locally produced ammunition in the latter role. Iran's 'Kaman' class fast attack craft must also have used their guns in the Gulf War, although Iraq for its part has yet to take delivery of six 76-mm armed 'Assad' class corvettes.

Specification
76-mm OTO Melara Compact
Calibre: 76 mm (3 in)
No. of barrels: one
Weight: 7.35 tons
Elevation: −15° to +85°
Muzzle velocity: 925 m (3,035 ft) per second
Projectile weight: 6.3 kg (13.9 lb)
Maximum rate of fire: 85-100 rpm (according to variant)
Maximum effective ranges: surface fire 8 km (5 miles), and anti-aircraft fire 5 km (3.1 miles)

Right: One of the most successful naval weapons in the post-war years, the 76-mm (3-in) OTO-Melara Compact gun mounting is in service with, or is being delivered to, 35 navies or more. It is manufactured under licence in the USA, Japan and Spain, and it has been extensively combat-tested by the Israeli navy.

Below: The light weight of the 76-mm Compact has enabled it to be installed on vessels displacing as little as 60 tons. It was mounted on the 'Pegasus' class hydrofoil USS Aquila, and the gun gives Aquila and her sisters considerable firepower, being able to fire at over 85 rounds per minute.

Below: With more than 60 built or projected, the US 'FFG-7' class is one of the most numerous frigate designs since the war. Unusually, the design placed the sole gun, a licence-built OTO-Melara Compact 76-mm, high up amidships. This is less than effective against sea-skimming missiles.

127-mm OTO Melara Compact gun

Design work for the **127-mm OTO Melara Compact** 54-calibre gun started in 1965 as a joint venture by OTO Melara with the Italian government. The first prototype was completed in May 1969 and the gun was adopted as the main armament for new-build Italian navy frigates and destroyers. The loading, ammunition, feeding and firing sequences are controlled by one man in the ship's opera-

tions room using a console. Ready-use ammunition is held in three 22-round loading drums below deck under the mount. This allows a choice between three different ammunition types, the gun's operator choosing the round appropriate to the action. The three drums are automatically reloaded via two hoists that are manually replenished in the main magazine. A drum can be reloaded even whilst the gun is

firing. The barrel itself is fitted with a muzzle brake. Apart from Italy the navies of Argentina, Canada, Iraq, Nigeria, Peru and Venezuela have guns of this type in service aboard frigates and destroyers.

Specification
127-mm OTO Melara Compact
Calibre: 127 mm (5 in)

No. of barrels: one
Weight: 37.5 tons
Elevation: −15° to +85°
Muzzle velocity: 807 m (2,648 ft) per second
Projectile weight: unknown
Total round weight: 32 kg (70.5 lb)
Maximum rate of fire: 45 rpm
Maximum effective ranges: surface fire 15 km (9.3 miles), and anti-aircraft fire 7 km (4.3 miles)

Left: OTO-Melara developed a compact, lightweight 127-mm (5-in) gun and turret for use as the main armament for frigates and destroyers. Blohm und Voss have adopted the gun for their 'Meko 360' class of destroyer, as seen here on Argentina's Almirante Brown.

Above: The major technical features of modern compact systems are the major use of light alloy structures, lightweight control mechanisms, and a higher rate of fire. This last feature requires an automatic loading sequence, with ready-use rounds close to hand and easily refillable.

ITALY

105-mm Breda SCLAR rocket-launcher

The **105-mm Breda SCLAR** naval rocket-launcher system normally consists of two 20-tube launchers for 105-mm (4.13-in) countermeasures or assault rockets, an Elsag fire-control unit and a magazine filled with SNIA rockets. The two launchers are mounted one on each side of the ship so that they provide as wide a coverage as possible. A remote-control facility on the fire-control unit allows them to be automatically trained and elevated to respond to any incoming threats detected by the ship's own ESM sensors. To meet any threat, mixed rocket type salvoes can be loaded into the launcher tubes, automatic selection of the type, fuse setting and launch sequence being undertaken by the operator on the remote fire-control console. If necessary the countermeasures rockets can be offloaded and replaced by a variant fitted with HE warheads for shore bombardment and defence suppression purposes.

About 1,000 SCLAR mountings have been built to date for the navies of Argentina, Ecuador, Iraq, Italy, Nigeria, Peru, Venezuela and West Germany. The other rocket types used include the 105LR-C long-range (up to 12 km/7.5 miles) chaff distraction, the 105MR-C medium-range (up to 5 km/

Above: the Breda 105-mm rocket-launcher is usually fitted to a ship as one of a pair, primarily for use as a launch system for countermeasures; high explosive warheads can be fitted for assault purposes.

Right: Developed from the 105-mm launcher, the multi-calibre assault launcher fires both 105-mm and 51-mm rockets. The servos of the training mechanisms are more carefully protected against adverse weather conditions than in the original system.

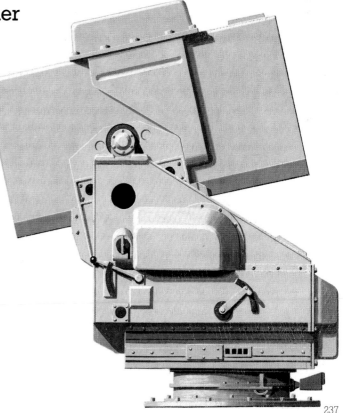

3.1 miles) chaff seduction and the 105LR-I illuminating with a maximum range of 4 km (2.5 miles).

Specification
SCLAR
Calibre: 105 mm (4.13 in)
No. of tubes per launcher: 20
Weight: 1.72 tons
Elevation: −5° to +60°
Rate of fire: 1 rocket per second
Rocket types: HE, chaff, illumination
Maximum range: 4-12 km (2.5-7.5 miles)

Seen aboard a 'Lupo' class frigate of the Italian navy, the Breda multi-calibre assault launcher retains the capacity to fire deception and countermeasure rockets from the 105-mm tubes. The 51-mm rockets are strictly for close range assault, however.

UK
Vickers 4.5-in Mk 8 gun

The Royal Navy has been using the 114-mm (4.5-in) weapon as its standard medium calibre gun since World War II. In the mid-1960s RARDE began design development of a fully automatic version to replace the semi-automatic Mk 6 twin turret. Based on the British army's Abbot gun, the radar-controlled **4.5-in Mk 8 gun**, as it became known, is a 55-calibre weapon fitted with a muzzle brake and fume extractor. The gun mounting itself is designed by Vickers and features a reinforced GRP gun shield with a simple ammunition feed system and remote power controls. A stockpile of

ready-use rounds can be accommodated at the mounting and fired remotely from the operations room with no crew closed up on the reloading system below decks. Five types of

Below: The Vickers 4.5-in Mk 8 mounting is currently in service with the Royal Navy aboard Type 42 and Type 82 destroyers as well as Type 21 and Batch 3 Type 22 frigates, and will be fitted to the new Type 23 'Duke' class of frigate.

fixed ammunition can be fired: chaff, surface practice, anti-aircraft practice HE (with impact, close proximity, distant proximity or delay-action fuses) and illuminating. Apart from the Royal Navy the Mk 8 is in service with the Argentine, Brazilian, Iranian, Libyan and Thai navies. The Mk 8 saw extensive combat service in the 1982 Falklands war, mainly in the shore bombardment and close-support roles for troops in contact with the enemy, but it is also credited with destruction of an Argentine supply ship when HMS *Alacrity* sank the *Isla de los Estados*.

Specification
Mk 8 gun
Calibre: 114.3 mm (4.5 in)

With a maximum range of 23 km (14.3 miles) and a sustained rate of fire of 25 rounds per minute, the Mk 8 can fire a variety of differing rounds, including high explosive with four different types of fuse (impact, close proximity, distant proximity and delayed action).

No. of barrels: one
Weight: not known
Elevation: −10° to +55°
Muzzle velocity: 870 m (2,854 ft) per second
Projectile weight: 21 kg (46.3 lb)
Maximum rate of fire: 25 rpm
Maximum effective ranges: surface fire 23 km (14.3 miles), and anti-aircraft fire 6 km (3.7 miles)

57-mm Bofors SAK gun

The 70-calibre **57-mm Bofors SAK Mk 1** dual-purpose gun can be used either in fully automatic remote-controlled or gyro-stabilized one-man local-control modes. The gun is housed in a plastic cupola and is designed for both surface and anti-aircraft fire. The barrel is liquid-cooled, whilst the feed system contains 40 ready-use rounds with another 128 rounds stowed in racks within the turret. The ammunition is of two types, a prefragmented round for use against aerial targets and a semi-armour-piercing round with a delay action fuse for use against surface targets. The turret can also be fitted with launching rails for 57-mm (2.24-in) illuminating rockets if required. The Mk 1 gun is in service with the navies of Sweden, Malaysia, Norway, Indonesia, Singapore, Thailand and Yugoslavia.

In the early 1980s a low-radar-signature variant, the all-purpose **57-mm Bofors SAK Mk 2**, was built. Using the same ammunition types it has a completely new automatic reloading system with 120 ready-use rounds in the cupola, and an improved electro-hydraulic remote-control system that greatly enhances the weapons accuracy against all types of targets, including sea-skimming anti-ship missiles. The Mk 2 is already in mass production for the navies of Sweden, Canada, Mexico and several unidentified countries.

Specification
SAK Mk 1
Calibre: 57 mm (2.24 in)
No. of barrels: one
Weight: 6 tons
Elevation: − 10° to +75°
Muzzle velocity: 1025 m (3,363 ft) per second
Projectile weight: 2.4 kg (5.3 lb)
Total weight of rounds: surface 6.8 kg (15 lb), and anti-aircraft 5.8 kg (12.8 lb)
Maximum rate of fire: 200 rpm
Maximum effective ranges: surface fire 13 km (8.1 miles), and anti-aircraft fire 5 km (3.1 miles)

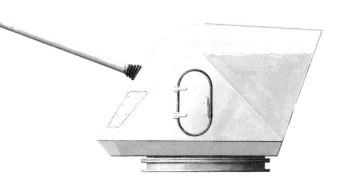

Right: Designed for combating both surface and aerial targets, the all-purpose Bofors 57-mm SAK Mk 2 is fitted to a completely automatic fire control system and is enclosed in a compact plastic turret to provide as low a radar signature as possible.

Below: The single 57 mm L/70 automatic gun mounting fitted to the 'Spica' class fast patrol boat is equipped with rocket-launching rails for 57-mm (2-in) rockets. The elevation arc of the gun is − 10° to +75°, rate of fire being as much as 200 rounds per minute.

Specification
SAK Mk 2
Calibre: 57 mm (2.24 in)
No. of barrels: one
Weight: 6 tons

Elevation: − 10° to +75°
Muzzle velocity: 1025 m (3,363 ft) per second
Projectile weight: 2.8 kg (6.2 lb)
Total weight of round: 6.5 kg (14.3 lb)

Maximum rate of fire: 220 rpm
Maximum effective ranges: surface fire 17 km (10.6 miles), and anti-aircraft fire 6 km (3.7 miles)

120-mm Bofors gun

The **120-mm Bofors** 46-calibre automatic gun was designed for use against surface and airborne targets. Housed in a 4-mm (0.16-in) thick steel turret, the gun has two ready-use magazines mounted on the elevating cradle, and these are manually filled from a hoist system from the main magazine. The alternative to the automatic control is a gyro-stabilized one-man local control console. For this telescopic sights are fitted, whilst the hoist, elevation and traverse mechanisms can be operated by hand. The gun barrel itself has an exchangeable liner, and is water-cooled to help prolong barrel life. At present only the Finnish and Indonesian navies have the gun in service on corvette- and frigate-sized vessels respectively. Sweden does not use guns of this calibre – it formerly operated an older, radar controlled 120-mm (4.7-in)

The first post-war destroyer design for the Swedish navy was armed with twin turrets for its 50-calibre 120-mm (4.7-in) guns. The Halland *is now deleted but the gun type is still active with the Dutch, Peruvian and Colombian navies.*

Naval Surface-to-Air Missiles

Silhouetted by the dawn, the twin Mk 26 launcher of the nuclear-powered cruiser USS Mississippi is loaded with two Standard SM-1 MR missiles.

Nowhere has the technological revolution affected warfare more than at sea. Today's warships fight with radar, computers and missiles to the extent that where fighting ships formerly bristled with light and heavy anti-aircraft guns, modern defences consist of a few solitary missile launchers.

During the period after World War II a vast array of research establishments, special trials ships, apparently unlimited money and groups of industrial contractors were employed to solve the problem of furnishing major surface combatants with a surface-to-air missile (SAM) defence that was able to go to sea.

Although the launcher and its missile were from an early stage seen to be the answer, it required considerable resources just for the peripheral equipment and redesigning of the ships to carry the systems. For example, most of the first-generation missiles literally had to have the launch vessels stripped to the framework and rebuilt just to accommodate the associated magazines, power supplies and electronic systems below decks; then provision had to be made for the launchers and radar equipment above decks. By the early 1960s these beam-riding area-defence missiles were overtaken by a second type specifically designed for short/medium-range defence of individual vessels, such systems being typified by the Tartar and Sea Cat systems. Surprisingly,

in all the 'brush wars' fought around the world it was not until the Vietnam War that the naval SAM was first fired in anger. This war allowed the area-defence weapon (in the form of the Talos and Terrier) to be fired on a number of occasions against North Vietnamese MiG aircraft, scoring a total of seven known kills. The short-range systems did not get their chance until the 1982 Falklands war, when dozens of Sea Dart, Sea Slug, Sea Wolf and Sea Cat missiles (as well as land-based Blowpipe and Rapier SAMs) were fired as part of a layered air defence network against Argentine aircraft. Although recent evidence suggests that the naval SAMs downed a combined total of only 11 aircraft, this weapon proved itself once and for all to be more efficient than the gun in anti-air warfare defence.

A British Aerospace Sea Dart missile is launched. Sea Dart, an area defence system, was used operationally for the first time in the 1982 South Atlantic conflict, shooting down at least five aircraft.

Naval Crotale

Derived from the ground-launched Crotale system, the **Naval Crotale** variant was designed as a self-defence missile for use by ships against medium-altitude, low-altitude and sea-skimming attacks by aircraft, helicopters and missiles. It can also be used against surface targets in an emergency. The standard **Naval Crotale 8B** version comprises a turret assembly with two co-axial units (one with eight ready-to-fire missiles in their container-launchers and the other supporting the fire-control radar and IR tracking systems), a shelter housing the electronic data-processing cabinets, and an operator's console in the combat operation centre for supervising the system and sending the fire orders. A new version, the **Modular Naval Crotale**, is available in four (**Model 4MS**) or eight (**Model 8MS**) round launcher turrets, and is designed to arm ships as small as 500 tons. The **Naval Crotale 8S** (also known as **EDIR**) has increased capability against cruise missiles and will replace earlier models aboard the 'Georges Leygues' and 'Tourville' classes and the carriers *Foch* and *Clemenceau*. The other main user is Saudi Arabia, whose 'Madina' class frigates have been fitted with the octuple model 8MS. In all the various Crotale SAM systems target acquisition and tracking is performed by the radar of the Naval Crotale system itself after it has been designated by the ship's sensors. Missile guidance is performed by an improved line-of-sight unit. For sea-skimming targets both the missile and target are tracked by a differential IR technique. Once in the vicinity of the target the warhead is detonated by an infra-red proximity fuse with a built-in time delay so that the prefragmented splinters formed by the detonation are concentrated to impact in the most vulnerable zone of the target. A total of 18 reload rounds is normally carried for the eight-round launchers.

Naval Crotale uses the same basic solid-fuelled Matra missile as the land-based version, having a Mach 2.5 performance and capable of tackling anti-ship missiles.

Specification
Naval Crotale 8S
Type: point-defence missile
Dimensions: length 2.89 m (9 ft 5.8 in); diameter 0.15 m (5.9 in); span 0.53 m (1 ft 8.9 in)
Weights: total round 85 kg (187 lb); warhead 15-kg (33-lb) HE-fragmentation
Performance: maximum speed Mach 2.3; range 0.7-13 km (0.43-8.08 miles) against helicopters and non-manoeuvring targets, or 0.7-8.5 km (0.43-5.28 miles) against manoeuvring targets, or 0.7-6.5 km (0.43-4.04 miles) against sea-skimming targets; altitude limits 4-5000 m (13-16,405 ft)

The destroyer Georges Leygues *is seen tied up alongside the wharf in Beirut. The eight-round Crotale launcher and its associated radar systems are prominent at the top of the photograph.*

Masurca

Developed in the mid-1950s, the **Masurca** is a wholly French-designed and French-built medium-range solid-propellant area-defence naval SAM for task force and carrier escorts. Only three French ships are equipped with the missile and its associated radar systems, namely the missile frigates *Duquesne* and *Suffren* and the cruiser *Colbert*. Each vessel has a 3D surveillance radar, a weapon-direction system, two independent fire-control radars and a twin-rail launcher with a 48-round magazine. Two types of guidance were developed for the definitive production version, the **Masurca Mk 2 Mod 2**, which used a command to line-of-sight beam-riding technique and **Mod 3** with semi-active radar homing. They entered service in 1964 and 1970 but only the later model remains in service, the former having been phased out in 1975. A solid-propellant booster unit is fitted, and in under 5 seconds this accelerates the missile to a speed of about Mach 3, at which point the sustainer motor takes over. During flight the missile follows a trajectory which is determined by proportional navigation as it keeps its antenna pointed at the target illuminated by one of the two fire-control radars. The Masurca system has undergone an extensive upgrading programme to increase its reliability and to improve its engagement envelope so that it can be used well into the 1990s.

Specification
Masurca Mk 2 Mod 3
Type: medium-range area-defence missile
Dimensions: length of missile 5.38 m (17 ft 7.8 in) and of booster 3.32 m (10 ft 10.7 in); diameter of missile 0.406 m

Originally a relatively primitive beam-riding command guidance missile, the Masurca is now, as the result of continuous development, a sophisticated SARH (semi-active radar homing) missile with a range of 50 km (31 miles).

Masurca (continued)

(1 ft 4 in) and of booster 0.57 m (1 ft 10.4 in); span of missile 0.77 m (2 ft 6.3 in) and of booster 1.50 m (4 ft 11.1 in)
Weights: missile 950 kg (2,094 lb); booster 1148 kg (2,531 lb); warhead 120 kg (264 lb) HE-fragmentation
Performance: maximum speed Mach 3; range 50 km (31 miles); altitude limits 30-23000 m (100-75,460 ft)

Masurca is an area defence missile developed in association with Matra. Currently being upgraded, the system will serve into the 1990s.

ITALY

Albatros

The **Albatros Mk 2** medium-range surface-to-air missile system uses the Aspide multi-role missile and can be integrated with various types of shipboard fire-control systems. It can engage anti-ship missiles of either the pop-up or diving type as well as the normal range of manoeuvring aircraft targets. The original **Albatros Mk 1** system developed in 1968-71 utilized the RIM-7H5 missile of the NATO Sea Sparrow project. Like the Sea Sparrow, the Aspide missile uses semi-active radar homing, the trajectory to the target being of the collision type with proportional navigation. Target-illumination is by a continuous-wave radar array which is part of the ship's electronic outfit. The launcher can either be a standard eight-round cell with associated reload magazine, or for ships down to 200 tons a four-round cell which can be reloaded if required via standard shipboard replenishment at sea facilities. Each missile is stored in its own canister that also serves as the launch tube. The missile is basically the same as the air-launched version but has cropped wings and fins. Since it was developed, the Albatros missile system has been adopted by at least 15 navies worldwide, including Argentina, Colombia, Ecuador, Egypt, Greece, Iraq, Italy, Japan, Libya, Morocco, Nigeria, Peru, Spain, Thailand and Venezuela.

Specification
Aspide
Type: point-defence missile

Above: Albatros has been developed by Selenia using Aspide missiles, which also serve as air-to-air weapons amongst other roles.

Dimensions: length 3.70 m (12 ft 1.7 in); diameter 0.203 m (8 in); span 0.80 m 2 ft 7.5 in)
Weights: total round 204 kg (450 lb); warhead 33-kg (72.75-lb) HE-fragmentation
Performance: maximum speed Mach 2.5+; range 18.5 km (11.5 miles); altitude limits 15-5000 m (50-16,405 ft)

Right: An Aspide missile is launched from the Albatros system of a 'Lupo' class frigate built in Italy for the Peruvian navy. Albatros has been adopted by 15 navies to date, including that of Italy.

Below: An Aspide missile is launched from the octuple launcher of an Italian 'Maestrale' class frigate. The Albatros system is replacing the NATO Sea Sparrow system in the vessels of the Italian navy.

Sea Cat

Designed and built by Short Brothers in the late 1950s, the **Sea Cat** was the first shipborne SAM system designed for close-range air defence in place of rapid-firing guns such as the 40-mm Bofors. The first guided trials took place in 1960, the initial shipboard trials following on board HMS *Decoy* in 1961. A series of full-scale shipboard trials before service acceptance was then undertaken in 1962 aboard the same ship, the missile system becoming known as the **Guided Weapon System (GWS) Mk 20** in the Royal Navy. The Sea Cat has a dual-thrust motor, four fixed fins, hydraulically-driven wings and a continuous-rod blast warhead with both delayed action contact and proximity fuses. The missile is guided by radio command and can be integrated with almost any type of sighting and fire-control system, as the continual improvement and updating programme in the Royal Navy has proved with the introduction into service of the **GWS Mk 21** and **GWS Mk 22** versions with different radars to give darkfire capabilities. The system is due to continue in service with the Royal Navy until the mid-1990s. The launcher used most often is a quadruple hand-loaded version, although some of the countries to which the missile has been exported use a lightweight triple unit. Since it entered production in the 1960s 18 navies have bought the missile, but it was not until the 1982 Falklands war that it was used in combat. There it proved to be a useful 'scare' defence, but its use against modern high-performance manoeuvring targets must now be somewhat in doubt. Current operator countries include Australia, Brazil, Chile, India, Indonesia, Iran, the Netherlands, New Zealand, Nigeria, Pakistan, and the United Kingdom.

Specification
Sea Cat
Type: point-defence missile
Dimensions: length 1.48 m (4 ft 10.3 in); diameter 0.1905 m (7.5 in); span 0.65 m (2 ft 1.6 in)
Weights: total round 68 kg (149.9 lb); warhead 15-kg (33-lb) HE-fragmentation
Performance: maximum speed Mach 1; range 5.5 km (3.4 miles); altitude limits 30-915 m (100-3,000 ft)

Above: Developed in the late 1950s, Sea Cat entered service as the Royal Navy's primary short-range air defence system in the early 1960s, replacing gun systems such as the 40-mm Bofors.

Right: Seen aboard the 'County' class missile destroyer HMS Antrim in the South Atlantic, Sea Cat first saw action in the battles around the Falkland Islands. While rapidly becoming less than effective against high speed targets, several Argentine aircraft were believed to have been destroyed by the system.

Below: Launched from the standard four-round launcher, Sea Cat is effective to about 5.5 km (3.4 miles) and is capable of Mach 1. Interceptions can be made between 30 and 915 m (100-3000 ft). Sea Cat is in service with some 15 navies, including that of Argentina.

Sea Dart

The **Guided Weapon System (GWS) Mk 30** otherwise known as the **BAe Sea Dart** was designed by British Aerospace in the 1960s as a third-generation area-defence naval SAM capable of engaging targets such as aircraft and missiles at both very high and, under certain circumstances, very low altitudes. The system was used operationally during the 1982 Falklands war, being officially credited with eight kills: a Puma helicopter, a Learjet 35A reconnaissance aircraft, a BAe Canberra B.Mk 62 bomber, one McDonnell Douglas A-4B Skyhawk, three A-4C Skyhawks, and tragically a single British Gazelle AH.Mk 1 helicopter, brought down in error. Two of

the Skyhawks were shot down at very low level, outside the missile's official performance envelope. The launcher is a twin unit and is coupled with two Type 909 target tracking and illuminator radars on the Type 42 (20 missiles) destroyers, 'Invincible' class aircraft carriers (20 missiles), and HMS *Bristol*

(40 missiles), the sole Type 82 class destroyer built. Sea Dart can also be used out to 25-30 km (15.5-18.6 miles) against surface targets if required. The system was also sold to Argentina for its two Type 42 destroyers, and this probably explains the low (25%) kill rate from the 31 missiles launched as

Sea Dart is an area defence missile, powered by a Rolls-Royce Odin ramjet with rocket booster for launch. The missile depicted has a cover over the ramjet intake.

the enemy already knew its performance capabilities. Guidance is of the semi-active homing type with associated proportional navigation. A ramjet engine powers the missile in flight after a solid-propellant booster unit has brought it up to the velocity required for the main engine to take over. Unfortunately, in the 1981 defence cuts a considerably improved **Sea Dart Mk 2** was cancelled: this was a version to combat the Soviet cruise missiles designed to go into a terminal dive from high altitude, and this politico-economic cut has left a serious gap in fleet defences for the period of the late

1980s and early 1990s. A **Lightweight Sea Dart** system has also been developed for ships down to 300 tons displacement: this uses deck-mounted container-launchers with simplified radars and fire-control units. The People's Republic of China planned to purchase this system as part of a modification package for its 'Luda' class destroyers, but the deal was cancelled because of funding problems.

In addition to arming the UK's Type 82 and Type 42 destroyers, Sea Dart is mounted on the three 'Invincible' class aircraft-carriers. It is also used by Argentina on their Type 42 destroyers. A lightweight system has been developed to arm vessels down to only 300 tons.

Specification
Sea Dart
Type: medium-range area-defence missile
Dimensions: length 4.36 m (14 ft 3.7 in); diameter 0.42 m (1 ft 4.5 in); span 0.91 m (2 ft 11.8 in)
Weights: total round 550 kg (1,213 lb); warhead HE-fragmentation
Performance: maximum speed Mach 3+; range 65 km (40.4 miles); altitude limits 30-18290 m (100-60,000 ft)

Sea Wolf

Conceived in 1962 and designed by British Aerospace, the **Sea Wolf** was originally developed as the replacement for the widely-fitted Sea Cat SAM system. Unfortunately, in the **Guided Weapon System Mk 25 Mod 0** devised for the Royal Navy, the weapons package proved so large that it could be fitted on warships only down to the size of 2,500 tons or so. In fact it was the room required to fit two complete manually-reloaded GWS Mk 25 systems with their attendant 30-round magazines and six-round launchers that helped to finalize the dimensions and displacement of the Type 22 frigates in excess of the Sea Dart-equipped Type 42 destroyers.

Sea Wolf is a fully automatic point-defence system with radio command to line-of-sight guidance coupled with radar differential or low light TV tracking. The missile's manoeuvrability and speed allows it to engage small Mach 2 sea-skimming missiles and aircraft with two-missile salvos in the most severe weather and sea states. During the Falklands war the Type 22 frigates HMS *Brilliant* and HMS *Broadsword*, together with the converted 'Leander' class frigate HMS *Andromeda* with only one launcher, used the missile operationally, one of the Type 22s acting as the close-range air-defence ship or 'goalkeeper' to the carriers. The first combat use was from the *Brilliant* on 12 May when the ship engaged a flight of four McDonnell Douglas A-4 Skyhawks, shooting down two and forcing a third to crash as it evaded a missile. The official list credits the Sea Wolf with five kills, although recent evidence now suggests it was only the three described above, plus a possible fourth. What actually came out of the war was that the system required a number of software upgrades to increase its reliability: on several occasions the computers associated with target-tracking broke lock because they had what was akin to a nervous breakdown when trying to differentiate between targets flying close together.

The modifications culminated in a successful trial whereby a Sea Wolf engaged and destroyed a sea skimming MM.38 Exocet anti-ship missile.

Several lightweight Sea Wolf systems have been developed, the **GWS Mk 25 Mod 3** with Type 911(1) dual frequency radar trackers being installed on the Batch 2 and Batch 3 Type 22 frigates. A vertical-launch Sea Wolf was demonstrated back in 1968 when it was considered a low priority programme. It is now being installed on the new Type 23 'Duke' class frigates as the **GWS Mk 26** with Type 911(2) radar trackers. Surprisingly, a development the Royal Navy has not adopted is the conversion of standard, four-round Sea Cat launchers to take Sea Wolf together with the fitting of suitable radar and electronics. For the 1990s, the advanced **GWS Mk 27** is under consideration. This is an evolutionary development of the vertical launch Mk 26, with an autonomous fire-and-forget terminal homing seeker for use against all aspect attacks and an increase in effective range to around 10 km (6.2 miles), giving limited area air defence coverage. To date, the Royal Navy is the only user of Sea Wolf.

Specification
Sea Wolf
Type: point-defence missile
Dimensions: length 1.90 m (6 ft 3 in); diameter 0.30 m (11.8 in); span 0.45 m (1 ft 5.7 in)
Weights: total round 82 kg (180.4 lb); warhead ? HE-fragmentation
Performance: maximum speed Mach 2+; range 6.5 km (4.04 miles); altitude limits about 4.7-3050 m (15-10,000 ft)

A Sea Wolf missile is launched from a Type 22 frigate. The missile is highly effective, but with ancillary radar, launch and command systems the Sea Wolf system is rather heavy, and to operate two launchers effectively the Type 22 frigates have to be larger than Type 42 destroyers.

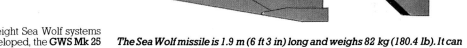

The Sea Wolf missile is 1.9 m (6 ft 3 in) long and weighs 82 kg (180.4 lb). It can be treated as a round of ammunition.

SA-N-1 'Goa' and SA-N-7 'Gadfly'

The two-stage, solid-propellant **SA-N-1 'Goa'** (Soviet designation M1) entered service in 1961 as the first Soviet naval SAM to be widely deployed with the fleet. It is derived from the ground-launched SA-3a 'Goa', and is considered to be an effective missile at low to medium altitudes, and in the surface-to-surface role out to the radar horizon. It is a medium-range area-defence weapon that is fired from a twin-arm launcher which is rotated to the 90° vertical position for reloading from an under-deck 16-round magazine. The four rectangular fins are folded until the missile leaves the launcher. An HE-fragmentation or 10-kiloton nuclear warhead can be fitted, the former having a 12.5-m (41-ft) lethal burst radius at low levels against targets the size of the McDonnell Douglas F-4 Phantom. Guidance is by radio command, although the latest up-rated versions of the 'Peel Group' naval fire-control radar array associated with the missile have been converted for semi-active terminal homing for use with the **SA-N-3b 'Goa'** variant. The 'Goa' is also used by India and Poland.

In 1981 the long-term replacement for the SA-N-1 system, the **SA-N-7 'Gadfly'** appeared fitted to the then new 'Sovremenny' class. Although the missile has not yet been seen, US sources claim that it is a navalized version of the Soviet army's Mach 3 SA-11 'Gadfly' system, and is very similar in appearance to the US Navy's Standard MR-1 SAM. The single rail, quick re-load launcher is associated with six or eight 'Front Dome' target-illumination radars for the missile's semi-active radar homing. The SA-N-7 has a conventional HE warhead and can engage targets between 30 m (100 ft) and 14000 m (46,000 ft) at ranges between a maximum of 28 km (17.4 miles) and a minimum of 3 km (1.86 miles).

Specification
SA-N-1 'Goa'
Dimensions: length 6.70 m (21 ft 11.8 in); diameter of missile 0.46 m (1 ft 6.1 in) and of booster 0.701 m (2 ft 3.6 in); span of missile 1.50 m (4 ft 11.1 in)
Weights: total round 946 kg (2,085.5 lb) for SA-N-1a and 950 kg (2,094.4 lb) for SA-N-1b; warhead 60-kg (132-lb) HE or 10-kiloton nuclear
Performance: maximum speed Mach 2.1; range 6-22 km (3.7-13.7 miles); altitude limits 90-15250 m (295-50,030 ft)

The first Soviet navy SAM to see wide service, the SA-N-1 'Goa' is thought to have been developed from the land-based system of the same name.

Below: A 'Kashin' class destroyer launches an SA-N-1 Goa. The engagement envelope of the Mach 2.1 missile is between 6 and 22 km (3.7-13.7 miles) at heights ranging from 90 to 15250 m (295-50,030 ft). The 60-kg (132-lb) warhead can be high explosive or low-yield nuclear.

Above: Visible behind the twin 130-mm gun mount on the Soviet destroyer Sovremenny, the single-rail launcher for the SA-N-7 is thought to be capable of rapid reloading and firing. The presence of six separate fire control radars implies a multiple target system.

Above: The twin-rail SA-N-1 launcher aboard a 'Kashin' class destroyer is roll-stabilized to give stable launch conditions in rough sea states. There are over 60 systems in use on 'SAM Kotlin', 'Kanin', 'Kynda', 'Kashin' and 'Kresta 1' class vessels, the last two classes having two twin launchers.

SA-N-3 'Goblet' and SA-N-6 'Grumble'

The two-stage solid-propellant **SA-N-3 'Goblet'** entered service in 1967 as the second-generation medium-range low/medium-altitude area-defence follow-on to the SA-N-1 'Goa' system in Soviet navy service. With improved anti-air warfare capabilities, the SA-N-3 can also be used in the surface-to-surface role out to the radar horizon. Unlike other contemporary Soviet navy SAMs it has no Soviet army equivalent, and is not derived from the SA-6 'Gainful' as often stated. The SA-N-3 may be fitted with either an HE-fragmentation or a 25-kiloton nuclear warhead, and is fired from a twin-arm

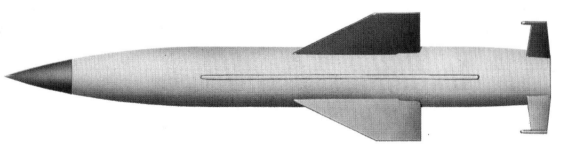

A generation farther on from the SA-N-1, the SA-N-3 'Goblet' is a Mach 2.8 missile that does not seem to have a land-based equivalent.

launcher, the system rotating to the vertical for reloading from an under-deck magazine. The proportion of missiles fitted with nuclear warheads in the ship's outfit has been assessed by some sources as 25 per cent. Guidance is by radio command via 'Head Light' series fire-control radar array. The 'Goblet' is fitted to 'Kresta II' and 'Kara' class missile cruisers as well as to the 'Moskva' and 'Kiev' classes of aviation ships.

In 1978 the replacement SA-N-6 'Grumble' system appeared on the 'Kirov' nuclear-powered cruiser class as part of what is now known to be a Soviet AEGIS-style SAM area-defence system for surface task groups. The single-stage missile is vertically launched from silos served by eight-round rotary magazines, and is an advanced high-performance SAM adapted from the Soviet army's SA-10 specifically to provide the navy with a missile that has extensive anti-cruise missile capabilities. Missile guidance is semi-active for the mid-course phase (with target-illumination from the 'Top Dome' radar) and then active radar for the terminal phase to give a much more accurate interception. The system has also entered service on the 'Slava' class missile cruisers. The 7m (22ft 11.6in) long solid-propellant Mach 6 missile has a 100kg (220lb) conventional HE warhead and can engage targets between 10 m (33 ft) and 27,500 m (90,000 ft) at ranges between 9.6 and 64 km (6 and 40 miles).

Specification
SA-N-3 'Goblet'
Type: medium-range area-defence missile
Dimensions: length 6.40 m (21 ft 0 in); diameter 0.70 m (2 ft 3.6 in); span 1.70 m (5 ft 6.9 in)
Weights: total round not known; warhead 150-kg (331-lb) HE or 25-kiloton nuclear
Performance: maximum speed Mach 2.8; range 6-30 km (3.7-18.6 miles) in early versions or 6-55 km (3.7-34 miles) in later versions; altitude limits 90-24500 m (295-80,380 ft)

Above: The large twin-rail launcher aboard 'Kresta II' class cruisers may be a dual purpose system, capable of firing SS-N-14 anti-submarine missiles as well as the SA-N-3. The system is also fitted to the 'Kiev', 'Kara' and 'Moskva' classes.

Right: The hatch covers over the vertical launch system aboard the Soviet cruiser Slava conceal eight-round rotary magazines for the SA-N-6 missiles carried. The SA-N-6 has also been fitted to the 'Kirov' class cruisers as an anti-missile system.

SA-N-4 'Gecko' and SA-N-9
USSR

The single-stage solid-propellant **SA-N-4 'Gecko'** entered service in the early 1970s as the Soviet navy's point-defence missile system for both large and small surface combatants. Based on the Soviet army's SA-8, the SA-N-4 uses a fully retractable twin-arm launcher with an 18-round under-decks missile magazine. The missile has an HE warhead and can be used out to its maximum range as a surface-to-surface missile in emergency. Its guidance is of the command type via the 'Pop Group' fire-control radar system associated with each launcher. Unlike other modern Soviet naval SAMs the 'Gecko' has been widely exported to a number of Soviet client states as part of the armament outfit for export versions of the 'Nanuchka' missile corvettes and 'Koni' class light frigates.

A new vertical-launch point-defence system was deployed in the 1980s aboard later 'Kiev' and 'Kirov' class vessels and 'Udaloy' class destroyers, associated with a radar system given the NATO reporting name 'Cross Swords'. The medium range, high-performance **SA-NX-9** is likely to have active or semi-active radar homing and a ceiling of some 18,250 m (60,000 ft).

Above: Little is known of the SA-N-9 system, other than the fact that it is a short- to medium-range system and may be active radar homing. First deployment is in the Udaloy large ASW destroyer, with pop-up systems fore and aft.

Right: In addition to the potent SA-N-6 in its vertical launchers, the Kirov has two 'pop-up' missile systems firing the point defence SA-N-4 'Gecko'. The two bandstand-like launcher covers are visible in front of and to either side of the bridge.

Specification
SA-N-4 'Gecko'
Type: point-defence missile
Dimensions: length 3.20 m (10 ft 6 in); diameter 0.21 m (8.25 in); span 0.64 m (2 ft 1.2 in)
Weights: total round 190 kg (418.9 lb); warhead 50-kg (110-lb) HE-fragmentation

Performance: maximum speed Mach 2; range 1.6-12 km (1-7.5 miles); altitude limits 50-13000 m (165-42,650 ft)

SA-N-5 'Grail'

USSR

The solid-propellant single-stage **SA-N-5 'Grail'** is the shipborne version of the Soviet army's shoulder-launched SA-7b short-range IR-homing SAM. The Soviets give the missile system the designation **9M32M** and the missile the designation **Strela 2M**. It is fitted aboard various small combatants, amphibious warfare vessels and auxiliary ships as a four-round pedestal mount with an adjacent reload locker containing a further four or eight launchers. The shoulder-launched version is also used by the Soviet Naval Infantry from the decks of amphibious warfare vessels and by other nations such as East Germany, Egypt, Israel and Syria from fast attack craft. The missile relies upon a pursuit interception to engage low-flying aircraft, and has proved especially effective against helicopters and slow-flying fixed-wing aircraft such as observation planes. A simple optical sight and tracker unit is used for both types of mounts, the IR

seeker being activated when the operator has acquired the target. An indicator light (denoting seeker acquisition) tells the operator when he is free to launch the missile. In order to defeat flare countermeasures, filters have been installed in the seeker. The SA-N-5 uses an increased-thrust propellant to give a greater range and speed in comparison with the earlier SA-7a.

Specification
SA-N-5 'Grail'
Type: point-defence missile
Dimensions: length 1.29 m (4 ft 2.8 in); diameter 0.07 m (2.76 in); span not known
Weights: total round 9.2 kg (20.3 lb); warhead 2.5-kg (5.5-lb) HE-fragmentation
Performance: maximum speed Mach 1.95; range 4.8 km (3 miles); altitude limits 45-4800 m (150-15,750 ft)

The SA-N-5 Grail is a simple adaptation of the SA-7 man-portable infra-red guided missile. The 'Polnocny' class landing ship shown has its two four-round launching posts amidships just ahead of the platform. On deck astern of the posts can be seen the reload lockers.

Terrier and Tartar

USA

The **Terrier** area-defence missile was developed from the technology involved in the Talos missile programme, but actually preceded that missile into service. Compared with Talos the Terrier was much more compact, being small enough to be fitted aboard the missile frigates or large destroyers that were being constructed to carry missile systems. Since the start of its development in 1949, the Terrier has evolved gradually over the years with only one major component at a time changed to produce new variants. The original Mach 1.8 beam-riding missile was designated **BW-0** (later **RIM-2A**) with range limits of 18.5 km (11.5 miles) and altitude limits of 1525-15240 m

One of the earliest generations of naval surface-to-air missiles, Tartar was supplied to the navies of the USA Australia, France, Italy, Japan, the Netherlands and the Federal Republic of Germany.

(5,000-50,000 ft). The next version, the **BW-1** (**RIM-2B**), was a re-engineered BW-0 but had no significant performance improvements in either range or altitude. The **BT-3** (**RIM-2C**) which entered service in 1956 had new tail controls, improved beam-riding guidance

and a new motor propellant. The improvements increased the velocity to Mach 3 and the range and maximum altitude limit by 50 per cent. This was rapidly followed by the **BT-3A** (**RIM-2D**), which added a surface-to-surface capability to the Terrier system when

Terrier has been largely superseded by Standard, but for many years it provided air defence for the US Navy. The RIM-2E, seen launched from the cruiser USS Josephus Daniels in 1973, had a maximum range in excess of 70 km (43 miles).

248

it entered service in 1958 and increased the SAM range to 37 km (23 miles). A nuclear version with the 1-kiloton yield W45 fission type warhead was also produced alongside this variant and designated **BT-3(N)**; in its redesignated **RIM-2D(N)** form this version is still in service on a number of US Navy ships equipped with the Standard SM-1/SM-2ER system. The last planned variant, the **HT-3 (RIM-2E)**, entered service one year earlier than the BT-3 and introduced continuous-wave semi-active homing as the guidance mode, which increased its low-altitude engagement capability and improved the single-shot kill capability figure by over 30 per cent compared with those of the beam-riding variants. The last HT-3 versions, delivered in the mid-1960s, were fitted with a new sustainer and power supply that raised the range to 74 km (46 miles); these missiles were then designated **RIM-2F**. Production of the Terrier ended in 1966 after some 8,000 rounds of all marks had been manufactured. The conventional warhead versions had by 1986 been superseded by variants of the Standard missile.

In 1952 a need was appreciated for a semi-active homing missile as a complement to the larger systems to engage low-flying targets and to replace the 127-mm (5-in) gun mount on a one-for-one basis. The result was the basic version of the Mach 1.8 **Tartar** missile **(RIM-24A)**, which was effective between ranges of 1.85 and 13.7 km (1.15 and 8.5 miles) and altitude limits of 15 and 16765 m (50 and 55,000 ft). However, a **Product Improved Tartar** was soon sought, the **Improved Tartar (RIM-24B)** version entering service in 1963. This had a range increase to 32.5 km (20.2 miles) and an upper altitude engagement limit of 21335 m

(70,000 ft). It also has a useful surface-to-surface anti-ship capability. About 6,500 rounds were produced, and most countries that were supplied with the type (Australia, France, Italy, Japan, the Netherlands and West Germany in addition to the USA) have now converted to the Standard missile.

Specification
RIM-2D(N) Terrier
Type: medium-range area-defence missile
Dimensions: length of missile 4.115 m (13 ft 6 in) and of booster 7.874 m (25 ft 10 in); diameter of missile 0.343 m (1 ft 1.5 in) and of booster 0.457 m (1 ft 6 in); span of missile 1.074 m (3 ft 6.3 in)
Weights: missile 535.2 kg (1,180 lb); booster 825.5 kg (1,820 lb); warhead W45 1-kiloton nuclear
Performance: maximum speed Mach 3; range 37 km (23 miles); altitude limits 150-24385 m (500-80,000 ft)

Specification
RIM-24B Improved Tartar
Type: medium-range area-defence missile
Dimensions: length 4.724 m (15 ft 6 in); diameter 0.343 m (13.5 in); span 0.610 m (2 ft 0 in)
Weights: total round 594.2 kg (1,310 lb); warhead ? HE
Performance: maximum speed Mach 1.8; range 32.3 km (20.1 miles); altitude limits 15-21335 m (50-70,000 ft)

First trials of the AEGIS air defence system used Tartar and Terrier missiles while awaiting development of the Standard. A Tartar missile is seen being launched from the trials ship USS Norton Sound against a supersonic Firebee drone.

USA
Standard

The semi-active radar homing conventional warhead **Standard** family of naval SAMs started development in the early 1960s as the replacement for the Terrier and Tartar systems. The latter's replacement was the **Standard SM-1MR (RIM-66A)**, and was designed with an engagement range of 46.35 km (28.8 miles) and an altitude of 45-15240 m (150-50,000 ft). The Terrier's replacement, designated **Standard SM-1ER (RIM-67A)** had a range of 74 km (46 miles) and altitude limits of 45-24385 m (150-80,000 ft). After entering service from 1968 onwards in ships undergoing refits and on new-build warships, both missiles have undergone several reliability improvement and performance update programmes. A new dual-thrust motor for the Standard SM-1MR produced the **RIM-66B** missile with a 45 per cent increase in maximum range and a 25 per cent increase in the upper altitude engagement limit. In most cases the changes that have been made have been incorporated as production 'Block' changes which have not given rise to any new designations. The most recent version of the SM-1MR, however, has been given the designation **RIM-66C or Standard SM-2MR** as it is the missile designed to operate with the AEGIS air-defence system. The AEGIS system allows for mid-course missile

guidance which extends the range of the Tartar-sized missile by 60 per cent to around 74 km (46 miles). A corresponding **Standard SM-2ER** variant or **RIM-67B** is not designed to be fired by AEGIS-equipped ships, although improvements in its booster technology adds a complete Mach number to its velocity to give a kinetic range far outside the current limits of an AEGIS type fire-control system. However, the improvements considerably enhance the weapons' capabilities against high-performance aircraft and missiles. Those ships equipped with Terriers and its Standard SM-1ER replacement have suitable fire-control systems and are getting the Standard SM-2ER.

A low-yield nuclear fission warhead, the W81, is under development for deployment with some 500 or so Standard SM-2MR and SM-2ER missiles from the mid-1980s onwards to replace the Terrier RIM-2D(N). Designated **Standard SM-2(N)**, the missile will become part

Latest in a line of missiles stretching back to the late 1940s, the Standard missile, in its SM-2 form, is used in the advanced AEGIS system.

Standard SM-2MR missiles are carried aboard the guided missile trials ships USS Norton Sound. The SM-2 version of the Standard missile   *almost doubles the range of the first model, and the greatly uprated electronics of the guidance system ensures improved performance.*

of the ship's normal missile outfit. All models currently have the same 97.4 kg (214.7-lb) conventional High Explosive warhead with contact and proximity fuzes. The US Navy uses all four versions of Standard, while the SM-1MR is also used by Australia, France, West Germany, Italy, Japan, the Netherlands and Spain.

Specification
RIM-66A Standard SM-1MR
Type: medium-range area-defence missile
Dimensions: length 4.47 m (14 ft 8 in) diameter 0.343 m (1 ft 1.5 in); span 0.914 m (3 ft 0 in)
Weights: total round 578.8 kg (1,276 lb)
Performance: maximum speed Mach 2+; range 46.25 km (28.75 miles); maximum altitude 15240 m (50,000 ft)

Specification
RIM-66B Standard SM-1MR
Type: medium-range area-defence missile
Dimensions: length 4.724 m (15 ft 6 in); diameter 0.343 m (1 ft 1.5 in); span 0.914 m (3 ft 0 in)
Weights: total round 608.7 kg (1,342 lb)
Performance: maximum speed Mach 2+; range 67 km (41.6 miles); maximum altitude 19050 m (62,500 ft)

Specification
RIM-66C Standard SM-2MR
Type: medium-range area-defence missile
Dimensions: length 4.724 m (15 ft 6 in); diameter 0.343 m (1 ft 1.5 in); span 0.914 m (3 ft 0 in)
Weights: total round 704 kg (1,553 lb)
Performance: maximum speed: Mach 2+; range 74 km (46 miles); maximum altitude 24385 m (80,000 ft)

Specification
RIM-67A Standard SM-1ER
Type: medium-range area-defence missile
Dimensions: length 7.976 m (26 ft 2 in); diameter 0.343 m (1 ft 1.5 in); span 0.914 m (3 ft 0 in)
Weights: total round 1306 kg (2,873 lb)
Performance: maximum speed Mach 2.5+; range 74 km (46 miles); maximum altitude 24385 m (80,000 ft)

Specification
RIM-67B Standard SM-2ER
Type: long-range area-defence missile
Dimensions: length 7.98 m (26 ft 2 in); diameter 0.343 m (1 ft 1.5 in); span 0.914 m (3 ft 0 in)
Weights: total round 1440 kg (3,172 lb)
Performance: maximum speed Mach 2.5+; range 150 km (93 miles); maximum altitude 30480 m (100,000 ft)

Off San Juan, the 'Belknap' class cruiser USS Wainwright *fires an SM-2ER missile. The extended range version of the Standard with the aid of the large booster motor is capable of ranges in the region of 150 km (93 miles), and the improved electronics and guidance enhance the performance considerably.*

Sea Sparrow

The **Basic Point Defense Missile System (BPDMS)** was developed in the early 1960s from the Sparrow air-to-air missile. The first **Sea Sparrow** was the **RIM-7E5** with expanding rod warhead and fired from the Mk 25 launcher, with the same semi-active radar homing as in the air-launched version. This was then reconfigured into the **RIM-7H** round and then the **RIM-7F** was used, based on the much improved AIM-7F. The semi-active radar-homing Sea Sparrow's performance was quite impressive as its engagement range was between 14.9 and 22.3 km (9.25 and 13.86 miles) depending upon the target's altitude, which could lie between 30 and 15240 m (100 and 50,000 ft). All versions were, however, considered deficient against low-flying cruise missiles which had by then become a major threat to US naval forces. In order to rectify this defect, low-altitude radar guidance and fusing capabilities were to be given to Block I RIM-7F missiles to enable them to hit targets below 15 m (50 ft), whilst Block II missiles were to get enhanced ECCM features. However, both fixes were dropped from the programme as the RIM-7F was superseded on the

The only missile defence carried by US Navy attack carriers is the Basic Point Defence Missile System, using Sea Sparrow missiles. The system has been in operation for some time, as this picture of USS John F. Kennedy *taken in the Mediterranean in 1969 demonstrates.*

Based on the AIM-7 Sparrow family of air-to-air missiles, the RIM-7 Sea Sparrow provides basic point defence for the US and NATO navies.

production line by the monopulse seeker equipped version, the **RIM-7M**. This incorporates the improvements introduced with AIM-7M and its new, improved blast-fragmentation warhead. The US Navy is deploying this missile in place of previous versions as fast as it can. The **NATO Sea Sparrow** differs from the BPDMS as it has fire-control systems that allow completely automatic engagements from target acquisition to missile impact. The missile used is the folding fin **RIM-7H5** version designed to fit the more compact eight-round launchers that NATO navies use. An **Improved PDMS** was introduced into the US Navy from 1973 onwards, and this has a much improved target-acquisition radar and data-handling system. The Sea Sparrow is operated by Belgium, Canada, Denmark, Greece, Italy, Japan, Norway, the Netherlands, Spain, the USA and West Germany.

Specification
RIM-7M Sea Sparrow
Type: point-defence missile

Dimensions: length 3.98 m (13 ft 1 in); diameter 0.203 m (8 in); span 1.02 m (3 ft 4 in)
Weights: total round 228.2 kg (503 lb);

warhead 40-kg (88-lb) HE-fragmentation
Performance: maximum speed Mach 3+; range 22.2 km (13.8 miles); altitude limits 8-15240 m (25-50,000 ft)

A Sea Sparrow missile is launched from its octuple box launcher aboard the amphibious command ship USS Mount Whitney.

USA
RAM

Interest in a short-range lightweight missile to complement the Phalanx close-in weapon system remained strong even after the Phalanx programme began in 1969. After considerable congressional pressure on the US Navy, the West German and Danish governments stepped in to save the programme from termination by signing memoranda of understanding to develop what by then was designated the **RIM-116A** or **Rolling Airframe Missile**, usually shortened as **RAM**, to arm both frigates and small combatants. The missile's unusual name is derived from the fact that it is spinning as it emerges from the launcher, after which fins are extended. Guidance is entirely passive, and initially uses a two-antenna broad-band radar seeker to point the terminal homing IR seeker head at the target. When this picks up the 'glint' of the target, the radar seeker is turned off as the IR guidance is considered much more accurate. The ship's fire-control system informs the missile's radar interferometer system of the frequency of the incoming target's active seeker head. The RAM employs the motor, fuse system and warhead of the Sidewinder air-to-air missile, the IR seeker of the Stinger surface-to-air missile, and the passive radar system described. A variety of launchers are planned including a 21-tube system (W. Germany), a lightweight eight-tube launcher (Denmark) or one five-round unit in each of the top two chambers of an octuple Sea Sparrow/ASROC launcher (US Navy). Sharply rising costs and limited success in trials to date has seen operational deployment deferred to the early 1990s.

Specification
RIM-116A RAM
Type: point-defence missile
Dimensions: length 2.794 m (9 ft 2 in); diameter 0.127 m (5 in); span 0.438 m (1 ft 5.25 in)
Weights: total round 72.1 kg (159 lb); warhead 10.2-kg (22.4-lb); HE-fragmentation
Performance: maximum speed Mach 2+; range 9.4 km (5.85 miles); altitude limits low to medium

The RAM, or Rolling Airframe Missile, employs components from both the Sidewinder AAM and the Stinger portable SAM, added to a passive radar seeker.

This is the first test launch of RAM over water, with only the nose of the missile out of the launch box but with the front fins already deploying.

Well on its way, the RAM missile accelerates towards its maximum velocity of Mach 2. The system is designed to complement the Phalanx 20-mm gun in providing comprehensive close-in anti-missile defence.

Modern Naval Anti-Aircraft Weapons

Typical of the light AA armament in use today, the EMERLEC-30 is designed to cope with air and surface targets, and possesses a limited anti-missile capability. The twin 30-mm Oerlikon cannon with associated below-deck magazine are typical, but less so is the enclosed operator's cabin.

The widespread introduction of the surface-to-air missile seemed for many years to signal the end of the anti-aircraft gun, both on land and at sea. Modern war has shown this to be a short-sighted attitude, the experience of large-scale air attack in the Falklands proving the value of the gun, especially in a balanced gun/missile defence.

It was not too long ago that the Royal Navy's experts on air defence were blithely stating that guns were no longer needed aboard ship, except for use in the 'junk-bashing' role, if at all. However, luckily for the Royal Navy and before it faced a real exponent on the use of anti-shipping air power, the Falklands war of 1982 against Argentina proved the folly of those sentiments once and for all. The anti-aircraft gun of whatever calibre proved to be a major component of the air defences used. Such guns could be relied upon to put up a fairly heavy barrage, and even if it was at times relatively inaccurate, this barrage was sufficient to discourage a fair number of Argentine pilots on bombing and rocket runs, while the hits the guns recorded resulted in two absolutely confirmed kills plus an unknown number of damaged aircraft that limped home to bases on the mainland.

For defence against the anti-ship missile, the Falklands war proved that the ideal situation is in fact a combination of fully automatic guns with short-range point-defence missiles, the combination effectively creating around the ship a 'no-go area' for fast-approaching attackers. The calibres in this field usually vary from 20 mm up to 30 mm because of the

high rate of fire required. The larger calibres are also represented, but for anti-missile work require sophisticated electronics coupled with the use of reliable proximity-fused fragmentation ammunition to ensure a kill.

It is interesting to note that the Soviets predated the Americans into this field with a CIWS (Close-In Weapon System) against missiles because of their experience of such weapons. The Western European navies, such as those of France and the UK, initially failed to show interest, preferring instead to concentrate on their missile systems. However, the latter country (together with several other NATO nations such as the Netherlands and Spain) have now adopted the CIWS as part of their naval armament. Surprisingly, relatively few other countries are following suit despite the combat experience to prove how useful such systems are.

Fitted with two Breda Compact Twin Naval Mount Type 70s, the Peruvian 'Lupo' class frigate Meliton Carvajal can utilize them in an integrated DARDO CIWS (Close-In Weapon System) for use against anti-ship missiles.

Breda Twin 30-mm Naval Mount

The **Breda Twin 30-mm Compact Naval Mount** is designed for export and uses two Mauser MK cannon set in a twin cradle within a turret. Some of the advanced features of the twin 40-mm L/70 mount described separately have been incorporated into the design to reduce reaction time to a minimum. The mount is completely automated, with sufficient ammunition reserves (2,000 belted ready-use rounds per mount) to meet both saturation and successive wave attacks without the need for human intervention to replenish stocks. Four versions are available to meet siting arrangements in various classes of warships. In each case the dimensions and weights have been reduced to the minimum to save top-weight. The ammunition is the same as that developed for the American GAU-8 tank-buster cannon, and comprises three basic types: an impact-fuzed HE-incendiary round, a depleted uranium penetrator AP-incendiary and a new

proximity fuzed frangible anti-aircraft round. A **Breda Single 30-mm** is also available weighing some 1330 kg (2,932 lb) fully loaded. It is easily fitted to small craft as their main armament or to corvettes and larger vessels as secondary weapons. Using a single Mauser Mk 30 gun it also fires the US developed GAU-8 type of ammunition.

Specification
Breda 30-mm
Calibre: 30 mm
Number of barrels: two
Elevation: −13° to +85°
Muzzle velocity: 1040 m (3,412 ft) per second
Effective range: 3000 m (3,280 yards)
Rate of fire: 1,600 rounds per minute
Weight: varies according to the ship type fitted
Number of rounds carried on mount: 2,000

The Breda Compact Twin 30-mm Naval Mount is now in production: first examples are for missile patrol craft of an unspecified customer. In the background is a 'Lupo' class frigate with twin 40-mm turret visible.

Above and below: The Breda Compact Twin 30-mm is fully automatic and is based on the advanced design features of the highly successful twin 40-mm system.

The general layout of the gunhouse and below-decks magazine for 2,000 ready-use rounds is seen in the cutaway drawings below. Already the Breda company has designed a single 30-mm naval mount along the same lines and firing the same GAU-8/A ammunition types.

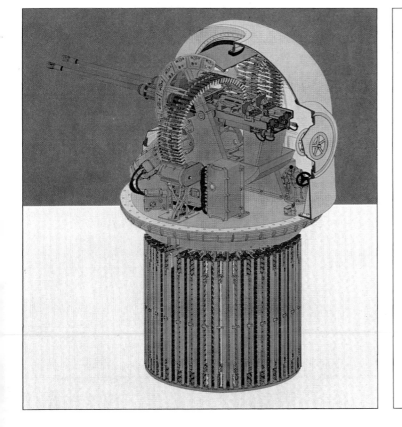

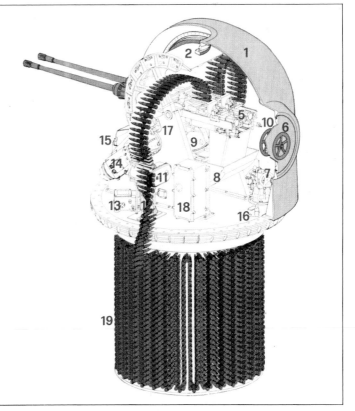

40-mm L/70 Breda Compact Twin Naval Mount Type 70

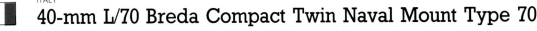

The 40-mm L/70 Breda Compact Twin Naval Mount Type 70 is a joint venture by Breda Meccanica Bresciana and Bofors to produce a system intended for point-defence use against aircraft and anti-ship missiles. The mount is fully automatic in operation, and features a high rate of fire with a considerable ready-use ammunition supply to the two guns, which are laid by remote-control high-performance servo-units. The mount is available in two versions, the **Type A** and **Type B**, which differ only in weights and the amount of ammunition carried in the turret's magazine (736 rounds in the Type A and 444 in the Type B). In each variant the magazine itself is divided in to two halves, each with hoist serving one barrel. Three types of ammunition are fired: 40-mm AP tracer, 40-mm HE direct action (with impact fuse) and 40-mm HE proximity-fused. Both turrets are in production and service with a number of navies worldwide, especially as secondary armament on missile craft. When the mount is coupled to a Selenia RTN-20X I/J-band fire-control radar with a direct electronic link to the ship's main surveillance radar and fire-control system, the weapon then forms part of the **Dardo** close-in weapon system designed specifically to counter high-speed late-detection attacks by anti-ship missiles. It does this by utilizing the turret's rapid-response characteristics and high rate of fire (together with proximity-fused ammunition) in order to ensure a kill. The Dardo CIWS is widely fitted in frigate-sized and larger vessels of the Italian navy, and the mounts have been sold to more than 20 nations worldwide, but particularly in the Middle East and in South America.

Specification
L/70 Breda Compact
Calibre: 40 mm
Number of barrels: two
Elevation: −13° to +85°
Muzzle velocity: 1000 m (3,281 ft) per second
Effective range: 3500-4000 m (3,830-4,375 yards) depending upon target type
Rate of fire: 600 rounds per minute
Weight: (with ammunition) Type A 7300 kg (16,093 lb), and Type B 6300 kg (13,889 lb)
Number of rounds carried on mount: see main text

The Omani navy missile boat Al Mansur mounts a 40-mm L/70 Breda Compact Twin Naval Mount Type 70 'B' forward, carrying a total of 444 rounds in its magazine below decks. The weapon can be used in both the air defence and surface attack roles, a flexibility important in smaller navies.

Left: The heavier twin 40-mm Breda Type A variant of the L/70 Type 70 mounting is used on larger warships, as it has a more capacious magazine with 736 ready-use rounds below decks and is some 1000 kg (2,205 lb) heavier. More than 20 navies have adopted the Type 70.

Above: The Ecuadorean corvette Esmerelda is typical of the general-purpose vessels in service with many navies. It is armed with Exocet SSMs and an OTO-Melara 76-mm dual-purpose gun in addition to the AA armament of Albatros missiles and the 40-mm L/70 Type 70 twin gun.

20-mm Meroka Close-In Weapon System

Developed by CETME, the **20-mm Meroka CIWS** consists of a turret with two rows each of six 20-mm automatic Oerlikon cannon, a PDS-10 control console which incorporates a digital fire-control computer, a RAN-12/L search and target-designation radar, and an on-mount PVS-2 monopulse Doppler I/J-band tracking radar with low-light thermal-imaging TV camera. The combined rate of fire of the barrels is some 9,000 rounds per minute,

although only 720 rounds are actually carried on the mount itself. An additional 240 rounds apiece are carried in each of three externally fitted boxes. It is estimated that each engagement will require up to ten 12-round salvos to destroy an incoming target, so a single system should be able to deal with five or six missiles before reloading. Fire-control is normally by radar, but optical/TV guidance is available for standby manual control. The twenty

systems ordered in place of more expensive foreign systems such as Phalanx will arm the carrier *Principe de Asturias*, (four systems) and one each for the six 'Descubierta' class frigates, the five new FFG-7 class frigates and the five 'Baleares' ASW class frigates. The latter had their Merokas fitted while undergoing mid-life refits from 1985 onwards. No export sales for Meroka are expected.

Specification
Meroka
Calibre: 20 mm
Number of barrels: 12
Elevation: not known
Muzzle velocity: 1200 m (3,937 ft) per second
Effective range: 2000 m (2,185 yards)
Rate of fire: 9,000 rounds per minute
Weight: 4500 kg (9,921 lb)
Number of rounds carried on mount: 1,440

30-mm anti-aircraft guns

The first Soviet 30-mm mount was the **AK-230** 60-calibre system which entered service in 1960 to replace the elderly 25-mm 60-calibre twin anti-aircraft gun on new-build major and minor warship classes. The small enclosed turret is usually known by the nickname Dalek because of its physical appearance. The two 30-mm cannon fitted are fully automatic in operation, and the barrels are water-cooled. The theoretical maximum rate of fire for the guns is 1,050 rounds per minute, but the maximum realistic rate to prevent damage is actually in the region of 200-240 rounds per minute. The guns are usually used in conjunction with a 'Drum Tilt' fire-control radar or a remote optical director. On the smaller ships fitted with the AK-230 an anti-surface role is also assigned to the type, the maximum effective range being 2500 m (2,735 yards). A shell weighing 0.54 kg (1.2 lb) is used. The system has been widely exported to Soviet-supplied states as the gun forms the main armament of the 'Osa' class missile craft.

To counter the threat of missile attack the Soviets developed the 30-mm weapon further to produce a 'Gatling' gun version with six 30-mm barrels inside a larger barrel-like cylinder in a similar shaped mount known by the designation **AK-630**. This is designed to fire at a fast rate as large a number of the 0.54-kg (1.2-lb) shells as possible, with high-density metal penetrators to destroy cruise missile sized targets at relatively close range. Usually

mounted in pairs with a 'Bass Tilt' fire-control radar, the mount is in service on the 'Kiev', 'Kara', 'Udaloy', 'Sovremenny', 'Slava' and 'Kresta II' classes, and has been retrofitted to several older ships. On smaller warships it is usually found as a single mount together with a larger-calibre gun and a fire-control radar. Each mount also has a remote fire-control optical director.

Specification
AK-230
Calibre: 30 mm
Number of barrels: two
Elevation: 0° to +85°
Muzzle velocity: 1000 m (3,281 ft) per second
Effective range: 2500 m (2,735 yards)
Rate of fire: 1,050 rounds per minute

Specification
AK-630
Calibre: 30 mm
Number of barrels: six
Elevation: 0° to +85°
Muzzle velocity: 1000 m (3,281 ft) per second
Effective range: 3000 m (3,280 yards)
Rate of fire: 3,000 rounds per minute

Right: Soviet distribution of CIWS is liberal, with vessels such as the nuclear-powered 'Kirov' class being equipped with up to eight 30-mm Gatling types, the four-stern turrets being shown here. The Soviets have developed a high-density penetrator round for the system.

Below: The 30-mm turret for twin automatic cannon is standard fit aboard Soviet light force units and is shown on the bow of a Soviet navy 'Osa I' class missile boat. The turret has also been exported widely to Soviet client states.

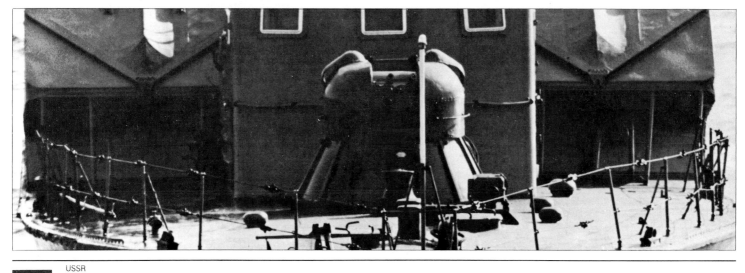

57-mm anti-aircraft guns

The oldest of the Soviet navy's **57-mm anti-aircraft guns** is a single-barrel 70-calibre mounting which can still be found on some 'Skory (Mod)' destroyers. This version was followed in the late 1950s by a twin-barrel version which is found on a number of the smaller warship classes such as the 'T-58' class patrol vessels and radar pickets. The final version of the weapon to appear was a quadruple mount with the barrels arranged in two superimposed pairs. All three systems can be controlled locally, the twin and quad guns using either 'Hawk Screech' or 'Muff Cob' fire-control radars to obtain target data for below-decks electronics. The guns fire a 2.8-kg (6.2-lb) shell which has in recent years

been fitted with a proximity fuse to increase its lethality against missile-type targets. The weapons can also be fired in the anti-surface target role, in which the maximum effective range is 8 km (5 miles).

In the early 1960s a new twin 57-mm 80-calibre water-cooled dual-purpose mount was introduced into service. This is fully automatic in operation from the below-decks ammunition handling room to the gun mount itself. Classes fitted with the gun include the 'Moskva', 'Kresta I', 'Kresta II', 'Poti', 'Grisha I/II/III'. 'Nanuchka', 'Turya', 'Ropucha', 'Ugra' and 'Berezina'. The fire-control radars used are the 'Muff Cob' or 'Bass Tilt' systems, while the ammunition fired is of the same type as used by the

70-calibre gun.

Specification
57-mm L/70
Calibre: 57 mm
Number of barrels: one, two or four
Elevation: 0° to +90°
Muzzle velocity: 1000 m (3,281 ft) per second
Effective range: 4500 m (4,920 yards)
Rate of fire: 120, 240 or 480 rounds per minute

'Kanin' class units of the Soviet navy have two 57-mm quadruple mountings located forward and have been supplied with new proximity-fused ammunition.

Specification
57-mm L/80
Calibre: 57 mm
Number of barrels: two
Elevation: 0° to +85°
Muzzle velocity: 1000 m (3,281 ft) per second
Effective range: 6000 m (6,560 yards)
Rate of fire: 240 rounds per minute

The twin 57-mm turret mounted aft on the Soviet 'Grisha III' class corvette was first introduced in the 1960s. Water-cooled, it is a fully automatic weapon with increased maximum range from that of its predecessor.

40-mm L/60 and L/70 Bofors automatic guns

The original **40-mm L/60 Bofors** automatic anti-aircraft gun was introduced into use during the period of World War II, and today is still in service with a number of navies. It may also be fitted to some new-build warships in a reconditioned form as it is no longer in production. Present-day construction is now devoted to the higher performance **40-mm L/70 Bofors gun** variant, which is operational worldwide with more than 30 navies. Three basic types of single barrel mountings for the L/70 are offered, these differing in the amount of automation provided. Gun control can be either local or remote, the latter using either a below-decks fire-control system or an above-decks optical director.

To increase the lethality of the older L/60, two new types of ammunition have been developed by the Swedes, a prefragmented HE (PFHE) round with a proximity fuse and an armour-piercing high-capacity tracer (APHC-T) round. The L/70 has its own family of ammunition which includes PFHE, HCHE, HE-tracer (HE-T) and practice types. The pulse-Doppler radar proximity fuses fitted to the two PFHE round types allows missile targets to be engaged, the L/60 version having an effective detonation distance of between 4.5 and 6.5 m (14.76 and 21.33 ft) and the L/70 round of between 1 and 7 m (3.28 and 22.97 ft) depending upon target size and type. The L/70 addi-

tionally forms part of the Italian Breda 40-mm single- and twin-barrel gun mounts, which are currently used by more than 20 navies.

Specification
L/60 Bofors
Calibre: 40 mm
Number of barrels: one
Elevation: −10° to +80°
Muzzle velocity: 830 m (2,723 ft) per second
Effective range: 3000 m (3,280 yards)
Rate of fire: 120 rounds per minute
Weight: varies, but typically between

1200 and 2500 kg (2,646 and 5,511 lb)
Number of rounds carried on mount: varies according to mount type

Specification
L/70 Bofors
Number of barrels: one
Elevation: −10° to +90°
Muzzle velocity: 1005-1030 m (3,297-3,379 ft) per second according to round type
Effective range: 4000 m (4,375 yards)
Rate of fire: 300 rounds per minute
Weight: (without ammunition) SAK 40L/70-350 2890 kg (6,371 lb), SAK 40L/

The original 40-mm L/60 Bofors was one of the principal air defence weapons of the US Fleet in the Pacific war. It served well into the 1970s and was last mounted on such vessels as the attack transport USS Sandoval, which is seen shadowed by a 'T-143' class minesweeper of the Soviet navy.

70-315 1700 kg (3,748 lb) and SAK 40L/70-520 3790 kg (8,355 lb)
Number of rounds carried on mount: SAK 40L/70-350 96, SAK 40L/70-315 96 and SAK 40L/70-520 144

The Breda/Bofors 40-mm L/70 naval mount with a Breda 144 round automatic feed device allows the number of men required on-mount to be reduced to two, with a third on standby to reload the feed mechanism during lulls in firing.

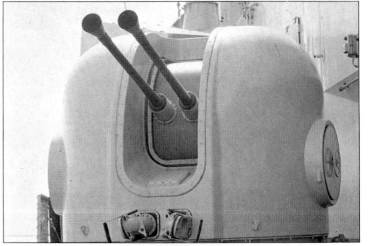

Among the most popular of Bofors mounts are those provided by Breda, the L/70 being used in both single and twin forms. The Compact Twin turret is currently in service or on order for more than 20 navies worldwide.

30-mm Goalkeeper Close-In Weapon System

The **30-mm Goalkeeper CIWS** naval air-defence system is an autonomous radar-directed short-range weapon designed for fully automatic defence against high-speed missile and aircraft. Built as a joint venture by the American company General Electric and the Dutch company Hollandse Signaalapparaten BV, the Goalkeeper has all its elements integrated on a single mount like the Phalanx system. The Goalkeeper consists of an I-band track-while-scan search-and-acquisition surveillance radar, a dual-frequency I/K-band tracking radar, fire-control electronics and a cannon with high rate of fire, namely the 30-mm seven-barrel GAU-8/A Sea Vulcan version of the aircraft Gatling gun. System operation is completely automatic from target detection, through target destruction and termination of the engagment, to detection of the next target. Missiles flying as low as 5 m (16 4 ft) have been successfully destroyed, and the tracking radar can also be used against high-elevation diving targets. For multiple attacks there is an automatic kill-assessment subsystem to assign target priorities. The AP discarding-sabot round has, instead of the original depleted-uranium penetrator, one made of a high-density tungsten alloy. For softer targets an HE-incendiary round is employed. A total of 1,190 rounds is carried in a linkless-feed/drum-storage system. To replenish this storage/feed arrangement a bulk loading system is used, but in an emergency manual reloading can be performed. The Goalkeeper system has been chosen by the Royal Netherlands navy for its 'Kortenaer', 'Jacob van Heemskerck' and future 'M' class frigates (one system each) and for the improved 'Poolster' class fast combat support ships. The Royal Navy has bought 15 Goalkeeper systems for installation on the 'Illustrious' class carriers (which will each have three systems), and the four 'Type 22 Batch 3' general-purpose frigates. More systems are likely to be ordered for the

Type 23 'Duke' class frigates now being built.

Specification
Goalkeeper
Calibre: 30 mm
Number of barrels: seven
Elevation: −25° to +85°
Muzzle velocity: 1021 m (3,350 ft) per second

Left: Goalkeeper is able to engage multiple targets, the system having demonstrated kills of simulated supersonic anti-ship cruise missiles at ranges of 500 m and 400 m respectively within about one second of switching target.

Effective range: 3000 m (3,280 yards)
Rate of fire: 4,200 rounds per minute
Weight: (with ammunition) 6730 kg (14,837 lb)
Number of rounds carried on mount: 1,190

Left: A Goalkeeper CIWS is seen on a test rig during the trials stage. At present the Royal Netherlands navy has ordered one prototype, two pre-production and 10 production systems for fitting to its warships, and the Royal Navy has ordered 15 for its latest warship classes.

Right: The 30-mm Goalkeeper CIWS uses a modified version of the seven-barrel GAU-8/A aircraft Gatling gun, with integrated fire control and search radars on the same mount.

30-mm TCM-30 Twin Naval Gun

Built by a subsidiary of Israel Aircraft Industries, the **30-mm TCM-30 Twin Naval Gun** consists of a pair of 30-mm automatic cannon and their feed systems mounted in a stabilized electrically-actuated turret capable of high angular accelerations. The cannon are 30-mm Oerlikon models, and are carried on a barrel-support system which reduces longer-range shot dispersion to a minimum. The turret's positioning and traverse velocity can be controlled from the ship's fire-control system. Five different types of ammunition can be used in the two 125-round linked-ammunition boxes that are located on the gun cradle. Two reserve magazines provide a further 40 rounds for the system. The TCM-30 prototype was tested aboard the 'Aliyah' class *Geoula*. The same gun has also been adapted for land use on a towed carriage and armoured fighting vehicles, as well as being employed in the **Spider II** air-defence artillery system. Under Israeli government regulations it is being offered for export.

The TCM-30 twin 30-mm naval air defence weapon was developed for export. The Israeli navy uses the much more sophisticated (and more expensive) American supplied Phalanx 20-mm CIWS, although they conducted the service trials for the new system.

Specification
TCM-30
Calibre: 30 mm
Number of barrels: two
Elevation: −20° to +85°
Muzzle velocity: 1080 m (3,543 ft) per second
Effective range: 3000 m (3,280 yards)
Rate of fire: 1,300 rounds per minute
Weight: (with ammunition) not known
Number of rounds carried on mount: 290

20-mm Naval Gun Type GAM-BO1 and 25-mm Naval Gun Type GBM-AO1

The single-barrel 20-mm **GAM-BO1** is a simple unpowered locally-operated mount that uses the Oerlikon-Bührle KAA automatic cannon. It is capable of engaging surface targets out to 2000 m (2,185 yards) and aircraft-sized targets out to 1500 m (1,640 yards). A night sight can be fitted if required. Over 20 navies use this weapon, including the Spanish navy's 'Lazarga' and 'Barcelo' class fast attack missile craft. The

Royal Navy's 'Invincible' class carriers; 'County', 'Type 42' and 'Type 82' destroyers; and 'Type 22 Batch 1/2' frigates each have two; and non-converted 'Leander Batch 3' class frigates (one apiece). The adoption of the gun by the Royal Navy was as a result of its experiences during the Falklands war.

For increased firepower there is the larger-calibre **25-mm GBM-AO1**, which is similar in characteristics to the GAM-BO1 system but mounts the 25-mm KBA-C02 cannon with a double belt feed. The engagement ranges are the same as those of the 20-mm cannon but the shell is heavier. Several unidentified navies have adopted this weapon.

Although a relatively simple weapon, the 20-mm Oerlikon Type GAM-BO1 has been chosen by a number of navies for its light weight and robustness. The Royal Navy uses it in conjunction with twin 30-mm mounts to boost close-range AA defences.

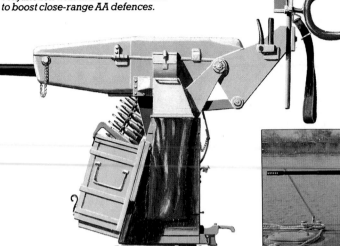

Below: Similar to the 20-mm weapon, the 25-mm GBM-AO1 fires a heavier shell. Its low weight makes it simple to instal aboard vessels down to the smallest of fast patrol craft, and no electrical power is required for operation.

Bottom: The widely-used 20-mm Oerlikon mounting of the World War II manual type is still in production and service worldwide. A more modern cannon and ring sighting system has been fitted, as on this gun in service with the Angolan navy aboard an ex-Portuguese 'Bellatrix' class patrol vessel.

Specification
GAM-BO1
Calibre: 20 mm
Number of barrels: one
Elevation: −15° to +60°
Muzzle velocity: 1050 m (3,444 ft) per second
Effective range: see text
Rate of fire: 600 rounds per minute
Weight: (with ammunition) 500 kg (1,102 lb)
Number of rounds on mount: 200

Specification
GBM-AO1
Calibre: 25-mm
Number of barrels: one
Elevation: −15° to +50°
Muzzle velocity: 1100 m (3,609 ft) per second
Effective range: see text
Rate of fire: 570 rounds per minute
Weight: (with ammunition) 600 kg (1,323 lb)
Number of rounds on mount: 200

30-mm Twin Anti-Aircraft Gun Type GCM-A

The Oerlikon-Bührle **30-mm Type GCM-A** is produced in three different versions: the **GCM-AO3-1** with an enclosed gunner's position, stabilized control and optional remote control from a fire-control system; the **GCM-AO3-2** which is essentially the same as the GCM-AO3-1 but with an open gunner's position; and the **GCM-AO3-3** without a gunner's position and thus fitted only for remote control. The 30-mm KCB cannon used in the GCM-AO3 is also used in the American twin 30-mm EMERLEC-30 and the British Laurence Scott (Defence Systems)

As is increasingly common, the GCM-A has been designed for fitment to small surface vessels. The model AO3-2, with an open gunner's station, weighs only 2560 kg (5,644 lb) complete, and can be operated both locally and by remote control.

single-barrel LS30B systems. As a direct result of the lack of close-range air-defence guns during the Falklands war, to augment secondary armament the Royal Navy purchased a number of licence-built GCM-AO3-2 mounts from the British company BMARC for fitting to its 'Type 82' and 'Type 42' class destroyers and to one of the LPD assault ships not in reserve. Unfortunately, the limited displacement of the 'Type 42s' means that the ship's boats have had to be landed to compensate for increased top-weight. Several other navies, including Egypt, Israel, Kenya, Tunisia and the United Arab Emirates have the system in service.

Specification
Type GCM-A
Calibre: 30 mm
Number of barrels: two
Elevation: − 10° to +75°
Muzzle velocity: 1080 m (3,543 ft) per second
Effective range: 3000 m (3,280 yards)
Rate of fire: 1,300 rounds per minute

Weight: (with ammunition) GCM-AO3-1 2910 kg (6,415 lb), GCM-AO3-2 2515 kg (5,545 lb) and GCM-AO3-3 2560 kg (5,644 lb)

Number of rounds carried on mount: GCM-AO3-1/2 500, and GCM-AO3-3 640

After its experience during the Falklands war, the Royal Navy bought a number of twin 30-mm GCM-A mounts fitted with Ferranti gyroscopic lead angle computing sights from BMARC Ltd to supplement its close-range anti-aircraft armament.

SWITZERLAND
35-mm Twin Anti-Aircraft Gun Type GDM-A

Similar in concept and design to the highly successful Oerlikon twin 35-mm Type GDF land-based anti-aircraft guns, the naval **35-mm Type GDM-A** is intended primarily for use against air attacks, but if required can also be used to engage surface targets at sea and on land. The stabilized mount is an all-weather system with its electronic control units located below decks. The cannon fitted are of the KDC model, which are fully automatic in operation. The turret has three possible modes of use: fully automatic with control exercised from either a below-decks fire-control system or an upper-deck optical aiming unit fitted with an auxiliary computer; local operator control with the gunner using a joystick and gyro-stabilized gunsight; and emergency manual control using two hand wheels and the gunsight when power to the mount is cut. Each of the cannon has 56 ready-use rounds, with another 224 rounds in total reserve. At least five countries use this turret on their

warships, namely Ecuador, Greece, Iran, Libya and Turkey.

Specification
Type GDM-A
Calibre: 35 mm
Number of barrels: two
Elevation: − 15° to +85°
Muzzle velocity: 1175 m (3,855 ft) per second
Effective range: 3500 m (3,830 yards)
Rate of fire: 1,100 rounds per minute
Weight: (with ammunition) 6520 kg (14,374 lb)
Number of rounds on mount: 336

Below: Produced as a private venture by OTO-Melara, the twin 35-mm OE/OTO mount uses the Oerlikon KDA 35-mm gun, which is similar to the KDC gun employed in the Swiss company's Type GDM-A system. At present only the Libyan navy has bought the mount for its 'Assad' class missile corvettes.

Above: The original Oerlikons were largely used as naval weapons, but the 35-mm KDC cannon used in the GDM-A is derived from a towed weapon developed in the late 1950s. The Italian model, known to Oerlikon as the GDM-C, uses a slightly heavier variant.

25-mm Seaguard Close-In Weapon System

The **25-mm Seaguard CIWS** naval air-defence system is an international project between companies from Italy, Switzerland and the United Kingdom. It consists of an above-decks tracker module, an independent search radar, a GMB-B1Z Sea Zenith mount with four KBB-R04/404 cannon, and a below-decks ammunition feed and operator's console with associated electronics. The sensor unit is fitted with a K-band radar, a forward-looking infra-red (FLIR) system and a laser sensor for the acquisition of missile-sized targets. Each of the cannon is independently fed from the below-decks ready-use supply, where sufficient rounds are available to engage 18-20 different targets without reloading. Typical engagement ranges are from 1500 m

(1,640 yards) down to 100 m (109 yards) against missiles and out to a maximum of 3500 m (3,830 yards) against aircraft. Ammunition types fired include an HE-incendiary round and a new Anti-Missile Discarding-Sabot (AMDS) round. If required the mount can be elevated to +127° to cover steep-diving targets. Three Seaguard CIWS systems are being fitted to each of the four 'Yavuz' class frigates being built at present for the Turkish navy.

Below: The first navy to adopt the 25-mm Seaguard CIWS is that of Turkey, which has ordered sufficient to arm four frigates currently under construction. Enough ammunition is provided on-mount to engage 18-20 targets without reloading.

Specification
Seaguard
Calibre: 25 mm
Number of barrels: four
Elevation: −20° to +127°
Muzzle velocity: 1355 m (4,446 ft) per second
Effective range: 100-3500 m (109-3,830 yards)

Rate of fire: 3,400 rounds per minute
Weight: (with ammunition) 5700 kg (12,566 lb)
Number of rounds carried on mount: 1,660

The obvious difference between Seaguard and most other close-in weapon systems is the provision of four barrels independently fed with ammunition, instead of a single rotary cannon. This allows for redundancy in the feed system.

20-mm Mk 15/16 Phalanx Close-In Weapon System

The General Dynamics Corporation **20-mm Phalanx Mk 15/16 CIWS** is a total weapons system which automatically carries out search and detection, target threat evaluation, tracking and firing against high-performance anti-ship missiles and aircraft as a 'last-ditch' defence. The Phalanx is built around the General Electric 20-mm M61A1 six-barrel 'Gatling' gun, and is hydraulically powered. Production started in late 1977, the first operational units being installed aboard the aircraft-carriers USS *Enterprise* and *America* during 1980. Current plans are for the US Navy to fit some 400 or more mounts in more than 250 ships, with frigates having only a single system and the 'Iowa' class battleships four. In order to enhance the Phalanx's capabilities a product-improvement programme is under way to increase the search-area and target-detection performance, and to provide for greater flexibility. By the end of 1984 220 Phalanxes had been installed aboard 125 US Navy ships, while a further 52 had been supplied to foreign buyers. Navies with Phalanx in service or on order include Australia, China, Canada, Greece, Israel, Japan, Saudi Arabia, Thailand and the United Kingdom. In the case of the last the systems were apparently ordered before the Falklands war for the 'Invincible' class carriers, with the first delivery being

accelerated to equip HMS *Illustrious*. At present the *Invincible* and *Illustrious* carry two, while the newly completed *Ark Royal* has three. In live firing trials undertaken by the US Navy and the Royal Navy the Phalanx has proved capable of detecting and destroying MM.38 Exocet anti-ship missiles that may threaten Royal Navy ships in any future conflict in the South Atlantic.

Specification
Phalanx Mk 15/16
Calibre: 20 mm
Number of barrels: six
Elevation: −25° to +80°
Muzzle velocity: 1097 m (3,600 ft) per second
Effective range: 500-1500 m (545-1,640 yards)
Rate of fire: 3,000 rounds per minute
Weight: (with ammunition) 6092 kg (13,430 lb)
Number of rounds on mount: 1,000 (latest Mk 16 version is believed to have 1,400-1,600)

The General Dynamics Phalanx uses a 20-mm six-barrel Gatling gun with magazine and integrated fire control radars on the same mount to produce a single modular weapon system package. It is fully automatic in operation, but manual override is possible.

EMERLEC-30 Twin 30-mm Mounting

The operator's cabin of the EMERLEC is environmentally controlled, with windscreen demisting and the option of local or remote control. The sighting station visible within the cabin is fitted with a reflex optical lens and a gyro-stabilizer together with the usual gun controls, and can be fitted with night sights and variable fire rate selection.

Access to the operator's cabin is between the cannon cradle assembly. The cannon cradles themselves allow an elevation between −18° and +84°.

The 30-mm Oerlikon automatic cannon fitted to the EMERLEC are of the KCB type, and are similar to those fitted to Oerlikon's own systems.

The KCB cannon can fire a range of ammunition, including the usual HE, incendiary and tracer rounds. It is also capable of firing a shell rejoicing under the title of APICT — Armour Piercing Incendiary Shell — with hardcore and tracer.

The mount is capable of a complete 360° turn, clockwise or anticlockwise, with elevation ranging between −18° and +84°. Traverse rate is 80° per second, as is elevation rate.

The weapon mount and training gear are all fitted into the mount above deck. Below deck the ammunition storage is arranged around a 2.75-m wide work area which is fitted with most of the system's electronics.

The training drive is located in a sponson above deck level, with access through sponson hatches. Elevating drives are in the main structure of the mount, inboard of the cannon cradle assemblies.

Access to the ammunition store is through below-deck panels. Reloading can be carried out by a single man, although a two-man loading team is recommended for maximum efficiency.

The EMERLEC-30 has 1,970 rounds of ready ammunition in the below-decks magazine, with 985 rounds per gun. All rounds of ready ammo can be fired even if ship's power is lost, and if the batteries are damaged there are hand crank mechanisms for fully-manual operation.

The electronics below decks comprise batteries, de-icing relays, servo systems, gun control relays and fire rate selection systems, as well as connections to the outside for remote or director control.

Designed and built by the Emerson Electric Company, the **EMERLEC-30 Twin 30-mm Mounting** was originally developed as the **EX-74 Mod O** for the US Navy to use aboard coastal patrol and interdiction craft. Based on two Oerlikon KCB cannon it has an environmentally controlled cabin for the gunner, day and/or night sights, and an integral below-decks magazine. The mount can also be operated by remote control using a standard shipboard fire-control system. In emergency an on-mount battery can provide all the power required to operate the guns and fire the full complement of ready-use ammunition carried. Manual gun controls are also fitted to provide further back-up if the battery fails. The mount has been in series production since 1976 and is known to be in service with the navies of Colombia, Ecuador, Ethiopia, Greece, Malaysia, Nigeria, the Philippines, South Korea and Taiwan. In most cases the fit has been to missile attack craft or large patrol boats. The mounting is also capable of being used in the surface-to-surface role.

Specification
EMERLEC-30
Calibre: 30 m
Number of barrels: two
Elevation: −15° to +80°
Muzzle velocity: 1080 m (3,543 ft) per second
Effective range: 3000 m (3,280 yards)
Rate of fire: 1,200 rounds per minute
Weight: (without ammunition) 1905 kg (4,200 lb)
Number of rounds on mount: 1,970

Below: Designed for anti-missile, anti-aircraft and surface fire, the EMERLEC-30 comprises two Oerlikon 30-mm cannon with associated sights, below-decks ready-use magazine and an enclosed operator's cabin.

Originally developed for US Navy coastal patrol and interdiction craft under the designation EX-74 Mod O, the EMERLEC-30 mounting was taken up for export by the Emerson Electric Company and has been sold to a number of countries.

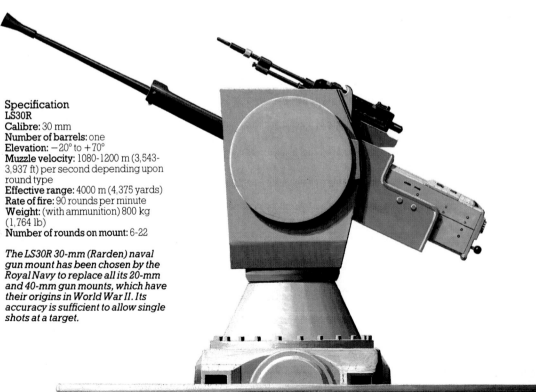

🇬🇧 UK
30-mm LS30R (Rarden) Naval Gun Mounting

The British firm Laurence Scott (Defence Systems) has developed a lightweight naval mounting for the RARDE-designed 30-mm Rarden automatic cannon. The gun is both power-driven and line-of-sight stabilized for use on small naval vessels as well as on large frigate or destroyer designs. An extensive series of tests were carried out by the Royal Navy both at sea (aboard the converted trials frigate HMS *Londonderry*) and on land (at the Fraser Gunnery Range at Portsmouth) to confirm the high accuracy of the weapon, which hit a 2-m^2 (21.5-sq ft) target some 80 per cent of the firing time at ranges between 1000 and 1300 m (1,095 and 1,420 yards) in good to poor visibility. If required the mount can be fitted with a predictor, image intensifier, IR camera and/or low-light TV camera for remote firing. The ammunition types used include HE, APSE and APDS rounds. The **LS30R** has been adopted for use by the Royal Navy, and an initial order for 25 mounts was intended for the new 'Duke' class frigates and to replace the old 20-mm Oerlikons and 40-mm Bofors in service. The first ships so fitted are the Offshore Patrol Vessels. The basic mounting can also be used with other types of 30-mm cannon such as the Oerlikon KCB and the Mauser Model F, in which case the designations become respectively **LS30B** and **LS30F**.

Specification
LS30R
Calibre: 30 mm
Number of barrels: one
Elevation: −20° to +70°
Muzzle velocity: 1080-1200 m (3,543-3,937 ft) per second depending upon round type
Effective range: 4000 m (4,375 yards)
Rate of fire: 90 rounds per minute
Weight: (with ammunition) 800 kg (1,764 lb)
Number of rounds on mount: 6-22

The LS30R 30-mm (Rarden) naval gun mount has been chosen by the Royal Navy to replace all its 20-mm and 40-mm gun mounts, which have their origins in World War II. Its accuracy is sufficient to allow single shots at a target.

Fire Control Systems

The problem with defending surface ships from aerial attack is that an aircraft provides a small target moving fast and unpredictably. The advent of sea-skimming missiles has compounded the problem, necessitating maximum efficiency in anti-aircraft systems.

The key to defending a surface combatant in modern naval warfare is the use of computerized command and control action-information systems located in a central operations room below decks. Here are co-ordinated all the data from the vessel's various sensors, inter-ship data-links, and weapon-control systems to build up an accurate set of plots of the tactical air, surface and sub-surface activity within a given volume round the platform. Once a potential threat is detected and determined to be hostile, then the appropriate weapon-control system is assigned to deal with it. In the case of a medium- to high-level aircraft or missile threat, initial detection may well be by the ship's long-range air-search radar, which uses a broad beam that scans through 360° every minute or so to indicate the presence but not the precise location of a possible target. The raw data from the search radar is then used by the relevant operations room personnel to key in a narrower-beam fire-control radar to the specified target in order to fix its flight direction and exact location. The information or target track thus gained is then fed into the computerized control system of a missile-launcher or anti-aircraft gun mount in order to direct the weapon in elevation and bearing so as to engage the incoming target. The computer then calculates the optimum engagement distance and for a gun the number and duration of burst. Such systems were in the majority amongst the Royal Navy ships in the Falklands, and could not cope very well with the Argentine low-level attacks coming out of the surrounding terrain when they operated close to shore.

To deal with this type of attack by low-flying aircraft, and with targets such as sea-skimming anti-ship missiles like the Exocet and the Soviet 'pop-up' SS-N-7, the conventional long-range and fire-control radars have to be replaced by a combined search and target-tracking set mounted on a completely automatic defence system with extremely rapid response times. There are a number of these 'last-ditch' close-in weapon systems now available, such as the 20-mm Phalanx, the 25-mm Skyguard and the 30-mm Goalkeeper. All are characterized by fully automatic operation from target detection to destruction, and once activated they will endeavour to shoot down all rapidly-closing targets in order of priority unless overridden by the operations room.

For those ships without the sophisticated electronics-equipped operations room and fire-control systems, reliance is placed back on optical detection and tracking devices. The oldest of which is the 'Mk 1 Eyeball' coupled with a simple ring and bead sight on the gun itself. The best example of this is the Royal Navy's elderly 20-mm Oerlikon cannon as currently used on most of its surface combatants. Further up the scale is the gyro-stabilized optical sight, while the ultimate is the fitting of low-light television or infra-red camera units which can be used in poor visibility and at night, a capability which was hitherto unavailable to air-defence guns unless they were directed by radar.

For the future, laser designators are already being tested both as a means to guide laser-homing shells and to give continuous and reliable ranging for close-in targets.

The Iraqis have produced their own anti-aircraft gun system based on four Yugoslavian 20-mm guns (derived from the 20-mm Oerlikon). Fire control is the simplest available, comprising the human eye and a simple sighting system with manual bearing and elevation controls.

Although the level of sophistication of fire-control systems is increasing rapidly, the 1982 Falklands war also demonstrated the fact that although such systems can be present aboard ship, there is still a need for as much firepower as can safely be carried by the ship to be brought to bear on the incoming target(s). Whether or not this weight of fire hits the target aircraft is not entirely relevant, as by its mere presence in the area of the target during the attack it can cause the pilot to lose his nerve and break off or delay weapons release sufficiently for them to miss. If the target is a missile, then the greater the weight of metal thrown at it the better the chance of hitting it hard enough to destroy it.

Where the fire-control system comes in, whatever its level of sophistication, is that it should ensure the guns be pointed in the correct direction at the right time and at roughly the correct elevation before the engagement begins. The Royal Navy learnt to its cost that it is no good having on paper some of the world's best available air-defence systems if the associated electronics are not capable of engaging manoeuvring targets but only those which appear like target drones, flying a straight and level course. These inadequacies should have by now been rectified in order for the Royal Navy to be capable of meeting a far more sophisticated threat in the form of the Warsaw Pact.

This 'Osa' class missile boat of the Egyptian navy is not typical in that its fire control system and associated 'Drum Tilt' radar (visible on the platform aft) control only the 30-mm guns. Comparable Western systems control guns, torpedoes and missiles, in addition to providing search and track facilities.

Fire Control Systems

Above: One of the two major elements in any fire control system is the radar. The Italian DARDO system employs the Orion RTN-20X radar, developed specifically for use with close-in weapon systems.

Above: The other main element is the computerized control centre in the ship. Typically, as in the Selenia example above, it will consist of an operator's console for the weapon system and a tactical data display.

Above: The Mk 92 FCS developed for the US Navy's PHM hydrofoil programme was designed for air and surface actions using guns and missiles. The system includes search radars, tracking radar, IFF and navigation radar as well as standard target illumination radar, and is integrated into a computerized command and control system.

Left: The price of failure – the charred hulk of HMS Sheffield after being struck by an Exocet missile. To avoid a similar fate the ships' fire control system must react in seconds to shoot down sea-skimming missiles.

Below: The Mk 86 gun fire control system fitted to the most recent US surface combatants can operate in several operational modes, including radar-directed surface fire, air action, anti-ship missile defence, visual surface fire and indirect short bombardment.

Modern Underwater Weapon Systems

The battle of the Atlantic in World War II led to enormous advances in underwater weapon systems and their associated sensors; since then both submarines and surface vessels have acquired increasingly complex rocket and missile systems with substantially longer ranges.

One of the more novel types of ASW weapon fielded to date has been the submarine-launched missile. SUBROC, launched from the torpedo tubes of attack submarines, carries a one-kiloton nuclear depth bomb as payload, which has a lethal radius of 5 to 8 km (3 to 5 miles).

There are two major types of anti-submarine projectiles, the proximity and the contact weapon. The former, typified by the depth charge which the Royal Navy first used in combat in 1916 during World War I, must carry an explosive charge large enough to damage a submerged target even at a considerable miss distance. The greatest lethal radius of weapons of this type is achieved by the nuclear depth charge, against which there is little defence, and which can destroy or severely damage targets within several thousand metres of its point of detonation. However, only the two great superpowers, the USA and USSR, actually have such weapons in large numbers, while their allied nations have them to a much lesser extent.

The second projectile type generally relies on much smaller warhead sizes, but must either be specifically guided onto its target or be used in such numbers that a hit is virtually guaranteed. The classic example of such a weapon is the World War II Hedgehog system. The intermediate case between the two is the lightweight ASW (anti-submarine warfare) homing torpedo, which with its great homing radius effectively covers the lethal distance of a nuclear weapon but needs close proximity or actual contact with the target to detonate. To bring such a weapon into the vicinity of a distant target very often requires a carrier platform which may be guided or unguided. Examples of these are respectively the Australian Ikara missile and the Soviet FRAS-1.

For the future, as sensor ranges increase, guided weapons will be developed with advanced-technology homing torpedo or nuclear payloads and ranges in excess of 50 km (31.1 miles). The first of these, the ASW-SOW, is already in the final design stages for deployment in the late 1980s to replace the elderly UUM-44A SUBROC missile aboard American SSNs.

The main development in ASW techniques in recent years has seen the use of a guided missile to carry a torpedo or depth bomb to within striking distance of a target. The Australian-developed Ikara system, with its lightweight torpedo payload, is typical of the types in use today.

Bofors 375-mm ASW rocket-launcher systems

The initial four-tube **Bofors 375-mm** (14.76-in) ASW rocket-launcher system was developed in the early 1950s, and became operational on Swedish navy destroyers in 1955-6. The ship's sonar provides target data for calculating the launcher elevation and bearing for firing. Single or multi-round salvoes can be fired, the ballistic shape of the rockets ensuring a predictable and accurate underwater trajectory. Once empty the launcher is automatically reloaded in three minutes from the magazine located directly beneath it. Three types of rocket can be used, these differing in the types of motor and fuse in order to give different operational characteristics. The four-tube launcher is no longer in production, but is still used by the navies of Colombia, Japan, Portugal, Sweden, Peru, Turkey and West Germany. France uses a six-tube variant built under licence by Creusot-Loire.

During 1969-72 a twin-tube variant, the **SR375**, was developed. This is still in production, and is used by Brazil, Egypt, India, Indonesia, Malaysia, Morocco, Nigeria and Spain. The total number of rounds in the twin-tube launcher magazine is 24, while for the four-tube launcher it varies from 36 on most ships to a maximum of 49 on the two Peruvian destroyer classes bought from the Dutch navy. The Swedish navy used its sole remaining four-tube system on the destroyer *Halland* dur-

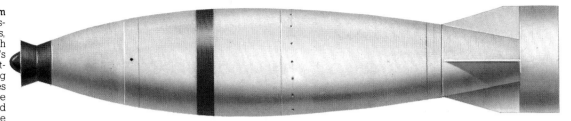

Above: The missiles fired from the Bofors 375-mm ASW launcher system have three different types of motor, giving a variety of ranges. Missile trajectory is flat to produce a short flight time, thus reducing the chances of successful evasive action by the target submarine.

ing the early 1980s when hunting suspected Soviet submarine intruders in coastal waters.

Specification
four-tube launcher
Calibre: 375 mm (14.76 in)
Weight: 7417 kg (16,352 lb)
Elevation: +15° to +90

two-tube launcher
Calibre: 375 mm (14.76 in)
Weight: 3861 kg (8,512 lb)
Elevation: 0° to +60°

Right: The magazine of the four-tube launcher is located directly underneath, and once available rounds have been expended the launcher is automatically replenished from below.

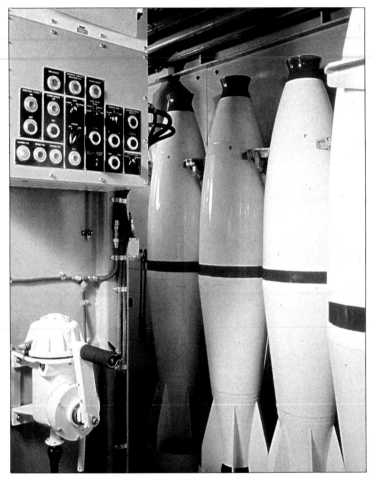

Rocket types:

	weight	length (time fuse/ proximity fuse)	HE charge	range
M/50	250 kg (551 lb)	2/2.05 m (6.56/6.73 ft)	100 kg (220 lb)	355-850 m (1,165-2,790 ft)
Erika	250 kg (551 lb)	2/2.05 m (6.56/6.73 ft)	107 kg (236 lb)	655-1635 m (2,150-5,365 ft)
Nelli	250 kg (551 lb)	2/2.05 m (6.56/6.73 ft)	80 kg (176 lb)	1580-3625 m (5,185-11,895 ft)

Notes:
1 The M/50 and Erika can use the Stidar time and impact fuse.
2 All three can use the Zambo proximity and impact fuse with an influence radius of 15 m (49 ft).

Below: The twin launcher variant, designated SR375, was developed between 1969 and 1972 and is still in production today. It is fitted to the warships of eight navies including those of Spain and India.

Below: The twin launcher can fire its missiles either separately or simultaneously, and the ballistic characteristics of the missile ensure the maintenance of an accurate trajectory once underwater.

Ikara anti-submarine missile

The initial design of the all-weather **Ikara** missile was undertaken by the Australian government, but when the Royal Navy expressed an interest in the system the programme became a joint one with British Aerospace to produce the variant known as **GWS Mk 40**. A further version, the **Branik**, was developed to meet the needs of the Brazilian navy. This last differs from both the Australian and Royal Navy systems in employing a special-purpose missile tracking and guidance unit (fully integrated into one of the launch platform's two fire-control computers) and a new lightweight semi-automated missile-handling system.

The Ikara is powered by a solid-fuel combined booster and sustainer rocket, and in all forms is launched on a bearing to bring it to a torpedo payload-dropping position near to the target. Data for the latter's position is supplied either by the launch platform's own sonar or by a remote data-linked source such as another ship or helicopter. The information received is used for a continuous update of the optimum drop zone position on the ship's fire-control computer, which then passes it (in the form of control commands by the ship's radio/radar guidance system) to the missile in flight. Once the Ikara arrives at the target area the torpedo (a lightweight Mk 44 or Mk 46, semi-enclosed in the missile body) is command-ejected via the communications link. The Ikara body then continues on, clearing the area and crashing, while the torpedo descends by parachute to achieve the best orientation and entry into the water and then to start its search pattern.

The ship classes fitted with the Ikara variants are the 'Niteroi' ASW frigate version of the Brazilian navy (four units with one launcher and 10 missiles); the 'Perth' class destroyers (three units each with two launchers and 24 missiles) and 'River' class frigates (six units each with one launcher and 24 missiles) of the Royal Australian Navy; the sole 'Type 82' destroyer HMS *Bristol* (with one launcher and 20 missiles) and the six remaining 'Leander Batch 1' class frigate conversions (each with one launcher and 14 missiles) of the Royal Navy; and the single 'Leander Batch 1' class conversion HMNZS *Southland* (ex-*Dido*) of the Royal New Zealand Navy.

A number of development programmes are in hand for the improvement of the Ikara system. An Italian/Australian team from OTO/Melara and the Australian Ministry of Defence is working

Ikara is a guided missile bearing a homing torpedo, the former flying to the approximate target area before releasing the homing torpedo to begin its search pattern. Initially developed by Australia, Royal Navy interest led to a version produced in a joint Australian/British programme.

on a **Modified Ikara** missile, with folding fins and the guidance system from the Otomat SSM. The Modified Ikara would be housed in a box launcher, and instead of the original payload would also be able to carry one of a number of new, advanced lightweight torpedoes. These could include the Swedish Type 42, the Italian A244/S or the advanced AS290, or the British Sting Ray. Using the Otomat guidance system means that a ship needs only one type of fire-control unit to manage both anti-ship (Otomat) and anti-submarine (Ikara) missions and so easing tactical and operational problems considerably. An Anglo/Australian programme is also underway (British Aerospace Naval Weapons Division being the UK partner) to develop the **Super Ikara** ASW weapons system. This will have a number of basing options, including shore platforms, offshore platforms such as oil rigs, and ships down to fast attack craft sizes. It will have some over-target loitering ability, and will also accept mid-course corrections from an ASW helicopter or a forward deployed surface vessel. Range is envisaged to be around 100 km (60 miles) with a payload of any of a number of modern lightweight torpedoes. Launched by a solid fuel booster, the missile will be sustained in flight by a small air breathing jet engine.

Left: Once Ikara is launched, its flight path is controlled from the ship's computer, which calculates the optimum position for the release of the torpedo. Once it is dropped the torpedo discards its parachute on reaching the sea, and dives to seek out its target while the missile flies on out of the target area.

Below: Ikara is launched from the Brazilian navy's Mk 10 frigate BNS Defensora. Brazilian Ikaras differ from the original system in employing a special-purpose missile-tracking and guiding unit, fully integrated into one of the two fire control computers.

Specification
Ikara
Dimensions: length 3.42 m (11.22 ft); wing span 1.52 m (4.99 ft); height 1.57 m (5.15 ft)
Weight: varies according to payload
Payload: lightweight ASW homing torpedo
Performance: maximum speed Mach 0.8; range 24 km (15 miles)

Malafon anti-submarine missile

The Société Industrielle d'Aviation Latécoère **Malafon** surface-to-subsurface winged missile started development in 1956, and by 1959 a total of 21 test launches had been completed. The first sea launch and guidance test took place in 1962, with full systems evaluation of over 20 launches taking place in 1964. The final operational trials took place in the following year.

The Malafon is primarily an ASW weapon, but can also be used to attack surface targets if required. Detection and designation for subsurface targets is provided by the ship's sonars, while for surface targets it is by radar. The

Malafon is ramp-launched, propulsion for the initial seconds of its flight being provided by two jettisonable solid-fuel boosters. Once these have been discarded the flight is unpowered, the gliding missile being stabilized by an automatic pilot and radio altimeter. In-

flight control is effected via a command radio link, the missile being tracked with the aid of flares attached to the wingtips. On reaching the drop-zone area, at a distance of some 800 m (875 yards) from the estimated target position, a parachute is deployed to slow

Malafon is a shipborne homing acoustic torpedo delivered to the target area by a command-guided missile. Although primarily intended as an ASW weapon, it can be used to engage surface targets.

the Malafon. This causes the 533-mm (21-in) L4 acoustic-homing torpedo payload to be ejected into the water to complete the attack.

Malafon is in service with the 'Tourville' and 'Suffren' classes and the *Aconit* and *La Galisonnière* destroyers, each having one launcher and 13 mis- siles. The missiles now have solid-state electronics in place of valves and will be operational to the end of the century.

Specification
Malafon
Dimensions: length 6.15 m (20.2 ft);

wing span 3.3 m (10.8 ft); diameter 0.65 m (2.13 ft)
Weight: 1500 kg (3,307 lb)
Warhead: L4 acoustic-homing torpedo
Performance: maximum speed low subsonic; range 13 km (8.1 miles)

Malafon is carried by 11 French vessels, in each case the fit consisting of a single launcher and 13 missiles. The DDG Duquesne carries her Malafon launcher forward of the four MM.40 Exocet launchers and immediately abaft the funnel/mast.

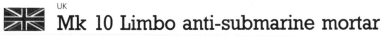

⚓ Mk 10 Limbo anti-submarine mortar

Developed by the Admiralty Underwater Weapons Establishment during the 1950s, the **Mk 10 Limbo** mortar entered service with the Royal Navy in the early 1960s. Still used by that service, the Limbo is also in service with the navies of Australia, Canada, Indonesia, India, Iran, Malaysia and Thailand. Although considered obsolete, the Limbo is in fact a very potent weapon in shallow water where acoustic homing torpedoes are at a distinct disadvantage. The ship's own sonar provides the target position data to a predictor unit which computes the mortar barrel elevation information and lateral tilt. The three-barrel mortar is then set and fired to give a pattern of three bombs fused to give a three-dimensional explosive burst around the target. The bombs use either a pre-programmed pressure fuse or a delay-action time fuse with the settings made by remote control through relays and uniselectors. The maximum engagement depth is 375 m (1,230 ft). Far Eastern sources indicate that there is also a proximity influence fused bomb, which has virtually an unlimited maximum depth. The mortar is reloaded in the horizontal plane (by pneumatic rammers) from a ready-use magazine located alongside the weapon. The Royal Australian Navy's version is of an improved local type which is quieter in operation, uses modern electrical solid-state control systems and requires only three crew instead of the seven normally used.

Specification
Mk 10 Limbo
Calibre: 305 mm (12 in)
Number of barrels: three
Bomb weight: 175 kg (385 lb)
Warhead: 92 kg (202.4 lb) HE
Performance: maximum depth 375 m (1,230 ft); range 0.9 km (0.56 miles)

Stabilized in pitch and roll by a metadyne system referenced to the ship's stable platform, Limbo fires a triple pattern of mortar bombs programmed to produce an explosive pattern in the predicted path of the target submarine. Maximum range is 900 m (985 yards).

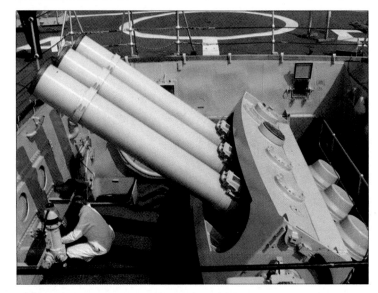

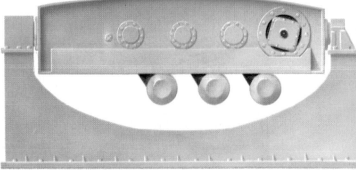

Above: Limbo has been in service with the Royal Navy for over 20 years, and is still in use despite being classified as obsolete. However, it remains a useful weapon in shallow waters that present difficulties for acoustic homing torpedoes. The Royal Australian Navy has at least updated its Limbo systems.

UUM-44A SUBROC submarine rocket

Development of the two-stage **UUM-44A SUBROC** submarine rocket began in 1958, the complete technical evaluation being finished by 1964. The first production rounds were delivered to the US Navy in the following year, and the average SSN basic load is four to six rounds. The SUBROC formed part of an advanced ASW system for its time.

Target heading and range data are determined by the submarine's onboard sonar suite. The co-ordinate data are then fed into the analogue Mk 113 fire-control system, which programmes an optimum flight profile into the missile's intertial guidance unit in terms of its course, speed and warhead separation point. The missile is then launched horizontally from the standard 533-mm (21-in) torpedo tube by normal means. At a safe distance from the submarine (and with the rocket not necessarily in the direction of the target) the solid-fuel rocket motor ignites and the weapon follows a short level path before pitching up and out of

the water. In both submerged and air-borne flight the SUBROC is steered by four jet deflectors. At the optimum payload-release point the 5-kiloton yield W55 warhead is released by a combination of explosive bolts and a thrust reversal deceleration system, and continues on a ballistic trajectory to the target area. Any minor course correction needed at this stage is performed by vanes on the depth bomb casing, which is cushioned to protect the arming and fusing mechanisms on impact with the water. The bomb then sinks to a preset depth, where a pressure fuse detonates it. The warhead has a lethal radius against submarines of

some 4.8-6.4 km (3-4 miles) from its detonation point.

Under current planning the 'SSN594' and 'SSN637' classes will carry SUBROC until they retire, while other classes such as the SSN688 class will have their digital fire-control systems modified to fire the weapon until the Sea Lance reaches service. The SUBROC fusing system allows for the weapon to be used against surface ships with a shallow water burst, and also against ships and land targets with an airburst.

Specification
UUM-44A SUBROC

Dimensions: length 6.71 m (22 ft); diameter 0.533 m (21 in)
Weight: 1814 kg (4,000 lb)
Warhead: 294.8-kg (650-lb) 5-kiloton yield W55 fission weapon
Performance: maximum speed Mach 1.5; range 56 km (35 miles)

SUBROC exits the water at the start of its flight, its rocket motor having ignited as soon as the missile was at a safe distance from the launch submarine. Target data has been fed into its inertial guidance system, the nuclear warhead allowing considerable leeway with its 6.4-km (4-mile) lethal radius.

Developed in the early 1960s, SUBROC is carried by the 'Permit' and 'Sturgeon' classes of attack submarine. Launched through a torpedo tube, its rocket motor blasts it out of the water and powers it on a flight of up to 56 km (35 miles) before it drops a 5-kiloton yield nuclear depth charge.

RUR-5A ASROC anti-submarine rocket

The all-weather day or night **RUR-5A ASROC** anti-submarine rocket was the result of combining the RAT-C rocket-thrown torpedo weapon with the concept of the rocket-thrown nuclear depth charge. The combination system called ASROC was to be a 9.1-km (5.65-mile) range ballistic rocket fired from a 12-round pepperbox launcher that was to be paired with the similar-range SQS-23 sonar. With the failure of the predecessor RAT-A the rocket had to be redesigned with a greater fin area and with launcher round capacity reduced to eight. The system entered operational service in 1962, the Mk 44 torpedo payload soon being upgraded to the more effective Mk 46 weapon. The nuclear option is the 1.5-kiloton yield W44 warhead on a Mk 17 nuclear depth charge. This option was tested as a complete system on 11 May 1962 from the destroyer USS *Agerholm* (DD826) during Operation 'Swordfish'. All target data are derived from the

ship's own sonars, and are then used to predict the elevation and bearing of the launcher to ensure an optimum launch position. The rocket follows a ballistic trajectory, the solid-fuel rocket motor being jettisoned at a predetermined point. The payload then continues towards the target position. If the payload is a homing torpedo the weapon is lowered into the water by parachute, while the nuclear depth charge is allowed to hit the water and sink to a preset depth for detonation. The nuclear variant can also be used against surface ships and land targets if required. The US Navy uses both

variants, and the conventional weapon is used also by Brazil, Canada, Greece, Italy, Japan, Pakistan, South Korea, Spain, Taiwan, Turkey and West Germany.

Vertical Launch ASROC entered production in 1987 for use with the US Navy's Mk 41 vertical launch system. This variant is 5.09 m (16.7 ft) long, 0.358 m (1.2 ft) in diameter, and weighs around 750 kg (1,650-lb). Launched with the aid of a solid fuel booster, the missile quickly performs a turn-over manoeuvre to bring it into the correct attitude for ballistic flight to the target location. The booster is then jettisoned

ASROC can carry either a Honeywell Mk 46 acoustic homing torpedo or a 1.5 kiloton yield W44 warhead on a Mk 17 nuclear depth charge. It is the primary ASW system carried by US Navy destroyers, cruisers and frigates.

and the weapon coasts until it starts the descent phase, when the airframe separates and the Mk 46 Mod 5 or the Mk 50 lightweight torpedo payload is released to descend by parachute. As it enters the water the nose cap shatters, the parachute is jettisoned and the torpedo begins its sonar search pattern. Maximum range for Vertical

Modern Underwater Weapon Systems

Launch ASROC is about 18km (11.25 miles). It will initially deploy aboard the US Navy's AEGIS cruisers, 'Arleigh Burke' class destroyers and will be retrofitted to the 31 'Spruance' class destroyers.

Specification
RUR-5A ASROC
Dimensions: length Mk 44 payload 4.57 m (15 ft) or Mk 46 payload 4.51 m (14.79 ft); wing span 0.845 m (2.77 ft); diameter 0.325 m (1.07 ft)
Weight: Mk 44 payload 434 kg (957 lb); Mk 46 payload 487 kg (1,073 lb)
Warhead: 192.8 kg (425 lb) Mk 44 or 230.4 kg (508 lb) Mk 46 Mod 1 lightweight homing torpedo, or 117.9 kg (260 lb) Mk 17 1.5-kiloton yield W44 fission weapon
Performance: maximum speed Mach 0.8; range 1.85-11.1 km (1.15-6.9 miles)

A 'California' class nuclear powered guided missile cruiser launches a torpedo carrying ASROC from her octuple launcher. Later cruisers have a dual ASW/SAM launcher system.

The mountain of water several kilometers beyond the destroyer USS Agerholm is the result of the first live firing of a nuclear-tipped ASROC which happened in May 1962.

Sea Lance anti-submarine warfare stand-off weapon (ASW-SOW)

The **ASW-SOW** was approved in 1980 as the 1990s long-range anti-submarine warfare system to succeed the SUBROC aboard US Navy attack submarines. Following a competitive concept phase, the team of Boeing with Gould Inc. and Hercules Aerospace was chosen to continue weapon development of the **Sea Lance**.

Following target designation by the digital Mk 117 fire-control system and sonars, the torpedo tube-launched missile is carried in a capsule to the surface before its single-stage solid-fuel rocket motor ignites. On clearing the surface of the sea, four small wrap-around fins at the rear of the rocket motor casing deploy automatically to stabilize the missile in flight. After booster burn-out the system is probably jettisoned, leaving the payload to follow a ballistic trajectory to the target zone, where after deceleration the warhead (either a Mk 50 Barracuda Advanced Lightweight Torpedo or a Mk 46 Mod 5) is released.

The Sea Lance will be capable of engaging targets out to at least the second convergence zone, which is at least twice the range of SUBROC. Originally it was conceived that the Sea Lance would also be surface-ship compatible, but technical and programme difficulties have resulted in a separate weapon based on an ASROC(VL). Primary platform for the Sea Lance will be the 'Los Angeles' class SSN, although older SSNs will be retrofitted as required.

Specification
Sea Lance ASW-SOW
Dimensions: length 6.25 m (20.5 ft);

Above: ASW-SOW is intended as the replacement for the obsolete SUBROC carried by US Navy attack submarines. Planned to enter service sometime in the late 1980s, the first vessels scheduled to receive it are the 'Los Angeles' class SSNs.

diameter 0.533 m (21 in)
Weight: 1403 kg (3,093 lb)
Warhead: 362.9-kg (800-lb) Mk 50 homing torpedo or nuclear depth charge
Performance: maximum speed Mach 1.5+; range 101-166.5 km (62.8-103.5 miles)

Above: An engineering model of Sea Lance is successfully launched by Boeing in Washington's Puget Sound. The production missile will carry either a Mk 50 Barracuda Advanced Lightweight Torpedo or an older Mk 46. The Sea Lance will have a speed of Mach 1.5 plus.

Below: How Boeing envisage the Sea Lance beginning its mission. After the missile exits the water, four small wrap-around fins at the rear of the rocket motor casing deploy automatically to stabilize it. A separate version is being developed for use by surface vessels.

USA

Mk 60 CAPTOR mine

The aluminium-case **Mk 60 CAPTOR** encapsulated torpedo mine is the US Navy's principal offensive anti-submarine warfare barrier weapon for use in the vicinity of deep-water routes that enemy submarines are likely to travel without escort.

CAPTOR is fitted with a detection and control unit (DCU) that is capable of detecting and classifying submarine targets over an estimated range of 1 km (0.62 miles) but gated to ignore surface traffic. There is, however, no identification friend or foe system, so friendly submarine units must be warned of any laying or spots where CAPTORs have already been deployed. The current operational life of the mine is believed to be six months underwater before self-neutralization devices are activated. The initial target detection is carried out by a passive sonar, while the optimum release time for the Mk 4 Mod 4 homing

torpedo payload (which is built with the latest Mod 5 NEARTIP improvements already implemented) is determined by a second (active) ranging set.

CAPTORS may be laid by surface ship, submarine or aircraft, the first platform requiring only an over-the-side boom or crane with a capacity of 1247 kg (2,750 lb) to ensure correct orientation of the mine when it hits the water. Any submarine with standard 533-mm (21-in) torpedo tubes can lay a CAPTOR, while aircraft deploy a parachute-equipped version. Likely wartime airborne delivery platforms include SAC Boeing B-52Hs, US Navy Lockheed P-3C Orions and possibly Lockheed C-130 Hercules transports.

After several years of problems the CAPTOR became fully operational in 1979, an improvement programme being initiated in the following year. A minimum of 2,500 CAPTORs are due to

enter the US Navy's inventory by the time production ends. The **Mk 66** is the practice version.

Specification
CAPTOR
Dimensions: length air/surface-launched 3.68 m (12.08 ft) or submarine-launched 3.51 m (11.5 ft); diameter 0.533 m (21 in)
Weight: air/surface-launched 1184 kg (2,610 lb) or submarine-launched 1069 kg (2,356 lb)
Payload: Mk 46 Mod 4 homing torpedo
Maximum depth: 915 m (3,000 ft)

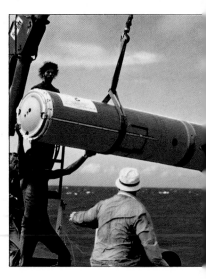

Right: CAPTOR mines can be deployed by an over-the-side boom or crane to ensure the correct orientation of the mine when it lands in the water. Submarines can launch CAPTOR through their torpedo tubes. Aircraft deploying these mines will include the Boeing B-52H.

The active component of CAPTOR consists of a Mk 46 Mod 4 lightweight torpedo, armed with a 43.5-kg (96-lb) shaped charge warhead designed to punch holes in pressure hulls. The ALWT (Advanced Lightweight Torpedo) currently under development may well be used in modified form in the future.

USA

Mk 67 submarine-launched mobile mine (SLMM)

The **Mk 67** SLMM dual anti-ship anti-submarine weapon is intended to provide the US navy submarine force with a capability for covert laying of ground influence mines in heavily defended and/or relatively inaccessible shallow waters. The platform used to perform the operation is a modified Mk 37 torpedo with its warhead and homing systems replaced by all the components needed to turn the weapon into a ground mine. Single and multi-influence fusing systems have been developed for this weapon and the new mines of the Quickstrike programme. At least 1,500 Mk 67s are required to meet current US Navy requirements. It is believed that a submarine will carry two Mk 67s in place of each standard 533-mm (21-in) sized weapon offloaded. At present all submarine classes up to the 'Los Angeles' class are fitted for minelaying, but it should be remembered that each submarine so loaded cannot carry many other weapons, thus effectively limiting its operational flexibility.

Specification
Mk 67 SLMM
Dimensions: length 4.09 m (13.4 ft); diameter 0.485 m (19 in)
Weight: 753 kg (1,660 lb)
Warhead: estimated 159-227 kg (350-500 lb) HE
Performance: speed 18 kts; maximum depth 100 m (330 ft); range 16.5 km (10.3 miles)

'Los Angeles' class attack submarines can carry two MK 67 mines in place of one standard 533-mm (21-in) torpedo. The Mk 67 mine gives US submarines the ability to lay ground-influence mines in heavily defended waters.

RBU anti-submarine rocket-launchers

Over the years the USSR has developed a number of multi-barrel rocket-launchers under the designation *Raketnaya Bombometnaya Ustaovka* (RBU), and these use the ahead-firing 'hedgehog' principle. The rockets are immune to torpedo countermeasures, and under certain circumstances can actually be used as anti-torpedo weapons if there is enough warning. All the rockets are fitted with dual contact and magnetic influence fuses. The most widely used version is the fully automatic 250-mm (9.84-in) **RBU6000**, which entered service in 1962. The 12-barrel launcher is arranged in a horseshoe shape with automatic fuse setting systems, and the rockets are fired in a paired sequence. The HE projectile weighs 70 kg (154 lb) overall, and loading is accomplished barrel by barrel with the launcher in the vertical position.

The RBU600 is usually fitted in conjunction with the fully automatic six-barrel 300-mm (11.81-in) **RBU1000** of the same date, but which uses a larger rocket with a 55-kg (121-lb) warhead.

Earlier systems of the RBU series include the 1957-vintage automatic 250-mm 16-barrel **RBU2500** with manual reloading; the 1958-vintage five-barrel 250-mm **RBU1200** with manual reloading, automatic elevation but manual training; and the 1960-vintage six-barrel manually reloaded **RBU600**. Most systems have three to five complete sets of reload rounds in the ship's magazines, while the rocket types are common to each calibre except that the RBU1200 fires an earlier type of rocket with a 34-kg (75-lb) HE warhead.

Practically all the Warsaw Pact navies use one or more RBU systems, and Soviet client states also use them widely. The People's Republic of China has taken some of the earlier designs and produced its own variants.

The 250-mm calibre rocket used in the various Soviet multiple launcher systems has a warhead weighing up to 55 kg (121 lb). These are not guided systems, the rockets being fired in patterns to bracket a target.

Specification
RBU series

weapon	calibre	range	barrel length	weights rocket	warhead
RBU6000	250 mm (9.84 in)	6 km (3.73 miles)	1.6 m (5.25 ft)	70 kg (154 lb)	21 kg (46.3 lb)
RBU2500	250 mm (9.84 in)	2.5 km (1.55 miles)	1.6 m (5.25 ft)	70 kg (154 lb)	21 kg (46.3 lb)
RBU1200	250 mm (9.84 in)	1.2 km (0.75 miles)	1.4 m (4.6 ft)	70 kg (154 lb)	34 kg (75 lb)
RBU1000	300 mm (11.81 in)	1 km (0.62 miles)	1.5 m (4.9 ft)	120 kg (265 lb)	55 kg (121 lb)
RBU600	300 mm (11.81 in)	0.6 km (0.37 miles)	1.5 m (4.9 ft)	120 kg (265 lb)	55 kg (121 lb)

Above: A Soviet 'Petya' class patrol vessel, on station in one of the Soviet navy's now regular forays into the waters around the Philippines, displays her twin 12-barrelled RBU 6000 rocket launchers, as well as the desire of Soviet sailors to get in as much sunbathing as possible.

Below: Soviet 'Krivak' class frigates have a considerable anti-submarine potential. Among the weapon systems carried are two of the ubiquitous 12-barrel RBU 6000 ASW rocket launchers, mounted ahead of the main bridge structure.

ASW rising mines and CAPTOR type mines

One of the most effective ASW weapons that the Soviets have in their inventory is the offensive rising mine. The weapon is designed primarily for use against submerged targets in areas adjacent to NATO submarine bases, at choke-points and on nuclear submarine deep-water transit routes. Of the two types so far identified, one is for use on the continental shelf (NATO reporting name **'Cluster Bay'**) and the other for use on the deeper continental ledge region (NATO reporting name **'Cluster Gulf'**). Both are tethered torpedo-shaped devices fitted with solid-fuel rocket propulsion units. Initial target detection is by passive sonar, precise target location then being fixed by transmissions from a second active sonar. If the target is confirmed as being within the vertical attack zone the tether is cut and the rocket motor ignited. The high upward speed allows the target very little time for evasion even if it detects the launch. Both mines can be used in an anti-ship role if required.

Since deploying the rising mine the Soviets are believed to have developed a mine similar in concept to the American CAPTOR, but with a 450-mm (17.7-in) acoustic-homing torpedo as the payload. Also primarily targeted against submarines, the mine allows strategic ASW mine barriers to be laid across choke-points in order to funnel NATO submarines into waiting surface and sub-surface ASW hunter-killer groups. Laid offensively in mixed

fields with rising mines, some of the homing torpedo payloads could be specifically tuned to attack the NATO deep-water mine-countermeasures vessels tasked with sweeping them. Primary delivery platforms for all three types are submarines, while barriers can be sown by surface ships and aircraft, the latter being ideally suited for renewing a field and as a fast reaction force.

Specification
rising mine
Type: moored acoustic influence
Laying depth: 600 m (1,970 ft)
Warhead: 225 kg (496 lb) HE
Weight: 1200 kg (2,646 lb)

CAPTOR type mine
Type: moored acoustic torpedo carrier
Laying depth: 750 m (2,460 ft)

Unlike the US Navy, the Soviet Union has a large force of conventionally powered submarines. These boats, such as this 'Tango' seen off the British Isles, would undoubtedly use their inherent quietness in laying mines at strategic points.

Payload: 450-mm (17.7-in) acoustic-homing torpedo
Weight: 1500 kg (3,307 lb)

FRAS-1 anti-submarine warfare rocket

The **FRAS-1** (Free Rocket Anti-Submarine) is an unguided single-stage solid-fuel ballistic weapon which was developed from the Soviet army's FROG artillery rocket series, and entered service in 1967. Target range and bearing data are obtained by the launch platform's own long-range low-frequency sonar sets. These data are then used to calculate the target's predicted course so that the launcher can be aimed to give the optimum rocket trajectory. The uncertainty of placing the rocket within a conventional weapon kill zone is considerably reduced by the use of a 15-kiloton yield pressure-fused nuclear depth charge as the payload. Recent information indicates that there is now a variant of the rocket fitted with a 450-mm (17.7-in) acoustic-homing torpedo as the payload for use in conventional conflicts. The launcher is designated the SUW-N-1 by NATO, and is similar in design to the surface-to-air launchers of the SA-N-1/3 series with twin rails. Only two classes are fitted with the system: the two 'Moskva' class helicopter cruisers and the four 'Kiev' class aircraft-carriers. In each case the system comprises one SUW-N-1 launcher on the forward end of the ship with a below-decks magazine of 20 rounds.

Specification (provisional)
FRAS-1
Dimensions: length 6.2 m (20.3 ft); wing span 1.3 m (4.3 ft); diameter 0.7 m (2.29 ft)
Weight: 800 kg (1,764 lb)
Warhead: 15-kiloton yield fission weapon or 450-mm (17.7-in) acoustic-homing torpedo
Performance: maximum speed Mach 1+; range 9.25-30 km (5.8-18.6 miles)

The bow view of the 'Kiev' class carrier Minsk operating in the East China Sea displays both the RBU6000 launchers and the twin launcher for the much larger FRAS-1 rockets. The missiles are launched on ballistic trajectories towards the target position (calculated from the target's course and speed).

The FRAS-1 (Free Rocket Anti-Submarine) is reputedly based upon the Soviet army's unguided FROG missile. The 30-km (18.6-mile) range and lack of guidance implies no great accuracy, but with a 15-kiloton nuclear warhead accuracy is not strictly essential.

USSR

SS-N-14 anti-submarine missile

The **SS-N-14 'Silex'** conceptually resembles the Australian Ikara and French Malafon in that a subsonic winged vehicle carrying a homing torpedo is guided to the proximity of a submerged target, whereupon the parachute-retarded payload is released into the water to make the final attack. In a brilliant piece of deception the Soviets managed to make NATO believe that this missile was in fact a tactical SSM. As part of this plan the first warships equipped with 'Silex' launchers went to sea in 1968, although the missile itself was not carried until 1974. The SS-N-14 also has a secondary anti-ship role. Carried in quadruple launchers of two distinct types, the 'Silex' forms the main ASW armament of the 'Kara', 'Kresta II' and 'Udaloy' class large ASW ships, and of the 'Krivak I' and 'Krivak II' series missile patrol ships. The guided missile cruiser *Kirov* also has on its forecastle a twin launcher which is reloadable from a 16-round magazine below decks. The large ASW vessels carry eight rounds, while the patrol boats only have four. The torpedo carried is believed to be of the 450-mm (17.7-in) acoustic-homing type with a 100-kg (220-lb) HE warhead. A variant with a nuclear depth bomb is also likely, with a yield of 2.5 kilotons. Guidance on the 'Kara'

and 'Kresta II' classes is effected by the SA-N-3 'Headlight' fire-control radars, while on the other platforms it is a dedicated 'Eye Bowl' radar director. Up to two missiles at a time can be guided. The minimum engagement range for any target type is said to be 7.4 km (4.6 miles).

Specification
SS-N-14
Dimensions: length 7.6 m (24.9 ft); wing span 1.1 m (3.6 ft); diameter 0.55 m (1.8 ft)
Weight: 1000 kg (2,205 lb)
Payload: 450-mm (17.7-in) acoustic-homing torpedo

The quadruple SS-N-14 missile launchers on either side of the bridge of a 'Kara' class crusier are an indication of the size of Soviet shipborne systems.

Performance: speed Mach 0.95; range 55 km (34.2 miles)

Left: The plethora of weapon and sensor systems common to all Soviet warships is dominated on this 'Krivak' class frigate (seen in the English Channel) by the massive quadruple bow launcher for four SS-N-14 missiles. The weapon is believed to be similar to the Malafon and Ikara systems.

Below: A close-up of the bridge and starboard quadruple missile launcher of the large anti-submarine dedicated destroyer Udaloy also shows one of the 'Eye Bowl' fire control radars associated with the SS-N-14 system (visible atop the bridge immediately above the massive missile containers).

SS-N-15 and SS-N-16 anti-submarine missiles

The **SS-N-15** submarine-launched anti-submarine missile entered operational service in 1972, and is believed to have been developed from technology gained by the GRU military intelligence service during operations against the American SUBROC system. Fired from standard 533-mm (21-in) torpedo tubes, the inertially guided solid-fuel rocket-powered SS-N-15 follows a short underwater path before breaking the surface to fly an airborne trajectory to the predicted target zone. On reaching this a nuclear depth bomb of 15-kiloton yield is released to continue on a ballistic course until it enters the water. The bomb then sinks to a preset depth, where its pressure fuse detonates the warhead. Soviet submarine types known to have been fitted with the missile system are the nuclear-powered 'Victor I', 'Victor II', 'Victor III', 'Sierra', 'Alpha', 'Akula', 'Mike', 'Charlie I', 'Charlie II', 'Papa' and 'Oscar' classes, plus the conventionally powered 'Tango' class.

In the mid-1970s a development of the SS-N-15 appeared in the form of the larger-calibre and longer-ranged inertially guided solid-fuel rocket-powered **SS-N-16**, which carries an acoustic-homing ASW torpedo as its payload in lieu of a nuclear depth bomb. Fired like the SS-N-15, it differs in that over the target area a parachute is used to lower the weapon to the water, where its protective nose cap is released. Once it has sunk to a preset depth the torpedo starts a programmed series of search manoeuvres, a terminal attack manoeuvre being used to engage any target encountered. Submarines fitted with this missile are believed to include the 'Victor II', 'Victor III', 'Sierra', 'Charlie II', 'Oscar',

'Mike' and 'Akula' classes. Both missile types have secondary anti-ship roles.

Specification
SS-N-15
Dimensions: length 6.5 m (21.3 ft); diameter 0.533 m (21 in)
Weight: 1900 kg (4,189 lb)
Warhead: 15-kiloton yield fission weapon

Performance: maximum speed Mach 1.5; range 37 km (23 miles)

SS-N-16
Dimensions: length 6.5 m (21.3 ft); diameter 650 mm (25.6 in)
Weight: 2150 kg (4,740 lb)
Warhead: 450-mm (17.7-in) acoustic-homing torpedo
Performance: maximum speed Mach 1.5; range 55 km (34.2 miles)

Believed to have been built from plans stolen from the US Navy, the SS-N-15 is fitted to Soviet nuclear boats as well as diesel-powered 'Tango' class vessels, seen here.

The 'Alpha' class, the fastest (and probably the most expensive) boats in the world, are known to have been fitted with the SS-N-15 SUBROC copy.

Depth charges and bombs

The **Cardoen AS-228** depth charge is a current example of the world's longest established anti-submarine weapon, which was first used in combat by the Royal Navy in World War I. The depth charge is a relatively simple weapon which can be rolled or catapulted into the sea by a thrower or mortar. It is generally fitted with a hydrostatic (pressure-activated) fuse that in modern depth charges allows targets to be engaged at depths between 30 and 500 m (100 and 1,640 ft). In appearance the depth charge can either be of conventional cylindrical shape or (as in the case of the AS-228) a streamlined teardrop with small fins for a faster sink rate.

The charges are dropped in patterns that are calculated to cover a volume notionally centred on the target in order to maximize the probability of its destruction. To improve lethality further the standard fuse on some charges can be replaced either with a magnetic- or acoustic-activated influence type, which gives virtually unlimited depth capability.

Surprisingly, in most Western navies the depth charge has gone out of favour except in its air-dropped variants for aircraft and helicopters. A typical example of this type is the British **Mk 11** series which has its origins in World War II. Fitted with a tail section that breaks off on impact with the water, the main body has an explosive charge armed by a hydropneumatic fusing system. These conventional air-dropped charges are complemented by nuclear models designed and built in the USA. These are used by the aerial ASW forces of the USA, UK and West Germany. The weapon used is the 5/10-kiloton yield **B57** tactical gravity bomb fitted with a depth pressure fuse. The Royal Navy also apparently uses an indigenously designed and built 1-kiloton yield ASW version of its **WE 177 Green Parrot** variable-yield bomb.

Depth charges of the classic World War II sort have largely gone out of fashion, with the notable exception of those arming the ASW helicopters which are in the front line of modern ASW effort. Aircraft such as the SH-3 Sea King of the US Navy are even capable of carrying nuclear weapons.

Specification
US Mk 16 Mod 0 (hydrostatic) and Mk 16 Mod 1 (acoustic) depth charges
Weight: 197.3 kg (435 lb)
Maximum depth: 762 m (2,500 ft); the Mod 1 has no limit

British Mk 11 Mod 3 air-dropped depth charge
Dimensions: length 1.40 m (4.6 ft); diameter 0.28 m (0.92 ft)
Weight: 144.7 kg (319 lb)

Warhead: 80 kg (176 lb) HE
Maximum depth: 90 m (295 ft)

US B57 Mod 1 air-dropped nuclear depth bomb
Dimensions: length 3.0 m (9.8 ft); diameter 0.374 m (1.23 ft)
Weight: 347 kg (765 lb)
Warhead: 5/10-kiloton yield W57 fission weapon
Maximum depth: about 1000 m (3,280 ft)

Cardoen's AS-228 depth charge is one of the last of the general purpose depth charges in the old style to be manufactured, and is launchable from surface ships and from the air. Most navies now reserve the depth charge as an helicopter weapon (except the very special case of the nuclear charge).

The sectioned model of British Aerospace's air-launched Mk 11 depth charge displays many of the features common to such weapons. The tail fins break off on impact with the water, allowing hydropneumatic arming. The Mk 11 is designed specifically for deployment from helicopters and MR aircraft.

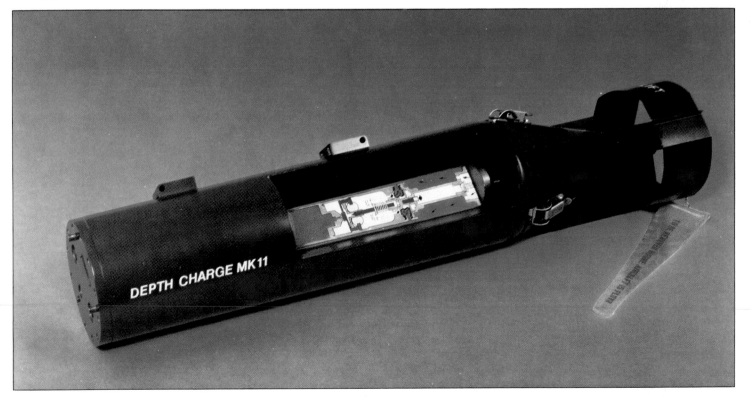

DEPTH CHARGE MK 11

Modern Underwater Weapons

The technological revolution of the last four decades has seen a profound change in the waging of war at sea, with the torpedo replacing the depth charge as the major anti-submarine weapon and the torpedo itself being complemented or in some cases replaced in the anti-shipping role by the guided missile.

The modern lightweight torpedo, in combination with the dedicated anti-submarine helicopter, has extended the capability of ASW vessels to an enormous extent. This is an American Mk 46 torpedo attached to an SH-3 Sea King helicopter, a combination common to several NATO navies.

With the advent into service of the British Sting Ray lightweight ASW torpedo in the early 1980s, the era of the intelligent (or 'smart') weapon arrived in the field of torpedo technology. Already the Americans are moving fast to close the gap by replacing their outmoded Mk 46 weapons by the 'smart' Mk 50, whilst both the Royal and US Navies are working to field as early as possible new heavyweight torpedoes (in the form of the Spearfish and Mk 48 ADCAP respectively) to counter the new generation of faster and deeper-diving Soviet nuclear submarines that have just entered service.

At the same time the Soviets took the opportunity of springing their own surprise in torpedoes in the form of their Type 65 long-range wake-homing anti-ship weapon of 609.6-mm (24-in) calibre aboard attack vessels. Such weapons are backed by a wide range of standard 533-mm (21-in) calibre steam- and electric-powered models (with speeds ranging from 28 kts up to 45 kts or so) including the only nuclear-armed torpedo left in service with any navy. The Soviets also deploy a wide variety of smaller weapons mainly for ASW use. Surprisingly, it is only in the last few years that any reports of wire-guided weapons in

service with the Soviets have surfaced, and to date these have not been substantiated.

Of the other torpedo-producing nations only Sweden has produced remarkably different designs. Its heavyweight Tp61 family is based on a hydrogen peroxide propulsion system of the type discarded by other Western countries such as the UK as being too dangerous to handle under operational conditions. And the Swedish lightweight Tp42 series is still the only Western torpedo of its class that can be guided by wire after an airborne launch.

For the next century there is the prospect of torpedo-like weapons used as robotic sub-surface vessels in the place of manned submarines. Such systems would be controlled from shore bases and form defensive barriers around friendly countries.

The launch of a modern heavyweight torpedo from a surface vessel has changed little from the method used by the destroyers and fast attack craft of World War II. What has changed, however, is the means by which the weapon is directed onto its target.

AEG-Telefunken Seal, Seeschlange, SST4 and SUT torpedoes

These AEG-Telefunken weapons constitute a complete family of heavyweight torpedoes. The electric-powered dual-speed **DM2A1 Seal** and the **DM1 Seeschlange** (Sea Snake) began development from 1958 onwards for the West German navy, and are currently in service aboard their 'Tp.205/206' submarines, whilst the Seal is also employed on some light forces' missile craft. There is a high degree of equipment commonality between the two weapons, the major difference being that the smaller ASW Seeschlange has only half the propulsive battery capacity of the anti-ship Seal. An active/passive homing head is fitted with a dual-core wire-guidance system that allows rapid changing between speeds, attack patterns and guidance modes in order to meet the needs of developing tactical situations.

The Seal was then taken as the model for the **Special Surface Target (SST) 4** torpedo, which except for certain features unique to West German operational requirements is comparable in dimensions, construction and capabilities to its predecessors. Used as the standard anti-ship weapon sold with export 'Type 209' submarines and West German missile craft, the SST4 is found in various NATO and South American navies, and was used operationally by the Argentine submarine *San Luis* during the 1982 Falklands war in several abortive torpedo attacks against Royal Navy task force ships.

The Seal was then further developed to produce the export **Surface and Underwater Target (SUT)** torpedo. As a dual-purpose ASW/anti-ship weapon capable of being launched from surface ships, submarines or shore positions, the SUT has the same shallow-water and deep-diving engagement capabilities of the other members of the family plus the same contact and magnetic proximity fusing systems. Like the SST4 it is in production for export with the 'Type 209' submarines.

Both West Germany and Norway are procuring the improved **DM2A3** or **Seal 3** heavyweight torpedo for their new 'Type 210/211' submarines. The Seal 3 is a dual-role, ASW and anti-ship wire-guided weapon which is expected to be in service in the late 1980s.

Countries operating AEG/Telefunken torpedoes are thought to include Argentina, Chile, Colombia, Ecuador,

A missile-armed Type 143 fast attack craft of the West German navy makes a test launch of an AEG/Telefunken Seal torpedo. One of a family of weapons, it is designed for the engagement of surface targets, and is fitted to Type 142 and 143 boats as well as aboard Type 206 submarines.

Greece, Indonesia, India, Peru and Venezuela.

Specification
Seeschlange
Dimensions: diameter 533 mm (21 in); length 4.15 m (13.62 ft), or 4.62 m (15.16 ft) with wire guidance casket
Weight: 800 to 900 kg (1,764 to 1,984 lb)
Warhead: 100-kg (220-lb) HE
Performance: speed 23 or 35 kts; range 14 or 6 km (8.70 or 3.73 miles)

Right: The Surface and Underwater Target (SUT) torpedo, seen being loaded aboard one of the widely exported 'Type 209' submarines.

Specification
Seal
Dimensions: diameter 533 mm (21 in); length 6.08 m (19.95 ft), or 6.55 m (21.49 ft) with wire guidance casket
Weight: 1370 kg (3,020 ft)
Warhead: 260-kg (573-lb) HE
Performance: speed 23 or 35 kts; range 28 or 12 km (17.40 or 7.46 miles)

Specification
SUT
Dimensions: diameter 533 mm (21 in); length 6.15 m (20.18 ft), or 6.62 m (21.72 ft) with wire guidance casket
Weight: 1414 kg (3,117 lb)

Warhead: 260-kg (573-lb) HE
Performance: speed 23 or 35 kts; range 28 or 12 km (17.40 or 7.46 miles)

Soviet sea mines

The USSR is the world's leading exponent of sea mine warfare, with over 400,000 of these weapons in its naval weapons inventory. The mine types used include small, medium and large defensive moored mines using contact, influence or antenna activating systems. Known types include the **YaRM** and **YaM** spherical contact mines for rivers and shallow waters, the **M08** and **KB** series contact mines for coastal waters, and the **KRAB** moored influence and **MAG** moored antenna mines for coastal and deeper continental shelf waters. All of these are likely to be in service with Soviet client states such as the other members of the Warsaw Pact, many nations in the Middle East, and also Vietnam and North Korea.

The offensive mines are mainly ground mines, of which the most important are the **AMD-500** and **AMD-1000** types (the number referring to the relevant mine's nominal weight in kilograms). The AMD-500 contains 300 kg (661 lb) and the AMD-1000 700 kg (1,543 lb) of HE. Using magnetic, acoustic, pressure or combination influence actuating systems, these weapons have also been widely exported, evidence being provided by recent wars in the Middle and Far East. The pressure types are almost certainly used only by the USSR and her most trusted Warsaw Pact partners, however, because of the possibility of technology compromise and the fact that in other hands they may well be used against their designers

eventually. A new type was retrieved by Royal Navy MCMV vessels after Libya mined the Red Sea in 1984.

There are also growing Soviet stocks of rising mines and underwater electrical potential mines for use in the offensive ASW role against NATO targets. The two types of rising mine available can also be used in a secondary anti-ship role. These two types are believed to be the **'Cluster Bay'** continental shelf and **'Cluster Gulf'** continental ledge types in NATO terminology. There is also a small stockpile of nuclear-armed mines with yields between 5 and 20 kilotons for use against very high-value targets.

The primary offensive minelaying platforms available to the Soviet navy are its conventionally-powered sub-

marines because of their covert laying capabilities. These would be backed by aircraft of the Soviet naval air force, whilst any defensive laying would be the responsibility of surface ship units.

Specification
M08
Dimensions: diameter 0.90 m (2.95 ft); maximum case length 6.096 m (20.00 ft)
Charge weight: 115 kg (253.5 lb)
Maximum laying depth: 130 m (427 ft)

Specification
KB1
Dimensions: diameter 0.9 m (2.95 ft); maximum case length 9.144 m (30.00 ft
Charge weight: 230 kg (507 lb)
Maximum laying depth: 275 m (902 ft)

Soviet torpedoes

Soviet torpedoes, like their Western counterparts, can be categorized into heavy and lightweight models for specific purposes. Of the former, two calibres are known: the standard 533 mm (21 in) and the relatively new 650 mm (25.6 in). The 533-mm (21-in) versions are thought to have been evolved from German World War II designs, and include straight- and pattern-running surface- and submarine-launched steam- or electric-powered models for anti-ship use, as well as acoustic/passive homing ASW/anti-ship versions. Surprisingly, most large modern surface combatants have multi-tube launchers for the ASW acoustic-homing versions. There is also a special 15-kiloton yield nuclear-armed non-terminal-homing 533-mm (21-in) torpedo in service on many of the submarines designed for use against high-value surface targets such as carriers or Very Large Crude Carriers. Similarly the huge 9.14-m (30-ft) long 650-mm (25.6 in) anti-ship **Type 65** torpedo has been introduced on board later-generation nuclear attack submarines for use against surface ship targets. It is believed to use wake-homing guidance methods and, with selectable 50- or 30-kt speeds, has ranges of 50 and 100 km (31 or 62 miles) respectively. With ranges like these, the Type 65 is being used to supplement the pop-up anti-ship cruise missile weapons of 'Charlie' class SSGNs, and the type's availability for the first time allows Soviet SSNs to fire torpedoes from outside the ASW screen of a convoy.

The standard Soviet lightweight torpedo (sub-, ship- and air-launched) is an electric powered 400-mm (15.75-in) weapon that has been in service for a number of years and is roughly equivalent to the US Navy's Type 46. This has been supplemented for air-launch by a 450-mm (17.7-in) weapon of similar speed which is thought to have a larger warhead and greater range to increase lethality. Both the air-launched weapons use parachutes

Above: The Vitse-Admiral Kulakov *is the second of the large ASW destroyers of the 'Udaloy' class. In addition to her ASW missiles and helicopters, she is armed with two quadruple 533-mm (21-in) torpedo tubes, one of which is visible astern of the aft funnel structure.*

to retard their entry into the water.

According to some reports there is also a short 400-mm (15.75-mm) anti-ship torpedo which is found aboard the first-generation 'Hotel', 'Echo' and 'November' class nuclear submarines in their stern tubes. The later-generation nuclear submarine classes apparently have had several of their standard 533-mm (21-in) calibre torpedo tubes fitted with liners to fire the ASW version of the same weapon.

The standard fusing system fitted to Soviet torpedoes is an active magnetic proximity device (to ensure detonation under the target's hull so as to break its back) with a secondary contact unit for a direct hit.

Above: The 'Alfa' class submarine is considerably shorter than other Soviet SSN designs, so it is unlikely to have been fitted to fire the massive 650-mm (25.6-in) torpedo reportedly in service with the Soviet navy although it may be armed with the strategic SS-N-21 cruise missile.

Below: Backbone of the Soviet anti-submarine force, the 'Krivak' class, like all major Soviet vessels, is fitted with torpedo tubes. The eight tubes abaft the bridge, in quadruple mounts port and starboard, probably fire acoustically-homing 533-mm (21-in) torpedoes.

Above: Photographed by a US Navy F-14 fighter, this 'Victor III' SSN has fouled the towed array sonar of a 'Spruance' class destroyer off the coast of Georgia. These large boats may be fitted with the extremely long-ranged 650-mm (25.6-in) torpedo, which allows attacks from as far as 100 km (62 miles).

FRANCE

DTCN L3, L4 and L5 torpedoes

The electric-powered 550-mm (21.7-in) calibre **L3** ship- or submarine-launched ASW homing heavyweight torpedo is currently in service with the French navy and was designed by the Direction Technique des Constructions Navales to attack submerged targets at depths up to 300 m (984 ft) and speeds from 0 to 20 kts. It is fitted with an AS-3T active acoustic guidance system that has a detection range of about 600 m (1,969 ft) in ideal conditions, and the warhead is detonated by an electro-magnetic proximity fusing system. A 533-mm (21-in) version with the same performance is available for export, length and weight being 4.318 m (14.17 ft) and 900 kg (1,984 lb). Apart from France, several of the countries (including Spain) which have bought 'Daphné' class submarines have also obtained the larger-calibre weapon.

Also in service with the French navy is the 533-mm (21-in) electric-powered **L-4** air-launched torpedo for use with helicopters, aircraft and the Malafon ASW missile. Fitted with an active acoustic-homing system, it describes a circular search path upon entering the water until its seeker acquires the target. The warhead is detonated either by an impact fuse or a proximity acoustic influence fuse. French L4s have recently been modernized to improve shallow-water performance and its 0/20-kt target capability from periscope depth to around 300-m (984-ft) deep cruising. A version for surface ship launching has also been developed: this has a length of 3.30 m (10.83 ft) and a weight of 570 kg (1,257 lb).

The most recent of the L-series torpedoes is the electric-powered **L5**, which is available in four versions. The dual-purpose ASW/anti-ship **L5 Mod 1** is carried by surface ships, whilst the similar-role but heavier **L5 Mod 3** is used by submarines. A single-role variant, the ASW **L5 Mod 4**, has been derived from the Mod 1 and is used solely by surface ships. A further ver-

The Sintra-Alcatel-built L3 is a conventional ship- or submarine-launched active acoustic homing anti-submarine torpedo. Unusually, it has a diameter of 550 mm (21.65 in) but has been offered in the more standard 533 mm (21 in) for export. It is in widespread French naval service.

sion of this has been developed for the export market as the **L5 Mod 4P** multi-role torpedo. All versions are fitted with a Thomson-CSF active/passive guidance system and are capable of various attack profiles including direct and programmed searches using either of the acoustic homing techniques available. Known operators of the L5 other than France include the Belgian navy (L5 Mod 3) and Spain (aboard submarines).

Specification
L3
Dimensions: diameter 550 mm (21.7 in); length 4.30 m (14.11 ft)
Weight: 910 kg (2,006 lb)
Warhead: 200-kg (441-lb) HE
Performance: speed 25 kts; range 7.5 km (4.66 miles)

Specification
L4
Dimensions: diameter 533 mm (21 in); length 3.033 m (9.95 ft), or 3.13 m (10.27 ft) with parachute pack
Weight: 540 kg (1,190 lb)
Warhead: 104-kg (229-lb) HE
Performance: speed 30 kts; range 5.5 km (3.4 miles)

Specification
L5
Dimensions: diameter 533 mm (21 in); length 4.40 m (14.44 ft)
Weight: (Mod 1) 1000 kg (2,205 lb), (Mod 3) 1300 kg (2,866 lb), (Mod 4) 920 kg (2,028 lb) and (Mod 4P) 930 kg (2,050 lb)
Warhead: 150-kg (331-lb) HE
Performance: speed 35 kts; range 9.25 km (5.75 miles)

Above: The L4 air-launched torpedo can function in shallow water against submarines manoeuvring at up to 20 kts. It also provides the warload for the Malafon ASW missile system, and a ship-launched version has been designed.

Below: The L5 series of multi-purpose torpedoes is fitted with Thomson-CSF active/passive homing heads, although the Mod 1 is intended for surface vessel use and the heavier Mod 3 version (shown here) equips submarines.

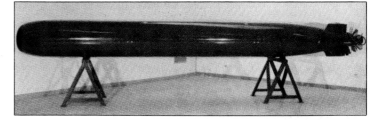

 FRANCE

DTCN F17 torpedo

The **F17** is the first wire-guided heavyweight torpedo to be used by the French navy. Designed for use against surface ships from submarines, the weapon can be employed either in the wire-guided mode or in an autonomous passive homing mode, the capability for instant switching between the two modes being provided on a control panel aboard the launch platform. The terminal attack phase is normally of the passive acoustic type under the torpedo's own internal control. A dual-purpose surface- or submarine-launched variant, the **F17P**, has also been developed for the export market, and has been bought by Saudi Arabia for use aboard its 'Madina' ('Type F2000') class frigates, and by Spain for use aboard its 'Agosta' and modernized 'Daphné' class submarines. The F17P differs from the basic F17 in having an active/passive acoustic-homing seeker which allows completely autonomous operation if required.

Specification
F17
Dimensions: diameter 533 mm (21 in);

length 5.914 m (19.40 ft)
Weight: 1410 kg (3,108 lb)
Warhead: 250-kg (551-lb) HE
Performance: speed 35 kts; range 18 km (11.18 miles)

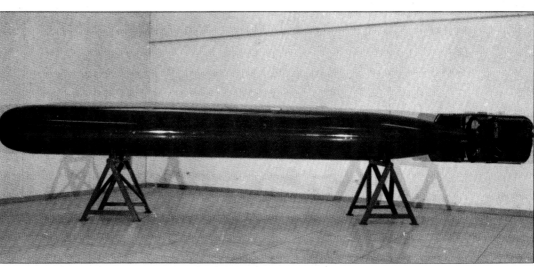

The wire-guided F17 heavyweight torpedo is an anti-shipping submarine-launched weapon, although an automatic homing head is standard. The F17P is a development capable of ship or submarine launch, and in addition to wire guidance is equipped for active or passive acoustic homing. In all the models, however, the terminal attack phase is usually autonomous.

Thomson-Sintra sea mines

Thomson-Sintra produces two types of operational sea mine. The **TSM3510** (or **MCC23**) is an offensive ground mine fitted with a multi-sensor fusing system based on two or all of the magnetic, acoustic and pressure actuating influences, and is shaped for launching from the standard torpedo tube of a submarine. The sensitivity of the fusing can be adjusted before laying to suit the depth of water and the type of target likely to be encountered. The mine is armed (by withdrawing two safety pins) before it is loaded into the tube and is activated by a preset timing delay to allow the submarine to clear the area. Two similarly shaped training mines, the **TSM3515** (**MCED23**) and the **TSM3517** (**MCEM23**), are also in service.

For defensive purposes there is the **TSM3530** (**MCT15**), which is a ground

As offensive mines have to be laid covertly, often in or near enemy waters, the most appropriate system for such work is the submarine. Hence the TSM 3510, in common with many other mines in production today, is designed to be ejected through standard torpedo tubes.

mine deployed from surface ships fitted with mine rails. It is checked in its descent to the sea bottom by a parachute-retarding device which ensures that correct orientation is achieved. It is armed by a preset timing delay which allows the laying platform to clear the area.

Both mines are in service with the French navy and have been sold abroad, especially the TSM3510 which is found in several of the countries that have purchased 'Daphné' class sub-

marines. Other users include Belgium, Brazil (from 'Oberon' SSKs), the Netherlands, Malaysia, Pakistan and Spain.

Specification
TSM3510
Dimensions: diameter 0.53 in (1.74 ft); length 2.368 in (7.77 ft)
Weight: 850 kg (1,874 lb)
Actuating sensors: any combination of magnetic, acoustic and pressure.

Specification
TSM3530
Dimensions: diameter 1.20 m (3.94 ft); length 1.10 m (3.61 ft)
Weight: 1200 kg (2,646 lb)
Actuating sensors: combination magnetic acoustic, magnetic pressure, acoustic pressure, or magnetic acoustic pressure

---

Marconi Sting Ray torpedo

Designed to supplement the American Mk 46 Mod 2 and to replace the Mk 44 torpedoes in British service, the **Marconi Sting Ray** lightweight torpedo was the sequel of the abortive Mod in-house lightweight Mk 30 and 31 programmes, which were cancelled in 1970. The Sting Ray is the first British torpedo to be developed entirely by private industry and incorporates a number of technical innovations. The weapon is capable of being launched from helicopters, aircraft and surface ships over a wide range of speeds and sea states and, as a result of its unique guidance system, can be used satisfactorily in both shallow and deep waters with an equally high single-shot kill probability. The former was demonstrated recently during a development trial shot when Sting Ray dropped from a BAe Nimrod of No. 42 Squadron hit and sank the decommissioned conventional submarine *Porpoise*, apparently whilst she was moored at periscope depth.

Although deployed operationally aboard several ships during the 1982 Falklands war, Sting Ray was not fired in anger and did not actually enter full-scale service with the Royal Navy and Royal Air Force until 1983. Since then the weapon has been sold to Thailand and Egypt. In terms of general performance it is similar to the Mk 46 though, it seems, the British torpedo has slightly deeper diving depth of 800 m (2,625 ft). The Sting Ray also possesses an onboard digital computer coupled to a multi-mode multi-beam active/passive sonar that effectively makes it a 'smart' weapon. Propulsion is by an electrically-driven pump-jet with a battery activated by sea water that ensures no speed loss as the depth increases. The warhead is of the directed-energy shaped-charge variety rather than blast type to ensure penetration of a Soviet submarine's double-hull construction.

In addition to its primary air-launch mode, Sting Ray will form a part of the ASW armament of several classes of Royal Navy surface combatant. The torpedoes will be launched from modified versions of the US Mk 32 triple tubes, as shown here in a trial launch from HMS Avenger.

Similar in size to the previous generation of lightweight torpedoes, the Marconi Stingray also has a similar performance. Where it differs is in the sophisticated guidance.

Specification (provisional)
Stingray
Dimensions: diameter 324 mm (12.75 in); length 2.6 m (8.52 ft)
Weight: 265.4 kg (585.2 lb)
Warhead: 40 kg (88 lb) shaped-charge HE
Performance: speed 45 kts; range 11.1 km (6.9 miles)

Right: The new generation of lightweight torpedo gives significant anti-submarine capability to relatively unsophisticated systems. The Britten-Norman Defender could carry Stingray and could use its sophisticated electronics to attack the most advanced of submarines.

UK
Marconi Mk 24 Tigerfish torpedo

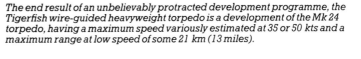

The origins of the **Mk 24 Tigerfish** heavyweight torpedo saga can be found as far back as 1959 in a British torpedo project codenamed 'Ongar'. By 1970 it was realized that the technology involved could not be handled solely by an in-house service approach, so the then Marconi Company was given the job of developing the weapon from 1972 onwards. This was five years after the originally envisaged in-service date. As a result of development and engineering problems the first version of the Tigerfish, the **Mk 24 Mod 0**, entered fleet service in 1974 with less operational capability than originally desired. It was only granted its full Fleet Weapon Acceptance certificate in 1979 after protracted evaluation.

To rectify the problems Marconi initiated development of a product-improved version, the **Mk 24 Mod 1**, during 1972 but this also encountered technical problems and finally entered limited service in mid-1978. By 1981 sufficient update kits were available to upgrade all the earlier Mod 0 weapons to this standard. Designed for submarine use against submerged (Mod 0 and 1) and surface (Mod 1) targets, the dual-speed electric-powered Tigerfish is guided in its initial stage by wire dispensed from both the submarine and the torpedo itself, using data derived from the launch platform's passive sonar sets. The roll-sta-

bilized (by retractable mid-body stub wings) torpedo is guided in this fashion up to the point where its own three-dimensional active/passive sonar seeker head and computer can take over for the attack on the target. At present only the Royal and Brazilian navies use Tigerfish. The dual-role **Mk 24 Mod 2** has longer range and enhanced guidance using Sting Ray seeker technology. Operational trials took place in 1986 from HM submarines *Conqueror* and *Trafalgar*.

Specification
Mk 24 Tigerfish
Dimensions: diameter 533 mm (21 in); length 6.464 m (21.2 ft)
Weight: 1547 kg (3,410 lb)
Warhead: 134-kg (295-lb) HE
Performance: speed 24 or 35 kts; Mod 1 range 21 or 13 km (13 or 8 miles), Mod 2 range 29 or 18 km (18 or 11.2 miles)

The Tigerfish is propelled by a two-speed electric motor driving a pair of contra-rotating propellers designed for high efficiency and low noise production.

The end result of an unbelievably protracted development programme, the Tigerfish wire-guided heavyweight torpedo is a development of the Mk 24 torpedo, having a maximum speed variously estimated at 35 or 50 kts and a maximum range at low speed of some 21 km (13 miles).

UK
Marconi Spearfish torpedo

Designed to meet Naval Staff Requirement 7525, the **Marconi Spearfish** is an advanced-capabilities wire-guided dual-role (ASW/anti-ship) heavyweight torpedo. It will be able to engage the new generation of Soviet high-speed deep-submergence submarines using a new HAP-Otto fuel-powered Sundstrand 21TP01 gas turbine engine with a pump-jet outlet to achieve speeds in excess of 60 kts (up to 70 kts on trials). The warhead is of the directed-energy shaped-charge type and is capable of penetrating the latest Soviet developments in submarine double-hull construction which can be found aboard the 'Oscar' SSGN and 'Typhoon' SSBN classes. To ensure that the weapon actually contacts the target's hull the installed guidance system uses technology developed originally for the Sting Ray lightweight tor-

pedo project. The computer will enable the torpedo to make its own tactical decisions during an engagement, optimizing the homing modes available to the underwater environment encountered and to the target's use of decoys and manoeuvring patterns.

Work on the development prototypes began in 1982, the first in-water trials taking place in the following year. Production deliveries are believed to be due in 1987, with operational capability scheduled for 1988-9.

Externally very similar to the Mk 24 Tigerfish wire-guided torpedo that it will eventually replace, the Marconi Spearfish is radically different internally and has a considerably enhanced performance.

Specification (provisional)
Spearfish
Dimensions: diameter 533 mm (21 in); length 8.5 m (27.9 ft)
Weight: 1996 kg (4,400 lb)
Warhead: 249-kg (550-lb) HE
Performance: speed 24 or 65 knots; range 36.5 or 22.9 km (22.7 or 14.25 miles)

Above: An early development model of the Spearfish is seen at the start of water trials. The torpedo guidance system is thought to make use of a digital computer (as in the Stingray), and the highly classified directed energy warhead is designed to cope with the latest Soviet submarines.

Left: Powered by an HAP-Otto fuelled gas turbine giving considerably more power density than electric motors, the Spearfish has achieved great speeds on trials, reaching more than 60 kts.

FFV Tp42 series torpedoes

Originally intended as the successor to the Royal Swedish navy's Tp41, the **Tp42** is the base model of a whole series of lightweight 400-mm (15.75-in) torpedoes built by FFV for the home market and for export. The basic model, the **Tp422**, entered service in mid-1983 and is intended primarily for ASW operations from the navy's small fleet of Boeing-Vertol 107 helicopters. It is unique amongst Western lightweight weapons in that it is capable of wire guidance after an air-launched delivery. The terminal attack phase is carried out by a passive sonar system. Propulsion is by an electric battery of the silver-zinc type, whilst the warhead is fitted with both proximity and contact fuses. The torpedo can be set to run at one of two speeds which are changeable after launch either via the guidance wire or as an instruction preprogrammed into the seeker unit. A similar model, the **Tp423**, is believed to be intended for launch from surface ships and submarines against submarine or ship targets. The export version of the Tp422/423 is known as the **Tp427**, and has internal/guidance changes which effectively introduce different sonar and proximity fuse frequencies in order not to compromise Swedish navy settings.

In 1984 the Swedish navy initiated a product improvement programme that has resulted in the **Tp431**, which entered production in 1987. This is designed to use new digital microprocessor guidance units and is optimized to attack the new generation of Soviet conventional submarines oper-ating in the quiet state in shallow waters. A new three-speed selectable propulsion system and increased guidance wire capacity have improved the maximum range of the weapon, at the slowest speed, by 33 per cent in comparison with the earlier Tp42 models. The equivalent export version is designated **Tp43XO** and will be able to use alternative propulsion systems if required. The lightest of the whole Tp432/43XO family will be the helicopter-launched variant which weighs 280 kg (617 lb), and because it has a smaller battery capacity this will have a maximum range in the order of 15-20 km (9.3-12.4 miles) at the slowest speed setting.

Specification
Tp422/427
Dimensions: diameter 400 mm (15.75 in); length 2.44 m (8.00 ft), or 2.60 m (8.53 ft) with wire guidance section
Weight: 298 kg (657 lb)
Warhead: 50 kg (110 lb) HE
Performance: speed 15 or 25 kts; range 20 or 10 km (12.43 or 6.21 miles)

Specification
Tp431/43XO
Dimensions: diameter 400 mm (15.75 in); length 2.60 m (8.53 ft), or 2.85 m (9.35 ft) with wire guidance section
Weight: 280 to 350 kg (617 to 772 lb)
Warhead: 45-kg (99-lb) HE
Performance: speed 15, 25 or 35 kts; range 30, 20 or 10 km (18.64, 12.43 or 6.21 miles)

Above: The Type 42 series are the only air launched torpedoes with wire guidance. Both Type 422 and Type 423 can have reduced charge warheads fitted. This would force intruding submarines (which Sweden has some experience of) to the surface.

Below: The advantage of lightweight torpedoes is that they can give a significant anti-submarine capability to the smallest of helicopters. The Type 422 has been launched from the Swedish navy's AB-206 helicopters, although the KV 107 (licence-built Boeing-Vertol CH-46) is the usual platform.

FFV Tp61 series torpedoes

Designed by FFV for use against surface ship targets, the Tp61 entered service in 1967 as a non-terminal-homing wire-guided heavyweight torpedo for use by surface ships, submarines and coastal defence batteries. In 1984 the longer-range **Tp613** entered service as the Tp61's successor with essentially the same propulsion system and a terminal homing seeker that utilizes an onboard computer to oversee the attack and, if necessary, to initiate previously-programmed search patterns at the target's predicted location. The computer also guides the torpedo to the latter point and initiates a search even if the guidance wire is broken. The torpedo's thermal propulsion system combines hydrogen peroxide with ethanol to power a 12-cylinder steam motor which produces an almost invisible wake signature. Compared with modern electrically-powered weapons at similar speed, the maximum range attainable is between three and five times greater.

The earlier Type 61 is in service with Norway and Denmark, though both are expected to order the **Type 617** torpedo. This 6.98 m (22.9 ft) long, 1850 kg (4,078-lb) weapon has been in service with the Swedish navy since 1984. It differs from the Tp613 in

The 'Hauk' class torpedo boat Gribb *of the Norwegian navy approaches an ammunition wharf. Currently equipped with Type 61 torpedoes, the Norwegians are expected to upgrade their force with the improved Type 617.*

Unlike most modern heavyweight torpedoes, the FFV Tp61 is not powered electrically but by a hydrogen-peroxide/ethanol driven engine. Such systems are more unstable than battery power, but of much higher performance.

internal software changes to give sonar and proximity fuse settings different from Swedish ones. Each Tp61 series torpedo can be left in its tube for up to four months without requiring overhaul.

Specification
Tp61
Dimensions: diameter 533 mm (21 in); length 7.025 m (23.05 ft)
Weight: 1796 kg (3,959 lb) or (Tp613) 1765 kg (3,891 lb)
Warhead: 250-kg (551-lb) HE
Performance: speed 45 kts; range 20 km (12.43 miles) or (Tp613) 30 km (18.64 miles)

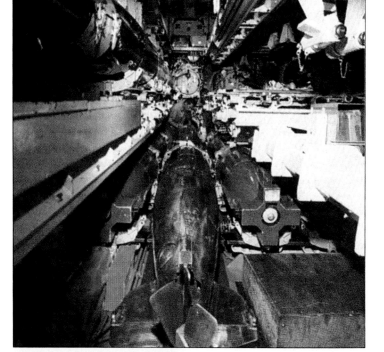

Snar, a 'Snogg' class fast attack craft, is fitted with four 533-mm (21-in) torpedo tubes in addition to Penguin anti-ship missiles. The torpedo and the missile have similar ranges and although the missile is much faster the torpedo does not appear on any radar screen.

Mk 37 torpedo

The original **Westinghouse Mk 37 Mod 0** heavyweight torpedo entered service in 1956 as a submarine- and surface ship-launched ASW acoustic-homing free-running torpedo. Fitted with studs along its sides, the 482.6-mm (19-in) calibre Mk 37 can be fired from standard 533-mm (21-in) torpedo tubes. As operational experience built up with the weapon, many Mod 0 torpedoes were refurbished and modified to bring them up to the **Mk 37 Mod 3** standard. Although useful in the ASW role these free-running weapons, which could dive to 300 m (985 ft), were not suited to really long sonar detection ranges as during the torpedo's run to a predicted target location it was possible that the target could perform evasive manoeuvres taking it out of the 640 m (2,100-ft) acquisition range of the weapon's seeker head. Thus wire guidance was fitted to the Mk 37 to produce the **Mk 37 Mod 1** version, which entered service in 1962 aboard American submarines. This was followed by the updated **Mk 37 Mod 2** conversion of Mod 1 weapons. Although the standard US Navy submarine-launched ASW torpedo for some 20 years, the Mk 37 is now found only aboard the diesel-electric boat USS *Darter*.

Many have been converted to Mk 67 submarine-launched mobile mine shells, whilst others have been put through major upgrading programmes before sale to other countries. The first such modification, in the mid-1970s, resulted in the **Northrop NT37C**, which incorporates a new thermo-chemical propulsion system based on that of the Mk 46 and has an anti-ship capability option. The NT37C is known to be in service with Canada and Israel aboard their submarine fleets. In 1979 Honeywell acquired the rights to the NT37C, and at the request of several NATO Mk 37 users further developed the weapon to the **Honeywell NT37E** standard which allows the fitting of several additional kits to produce **NT37E Mod 2** and **NT37E Mod 3** conversions of the basic Mk 37 variants. In general terms these new variants display a 40 per cent increase in speed, a 150 per cent increase in range, an 80 per cent increase in endurance and a 100 per cent increase in seeker detection range in comparison with the original Mk 37 models. At least 16 countries are known to use the various versions of the Mk 37 family including the above, plus West Germany, Spain, Argentina and the Netherlands.

Specification
Mk 37
Dimensions: diameter 484.6 mm (19 in); length (Mod 0 and 3) 3.52 m (11.55 ft) or (Mod 1 and 2) 4.09 m (13.42 ft)
Weight: (Mod 0 and 3) 649 kg (1,430 lb) or (Mod 1 and 2) 767 kg (1,690 lb)
Warhead: 150-kg (330-lb) HE
Performance: speed 16 or 24 kts; range (Mod 0 and 3) 16.5 or 7.3 km (10.25 or 4.5 miles), or (Mod 1 and 2) 8.7 km (5.4 miles)

Specification
NT37E
Dimensions: diameter 484.6 mm (19 in); length (Mod 2) 4.506 m (14.78 ft) or (Mod 3) 3.946 m (12.95 ft)
Weight: (Mod 2) 748 kg (1,650 lb) or (Mod 3) 640 kg (1,412 lb)
Warhead: 150-kg (330-lb) HE
Performance: speed 22.4 or 33.6 kts; range (Mod 2) 21.7 km (13.5 miles) or (Mod 3) 18.3 km (11.4 miles)

Above: Dutch seamen manoeuvre the long, heavy bulk of a NATO standard NT37 torpedo into one of the forward tubes of a 'Dolfijn' class submarine. The original Mk 37 entered service in the 1950s, but progressive modifications by Westinghouse and Northrop have upgraded the weapon's capability to an enormous extent.

Left: In its anti-ship version the NT37 can be programmed to explode on contact or be fitted with an acoustic proximity fuse. By adjusting the running depth this can ensure detonation immediately under the target, so breaking the ship's back. Had the trial torpedo seen here been armed, the explosion would have occurred immediately under the engines.

Mk 44, Mk 46 and Mk 50 torpedoes

The **Mk 44 Mod 0** lightweight torpedo was selected for production in 1956 and in the following year became the payload for the new ASROC ASW missile as well as the standard US Navy ship- and air-launched lightweight torpedo. The weapon is electrically powered, and utilizes a seawater-activated battery and an active-homing seeker with a detection range of 585 m (1,920 ft). A slightly modified version, the **Mk 44 Mod 1**, was produced at a later date, and this model differed only in internal details. Several countries procured the weapon, but most have now replaced it with the Mk 46 although some like the UK have kept stocks because of the Mk 44's better shallow-water performance than its successor. The US Navy replaced it completely from 1967 onwards by the **Mk 46**.

The active/passive acoustic-homing Mk 46 programme began in 1960, the first production rounds of the air-launched **Mk 46 Mod 0** variant being delivered in 1963. The new torpedo achieved twice the range of the Mk 44, could dive deeper (460 m/1,500 ft versus 300 m/984 ft) and was 50 per cent faster (45 kts versus 30 kts) because of the use of a new type of propulsive system. In the Mod 0 this was a solid-fuel motor, but as a result of maintenance difficulties it had to be changed to the Otto-fuelled thermo-chemical cam engine in the follow-on **Mk 46 Mod 1** (which first entered service in 1967 for use in ASROC, surface ship and some airborne launching purposes) and the **Mk 46 Mod 2** that first appeared in 1972. There was no Mod 3, so the next variant to see service was the **Mk 46 Mod 4** intended specifically for use as the payload for Mk 60 CAPTOR mines. However, because of Soviet submarine developments (primarily in the area of anechoic hull coatings to degrade active sonar acoustic transmissions) the US Navy had to develop a modification kit with new guidance and control units, engine improvements and an enhanced sonar transducer to restore the 33 per cent loss in the 550-m (1,800-ft) detection range suffered by Mk 46s when encountering such coatings. Known by the title **NEARTIP** (NEAR-Term Improvement Program), the **Mk 46 Mod 5** is being procured both as new-build weapons and as conversions of the earlier Mod 1 and Mod 2 weapons.

Other users of the Mk 46, mostly Mods 2 and 5, include Australia, Brazil, Canada, Ecuador, France, West Germany, Greece, Indonesia, Iran, Israel (Mod 1), Italy, Morocco, the Netherlands, New Zealand, Pakistan (Mod 1), Saudi Arabia, Spain, Turkey, Taiwan and the UK. The Mk 46 was used by the Royal Navy on a number of occasions during the Falklands war with inconclusive results, although the threat of Mk 46s did help in the damaging and subsequent grounding of the Argentine submarine *Santa Fé* off South Georgia.

The replacement for the Mk 46 in US Navy service is the **Advanced Lightweight Torpedo (ALWT)**, which has now been given the designation **Mk 50 Barracuda** following a competitive evaluation. Fitted with a directed-energy shaped-charge warhead, the Mk 50 is roughly the same size and weight as the Mk 46 but will be faster at 55+ kts and be able to dive deeper (to 600 m/1,970 ft). It will also have a new stored chemical-energy propulsion system with a closed-cycle steam turbine in conjunction with a pump-jet arrangement. An onboard computer and advanced active/passive sonar will give the weapon 'smart' capabilities similar to those of the British Sting Ray. Programme delays mean it will not reach IOC until well into the 1990s.

Specification
Mk 44
Dimensions: diameter 324 mm (12.75 in); length (Mod 0) 2.54 m (8.33 ft) or (Mod 1) 2.57 m (8.44 ft)
Weight: (Mod 0) 192.8 kg (425 lb) or (Mod 1) 196.4 kg (433 lb)
Warhead: (Mod 0) 34-kg (75-lb) HE or (Mod 1) 33.1-kg (73-lb) HE
Performance: speed 30 kts; range 5.5 km (3.4 miles)

Specification
Mk 46
Dimensions: diameter 324 mm (12.75 in); length 2.6 m (8.5 ft)
Weight: (Mod 0) 257.6 kg (568 lb) or (Mod 1, 2, 4 and 5) 230.4 kg (508 lb)
Warhead: 43.1-kg (95-lb) HE
Performance: speed 40/45 kts; range 11 km (6.8 miles) at 15-m (50-ft) depth or 5.5 km (3.4 miles) at 457-m (1,500-ft) depth

Specification (provisional)
Mk 50 Barracuda
Dimensions: diameter 324 mm (12.75 in); length 2.9 m (9.5 ft)
Weight: 362.9 kg (800 lb)
Warhead: 45.4-kg (100-lb) shaped-charge HE
Performance: speed 55+ kts; range 13.7 km (8.5 miles)

More than 9,000 Mk 46 lightweight torpedoes have been produced by Honeywell for service with the US Navy and the naval forces of more than 20 other countries. It is launched from the air, the surface and by ASROC.

Above: The development of the dedicated anti-submarine helicopter, together with the lightweight acoustic homing torpedo, has immensely extended ASW radius. This Mk 46 torpedo, dropped by an SH-3A Sea King, is deploying a parachute to retard its speed.

Right: A Mk 46 torpedo is launched from one of the triple torpedo tubes fitted to all of the cruisers, destroyers and frigates of the US Navy.

The Israeli navy is one of several that have acquired Mk 46 torpedoes, and some of the 36 'Dabur' class coastal patrol craft operating in the Mediterranen and the Red Sea have been equipped with a pair of single tubes.

Mk 48 torpedo

The **Mk 48** heavyweight torpedo is the latest in a long line of US Navy 533-mm (21-in) calibre submarine-launched weapons. As a long-range selectable-speed wire-guided dual-role (ASW/anti-ship) weapon it replaced both the Mk 37 series wire-guided ASW torpedo and the US Navy's only nuclear-armed torpedo, the anti-ship Mk 45 ASTOR fitted with a 10-kiloton yield W34 warhead. Development of the Mk 48 began in 1957 when feasibility studies were initiated to meet an operational requirement eventually issued in late 1960. The weapon was intended as both a surface- and submarine-launched torpedo, but the former requirement was dropped when surface-launched weapons went out of favour. Two versions were produced to meet the range and speed performance figures needed to engage a 35-kt submerged target: the **Westinghouse Mk 48 Mod 0**, which used a gas turbine and was subsequently refined to the proposed production **Mk 48 Mod 2** variant, and the **Gould Mk 48 Mod 1** which used an Otto-fuelled piston (swashplate) engine and a redesigned acoustic-homing system. The latter was chosen for mass production, operational capability being achieved in 1972.

The next version to be built was the

The Mk 48 torpedo is carried by all US attack and ballistic missile submarines, a continual process of development having enhanced its performance in line with that of Soviet submarines in the past 15 years.

Mk 48 Mod 3, which had the same 762-m (2,500-ft) depth capability as the Mod 1 but introduced a new two-way TELECOM (rather than one-way) wire-guidance communication link that allowed the torpedo head to transmit its search data back to the launch platform for more accurate processing to produce what was in effect a track-via-torpedo guidance mode.

From 1980 most weapons were upgraded to the standard of the **Mk 48 Mod 4** which entered service that year. This has the same TELECOM facilities of the Mod 3, enhanced speed (to 55 kts) and depth (to 915 m/3,000 ft) capabilities, plus an additional fire-and-forget mode which can be initiated if the torpedo's own noise masks the launch submarine's passive sonar detection sets.

By 1978, because of an increasing awareness of the latest Soviet submarine capabilities in the area of speed and diving depth, an **ADvanced CAPability (ADCAP)** version of the Mk 48, the **Mk 48 Mod 5**, entered development. A new higher-powered sonar was fitted both to improve the target acquisition range from the current 3660 m (12,000 ft) and to reduce the effect of enemy decoys and anechoic coatings. The sonar is electrically steered to decrease the need for the torpedo to manoeuvre in the search phase. Together with a larger fuel load, this gives the new variant a longer range (using the same propulsion system) and a new under-ice capability. Further modifications are at present being researched to give an **Upgraded ADCAP** weapon for the next

decade: these developments include improved anti-ship homing features, an even greater maximum diving depth and a higher target speed engagement envelope. The ADCAP Mk 48 Mod 5 entered service in 1986 with several hundred more planned by 1990. The only foreign users of the Mk 48 (all Mod 4) are Australia, Canada and the Netherlands.

Specification
Dimensions: diameter 533 mm (21 in); length 5.8 m (19.17 ft)
Weight: 1579 kg (3,480 lb)
Warhead: 294.5-kg (650-lb) HE
Performance: speed (Mod 1 and 3) 48 kts, (Mod 4) 55 kts or (Mod 5) 60 kts; range (Mod 1 and 3) 32 km (20 miles), (Mod 4) 28 km (17.5 miles) or (Mod 5) 38 km (23.75 miles)

Above: Crewmen aboard the 'Sturgeon' class nuclear attack submarine USS Pargo carefully receive a Mk 48 Mod 1 torpedo into the torpedo room. Most current American SSNs have reduced torpedo armament to allow for missiles such as Subroc, Harpoon and Tomahawk, or tube-launched mines.

Above left: A Mk 48 torpedo is lowered into the torpedo room of the nuclear-powered ballistic missile submarine USS Stonewall Jackson at the Naval Submarine Support base at Kings Bay, Georgia. These submarines are armed with torpedoes for self-protection only.

Left: An artist's impression of the last stage in the life of a Mk 48, with the onboard sonar homing in on the hapless target at a maximum speed of close to 60 kts.

Whitehead Motofides A184 and A244 torpedoes

The **A184** is a dual-purpose ASW/anti-ship heavyweight wire-guided torpedo produced by Whitehead Motofides and carried by Italian navy submarines and surface ships. It has also been exported to Peru and Taiwan, for her 'Guppy II' and 'Zwaardvuis' class submarines. The panoramic active/passive acoustic-homing head controls the torpedo's course and depth in the final attack phase whilst the initial wire guidance uses the launch platform's own sonar sensors to guide the weapon up to the point of acoustic acquisition. Like most modern electrically-powered torpedoes the A184 is fitted with a silver-zinc battery and has dual speed capabilities (low speed for the passive hunting phase and high speed for the terminal attack or active phase).

To complement the A184 and replace the American Mk 44 for operations in the notoriously difficult ASW environment of the Mediterranean the lightweight **A244** was developed. This is an electrically-driven weapon suitable for use by aircraft, helicopters or surface ships in normal or shallow waters. In its original form it was fitted with a Selenia AG70 homing head, but the latest variant, the **A244/S**, has an advanced homing seeker. Using special signal-processing techniques, this allows both active and passive operations which can discriminate between a real target and decoys. The A244 series has been sold to a number of countries including Argentina, Ecuador, India, Indonesia, Iraq, Libya, Nigeria, Peru and Venezuela. Whitehead is currently working on a replacement weapon for the A244 series, the 50-kt high-performance **A290**, which uses seeker technology derived from the A244/S weapon and a polymo-

Capable of submarine or surface launch, the Whitehead A184 is capable of engaging both submarine and surface targets. Wire-guided, it is capable of operating at great depths and in a two-speed mode.

tor pumpjet propulsion system. Production of this advanced lightweight torpedo is due to start in the early 1990s.

Specification
A184
Dimensions: diameter 533 mm (21 in); length 6.00 m (19.69 ft)
Weight: 1265 kg (2,789 lb)
Warhead: 250-kg (551-lb) HE
Performance: 24 or 36 kts; range 25 or 10 km (15.53 or 6.21 miles)

Specification
A244/S Mod 0/1
Dimensions: diameter 324 mm (12.75 in); length 2.70 m (8.86 ft)
Weight: 221 kg (487 lb)
Warhead: 45.4-kg (100-lb) HE
Performance: speed 37 kts; range 6.5 km (4.04 miles)

Right: Designed for launch from surface ships, helicopters and aircraft, the A244 is capable of both active and passive operations, in a wide variety of attack patterns.

Below: The A184 is the latest heavyweight product of one of the world's oldest torpedo manufacturers. As with most modern torpedoes, it is electrically powered.

The Mediterranean is a very difficult environment for the effective use of torpedoes, and the A244 has been designed with that fact in mind to replace the US-built Mk 44 in Italian service.

Whitehead lightweight torpedoes, like many other western types, can be launched from the ubiquitous Type 32 triple tube launcher developed for the US Navy.

World
Navies

ALBANIA

Strength: 3,250
Fleet includes: 2 or 3 patrol submarines, up to 44 fast attack craft (torpedo), 6 fast attack craft (gun), 2 large patrol craft, 2 ocean minesweepers, 6 inshore minesweepers, c.30 miscellaneous types

ALGERIA

Strength: 8,000 (including Coastguard)
Fleet includes: 2 patrol submarines, 3 frigates, 4 corvettes, 11 fast attack craft (missile), 1 large patrol craft, 24 Coastguard patrol craft, 2 ocean minesweepers, 3 landing ships, 30+ miscellaneous types

ANGOLA

Strength: 1,500
Fleet includes: 4-6 fast attack craft (missile), 3-5 fast attack craft (torpedo), c.12 patrol craft, 3-4 landing ships, 5 landing craft, up to 8 miscellaneous types
1 MR aircraft

ARGENTINA

Strength: 18-20,000 (including Marines)
Fleet includes: 4 patrol submarines (3 building), 1 light aircraft carrier, 6 destroyers, 5 frigates (4 under construction), 2 fast attack craft (gun), 2 (possibly non-opertional) fast attack craft (torpedo), up to 60 patrol craft (including *Prefectura Naval* vessels), 6 coastal MCM vessels, 1 landing ship, 12+ landing craft, 4 supply ships, 2 tankers, 26 miscellaneous types
60+ fixed wing aircraft
20+ helicopters
Note: Due to cost constraints the Argentine armed forces have contracted considerably. A number of vessels are reportedly for sale, including most of those under construction in Argentine shipyards.

AUSTRALIA

Strength: 16,000
Fleet includes: 6 patrol submarines, 3 destroyers, 10 frigates (2 building), 21-24 patrol craft (2 building), 3 coastal MCM vessels, 1 landing ship, 6 large landing craft, 1 depot ship, 1 replenishment tanker, 100 miscellaneous types.
30+ helicopters (16 on order)

The Australian 'Oberon' class submarine HMAS Otama *is seen at Sydney.*

AUSTRIA

Strength: less than 50 personnel
Fleet includes: 12 river patrol craft

BAHAMAS

Strength: less than 500 (Coastguard para-military)
Fleet includes: 10 patrol craft (3 on order), 3 support craft

BAHREIN

Strength: c.300
Fleet includes: 2 fast attack craft (missile) (2 on order), 2 fast attack craft (gun), 15+ small patrol craft, 1 landing craft, 3 miscellaneous types

BANGLADESH

Strength: c.6,000
Fleet includes: 3 frigates, 4 fast attack craft (missile), up to 4 fast attack craft (torpedo), up to 15 fast attack craft (gun), c.12 patrol craft (5 more on order), 7 miscellaneous types
Note: shortage of spares may mean some vessels are unserviceable

BARBADOS

Strength: 120
Fleet includes: 6 patrol craft

BELGIUM

Strength: 4,600
Fleet includes: 4 frigates, 8 ocean MCM vessels (10 or more planned or building), 6 coastal MCM vessels, 14 inshore MCM vessels, 2 support vessels, 20 miscellaneous types
3 helicopters (5 SAR helicopters are also operated jointly with the Air Force)

BELIZE

Strength: 40 personnel (Army Maritime Wing)
Fleet includes: 4 patrol craft

BENIN

Strength: 100-150
Fleet includes: 2 fast attack craft (torpedo), up to 4 patrol craft

BOLIVIA
Strength: 3,600 (including Marines)
Fleet includes: c.40 river and lake patrol boats, 1 transport
3-4 aircraft

BRAZIL
Strength: 46,000+ (including Marines)
Fleet includes: 8 patrol submarines (2 building), 1 light aircraft carrier, 10 destroyers, 6 frigates, 9 corvettes (2 building), 6 river patrol ships, 6 patrol craft, 6 coastal MCM vessels, 2 landing ships, 35 landing craft, 2

The island of Bahrein has a small fleet of craft such as the Al Riffa.

repair ships, 4 tankers, c.95 miscellaneous types
60+ helicopters

BRUNEI
Strength: 446
Fleet includes: 3 fast attack craft (missile), 6 patrol craft, 24 fast and river assault boats, 2 landing craft, 3 utility craft

The Brazilian GP frigate Liberal is a variant of the 'Niteroi' ASW class.

BULGARIA

Strength: 8,500
Fleet includes: 2/3 patrol submarines, 2 frigates, 3 corvettes, 6 fast attack craft (missile), 6 fast attack craft (torpedo), 11 patrol craft, 2 ocean MCM vessels, 9 coastal MCM vessels, c.22 inshore and river minesweepers, c.25 large landing craft, 1 replenishment vessel, 3 tankers, 26 other craft
18/20 helicopters.

BURMA

Strength: 7/10,000 (including Marines)
Fleet includes: 4 corvettes, 65+ gunboats and river patrol craft, several ex-US landing craft (used as gunboats), 1 support craft, 15 miscellaneous types

CAMEROON

Strength: 350
Fleet includes: 2 fast attack craft (missile) (only 1 with missiles), 2 fast attack craft (gun), c.14 patrol craft, 6/7 landing craft, 11 miscellaneous types

CANADA

Strength: 13,400 (Maritime component of Canadian Armed Forces)
Fleet includes: 3 patrol submarines (up to 12 SSNs planned), 4 destroyers (6 building or planned), 19 frigates, 13 patrol craft, 1 support ship, 3 replenishment vessels, 1 tanker, 50+ miscellaneous types.
33 MR aircraft
35+ ASW helicopters

CHILE

Strength: 29/30,000 (including Marines)
Fleet includes: 4 patrol submarines, 8 destroyers, 2 frigates, 3 corvettes, 2 fast attack craft (missile), 4 fast attack craft (torpedo), 10 patrol craft, 3 landing ships, 2 large landing craft, 1 depot ship, 3 tankers, 24 miscellaneous types
20+ aircraft (c.10 MR/SAR)
c.20 helicopters

CHINA (People's Republic)

Strength: 350,000 (including Marines)
Fleet includes: 2 nuclear-powered ballistic missile submarines (4[?] more planned), 1 diesel-powered ballistic missile submarine, 3 nuclear-powered attack submarines (3[?] more planned), 100+ patrol submarines, 15 destroyers (4[?] building), 31 frigates (8+ building or planned), c.250 fast attack craft (missile), c.190 fast attack craft (torpedo), c.360 fast attack craft (gun), 200+ patrol craft, 24-30 ocean MCM vessels, 80+ inshore MCM vessels, 4 assault transport ships, c.60 landing ships (2 or 3 building), c.550 large and medium landing craft, 16 depot and repair ships, 24 replenishment and supply ships, 34 tankers, c.500 miscellaneous types
c.800 combat aircraft
c.20 MR flying boats
c.90 helicopters

COLOMBIA

Strength: 9,000+ (including Marines)
Fleet includes: 2 patrol submarines, 2 midget submarines, 1 destroyer, 4 frigates, 4 patrol ships, 6 gunboats, 25+ patrol craft, 1 tanker, 36 miscellaneous types (including Coast Guard)
4 helicopters

Above: The Cuban intelligence collector Isla de la Juventud was once a trawler.

Below: The Peoples Republic of China operates vast numbers of coastal craft.

Niels Juel (*F 354*) *is name ship of a class of three light frigates designed in Britain and built in Denmark.*

CONGO
Strength: 200
Fleet includes: 6 fast attack craft (gun) (four more non-opertional), 10 patrol craft, up to 12 miscellaneous craft

COSTA RICA
Strength: 90 (para-military, part of Civil Guard)
Fleet includes: 9+ patrol craft.

CUBA
Strength: c.13,000
Fleet includes: 3 patrol submarines, 2 frigates, 23 fast attack craft (missile), 17-20 fast attack craft (torpedo), 30+ fast attack craft (gun), 20[?] patrol craft, 2-4 coastal minesweepers, 10-11 inshore minesweepers, 2 landing ships, 7 landing craft, 1 intelligence collector, 35+ miscellaneous types (including Coast Guard)
30+ helicopters (may be operated by Air Force personnel)

DENMARK
Strength: c.6,000 (not including 9,000 active reserve and Home Guard)

Fleet includes: 4 patrol submarines (3, possibly 6 more to be leased), 8 frigates, 10 fast attack craft (missile), 6 fast attack craft (torpedo), c.30 patrol craft, 7 minelayers, 6 coastal minesweepers, 24 miscellaneous types
8 helicopters

DOMINICAN REPUBLIC
Strength: 4,000-4,500 (including naval infantry)
Fleet includes: 1 frigate, 5 corvettes, 10-15 patrol craft, 1 landing ship, 2 landing craft, 2 tankers, 17 miscellaneous types

ECUADOR
Strength: 4,000-4,500 (including Marines)
Fleet includes: 2 patrol submarines, 1 destroyer, 1 frigate, 6 corvettes (of which one was damaged seriously by fire in 1985), 6 fast attack craft (missile), 9-10 patrol craft, 1 landing ship, 32 miscellaneous types (including Coast Guard)
6+ aircraft
2 helicopters

EGYPT

Strength: 20,000
Fleet includes: 12 patrol submarines, 3 destroyers (four more ordered), 6 frigates, 32 fast attack craft (missile), c.12 fast attack craft (torpedo), c.20 fast attack craft (gun or multiple rocket armed), 40+ patrol craft, 10 ocean minesweepers, 2-4 inshore minesweepers, 3 landing ships, 24 landing craft, 80+ miscellaneous vessels (including Coast Guard)
6 ASW helicopters

EL SALVADOR

Strength: c.1,200 (including over 800 Marines and Commandos)
Fleet includes: 7-10 patrol craft, 10-12 motor launches

EQUATORIAL GUINEA

Strength: 100-150
Fleet includes: 1 fast attack craft (torpedo), 3 patrol craft

ETHIOPIA

Strength: c.2,500-3,000
Fleet includes: 2 frigates, 4 fast attack craft (missile), 3 fast attack craft (torpedo), 12 patrol craft, 2 landing ships, 6 landing craft
Note: about 50% of the inventory is thought to be unserviceable

FIJI

Strength: 170
Fleet includes: 3 coastal minesweepers, 3 miscellaneous types

FINLAND

Strength: 2,700
Fleet includes: 2 corvettes, 9 fast attack craft (missile), 6 fast attack craft (gun), 10 patrol craft, 3 minelayers, 13 inshore minesweepers and minesweeping boats, 14 landing craft, 3 support vessels, c.80 miscellaneous vessels (including Frontier Guard)

FRANCE

Strength: 68,000 (including Naval Air and Naval Commandos)
Fleet includes: 6 nuclear-powered ballistic missile submarines, 1 diesel-powered missile submarine, 4 nuclear-powered attack submarines (2 building), 12 patrol submarines, 2 aircraft carriers (1 nuclear-powered carrier building, 1 planned), 1 helicopter carrier/training ship, 1 cruiser, 19 destroyers (6 building), 25 frigates (3 building or ordered), 4 fast attack craft (missile), 10 fast attack craft (missile/gun), 3 patrol craft, 16 ocean MCM vessels (4 building), 5 coastal minesweepers, 2 assault ships (1 building), 4 landing ships, 11 large landing craft, 36 landing craft, 6 depot/repair ships, 4 replenishment ships, 3 tankers, 9 supply ships, 200+ miscellaneous types (including Coast Guard vessels)
100 combat aircraft
70+ MR aircraft (land and carrier based)
80+ helicopters

Below: The nuclear ballistic missile submarine L'Inflexible commissioned into the French Navy in 1985.

Right: France operates a pair of aircraft carriers. This is the Clemenceau, seen off the Cote d'Azur.

GABON

Strength: 200
Fleet includes: 1 fast attack craft (missile) with 2 on order, 3 fast attack craft (gun), 3 patrol craft, 10 small patrol craft, 1 landing ship, 3 landing craft

GERMAN DEMOCRATIC REPUBLIC

Strength: 14,500
Fleet includes: 3 frigates, 20 corvettes, 10 fast attack craft (missile), 46 fast attack craft (torpedo), 28 coastal minesweepers, 12 landing ships, 2 light replenishment ships, 6 support ships, 10 tankers, 3 intelligence ships, 50+ miscellaneous types (including Frontier Guard) c.20 helicopters

GERMAN FEDERAL REPUBLIC

Strength: 38,000
Fleet includes: 24 patrol submarines (6 on order), 7 destroyers, 9 frigates (2 on order), 5 corvettes, 40 fast attack craft (missile), 39 coastal MCM vessels (22 building or planned), 20 inshore minesweepers, 50 landing craft, 12 depot ships, 12 support ships, 8 replenishment tankers, c.80 miscellaneous vessels (including Coast Guard)
96+ combat aircraft
40 MR and utility aircraft
36 helicopters

GHANA

Strength: 1,000+
Fleet includes: 2 corvettes, 4 fast attack craft (gun), 6 patrol craft

A Soviet built 'Shershan' fast attack craft of the navy of the German Democratic Republic is seen at speed on exercise in the Baltic. The East Germans operate closely with the Soviet navy.

GREECE

Strength: 19,500
Fleet includes: 10 patrol submarines, 14 destroyers, 6 frigates, 14 fast attack craft (missile), 10 fast attack craft (torpedo), 11 patrol craft, 2 minelayers, 15 coastal minesweepers, 1 assault ship, 12 landing ships, 2 large landing craft, 68 medium and small landing craft, 1 depot ship, 6 tankers, 100+ miscellaneous types (including Coast Guard vessels)
23 helicopters

GUATEMALA

Strength: 1,000 (including 650 Marines)
Fleet includes: c.10 coastal patrol craft, 3 landing craft, numerous river patrol craft and motor launches

GUINEA

Strength: 600
Fleet includes: 18 fast attack craft (gun), 20 patrol craft, 2 landing craft

U 29 is a Type 206 submarine operated by the Federal Republic of Germany. These very quiet boats were the precursors of a highly successful series of submarines built for export, although only the German boats are built from high-tensile, non-magnetic steel.

GUINEA-BISSAU
Strength: 275
Fleet includes: 6 fast attack craft (patrol), 11 patrol craft, 4 landing craft

GUYANA
Strength: 150
Fleet includes: 15 patrol craft, 1 landing craft

HAITI
Strength: 300
Fleet includes: 14 patrol craft

HONDURAS
Strength: 500 (including 300 Marines)
Fleet includes: 11 coastal patrol craft, 8 river patrol craft

HONG KONG
Strength: 2,700 (Hong Kong Police Marine)
Fleet includes: 2 command craft, 60 patrol craft

HUNGARY
Strength: 600 (Army Danube Flotilla)
Fleet includes: 25 patrol craft, 25+ riverine MCM vessels, c.30 miscellaneous riverine types

ICELAND
Strength: 120 (Coast Guard)
Fleet includes: 4 large patrol vessels
2 helicopters
2 SAR aircraft

INDIA
Strength: 47,000
Fleet includes: 10 patrol submarines (7 building), 2 light aircraft carriers, 3 cruisers (building), 1 training cruiser, 4 destroyers (3 building), 25 frigates, 6 corvettes (11 building or on order), 14 fast attack craft (missile), 7 fast attack craft (gun) with 6 on order, 1 patrol craft, 10 ocean minesweepers (2 on order), 13 coastal and inshore MCM vessels (3 in order), 10 landing ships (4 building or on order), 4 landing craft (4 on order), 3 depot and repair ships, 7 tankers, 55+ miscellaneous types (including Coast Guard vessels)
19 combat aircraft (8 more ordered)
25 MR & ASW aircraft
50+ helicopters

INDONESIA
Strength: 35,800 (including Marines)
Fleet includes: 2 patrol submarines, 16 frigates, 4 fast attack craft (missile) (4 ordered or being built), 2 fast attack craft (torpedo), 4 fast attack craft (gun), 23 patrol craft, 5 patrol jetfoils (6 on order), 3 ocean minesweepers (2 building), 15 landing ships, 60+ landing craft, 4 depot ships, 5 tankers, 14 Army transports, 1 Army landing ship, 20 Army landing craft, 6 Air Force cargo ships, 70+ Customs craft, 29 large Police patrol craft, 45 miscellaneous vessels
16 combat aircraft
34+ other aircraft
5 amphibious flying boats
c.30 helicopters

IRAN
Strength: 20,000 (including Marines)
Fleet includes: 3 destroyers, 4 frigates (possibly only 3 in service), 1[?] corvette, 8[?] fast attack craft (missile) (out of 12, 4 reported sunk by Iraq and only 3[?] of remainder serviceable), 2[?] patrol craft (5 reported

Indonesia has a myriad of islands to patrol, and amongst the types used with some success are converted Boeing 737 airliners and a number of Boeing Jetfoils.

sunk), 50+ armed speed boats (manned by Revolutionary Guards), 1 or 2 MCM vessels (3 or 4 reported sunk), 4 landing ships, 1 landing craft, 2[?] Air Cushion Vehicles (12 more reported destroyed), 5 support vessels, 40[?] miscellaneous types
2[?] MR aircraft
12[?] helicopters
Note: all figures tentative – losses in the war with Iraq are difficult to verify

IRAQ
Strength: 5,000
Fleet includes: 4 frigates (delivery held up due to the war), 6 corvettes (delivery held up due to the war), 8[?] fast attack craft (missile), 5[?] fast attack craft (torpedo), 10[?] patrol craft, 2 ocean minesweepers, 6 inshore minesweepers, 6[?] landing ships, 1 replenishment tanker, c.10 miscellaneous craft
Note: all figures tentative – losses in the war with Iran are difficult to verify

IRELAND
Strength: c.1,000
Fleet includes: 5 patrol ships, 2 coastal minesweepers
2 MR aircraft
2 helicopters

ISRAEL
Strength: c.6,000 (including Naval Commandos)
Fleet includes: 3 patrol submarines, 2 corvettes (building), 30 fast attack craft (missile), 3 patrol hydrofoils (missile), 45 coastal patrol craft, 3 landing ships, 9 landing craft, 5 miscellaneous types
3 MR aircraft

Israel's navy does not have to travel far to meet with potential enemies, and small patrol craft have an important place in its force. The 'Dvora' class, armed with a pair of Gabriel anti-ship missiles, are some of the world's smallest practical missile boats.

ITALY
Strength: 45,000 (including Marines)
Fleet includes: 12 patrol submarines, 1 light aircraft carrier, 1 helicopter carrier, 2 cruisers, 4 destroyers (2 on order), 14 frigates, 8 corvettes (11 building or ordered), 2 fast attack craft (convertible), 7 fast attack hydrofoils (missile), 8 ocean MCM vessels, 21 coastal MCM vessels, 5 inshore MCM craft, 2 replenishment tankers, 100+ miscellaneous types. Government Maritime forces operate 127 Port Captain launches, and the Ministry of Finance controls nearly 500 small and medium patrol craft
32 MR aircraft
110 helicopters

IVORY COAST
Strength: 700
Fleet includes: 4 fast attack craft (missile), 9 patrol craft, 1 landing ship, 2 landing craft

JAMAICA
Strength: 170
Fleet includes: 6 patrol craft

JAPAN
Strength: 57,000 (including 12,000 Maritime Safety Agency)
Fleet includes: 16 patrol submarines (2 building or ordered), 37 destroyers (7 building), 18 frigates (2 ordered), 5 fast attack craft (torpedo), 12 patrol craft, 1 coastal minelayer, 32 coastal minesweepers, 6 minesweeping boats, 2 MCM support ships, 8 landing ships, 37 landing craft, 1 replenishment ship, 1 replenishment tanker, 24 small tankers, c.600 miscellaneous vessels (including 500+ Maritime Safety Agency craft)
100+ MR aircraft
25 flying boats
135+ helicopters (including 35 Maritime Safety aircraft)
c.125+ miscellaneous aircraft (including Maritime Safety Agency types)

JORDAN
Strength: 300 personnel
Fleet includes: 9 patrol craft

KAMPUCHEA
Ten years ago the Kampuchean Navy had some 11,000 personnel (mostly a large Marine Corps). How many of the 40 or so riverine and coastal patrol craft left behind by the American backed regimes are operational is hard to say. It is believed that more equipment has been ordered from the USSR via Vietnam, and deliveries are thought to include 1 fast attack craft (patrol), 2 fast attack hydrofoils, 4 river patrol craft, 2 landing craft.

Maestrale is nameship of a class of eight frigates built for the Italian Navy. Fast and well armed, the 'Maestrales' are a notable improvement on the preceding 'Lupo' class.

KENYA

Strength: c.650
Fleet includes: 4 missile patrol craft (2 fast attack craft on order), 5 patrol craft

KOREA, DEMOCRATIC PEOPLE'S REPUBLIC (North)

Strength: 35,000
Fleet includes: 19 patrol submarines, 4 frigates, 38 fast attack craft (missile), 140+ fast attack craft (torpedo), 160+ fast attack craft (gun), c.80 patrol craft, 6+ landing ships, 130 landing craft, 100 miscellaneous types

KOREA, REPUBLIC OF (South)

Strength: 49,000 (including 20,000 Marines)
Fleet includes: 1 coastal submarine (more building), 11 destroyers, 6 frigates (2 on order), 16 corvettes (8 on order), 11 fast attack craft (missile), 62 fast attack craft (patrol), 6+ large patrol craft, 8 MCM vessels, 15 landing ships, 17 landing craft, 2 supply ships, 6 tankers, c.40 miscellaneous types (including 30 Coast Guard craft)
20+ MR/ASW aircraft
10 Marine Corps aircraft
12+ Marine Corps helicopters

KUWAIT

Strength: 1,100
Fleet includes: 8 fast attack craft (missile), 65 coastal patrol craft, 3 amphibious support ships, 7 large landing craft, 10 miscellaneous types

LAOS

Strength: 1,700
Fleet is known to include 22 riverine craft. The Soviet Union may have supplied as many as 40 craft for operations on the Mekong.

LEBANON

The rump of the Lebanese Navy is a Christian force which has some 300 personnel operating 4 patrol craft and 2 landing craft. There are 8 customs patrol craft which may be under naval control though 1 may have been stolen by the Christian Lebanese Forces Militia (otherwise known as the Phalange), The Phalange has three patrol boats, and the Progressive Socialist Party (Druze) has about 18 small craft.

LIBERIA

Strength: 450
Fleet includes: 6 coastal patrol craft

LIBYA

Strength: 5,000
Fleet includes: 6 patrol submarines, 6 mini-submarines, 1 frigate, 8 corvettes, 25 fast attack craft (missile) with four more planned, 14 fast attack craft (gun/missile) which may be attached to the customs service, 7 patrol craft, 6 ocean minesweepers, 1 logistic support ship, 5 landing ships, 20 landing craft, 10+ miscellaneous craft (Libya is known to use roll-on/roll-off merchant ships for covert minelaying)
c.20 helicopters

Japan has a powerful force of destroyers and frigates, such as the Kikuzuki, providing a notable ASW capability (though anti-air weapons can be weak).

MADAGASCAR
Strength: 600 (including Marines)
Fleet includes: 1 large patrol craft, 1 landing ship, 7 landing craft, 6 miscellaneous types

MALAYSIA
Strength: 11,000
Fleet includes: 4 frigates, 2 patrol ships, 8 fast attack craft (missile) with four more on order, 6 fast attack craft (gun), c.102 patrol craft (including 80+ craft operated by the Malaysian Police and the Royal Malaysian Customs Service), 4 MCM vessels, 2 landing ships, 30+ landing craft, 3 logistic support ships, c.9 miscellaneous types

MALDIVES
Strength: not known
Fleet includes: 4 patrol craft, 4 landing craft, 3 armed trawlers

MALI
Strength: 50
Fleet includes: 3 river patrol craft

MALTA
Strength: 775 (entire armed force, which includes a marine section)
Fleet includes: 15 patrol craft

MAURITANIA
Strength: 320
Fleet includes: 8 patrol craft

MEXICO
Strength: 23,600 (including 4,500 Marines)
Fleet includes: 3 destroyers, 6 frigates, 28 patrol ships, 40+ patrol craft, 19 coastal and river patrol boats, 2 landing ships, 6 small landing craft, 20 miscellaneous types
20+ aircraft
9-12 amphibious flying boats
15 helicopters

MOROCCO
Strength: 6,000 (including 1,000 Marines)
Fleet includes: 1 frigate, 4 fast attack craft (missile) with 6 building, 4 fast attack craft (gun), 13 patrol craft, 3 landing ships, 1 large landing craft, 2 transport ships. Customs/Coast Guard operate 12 patrol craft (20+ on order)

MOZAMBIQUE
Strength: 800
Fleet includes: 30 patrol craft (9 on order), 2 or 3 amphibious craft, 5 other craft

NETHERLANDS
Strength: 16,800 (including 2,800 Marines)

Organized intrusions into Mexican fishing grounds, plus the need to protect the offshore oil fields, have increased the importance of the country's navy in recent years. Heriberto Jara Corona is one of 31 'Azteca' class large patrol boats armed with one 40-mm (1.57-in) and one 20-mm (0.78-in) gun.

Fleet includes: 4 patrol submarines (four more on order), 16 frigates (4 building), 4 corvettes on order, 3 patrol craft, 15 ocean MCM vessels, 12 coastal MCM vessels, 20+ landing craft, 2 fast combat support ships, 50+ miscellaneous types (including army vessels)
15 MR aircraft
22 helicopters

NEW ZEALAND
Strength: 2,750
Fleet includes: 4 frigates, 8 patrol craft, 8 miscellaneous craft
7 helicopters

NICARAGUA
Strength: c.1,000
Fleet includes: 25 patrol craft, 6 inshore minesweepers, 1 landing craft

NIGERIA
Strength: 5,000
Fleet includes: 2 frigates (1 used for training), 4 corvettes, 6 fast attack craft (missile), 9 large patrol craft, 14 inshore patrol craft, 2 MCM vessels, 2 landing ships, 2 landing craft, 150+ miscellaneous types (including police launches)
3 helicopters

NORWAY
Strength: 8,000 (including almost 2,000 manning coastal artillery)
Fleet includes: 14 patrol submarines (at least six more on order), 5 frigates, 2 corvettes, 33 fast attack craft (missile), 6 fast attack craft (missile/torpedo), 8 fast attack craft (torpedo) in reserve, 3 patrol craft, 3 minelayers, 10 coastal minesweepers, 7 large landing craft, 31 miscellaneous vessels (including Coast Guard)
6 helicopters (air force operated aboard Coast Guard vessels)

OMAN
Strength: 2,000
Fleet includes: 5 fast attack craft (missile), 4 fast attack craft (gun), 4 patrol craft, 2 landing ships, 5 landing craft, 28+ miscellaneous vessels (including Royal Oman Police craft)

PAKISTAN
Strength: 15,500
Fleet includes: 6 patrol submarines, 3 midget submarines, 8 destroyers, 8 fast attack craft (missile), 12 fast attack craft (gun), 4 fast attack hydrofoil (torpedo), 6 patrol craft, 3 MCM vessels, 2 landing craft, 1 training/AA cruiser, 11 miscellaneous types
4 MR/utility aircraft
10 helicopters

Above: The 'Kortenaer' class frigate Callenburgh (F 808) leads the large frigate Tromp (F 801) in the North Sea. The highly efficient Dutch fleet maintains at least two ASW groups for operations in the North Sea and the North Atlantic.

Right: Oslo is the nameship of a class of five Norwegian frigates built in the 1960s with US assistance. The design is based on that of the US Navy's 'Dealy' destroyer escort class, but substantially modified for service in the challenging Norwegian conditions.

PANAMA
Strength: 500
Fleet includes: 2 large patrol craft, 6 coastal patrol craft, 3 landing ships, 3 landing craft, 3 miscellaneous types

PAPUA NEW GUINEA
Strength: 400
Fleet includes: 5 large patrol craft (4 on order), 2 landing craft, 1 tug, 9 miscellaneous craft

PARAGUAY
Strength: 2,000 (including 500 Marines)
Fleet includes: 3 river defence vessels, 3 corvettes (ex-minesweepers), 7+ patrol craft, 1 landing ship, c.19 miscellaneous vessels
Note: most of Paraguay's craft date from the Second World War or before, some having been in service for almost 80 years

PERU
Strength: 27,000 (including Marines)
Fleet includes: 12 patrol submarines, 2 cruisers, 10 destroyers, 4 frigates, 6 fast attack craft (missile), 27 patrol craft (including some 24 Coast Guard craft), 4 lake patrol craft, 5 river gunboats, 9 landing vessels, 5 tankers, 33 miscellaneous craft
30 aircraft
22 helicopters

PHILIPPINES
Strength: 26,000 (including Coast Guard and 9,500 Marines)
Fleet includes: 2 destroyers (on order), 7 frigates, 10 corvettes, 3 fast attack craft (missile) (building), 13 large patrol craft (6 on order), 135 medium and small patrol craft (including Coast Guard vessels), 31

Above: The Peruvian navy has six PR-72P fast attack craft built by SFCN in France. Displacing 560 tons at full load, they carry four Exocet SSMs in single cells as well as a useful gun armament.

landing ships, 70+ landing craft, 3 repair ships, 2 tankers, c.40 miscellaneous craft
13 SAR/MR aircraft
10 helicopters

Below: João Coutinho is the nameship of a six-strong class of Portuguese frigates, of which three were built in West Germany and three in Spain.

POLAND
Strength: 19,000
Fleet includes: 5 patrol submarines, 1 destroyer, 4 corvettes, 12 fast attack craft (missile), 7 fast attack craft (torpedo), 23 large patrol craft (including 15 Coast Guard vessels), 54 coastal patrol craft (Coast Guard manned), 24 ocean MCM vessels, 6 coastal MCM vessels, 23+ minesweeping boats, 23 large landing craft, 20+ medium and small landing craft, 2 intelligence collectors, 7 tankers, 70+ miscellaneous craft
95 combat aircraft (80 fighters, 15 light bombers)
40 helicopters

PORTUGAL
Strength: 14,500 (including Marines)
Fleet includes: 3 patrol submarines, 17 frigates (3 on order), 10 large patrol craft, 24 coastal patrol craft, 4 coastal minesweepers, 16 landing craft, 1 tanker, 11 miscellaneous craft

QATAR
Strength: 700 (including Maritime Police)
Fleet includes: 3 fast attack craft (missile), 6 large patrol craft, 40+ inshore and small patrol craft

ROMANIA
Strength: 8,000
Fleet includes: 2 destroyers, 3 frigates, 3 corvettes, 6 fast attack craft (missile), 20+ fast attack craft (gun), 20+ fast attack craft (torpedo), 20+ fast attack hydrofoils (torpedo), 3 large patrol craft, 1 large river monitor, 40+ river patrol craft, 2 minelayers, 4 coastal minesweepers, 32 inshore minesweepers, 3 landing craft, 2 support ships, 3 tankers, c.30 miscellaneous craft
6 helicopters

SAUDI ARABIA
Strength: 12,000 (including 8,500 Frontier Force and Coast Guard)
Fleet includes: 4 frigates, 4 corvettes, 9 fast attack craft (missile), 3 fast attack craft (torpedo), 1 large patrol craft, c.180 coastal patrol craft (including 130 Frontier Force/Coast Guard), 300 inshore patrol craft (Frontier Force/Coast Guard manned), 24 air cushion vehicles, 2 patrol hydrofoils, 4 MCM vessels, 3 landing ships, 16 landing craft, 2 replenishment tankers, c.40 miscellaneous types
2 aircraft
24 helicopters

SENEGAMBIA
Strength: 750 (700 in Senegal, 50 in The Gambia)
Fleet includes: 12 patrol craft, 4 landing craft (1 on order), 17 armed coastal craft (customs service manned)

SEYCHELLES
Strength: 100
Fleet includes: 5 patrol craft, 1 landing craft

SIERRA LEONE
Strength: 100 (Coast Guard)
Fleet includes: 2 patrol boats, 3 landing craft

The Saudi frigate Madina is one of the most capable ships in the Gulf.

SINGAPORE
Strength: 4,000
Fleet includes: 6 fast attack craft (missile), 6 fast attack craft (gun), 12 patrol craft, 2 coastal minesweepers, 6 landing ships, 8 landing craft, 65 miscellaneous craft (including 60 police craft)

SOLOMON ISLANDS
Strength: not known
Fleet includes: 3 patrol craft

SOMALI REPUBLIC
Strength: 700
Fleet includes: 2 fast attack craft (missile), 8 fast attack craft (torpedo), 5 patrol craft, 5 landing craft

SOUTH AFRICA
Strength: 9,000 (including Marines)
Fleet includes: 3 patrol submarines, 1 frigate, 12 fast attack craft (missile), 5 large patrol craft, 30+ small patrol craft, 10 MCM vessels, 2 replenishment ships, 12 miscellaneous craft

SPAIN
Strength: 65,000 (including Marines)
Fleet includes: 8 patrol submarines, 2 light V/STOL aircraft carriers, 10 destroyers, 12 frigates (4 on order), 4 corvettes, 12 fast attack craft, 20+ large patrol craft and 110+ coastal/inshore patrol craft (including 10 large, 40+ small patrol craft operated by the Maritime Surveillance Force of the Ministry of Transport), 4 ocean MCM vessels, 8 coastal MCM vessels, 4 landing ships, 25+ landing craft, 2 amphibious transports, 1 replenishment tanker, 138 miscellaneous craft
10 combat aircraft (12 on order)
7 other aircraft
40+ helicopters (18 ASW helicopters on order)

SRI LANKA
Strength: 3,500
Fleet includes: 6 fast attack craft (gun), 2 large patrol craft, 28 coastal patrol craft, 2 landing craft, 9 miscellaneous craft

Above: South Africa has obtained a great deal of hardware and military technology from Israel. The South African 'Minister' class fast attack craft are copies of the Israeli 'Reshef' class, and are armed with licence built Gabriel anti-ship missiles, known locally as the Skorpioen.

Below: Spain has developed its own unique close-in weapon system. The Meroka multi-barrelled gun was tested aboard the 'Lazaga' class fast attack craft Cadarso before being put into production for major units of the Spanish navy.

SUDAN
Strength: 2,000
Fleet includes: 2 fast attack craft (missile), 12 patrol craft (6 on order), 2 landing craft
Note: serviceability of all equipment is doubtful

SURINAME
Strength: 160
Fleet includes: 10 patrol craft

SWEDEN
Strength: 9,650 (including Coast Artillery)
Fleet includes: 13 patrol submarines (3 building), 2 missile corvettes (4 building), 28 fast attack craft (missile), 4 fast attack craft (torpedo), 32 coastal patrol craft, 3 large minelayers, 13 coastal minelayers, 22 inshore minelayers, 15 MCM vessels, 18 inshore MCM vessels (6 on order), 125+ landing craft, 1 intelligence ship, 3 tankers, 3 support ships, c.180 miscellaneous craft
20 helicopters

SWITZERLAND
The Swiss army controls some 11 lake patrol craft

SYRIA
Strength: 2,500
Fleet includes: 2 patrol submarines, 2 frigates, 3 corvettes, 22 fast attack craft (missile), fast attack craft (torpedo), 6 patrol craft, 2 ocean MCM vessels, 2 coastal MCM vessels, 4 inshore MCM vessels, 3 landing ships, 1 diver support ship

TAIWAN
Strength: 38,000
Fleet includes: 4 patrol submarines, 23 destroyers (some in reserve), 9 frigates, 4 corvettes, 60+ fast attack craft (missile) with a further 10 on order or building, c.46 patrol craft (including 18 armed Customs craft), 13 MCM vessels, 3 amphibious assault ships, 26 landing ships, 430 landing craft, 1 repair ship, 4 transports, 7 tankers, 50+ miscellaneous craft
12 helicopters (10 on order)

TANZANIA
Strength: c.750
Fleet includes: 6 fast attack craft (gun), 4 fast attack hydrofoil (torpedo), 12 patrol craft, 6 landing craft, 2 miscellaneous craft

THAILAND
Strength: 40,000 (including Naval Air and 20,000 Marines)
Fleet includes: 6 frigates, 3 corvettes (on order), 6 fast attack craft (missile), 3 fast attack craft (gun), 1 fast attack hydrofoil, c.100 patrol craft, 6 MCM vessels, 9 coastal and inshore MCM vessels, 10 landing ships, 54 landing craft, 1 transport, 5 tankers, 13 miscellaneous vessels
60 aircraft (including some 30 light observation types)
11 helicopters

TOGO
Strength: 100
Fleet includes: 2 coastal patrol craft

TONGA
Strength: c.100
Fleet includes: 2 patrol craft and 1 landing craft

Above: Hugin *is a Norwegian designed craft operated by Sweden. Baltic operational conditions has seen Sweden put large numbers of such fast attack craft into service.*

Below: Sweden is like other Baltic navies in the emphasis it places on offensive and defensive mine warfare. Arkö *is one of a class of nine wood-built coastal minesweepers.*

TRINIDAD AND TOBAGO
Strength: 600 (Coast Guard)
Fleet includes: 6 large patrol craft, 13 coastal patrol craft (including 6 police craft), 4 miscellaneous craft

TUNISIA
Strength: 3,500
Fleet includes: 1 frigate, 6 fast attack craft (missile) with two on order, 2 fast attack craft (gun), 2 fast attack craft (patrol), 1 patrol ship, 4 large patrol craft, 14 coastal patrol craft, 1 tug

TURKEY
Strength: 55,000 (including Coast Guard and Marines)
Fleet includes: 17 patrol submarines, 13 destroyers, 4 frigates (4 on order), 14 fast attack craft (missile), 11 fast attack craft (torpedo), 1 fast attack craft (gun), c.75 patrol craft (including 45 Coast Guard), 7 minelayers, 22 coastal minesweepers, 4 inshore minesweepers, 8 inshore minehunters, 7 landing ships, 70+ landing craft (12 on order), 2 repair ships, 4 depot ships/tenders, 10 tankers, 40 cargo and transport craft (including 4 Coast Guard vessels), 50+ miscellaneous craft
15 aircraft
6 helicopters

UNION OF SOVIET SOCIALIST REPUBLICS
Strength: 5.500,000 (including Strategic, Naval Air, Naval Infantry and Coastal Artillery personnel)
Fleet includes: 63+ nuclear-powered ballistic missile submarines, 15 diesel-powered ballistic missile submarines, 51 nuclear-powered guided missile submarines, 17 diesel-powered guided missile submarines, 85+ nuclear-powered attack submarines (including SSBN conversions), c.150 patrol submarines, 12 other submarines (including command, training, rescue, and research boats), c.70 patrol submarines in reserve, 2 nuclear-powered aircraft carriers (building), 4 V/STOL aircraft carriers, 2 large nuclear-powered cruisers (at least 1 building), 2 helicopter cruisers, 34 cruisers, 75 destroyers, 10 destroyers in reserve, 80+ frigates, 118+ light frigates, 48 missile corvettes, c.100 fast attack craft (missile), 17 fast attack hydrofoils (missile), 180 fast attack craft (patrol), 40+ fast attack hydrofoils (patrol), 10 fast attack craft (torpedo), 17 patrol ships, 15 patrol craft (some operated by the KGB), 110+ river patrol craft, 10 radar pickets, 3 minelayers, c.130 ocean MCM vessels, c.150 coastal MCM vessels, c.110 inshore MCM vessels and minesweeping boats, 2 amphibious assault ships, 75 landing ships, 120 landing craft, c.80 air cushion vehicles, 28 replenishment tankers, 45 support tankers, c.85 depot, repair and support ships, 62 intelligence collectors, 480 major miscellaneous vessels including civilian manned research ships.
The 1,900 vessels of the Soviet merchant fleet are subordinate to the navy, many having naval commanders. They include roll-on/roll-off ships, barge carriers (including one large nuclear-powered example), and passenger liners. The massive and well equipped Soviet fishing fleet is another considerable asset.
Naval Aviation has 400 bombers, 150 frigates and fighter/bombers, over 200 ASW aircraft, over 170 MR aircraft, c.300 other aircraft (including transport, tanker and training types), and over 300 helicopters.
The KGB (*Komitet Gosudarstvennoy Bezopasnosti*, or Committee for State Security) controls over a dozen frigates and more than 250 patrol craft which are used for border security duties.

Below: This 'Kynda' class cruiser of the Soviet Pacific Fleet is refuelling from the replenishment tanker Boris Chilikin off Hawaii.

Right: The mightily impressive Kirov was the first of a series of very large nuclear powered cruisers built for the Soviet navy.

UNITED ARAB EMIRATES

Strength: 1,500 (not including Coast Guard)
Fleet includes: 6 fast attack craft (missile), 9 patrol craft, 2 support craft, 57 coastal patrol craft (Coast Guard manned), 10 miscellaneous craft

UNITED KINGDOM

Strength: 69,000 (including Fleet Air Arm and Marines)
Fleet includes: 4 nuclear-powered ballistic missile submarines (1 building), 16 nuclear-powered attack submarines (3 building), 11 patrol submarines (4 on order or building), 3 light V/STOL aircraft carriers, 13 destroyers, 40 frigates (4 on order or building), 30 patrol vessels, 37+ MCM vessels, 10 coastal minesweepers, 2 amphibious assault ships, 6 logistic landing ships, 70+ landing craft (including 39 Army, 18 Marine operated), 4 large replenishment vessels (1 building), 14 replenishment tankers, 6 repair/support ships, c.200 miscellaneous vessels
50+ combat aircraft
c.70 other aircraft
c.280 helicopters

UNITED STATES OF AMERICA

Strength: 795,000 (including Naval Air and 200,000 Marines)
Fleet includes: 36 nuclear-powered ballistic missile submarines, 97 nuclear-powered attack submarines, 5 nuclear-powered transport/research submarines, 4 patrol submarines, 5 nuclear-powered aircraft carriers (2 on order), 10 aircraft carriers, 4 battleships, 9 nuclear-powered cruisers, 22 cruisers (15 on order), 68 destroyers (1 building),

106 frigates (5 on order, 6 in reserve), 7 fast attack hydrofoils (missile), c.100 small patrol craft, 4 ocean MCM vessels (4 on order, 18 in reserve), 12 coastal MCM vessels (on order), 4 command ships, 5 large amphibious assault ships (1 building), 30 amphibious assault ships (5 on order), 18 landing ships, 5 amphibious cargo ships, 50+ large landing craft, c.60 utility landing craft, many smaller landing craft, 12 air-cushion landing craft (28 on order or building), 5 fast combat support ships, 13 ammunition replenishment ships, 10 combat stores ships, 25 oilers/replenishment oilers, 22 tenders/repair/depot ships, 9 ocean surveillance ships (17 building or planned), 500+ miscellaneous Navy, Military Sealift Command, Strategic Reserve and Prepositioning Ships
Navy Aviation control some 7,000 aircraft including 2,500 combat aircraft (including Marine Corps), 300 helicopters (MCM, ASW, transport, utility), 100+ Marine Corps attack helicopters and 450+ Marine Corps assault and transport helicopters
The United States Coast Guard comes under Navy control in time of war. Its 43,000 personnel man 49 patrol ships (high- and medium-endurance cutters), 90+ patrol craft and 110+ miscellaneous craft (ranging from 11,000 ton ice-breakers down to riverine buoy-tenders)

Below: The British Ikara armed ASW frigate Ajax is seen in company with the 'Krivak' class large anti-submarine ship in the North Sea. The Soviet vessel is notable for its heavy weapon and sensor fit.

Right: An 'Invincible' class light aircraft carrier steams at the head of a British ASW force in the Atlantic. The Phalanx CIWS system was added as a result of the lessons of the Falklands.

Left: The almost unbelievable power of a modern US carrier such as USS John F. Kennedy is contained in the 80 or more modern combat aircraft she carries.

Above: The US Navy has a pair of specially built command ships developed from the hull design of the Iwo Jima class. USS Blue Ridge serves as flagship to the US Seventh Fleet.

URUGUAY

Strength: 6,600 (including Naval Air, Naval Infantry)
Fleet includes: 3 frigates, 1 corvette, 8 patrol craft, 7 landing craft, 1 tanker, 3 miscellaneous craft
23 aircraft
2 helicopters

VENEZUELA

Strength: 8,000 (including Naval Air, Marines and Coast Guard)
Fleet includes: 3 patrol submarines, 8 frigates (including 2 Coast Guard patrol ships), 2 Coast Guard fast attack craft (missile), 4 Coast Guard fast attack craft (gun), 2 Coast Guard patrol craft, 60+ coastal patrol craft (manned by the National Guard), 5 landing ships, 14 landing craft, 3 transport/cargo vessels, 17 miscellaneous craft
20 aircraft
6 helicopters

VIETNAM

Strength: 40,000 (including 27,000 Naval Infantry)
Fleet includes: 6 or 7 frigates/patrol ships, 8 fast attack craft (missile), 16 fast attack craft (torpedo), 5 fast attack hydrofoils (torpedo), 40+ patrol craft, 1 coastal MCM vessel, 1 inshore MCM vessel, 10 minesweeping boats, 9 landing ships, 30+ landing craft, 3 miscellaneous craft.
Vietnam has an enormous fleet of vessels lying idle, including many obtained from the South after the 1975 conquest together with Chinese supplied vessels. There are believed to be 160 fast attack and patrol craft, up to 600 riverine craft, 100 landing craft, and 110 miscellaneous craft currently non-operational.

YEMEN, ARAB REPUBLIC (North)

Strength: 550
Fleet includes: 5 patrol craft, 12 small patrol craft, 2 inshore minesweepers, 4 landing craft

YEMEN, PEOPLE'S DEMOCRATIC REPUBLIC (South)

Strength: 1,000
Fleet may include: 8 fast attack craft (missile), 2 fast attack craft (torpedo), 8 patrol craft, 1 landing ship, 3 large landing craft, 6 small landing craft
Note: most naval equipment was severely damaged if not destroyed during the short civil war of 1986.

YUGOSLAVIA

Strength: 13,000 (including Marines and Coast Defence troops)
Fleet includes: 7 patrol and training submarines, 2 mini-submarines, 3 frigates (1 building), 4 corvettes (9 on order), 16 fast attack craft (missile), 15 fast attack craft (torpedo), 27 large patrol craft (including 9 Frontier Guard craft), 60+ medium and small patrol craft, 4 coastal minehunters, 10 inshore minesweepers, 20+ river minesweepers, 30+ landing craft, 6 transports, 6 tankers, 26 miscellaneous craft
20 helicopters

ZAIRE

Strength: 1,500 (including 600 Marines)
Fleet includes: 4 fast attack craft (gun), 3 fast attack craft (torpedo), 4 patrol hydrofoils, 30 small patrol craft

Index

Index

The publishers would like to thank the following individuals and organizations who have supplied photographs used in this book:

Aérospatiale; Associated Press; Bell Aerospace Textron; Boeing; Bofors; Brazilian Navy; Breda; British Aerospace; British Hovercraft; British Ministry of Defence; Central Office of Information, London; Chinese Navy; Contraves; DCAN; ECPA Paris; Emerson Electric; FFV; Finnish Navy; General Dynamics; Hollandse Signaalapparatan; Israel Aircraft Industries; Israel Defence Force; Japan Maritime Self-Defence Force; Kongsberg; Lürssen; Laurence Scott; Marconi; MARS, Lincs.; MBB; McDonnell Douglas; Oerlikon-Bürhrle; OTO-Melara; Pilot Press; Edward Rasen; Royal Air Force; Royal Australian Navy; Royal Navy; Royal Netherlands Navy; Royal Norwegian Navy; SAAB-Bofors; Selenia; Shorts; Spanish Navy; Swedish Navy; US Department of Defense; US Navy; Westland Helicopters; Lt. K.P. White; Whitehead Motofides; Xinhua News Agency